Retracing
the
Past

Retracing
the
Past

Readings in
the History of the American People

VOLUME TWO · SINCE 1865

Second Edition

EDITORS
GARY B. NASH
University of California, Los Angeles

RONALD SCHULTZ
University of Wyoming

1817

HARPER & ROW, PUBLISHERS, New York
Grand Rapids, Philadelphia, St. Louis, San Francisco,
London, Singapore, Sydney, Tokyo

Sponsoring Editor: Lauren Silverman
Art Direction: Heather A. Ziegler
Cover Coordinator: Mary Archondes
Cover Design: A Good Thing, Inc.
Photo Research: Joan Scafarello
Production: Willie Lane

Cover Illustration: William Glackens 1870–1938, *Park on the River,* circa 1902. Oil on canvas, 65.8 × 81.3 (25⅞ × 32). The Brooklyn Museum. Dick S. Ramsay Fund.
Part-Opening Illustrations: Page 1: *The Ironworkers' Noontime* by Thomas Pollock Anshutz, 1880. The Fine Arts Museums of San Francisco, Gift of Mr. and Mrs. John D. Rockefeller, 3rd. **Page 93:** *Construction Steel Workers* by Reginald Marsh, 1924. Private Collection. Photograph Courtesy of Hirshl & Adler Galleries, New York. **Page 201:** *Firing Room* by Jamie Wyeth, 1969. Courtesy NASA, Washington, D. C. Photograph Bara King Photographic, Inc.

RETRACING THE PAST: Readings in the History of the American People, Volume Two, Since 1865, Second Edition.
Copyright © 1990 by Harper & Row, Publishers, Inc.

Library of Congress Cataloging-in-Publication Data

Retracing the past : readings in the history of the American people
    editors, Gary B. Nash, Ronald Schultz. — 2nd ed.
        p.   cm.
      Contents: v. 1. To 1877 — v. 2. Since 1865.
      ISBN 0-06-044744-3 (v. 1). — ISBN 0-06-044745-1 (v. 2)
      1. United States—History. I. Nash, Gary B. II. Schultz,
Ronald, 1946-   .
    E178.6.R45   1990
    973—dc20
                                                    89-20053
                                                    CIP

89 90 91 92 9 8 7 6 5 4 3 2 1

CONTENTS

PART THREE
A RESILIENT PEOPLE 201

PREFACE

This two-volume reader has been constructed to accompany the second edition of *The American People: Creating a Nation and a Society* (New York: Harper & Row, 1990), but we hope it will also prove a useful supplement to other books in American history. The essays have been selected with three goals in mind: first, to blend political and social history; second, to lead students to a consideration of the role of women, ethnic groups, and laboring Americans in the weaving of the nation's social fabric; and third, to explore life at the individual and community levels. The book also means to introduce students to the individuals and groups who made a critical difference in the shaping of American history or whose experience reflected key changes in their society.

A few of the individuals highlighted are famous—Benjamin Franklin, Abraham Lincoln, and Jackie Robinson, for example. A number of others are historically visible but are not quite household names—Squanto, Tecumseh, Samuel Gompers, W. E. B. Du Bois, John Muir, and Elizabeth Blackwell. Some will be totally unknown to students, such as "Long Bill" Scott, a Revolutionary soldier, and Absalom Jones, who bought his way out of slavery and became a leader of Philadelphia's free African Americans after the American Revolution. Often the focus is on groups whose role in history has not been adequately treated—the Chinese in the building of the transcontinental railroad, the grass-roots black leaders during Reconstruction, and the Hispanic agricultural laborers of this century.

Some of the essays chosen take us inside American homes, farms, and factories, such as the essays on the Springer family of Delaware farmers before the Civil War and the transcontinental migrants of the nineteenth century. Such essays, it is hoped, will convey an understanding of the daily lives of ordinary Americans, who collectively helped shape their society. Other essays deal with the vital social and political movements that transformed American society: the debate over the Constitution in the 1780s; abolitionism and reform in the antebellum period; populism and progressivism in the late nineteenth and early twentieth centuries; and the civil rights and women's movements of our own times.

Readability has been an important criterion in the selection of these essays. An important indicator of readability, in turn, is how vividly and concretely the past has been brought alive by the authors. The main objective has been a palpable presentation of the past—one that allows students to sense and feel the forces of historical change and hence to understand them.

Gary B. Nash
Ronald Schultz

Retracing
the
Past

PART ONE
AN INDUSTRIALIZING PEOPLE

1

BLACK RECONSTRUCTION LEADERS AT THE GRASSROOTS

ERIC FONER

The end of the Civil War in 1865 opened the question of the position of the freedman in American society. Now that they were no longer slaves, would black Americans be allowed the same rights as white citizens? Should black males be allowed to vote? To serve on juries? To hold office? To own property? The Fourteenth and Fifteenth Amendments to the Constitution provided one answer to these questions: they gave to the freedman all of the rights of American citizenship including the right to vote.

But constitutional principle was one thing and southern practice another. Through intimidation and violence, southern whites sought to maintain the old system of racial domination and white supremacy that had prevailed in the prewar South. Throughout the region, blacks were beaten for attempting to vote, black political leaders were assassinated, and the Klu Klux Klan was organized with the object of keeping blacks "in their place." By the late 1860s it was clear that white southerners were determined to prevent any change in their system of racial privilege and power.

However, the history of Reconstruction was not only a story of black suppression and white domination. Wherever they could, freedmen reestablished the family and kinship ties they had lost during slavery. Meanwhile, thousands of ex-slaves flocked to urban areas in search of employment, and others purchased land and livestock in order to establish their economic independence. Most important, with citizenship rights guaranteed by the Constitution and the Union Army, southern blacks eagerly embraced politics as a means to gain an equal place for themselves in American society. From a series of black political conventions held in the early years of Reconstruction emerged a group of local black leaders who spoke for the rights of freedmen, not only to economic opportunity and political and legal equity, but to the possession of confiscated Confederate land. In this essay, Eric Foner tells the story of these grass-roots leaders and in the process reveals the hopes and dreams of freedmen and -women as well as the limits of black Reconstruction.

Chapter 11 in Leon Litwack and August Meier, eds., *Black Leaders of the Nineteenth Century* (Urbana, Ill.: University of Illinois Press, 1988). Reprinted by permission of Eric Foner and University of Illinois Press.

In November 1869, in Greene County, Georgia, disguised Klansmen forced Abram Colby into the woods "and there stripped and beat him in the most cruel manner, for nearly three hours." Born a slave and freed in 1851, Colby earned his living as a minister and barber. Since the end of the Civil War he had taken an active part in black political life, organizing "one of the largest and most enthusiastic" branches of Georgia's Equal Rights Association in 1866 and winning election to the state legislature two years later. According to the local agent of the American Missionary Association, Colby was whipped because he had recently appealed to Governor Rufus Bullock to protect the county's black population, and his assailants "had besides, as they said, many old scores against him, as a leader of his people in the county." Eighteen months later South Carolina Klansmen whipped Samuel Bonner, an unassuming black sharecropper, along with his mother and sister. Before the assault Bonner was asked if he were a Republican. "I told them," he later recalled, "I was that, and I thought it was right."

Minor episodes in the history of Reconstruction, these incidents nonetheless illuminate larger themes of its political culture and the nature of grass-roots black leadership. Colby exemplifies the humble social status of local black leaders; although free before the Civil War, he was illiterate and, according to the 1870 census, owned no property. His experience in the legislature reveals the fragility of black-white cooperation in Reconstruction politics, for white Republicans were among those who voted to expel Colby and other blacks. Bonner's willingness to assert his convictions in the face of violence epitomizes the depth of commitment that animated the Reconstruction black community. These small dramas guide us into the world of local black politics, its organization, ideology, and leadership during Reconstruction.

Southern black politics, of course, did not begin with the Reconstruction Act of 1867, as Abram Colby's career illustrates. Before the end of the Civil War, black political organizations had appeared in such Union-occupied areas as New Orleans. And in 1865 and 1866, in black conventions throughout the southern states, future Reconstruction leaders like James T. Rapier and William H. Grey first came into prominence. By and large, however, the tone of these early conventions was moderate. Throughout the South, 1865 was a year of labor conflict, with freedpeople refusing to sign contracts and some seizing plantations and staking a claim to the soil. But the free-born mulattoes, ministers, and northern blacks who dominated the conventions all but ignored the land question.

Whatever the accomplishments of these conventions (and one delegate told the 1866 gathering in Tennessee that his constituents believed "we do nothing but meet, pass resolutions, publish pamphlets, and incur expenses"), the process of selecting delegates politicized black communities. Some delegates were elected by local mass meetings; others were sent by churches, clubs, and black army units stationed in the South. In the fall of 1866, two black men held "a regular canvass" in Greene County, North Carolina; an organized election followed to choose a delegate to the state's second black convention. The local chapters of the Georgia Educational Association, established at the state's January 1866 black convention, became "schools in which the colored citizens learn their rights." Nonetheless, this first phase of political organization was spotty and uneven—large areas of the black belt remained untouched by organized political activity.

It was in 1867, the *annus mirabilis* of Reconstruction, that a wave of political activism swept across the black belt. Itinerant lecturers, black and white, brought their message into the heart of the rural South. A black Baptist minister calling himself Professor J. W. Toer toured parts of Georgia and Florida "with a magic lantern to exhibit what he calls the progress of reconstruction. . . . He has a scene, which he calls 'before the proclamation,' another 'after the proclamation' and then '22nd Regt. U.S.C.T. Duncan's Brigade." Voting registrars held public meetings to instruct blacks on the nature of American government and "the individual benefits of citizenship in the nation and in the state." In Monroe County, Alabama, where no black political meetings had occurred before 1867, freedpeople crowded around the registrar shouting "God bless you," "Bless God for this." Throughout the South there were complaints of blacks neglecting plantation labor: "they stop at any time and go off to Greensboro or any other place to attend a political meeting" complained a white Alabamian. So great was the enthusiasm for politics that, as one former slave minister later wrote, "politics got in our midst and our revival or religious work for a while began to wane." Although suffrage was restricted to men, black women and even children often played a vocal part in political gatherings. One plantation manager summed up the situation: "You never saw a people more excited on the subject of politics than are the negroes of the south. They are perfectly wild."

The meteoric rise of black political activity was reflected in the growth of the Union League. Few developments of this period are more tinged with irony than the metamorphosis of a loyalist club, developed among the respectable middle classes of the Civil War North, into the political expression of impoverished freedpeople. An earlier generation of historians tended to dismiss the Union League by portraying it as a vehicle through which carpetbaggers manipulated the votes of gullible blacks, who were attracted to its meetings by secret passwords and colorful initiation rites. In fact, its purposes were far more complex: the league served simultaneously as "a political school for the people," as a North Carolina teacher described it, a vehicle for the emergence of a greatly expanded class of black political leaders, and an institutional structure blacks could utilize for their own purposes and through which they could articulate their own aspirations.

Even before 1867, local Union League branches had sprung up among blacks in some parts of the South, and the order had spread rapidly among Unionist whites in the Alabama, Georgia, and Tennessee hill country. In 1867, as blacks poured into the league, many white members either withdrew or formed segregated local chapters. Many local leagues were all-black or all-white, but integrated leagues also existed, in which black and white Republicans achieved a remarkable degree of interracial harmony. In Union County, North Carolina, a racially mixed league met "in old fields, or in some out of the way house, and elected/ed/ candidates to be received into their body."

By the end of 1867 it seemed that virtually every black voter in the South had enrolled in the Union League, the Loyal League, or some equivalent local political organization. Meetings were generally held in a black church or school, or at the home of some prominent black individual, or, if necessary, secretly in woods or fields. In Paulding, Mississippi, a hundred or more blacks, along with a few whites, met monthly at the home of Jim Cruise, a black house carpenter. Usually, a Bible and a copy of the Declaration of Independence and the Constitution lay on a table, a minister opened the meeting with a prayer, new members took an initiation oath, and there were pledges to support the Republican party and uphold the principle of equal rights.

The main function of these meetings, however, was political education. "We just went there," related Henry Holt, an illiterate black league member from North Carolina, "and we talked a little; made speeches on one question and another." Republican newspapers were read aloud, candidates were nominated for office, and political issues were debated. One racially mixed league discussed at various meetings the organization of a July 4 celebration, cooperation between the league and the Heroes of America (a secret white Unionist organization dating from the Civil War), and issues like disfranchisement, debt relief, and public education which were likely to arise at the forthcoming constitutional conventions. In Maryville, Tennessee, the Union League held weekly discussions on the issues of the day— the impeachment of President Johnson, the national debt, and such broader questions as, Is the education of the female as important as that of the male? Should students pay corporation tax? Should East Tennessee be a separate state? Although mostly white in membership in a county only one-tenth black, this league called for Tennessee to send at least one black to Congress. In 1868 its members elected a black justice of the peace and four blacks to the seven-member city commission.

It would be an error, however, to assume that the Union leagues were "political" only in the sense of electoral politics. Their multifaceted activities reflected what might be called the politicization of everyday life during Reconstruction. Colleton County, South Carolina, league members (led by a freedman with the venerable Palmetto State name Wade Hampton) marched in a body to the local magistrate demanding the arrest of a white man who had injured a black with a slingshot. A local North Carolina league official—a minister describing himself as "a poor Colord man"—proposed to Governor Holden that the league "stand as gardians" for blacks who "don't know how to make a bargain . . . and see that they get the money." In Alabama's black belt, league organizer George W. Cox was besieged by freedpeople requesting information about suing their employers, avoiding fines for attending political meetings, and ensuring a fair division of crops at harvest time. Two of the most militant collective actions by blacks during Georgia Reconstruction, the Ogeechee uprising of 1869 and Cudjo Fye's "rebellion" of 1870, were sparked by the arrest of league members by white authorities.

In 1867 and 1868 Union League activity reached its zenith. By 1869 it had begun to decline in many parts of the South, disrupted by Klan violence or absorbed into the burgeoning apparatus of the Republican party. "It

is all broke up," said one black member from Graham, North Carolina, an area of rampant Klan activity. In Texas, Republican chieftain James Tracy moved to assimilate the leagues into a more disciplined party structure, evoking strong protests from militant black leaders like the legislator Matthew Gaines. But in wide areas of the black belt, the tradition of local political organization embodied in the leagues persisted throughout Reconstruction. Sometimes the names changed, but the structure and purposes remained the same. In Abbeville County, South Carolina, the Union League was succeeded by The Brotherhood, the United Brethren, and finally, in 1875, the Laboring Union; as former slave A. J. Titus explained, "they was all laboring men, you see." In the Vicksburg region a successor to the Union League, called the "council" by blacks, met until 1874 to discuss self-protection and Republican politics. Its members, armed with pistols and shotguns, unsuccessfully resisted white efforts to oust black sheriff Peter Crosby in the Vicksburg crisis of December 1874.

In this hothouse atmosphere of political mobilization, the Union leagues generated a new class of local black political leaders. Local leaders in the black belt, where few free blacks had lived before the Civil War, and especially outside Louisiana and South Carolina, with their large and politically active freeborn communities, tended to be former slaves of very modest circumstances. Many were teachers and preachers or other individuals who possessed a skill of use to the community. Former slave Thomas Allen, a Union League organizer elected to the Georgia legislature, was a propertyless Baptist preacher, shoemaker, and farmer. But what established him as a leader was literacy: "In my county the colored people came to me for instructions, and I gave them the best instructions I could. I took the New York Tribune and other papers, and in that way I found out a great deal, and I told them whatever I thought was right." In occupation, the largest number of local black leaders appear to have been artisans, men whose skill and independence marked them as leaders but who were still deeply embedded in the life of the black community. There were others, apparently lacking in distinctive attributes of status, respected for personal qualities—oratorical ability, a reputation for moral standing, or simply good sense, honesty, or a concern for the welfare of their neighbors. Calvin Rogers, a black constable murdered by the Florida Klan, was described by another freedman as "a thorough-going man; he was a stump speaker, and tried to excite the colored people to do the right thing. . . . He would work for a man and make him pay him." Others were men who had achieved prominence as slaves before emancipation, like Louisiana justice of the peace Hamilton Gibson, a "conjurer."

In his study of social and political organizations among Memphis blacks, Armstead Robinson has identified a fairly sharp distinction between political leaders, who tended to be prosperous and light of skin, and religious/benevolent leaders, who were generally unskilled former slaves. In the less-stratified rural black belt, however, lines of occupation and social function frequently overlapped: preachers and teachers earned their living in part as artisans or laborers, politicians helped establish churches, meetings of fraternal organizations discussed political events, and Union leagues raised money for black schools. This was a world suffused with politics, in which local leaders gave articulate expression to the multiplicity of grievances and the timeless aspirations of their humble constituents.

In Union leagues, Republican gatherings, and impromptu local meetings, black and white Republicans in these years debated the basic question of the polity—What was the meaning of freedom and citizenship in republican America? Black leaders drew upon a broad range of experiences and ideas, some derived from slavery itself and others grounded in the traditions of the larger society, in defining the bounds of black politics. The language of American republicanism suffused black political culture. As Rev. J. M. Hood put it at the

North Carolina Constitutional Convention of 1868, "the colored people had read . . . the Declaration /of Independence/ until it had become part of their natures." A petition of eleven Alabama blacks complaining in 1865 of contract frauds, injustice before the courts, the refusal of whites to rent land to freedpeople, and other abuses, concluded with a revealing masterpiece of understatement: "this is not the pursuit of happiness." And ten years later, a group of Louisiana freedpeople felt it appropriate to open their petition for the removal of a hostile local official with these well-known words: "We the people of Louisiana in order to establish justice, insure domestic tranquility, promote the general welfare . . . do ordain and establish this Constitution."

There was much more here than simply accustomed language; blacks, freeborn and slave, were staking their claim to equal citizenship in the American republic. To them the republican inheritance implied the rights to vote and to education, the free exercise of religion, access to the courts, and equal opportunity in all the avenues of economic enterprise—every right already enjoyed by whites. As one black delegate to the Virginia Constitutional Convention put it, no civil right "ever enjoyed by citizens prior to the year 1861" could now justifiably be denied to blacks. Anything less would be a violation of the principles upon which the nation had been founded. As Louisiana's Oscar J. Dun insisted, "it is the boast and glory of the American republic that there is no discrimination among men, no privileges founded upon birth-right. There are no hereditary distinctions." Continued proscription of blacks, Dunn warned, would undermine the republic and "open the door for the institution of aristocracy, nobility, and even monarchy."

At their most utopian, blacks in Reconstruction envisioned a society purged of all racial distinctions. This did not mean the abandonment of race consciousness—there is abundant evidence that blacks preferred black teachers for their children as well as black churches and ministers. But in the polity, blacks, who had so long been proscribed because of their color, defined equal citizenship as color-blind. Thomas Bayne told the Virginia Constitutional Convention that his constituents expected him to help draft a constitution "that should not have the word black or white anywhere in it." Politicians seeking to arouse a sense of racial self-consciousness sometimes found black audiences unreceptive to their message. Martin Delany, the "father of black nationalism," discovered in South Carolina that it was "dangerous to go into the country and speak of color in any manner whatever, without the angry rejoinder, 'we don't want to hear that; we are all one color now." He was astonished to find that the freedpeople did not share his belief in the necessity of electing blacks (particularly Martin Delany) to office. Rather, they believed "that the Constitution had been purged of color by a Radical Congress."

The black claim to equal citizenship was grounded in more than a restatement of republican principles, however. Repeatedly in Reconstruction it was linked as well to black participation in the Civil War. Indeed, while blacks revered Lincoln as the Great Emancipator, it was also an article of faith that they had helped emancipate themselves. "They say," an Alabama planter reported in 1867, "the Yankees never could have whipped the south without the aid of the negroes." At the same time, the secular claim to citizenship was underpinned by a religious messianism deeply rooted in the black experience. As slaves, blacks had come to think of themselves as analagous to the Jews in Egypt, an oppressed people whom God, in the fullness of time, would deliver from bondage. They viewed the Civil War as God's instrument of deliverance, and Reconstruction as another step in a divinely ordained process. Black religion reinforced black republicanism, for, as Rev. J. M. P. Williams, a Mississippi legislator, put it in an address to his constituents in 1871, "my dear friends, remember this, of one blood God did

make all men to dwell upon the face of the whole earth . . . hence, their common origin, destiny and equal rights." Even among nonclerics, secular and religious modes of political discourse were virtually interchangeable. One example is a speech by North Carolina black Edwin Jones, as reported by a justice of the peace in 1867: "He said it was not now like it used to be, that . . . the negro was about to get his equal rights. . . . That the negroes owed their freedom to the courage of the negro soldiers and to God. . . . He made frequent references to the II and IV chapters of Joshua for a full accomplishment of the principles and destiny of the race. It was concluded that the race have a destiny in view similar to the Children of Israel."

Republicanism, religious messianism, and historical experience combined to produce in black political Reconstruction culture a profound sense of identification with the American polity. The very abundance of letters and petitions addressed by ordinary freedpeople to officials of the army, the Freedmen's Bureau, and state and federal authorities revealed a belief that the political order was open to black participation and persuasion. Blacks enthusiastically embraced that hallmark of the Civil War era, the rise of an activist state. With wealth, political experience, and tradition all mobilized against them in the South, blacks saw in political authority a countervailing power. On the local and state level, black officials pressed for the expansion of such public institutions as schools and hospitals. And in proposing measures (generally not enacted) for free medical care and legal assistance for the poor, government regulation of private markets, restrictions on the sale of liquor, and the outlawing of fairs and hunting on Sunday, they revealed a vision of the democratic state actively promoting the social and moral well-being of its citizenry.

It was the national government, however, that blacks ultimately viewed as the guarantor of their rights. Those whose freedom had come through the unprecedented exercise of federal authority were utterly hostile to theories of state rights and local autonomy. As Frederick Douglass put it, until Americans abandoned the idea of "the right of each State to control its own local affairs, . . . no general assertion of human rights can be of any practical value." Blacks did not share fears of "centralism" common even in the Republican party; like white Radical Republicans, black leaders found in the guarantee of republican government—the "most pregnant clause" of the Constitution, Robert B. Elliott called it—a grant of federal power ample enough to promote the welfare and protect the rights of individual citizens. Throughout Reconstruction, black political leaders supported proposals for such vast expansions of federal authority as James T. Rapier's plan for a national educational system, complete with federally mandated textbooks.

The course of events during Reconstruction reinforced this tendency to look to the national government for protection. The inability of state and local authorities to control violence prompted demands for federal intervention. "We are more slave today in the hand of the wicked than we were before," read a desperate plea from five Alabama blacks. "We need protection . . . only a standing army in this place can give us our right and life." Blacks enthusiastically supported the Enforcement Acts of 1870 and 1871 and the expansion of the powers of the federal judiciary. One black convention went so far as to insist that virtually all civil and criminal cases involving blacks be removable from state to federal courts, a mind-boggling enhancement of federal judicial authority. To constitutional objections, most blacks would agree with Congressman Joseph Rainey: "Tell me nothing of a constitution which fails to shelter beneath its rightful power the people of a country."

Republican citizenship implied more than political equality overseen by an active state, however. It helped legitimize the desire for land so pervasive among the freedpeople, for a society based upon a landed aristocracy and a large propertyless lower class could not be considered truly republican. "Small estates are the real element of democracy," wrote the *New Orleans Tribune.* "Let the land go into the hands of the actual laborers."

In 1865 and 1866 the claim to land found little expression at statewide black conventions. In 1867, however, the situation was very different. At the grass roots, demands for land among blacks and, in some areas, poor whites animated early Republican politics. The advent of suffrage and Thaddeus Stevens's introduction of a confiscation bill in the House rekindled expectations that had, in most areas, subsided after January 1866. A northern correspondent reported that "Thad Stevens' speech has been circulated among those of them who can read and fully expounded to those of them who cannot." As southern Republican parties were organized in the spring of 1867, virtually every convention found itself divided between "confiscation radicals" and more moderate elements. In Mississippi, a black delegate proposed that the party commit itself to the confiscation of Confederate estates and their distribution to freedpeople. At a black mass meeting in Richmond, a freedman announced that large holdings belonging to rebels should be confiscated for the benefit of poor, loyal blacks. The issue was most divisive in North Carolina, where local demands for land were voiced by both black Union leagues and loyalist whites in the Heroes of America. One delegate told the state Republican convention, "the people of this State have a hope in confiscation, and if that is taken away the Republican party /will/ give away the power they have gained."

The outcome of the confiscation debate reveals a great deal about the limits within which black politics could operate during Reconstruction. No state convention endorsed the idea, although a few called for planters voluntarily to sell land to impoverished freedmen. The obstacles to confiscation were indeed immense. National Republican leaders, including long-time Radicals like Henry Wilson, publicly condemned Stevens's initiative. "Let confiscation be, as it should be, an unspoken word in your state," Wilson advised North Carolina black leader James H. Harris. Democratic victories in the 1867 northern elections reinforced the conviction that Reconstruction had gone far enough; more radical policies would jeopardize Republican electoral chances in 1868 and beyond.

Even among southern Republicans there was strong opposition to the confiscation idea. Most white Republican leaders were committed to what Mark Summers calls the "Gospel of Prosperity," believing that their party's prospects hinged on a program of regional economic development and diversification. While envisioning the eventual demise of the plantation system, this "gospel" called for respect for individual enterprise and desired to encourage northern investment in the South, both seemingly incompatible with confiscation. Then, too, most white Republicans fully embraced the free labor ideology, insisting that while possession of land was unquestionably desirable, the freedpeople, like all Americans, would have to acquire it through hard work. Alabama carpetbagger C. W. Dustan solemnly announced that lands "cannot be owned without being earned, they cannot be earned without labor. . . ." (Dustan did not exactly follow this free labor prescription in his own life: he acquired a sizable holding by marrying the daughter of a Demopolis planter.)

Of course, as Thomas Holt has demonstrated, the black community itself was divided on the land question. The free labor ideology, with its respect for private property and individual initiative, was most fully embraced by two sets of black leaders—those from the North and the better-off southern free Negroes. Prominent northern blacks like Jonathan Gibbs and James Lynch would insist during Reconstruction that the interests of labor and capital were identical. Among "black carpetbaggers" only Aaron A. Bradley became actively involved in the land struggles of the freedpeople. So, too, the free black leadership

of Charleston and New Orleans rejected confiscation. At Louisiana's Republican state convention, "all the freedmen, *save one,* were in favor of confiscation, and the measure would have been adopted . . . had it not been for the energetic exertions of the white and free born colored members." Their own experience convinced successful free blacks that freedpeople required not government largesse but only an equal chance.

I have dwelt at length on the years 1867 and 1868, not only because of the remarkable political mobilization of the black community, but because many of the dilemmas that would confront black political leaders were by then already fully evident. In utopian aspirations for a New South with a reconstructed racial and economic order, these years revealed the radical potential inherent in Reconstruction. But the fate of the confiscation debate presaged the rapid waning of the radical impulse, both nationally and in the South. Increasingly, black politics took on a defensive cast; in place of demands for a fundamental restructuring of southern society, politics came to revolve around preserving what gains had been achieved and making the existing order operate fairly (a difficult task at best in a plantation society).

Comprising the vast majority of Republican voters, blacks would remain junior partners within the party. Even in Louisiana they would be barred from the most important positions; as one prominent black there complained in 1874, "we share, neither . . . in the control of the government which we have created, nor participate in the patronage resulting from political victories we have won." Only in Mississippi and South Carolina would blacks come to play a dominant role in shaping Reconstruction policy. But even there, politics never escaped a "colonial" pattern—the interests of the national Republican party always took precedence over the needs of the localities. Unable to establish their own legitimacy in the eyes of their powerful opponents, the survival of the new southern governments ultimately rested on federal support. Thus, the boundaries of Reconstruction were determined in Washington. As Albert T. Morgan observed of Mississippi, "three-fourths of the republican members of the Legislature regard themselves as still under the control and dominion of *Congress* as the supreme government. They can hardly settle our per diem without the feeling of *subserviency to Congress.*"

As Reconstruction wore on, black political leaders were caught in a web of seemingly insoluble dilemmas. The few black congressmen had to choose between supporting national economic policies like a deflationary monetary program, arguably detrimental to the interests of their constituents, and joining Democrats in opposition, which would further alienate northern Republican support. Their broad conception of federal authority was increasingly out of step with a national party described by U.S. Attorney General Amos T. Akerman as "anxious for an end of Southern troubles" and convinced that "Southern Republicans must cease to look for special support to Congressional action." By the mid-1870s it was well understood in the South that the remaining Republican states could expect no help from federal authorities. Former slave Jerry Thornton Moore, president of a local Republican club in Aiken County, South Carolina, was told by his white landlord that Democrats planned to carry the 1876 elections "if we have to wade in blood knee-deep." "Mind what you are doing," Moore responded; "the United States is mighty strong." Replied the white man, "but, Thornton, . . . the northern people is on our side."

Increasingly abandoned by the national party, black politicians had nowhere to turn. Democrats offered even less than Republicans, and at any rate, black voters refused to countenance independent politics. When Alabama legislator C. S. Smith proposed to the 1876 national black convention that blacks declare their political autonomy, he won hearty applause inside the hall, but "colored men on street corners" spoke of cutting his throat.

Blanche K. Bruce earned a grass-roots reputation as a "conservative negro" for a Senate speech condemning Republican indifference to the plight of southern freedpeople. When Edward Shaw, a prominent Memphis black leader, ran for Congress in 1870 against the white Republican incumbent, he received only 165 votes. The 1870s did witness a rise in black political assertiveness and an increase (where Reconstruction survived) in the number of blacks holding office, but this could only take place within the context of the Republican party.

At the local level, numerous enclaves of genuine black political power existed during Reconstruction. Reporter Edward King, traveling across the South in 1873 and 1874, encountered many examples of black officeholding—black aldermen and city councilmen in Petersburg, Houston, and Little Rock; parish jury members in Louisiana; black magistrates in the South Carolina low country. Hundreds, perhaps thousands of blacks held positions ranging from constable to school board official, tax assessor, and sheriff. Their numbers were fewest in states like Georgia and Florida, where conservative Republicans had drafted constitutions centralizing appointive power in the hands of the governor, and most extensive in South Carolina and Mississippi. About a third of Mississippi's black population lived in one of the thirteen counties that elected a black sheriff, the official who collected taxes, appointed registrars, and controlled selection of juries.

The existence of black and sympathetic white local officials often made a real difference in the day-to-day lives of the freedpeople, ensuring that those accused of crimes would be tried before juries of their peers (who, whites complained, often refused to convict in cases of vagrancy or theft) and enforcing fairness in such prosaic aspects of local government as road repair, public employment, and poor relief. In Louisiana, blacks, whites, and Chinese were employed to repair the levees, and, in a startling departure from traditional practice, all received the same wages. As the chief engineer reported, "our 'Cadian friends were a little disgusted at not being allowed double (colored) wages, and the Chinamen were astonished at being allowed as much and the American citizens of African descent were delighted at being *'par.'* " Any doubt as to the importance of sympathetic local officials is quickly dispelled by a glance at the conduct of local government in counties remaining under Democratic control (as well as some localities dominated by conservative white Republicans.) In such areas blacks persistently complained of exclusion from juries, discrimination in tax assessment and collection, and an inability to obtain justice before the courts. In one Democratic Alabama county in 1870, a black woman brutally beaten by a group of white men was forced to raise $16.45 for court costs before the judge released the offenders and instructed the injured woman to drop the matter or face a jail sentence. This state of affairs harked back to the mockery of justice practiced in southern courts during Presidential Reconstruction and looked ahead to the situation that would obtain under the Redeemers.

For some black politicos, as for many whites in nineteenth-century America, official positions became a means of social advancement. Politics was one of the few areas of dignified work open to black men of talent and ambition, and compared with other employment opportunities, the rewards of even minor office could seem dazzlingly high. The thirteen dollars per diem earned by members of the Louisiana Constitutional Convention, or the seven dollars per day plus mileage paid to North Carolina legislators, far outstripped the wages most blacks could ordinarily command. More important offices garnered far higher rewards—sheriffs could earn thousands of dollars in commissions and fees, and state officeholders were handsomely paid during Reconstruction. Blacks consistently opposed attempts to reduce the pay of officials. As one black put it at the Virginia Constitutional Convention, "the salary is none too great. Many of us have no incomes." And, at any rate, as another black delegate observed, "all our troubles have arisen from not paying people for their services."

Some black politicians translated official positions into significant personal gain. Josiah Walls, a Florida congressman, was able to acquire a large estate formerly owned by Confederate general James H. Harrison, and Senator Blanche K. Bruce accumulated a fortune in real estate. Louisiana lieutenant governor C. C. Antoine owned an expensive racehorse whose earnings were considerable. On a less-exalted level, about one-third of the forty-six blacks who served in the Virginia legislature used their salaries to purchase land. Like white politicos, some black officials were less than scrupulous in the pursuit of wealth. P. B. S. Pinchback, who lived in luxury in New Orleans, told a reporter that his wealth derived from "speculation upon warrants, bonds and stocks." Pinchback forthrightly admitted that inside information enabled his speculations to succeed: "I belonged to the General Assembly, and knew about what it would do. . . . My investments were made accordingly."

For most black leaders, however, politics brought little personal wealth. Even the most prominent found it difficult to translate political standing into a real share in the economic resources of their states. A Charleston streetcar company formed by leading black politicians and chartered by the state failed, as did the Mississippi River Packet Company organized by Pinchback, Antoine, and others. The black community was too poor to subscribe capital to such endeavors, and whites shunned them entirely.

Far from being a vehicle for social mobility, politics in many cases entailed devastating financial loss. Former slave Henry Johnson, a South Carolina Union League and militia leader, was a bricklayer and plasterer by trade. "I always had plenty of work before I went into politics," he remarked, "but I have never got a job since. I suppose they do it merely because they think they will break me down and keep me from interfering with politics." Jefferson Long, a Macon tailor, had commanded "much of the fine custom of the city" before embarking upon a career that would take him briefly to Congress. However, "his stand in politics ruined his business with the whites who had been his patrons chiefly." Robert Reed, a black Alabama legislator, was told by local whites "that there is not a white man in the State that can beat me farming, and if I kept out of politics I would be the richest man in the State." Reed did not stop political organizing, but the costs of such commitment could be high. When North Carolina black leader A. H. Galloway, a former soldier, brick mason, and state legislator, passed away in 1870, a black newspaper commented, "He died poor, very poor."

Loss of livelihood was not the most serious danger black political leaders had to face. Political violence, so pervasive in large portions of the Reconstruction South, was often directed precisely at local leaders—black officeholders, Union League organizers, and militia captains. As Emanuel Fortune, himself driven from Jackson County, Florida, by the Klan, explained, "the object of it is to kill out the leading men of the republican party. . . . They have never attacked any one but those who have been somewhat prominent in the party, men who have taken prominent stands." At least 10 percent of the black delegates to the 1867–68 constitutional conventions were victims of violence, including six actually murdered. Other assassination victims included men like Richard Burke, an Alabama preacher, schoolteacher, legislator, and Union League officer, and Wyatt Outlaw, Republican organizer in Alamance county, North Carolina. During the mid-1870s Redemption campaigns, political violence claimed the lives of black constables and justices of the peace in Issaquena County, Mississippi, and black militiamen and local officials in Hamburg, South Carolina, among many others. For every leader murdered, many more were driven from their homes. To remain politically active in such circumstances

required a rare degree of personal courage and the kind of integrity epitomized by former slave David Graham, a deputy U.S. marshal in South Carolina, who told a congressional committee: "The white people liked me very well until I got into politics, and they have hated me ever since. . . . I heap rather farm than be in politics; politics is the most disgusting thing I was ever in in my life. I can't sleep in my house only part of the time. I want to get out of politics, but here I is; these other leading fellows can't get along without me."

Violence devastated the Republican party in many a local community. After a series of outrages in Union County, South Carolina, one black commented, "the Republican party, I may say, is scattered and beaten and run out. . . . They have no leaders up there—no leaders." The reign of terror in Yazoo County, Mississippi, in 1875, according to one black official, "got the republicans so demoralized that we did not know what to do. We had no leaders. Every leader had been run out of the town and out of the county. They did not know what to do, so they just 'hung up.' "

Indeed, it might be argued that the black community was more dependent on its political leadership, more vulnerable to the destruction of its political infrastructure by violence, than the white community. Local black leaders played such a variety of roles in schools, churches, and fraternal organizations, as well as politics, that the killing or exiling of one man affected a multiplicity of areas. For a largely illiterate constituency, local leaders were bridges to the larger world of politics, indispensable sources of political information and guidance. They were also looked to for assistance in contract disputes, advice about the marketing of crops, and all sorts of other issues. John R. Lynch later recalled how, when he served as a Mississippi justice of the peace, free blacks "magnified" his office "far beyond its importance," bringing him complaints ranging from disputes with their employers to family squabbles. Black officials epitomized the revolution that seemed to have put the bottom rail on top, the openness of the new political order to black influence. Their murder or exile inevitably had a demoralizing impact upon their communities.

Alone among the nations that abolished slavery in this hemisphere, the United States accorded its former slaves legal and political equality within a few years after emancipation. The unprecedented character of this development, the sense among blacks that their newly won rights were constantly at risk, the refusal of large numbers of Democrats to acknowledge freed blacks as part of the "political nation," helps explain the abnormal aspects of Reconstruction politics—the high degree of political mobilization in the black community, the burdens placed upon black leaders by their constituents, and the widespread use of violence and economic coercion as political weapons.

In the spring of 1868 a northern correspondent, reporting on election day in Alabama, captured the sense of hope with which Reconstruction opened, the conviction among the enfranchised black voters that politics could indeed change their lives. "In defiance of fatigue, hardship, hunger, the threats of employers," blacks had flocked to the polls. Not one in fifty wore an "unpatched garment," few possessed a pair of shoes, yet they stood for hours in line in a "pitiless storm." Why? "The hunger to have the same chances as the white men they feel and comprehend. . . . That is what brings them here" to vote. With the overthrow of Reconstruction, politics could no longer serve as an effective vehicle for expressing such aspirations. The emerging black political class was devastated by Redemption—murdered or driven from their communities by violence or deprived of the opportunity to hold office, except in a few exceptional areas of the South. Black politicians ceased to exercise real power, apart from a handful of men dependent on federal patronage and on prominent politicos who advised Republican presidents on token appointments for blacks. Men of ambition in the black community now found other outlets for their talents, whether in education, business, the church, or the professions. Nearly a century would pass before the southern black community was again as fully galvanized at the grass roots by political activity.

2

THE CHINESE LINK A CONTINENT AND A NATION

JACK CHEN

It is an historical commonplace that America is a nation of immigrants. From the original settlers of Jamestown in 1607 to the Hispanic and Asian immigrants of the 1980s new Americans have loomed large in the national experience. But while immigration has always played an important role in American life, its impact was perhaps greatest during America's industrial revolution of the nineteenth century. From the 1820s, when 100,000 men, women, and children entered the United States, to the first decade of the twentieth century, when 8.2 million landed on American shores, more than 33 million immigrants came to the United States and helped build it into the world's premier industrial power.

Among these millions of immigrants, one group has received scant attention—the Chinese peasants, almost entirely males, who came to America as contract laborers to provide agricultural labor for California's central valley and to build railroads and levees in the West. Unlike European immigrants who arrived as free men and women in New York and other eastern cities, the Chinese who landed in San Francisco were bound to the mercantile companies that acted as labor contractors and had advanced them the cost of their fare. Under this contract system, one of the Six Companies in San Francisco negotiated with an employer and agreed to provide workers at an agreed-upon rate. The Companies were then responsible for the supply, supervision, and discipline of the contract laborers.

As Jack Chen shows in this essay, these Chinese contract laborers braved the harshest of conditions to fulfill their contract to build America's first transcontinental railroad. Employing skills in excavation and the use of explosives which they had brought from China, these Chinese workingmen carved a path through the solid granite of the Sierra Nevada range that opened the West to the remainder of the nation.

The expansion of the railroad system in the United States was astonishingly swift. England had pioneered the building of railways and for a time was the acknowledged leader in the field, but from the moment the first locomotive was imported into the United States in 1829 the farsighted saw railways as the obvious solution for transport across the vast spaces of the American continent. By 1850, 9,000 miles of rails had been laid in the eastern states and up to the Mississippi. The California Gold Rush and the opening of the American West made talk about a transcontinental line more urgent. As too often happens, war spurred the realization of this project.

The West was won. California was a rich and influential state, but a wide unsettled belt of desert, plain, and mountains, separated it and Oregon from the rest of the states. As the economic separation of North and South showed, this situation was fraught with danger. It could lead to a political rift. In 1860, it was cheaper and quicker to reach San Francisco from Canton in China—a sixty-day voyage by sea—than from the Missouri River, six months away by wagon train. The urgent need was to link California firmly with the industrialized eastern states and their 30,000 miles of railways. A railway would cut the journey to a week. The threat of civil war loomed larger between North and South over the slavery issue. Abraham Lincoln's Republican administration saw a northern transcontinental railway as a means to outflank the South by drawing the western states closer to the North. In 1862, Congress voted funds to build the 2,500-mile-long railway. It required enormous resourcefulness and determination to get this giant project off the drawing boards. Not much imagination was required to see its necessity, but the actual building presented daunting difficulties. It was calculated that its cost would mount to $100 million, double the federal budget of 1861.

It was Theodore Judah, described by his contemporaries as "Pacific Railroad Crazy," who began to give substance to the dream. An eastern engineer who had come west to build the short Sacramento Valley Railroad, he undertook a preliminary survey and reported that he had found a feasible route crossing the Sierra by way of Dutch Flat. But the mainly small investors who supported his efforts could not carry through the whole immense undertaking. With rumors of civil war between North and South, San Francisco capitalists, mostly Southerners, boycotted the scheme as a northern plot, and pressed for a southern route. Then the Big Four, Sacramento merchants, took up the challenge: Leland Stanford as president, C. P. Huntington as vice-president, Mark Hopkins as treasurer, and Charles Crocker, in charge of construction, formed the Central Pacific Railway Company. Judah was elbowed out.

The Big Four came as gold seekers in 1849 or soon after but found that there was more money to be made in storekeeping than in scrabbling in the rocks in the mountains. As Republicans, they held the state for the Union against the secessionists. Leland Stanford, the first president of the Central Pacific, was also the first Republican governor of California.

The beginnings were not auspicious. The Union Pacific was building from Omaha in the East over the plains to the Rockies, but supplies had to come in by water or wagon because the railways had not yet reached Omaha. The Civil War now raged and manpower, materials and funds were hard to get. The Indians were still contesting invasion of their lands. By 1864, however, with the Civil War ending, these problems were solved. The UP hired Civil War veterans, Irish immigrants fleeing famine and even Indian women, and the line began to move westward.

The Central Pacific, building eastward from Sacramento, had broken ground on January 8, 1863, but in 1864, beset by money and labor problems, it had built only thirty-one miles of track. It had an even more intractable manpower problem than the UP. California was sparsely populated, and the gold mines, homesteading, and other lucrative employments offered stiff competition for labor. Brought to the railhead, three out of every five men quit immediately and took off for the better prospects of the new Nevada silver strikes. Even Charles Crocker, boss of construction and raging like a mad bull in the railway camps, could not control them. In the winter of 1864, the company had only 600 men working on the line when it had advertised for 5,000. Up to then, only white labor had been recruited and California white labor was still motivated by the Gold Rush syndrome. They wanted quick wealth, not hard, regimented railway work. After two years only fifty miles of track had been laid.

James Strobridge, superintendent of construction, testified to the 1876 Joint Congressional Committee on Chinese Immigration: "/These/ were unsteady men, unreliable. Some would not go to work at all. . . . Some would stay until pay day, get a little money, get drunk and clear out." Something drastic had to be done.

In 1858, fifty Chinese had helped to build the California Central Railroad from Sacramento to Marysville. In 1860, Chinese were working on the San Jose Railway and giving a good account of themselves, so it is surprising that there was so much hesitation about employing them on the Central Pacific's western end of the first transcontinental railway. Faced with a growing crisis of no work done and mounting costs, Crocker suggested hiring Chinese. Strobridge strongly objected: "I will not boss Chinese. I don't think they could build a railroad." Leland Stanford was also reluctant. He had advocated exclusion of the Chinese from California and was embarrassed to reverse himself. Crocker, Huntington, Hopkins, and Stanford, the "Big Four" of the Central Pacific, were all merchants in hardware, dried goods, and groceries in the little town of Sacramento. Originally, they knew nothing about railroad building, but they were astute and hard-headed businessmen. Crocker was insistent. Wasted time was wasted money. The CP's need for labor was critical. The men they already had were threatening a strike. Finally fifty Chinese were hired for a trial.

BUILDING THE TRANSCONTINENTAL RAILROAD

In February 1865, they marched up in self-formed gangs of twelve to twenty men with their own supplies and cooks for each mess. They ate a meal of rice and dried cuttlefish, washed and slept, and early next morning were ready for work filling dump carts. Their discipline and grading—preparing the ground for track laying—delighted Strobridge. Soon fifty more were hired, and finally some 15,000 had been put on the payroll. Crocker was enthusiastic: "They prove nearly equal to white men in the amount of labor they perform, and are much more reliable. No danger of strikes among them. We are training them to all kinds of labor: blasting, driving horses, handling rock as well as pick and shovel." Countering Strobridge's argument that the Chinese were "not masons," Crocker pointed out that the race that built the Great Wall could certainly build a railroad culvert. Up on the Donner Pass today the fine stonework embankments built by the Chinese are serving well after a hundred years.

Charles Nordhoff, an acute observer, reports Strobridge telling him, "/The Chinese/ learn all parts of the work easily." Nordhoff says he saw them "employed on every kind of work. . . . They do not drink, fight or strike; they do gamble, if it is not prevented; and it is always said of them that they are very cleanly in their habits. It is the custom, among them, after they have had their suppers every evening, to bathe with the help of small tubs. I doubt if the white laborers do as much." As well he might. Well-run boardinghouses in California in those days proudly advertised that they provided guests with a weekly bath.

Their wages at the start were $28 a month (twenty-six working days), and they furnished all their own food, cooking utensils, and tents. The headman of each gang, or sometimes an American employed as clerk by them received all the wages and handed them out to the members of the work gang according to what had been earned. "Competent and wonderfully effective because tireless and unremitting in their industry," they worked from sun-up to sun-down.

All observers remarked on the frugality of the Chinese. This was not surprising in view of the fact that, with a strong sense of filial duty, they came to America in order to save money and return as soon as possible to their homes and families in China. So they usually dressed poorly, and their dwellings were of the simplest. However, they ate well: rice and vermicelli (noodles) garnished with meats and vegetables; fish, dried oysters, cuttlefish, bacon and pork, and chicken on holidays, abalone meat, five kinds of dried vegetables, bamboo shoots, seaweed, salted cabbage, and mushroom, four kinds of dried fruit, and peanut oil and tea. This diet shows a considerable degree of sophistication and balance compared to the beef, beans, potatoes, bread, and butter of the white laborers. Other supplies were purchased from the shop maintained by a Chinese merchant contractor in one of the railway cars that followed them as they carried the railway line forward. Here they could buy pipes, tobacco, bowls, chopsticks, lamps, Chinese-style shoes of cotton with soft cotton soles, and ready-made clothing imported from China.

On Sundays, they rested, did their washing, and gambled. They were prone to argue noisily, but did not become besotted with whiskey and make themselves unfit for work on Monday. Their sobriety was much appreciated by their employers.

Curtis, the engineer in charge, described them as "the best roadbuilders in the world." The once skeptical Strobridge, a smart, pushing Irishman, also now pronounced them "the best in the world." Leland Stanford described them in a report on October 10, 1865, to Andrew Johnson:

> As a class, they are quiet, peaceable, patient, industrious, and economical. More prudent and economical /than white laborers/ they are contented with less wages. We find them organized for mutual aid and assistance. Without them, it would be impossible to complete the western portion of this great national enterprise within the time required by the Act of Congress.

Crocker testified before the congressional committee that "if we found that we were in a hurry for a job of work, it was better to put on Chinese at once." All these men had originally resisted the employment of Chinese on the railway.

Four-fifths of the grading labor from Sacramento to Ogden was done by Chinese. In a couple of years more, of 13,500 workers on the payroll 12,000 were Chinese. They were nick-named "Crocker's Pets."

APPRECIATING CHINESE SKILLS

The Chinese crews won their reputation the hard way. They outperformed Cornish men brought in at extra wages to cut rock. Crocker testified,

> They would cut more rock in a week than the Cornish miners, and it was hard work, bone labor. /They/ were skilled in using the hammer and drill, and they proved themselves equal to the very best Cornish miners in that work. They were very trusty, they were intelligent, and they lived up to their contracts.

Stanford held the Chinese workers in such high esteem that he provided in his will for the permanent employment of a large number on his estates. In the 1930s, some of their descendants were still living and working lands now owned by Stanford University.

The Chinese saved the day for Crocker and his colleagues. The terms of agreement with the government were that the railway companies would be paid from $16,000 to $48,000 for each mile of track laid. But there were only so many miles between the two terminal points of the projected line. The Union Pacific Company, working with 10,000 mainly Irish immigrants and Civil War veterans, had the advantage of building the line through Nebraska over the plains and made steady progress. The Central Pacific, after the first easy twenty-three miles between Newcastle and Colfax, had to conquer the granite mountains and gorges of the Sierra Nevada and Rockies before it could emerge onto the Nevada-Utah plains and make real speed and money. The line had to rise 7,000 feet in 100 miles over daunting terrain. Crocker and the Chinese proved up to the challenge. After reaching Cisco, there was no easy going. The line had to be literally carved out of the Sierra granite, through tunnels and on rock ledges cut on the side of precipices.

Using techniques from China, they attacked one of the most difficult parts of the work: carrying the line over Cape Horn, with its sheer granite buttresses and steep shale embankments, 2,000 feet above the American River canyon. There was no foothold on its flanks. The indomitable Chinese, using age-old ways, were lowered from above in rope-held baskets, and there, suspended between earth and sky, they began to chip away with hammer and crowbar to form the narrow ledge that was later laboriously deepened to a shelf wide enough for the railway roadbed, 1,400 feet above the river.

Behind the advancing crews of Chinese builders came the money and supplies to keep the work going. This was an awesome exercise in logistics. The Big Four, unscrupulous, dishonest, and ruthless on a grand scale, were the geniuses of this effort. The marvel of engineering skill being created by Strobridge and his Chinese and Irish workers up in the Sierra was fed by a stream of iron rails, spikes, tools, blasting powder, locomotives, cars, and machinery. These materials arrived after an expensive and hazardous eight-month, 15,000-mile voyage from East Coast ports around Cape Horn to San Francisco, thence by river boat to Sacramento, and so to the railhead by road.

The weather, as well as the terrain, was harsh. The winter of 1865–1866 was one of the severest on record. Snow fell early, and storm after storm blanketed the Sierra Nevada. The ground froze solid. Sixty-foot drifts of snow had to be shoveled away before the graders could even reach the roadbed. Nearly half the work force of 9,000 men were set to clearing snow.

In these conditions, construction crews tackled the most formidable obstacle in their path: building the ten Summit Tunnels on the twenty-mile stretch between Cisco, ninety-two miles from Sacramento and Lake Ridge just west of Cold Stream Valley on the eastern slope of the summit. Work went on at all the tunnels simultaneously. Three shifts of eight hours each worked day and night.

The builders lived an eerie existence. In *The Big Four,* Oscar Lewis writes,

> Tunnels were dug beneath forty-foot drifts and for months, 3,000 workmen lived curious mole-like lives, passing from work to living quarters in dim passages far beneath the snow's surface. . . . *[There]* was constant danger, for as snows accumulated on the upper ridges, avalanches grew frequent, their approach heralded only by a brief thunderous roar. A second later, a work crew, a bunkhouse, an entire camp would go hurtling at a dizzy speed down miles of frozen canyon. Not until months later were the bodies recovered; sometimes groups were found with shovels or picks still clutched in their frozen hands.

On Christmas Day, 1866, the papers reported that "a gang of Chinamen employed by the railroad were covered up by a snow slide and four or five *[note the imprecision]* died before they could be exhumed." A whole camp of Chinese railway workers was enveloped during one night and had to be rescued by shovelers the next day.

No one has recorded the names of those who gave their lives in this stupendous undertaking. It is known that the bones of 1,200 men were shipped back to China to be buried in the land of their forefathers, but that was by no means the total score. The engineer John Gills recalled that "at Tunnel No. 10, some 15–20 Chinese [again, note the imprecision] were killed by a slide that winter. The year before, in the winter of 1864–65, two wagon road repairers had been buried and killed by a slide at the same location."

A. P. Partridge, who worked on the line, describes how 3,000 Chinese builders were driven out of the mountains by the early snow. "Most . . . came to Truckee and filled up all the old buildings and sheds. An old barn collapsed and killed four Chinese. A good many were frozen to death." One is astonished at the fortitude, discipline and dedication of the Chinese railroad workers.

Many years later, looking at the Union Pacific section of the line, an old railwayman remarked, "There's an Irishman buried under every tie of that road." Brawling, drink, cholera, and malaria took a heavy toll. The construction crew towns on the Union Pacific part of the track, with their saloons, gambling dens, and bordellos, were nicknamed "hells on wheels." Jack Casement, in charge of construction there, had been a general in the Civil War and prided himself on the discipline of his fighting forces. His work crews worked with military precision, but off the job they let themselves go. One day, after gambling in the streets on payday (instigated by professional gamblers) had gotten too much out of hand, a visitor, finding the street suddenly very quiet, asked him where the gamblers had gone. Casement pointed to a nearby cemetery and replied, "They all died with their boots on." It was still the Wild West.

It is characteristic that only one single case of violent brawling was reported among the Chinese from the time they started work until they completed the job.

The Central Pacific's Chinese became expert at all kinds of work: grading, drilling, masonry, and demolition. Using black powder, they could average 1.18 feet daily through granite so hard that an incautiously placed charge could blow out backward. The Summit Tunnel work force was entirely composed of

Chinese, with mainly Irish foremen. Thirty to forty worked on each face, with twelve to fifteen on the heading and the rest on the bottom removing material.

The Donner tunnels, totaling 1,695 feet, had to be bored through solid rock, and 9,000 Chinese worked on them. To speed the work, a new and untried explosive, nitroglycerin, was used. The tunnels were completed in November 1867, after thirteen months. But winter began before the way could be opened and the tracks laid. That winter was worse than the preceding one, but to save time it was necessary to send crews ahead to continue building the line even while the tunnels were being cut. Therefore, 3,000 men were sent with 400 carts and horses to Palisade Canyon, 300 miles in advance of the railhead. "Hay, grain and all supplies for men and horses had to be hauled by teams over the deserts for that great distance," writes Strobridge. "Water for men and animals was hauled at times 40 miles." Trees were felled and the logs laid side by side to form a "corduroy" roadway. On log sleds greased with lard, hundreds of Chinese manhandled three locomotives and forty wagons over the mountains. Strobridge later testified that it "cost nearly three times what it would have cost to have done it in the summertime when it should have been done. But we shortened the time seven years from what Congress expected when the act was passed."

Between 10,000 and 11,000 men were kept working on the line from 1866 to 1869. The Sison and Wallace Company (in which Crocker's brother was a leading member) and the Dutch merchant Cornelius Koopmanschap of San Francisco procured these men for the line. Through the summer of 1866, Crocker's Pets—6,000 strong—swarmed over the upper canyons of the Sierra, methodically slicing cuttings and pouring rock and debris to make landfills and strengthen the foundations of trestle bridges. Unlike the Caucasian laborers, who drank unboiled stream water, the Chinese slaked their thirst with weak tea and boiled water kept in old whiskey kegs filled by their mess cooks. They kept themselves clean and healthy by daily sponge baths in tubs of hot water prepared by their cooks, and the work went steadily forward.

Crocker has been described as a "hulking, relentless driver of men." But his Chinese crews responded to his leadership and drive and were caught up in the spirit of the epic work on which they were engaged. They cheered and waved their cartwheel hats as the first through train swept down the eastern slopes of the Sierra to the meeting of the lines. They worked with devotion and self-sacrifice to lay that twenty-odd miles of track for the Central Pacific Company in 1866 over the most difficult terrain. The cost of those miles was enormous—$280,000 a mile—but it brought the builders in sight of the easier terrain beyond the Sierra and the Rockies. Here costs of construction by veteran crews were only half the estimated amount of federal pay.

By summer 1868, an army of 14,000 railway builders was passing over the mountains into the great interior plain. Nine-tenths of that work force was Chinese. More than a quarter of all Chinese in the country were building the railway.

When every available Chinese in California had been recruited for the work, the Central Pacific arranged with Chinese labor contractors in San Francisco to get men direct from China and send them up to the railhead. It was evidently some of these newcomers who fell for the Piute Indian's tall tales of snakes in the desert "big enough to swallow a man easily." Thereupon "four or five hundred Chinese took their belongings and struck out to return directly to Sacramento," reports the *Alta California.* "Crocker and Company had spent quite a little money to secure them and they sent men on horseback after them. Most of them came back again kind of quieted down, and after nothing happened and they never saw any of the snakes, they forgot about them." At least one Chinese quit the job for a similar reason. His daughter, married to a professor of Chinese art, told me that her father had worked on the railway but quit because "he was scared of the bears." He later went into domestic service.

By September 1868, the track was completed for 307 miles from Sacramento, and the crews were laying rails across the plain east of the Sierra. Parallel with the track layers went the telegraph installers, stringing their wires on the poles and keeping the planners back at headquarters precisely apprised of where the end of the track was.

THE GREAT RAILWAY COMPETITION

On the plains, the Chinese worked in tandem with all the Indians Crocker could entice to work on the iron rails. They began to hear of the exploits of the Union Pacific's "Irish terriers" building from the east. One day, the Irish laid six miles of track. The Chinese topped this with seven. "No Chinaman is going to beat us," growled the Irish, and the next day, they laid seven and half miles of track. They swore that they would outperform the competition no matter what it did.

Crocker taunted the Union Pacific that his men could lay ten miles of track a day. Durant, president of the rival line, laid a $10,000 wager that it could not be done. Crocker took no chances. He waited until the day before the last sixteen miles of track had to be laid and brought up all needed suplies for instant use. Then he unleashed his crews. On April 28, 1869, while Union Pacific checkers and newspaper reporters looked on, a combined gang of Chinese and eight picked Irish rail handlers laid ten miles and 1,800 feet more of track in twelve hours. This record was never surpassed until the advent of mechanized track laying. Each Irishman that day walked a total distance of ten miles, and their combined muscle handled sixty tons of rail.

So keen was the competition that when the two lines approached each other, instead of changing direction to link up, their builders careered on and on for 100 miles, building lines that would never meet. Finally, the government prescribed that the linkage point should be Promontory, Utah.

Competition was keen, but there seems to be no truth in the story that the Chinese and Irish in this phase of work were trying to blow each other up with explosives. It is a fact, however, that when the two lines were very near each other, the Union Pacific blasters did not give the Central Pacific men timely warning when setting off a charge, and several Chinese were hurt. Then a Central Pacific charge went off unannounced and several Irishmen found themselves buried in dirt. This forced the foremen to take up the matter and an amicable settlement was arranged. There was no further trouble.

On May 10, 1869, the two lines were officially joined at Promontory, north of Ogden in Utah. A great crowd gathered. A band played. An Irish crew and a Chinese crew were chosen to lay the last two rails side by side. The last tie was made of polished California laurel with a silver plate in its center proclaiming it "The last tie laid on the completion of the Pacific Railroad, May 10, 1869." But when the time came it was nowhere to be found. As consternation mounted, four Chinese approached with it on their shoulders and they laid it beneath the rails. A photographer stepped up and someone shouted to him "Shoot!" The Chinese only knew one meaning for that word. They fled. But order was restored and the famous ceremony began; Stanford drove a golden spike into the last tie with a silver hammer. The news flashed by telegraph to a waiting nation. But no Chinese appears in that famous picture of the toast celebrating the joining of the rails.

Crocker was one of the few who paid tribute to the Chinese that day: "I wish to call to your minds that the early completion of this railroad we have built has been in large measure due to that poor, despised class of laborers called the Chinese, to the fidelity and industry they have shown." No one even mentioned the name of Judah.

The building of the first transcontinental railway stands as a monument to the union of Yankee and Chinese-Irish drive and know-how. This was a formidable combination. They all complemented each other. Together they did in seven years what was expected to take at least fourteen.

In his book on the building of the railway, John Galloway, the noted transportation engineer, described this as "without doubt the greatest engineering feat of the nineteenth century," and that has never been disputed. David D. Colton, then vice-president of the Southern Pacific, was similarly generous in his praise of the Chinese contribution. He was asked, while giving evidence before the 1876 congressional committee, "Could you have constructed that road without Chinese labor?" He replied, "I do not think it could have been constructed so quickly, and with anything like the same amount of certainty as to what we were going to accomplish in the same length of time."

And, in answer to the question, "Do you think the Chinese have been a benefit to the State?" West Evans, a railway contractor, testified, "I do not see how we could do the work we have done, here, without them; at least I have done work that would not have been done if it had not been for the Chinamen, work that could not have been done without them."

It was heroic work. The Central Pacific crews had carried their railway 1,800 miles through the Sierra and Rocky mountains, over sagebrush desert and plain. The Union Pacific built only 689 miles, over much easier terrain. It had 500 miles in which to carry its part of the line to a height of 5,000 feet, with another fifty more miles in which to reach the high passes of the Black Hills. With newly recruited crews, the Central Pacific had to gain an altitude of 7,000 feet from the plain in just over 100 miles and make a climb of 2,000 feet in just 20 miles.

All this monumental work was done before the age of mechanization. It was pick and shovel, hammer and crowbar work, with baskets for earth carried slung from shoulder poles and put on one-horse carts.

For their heroic work, the Chinese workmen began with a wage of $28 a month, providing their own food and shelter. This was gradually raised to $30 to $35 a month. Caucasians were paid the same amount of money, but their food and shelter were provided. Because it cost $0.75 to $1.00 a day to feed a white unskilled worker, each Chinese saved the Central Pacific, at a minimum, two-thirds the price of a white laborer (1865 rates). Chinese worked as masons, dynamiters, and blacksmiths and at other skilled jobs that paid white workers from $3 to $5 a day. So, at a minimum, the company saved about $5 million by hiring Chinese workers.

Did this really "deprive white workers of jobs" as anti-Chinese agitators claimed. Certainly not. In the first place, experience had proved that white workers simply did not want the jobs the Chinese took on the railroad. In fact, the Chinese created jobs for white workers as straw bosses, foremen, railhandlers, teamsters, and supervisors.

The wages paid to the Chinese were, in fact, comparable to those paid unskilled or semi-skilled labor in the East (where labor was relatively plentiful), and the Chinese were at first satisfied. Charles Nordhoff estimated that the frugal Chinese could save about $13 a month out of those wages. The *Alta California* estimated their savings at $20 a month and later, perhaps, as wages increased, they could lay aside even more. With a bit of luck, a year and a half to two years of work would enable them to return to China with $400 to buy a bit of land and be well-to-do farmers.

But the Chinese began to learn the American way of life. On one occasion in June 1867, 2,000 tunnelers went on strike, asking for $40 a month, an eight-hour day in the tunnels, and an end to beating by foremen. "Eight hours a day good for white man, all same good for Chinese," said their spokesman in the pidgin English common in the construction camps. But solidarity with the other workers was lacking, and after a week the strike was called off when the Chinese heard that Crocker was recruiting strikebreakers from the eastern states.

When the task was done, most of the Chinese railwaymen were paid off. Some returned to China with their hard-earned savings, and the epic story of building the Iron Horse's pathway across the continent must have regaled many a family gathering there. Some returned with souvenirs of the great work, chips of one of the last ties, which had been dug up and split up among them. Some settled in the little towns that had grown up along the line of the railway. Others took the railway to seek adventure further east and south. Most made their way back to California and took what jobs they could find in that state's growing industries, trades, and other occupations. Many used their traditional and newly acquired skills on the other transcontinental lines and railways that were being swiftly built in the West and Midwest. This was the start of the diaspora of the Chinese immigrants in America.

The Union and Central Pacific tycoons had done well out of the building of the line. Congressional investigation committees later calculated that, of $73 million poured into the Union Pacific coffers, no more than $50 million could be justified as true costs. The Big Four and their associates in the Central Pacific had done even better. They had made at least $63 million and owned most of the CP stock worth around $100 million and 9 million acres of land grants to boot.

Ironically, the great railway soon had disastrous results for the Chinese themselves. It now cost only $40 for an immigrant to cross the continent by rail and a flood of immigrants took advantage of the ease and cheapness of travel on the line the Chinese had helped to build. The labor shortage (and resulting high wages) in California turned into a glut. When the tangled affairs of the Northern Pacific line led to the stock market crash of Black Friday, September 19, 1873, and to financial panic, California experienced its first real economic depression. There was devastating unemployment, and the Chinese were made the scapegoats.

BUILDING OTHER LINES

The expansion of the railroads was even faster in the following decade. In 1850, the United States had 9,000 miles of track. In 1860, it had 30,000. In 1890, it had over 70,000 miles. Three years later, it had five transcontinental lines.

The first transcontinental railway was soon followed by four more links: (1) the Southern Pacific–Texas and Pacific, completed in 1883 from San Francisco to Texas by way of Yuma, Tucson, and El Paso; (2) the Atchison, Topeka, and Santa Fe, completed in 1885 from Kansas City to Los Angeles via Santa Fe and Albuquerque; (3) the Northern Pacific completed in 1883 from Duluth, Minnesota, to Portland, Oregon and; (4) the Great Northern (1893). The skill of the Chinese as railroad builders was much sought after, and Chinese worked on all these lines. Some 15,000 worked on the Northern Pacific, laying tracks in Washington, Idaho, and Montana; 250 on the Houston and Texas line; 600 on the Alabama and Chattanooga line; 70 on the New Orleans line. Nearly 500 Chinese were recruited for the Union Pacific even after the lines were joined. Many worked in the Wyoming coal mines and during the summer months doubled as track laborers. They carried the Southern Pacific lines over the burning Mojave Desert. They helped link San Francisco with Portland in 1887.

The Canadian Pacific seized the chance to enlist veteran Chinese railwaymen from the Southern Pacific and Northern Pacific railroads and also brought Chinese workers direct from China. In 1880, some 1,500 were working on that line, increasing to 6,500 two years later. Casualties were heavy on this line. Hundreds lost their lives while working on it.

Chinese railwaymen helped on the Central and Southern Pacific's main line down the San Joaquin Valley in 1870 and 1871. They worked on the hookup to Los Angeles and the loop with seventeen tunnels over the Tehachapi Pass completed in 1876. On this line, 1,000 Chinese worked on the 6,975-foot San Fernando Tunnel, the longest in the West. This rail link between San Francisco and Los Angeles, tapping the rich Central Valley, played a major role in the development of California's agriculture, later its biggest industry. They worked on the line north from Sacramento along the Shasta route to Portland, which was reached in 1887. In 1869, the Virginia and Truckee line employed 450 Chinese, veterans of the Central Pacific, to grade its track. When the Virginia and Truckee's Carson and Colorado branch line was planned from Mound House to Benton, its tough manager Yerington arranged with the unions for the grading to be done by white labor to Dayton and by Chinese from Dayton on south. "If the entire line had to be graded by white labor, I would not think of driving a pick into the ground, but would abandon the undertaking entirely," he said.

Chinese laborers worked on the trans-Panamanian railway, which linked the Pacific and the Atlantic before the Panama Canal was completed. This railway played a major role in speeding up the economic development of the United States, but it was not built without sacrifice: hundreds of the Chinese builders died of fever and other causes during its construction.

This by no means completes the list of contributions of the Chinese railway workers. The transcontinental lines on which they worked "more than any other factor helped make the United States a united nation," writes the *Encyclopedia Britannica* ["Railways"]. They played a major role in building the communications network of iron roads that was the transport base of American industrial might in the twentieth century.

Speaking eloquently in favor of the Chinese immigrants, Oswald Garrison Villard said,

I want to remind you of the things that Chinese labor did in opening up the Western portion of this country. . . . [They] stormed the forest fastnesses, endured cold and heat and the risk of death at hands of hostile Indians to aid in the opening up of our northwestern empire. I have a dispatch from the chief engineer of the Northwestern Pacific telling how Chinese laborers went out into eight feet of snow with the temperature far below zero to carry on the work when no American dared face the conditions.

And these men were from China's sun-drenched south, where it never snows.

In certain circles, there has been a conspiracy of silence about the Chinese railroadmen and what they did. When U.S. Secretary of Transportation John Volpe spoke at the "Golden Spike" centenary, not a single Chinese American was invited, and he made no mention in his speech of the Chinese railroad builders.

3

FEMINISM, PROFESSIONALISM, AND GERMS: THE THOUGHT OF MARY PUTNAM JACOBI AND ELIZABETH BLACKWELL

REGINA MARKELL MORANTZ

Many historians locate the beginning of American feminism with the Seneca Falls Convention of 1848. There a group of men and women gathered to discuss ways of achieving full equality for American women and founded the first American women's movement. The legacy of Seneca Falls was a collective approach to women's equality, an approach that eventually led to the formation of the American and the National Women Suffrage Associations after the Civil War.

But, as Regina Markell Morantz points out in this essay, collective organization was not the sole path toward women's equality in nineteenth-century America. For Elizabeth Blackwell, the nation's first college-trained and licensed female physician, feminism could also be served by opening occupations hitherto closed to women. Struggling against social prejudice and personal adversity, Blackwell forcefully established the claim that women were the equals of men in the practice of medicine and in other male-dominated professions as well. Yet for some early female physicians, such as Mary Putnam Jacobi, Blackwell's intuitive approach to the study of medicine and her notion of the ameliorative role of the woman physician were far too reminiscent of traditional American views of women. For Jacobi, science was blind to the gender of its practitioners, and men and women thus had an equal purchase on the study and practice of clinical medicine. As Morantz reveals, while Blackwell and Jacobi agreed on many points, their thinking diverged radically on such contemporary questions as the scientific basis of medical practice and the social role of female physicians. Prefiguring issues debated by feminists today, the dispute between Jacobi and Blackwell went far beyond questions of etiology (the study of the causes of disease) to pose the broader question of whether professional women ought to follow the same roles set for professional men.

From *American Quarterly* 34(5): 459–78, Copyright 1982. Reprinted by permission of *American Quarterly,* the author, and the American Studies Association.

On Christmas Day, 1888, Dr. Mary Putnam Jacobi sat at her desk to write a long, frank, and remarkably revealing letter to Elizabeth Blackwell. Although Blackwell was several years her senior, both women belonged to the pioneer generation of women physicians. Blackwell, the first woman to receive a medical degree in the United States, had founded both a hospital and a medical school for women—the New York Infirmary for Women and Children—where Jacobi had been an attending physician and professor of materia medica and therapeutics since 1870. Yet the two women never knew each other well. In 1869, shortly after she established the Woman's Medical College of the New York Infirmary, Blackwell left America and took up permanent residence in England, where she believed she could accomplish more in behalf of women physicians. She consigned the school to the competent administration of her sister Emily (also a physician), and an able faculty, which included Jacobi, a handful of recent graduates, and a few young but sympathetic male physicians.

Both women had fine reputations and were recognized leaders among the rapidly expanding ranks of women physicians. Yet though they admired each other deeply, it is also clear that their cordiality and mutual respect was enhanced rather than hampered by the geographical distance between them. No two temperaments could have differed more profoundly. Jacobi had not a trace of sentimentality about her. Her quick and penetrating intellect cut to the core of things with a rapidity that left lesser minds bewildered. No one valued rational thinking more highly; no one remained more frustrated with mushy generalities that could not be grounded in empirical investigation and factual analysis. Jacobi chose medicine out of a love for scientific rationalism. She adored chemistry and pursued medical study with the joyous abandon of a mind comfortably at home with its rigors. While attending the Ecole de Medicine in Paris she once sheepishly confessed to her mother that "immersion in technical studies is like ar-

senic eating,—once begun, you must go on, and at a continually increasing dose. I am really astonished to find how this absorption grows upon me."

Blackwell, in contrast, was nothing if not sentimental. She entered medicine with a perfectionist conception of morality and her own role in the moral universe. Believing that the realm of medicine and health must be a fundamental area of concern for the reformer, she wrote in 1889, "The progress and welfare of society is more intimately bound up with the prevailing tone and influence of the medical profession than with the status of any other class of men." Indeed, Victor Robinson, a younger physician who knew and admired her, called her a "Swedenborgian-theosophical-theological-Christian-metaphysician, instead of just an unadulterated scientist."

To the amused Robinson such failings could be tolerated in great pioneers. But, as Jacobi formulated her thoughts on Christmas morning in 1888, she realized that Blackwell's thinking raised her "antagonistic hairs" particularly because the woman was a pioneer. Sentimentality hurt the cause. Blackwell's preoccupation with the abstract struggle to make a place for women in medicine, Jacobi complained, never allowed her to descend from her vision "into the sphere of practical life within which, that vision if anywhere must be realized. You left that for others to do." What rankled Jacobi most was Blackwell's dominant "mental habit—principle,—or method, . . . the well known Transcendental method of arriving at conclusions by the force of meditative insight, and then refusing to submit these to tests of verification. Indeed," Jacobi continued upon further reflection,

it is the latter omission I really object to: the Transcendental vision probably always comes first in all large generalizations. . . . But whether these are to stand as effective truths or not depends upon how far they can bear the tests of close conflicts with facts, with innumerable details: how they can sustain the onslaught of argument and criticism. Your sex, your age, and your cast of mind render all this difficult. . . . You resemble your sister Anna sufficiently to prefer to remain within the sphere of large, often half mystical assertion.

What mystified and frustrated Jacobi was Blackwell's inattention to clinical medicine. "You have always disliked, ignored and neglected medicine!" she wrote, and the "one real occasion where from your position you should have shown me much, yet failed to show me anything, was when I began to study medicine under your direction in New York." Jacobi could sympathize with the "immense" obstacles in the way of Blackwell's reading and being taught medicine at mid-century, but she confessed she had always suspected that her friend's "greatest real difficulty" was "your own intense indifference to the work."

The differences between the two women were partly temperamental. Yet in the last third of the nineteenth century they also reflected tensions within the medical profession created by the new discoveries in immunology and bacteriology. In the decade or so between the time that Blackwell received her medical degree in 1849 and Jacobi entered the Woman's Medical College in Philadelphia in 1864, medicine as an occupation began to merge with medicine as a science. Certainly Jacobi's exposure to the new ideas as a student rather than as a young practitioner may account for the younger woman's greater openness to change. Yet the debate over the role of the physician in specific areas of reform—a debate intensified by findings in the laboratory—was never wholly generational, nor was it ever confined solely to the female portion of the profession.

Yet Jacobi and Blackwell disagreed not only over bacteriology; they also represented variant traditions among women physicians, and their divergences led them on occasion to view the role of the woman physician from slightly different perspectives as well. For both these reasons their lives will be ex-

plored in this essay. Women physicians, by nature of their being physicians, ranged themselves on different sides of the controversies shared by their medical brethren. Yet by virtue of their being women, they also faced dilemmas from which their male colleagues were spared. Most of these centered around the fact of their womanhood and its meaning with regard to their larger connection with the profession.

* * *

One of the most bewildering controversies to twentieth-century observers remains the reluctance of many nineteenth-century physicians and public health advocates to accept the discoveries of the bacteriologists. How could such men and women persist in speaking of "effluvia," "miasma," and "filth" when the precise experimentation of Pasteur, Koch, and their followers had, by reproducing various diseases in the laboratory and identifying various "germs," ushered in the concept of "specific etiology?"

To make sense of the sanitarians' objections we must remember that bacteriological concepts called into question an older and deeply internalized view of disease which was holistic in its scope, moralistic in its implications, and fundamentally religious in its point of departure. In the minds of many sanitarians, Elizabeth Blackwell included, health was the natural order of things, a gift to be enjoyed by people if they governed their lives wisely and well. Disease was neither the arbitrary visitation of an angry God nor the quixotic outcome of blind fate, but rather the inevitable result of one's violation of the laws of nature made manifest by a benevolent deity. Disease, so often equated in their cosmology with sin, was permitted by God to exist, but conscience and revelation on the one hand and reason and science on the other were the tools provided by Him for men and women to combat these evils. The task of medicine was to reveal and teach the laws by which people could ensure the proper balance between environment and individual behavior.

From our perspective, nineteenth-century sanitarians may have been scientifically naive, but their ideas exhibited an internal consistency that linked together a perfectionist world view with the more personal concerns of men and women interested in active and dramatic social reform. They reasoned that since disease was always accompanied by ugliness, want, and pollution, health could be achieved by replacing these modern blights with the pure food, air, water, and pleasant surroundings enjoyed in the preindustrial age.

To be sure, the tension between environmentalism and the concept of specific etiology, which agitated the medical community at the end of the nineteenth-century both in America and abroad, generally represented different points of view on a continuum rather than a conflict between two opposing camps. As early as the 1840s and 1850s individual physicians spoke of "germs," and used the term to identify a cause of disease that defied mere cleanliness and purity and suggested further that conscience and clean living were not always enough. Enlightened American physicians like Lemuel Shattuck or Henry Ingersoll Bowditch, for example, carefully balanced traditional sanitation theory, with its emphasis on filth, against new concepts pointing to a specific microbial invader. Nevertheless, the social implications of the two poles of thought can be usefully contrasted. Blackwell, perhaps because her scientific opinions exhibited none of the subtlety of contemporaries like Shattuck, Bowditch, or Mary Putnam Jacobi, stands as an appropriate representative of an older, more conservative tradition, still unmoved by the startling new discoveries of laboratory experimentation.

One clue to Blackwell's thinking lies in the fact that her interest in moral reform antedated her attraction to medicine. In part this was due to her remarkable family background. The children of the abolitionist Samuel Blackwell immersed themselves in the traditions of Christian perfectionism and reformist activity. Elizabeth's brothers, Henry and Samuel, supported antislavery and women's rights: the former married the feminist Lucy Stone and the latter married Antoinette Brown, the first formally ordained woman minister in the United States. Sister Emily also became a physician, and another sister, Anna, a poet and translator. Several family members dabbled in spiritualism. Blackwell's approach to medical issues confidently bore the stamp of her family's progressive tendencies.

The idea of studying medicine did not come easily to Blackwell, for she admitted in her autobiography that as a young adult she "hated everything connected with the body" and "the very thought of dwelling on . . . its various physical ailments filled me with disgust." Yet other circumstances pushed her toward her life's work. One was her burning desire for engrossing, ennobling activity. When a close friend dying of what was probably uterine cancer urged upon Blackwell the thought that her worst sufferings would have been alleviated had she been treated by a woman physician, Elizabeth could no longer "put the idea . . . away." She knew even then that the term "female physician" referred primarily at that time to abortionists, the most notorious of whom was New York's Madame Restell. Such misuse of female power directly offended her growing mystical fascination with what she later termed "the spiritual power of maternity." The Madame Restells of the world represented "the gross perversion and destruction" of womanhood, and "utter degradation of what might and should become a noble position for women." With determination she concluded to do what she could to "redeem the hells, . . . especially the one form of hell thus forced upon my notice."

Blackwell seems to have consciously chosen a life that would protect her from marriage and intimacy with men. Her autobiography reveals that her choice of career came in part from her susceptibility to the "disturbing influence exercised by the other sex." Although she was constantly "falling in love," she shrank from the implications of those feelings, "repelled" by the idea of intimacy and a "life association." Soon after seizing upon the idea of medical practice, she confided to her journal:

> I felt more determined than ever to become a physician, and thus place a strong barrier between me and all ordinary marriage. I must have something to engross my thoughts, some object in life which will fill this vacuum and prevent this sad wearing away of the heart.

Blackwell often used a traditionally religious vocabulary to articulate these goals. She turned for aid "to that Friend with whom I am beginning to hold true communion," and shortly after she began preparing for her future course her fears and doubts were dispelled by a mystical experience which left her confident that her individual work was divinely inspired and "in accordance with the great providential ordering of our race's progress." This conversion of religious impulses into paths of professional activity was characteristic of many sanitarians during the antebellum period, both in America and in England.

Similar themes pervaded Blackwell's writings as she formulated her two major concerns, the role of the physician in society and the place of women in the profession. Because her approach to disease was holistic, she argued that the physician had more to do than cure. She constantly spoke of the union of the spiritual and the physical, warning her students frequently against the dangers of materialism. "True science," she wrote, "supports the noblest intuitions of humanity, and its tendency is to furnish proof suited to our age of these intuitions." When "the recognition of the higher facts of consciousness is obscured, and the physician is unable to perceive life more real than the narrow limits of sensation," she warned, the loss to practical medicine was "immense."

The bacteriologists obscured "the higher facts of consciousness" because bacteriology *appeared* to develop at the expense of sanitation, hygiene, preventive medicine, and most important, morality itself. By equating disease with a specific microbial invader, laboratory scientists seemed to be challenging the older view of health as equilibrium and threatening the work of those reformers who supported massive sanitary measures to remove the filth, want, and pollution that they believed caused disease. The traditional art of medicine, whose monistic pathologies bid the physician treat only after a careful balance of emotional, environmental, and physio-psychological factors, was rendered obsolete. Not laboratory experimentation, dissented Blackwell, but "pure air, cleanliness, and decent house-room secured to all . . . form the true prophylaxis of smallpox." "The arbitrary distinction," she continued elsewhere, "between the physician of the body and the physician of the soul . . . tends to disappear as science advances."

Blackwell continued to explore these themes when she turned her attention to the role of women in the profession. In 1889 she wrote that the sense of right and wrong must constantly govern medical research and practice, "the Moral must guide the Intellectual, or there is no halting-pace in the rapid incline to error." Because she believed that women innately exhibited a higher moral sense than did men, she saw the role of medical women as integral to the proper and healthy progress of the profession as a whole. Indeed, a "distinguishing characteristic" of the nineteenth century, she argued, was the "increasing devotion of women to the relief of social suffering" through the "spiritual power of maternity." By this she meant

> the subordination of self to the welfare of others; the recognition of the claim which helplessness and ignorance make upon the stronger and more intelligent; the joy of creation and bestowal of life; the pity and sympathy which tend to make every woman the born foe of cruelty and injustice.

Women were accomplishing great deeds. Such "spiritual mothers of the race," she judged "often more truly incarnations of the grand maternal life, than those who [were] technically mothers in the lower physical sense."

Women physicians, she argued, had to monitor medical progress so that it did not violate moral truth. "Whatever revolts our moral sense as earnest women," she reminded her students, "is not in accordance with steady progress . . ." and "cannot be permanently true." It was through the "moral, guiding the intellectual," that the "beneficial influence of women in any new sphere of activity" would be felt.

Bacteriology and its penchant for vaccination offended Blackwell because its concept of specific etiology undermined her sense of the moral order. A concomitant of modern laboratory science, animal experimentation represented something much worse: the triumph of the intellect over morality. Blackwell probably opposed vaccination primarily because early in her practice she lost a young child whom she had vaccinated against small pox. Vivisection, however, represented to her an attempt to do good by evil means. Animal experimentation, she felt, hardened the heart, blunted the moral sense, and injured the "intelligent sympathy with suffering" which was the mark of a good physician. Ultimately it led to the dangerous habit of treating the poor and helpless with indifference, by regarding them merely as "clinical material." Blackwell regretted this tendency particularly among younger physicians, and she felt it the responsibility of women doctors to discourage such inhumane practices. In 1891 she addressed a letter of protest to the Alumnae Association of the Woman's Medical College of the New York Infirmary in which she opposed their endowment of a new experimental laboratory. She reminded her female colleagues of their "duty" as potential mothers to oppose the cruelty and narrow materialism of which, to her mind, the new laboratory was symbolic.

Blackwell even connected the corruption of the moral sense resulting from "unrestrained experiment on the lower animals" to the increase in gynecological surgery at the end of the century. To her, ovariotomy represented "mutilation" and was especially heinous because it rendered women incapable of having children. Again she looked to women physicians to remind the profession that "moral error may engender intellectual error," and talked often of returning to the United States to rally women's attention on these issues.

Fascinated and energized by recent events in laboratory medicine, Mary Putnam Jacobi could muster little enthusiasm for Blackwell's views. In her private life she too confronted the moral dilemmas of the reformer, and she enthusiastically supported numerous meliorist efforts, including the Consumer's League, woman's suffrage, and the reform of primary education in the direction of manual training and physical culture. Yet though she understood that the pursuit of truth could never be divorced totally from moral life, she approached the acquisition of medical knowledge as something quite independent of morality. Believing in science with an earnestness that was almost religious, she nevertheless remained uncomfortable with Blackwell's traditional religious vocabulary, and she viewed scientific research as an absolute good because it added to the fund of human knowledge.

As a young medical student, Jacobi had written her mother that her vision of Heaven was "simply the Region of Pure Thought" emancipated from "the overwhelming dominion of personal emotion and instinct." Her desire to pursue a scientific career developed early and she hesitated only when deciding whether to concentrate on medical practice or laboratory research. The oldest daughter of the publisher George Palmer Putnam, Jacobi, like Blackwell, received considerable support from her family. Although the Putnams were not active reformers, they were nevertheless New Englanders who remained sympathetic to the meliorist causes of the day. Mary's Aunt Elizabeth Peabody, for example, kept her in touch with every new social "ism." Yet Mary remained too hardheaded and practical to identify herself with trends and fads. She once wrote to her mother, "I detest vulgarity, pretention, . . . inanity, twaddle, insipidity and pretention in velvet. I will have none of either. No homeopaths, no spiritualists, few 'female' orators. . . ."

The Putnams were not pleased with their daughter's choice of career, but their disappointment did not hinder their providing emotional and material support. Jacobi's father considered medical science to be a "repulsive pursuit," but nevertheless took great pride in Mary's success. He begged only that she shun the company of "strong-minded women! . . . (your self-will and independence . . . are strong enough already)," and that she preserve her "feminine character." "Be a lady from the dotting of your i's to the color of your ribbons," he wrote to her in 1863, soon after she began her studies at the Woman's Medical College of Pennsylvania, "and if you must be a doctor and a philosopher, be an attractive and agreeable one."

Jacobi appreciated and respected her parents' advice because she understood the significance of their liberalism with regard to her aspirations. "You have always been such a dear good father . . . ," she once wrote to George Putnam. "The more I see of other people's way of doing, the more highly I value the large liberty in which you have always left me. It has occasioned certain mistakes, but on the whole, the advantage has infinitely outweighed the disadvantage. I do not see how I could have lived without it."

Their tolerance of her plans was indeed remarkable for Victorian parents. Jacobi was headstrong, and she spent long years stubbornly pursuing her goals—years that the oldest girl of an upper middle-class New York family might have passed making more of a contribution to home life as daughter, sister, and, eventually, wife. After receiving a degree

in 1863 from the New York College of Pharmacy, Jacobi attended the Woman's Medical College of Philadelphia and was graduated a year later, the only student in the history of the school to write her thesis in Latin. She spent the next several months studying clinical medicine with Marie Zakrzewska and Lucy Sewall at the New England Hospital for Women and Children. Yet neither experience satisfied her thirst for formal medical training, and in 1866 she left the United States for France, where she hoped to be admitted to the Ecole de Medicine in Paris. Looking back on this decision in 1871, she wrote to her mother:

> I cannot do a thing half way. When I was in Boston, Lucy Sewall considered me stupid, because I could not do things without having studied them, and could not accept her methods without question. In Paris, I am considered one of the most successful students, because I have been able to "go the whole horse." Explain it as you may, I always find the whole of a thing easier to manage than the half.

Jacobi's time in Paris testified to her persistence and determination. Although she immediately began attending hospital clinics, lectures, and laboratories, it took her two years of dogged perseverance to achieve her goal of admission to the Ecole. Characteristically, she passed her examinations with high honors and won a bronze medal for her graduating thesis in 1871.

In Paris, Jacobi pursued the most advanced medical science of her day. Soon after her arrival there she wrote enthusiastically to her mother, "I have a fair prospect here of becoming a thoroughly educated physician," adding that "unless I am, I certainly will never undertake to practice medicine." Her commitment to the laboratory made it natural that she would welcome the discoveries of the bacteriologists and seek to stay abreast of their findings. She perceived early that opportunities for medical study in America did not begin to compare with those abroad. In another letter to her mother she spoke of New York City's inadequacies:

> I have already sufficient terror of the demoralization imminent from the atmosphere of New York, with its very slack interest in medical science or progress, its deficient libraries, badly organized schools and hospitals, etc. I am doing my best to accumulate a sufficient fund of original force to make headway against these adverse influences, and to subordinate them to my purposes, instead of allowing them to subordinate me.

Yet at the same time Jacobi shunned opportunities for practicing medicine that would take her out of the mainstream, as inadequate as it was. She would not even consider teaching at the Woman's Medical College in Philadelphia, which she believed to be sincere, but deficient, and when offered the position of resident physician at one of the women's colleges she remarked that such isolation from the medical world would be "suicidal."

In 1871 Jacobi returned to New York to join the faculty of the Woman's Medical College of the New York Infirmary as professor of therapeutics and materia medica. She also set up private practice, feeling satisfied that "few young physicians could have a better opening." Family considerations and a sense of duty determined the subordination of chemistry—her first love—to private practice. As she explained to her mother, "After all the sacrifices you have made . . . I see more chance of satisfying you if I am a practical physician than if, without fortune, I try to become a scientific chemist."

Plunging herself into the world of New York medicine, Jacobi fulfilled her ambitions to become a first-rate physician and scientist. She became the first woman to be admitted to the New York Academy of Medicine and later chaired their section on neurology. She gained admission to numerous other medical societies as well and sustained her interest in research by publishing 9 books and over 120 medical articles. The respect of her male colleagues was never in doubt. One younger member of the Pathological Society, for example, remembered her as a woman

> whose knowledge of pathology was so thorough, whose range of the literature was so wide and whose criticism was so keen, fearless and just that in our discussions, we felt it prudent to shun the field of speculation and to walk strictly in the path of demonstrated fact.

Perhaps Jacobi's successes in the male professional world were due at least in part to her willingness to accept men as equals—no more, no less. Certainly Jacobi did not share Blackwell's ambivalence toward romantic attachments to men, and her private correspondence never reveals the mistrust of marriage characteristic of many accomplished women of her generation. Nevertheless, she sought in a mate a rare thing in the nineteenth century—an intellectual and spiritual companion who could fully support her commitment to her work. Although she had a passionate nature, she was prepared to forgo marriage if she did not find such a man and broke two engagements before she joined the ranks of New York's professional medical elite. While still in Paris she had written on the subject of marriage to her mother:

> I have no particular desire to marry at any time; nevertheless, if at home, I should ever come across a physician, intelligent, refined, more enthusiastic for his science than me, . . . I think I would marry such a person if he asked me, and would leave me full liberty to exercise my profession.

Fortunately, Jacobi did meet such a man. In 1873 she became the wife of Dr. Abraham Jacobi, a German-Jewish refugee from the revolutionary upheavals of 1848. Jacobi was already one of the most distinguished physicians in America and has often been called the father of modern pediatrics. The couple shared common medical interests and collaborated occasionally. Although the marriage was often stormy, it remained a relationship of equals, despite Jacobi's assuredly ironic remark to her students that "it is desirable that every woman remain as inferior to her own husband as may be feasible and convenient."

Jacobi's personal and professional history made her understandably impatient with Blackwell's rigid theorizing, and glimpses of irritability appear in her comments concerning Blackwell's proposed trip to America. On Blackwell's antivivisectionism she remarked coolly, "Of course . . . you know . . . I should oppose you," adding with humor and a touch of wistful regret that a campaign among women physicians would be useless because "I am tolerably confident that I am the only woman in the United States who experiments on animals!"

As for the "problem" of gynecological surgery, Jacobi was less polite: "When you shudder at 'mutilation,' " she wrote,

> it seems to me you can never have handled a degenerated ovary or a suppurating Fallopian tube—or you would admit that the mutilation had been effected by disease,—possibly by the ignorance or neglect of a series of physicians, before the surgeon intervened. You always seem so much more impressed with the personalities,—sufficiently faulty,—of doctors, than with the terrific difficulties of the problems they have to face. . . . There has been much reprehensible malpractice. But I do not see that malpractice which may render a woman incapable of bearing children differs . . . from the malpractice which may result in the loss of a limb or of an eye. *There is not such special sanctity about the ovary!*

To Blackwell's suggestion that women physicians ought to avoid performing gynecological surgery she retorted, "And why should not women be delighted if they succeed in achieving a difficult and useful triumph in technical medicine," adding that she did not feel women physicians should be urged to strike out for

independent views until they had "demonstrated an equality of achievement in the urgent practical problems,—*not of sociology but of medicine.*" The chief task of women physicians, she believed, was not the fostering of morality ("sociology"), but "the creation of a scientific spirit" among them.

* * *

In the end, their divergent attractions to the potentialities inherent in medical practice led Blackwell and Jacobi to differ most intensely on the question of the role of women in medicine. Historians have long maintained that much of the rhetoric mustered in defense of women's medical education fell into two broad categories which occasionally contradicted each other. The first set of arguments, which paralleled Jacobi's brand of feminism, emphasized woman's right to self-development and her ability to make a contribution to clinical medicine equal to any man's. Proponents downplayed the physical and psychological handicaps allegedly endured by the female sex and openly challenged the tenet of Victorian culture that relegated women to the private and the family spheres. No longer were all women necessarily hampered by family responsibilities; a select few could practice medicine in lieu of family and career. These arguments drew their strength primarily from abstract concepts of justice and equality.

Blackwell's thought derived from a second, more popular set of beliefs emphasizing not the essential identity between men and women, but their differences. This approach adapted itself more readily to Victorian mythology regarding separate sexual spheres. Women should become physicians because they exhibited unique qualities that would allow them to make a distinct contribution to the profession.

Indeed, a central theme in the story of women in medicine—the tension between "feminism" and "morality" on the one hand and "professionalism" and "science" on the other—has plagued women physicians up until the present day. Nor have other women professionals escaped such conflicts. In a society that has continued to emphasize woman's primary maternal role, the stepping out of prescribed avenues of endeavor has inevitably involved for its participants some explanation of purpose. Did women have the right to pursue professional goals, usually considered masculine, with the same vigor as their male colleagues and for similar reasons of self-interest and personal fulfillment? Was the goal of equality legitimate for women, or need they contribute as well to some higher female mission? What obligations did women professionals have to other women, or to "female values" in general? Must women emulate the professionalism of men, or seek to temper dominant male values by asserting their uniquely feminine characteristics?

Blackwell's writings underscored the singular capabilities of women as physicians and led to a peculiar kind of female chauvinism. The purpose of teaching women medicine was not to convert them into "physicians rather inferior to men," but to occupy "positions which men cannot fully occupy," and exercise "an influence which men cannot wield at all." Those positions had mainly to do with women, children, and the family. Women physicians must bring science to bear on daily life. This could be done best as family physicians, obstetricians, public health advocates, and teachers of preventive medicine and hygiene, because it was in these areas that women could excel. Other branches of medicine reeked to Blackwell of the tyranny of male authority unmitigated by the dictates of conscience. She cautioned her students against the "blind acceptance of what is called 'authority' in medicine," which she equated with the "male intellect." "It is not blind imitation of men, nor thoughtless acceptance of whatever may be taught by them that is required," she wrote. Women students, she regretted, were as yet too "accustomed to accept the government and instruction of men as final, and it hardly

occurs to them to question it." They must be taught that "methods and conclusions formed by one-half of the race only, must necessarily require revision as the other half of humanity rises into conscious responsibility."

In advocating this position Blackwell voluntarily set herself and women physicians apart from the mainstream of professional developments. Rather than assimilate women into the larger group, she preferred to give them special responsibilities in order to achieve what she believed was a higher social and moral purpose. Women physicians were to be "in" the profession, but not "of" it.

This stress on the primacy of the maternal qualities of sympathy and instinct troubled Jacobi because she objected to female-centered, moralistic, and separatist standards for women. Her concern for objective science and the centrality of intellectual endeavor remained fundamentally universalist and assimilationist. For Jacobi, the physician dwelt in two realms, the intellectual and the practical. Although she admitted that moral considerations occasionally entered into the equation, she hailed the liberation of science from the mystic and demonic influences of the past and believed that the physician should deal with rational concepts based on objective knowledge. Ideally his business was to "take conditions which science has abstracted for the purpose of thought and to recombine them for the purpose of life. In the absence of the physician there would be no one to do this. . . ." Thus the physician was the link between theory and practice. Moral issues were often beside the point. The intrinsic difficulty in medicine, she wrote, was not moral, but remained "the great mass of facts which it is necessary to know" and "the variety of sciences which must be understood in order to interpret these facts."

Where Blackwell emphasized sympathy and compassion and identified such qualities with women, Jacobi spoke rarely of exclusively feminine contributions to medical practice. Having a sympathetic nature, she argued, did not necessarily make one a good physician. He or she must be interested primarily in the facts. In the end, she wrote, unless "the interest in the disease be not habitually greater than the interest in the patient," the patient would surely suffer. She saw women participating in the profession, not as a distinct entity unto themselves, but as separate individuals united with men by objective, demonstrable, and professional criteria in the search for truth. "Indeed," she cautioned her students in 1883, "you are liable to be so much and so frequently reminded that you are women physicians, that you are almost liable to forget that you are, first of all, physicians."

Jacobi did not reject entirely the notion that women had special strengths, although it is apparent that she believed such characteristics were acquired rather than innate. She admitted, for example, that "it is impossible to deny that women are intrinsically more suitable than men to take charge of insane women," because of their "superior kindness and conscientiousness." She quarreled little with the common wisdom that "tact, acuteness, and sympathetic insight [were] natural to women." Indeed, while stressing the importance of first-rate training she graciously conceded that "the special capacities of women as a class for dealing with sick persons are so great, that in virtue of them alone hundreds have succeeded in medical practice, though most sufficiently endowed with intellectual or educational qualifications."

Yet despite women's unique skills, Jacobi insisted that they be fully integrated into the profession. She deplored the tendency of women doctors "to nestle within a little circle of personal friends and to accept their dictum as the ultimate law of things." Their role must not be supplementary or distinctive; inevitably skilled women physicians should displace inferior men. There was nothing earthshaking about women competing with men: "Since society is, numerically speaking, already supplied with quite enough doctors," she wrote, "the only way in which women physicians can possibly gain any footing is by displacing a certain number of men." In order to do so, of course, they needed to be either equal or superior, and this meant receiving a better medical education than had yet been possible.

While Blackwell urged women to specialize, Jacobi continuously cautioned women not to concentrate in obstetrics and gynecology, but to devote themselves to a "liberal study of the whole field." Treating women and children should be used only "as a stepping-stone to general medicine." If women "do not obtain a foothold" there, if they "content themselves with claiming this little corner," she warned, "they will never really gain a high place even there. . . ."

Although Jacobi remained suspicious of separatism, she also conceded that since the "opposition to women students and practitioners of medicine has been so bitter, so brutal . . . so multiple in its hypocrisy," women did have common interests as an oppressed class. She repeatedly prescribed grit and hard work in the face of discrimination: "I have always advised you . . . to so saturate and permeate your consciousness with the feeling for medicine," she told the graduating class of the Woman's Medical College of the New York Infirmary in 1883, "that you would entirely forget that public opinion continued to assign you to a special, and on the whole, inferior" position. She even urged students to forget that they "have in any way braved public opinion." "Acclimate," she implored, "as quickly and as thoroughly as possible" to your "new place," and don't "keep dawdling on the threshhold to forever remind yourselves and everyone else that you have just come in." Medicine remained too demanding a profession for conscientious doctors to allow themselves to be concerned with problems of "social status." If you do not find the facts of medicine more interesting than any other facts," she cautioned, "you are not fit to be physicians."

Yet if Jacobi lost her patience with those who "dawdled on the threshold," the "monopoly" that excluded "one half of the race [from] the advantages of education and the facilities of increased life which that confers" rankled even more. She was not naive; she knew such opposition could be removed only after "much effort, individual and collective, persistent, patient, farsighted, indomitable." Thus she devoted considerable time and effort to examining the practical difficulties involved in assimilating women into the male professional world. For her the most obvious problem remained what she knew was "the most delicate": "actually raising to an equality the class which hitherto has been really inferior."

In acknowledging and working to overcome women's shortcomings, Jacobi and Blackwell remained of one mind. Indeed, one suspects that however substantial were their disagreements on theoretical points, practical issues of strategy continuously drew them together. Both women deplored women's inferior preparatory education, an education that rendered them deficient in intellectual initiative, dependent on authority, and apathetic—all qualities that Jacobi perceptively labeled characteristics of the subordination of "colonial life." In order to rectify such disadvantages, she wrote, medical women must combine as a class to remove the obstacles that have blocked their progress. Their first task was to create among themselves a "scientific spirit," by improving medical education for women and encouraging "free, self-sustained, self-reliant intellectual activity." Jacobi hoped that this "gradual progress in mental culture" would improve "mental initiative" in women and hopefully render them equal to men "in every work that both undertake."

Blackwell had no quarrel with these points. She agreed that the barriers to women's equal access to quality medical education must be removed as quickly as possible, and she understood that only thorough scientific training would promote women's success. Both women hoped that the unique opportunities offered by the Woman's Medical College of the New York Infirmary would begin to alleviate some of these difficulties. The two stood united as well in the battle to widen women's opportunities for clinical experience and professional association, and both, for different reasons, enthusiastically welcomed the advance of medical coeducation. Yet where Jacobi's brand of feminism strived to minimize the differences between men and women and to integrate female physicians into the profession as rapidly as possible, Blackwell adhered to the very end to a vision of the woman doctor's unique contribution. This was true at least in part because her concept of disease was linked to her notions of morality and her belief that authentic moral understanding depended on female intuition. Such assumptions allowed her to equate bacteriology with male science and its triumph with the victory of the male principle over the female. That such a victory would lead inevitably to the denigration of intuition and morality in medicine was deplorable enough, but the final and most egregious consequence would be that women would be deprived of their power, purpose, and unique advantage in the profession—and this at the very moment when civilized society was beginning at long last to afford them a role appropriate to their highest capacities.

Blackwell's suspicions of "ignorant male domination" caused her to worry that women physicians accepted male models uncritically. "The only disappointment which comes to me now, as I draw towards the close of a life full of joy and gratitude," she mused in 1889,

> is the surprise with which I recognize that our women physicians do not all and always see the glorious moral mission, which as women physicians they are called on to fulfill. It is not by simply following the lead of male physicians, and imitating their practices, that any new and vitalizing force will be brought into the profession.

* * *

As first-generation women physicians, Jacobi and Blackwell shared similar goals as well as the common experience of being pioneers. Their differences on the issue of women appear in retrospect less pronounced than their broad areas of agreement. Each struggled defiantly in her own way with the humiliating effects of discrimination, while holding fast to an objective that sought to broaden the sphere of constructive activity for all women. Both saw the role of women in medicine idealistically, in the sense that they rejected its pursuit on the grounds of self-interest and emphasized instead the physician's larger social responsibilities. Jacobi, for example, once declared to her mother that "I look upon a rich physician with as much suspicion as a rich priest." In 1889 Blackwell wrote in the same vein, "I say emphatically that anyone who makes pecuniary gain the chief motive for entering upon a medical career is an unworthy student: he is not fit to become a doctor." Both women believed that the success of women in the profession had immense importance for the general success of women "in every other department of society." On questions of strategy too, they were usually of one mind: both struggled to widen the access of medical women to superior scientific training and to increase their professional and clinical opportunities. Nevertheless, the two women represented distinct approaches to the problem of women in medicine, and their differences were passed on to succeeding generations of professional women.

Versions of Blackwell's argument remained the most popular in the public and private rhetoric of women physicians. However committed privately were later generations of women doctors to abstract concepts of equal justice, the Blackwellian tradition, with its glorification of woman's uniqueness, meshed more easily with familiar cultural verities. Male supporters, too, felt more at ease with the idea that women would not so much compete with them as concentrate their energies in what came to be known as "feminine preserves"— public health and social morality, child hygiene and maternal care, institutional work, industrial medicine, and public school and university teaching and counseling.

In 1926 the Woman's Medical College of Pennsylvania issued a pamphlet designed to encourage women to pursue a medical career. Its very title, *Natural Guardians of the Race,* illustrates how little the arguments had changed since Blackwell first spoke of the "spiritual power of maternity." Women "will always be necessary in medicine" the pamphlet maintained, because of "their special qualifications for definite fields of practice." Such fields were "child care," the "care of women, foreign medical missionary work," and "the field of research," for which "women have displayed peculiar aptitude" because of their "natural bent for painstaking accuracy and detail."

This bulletin and others like it suggest that until well into the twentieth century women physicians needed extraordinary reasons to justify their deviation from social norms, and still viewed themselves as a special group within the medical establishment. Not until the profound cultural changes of the 1960s brought about by the black and women's liberation movements did abstract concerns for equality and justice in the rhetoric of medical women take equal place beside the Blackwellian emphasis on women's unique capabilities.

Although the fact of their womanhood was central to them both, Jacobi and Blackwell differed in the final analysis on medical issues that went well beyond questions of gender. The achievements of the bacteriologists and the introduction of the concept of specific etiology have been among the most constructive forces in modern medicine for almost a century. Yet the scientific medicine that has flourished since 1900 has done so increasingly at the expense of a holistic approach to the problem of illness. In many respects the worst fears of Elizabeth Blackwell concerning the neglect of psychological, environmental, social, and personal factors have come to pass. Doctors no longer treat the whole patient; they concentrate merely on the disease. Medical science has become increasingly and aggressively masculine. The nurturant aspects of nineteenth-century practice, with its heavy emphasis on intuition, sympathy, and art, have all but disappeared. From the perspective of the nineteenth-century, Jacobi's enthusiasm for laboratory science and her identification with the most revolutionary and dramatic achievements of her profession seem progressive and refreshing. Blackwell's ideas, heavy with religious overtones and convoluted personal idiosyncrasies, appear reactionary, uninformed, and annoyingly short-sighted. Yet the passage of time has gradually revealed to us the shocking limitations of laboratory science. Once again we must return full circle to deal with factors in disease causation that cannot be measured, recorded, or re-created in an experimental setting.

To be sure, the contemporary interest in holistic approaches to disease is something very different from the kind of position Elizabeth Blackwell occupied a century ago, and could, in fact, have come about only after the supremacy of scientific reductionism in medicine. However, in the midst of such an about-face, Blackwell's vision seems almost prophetic as she mused to a friend in 1853:

> I hope some day to arrange a hospital on truer principles than any that we have yet seen—but in thinking of this subject, I feel continually the want of the *Science* of reform, which I believe is as yet unknown—I should want my hospital to be a center of Science, and of moral growth—in the scientific department I should be puzzled to know how far I ought to unite men and women—In the future I have no doubt that the two sexes, in varying proportions, will unite in every act of life—but now there are difficulties both in their separation and their combination. . . . I should want also in my Hospital to cure my patients spiritually as well as physically, and what innumerable aids that would necessitate! I must have the church, the school, the workshop . . . to cure my patients—a whole society, in fact. . . .*

4

LEGACIES OF THE DAWES ACT: BUREAUCRATS AND LAND THIEVES AT THE CHEYENNE-ARAPAHO AGENCIES OF OKLAHOMA

DONALD J. BERTHRONG

Throughout the nineteenth century, successive generations of social reformers and government administrators sought to make Native Americans part of white America. But by the turn of the twentieth century it was clear that these attempts at assimilation had largely failed. Although dispossessed of their ancestral lands and confined to isolated reservations, Native Americans steadfastly refused to relinquish their ancient way of life. Frustrated by this legacy of failure, in 1877 Congress passed the Dawes Act, which set in motion a comprehensive reorganization of government policy regarding Native Americans.

Prior to the Dawes Act Congress had been content to allow Native Americans to retain communal ownership of tribal lands. Now with passage of the act, these communal lands were removed from tribal control, converted into private property, and divided into small family plots. By giving each Native American family its own land, congressional reformers hoped to remake supposedly "lazy" Indians into productive American farmers.

In this essay, Donald J. Berthrong recounts the impact of the Dawes Act on the Cheyenne and Arapaho people of Oklahoma. Against the best intentions of reformers and bureaucrats, the parceling of communal land only weakened the Native American position in the Southwest as unscrupulous white land speculators used fraud, coercion, and cultural misunderstanding to appropriate "surplus" Indian land. Blinded by their ethnocentrism, pro-Dawes reformers and administrators had only succeeded in pushing Native Americans further into poverty and cultural dislocation.

From *Arizona and the West* 21:335–54 (1979). Reprinted by permission.

During the Progressive Era, the ideals of nineteenth-century Christian reformers continued to influence the Indian policy of the United States. Assimilation of Native Americans into the mainstream of American life remained the principal goal. However, in implementing the larger outlines of Indian policy, both reformers and government officials invariably encountered obstacles. One of the major obstacles that blocked progress was the leasing of Indian allotments. The Dawes Act of 1887 had made allotments to tribesmen who instead of starting small farms had leased their land and soon were drawing a substantial income from farmers and ranchers. Reformers, imbued with the work ethic, pronounced this arrangement an evil and reasoned that if the Indians owned less land, they would be forced to gain a livelihood directly from farming or some other employment. If allotted land were sold, the money obtained could be used to buy farm machinery, provide houses, and generally assist an Indian begin farming. To achieve such a program, Congress enacted legislation between 1902 and 1910 which permitted the sale of all Indian lands allotted under the Dawes Act. Poorly administered by misguided bureaucrats, these statutes created myriad opportunities for whites to defraud Indians of their land and property. By 1921 more than one half of the individuals within tribes affected by the Dawes Act were landless, rural, and economically devastated people. The impact of this national disgrace was vividly illustrated by the alienation of Indian lands on the Cheyenne-Arapaho Reservation in Oklahoma during these years.

Christian reformers and humanitarians, allied with government officials, believed by 1900 that the "Indian question" would soon be solved. Their naive assumption resulted from the anticipated efficacy of the General Allotment (Dawes) Act of 1887. Key features of the act provided for the allotment of reservation land, the eventual sale of non-allotted land to whites, and citizenship for all Indian allottees. Allotted land would remain in trust for twenty-five years. While the federal government served as trustee for these allotments and other restricted Indian lands, the benefits of private property and citizenship would be supplemented by vocational education emphasizing farming, stock raising, and manual skills, and by religious instruction stressing individualism over tribalism. In a generation, it was assumed, Indians would possess all the requisites for full participation in American society. Labor, thrift, and the accumulation of private property would swiftly transform tribesmen into self-supporting farmers and stockmen who would have no need for federal paternalism.

Congress, responding to Western land demands, had enacted legislation to implement the intent of the Dawes Act. A clause in the Indian Appropriation Act passed in March of 1889 authorized the appointment of a commission to negotiate with various tribes for lands in central and western Indian Territory. The Unassigned (Oklahoma) District was opened on April 22, 1889, and quickly occupied by land seekers. A year later, on May 2, 1890, Congress created the Territory of Oklahoma and immediately sought to expand the new political unit by opening land on adjoining Indian domains. To accomplish this objective, a three-man commission chaired by David H. Jerome in June initiated talks to implement the allotment program and purchase unoccupied reservation land.

The Jerome Commission met with the Southern Cheyennes and Arapahoes during July and October of 1890. Hard bargaining, threats, deception, and bribery were employed to break down the resistance of several Cheyenne and Arapaho chiefs to the concept of allotment and loss of unused land. When the cession agreement was worked out, every Cheyenne and Arapaho listed on the 1891 tribal roll would be allotted a one hundred sixty acre homestead—eighty acres each of crop and grazing land—and the surplus land would be sold to the government. In time, when the allotting process was completed,

3,294 Cheyennes and Arapahoes had acquired a total of 529,682 acres of land, out of slightly more than four million on the reservation, to be held in trust for twenty-five years by the government. Approximately 3,500,000 surplus acres of their reservation was signed over to the federal government for $1,500,000. Of that sum $500,000 was distributed to tribal members in per capita payments, while $1,000,000 was deposited at five percent interest in the United States Treasury for the tribes' benefit.

Even before the Cheyennes and Arapahoes had accepted the allotment program, Congress began modifying the Dawes Act. The modification was necessary because, in setting aside allotments, the 1887 statute made every conveyance or contract touching trust lands "absolutely null and void" during the trust period. On March 10, 1890, Senator Henry L. Dawes, the sponsor of the original act, introduced a bill to authorize Indians, subject to the approval of the Secretary of Interior, to lease their allotments. In 1891 statutory authority to lease land was extended to allottees who "by reason of age or other disability" could not personally benefit from the occupation or cultivation of the allotment. Congress broadened the leasing criteria in 1894 by amending the defining phrase to read, "by reason of age, disability or inability," and by extending the lease periods.

With these modifications, Indian agents began arranging leases. By 1900 approximately 1,100 leases had been signed for the Cheyennes and Arapahoes, who realized $42,-120.83 for the 1899—1900 fiscal year. These leases, which covered approximately one third of their allotted land, increased Cheyenne-Arapaho income by slightly more than 40 percent. Leasing of allotments was more prevalent at the Cheyenne-Arapaho Agency than in other jurisdictions in 1900, when it was estimated that 13 percent of land allotted to all tribes was leased.

The Dawes Act, however, did not eliminate tribalism. Allotted Indians continued to live together in extended families and small villages,

resisting the white man's education, Christianity, family structure, and concept of private property. Furthermore, marginal soil fertility and rainfall, minimal capacity to operate agricultural machinery, and deep aversion to agricultural labor prevented most tribesmen from becoming farmers. A Cheyenne-Arapaho Indian agent reported that eight years after allotment only 15 to 18 percent of the adult male population was "actually occupying and cultivating their own lands." Other tribal members were dependent upon rations, per capita payments from interest on funds deposited in the United States Treasury, and lease income. An insignificant fraction of tribal adults was gainfully employed at the agency or as clerks in traders' stores. Commissioner William A. Jones complained in 1900 that the widespread practice of leasing Indian allotments undermined the goals of the Dawes Act. "The Indian," wrote Jones, "is allotted and then allowed to turn over his land to whites and go on his aimless way." Leases not only fostered "indolence with its train of attendant vices," but also provided white settlers and realtors an effective means to exploit Indian lands. When an allottee became discouraged by unsuccessful efforts to farm, he usually leased his land and returned to camp life.

The sale of allotted lands soon was being pushed. If lease income permitted Indians to live without engaging in physical labor, then legislation amending the Dawes Act was necessary. A lease only temporarily abridged an allottee's property rights, but if this land could be removed from a trust status and opened for sale, Indians would have less land to lease. Indians could use the money derived from the sale of whole or partial allotments to aid in building houses, barns, and fences; buying draft animals, cattle, and swine; and providing the necessities of life while bringing smaller and more manageable acreage into cultivation. Congress would also be relieved of approving larger appropriations to support Indians.

Westerners also wanted to see Indian allotments sold to whites. The editor of a newspaper in Watonga, the seat of Blaine County, Oklahoma Territory, alleged that 69 percent of the original Cheyenne and Arapaho allottees were dead and their land was idle and unproductive. Nothing, the editor argued, could benefit Blaine County more than to have those allotments belonging to "dead Indians" owned and cultivated by white farmers.

In 1902 the Dawes Act was modified to free inherited allotments from trust status. According to the act, when an allottee died his homestead would be held in trust for his heir or heirs for the remainder of the twenty-five-year trust period. However, tucked obscurely into the Indian Appropriation Act of 1902 was a little-discussed provision which altered this requirement. Section 7 stated that adult heirs "of any deceased Indian to whom a trust or other patent containing restrictions upon alienation has been or shall be issued for lands allotted to him may sell and convey lands inherited from such decedent."

Congress also responded to pressure from Western townsite promoters to approve alienation of allotted land. In March of 1903, the Secretary of Interior was "authorized and directed" to dispense patents in fee (unrestricted titles) for eighty acres each in four Cheyenne allotments. These lands were covered by restricted patents issued in 1892 to No-wa-hi, Darwin Hayes, Red Plume, and Shoe. Their property had become extremely valuable because it lay adjacent to the intersection of four railroads, including branch lines of the Rock Island and Frisco railroads. Despite the provisions of the Dawes Act, Congress was prevailed upon to vote under Section 9 of the Indian Appropriation Act to free 320 acres of allotted land belonging to the four Cheyennes from all "restrictions as to the sale, encumbrance or taxation" of the specified tracts. The Indians received $6,200 for their tracts. When divided into town lots, the land was sold for more than $150,000 by Thomas J. Nance, who had obtained title to the four tracts. While the acreage involved in this case was small, Con-

gress willingly had set aside provisions of the Dawes Act to satisfy the economic ambitions of Western entrepreneurs.

When Congress began debating the need for a major modification of the Dawes Act, reformers, legislators, and Western residents expressed differing feelings regarding goals. Reformers saw no harm in issuing fee patents for allotments to those Indians who by reason of education, intelligence, industry, and thrift appeared competent to manage their own economic affairs without supervision of the Bureau of Indian Affairs (BIA). Legislators hoped that Indians who received fee patents would drift away from their people and into white society, so that congressional appropriations supporting Indian affairs could be reduced. Westerners knew that few allotted Indians, regardless of competency criteria, would be sufficiently adroit in business matters to protect their unrestricted property.

The Burke Act of May 8, 1906, significantly modified the Dawes Act. Under this legislation, competent Indians, at the discretion of the Secretary of Interior, could be issued fee patents freeing their allotments from all restrictions "as to sale, encumbrance or taxation," except that the land was not liable for any debt contracted before the issuance of the unrestricted patent. The new law also stipulated that thereafter citizenship would be granted only to Indians who received fee patents for their allotments. Those allottees with restricted property still needed BIA supervision, and remained "subject to the exclusive jurisdiction of the United States" until they were issued a fee patent.

Less than a year after the passage of the Burke Act, Congress made possible the additional alienation of allotted land. The 1907 Indian Appropriation Act included a section which permitted non-competent Indians to sell both their original allotments and inherited land under rules and regulations promulgated by the Secretary of Interior. Funds obtained from land sales were to be used for the benefit of non-competent allottees or heirs, under the supervision of the Commissioner of Indian Affairs.

Thus, two decades after the passage of the Dawes Act, every square inch of land used and occupied by Indians was subject to alienation. How much land Indians would retain depended upon the rapidity with which the Dawes Act and its modifying legislation would be applied administratively to Indian tribes or individuals.

In part, the land base of Indians diminished because reformers and government officials were blinded by their ideologies. They tied the destiny and lives of Indians to white institutions, regardless of the Indians' ability or desire to adapt to a new way of life. It was disturbing to see Indians living on reservations or allotments without labor. If Indians dissipated their funds and resources, they would be forced, one Commissioner of Indian Affairs commented, "to earn their bread by labor." Albert K. Smiley, long influential in the Lake Mohonk Conference and on the Board of Indian Commissioners, expressed similar sentiments in 1905, when he wrote: ". . . work is the saving thing for the Indians. We have coddled them too much. . . . Put them on their mettle; make them struggle, then we will have some good Indians." Reformers and government officials agreed that assimilation and termination must be the goals of Indian policy, even though many Indians would suffer, "fall by the wayside and be trodden underfoot."

Although some Indian Service field personnel were cautious in stripping land from Indians, pressures grew for the sale of Indian land. Old or incapacitated Indians needed money for life's necessities, young heirs of original allottees required money for education, Indians attempting to farm needed homes, teams, machinery, and barns. Policy changes by the BIA, meanwhile, made alienation easier, and agency administrators who were indifferent to the Indians' interests or who profited by corrupt acts willingly acquiesced to white pressure for the sale of valuable allotments.

Since land was the only significant capital resource the Indians possessed, its retention was imperative. Unlike white Americans, Indians could not replenish their capital resources for a number of reasons: limited employment opportunities; inadequate and inappropriate education; a high incidence of debilitating diseases; an inability to protect property through legal actions; a hostile white population that preyed upon their property; and a tenacious Indian adherence to traditional social and cultural customs. The Cheyennes and Arapahoes of Oklahoma, for example, were systematically impoverished as the Dawes Act and subsequent legislation affected young and old, healthy and infirm, competent and non-competent tribal members alike. Once the act was applied to tribal lands, the allotted land base continued to decrease until many tribal members became landless and indigent. Would the reformers have insisted upon their legislative program if they had known its consequences? If Albert K. Smiley's 1905 judgment reflected the opinion of other like-minded reformers, the answer, deplorably, would have been yes!

Beginning in 1908, Cheyenne and Arapaho chiefs protested the sale of allotments. Cloud Chief, Little Bear, and Big Wolf, Cheyenne chiefs from the Darlington Agency, insisted that "it isn't right for old Indians and young ones to draw patents in fee, it makes /them/ worse and poor." According to Indian customs, complained the chiefs, "those who have secured patents to their land, sold them and wasted the proceeds, are without home and food . . . /and/ the burden of their existence would fall upon those who have held their lands." The chiefs fully comprehended the detrimental economic impact upon other members of extended families when allotments were alienated. In May of 1909 tribal representatives presented their objections to Washington bureaucrats. The discussion ranged over many topics, but the land question was of greatest concern, especially to the older, uneducated chiefs. Mower, a Dog Soldier chief from the Cantonment Agency, best expressed the attitudes of the traditional chiefs when he asked Acting Commissioner R. G. Valentine to tighten rather than remove restrictions "because we don't know how to use our money, and speculators take money from us. . . . They are standing ready to grab our land and money the moment it is in our possession."

Arapaho spokesmen stated that some tribesmen desired increased land sales to relieve existing hardships for their families. The ration system had been abolished and allotted Indians were dependent upon tribal or individual income to survive. Cleaver Warden, a Carlisle-educated Arapaho and peyote leader, favored increased land sales to alleviate poverty among families that could not live upon lease income and distributions from the sale of inherited land. Warden argued that an Indian should be "treated like a white man and let him suffer the consequences if he does make a mistake." Frank Harrington, another educated Arapaho from Cantonment, suggested that five members from each of the two tribes could be appointed as a committee to screen fee patent applications. Since the Cheyennes and Arapahoes knew the personal habits and abilities of their people, committee members should determine whether applicants were competent to manage their money and property and could advise a superintendent concerning endorsements.

Regardless of educational status, all Cheyenne and Arapaho delegates insisted that their people needed more money in order to buy the necessities of life. Families could not subsist on the ten-dollar disbursements each month from the restricted Individual Indian Accounts. Little Raven, an Arapaho chief, informed Commissioner Valentine that Indians without money signed promissory notes to cover the costs of food and clothing purchases. When the notes could not be redeemed, merchants foreclosed on the Indians' non-trust property. To increase the amount of money available, all Cheyenne and Arapaho delegates advocated that more Indians be allowed to lease their land and receive the income directly from the lessee. Negotiating leases and

expending their own money, it was suggested, would enhance the Indians' ability to deal with the white community.

Leasing of land independent of governmental supervision would not have solved the economic problems of the Cheyennes and Arapahoes. Even if lease and other incomes were maximized, the average annual per capita income for all Cheyennes and Arapahoes at this time would have been approximately $160. Only a few fortunate individuals, or families with multiple inherited allotments, lived far above subsistence level. Since Congress accepted the reformers' view that lease income hindered the inculcation of steady work habits and agreed that Indians should support themselves, the sale of original or inherited allotments was the only means of preventing starvation. But the amount of allotted land was finite, and land sales merely postponed the day of permanent poverty and deprivation.

The May 1909 conference prompted the Indian Office to send Indian Inspector Edgar A. Allen to investigate how Indian policy was affecting the welfare of the Cheyennes and Arapahoes. Allen's report, confined to the Darlington Agency, was shocking. He found that ninety-seven fee patents had been issued to the "most promising allottees" to test their capacity to manage their property, and at the time of his report in November all but two of the patentees had sold their land—in most instances, at far below market value. Furthermore, they had signed over title to cancel debts or in exchange for horses, buggies, and other merchandise at inflated prices, and had received little cash for their land. None of the property acquired remained in their possession, and few permanent improvements were visible on their remaining lands. "The granting of these patents," Allen concluded, "brings joys to the grafter and confidence man and abject poverty to the Indian. No good reasons exist from the standpoint of Indian welfare, for removing restrictions from another allotment, in advance of the trust period. The most capable do not desire such action."

Many Cheyennes and Arapahoes were in dire need by November of 1909, despite the sale of almost 22 percent of all inherited and original allotments and extensive land leasing. Without funds or credit, Indians had "nothing to tide them over during the cold weather." Even Indian farmers were in straits. Corn crops, for example, for the 1909 season produced only from five to twenty bushels per acre because of hot, dry weather. Agency Superintendent C. E. Shell apologetically explained that he had never favored issuing fee patents; his recommendations had simply conformed to Indian Office instructions. No more fee patents should be approved, Shell recommended, unless exceptional circumstances existed.

Commissioner Valentine saw no immediate reason to change existing policy by "laying down hard and fast rules." He merely cautioned the Darlington superintendent to give fee patent applications "more careful scrutiny and recommend only those who have shown by past performances that they are qualified to care for their own affairs." Investigations in 1911 at agencies where fee patents had been issued revealed that 60 percent of all Indians who had received fee patents had sold their land and wasted the sale money. Valentine, annoyed by the "carelessness and incompetence" of Indians who had received fee patents, maintained that any "liberal policy of giving patents in fee would be strictly at cross-purposes with other efforts of the Government to encourage industry, thrift and independence."

Valentine's land-sale program shifted from issuance of fee patents to competent tribesmen to the alienation of inherited land and the trust land of non-competent allotted Indians. Since those lands could be sold under governmental supervision, he maintained that prices would be equitable and the proceeds would remain on deposit for the Indians' benefit as restricted funds. Valentine also judged that leasing was injurious to the Indians' welfare. Only if an Indian had begun to farm and needed lease money to attain full production on the cultivated portion of an allotment should leasing be recommended. Even then, Valentine believed that if market conditions were favorable, it might still be more advantageous to sell land and use the money for permanent improvements on the remaining trust land.

The lack of agricultural progress by the Cheyennes and Arapahoes disturbed Valentine. At the Cantonment Agency he noted that only 2,587 acres were cultivated out of a total of 92,859 acres of trust land, while 80,320 acres were leased to non-Indians. He encouraged Superintendent Walter G. West to expedite the sale of inherited land to provide agency Indians with funds to improve their farming operations. Even if a family had not inherited land, portions of original allotments should be sold to buy farming equipment.

Such recommendations reflected Valentine's bureaucratic blindness. The Cheyennes and Arapahoes of Cantonment were the least likely groups of the two tribes to adapt to agriculture. After two decades of BIA efforts to implant the work ethic in these tribesmen through agricultural pursuits, their per capita cultivated acreage in 1912 was 3.38 acres. Agricultural machinery purchased for them would be abandoned, stolen, sold, or mortgaged, despite laws which prohibited the disposal of trust property. Therefore, if their agricultural land was sold, lease money would diminish and the Indians would be forced to work, thereby fulfilling the reformers' ideals, or starve.

Superintendent West hoped that younger Cheyennes and Arapahoes would become productive citizens after they were provided with farming machinery. More than 50 percent of the tribal population at the Cantonment Agency still lived in tipis and in camps consisting of from two to fifteen families. Some would fail to earn a living after their lands were sold, but West rationalized that "in any case, the Government will have done its part and the Indians will be no worse off than he [sic] would otherwise be . . . /and/ will be benefited by the experience afforded them." Toward the older people, West was more compassionate. He optimistically predicted that the government could "conserve their health and make them as comfortable and happy as possible during the remainder of their days." When lease income of an elderly person was insufficient, West suggested the use of tribal shares and the sale of trust lands, reserving only enough land for the elderly to live on and to raise a garden.

During the administration of Woodrow Wilson, the onslaught against allotted lands increased. No new legislation was necessary; the reformers had provided all administrative statutory authority required to strip land and property from allotted Indians. This power was seized by Franklin K. Lane, a Californian, and Cato Sells, a Texan, who as President Wilson's Secretary of Interior and Commissioner of Indian Affairs, respectively, viewed Indian affairs from a pro-Western perspective. Arable land in the public domain was becoming less plentiful immediately before and during World War I, making unused Indian allotments attractive to non-Indian land speculators, farmers, and ranchers. The policies of the Theodore Roosevelt and William Howard Taft administrations of selling Indian allotments required only different emphases to decimate further the land base of many allotted tribes.

Cheyenne and Arapaho chiefs and spokesmen quickly perceived that more of their people were receiving fee patents and selling trust land. They were also worried that tribal restrictions would not be renewed in 1917, when their twenty-five-year trust period expired. When Wolf Chief, an uneducated Cheyenne chief from the Seger Agency, heard in 1914 that Commissioner Sells intended to turn the Cheyennes and Arapahoes "loose to be civilized," he began "to moan aloud" and traveled to Washington to protest Sells's proposal. To Assistant Commissioner E. B. Meritt, Wolf Chief insisted that his people were not prepared to be severed from governmental supervision. "I am kind of afraid," Wolf Chief explained, "to take the white man's ways yet—I don't know how to write, I don't know how to manage my affairs the white man's way . . . when I look around amongst my tribe, my people, my school children—none of them are able to work like the white man, none of them can be doctors, none lawyers, none clerks in stores, and other work like that—they are too far behind yet." Alfrich Heap of Birds, a Carlisle graduate, told Meritt: "Some of our school boys thought they were educated enough to manage their own affairs and they received patents to their lands. As soon as the white man saw this they jumped on them and took all their land and money. Today they have nothing."

Evidence abounds that few Cheyennes and Arapahoes were prepared to be declared competent under the 1906 Burke Act. During a 1916 inspection tour of the Concho Agency, Supervisor H. G. Wilson learned that none of the 173 persons who had been issued fee patents since 1906 retained any of their allotted land. Only one patentee had invested his money by purchasing other land and buying good livestock. The others had sold their allotments for less than market value and spent the money for unneeded merchandise. Wilson recommended that the Cheyenne and Arapaho land "be held in trust for them for many years to come."

Ignoring information received from field personnel, Commissioner Sells in January of 1917 sent a competency board to the four Cheyenne-Arapaho agencies to prepare a list of Indians to whom fee patents should be issued. While the board members were en route to Oklahoma, a Cheyenne-Arapaho delegation made a futile appeal to Commissioner Meritt to have the board's proceedings delayed. Victor Bushyhead, a Haskell-educated Cheyenne, explained that even the younger educated people were not able to assume control of their land and money. "We young people," Bushyhead declared, "are always tempted to fall back and adopt the customs of the older people. We realize that if we were given . . . the right of conducting our own business affairs and our land turned over to us, that then all of our property and money would fall into the hands of grafters. We are not ready to prepare ourselves to compete with civilized people in a business way." Commissioner Sells made no concessions to the delegation, indicating only that he would recommend a ten-year extension of the trust period for those judged noncompetent. The younger people and mixed-bloods would have to take their chances with white merchants, bankers, and lawyers.

On January 19, 1917, the competency board began hearings on the "business competency" of the Cheyennes and Arapahoes. The board was concerned primarily with the level of education, the amount and value of trust land, the degree of Indian blood, employment, the number of dependents, marital status, and the ability of the Indians to read, write, and speak English. At the conclusion of the hearings, the board recommended that 177 Cheyennes and Arapahoes be issued fee patents. By executive order on April 4, 1917, President Wilson directed that 167 patents be issued from the list the board submitted.

The allottees recommended as competent had attained at least a fourth or fifth grade education. A significant fraction had attended programs at non-reservation schools such as Carlisle, Haskell, Chilocco, and Hampton. Of the individuals recommended for fee patents, 26.5 percent were of mixed Indian, white, black, or Mexican ancestry, and 73.5 percent were full-blood Indians.

The board's criteria of business competency were unclear. A few Indians recommended for fee patents worked as laborers, store clerks, held agency positions, or were craftsmen. A large majority of the younger people, however, pursued no vocation and lived on lease money. Among the fee patents subsequently issued, 54 percent were for full allotments, while 46 percent were issued for fractional allotments to individuals whose land had been partially patented or sold under the non-competency provisions of the 1907 Indian Appropriation Act. Individuals on the board's

fee patent list frequently retained inherited land or a portion of their original allotment, while a spouse's land often continued to be restricted. Of the 167 whose restrictions on land were removed, 76.5 percent were between the ages of twenty-one and thirty-nine. Regardless of age, 58.2 percent refused to sign applications for the removal of restrictions from their land. As the board's journal and recommendations indicate, little consideration was given to the allottee's previous record of handling his or her money and property.

The fears of the Cheyenne and Arapaho chiefs and spokesmen soon became realities. Land thieves, grafters, merchants, bankers, lawyers, and realtors prepared to profit handsomely from land which the Cheyennes and Arapahoes would be free to sell. An estimated $660,000 worth of land was available for plundering. Superintendent J. W. Smith of the Seger Agency warned Commissioner Sells that many younger Indians had purchased automobiles, giving the dealers undated mortgages on their lands which could be recorded after the fee patents had been received. If the "reckless disposition" of the money affected only the young men, Smith complained, he would not protest so vigorously. But in many instances the Indians were the "father/s/ of several children and most often have wives who do as much as they can to discourage such practices." W. W. Scott, superintendent at Concho and a competency board member, although displeased, was not as indignant as Smith at what was transpiring with the patented land. Scott also had learned that many Indians had "pledged" or mortgaged their allotments in anticipation of receiving a fee patent. In a matter of a few weeks after the patents had been received, Superintendent Smith claimed that all patented land had been sold. The Indians rarely acquired full value for their land, and spent their money for automobiles and other purchases which soon disappeared from their possession.

On April 17, 1917, Commissioner Sells announced a new Indian policy. Among all allotted tribes, any individual of one-half or more white ancestry, every Indian twenty-one years of age or older who had completed a full course of instruction in a government school, and all other Indians judged to be as competent as the "average whiteman" would be given "full control of his property and have all his lands and money turned over to him, after which he will no longer be a ward of the government." Sells decreed the sale of land for non-competent Indians to increase, liberalized regulations controlling the sale of inherited land, and encouraged land sales for the "old and feeble." He also permitted an accelerated use of tribal funds and Individual Indian Account money. The depletion of the Indian land base quickened even more when Indians who escaped the judgments of competency boards had trust restrictions removed from their property and money. Although Sells described his program as the "beginning of the end of the Indian problem," the reverse was correct. Once the land sales closed and the money received was expended, allotted Indians and their dependents faced lives of endless poverty.

Wherever allotted Indians lived, whites schemed to defraud them of their holdings. One center of white conspirators was the small community of Watonga, around which hundreds of Cheyenne and Arapaho allotments were concentrated in Blaine and adjacent counties. As early as 1908, Thompson B. Ferguson, former governor of the Territory of Oklahoma and editor and publisher of the Watonga *Republican,* warned that "sharks . . . have commenced to lay plans to beat the Indians out of their lands." At the heart of the ring of land thieves was Ed Baker, a Blaine County lawyer and judge, who was assisted by livestock dealers, merchants, bankers, county officials, four or five Cheyennes and Arapahoes, and at least one agency superintendent. Baker ingratiated himself with Cheyennes and Arapahoes by acting as their attorney for moderate fees in criminal and civil suits before local courts. He also loaned money at ten percent interest to Indians whom he believed would be granted fee

patents, keeping complete records of their indebtedness to him.

Baker never loaned Indians more than one half of the value of the land for which a fee patent would be issued. When Indians first obtained money from him, the attorney secured their signatures on undated mortgages which were recorded against their land and dated at a later time. The Indian spent the borrowed money for horses and merchandise (at highly inflated prices), feasts for his friends, and trips to visit relatives in Wyoming or Montana. When the mortgage fell due and Baker demanded repayment, the Indian had run through all of the money and could not borrow more from any source. Threatening foreclosure, Baker obtained the individual's signature to a deed to the patented land for a small additional sum. Merchants who cooperated with Baker sold the Indian's horses, buggies, wagons, and other goods valued higher than the amount borrowed from Baker, obtaining a promissory note for the difference. When a note fell due and the Indian was unable to redeem it, the merchant foreclosed and seized the chattel property before a cooperative county court.

From 1908 to 1917, Baker cleverly concealed his operations and avoided damaging legal actions. Only once, in 1914, was he sued successfully in a county court and forced to pay partial restitution for an illegal sale of two horses which were trust property. Prior to 1917, investigations by agency superintendents and BIA personnel dispatched from Washington failed to accumulate sufficient evidence against Baker and his fellow conspirators to present before a grand jury or a federal court. Following the 1917 hearings of the Cheyenne and Arapaho Competency Board, and Commissioner Sells's widespread issuance of fee patents, Baker's successful evasion of serious legal action emboldened him to embark upon numerous fraudulent ventures. Eventually, his activities and those of his friends became too flagrantly criminal for even Sells to ignore. Indian Inspector H. S. Traylor was sent to the

Concho and Cantonment agencies to initiate another investigation of Baker. Traylor obtained sufficient evidence from R. H. Green, a wealthy white farmer, to prosecute. Baker had double-crossed Green on an arrangement to acquire a valuable fee patented allotment. The irate farmer's testimony and the evidence Inspector Traylor gathered induced a grand jury to indict Baker for conspiracy to defraud the United States Government in its capacity as trustee of restricted Indian land and property.

The grand jury indictment led to a criminal case tried in the United States District Court for the Western District of Oklahoma. Tried with Baker were Ernie Black, a forty-five-year-old, full-blood Cheyenne educated at Carlisle, and W. W. Wisdom, a former superintendent of the Cantonment Agency. The United States attorney, using evidence compiled by Inspector Traylor and testimony of Cheyennes and Arapahoes and BIA employees, demonstrated that Baker and Black had defrauded the federal government through purchases of scores of patented Indian allotments for grossly unfair considerations. Baker and Black on June 13, 1919, were found guilty as charged. Baker was sentenced to four months in jail and fined $1,000, while Black received a two-month jail sentence and a $250 fine. Baker appealed his conviction, but the district court's verdict was affirmed in the September 1921 term of the United States Court of Appeals, Eighth Circuit. The judicial victory, however, did not restore one acre or one dollar to the Cheyennes and Arapahoes who had lost their land, money, and property to Baker and other looters.

In an attempt to recover the lost allotments, or their monetary value, four actions in equity were brought in 1919 before the United States District Court. Baker and secondary purchasers—a banker and insurance companies who had loaned money to Baker—were named defendants in the legal actions. The court returned a judgment against Baker alone, forcing the four Indian plaintiffs to look to the lawyer for recovery of their land or money. The secondary purchasers, the banker who certainly had full knowledge of Baker's operations and the insurance companies, were held by the court to be innocent and not liable to share in any judgment against Baker. In 1920 Baker moved from Oklahoma to Missouri, where in 1925 he stated that he was unable to pay the judgment handed down against him. Inquiries into Baker's financial status confirmed that he owned no property and that all of his family's assets, including his home, were registered in his wife's name. Although judgments were rendered against Baker for his crimes, the lawyer never repaid one cent of the money he had defrauded from over one hundred Cheyennes and Arapahoes.

The economic potential of the Cheyennes and Arapahoes was severely crippled during Cato Sells's administration. A total of 181,500 acres, or 34.3 percent, of all their allotted land was alienated. By adding land sold during the Roosevelt and Taft administrations, 297,214 acres, or 56.3 percent of all land allotted to the tribes, had passed from their possession. Criticism of Sells's policies surfaced in 1921, when the Board of Indian Commissioners concluded that the actions of the competency boards seemed to be "a shortcut to the separation of freed Indians from their land and cash." What happened to the Cheyennes and Arapahoes, unfortunately, also occurred at other Western agencies. With less land to sell and reduced demand during the 1920s, allotted land sales declined sharply. Because much of the productive agricultural land had been sold, income from leases and crops decreased at the Cheyenne and Arapaho agencies. And since Individual Indian Accounts were depleted even before Sells left office in 1921, the economic future of the tribesmen was bleak.

The attempt to transform the Cheyennes and Arapahoes into self-sufficient farmers and stock raisers during the Progressive Era had been a failure. The Dawes Act and its modifications led directly to the destruction of a viable land base for the two tribes, and bureaucrats wasted little sympathy on Indians when their land and money slipped away. Horace G.

Wilson, supervisor of farming, commented with remarkable callousness in early 1919 that some Cheyennes and Arapahoes were "probably better off now than they were before, as they made little or no use of their lands, and now that the land is gone and they receive no rentals, they are compelled to go to work." Land thieves such as Ed Baker, ready to defraud the Indians, profited from the blind adherence of reformers and bureaucrats to the work ethic. Misguided idealism, crippling legislation, destructive Indian policy and BIA regulations, hostile or indifferent courts, and white greed sapped the economic vitality of the Cheyenne and Arapaho peoples. That they have survived and multiplied in the twentieth century in spite of the policies of reformers and bureaucrats is a singular testament to their inner strength and a way of life based upon time-honored customs and spiritualism.

5

POPULIST DREAMS AND NEGRO RIGHTS: EAST TEXAS AS A CASE STUDY

LAWRENCE C. GOODWYN

The last decade of the nineteenth century was a time of upheaval in a century marked by unprecedented change. In the Northeast, mammoth factories and the immigrants who labored in them dominated the cities of America's industrial heartland. Throughout the country an ever-growing network of railroads connected even outlying regions to the burgeoning metropolises of the nation. And in these metropolises, financial and industrial cartels, monopolies, and holding companies exercised an economic and political influence unparalleled in American life.

Facing these changes were workers and farmers. American workers responded to the growing power of industrial capitalism with the collective power of their numbers and struggled with their employers over control of the workplace and the process of production itself. For their part the small farmers of the South and Midwest responded by forming organizations to fight discriminatory railroad freight rates and to challenge the power of eastern banks to yoke them to a cycle of unending indebtedness.

In the South the farmer's protest was embodied in the Southern Farmers' Alliance and its successor, the Populist or People's party, which sought to forge an alliance between black and white small farmers that would reinstate the power of the small producer in American society. As Lawrence Goodwyn shows in this essay, this Populist ideal followed a path fraught with danger. Faced with a resurgent white supremacist movement and mounting southern terrorism directed against its black members, the Populist movement found itself unable to protect its unique interracial coalition. Racism had again triumphed in America. Yet the idea of an interracial radical movement did not die with the decline of Populism; it took root after 1910 in the southern and western branches of the Socialist party, which elected local and state officials to represent the interests of small farmers and rural workers much as the Populists had done before them.

From *American Historical Review* 76:1435–56 (1971). Reprinted by permission.

Nearly a century later the Populist decade lingers in historical memory as an increasingly dim abstraction. The very word "Populism" no longer carries specific political meaning. It is now invoked to explain George Wallace, as it was used to explain Lyndon Johnson in the sixties, Joe McCarthy in the fifties, and Claude Pepper in the forties. Though afflicting principally the popular mind, this confusion is at least partly traceable to those historians who have insisted on concentrating on Populism as exhortation, so that Ignatius Donnelly's utopian novels or Mary Lease's pronouncements on the respective uses of corn and hell become the explanatory keys to agrarian radicalism. For scholars who mine political movements with a view to extracting cultural nuggets, the focus has been chiefly upon the word, not the deed; in the process the agrarian crusade has become increasingly obscure.

Much of the difficulty centers on the subject of race. There is essential agreement that, on economic issues, Populists were men of the Left, primitive to some, prophetic to others, but leftists to all. But did their banner indicate a highly selective nativist radicalism for whites only, or did they grapple with the inherited legacies of the caste system as part of an effort to create what they considered a more rational social and economic order? The analysis of Populist rhetoric has left us with contradictory answers.

While party platforms can be useful tools in determining professed attitudes, the gap between asserted ideals and performance is sufficiently large to defeat any analysis resting on the implicit assumption that political manifestos have an intrinsic value apart from the milieu in which they existed. In America the distance between assertion and performance is especially evident in matters of race; as a result, on this issue above all, the context of public assertions is central to the task of their political evaluation. An inquiry into the murkiest corner of Populism, interracial politics, should begin not merely with what Populists said but what they did in the course of bidding for

power at the local level. What was the stuff of daily life under Populist rule in the rural enclaves where the third party came to exercise all the authority of public office, including police authority? What can we learn not only about Populist insurgency but also about the orthodoxy the third party opposed?

Grimes County, Texas, was one of many counties scattered across the South and West where the People's party achieved a continuing political presence in the latter part of the nineteenth century. Located some sixty miles north of Houston in the heart of what the natives call the Old South part of Texas, Grimes County displayed the cotton-centered economy typical of rural East Texas in 1880. Its largest town, Navasota, contained 1,800 persons in 1890 and its second largest town, Anderson, the county seat, only 574 persons as late as 1900. Farms in Grimes County ranged from plantation size in the rich bottomland country of the Brazos River on the county's western border to small, single-family agricultural units on the poorer land of the northern part of the county. The 1890 census revealed a county population of 21,312, of which 11,664 were black.

Populism in Grimes County is the story of a black-white coalition that had its genesis in Reconstruction and endured for more than a generation. In time this coalition came to be symbolized by its most enduring elected public official, Garrett Scott. The Scotts had roots in Grimes County dating back before the Civil War. Their sons fought for the Confederacy and returned to face a postwar reality by no means unique in the South; possessing moderately large holdings of land but lacking necessary capital to make it productive, the Scotts did not achieve great affluence. During the hard times that continued to afflict undercapitalized Southern agriculture through the 1870s Garrett Scott became a soft-money agrarian radical. His stance was significant in the political climate of Grimes County in the early 1880s. During Reconstruction Negroes in the county had achieved a remarkably stable local Republican organization, headed by a number of resourceful black leaders. When Reconstruction ended and white Democrats regained control of the state governmental machinery in Texas, Grimes County blacks retained local power and sent a succession of black legislators to Austin for the next decade. The local effort to end this Republican rule took the usual postwar Southern form of a political movement of white solidarity under the label of the Democratic party. In supporting the Greenback party Garrett Scott not only was disassociating himself from the politics of white racial solidarity, he was undermining it.

In 1882 a mass meeting of various non-Democratic elements in Grimes County nominated a variegated slate for county offices. Among the candidates were black Republicans, "lily-white" Republicans, and Independent Greenbackers. Garrett Scott was on the ticket as the Independent Greenback candidate for sheriff. Not much is known about the racial climate in Grimes County in 1882, but it must not have been wholly serene, because the "lily-white" nominee for county judge, Lock MacDaniel, withdrew from the ticket rather than publicly associate with black candidates. Garrett Scott did not withdraw, and in November he was elected. Also elected, as district clerk, was a black man who became a lifelong political ally of Scott, Jim Kennard. Thus began an interracial coalition that endured through the years of propagandizing in Texas by the increasingly radical Farmers Alliance and through the ensuing period of the People's party. The success of the coalition varied with the degree of white participation. After the collapse of the Greenback party in the mid-eighties visible white opposition to the Democratic party declined for several years before Grimes County farmers, organized by the Alliance, broke with the Democracy to form the nucleus of the local People's party in 1892. Scott and Kennard were the most visible symbols of the revitalized coalition, but there were others as well. Among them were Morris Carrington, a Negro school principal, and Jack Haynes, both staunch advocates of Populism in the black community, as well as J. W. H. Davis and J. H. Teague, white Populist leaders. These men led the People's party to victory in the county elections of 1896 and again in 1898.

A subtle duality creeps into the narrative of events at this point. To the world outside Grimes County in the 1890s, to both Populist and Democrats, Garrett Scott was simply another Populist officeholder, distinguished for his antimonopoly views and his generally radical approach to monetary policy. To his white supporters within Grimes County he was doubtless respected for the same reasons. But to the Democrats of Grimes County the sheriff symbolized all that was un-Southern and unpatriotic about the third party. Under Populist rule, it was charged, Negro school teachers were paid too much money; furthermore, in Scott's hands the sheriff's office hired Negro deputies. The two Democratic newspapers in Navasota were fond of equating Populist rule with Negro rule and of attributing both evils to Scott. The Navasota *Daily Examiner* asserted that "the Negro has been looking too much to political agitation and legislative enactment.... So long as he looks to political agitation for relief, so long will he be simply the means of other men's ambition." To the Navasota *Tablet* Scott was simply "the originator of all the political trouble in Grimes County for years." Both these explanations oversimplify Grimes County politics. The political presence and goals of blacks were definite elements of local Populism, as was, presumably, the personal ambition of Garrett Scott. But the Populists' proposed economic remedies had gained a significant following among the county's white farmers, and this was of crucial importance in inducing white Populists to break with Democrats and ally themselves with blacks. Garrett Scott was a living embodiment of white radicalism; he did not cause it. Beyond this the political cohesion of blacks was a local phenomenon that had preceded Scott's entry into Grimes County politics and had remained relatively stable since the end of the war. The ease with which Democratic partisans saw the fine hand of Garrett Scott in Negro voting was more a reflection of their own racial presumptions than an accurate description of the political dynamics at work in the county.

Through the election of 1898 Democrats in Grimes County had labored in vain to cope with the disease of Populism among the county's white farmers. Finally, in the spring of 1899, the Democrats moved in a new direction. The defeated Democratic candidate for county judge, J. G. McDonald, organized a clandestine meeting with other prominent local citizens and defeated Democratic office seekers. At this meeting a new and—for the time being—covert political institution was created: the White Man's Union. A charter was drawn providing machinery through which the Union could nominate candidates for county offices in elections in which only White Man's Union members could vote. No person could be nominated who was not a member; no person could be a member who did not subscribe to these exclusionary bylaws; in effect, to participate in the organization's activities, so adequately expressed in its formal title, one had to support, as a policy matter, black disfranchisement. Throughout the summer and fall of 1899 the White Man's Union quietly organized.

Writing years later McDonald explained that care was taken not to launch the organization publicly "until the public attitude could be sounded." By January 1900 the covert organizing had been deemed sufficiently successful to permit the public unveiling of the White Man's Union through a long story in the *Examiner.* During the spring the *Examiner's* political reporting began to reflect a significant change of tone. In April, for example, the *Examiner's* report of a "quiet election" in nearby Bryan noted that friends of the two mayoral candidates "made a display of force and permitted no Negroes to vote. All white citizens went to the polls, quietly deposited their ballots for whom they pleased and went on about their business." The *Examiner* had progressed from vague suggestions for disfranchisement to ap-

proval of its forcible imposition without cover of law.

The first public meetings of the White Man's Union, duly announced in the local press, occupied the spring months of 1900 and were soon augmented by some not-quite-so-public night riding. The chronology of these events may be traced through the denials in the local Democratic press of their occurrence. In July the *Examiner* angrily defended the county's honor against charges by the Negro Baptist State Sunday School Conference that the county had become unsafe for Negroes. The Austin *Herald* reported from the state's capital that the Sunday School Board, "after mature thought and philosophical deliberation," had decided to cancel its annual meeting scheduled for Navasota. The *Examiner* cited as "irresponsible slush" the charge that Negroes were being threatened and told to leave the county, but within weeks reports of just such events began cropping up in the *Examiner* itself. One example of terrorism left no one in doubt, for it occurred in broad daylight on the main street of the county seat: in July Jim Kennard was shot and killed within one hundred yards of the courthouse. His assailant was alleged to be J. G. McDonald.

Intimidation and murder constituted an even more decisive assault on the People's party than had the ominous bylaws of the White Man's Union. The Populist leadership recognized this clearly enough, and Scott went so far as to attempt to persuade Southern white farmers to shoulder arms in defense of the right of Negroes to vote. Beyond this we know little of the measures attempted by the local Populist constabulary to contain the spreading terrorism. A well-informed member of the Scott family wrote a detailed account of these turbulent months, but the manuscript was subsequently destroyed. In the early autumn of 1900 members of the White Man's Union felt sufficiently strong to initiate visits to white farmers with a known allegiance to the People's party. Under such duress some of these farmers joined the White Man's Union.

In August the Union, aided by a not inconsiderable amount of free publicity in the local press, announced "the Grandest Barbecue of the Year," at which the "working of the White Man's Union" would be explained to all. The leadership of the People's party objected to announced plans to include the local state guard unit, the Shaw Rifles, in the program. After some discussion the Texas adjutant general, Thomas Scurry, placed at the discretion of the local commander the question of the attendance of the Shaw Rifles in a body. The commander, Captain Hammond Norwood, a leading Navasota Democrat and a member of the White Man's Union, exercised his option, and the Shaw Rifles appeared en masse at the function. Populist objections were brushed aside.

Shortly after this well-attended barbecue had revealed the growing prestige of the White Man's Union as well as the inability of the People's party to cope with the changing power relationships within the county, a black exodus began. People left by train, by horse and cart, by day and by night. The *Examiner,* with obvious respect for the new political climate its own columns had helped engender, suggested elliptically that the exodus could produce complications. Some citizens, said the *Examiner,* "are beginning to feel a little nervous as the thing progresses, and lean to the idea that the action will bring on detrimental complications in the labor market."

The next day, however, the paper printed a public address that it said had been "ordered published by the executive committee of the White Man's Union in order to combat the many reports that are calculated to injure the Union." After reaffirming the Union's intent to end "Negro rule" in the county, the report concluded with a message "to the Negroes":

> Being the weaker race, it is our desire to protect you from the schemes of those men who are now seeking to place you before them. . . . Therefore, the White Man's Union kindly and

earnestly requests you to keep hands off in the coming struggle. Do not let impudent men influence you in that pathway which certainly leads to trouble. . . . In the future, permit us to show you, and convince you by our action, that we are truly your best friends.

Fourteen days later a black Populist leader, Jack Haynes, was riddled with a shotgun blast by unknown assailants. He died instantly in the fields of his cotton farm.

The White Man's Union held a rally in Navasota two nights later that featured a reading of original poetry by one of the Union's candidates, L. M. Bragg. The verse concluded:

> *Twas nature's laws that drew the lines*
> *Between the Anglo-Saxon and African races,*
> *And we, the Anglo-Saxons of Grand Old*
>   *Grimes,*
> *Must force the African to keep his place.*

Another White Man's Union rally held in Plantersville the same week displayed other Union candidates whose conduct won the *Examiner*'s editorial approval: "They are a solid looking body of men and mean business straight from the shoulder." Apparently this characterization of the Plantersville speakers was not restricted to approving Democrats; Populists, too, responded to events initiated by the men who "meant business." In October the Plantersville school superintendent reported that only five white families remained in his school district and that all the Negroes were gone. The superintendent stated that twelve white families had left that week, and "the end is not in sight."

Amid this wave of mounting terror the People's party attempted to go about its business, announcing its nominating conventions in the local press and moving forward with the business of naming election judges and poll watchers. But there were already signs of a fatal crack in Populist morale. The People's party nominee for county commissioner suddenly withdrew from the race. His withdrawal was announced in the *Examiner,* and no explanation was offered.

Throughout the late summer and autumn of 1900 the demonstrated power of the White Man's Union had protected McDonald from prosecution in the Kennard slaying. Nothing short of a war between the Populist police authority and the White Man's Union could break that extralegal shield. An exasperated and perhaps desperate Garrett Scott angrily challenged a White Man's Union official in October to "go and get your Union force, every damn one of them, put them behind rock fences and trees and I'll fight the whole damn set of cowards." That Scott had to use the first person singular to describe the visible opposition to the Union underscores the extent to which terror had triumphed over the institutions of law in Grimes County. By election eve it was clear that the Populist ticket faced certain defeat. The third party had failed to protect its constituency. White Populists as well as black were intimidated. Many would not vote; indeed, many were no longer in the county.

Over 4,500 votes had been cast in Grimes in 1898. On November 6, 1900, only 1,800 persons ventured to the polls. The People's party received exactly 366 votes. The Populist vote in Plantersville fell from 256 in 1898 to 5 in 1900. In the racially mixed, lower-income precinct of south Navasota the Populist vote declined from 636 to 23. The sole exception to this pattern came in a geographically isolated, lower-income precinct in the extreme northern part of the county that contained few Negroes and thus, presumably, fewer acts of terrorism. The Populist vote in this precinct actually increased from 108 to 122 and accounted for one-third of the countywide vote of 366. In north Navasota, also almost all white but not geographically isolated from the terror, the Populist vote declined from 120 to 3. An additional element, nonstatistical in nature, stamped the election as unusual. The underlying philosophy of the South's dominant political institution, the Democratic party, has perhaps never been expressed more nakedly than

it was in Grimes County in 1900 when "the party of white supremacy," as C. Vann Woodward has called the Southern Democracy, appeared on the official ballot as the White Man's Union.

On the way to its landslide victory the Union had grown more self-confident in its willingness to carry out acts of intimidation and terrorism in defiance of the local Populist police authority. Now that that authority had been deposed and a sheriff friendly to the White Man's Union had been elected, would terrorism become even more public?

On November 7, 1900, the morning after the election, a strange tableau unfolded on the streets of Anderson, the tiny county seat. Horsemen began arriving in town from every section of the county, tied their horses all along the main street, and occupied the second floor of the courthouse. In a nearby house Garrett Scott's sister, Cornelia, and her husband, John Kelly, watched the buildup of Union supporters on the courthouse square, not fifty yards from the sheriff's official residence on the second floor of the county jail. They decided the situation was too dangerous to permit an adult Populist to venture forth, so the Kellys sent their nine-year-old son with a note to warn Scott not to appear on the street.

At about the same time that this mission was carried out Garrett Scott's younger brother, Emmett Scott, came into town from the family farm, rode past the growing clusters of armed men, and reined up in front of the store belonging to John Bradley, his closest friend in town. Bradley was a Populist but, as befitting a man of trade, a quiet one. His store was adjacent to the courthouse.

Cornelia Kelly's son found the sheriff at Abercrombie's store across the street from the jail and delivered the warning note. As Scott read it an outbreak of gunfire sounded from the direction of Bradley's store. Scott stepped to the street and peered in the direction of the fusillade. Rifle fire from the second floor of the courthouse immediately cut him down. Upon hearing the gunfire Cornelia Kelly ran out of her house and down the long street toward the courthouse. The gunsights of scores of men tracked her progress. Seeing her brother's body in the street she turned and confronted his attackers. "Why don't you shoot me, too," she yelled, "I'm a Scott." She ran to her brother and, with the assistance of her son, dragged him across the street to the county jail. He was, she found, not dead, though he did have an ugly wound in his hip. Inside Bradley's store, however, three men were dead—Emmett Scott, Bradley, and Will McDonald, the son of a Presbyterian minister and a prominent member of the White Man's Union. McDonald had shot Scott shortly after the latter had entered the store; the two men grappled for the gun, and the fatally wounded Scott fired one shot, killing McDonald. Bradley was killed either by a shot fired from outside the store where Union forces had gathered near the courthouse or by a stray bullet during the struggle inside.

The siege of Anderson continued for five days, with the wounded sheriff and his deputies—black and white—in the jail and the White Man's Union forces in the courthouse. Shots crossed the fifty yards between the two buildings intermittently over the next several days. On the evening of the fatal shooting another member of the Scott clan, Mrs. W. T. Neblett, had left Navasota for Austin to plead with the governor, Joseph D. Sayers, for troops. On Friday she returned, accompanied by the adjutant general of the State of Texas, Thomas Scurry—the same official who had earlier acquiesced in the participation of the state guard in the White Man's Union barbecue. After conferring with the contending forces Scurry pondered various methods to get the wounded Scott out of town and into a hospital; gangrene had set in. For protection, Scurry suggested that he be authorized to select a group of twenty prominent citizens of Navasota to escort the sheriff from the jail to the railroad station. Since most of the "prominent citizens" of Navasota were members of the White Man's Union, it is perhaps under-

standable that Scott declined this offer. The adjutant general then suggested that the Shaw Rifles be employed as an escort. This idea was respectfully declined for the same reason. Asked what he would consider a trustworthy escort, the wounded sheriff suggested a state guard unit from outside the county.

On Saturday, four days after the shooting, a company of Houston light infantry of the Texas Volunteer State Guard detrained at Navasota and marched the eleven miles to Anderson. On Sunday morning Garrett Scott was placed on a mattress, the mattress put in a wagon, and the procession began. In the wagon train were most of the members of the large Scott clan— Emmett Scott's widow and children, the Kelly family, and the Nebletts, all with their household belongings piled in wagons. A file of infantrymen marched on either side as the procession formed in front of the jail, moved past hundreds of armed men at the courthouse and onto the highway to Navasota, and then boarded a special train bound for Houston.

Thus did Populism leave Grimes County. From that day in 1900 until well after mid-century Negroes were not a factor in Grimes County politics. J. G. McDonald regained his judgeship and served for many years. The White Man's Union continued into the 1950s as the dominant political institution in the county. None of its nominees, selected in advance of the Democratic primary, was ever defeated. The census of 1910 revealed the extent of the Negro exodus. It showed that Grimes County's Negro population had declined by almost thirty per cent from the 1900 total. School census figures for 1901 suggest an even greater exodus.

To this day the White Man's Union, as a memory if no longer as an institution, enjoys an uncontested reputation among Grimes County whites as a civic enterprise for governmental reform. In this white oral tradition the general events of 1900 are vividly recounted. Specific events are, however remembered selectively. The exodus of Negroes from the county is not part of this oral tradition, nor is the night riding of the White Man's Union or the assassination of the Negro Populist leaders.

As for Garrett Scott, he endured a long convalescence in a San Antonio hospital, regained his health, married his nurse, and moved to a farm near Houston. He retired from politics and died in his bed. He is remembered in the oral tradition of the black community as the "best sheriff the county ever had." Kennard and Haynes were killed because they "vouched" for Scott among Negroes. In this black oral tradition the Negro exodus plays a central role. It is perhaps an accurate measure of the distance between the races in Grimes County today that two such contradictory versions of famous events could exist side by side without cross-influence.

To these two oral traditions a third must be added—the Scott tradition. The Scotts were, and are, a proud family. One by one, as they died, they were brought home to be buried in the family plot in the Anderson cemetery, little more than a mile from the site of the bloody events of 1900. Tombstones of female members of the clan bear the Scott middle name, defiantly emblazoned in marble. Edith Hamilton of Richards, Grimes County, was ten years old in November 1900 and remembers vividly the day her nine-year-old brother carried her mother's message to Garrett Scott. She remembers the defiance of her mother, the political commitment of her father, the acts of intimidation by the White Man's Union, the Negro exodus, and what she calls the "intelligence of Uncle Garrett." "They said that Uncle Garrett was a nigger-lover," recalls Mrs. Hamilton. "He wasn't a nigger-lover, or a white-lover, he just believed in being fair to all, in justice."

The Scott oral tradition—similar to the black oral tradition and at odds with the white tradition—is virtually the only legacy of the long years of interracial cooperation in Grimes County. Beyond this the substance of political life that came to an end in Grimes County in 1900 cannot be measured precisely from the available evidence. Very little survives to provide insight into the nature of the personal relationship that existed between Garrett Scott and Jim Kennard, between any of the other Populist leaders of both races, or between their respective constituencies. Scott and his third-party colleagues may have been motivated solely by personal ambition, as the White Man's Union charged; on the other hand, the impulses that made them Populists in the first place may have led them toward public coalition with blacks. It is clear that such stridently white supremacist voices as the Navasota *Tablet* were unable to project any reason other than personal ambition to explain the phenomenon of white men willingly associating themselves politically with black men. To what extent this attitude reflected Populist presumptions is another question. White Populists and black Republicans shared an animosity toward the Southern Democracy that grew in intensity during the bitter election campaigns of the 1890s. Democratic persistence in raising the cry of "Negro domination" to lure Populist-leaning voters back to the "party of the fathers" was effective enough to keep white Populists on the defensive about the race issue throughout the agrarian revolt in the South. The circumstance of a common political foe nevertheless provided Populists and Republicans with a basis for political coalition that was consummated in a bewildering variety of ways—and sometimes not consummated at all. The stability of local black organizations and their demonstrated capacity to withstand Democratic blandishments or acts of intimidation were only two of the factors governing the complex equation of post-Reconstruction interracial politics. A stable, local black political institution existed in Grimes County, and its enduring qualities obviously simplified the organizational task confronting Garrett Scott. What might be regarded as "normal" Bourbon efforts to split blacks from the Populist coalition—mild intimidation, petty bribery, campaign assertions that the Democrats were the Negroes' "best friends," or a combination of all three—failed to achieve the desired results in Grimes County in the 1890s.

The precise reasons are not easily specified. The Navasota *Tablet,* seeing the world through lenses tinted with its own racial presumptions, ascribed the credit for Negro political cohesion solely to the white sheriff. In the face of all Democratic stratagems, the third party's continuing appeal to Negroes was, in the *Tablet*'s view, a thing of "magic." A white supremacist view does not automatically exclude its holder from rendering correct political analyses on occasion, and it is possible that the *Tablet*'s assessment of the cause of Negro political solidarity was correct; however, such an analysis does not explain how the Negro Republican organization was able to send a succession of black legislators to Austin in the 1870s and 1880s, before Garrett Scott became politically active. It seems relevant that when Grimes County Democrats decided upon an overt campaign of terrorism, the men they went after first were the leading black spokesmen of Populism in the county rather than the third party's white leadership. To this extent the actions of Democratic leaders contradicted their public analysis of the causal relationships inherent in the continuing Populist majorities.

Before they indulged in terrorism the Democrats already possessed another method of splitting the Populist coalition: regaining the loyalty of white Populists. Against the historic Democratic campaign cry of white supremacy, the People's party had as its most effective defense the economic appeal of its own platform. The persuasiveness of Populism to white farmers in Grimes County was confirmed by newspaper accounts of the public reaction to the Populist-Democratic debates that occurred during the years of the agrarian uprising. While the reports in the *Examiner* were uniformly partisan and invariably concluded that Democratic spokesmen "won" such debates hands down, the papers conceded that Populist speakers also drew enthusiastic responses from white residents. The absence of reliable racial data by precincts renders a statistical analysis of the Populist vote in Grimes County impossible; however, the fragmentary availa-

ble evidence suggests that the People's party was generally able to hold a minimum of approximately thirty per cent of the county's white voters in the four elections from 1892 to 1898 while at the same time polling approximately eighty to ninety per cent of the Negro electorate. The inability of the Democratic party to "bloc vote" the county's white citizenry, coupled with the party's failure to win black voters by various means or, alternatively, to diminish the size of the Negro electorate, combined to ensure Democratic defeat at the polls. The fact merits emphasis: both the cohesion of black support for the People's party and the maintenance of substantial white support were essential to the local ascendancy of Populism.

This largely deductive analysis, however, reveals little about the internal environment within the third-party coalition during the bitter struggle for power that characterized the decade of Populist-Democratic rivalry. However scrutinized, the bare bones of voting totals do not flesh out the human relationships through which black and white men came together politically in this rural Southern county. In the absence of such crucial evidence, it seems prudent to measure the meaning of 1900 in the most conservative possible terms. Even by this standard, however, a simple recitation of those elements of Grimes County politics that are beyond dispute isolates significant and lasting ramifications.

An indigenous black political structure persisted in Grimes County for thirty-five years following the Civil War. Out of his own needs as a political insurgent against the dominant Southern Democratic party, Garrett Scott decided in 1882 to identify his Greenback cause with the existing local Republican constituency. Once in office as sheriff he found, among other possible motives, that it was in his own self-interest to preserve the coalition that elected him. It is clear that the style of law enforcement in Grimes County under Scott became a persuasive ingredient in the preservation of black support for the People's party.

The presence of black deputy sheriffs and Scott's reputation within the black community seem adequate confirmation of both the existence of this style and its practical effect. The salaries paid Negro school teachers constituted another element of third-party appeal. Comparisons with white salaries are not available, but whatever black teachers received, partisans of the White Man's Union publicly denounced it as "too much." It is evident that Grimes County Negroes supported the People's party for reasons that were grounded in legitimate self-interest—an incontestable basis for political conduct. The point is not so much that the county's Negroes had certain needs, but that they possessed the political means to address at least a part of those needs.

From this perspective the decisive political event of 1900 in Grimes County was not the overwhelming defeat of the local People's party but the political elimination of that part of its constituency that was black. Scott was valuable to Negroes in short-run terms because he helped to translate a minority black vote into a majority coalition that possessed the administrative authority to improve the way black people lived in Grimes County. In the long run, however, it was the presence of this black constituency—not the conduct of a single white sheriff nor even the professed principles of his political party—that provided the Negroes of the county with what protection they had from a resurgent caste system. As long as Negroes retained the right to cast ballots in proportion to their numbers they possessed bargaining power that became particularly meaningful on all occasions when whites divided their votes over economic issues. Disfranchisement destroyed the bargaining power essential to this elementary level of protection. Arrayed against these overriding imperatives for Negroes such questions as the sincerity of Garrett Scott's motives fade in importance. Whatever the sheriff's motives, both the political realities that undergirded the majority coalition and Scott's ability to respond to those realities shaped a course of government conduct under the People's party that was de-

monstrably of more benefit to Negroes than was the conduct of other administrations before or since. The permanent alteration of those realities through black disfranchisement ensured that no other white administration, whether radical, moderate, or opportunistic, would be able to achieve the patterns in education and law enforcement that had come to exist in the county under Populism. Stated as starkly as possible, after 1900 it was no longer in the interest of white politicians to provide minimal guarantees for people who could not help elect them.

Beyond this crucial significance for the county's black people, disfranchisement also institutionalized a fundamental change in the political environment of whites. More than a third party passed from Grimes County in 1900; in real political terms an idea died. Though a new political idea invariably materializes in democratic societies as an expression of the self-interest of a portion of the electorate, the party that adopts the idea in the course of appealing for the votes of that sector of the electorate inevitably is placed in the position of having to rationalize, defend, explain, and eventually promote the idea. If the concept has substance, this process eventually results in the insinuation of the idea into the culture itself. In this sense it is not necessary to know the precise depth of the commitment to Negro rights of the Grimes County People's party to know that the *idea* of Negro rights had a potential constituency among white people in the county as long as black people were able to project its presence through their votes. Given the endurance of this real and potential constituency, one could reasonably intuit that twentieth-century politics in Grimes County would have contained one, or a dozen, or a thousand Garrett Scotts—each more, or less, "sincere" or "ambitious" than the Populist sheriff. Disfranchisement destroyed the political base of this probability. A political party can survive electoral defeat, even continuing defeat, and remain a conveyor of ideas from one generation to the next. But it cannot survive the destruction of its constituency, for the party itself then dies, taking with it the possibility of transmitting its political concepts to those as yet unborn. It is therefore no longer possible to speak of two white political traditions in Grimes County, for the White Man's Union succeeded in establishing a most effective philosophical suzerainty. Seventy years after disfranchisement Mrs. Hamilton can recall the racial unorthodoxy of Uncle Garrett; she cannot participate in such activity herself. "The Negro people here don't want this school integration any more than the whites do," she now says. "They're not ready for it. They don't feel comfortable in the school with white children. I've talked to my maid. I know."

While Garrett Scott's memory has been preserved, the local presence of the creed of his political party died with the destruction of that party. There has been literally no political place to go for subsequent generations of Scotts and Teagues, or Kennards and Carringtons. This absence of an alternative political institution to the Democratic party, the party of white supremacy, has been a continuing and unique factor in Southern politics. The circumstance is based on the race issue, but in its long-term political and social implications it actually transcends that issue.

The Populist era raises a number of questions about the interaction of the two races in the South, both within the third party and in the larger society. It is widely believed, by no means merely by laymen, that after the failure of Reconstruction meaningful experiments with the social order were finished in the South and that the aspirations of blacks were decisively thwarted. The example of Grimes County suggests, however, the existence of a period of time—a decade perhaps, or a generation—when nascent forms of indigenous interracial activity struggled for life in at least parts of the old Confederacy. Was some opportunity missed and, if so, how? How widespread through the South, and the nation, was this opportunity?

The White Man's Union was organized and led by men who considered themselves the "best people" of the South. If this attitude was typical, major adjustments must be made in our understanding of precisely how, and for what reasons, the antebellum caste system, in altered form, was reinstitutionalized in Southern society a generation after the formal ending of slavery. Was the "red-neck" the source of atrocity, or was he swept along by other stronger currents? And what of the Populist role? To what extent was agrarian racial liberalism in Texas traceable to an overall philosophy within the third-party leadership? Through what intuition of self-interest did the radical organizers of the Farmers Alliance, the parent institution of the People's party, accept the political risks of public coalition with blacks? What were their hopes and fears, and where did they falter? And, finally, what does the substance of their effort tell us about the Democrats in the South and the Republicans in the North who opposed them?

Answers to these questions rest, in part, on detailed knowledge of such events as those in Grimes County, but they require more than compilations of local histories, just as they assuredly require more than cultural assessments based on novels, speeches, and party manifestoes considered apart from their organic milieu. These answers will not provide much of a synthesis—Populism was too diverse, too congregational, and too ideologically thin—but they should tell us more about the larger society that, along with the Populists, failed to erect the foundations for a multiracial society in the nineteenth century. As the inquiry proceeds, it should be remembered that Populism perished before developing a mature philosophy—on race, on money, or on socialism. One must generalize, therefore, not only from contradictory evidence but, more important, from incomplete evidence. An analogy, doubtless unfair, could be made with the plight that would face modern historians of Marxism had that movement been abruptly truncated at the time, say, of the Brussels Conference in 1903. Who could have predicted on the evidence available to that date the Stalinist reign of terror that evolved from the mature, victorious revolutionary party of 1917? By the same token sweeping generalizations about what Populist radicalism could have become are not only romantic but historically unsound.

It should be sufficient to observe that in the long post-Reconstruction period—a period not yet ended—during which the social order has been organized hierarchically along racial lines, Populism intruded as a brief, flickering light in parts of the South. For a time some white Southerners threw off the romanticism that has historically been a cover for the region's pessimism and ventured a larger, more hopeful view about the possibilities of man in a free society. Under duress and intimidation this public hope failed of persuasion at the ballot box; under terrorism it vanished completely.

The Grimes County story dramatically illustrates this failure, but in the insight it provides into the underlying politics of black disfranchisement and the achievement of a monolithic one-party political environment in the American South it is not unique. Other Populists in East Texas and across the South—white as well as black—died during the terrorism that preceded formal disfranchisement. In Texas the extraparliamentary institutions formed by white Democrats to help create the political climate for disfranchisement bore a variety of local names: the Citizens White Primary of Marion County; the Tax-Payers Union of Brazoria County; the Jaybird Democratic Association of Fort Bend County; and the White Man's Union of Wharton, Washington, Austin, Matagorda, Grimes, and other counties. The available historical material concerning each of these organizations comes largely from the founders themselves, or their descendants, reflecting an incipient or a mature oral tradition—one oral tradition. The secondary literature based on these accounts, including scholarly works used in graduate schools as well as primary and secondary textbooks, is correspondingly inadequate.

A surprising amount of uninterpreted mate-

rial from violently partisan white supremacist sources has found its way into scholarly literature. One example from the Grimes experience pertains directly to the scholarly characterization of Negro political meetings during the Populist era. It is worth attention as an illustration of the impact of white supremacist modes of thought on modern scholarship. The sunup-to-sundown work routine of Southern farm labor obviously precluded daytime political meetings. Accordingly, Kennard, Haynes, and Carrington campaigned among their black constituents by holding political meetings in each of the towns and hamlets of the county at night. Democratic partisans termed these rallies "Owl Meetings" and characterized black Populist leaders as " 'fluence men." Drawing upon their own party's time-honored campaign technique with Negroes, Democrats further asserted that owl meetings were more concerned with sumptuous banquets and whisky than with politics. If partisans of white supremacy had difficulty finding reasons for white acceptance of political coalition with blacks, they were culturally incapable of ascribing reasons for Negro support of the third party to causes other than short-run benefits in terms of money and alcohol. The point is not that Democrats were always insincere in their descriptions (as white supremacists they were quite sincere), but that scholars have subsequently accepted such violently partisan accounts at face value. The darkly sinister picture of " 'fluence men" corrupting innocent blacks with whisky at surreptitious owl meetings served to justify, at least to outsiders, the use of terrorism as the ultimate campaign technique of Democratic interracial politics. This sequential recording of events has found its way into scholarly monographs that otherwise demonstrate no inherent hostility to the Populistic inclinations of Southern farmers, black or white. In *The People's Party in Texas* Roscoe Martin precedes his brief allusion to the White Man's Union with a resumé of owl meetings and " 'fluence men" that reflects in detail the bias of white supremacist sources. Other scholars writing broadly about Gilded Age politics have routinely drawn upon such monographs as Martin's, and by this process " 'fluence men" have materialized as an explanation of Negro political insurgency in the nineties. In the heat of local political combat, however, Democratic leaders often were able to face a wholly different set of facts in the course of persuading their followers, and the citizenry as a whole, to adjust to the necessity of terrorism. As the time approached for actual precinct campaigning in Grimes County in the autumn of 1900, the executive board of the White Man's Union published a notice of the Union's intentions, climaxed by a "fair distinct warning" to the county's Negro leadership. The statement is revealing—not only of the transformation visited upon normal campaign practices when they were viewed through the cultural presumptions of white supremacy but also of the dangers of uncritical acceptance of such perspectives by scholars relying upon monoracial sources. The notice read in part:

> The Union is largely composed of the best citizens of the county. . . . They are the tax payers, representing the worth, the patriotism, the intelligence, and the virtues of the county. . . . We are not fighting any political party or individuals, but only those who band together under any name, who seek to perpetuate negro rule in Grimes County. *[Good citizens]* are astounded at the manner in which the children's money has been expended. Colored teachers with fat salaries and totally incompetent have been appointed for political "fluence." Our white teachers, male and female, enjoy no such fat salaries as these colored politicians or these sweet colored girls. . . . One of the most corrupting practices in the past has been the system of Owl Meetings which has been in vogue for years. . . . This is the school and hot bed where the negro politician received his inspiration, and riding from one end of the county to the other as an apostle of his race, corrupting his own people who may be in the honest pathway of duty. We give fair warning that any effort to continue these Owl Meetings—by the appointment of special deputies sheriffs to organize

and carry them on—will be prevented. No threat of shotguns will deter us from the discharge of this duty.

Even without recourse to other perspectives this view of the existing political situation in Grimes County contains serious internal contradictions. Black Populist leaders were "incompetent" but as "apostles of their race" they had been so effective that their efforts needed to be stopped. Black teachers were paid "fat salaries" solely for political reasons, but among those receiving such gross patronage were "sweet colored girls," who obviously were not conducting owl meetings. The assertion that black teachers were actually paid more than white teachers must be rejected out of hand. In addition to the compelling fact that such an arrangement would have constituted poor political behavior on the part of a third party strenuously endeavoring to hold a substantial portion of the white vote and the further reality that such expenditures were unnecessary since parity for blacks in itself would have represented a notable accomplishment in the eyes of Negro leaders, Democrats had access to the records of all county expenditures and no such charge was ever leveled, much less documented, at any other time during the Populist decade. Whites complained that Negro teachers received "too much," not that they received more than white teachers. In any case, it seems necessary only to observe that American political parties have routinely utilized night gatherings without having their opponents characterize them as owl meetings and that persons who benefited from incumbency were not presumed to be acting in sinister ways when they campaigned for their party's re-election. The only thing "special" about Garrett Scott's deputies was that some of them were black. Viewed as some sort of black abstraction Jim Kennard might appear convincing as a shadowy " 'fluence man," but as an intelligent and determined voice of the aspirations of Negro people he merits scholarly attention from perspectives not bounded by the horizons of those who murdered him. To an extent that is perhaps not fully appreciated, decades of monoracial scholarship in the South have left a number of Jim Kennards buried under stereotypes of one kind or another. They sometimes intrude anonymously as " 'fluence men," but they simply do not appear as people in books on Southern politics.

This circumstance suggests that not only the broad topic of interracial life and tension but the entire Southern experience culminated by disfranchisement needs to be tested by a methodology that brings both black and white sources to bear on the admittedly intricate problem of interpreting a free society that was not free. At all events, evidence continues to mount that monoracial scholarship, Northern and Southern, has exhausted whatever merit it possessed as an instrument of investigating the variegated past of the American people. The obvious rejoinder—that written black sources do not exist in meaningful quantity—cannot, of course, be explained away; at the same time, this condition suggests the utility of fresh attempts to devise investigatory techniques that offer the possibility of extracting usable historical material from oral sources. The example of the erroneous report in the Navasota *Examiner* of Morris Carrington's death illustrates, perhaps as well as any single piece of evidence, not only the dangers inherent in relying on such "primary sources" for details of interracial tension in the post-Reconstruction South but also the value of received oral traditions in correcting contemporary accounts. Nevertheless, the problem of evaluating such source material remains; white and black versions of the details of racial conflicts are wildly contradictory. When they are measured against other contemporary evidence, however, the interpretive problem becomes considerably less formidable; indeed, the task of penetrating the substance behind partisan contemporary accounts may be lessened through recourse to available oral sources, as I have attempted to demonstrate.

Since much of the *Realpolitik* of the South, from Reconstruction through the modern civil rights movement, rests on legal institutions that, in turn, rest on extralegal methods of intimidation, the sources of political reality may be found less in public debate than in the various forms of intimidation that matured in the region. However determined a historian may be to penetrate the legal forms to reach this extralegal underside of the political culture of the South he is, in our contemporary climate, blocked off from part of his sources by his skin color. For black scholars there are limits to the availability both of courthouse records in the rural South and of responsive white oral sources. There are corresponding limits to the information white scholars can gain from interviews in black communities. Here, then, is fertile ground for scholarly cooperation. Methods of achieving this cooperation need to be explored. In its fullest utilization the subject is not black history or Southern history but American history.

6

SAMUEL GOMPERS AND THE RISE OF AMERICAN BUSINESS UNIONISM

JOHN H. M. LASLETT

The American labor movement began among independent skilled artisans who sought to protect their way of life from the incursions of industrial capitalism. But while the craft focus of American labor unions was a source of real strength, it also proved to be a liability. As industrial capitalism expanded rapidly after the Civil War, the ranks of unskilled, immigrant workers expanded as well. Often possessing neither skills nor craft traditions, this growing body of immigrant workers performed the most menial and repetitive industrial tasks while working under the worst conditions and receiving the lowest rates of pay. By the end of the nineteenth century, America supported a segmented labor market in which native-born and northern European immigrant workers held the best and highest paying jobs, while southern European, Asian, black, and women workers occupied the lowest rungs of the occupational ladder.

As John H. M. Laslett reveals in this biographical sketch of Samuel Gompers, founder and early leader of the American Federation of Labor, the craft orientation of the turn-of-the-century labor movement served to reinforce this segmented labor market. By limiting membership to those holding traditional skills, craft unions were able to obtain high wages and good working conditions for the upper tier of the industrial workers, but only at the expense of those at the middle and bottom of labor's ranks, who were left without effective organization. More than any other American labor organization, the American Federation of Labor came to symbolize this exclusive, craft-oriented form of unionism. Rather than bringing the millions of second- and third-tier workers into their union ranks, Gompers and the American Federation fought to maintain the privileges of its members by limiting its goals to purely economic issues and, after the turn of the century, by joining in partnership with the developing American state. In this essay, Laslett attempts to explain the complex motivations of Samuel Gompers by placing his idea of "business unionism" within the context of the contradictory realities faced by the labor movement in the era of monopoly capitalism.

Chapter 3 in Melvyn Dubofsky and Warren Van Tine, eds., *Labor Leaders in America* (Urbana, Ill.: University of Illinois Press, 1987). Reprinted by permission of John H. M. Laslett and University of Illinois Press.

No figure has been more important in the development of the American labor movement than Samuel Gompers. Beginning in obscurity, he rose to become a confidant of presidents, politicians, and businessmen. More than any other leader, he was responsible for bringing organized labor out of the shadows of obscurity to a place near the center of American political and economic life. He did this by articulating the singular trade union philosophy of the American Federation of Labor (AFL), which he helped found and of which he remained president almost continuously from 1886 to 1924. This philosophy eschewed the socialism and independent labor politics of most European labor movements. Instead, it upheld a form of "pure and simple" or business unionism that concerned itself primarily with advancing the immediate economic interests of workers in terms of wages, hours, and conditions of work.

By 1913 Gompers was influential enough internationally to propose the establishment of an International Federation of Trade Unions. Simultaneously, he exerted considerable influence over the labor movements in both Puerto Rico and Mexico, and during the First World War he became a crucial figure in mobilizing working people behind President Wilson's policies. In 1919 the AFL, which had begun with less than three hundred thousand members, reached almost 3 million. When Gompers died a self-proclaimed patriot in San Antonio, Texas, on December 3, 1924, his casket was drawn to the railroad station on a flag-draped military caisson furnished by the U.S. War Department.

But aside from his obvious role in union building, there is surprisingly little agreement among Samuel Gompers' biographers as to the precise nature of his achievement. Almost universally, commentators have expressed either unstinting praise or barely concealed contempt. To his research assistant, Florence Thorne, Gompers was an "American statesman" of the first rank; to labor historian John R. Commons, he was an intellectual innovator

to be put alongside Karl Marx; and to sociologist Daniel Bell, he was a man who "with driving force, created the American labor movement in his own stubborn and pragmatic image."

Perhaps the most important of Gompers' detractors is Bernard Mandel, who has written the most comprehensive biography. Yet his approach, like that of Gompers' admirers, is essentially ideological. Impatiently rejecting the idea that Gompers' leadership may have been, at least in part, an accurate reflection of the interests of the skilled workers who made up the AFL, Mandel condemns Gompers for his ambition, for his hostility towards socialism and industrial unionism, and for the exclusive, aristocratic brand of labor unionism that he allegedly foisted upon the AFL. Stuart Kaufman, the most thoughtful analyst of Gompers' early life, recognizes the radicalism of his youth. Yet by ending his study in 1896, Kaufman provides us with no effective means of explaining Gompers' transition to conservatism. Philip S. Foner notes the transition but dismisses Gompers as a labor bureaucrat and a cynical opportunist who abandoned his radical opinions when they no longer advanced his career. According to Foner, Gompers spent most of his years as AFL president practicing "class collaboration on behalf of the bourgeoisie."

Seen in the overall context of the American labor tradition, these negative evaluations contain more truth than the eulogistic ones. Both the Knights of Labor, which preceded the AFL, and the Congress of Industrial Organizations (CIO), which broke away from it, reflected a broader and in many ways more accurate conception of American labor militancy than did the AFL. Yet to attribute its dominance, even though it was only temporary, to the self-conscious manipulation of one man, or even a group of men, strains credulity. For one thing, such a mechanistic approach ignores the personality of Gompers himself. It is true that Gompers was ambitious—what pioneering leader is not?—as well as being self-righteous, bigoted, and increasingly rigid in his later years. Yet he was also scrupulously honest, willing to drive himself to exhaustion in the cause of trade unionism as he saw it, and capable of great personal courage when a principle he believed in was at stake.

For many years, also, the personal rewards to be gained from high union office were rarely sufficient to tempt large numbers of skilled workers to leave the workbench simply for the purpose of self-aggrandizement. At the beginning, Gompers ran the central office of the AFL from his own New York apartment, at a salary considerably less than he had been earning as a skilled cigarmaker. In the mid-1880s, too, the Knights of Labor was considerably larger than the Federation of Organized Trades and Labor Unions (FOTLU), the AFL's immediate predecessor. It, not Gompers' organization, seemed to be the wave of the future. In fact, it was not until after 1896 that the future of the AFL was assured; and it was not until after the First World War that Gompers could afford to purchase a home of his own. None of this squares with the modern picture of the business unionist as a bloated bureaucrat living off the earnings of a hard-working union membership.

Daniel Bell's assertion that Gompers "created the labor movement in his own stubborn and pragmatic image" is misleading not only because it ignores the role played by the great mass of rank-and-file workers in building the labor movement, both in the AFL and outside it, whose views were often at variance with those of the Old Man, as Gompers came to be called; it also exaggerates the extent of his personal power. It does this because at the time of its founding, as well as for much of its subsequent career, the AFL was a federation of previously established trade unions such as the Carpenters, Iron Moulders, Cigarmakers, and Printers, who were jealous of their sovereignty, and which the executive council could do little to control. At the turn of the century, for example, Gompers lost a thirteen-year-old struggle to establish a separate strike fund that the AFL could use to aid its striking members.

Thus attacks on him for refusing to commit the AFL to a sympathy strike in support of Eugene Debs's American Railway Union at the time of the Pullman strike in 1894, or for failing to make a success of the 1919 steel strike, must be tempered with the knowledge that for much of its early history the federation was too small and vulnerable to have decisively affected the outcome of these events.

My purpose in this essay, therefore, is neither to pillory nor to eulogize Gompers further, a preoccupation that can only serve to further distort his place in history. Instead I shall attempt to explore, and perhaps to reconcile, some of the conflicting views about Gompers' leadership by placing the development of his opinions in the political and economic environment in which he grew to maturity. I shall also try to judge his behavior in terms of the influences to which he was subject and in terms of the choices that were realistically open to him, not in terms of some preconceived political standard.

During Samuel Gompers' earliest years, both in London and New York, he was forced to struggle with genuine poverty; and he worked in a trade that was even more subject to the vagaries of technological innovation and international capitalist development than most other skilled occupations of the mid-Victorian era. Gompers was born on January 26, 1850, to Dutch-Jewish immigrant parents, in a crowded cigarmakers' tenement building in London's East End. At age ten young Sam was forced to leave school to help supplement the family's income, first as a shoemaker's apprentice and then in a cigarmaker's shop in Bishopgate Street. As he sat at the worktable cutting and rolling the tobacco, Gompers sang such popular songs as "The Slave Ship," which expressed sympathy for American blacks, and "To the West," which according to his autobiography created his "feeling for America" and "his desire to go there."

Economic deprivation soon turned this desire into a reality. In 1862 the United States levied duties on European tobacco products, severely depressing the London cigar trade and rendering Solomon Gompers' income inadequate to support his rapidly growing family. The Cigarmakers' Society of England, like other British trade unions of the time, established an emigration fund, and in June 1863 the Gompers family left for New York. They arrived during the course of the racially motivated, Civil War anti-draft riots that spread near the docks; young Samuel remembered his father shaking hands with a black seaman as they left the ship, causing a crowd of angry onlookers to threaten him with a lynching. For approximately the next twenty years Gompers continued to work at his trade, moving from one cigar shop to another, engaging in trade union activities, and living at the margin of poverty even after he married Sophia Julian, also a London-born émigré who worked in his shop stripping tobacco leaves.

The world of work that the young Samuel Gompers entered was a cut beneath the relatively safe, respectable existence that still characterized such skilled occupations as printing, iron molding, or carpentry in both England and America. All of his life, Gompers remained proud of his ability to roll a cigar, even though in the London home of his parents we catch occasional glimpses of the petty bourgeois lifestyle that some of his more affluent relatives had known in Holland. Although a desire for further education was clearly present in Samuel's attendance at night classes at New York's Cooper Union, in his personal life he manifested few of the other attributes of the self-improving artisan. He was not religious; he drank quite heavily; and he put little money away in the form of savings for the future. In fact, if anything, when he arrived in the United States both his own family and the trade that he practiced were downwardly, rather than upwardly, mobile. In the early 1870s the sweated, tenement system of cigar production was introduced on an even larger scale in New York than it had been in London. By 1877 half of the New York trade's production came out of sev-

enty large units. This was a small proportion of the approximately 1,400 cigar firms in the city, the great bulk of which were family-style tenement shops. The evils of the tenement system made a deep impression on Gompers, and one of his first political aims was to abolish it.

Two further developments exacerbated the situation. One was the arrival of large numbers of unskilled Bohemian workers in the trade, who mostly worked in the tenements and who by virtue of their peasant background had different values from the skilled German, Dutch, and English immigrants who had hitherto dominated cigarmaking. The other was the introduction of the cigar mold, a mechanical press that enabled manufacturers to break down the skilled craft into two distinct stages, bunch-making and rolling, and to employ unskilled immigrants at lower wages. As a child in London, Gompers had already witnessed the human impact of mechanization on the neighboring Spitalsfields silk workers. One of his "most vivid early recollections" was the tramp of unemployed men walking the streets for work. Now he was faced with a similar problem in his own trade. The 1870 Cigarmakers International Union (CMIU) convention prohibited union members from working with bunchmakers, and in the early 1870s many cigarmakers struck unsuccessfully against the introduction of the cigar mold into their shops. Though some Bohemian cigarmakers later organized Local 90 of the CMIU, most were at first ineligible to join the International because of their system of work.

The initial effect of these experiences was to radicalize the young Gompers. His early poverty caused him to sympathize with the toiling masses long after he had left the cigarmaker's bench; the mechanization of his trade laid the foundations for his life-long preoccupation with defending the skills of the hand craftsman; his family's enforced migration, coupled with working alongside Bohemians, Germans, and other immigrants at the cigarmaker's bench, stirred his early internationalism; and his father's evident pro-abolitionist stand when the family first came to America suggested an initial sympathy for the America Negro that remained with him throughout his first years as an AFL leader. Gompers' formal acquaintance with socialist ideas came in the years just after 1873, when he began working in the cigar shop of David Hirsch, a political immigrant from Hamburg, Germany. Here, Gompers later wrote, he read "all the German economic literature that I could lay hands on—Marx, Engels, Lassalle, and the others." Soon he was attracted to the ideas of the First Marxist International.

Although he claimed in his autobiography that he never joined the First International or any other socialist organization, the attraction was in many ways a natural one. The First International had been founded in his native city of London, in 1864, to strengthen trade unionism, restrict the international migration of contract labor, and express sympathy and support for oppressed peoples everywhere—all causes with which he could identify. In David Hirsch's shop, and in the Economic and Sociological Club that met in a room above a nearby saloon, Gompers was influenced by a number of leading socialist émigrés who had been active in the different national branches of the First International in Europe and whose views commanded respect. Among them were Hirsch himself; J. P. McDonnell, an Irish Fenian who had worked beside Marx in London as secretary of the First International; and Gompers' fellow cigarmaker Ferdinand Laurell, who had served as secretary of the Scandinavian section of the First International until he was forced into exile in the United States.

Ferdinand Laurell was Gompers' particular tutor, translating a copy of the *Communist Manifesto* for him and interpreting it "paragraph by paragraph." But Gompers was influenced also through such pamphlets as *Praktische Emanzipationswinke* by Carl Hillman, a socialist from Saxony who, unlike the Lassallean school of German socialism that emphasized political action, laid particular stress on the trade unions' role in the emancipation of the working class. Hillman argued that working-class organizations, established on a bedrock of sound financial benefits, strong trade union journals, and the pursuit of ameliorative legislation, could become the instruments of the workers' education and power. These ideas became the common stock of the Marxist trade union wing of the First International in New York, and they were incorporated into Gompers' own philosophy.

Other incidents also occurred in these early years that appeared to strengthen Gompers' commitment not simply to radical ideas but also to the kind of broadly based, inclusive unionism that he was later to reject. In the summer of 1872 Adolph Strasser, the Hungarian bunch-maker who was later to head the CMIU, established the independent United Cigarmakers as a vehicle for organizing the unskilled German and Bohemian mold- and bunch-makers who were not yet permitted into the International. Its membership was open to all "regardless of sex, method, or place of work, or nationality"; thus it accepted female as well as male immigrant workers. In November 1875 Gompers engineered the acceptance of the United Cigarmakers into the CMIU as Local 144, which for many years remained his own local union. In October 1877, partially as a response to the great railroad strike that swept the country in the summer of that year, over ten thousand New York cigarmakers came out in a general cessation of work. Gompers did not oppose this shutdown, as he was later to do in the Pullman and other mass strikes. On the contrary, in order to provide employment for evicted cigarmakers, as well as to raise strike funds, he resigned his job at Hirsch's, became superintendent of a union-operated cigar factory, and was blacklisted for four months when the strike failed.

Hence it is not surprising to find that at this point in his life Gompers, unlike Powderly and the leaders of the Knights of Labor, who did not accept a class conflict model of the labor movement, fully endorsed the Marxist concept of class struggle. "From my earliest understanding of the conditions that prevail in the industrial world," he wrote later, "I have been convinced and I have asserted that the economic interests of the employing class and those of the working-class are not harmonious. . . . There are times when for temporary purposes, interests are reconcilable; but they are temporary only."

That this belief—as well as an early willingness to accept the need for a broadly based, industrywide form of trade unionism—was not an abberation can be seen in Gompers' support for the call, put out by the FOTLU, to urge a general strike of workers in behalf of the eight-hour day to take place no later than May 1, 1886. It can also be seen in his 1888 recommendation, as president of the fledgling AFL, that the federation remodel itself on the basis of industrial divisions that would hold their own conventions, legislate on subjects of interest to their own trades and industries, and be represented by a proportionate number of delegates to the AFL. This proposal was rejected by the more conservative leaders of the craft unions, suggesting once again the exaggerated nature of Daniel Bell's claim that Gompers created the labor movement in his own image. Up until the later 1880s, his radicalism even appeared to extend into politics. In the 1876 and 1880 presidential elections, Gompers voted for the candidates of the Greenback-Labor party, and although he resisted committing the AFL to independent labor politics, in the fall of 1886 he campaigned on behalf of the Single-Taxer Henry George in his bid to become mayor of New York.

But at the same time that his early experiences were propelling Samuel Gompers towards a radical interpretation of the role of the labor movement and of the workers' position under capitalism, other pressures that pulled him in the opposite direction were at work on him. Seen from this perspective the issue becomes not, as Philip Foner and Stuart Kaufman define it, whether there was a difference between the radical Gompers of the pre–1890 years and the conservative Gompers of the later period. The important issue is to establish what were the influences that drew him away from the radicalism of his youth, and why in the end these influences predominated.

Paradoxically, part of the answer lies in the narrow and historically dated view of Marxism held by the European émigré socialists in the Cigarmakers International Union, in the First International, and in the New York labor movement with whom Gompers associated in the 1870s and the 1880s. These men had little knowledge of, and even less sympathy with, the indigenous traditions of American political reform represented by greenbackism, by land and currency reform, and by the ideals of co-operation. Brought up with the proletarian orientation of classical Marxism, which saw the factory working-class as the only one capable of presenting a fundamental challenge to industrial capitalism, Friedrich A. Sorge and the other German leaders of the First International in New York considered the demands of the native-born American reformers to be middle-class nostrums that interfered with the organization of workers at the workplace. It was this that should be the primary, if not the exclusive, function of the labor movement. In 1872 Sorge expelled the largely native-born Section 12 from the First International. Its members included third-party-oriented Victoria Woodhull and Tennessee Claflin, two ardent women suffragists and preachers of free love, as well as elements of the New Democracy or Political Commonwealth, a group of intellectuals who believed that socialism could be legislated politically by the simple device of a popular referendum. These people, Sorge stated, had improperly intruded themselves into the labor movement "either for intellectual purposes or for advancing some hobbies of their own," instead of advancing the interests of the urban working-class.

Gompers agreed with this analysis. "The labor movement holds it as a self-evident maxim," he wrote some years later, "that the emancipation of the working-class must be achieved by the working-classes themselves. There is no doubt that men with the best of intentions outside of the ranks of labor can aid the movement. We court their . . . sympathy . . . but cannot give into their hands the direction of the affairs which rightfully belong and must be exercised by the wage workers." In such statements we find much of the basis for Gompers' subsequent hostility towards the Knights of Labor and towards populism and other agrarian movements, as well as the seeds of his anti-intellectualism. One of his most persistent criticisms of the Knights of Labor was that its concept of the producing classes permitted it to include agricultural laborers, petty bourgeois shopkeepers, and even small businessmen as part of the labor movement. Similarly, he attacked the People's party of the mid-1890s and attempted to prevent political support being given to it by rank-and-file trade unionists—despite the widespread participation of those who rejected his views—because it did not consist of urban wage workers. "Composed, as the People's Party is," he wrote in July 1892, "mainly of employing farmers without any regard to the interests of the . . . mechanics and laborers of the industrial centres, there must of necessity be a divergence of purposes, methods, and interests."

But Gompers had expressed similar opinions many years before this. Some of them, in fact, were formulated as early as 1874. In the winter of that year the severity of unemployment due to the industrial depression led a Committee on Public Safety formed by First International leaders in New York to plan a mass demonstration of protest in Tompkins Square. At the last minute the city authorities, fearing a mass uprising of the sort that had occurred three years earlier in the Paris Commune, cancelled permission for the meeting. The more radical members of the committee, however, refused to call it off, with the result that on January 13 mounted police charged into the crowd, inflicting many injuries. Gompers, who was present only as a bystander,

was dismayed by the results. "I saw the dangers of entangling alliances with intellectuals who did not understand that to experiment with the labor movement was to experiment with human life," he later wrote. "I saw that leadership in the labor movement could be safely entrusted only to those into whose hearts and minds had been woven the experiences of earning their bread by daily labor."

Not long after this, Gompers and his associates in the Economic and Sociological Club identified the shorter working day as the first essential step in bettering industrial conditions. Later on, this formed the basis of the eight-hour day campaign, which reached its peak in 1886 and was intimately connected with the founding of the AFL. Gompers felt that the eight-hour day could only be achieved by trade union rather than by legislative action. Hence in discussing this issue, as well as other practical steps that could be taken to improve the lot of New York's workingmen, Gompers and Adolph Strasser of the Cigarmakers Union, as well as Peter McGuire of the Carpenters, found themselves increasingly at odds with the more politically-oriented radicals, most of them outside the First International, which wished to subordinate the economic activities of trade unions to socialist party activism. In July 1876, a few days after delegates attended what turned out to be the last convention of the First International held in America, a unity conference of disparate socialist groups met in Philadelphia and formed the Workingmen's party of the United States (WPUS), known as of 1877 as the Socialist Labor party (SLP). Although active on the fringes of the New York, American (i.e., English-speaking) section of the WPUS, Gompers and his associates came more and more to reject "Socialist partyism" as the instrument of change, identifying instead "trade unions, amalgamated trade unions, and national or international amalgamation of all labor unions," as the road to the future.

In the mid-1870s Gompers and Strasser also began advocating the introduction of benefit systems and tighter administrative control into their unions. They were first introduced into CMIU Local 144, then later in the national Cigarmakers' organization. The benefit idea, which was henceforth mandatory on all Cigarmakers' locals throughout the country, was begun in 1880 with the creation of separate strike and death funds. It was extended five years later with the addition of a strike benefit. Later, a pension fund was added. An "equalization of funds" system was also adopted. This made possible the transfer of funds from a prosperous local to one in distress, thereby increasing the availability of funds to organize new workers. And finally, as a result of a constitutional amendment passed in 1885, the CMIU placed much of the power to call strikes in the hands of the international executive board.

In all of these activities, which lasted from approximately 1873 into the 1880s and 1890s, Gompers and his fellow trade unionists believed themselves to be both innovators and followers of the precepts of Karl Marx. In establishing the high-dues, high-benefits form of trade unionism in Local 144 of the CMIU in the mid–1870s, Gompers and Strasser saw themselves elaborating "a new movement," which was being "born out of the experience of the old." At the same time, by asserting the primacy of trade union action and by rejecting the attempt of theoretically inclined radicals to dominate the labor movement, Gompers believed himself to be acting according to Marx's own precepts. In a limited tactical sense, he had some justification for this view. Gompers' statements about the need for the working-class to emancipate itself accorded with classical Marxist doctrine; the General Council of the First International in London, which was dominated by Marx's circle, had endorsed Sorge's ousting of the politically-oriented Section 12 in New York; and as late as 1891 Friedrich Engels upheld Gompers' refusal to permit the American Marxist SLP to secure indirect representation in the AFL via its association with the Central Labor Federation of New York.

In reality, however, Gompers' claims on both these points were somewhat specious. At best they reflected a rather superficial and relatively fleeting moment in the development of Marxism in the 1860s. This was a period when the revolutionary tide that had flowed so strongly in 1848 had temporarily ebbed, when the "new model" craft unions had come to dominate the British labor movement, and when the passage of the Ten Hours Act and the agitation for parliamentary reform in England dictated that pressure group tactics, rather than the immediate establishment of an independent working-class political party, constituted the best strategy.

But this was a tactical road only. That Marx had not given his approval to the English "new model" unionism as the optimal type of labor organization was demonstrated clearly in 1867 when he criticized them for seeking to prove their respectability before the British Royal Commission on Trade Unions, saying they had "offered up the principle of Trade Unionism on the altar of middle-class legitimisation." Throughout, Marx and most European members of the First International continued to believe in a further and more important role for trade unions. This was to educate workers into a revolutionary mentality in such a way that they would be willing and able to commit themselves to overthrowing the capitalist system as a whole.

Gompers' claim to have acted as an innovator in introducing the high-dues, high-benefit system into Local 144 of the CMIU—and which John R. Commons evidently believed Gompers to have elucidated for the first time—also had little substance. For in practice the "new movement" he advocated represented little more than the reproduction on the American continent of the mid-Victorian "new model" form of English trade unionism that had first been introduced at the national level in 1851 by the Amalgamated Society of Engineers. This form of unionism involved amalgamating into one organization the collective bargaining and "friendly benefit" features of trade unionism that in Britain had hitherto been kept largely separate, under a system of tight administrative control. Gompers himself was even explicit about the derivative nature of his reforms. In his own autobiography he revealed that he had "gathered all the information I could get on the benefits provided by the British trade unions" and discussed them with fellow members of Local 144 before actually introducing them. Strasser was skeptical at first, but then he too, as president of the CMIU after 1877, turned to the British model, examining in particular the benefit features of the Amalgamated Society of Carpenters and Joiners. He became "convinced that their Protective and benevolent . . . character" was the "secret of the growth and power of trade unions in England."

Just how did Gompers' growing anti-intellectualism, coupled with his espousal of English-style "new model" unionism, propel him toward a more conservative position? The answer to the first half of the question is not difficult to find. Virtually all successful socialist movements have been built around an alliance of some kind between trade unionists and intellectuals, in a format that by the end of the 1890s Gompers was increasingly unwilling to countenance. Thus in deliberately cutting himself off, and—insofar as he was capable of doing—cutting the AFL itself off, from the advice and counsel of theoretically inclined persons both inside the labor movement and outside of it, Gompers was dissociating the trade unions from socialists and others who advocated independent labor politics. Later on, this distrust was extended to welfare workers and research experts, although this particular prejudice was softened somewhat during and after the First World War when Gompers came into closer contact with such persons, particularly those who because of the war and the Russian Revolution had become antisocialist. Nevertheless, throughout the latter part of his life he characteristically expressed doubts concerning the sincerity of anyone who did not work with their hands, calling them "careerists," "faddists," or "professional friends of labor." "Intellectuals usually suspend their labor programs from sky hooks," he wrote in the *American Federationist* in May 1918. "Their practical efforts are confined to criticizing the achievement and methods of workingmen. They can find nothing good in the practical structure of labor organizations which workers have built upon solid foundations upon the ground where labor problems exist."

The answer to the second half of the question is more difficult. It must be remembered that the English system of high dues and high benefits, and the increased amount of authority that was accorded to the officials who were introduced to administer them, was first established in order to provide Local 144, and later the CMIU as a whole, with sufficient discipline and financial strength to survive the depression of 1873–77, which decimated most other trade unions. Seen from this point of view, these reforms unquestionably paid off. The CMIU's national membership, which in 1877 had fallen to as little as 1,016, had by 1901 reached a total of more than 30,000. Its benefit system and large treasury were admired by other craft unions and were used widely as a model of what by then had become publicly known as business unionism. Nor did there appear to be anything inherently conservatizing in the adoption of benefit systems as such. Indeed, it might be argued that such systems could just as readily be used to fund large, class-based trade unions as they could be to defend the interests of small groups.

But the effect, if not the intention, of these changes was conservatizing in several aspects. In the first place, by explicitly making financial advantage rather than social idealism the basis for trade union loyalty, it reinforced those tendencies toward respectability and material success that were already present among many of the skilled artisans with whom Gompers habitually associated. Secondly, the act of leaving the workman's bench to become a paid official, the need for a hierarchical system of authority that the centralized system of administering AFL unions necessitated, and the sense of caution that preserving significant financial reserves induced, all tended to undermine the proletarian outlook with which many trade union leaders began their careers and encouraged them to identify with each other rather than with the workmates they had left behind.

Gompers was even more subject to such pressures than were most other AFL leaders, because he was responsible for administering a much larger bureaucracy than most of his colleagues, as well as for spending a greater proportion of his time in the company of businessmen and politicians, a fact that inevitably affected his outlook. The presence of rabbis, merchants, and even inventors and poets among his forebears also suggests that Gompers' eagerness to collaborate, as president of the AFL, with statesmen and business leaders may have reflected at some level a desire to retrieve the fortunes of a family that had earlier been declassé. Whatever truth there may be in this, there seems to be little doubt that Gompers' own sense of militancy, his willingness to take risks in supporting large-scale strikes, and his willingness, also, to put the financial resources of the AFL at the disposal of those who sought to organize the great mass of unskilled and semiskilled workers were significantly diminished by the way of life he came to adopt when he turned from a labor agitator into a labor administrator.

This last point brings up the third, and by far the most serious, consequence of the high-dues, high-benefit system that by 1900 had become characteristic of most unions in the AFL. This was the fact that the payment of high dues, which in the case of the cigarmakers had by 1896 reached the sum of thirty cents per month, was beyond the reach of the majority of the American work force, even if they could qualify for the apprenticeship system that many unions helped introduce into their trades. Significant additional payments were also made necessary by special levies and by high initiation fees. These high dues were not, in themselves, inappropriate, because employer opposition often made major expenditures necessary in order to protect the immediate, and legitimate, self-interests of skilled craftsmen. Nor were they by any means confined to the United States. But the logic implied by the American version of the English "new model" unionism, which Gompers and Strasser initially introduced, in the words of the one historian, was to close the trade unions "to all but the thriftier and better-paid artisans."

The preceding section has provided a basis for understanding Samuel Gompers' pragmatism, his anti-intellectualism, and his determination, stemming initially from his own misconceptions about the nature of Marxism, to keep the AFL free from the kind of entangling alliances with other elements in society that would have been necessary if it was to develop into a broad-ranging social movement. But by itself, this analysis does not fully explain the conservatism of Gompers' later years. In particular, it does not take into account Gompers' nativist attitudes towards the new, peasant immigrants who by 1885 were pouring into the United States; his espousal of the doctrine of political voluntarism; his growing preoccupation with trade autonomy in opposition to industrial unionism; or the bitter hostility (as opposed to personal disassociation) that he displayed towards socialists and other radicals in the period after 1900. Nor does Gompers' early development enable us to explain why, after the turn of the century, he showed a willingness to cooperate with the National Civic Federation and with other elements of the business community. This was a course that during the 1877 cigarmakers' general strike he would undoubtedly have shunned. On the other hand, some elements of his later conservatism were consistent with his earlier opinions. For example, he remained skeptical about the desirability of abolishing large-scale trusts on the ground that they were part of the logic of the development of capitalism. This was very similar to the position taken by moderate socialists in both Germany and Great Britain after the turn of the century.

But by no means did all of Gompers' other attitudes display such consistency. In his earliest years as a labor leader, for example, Gompers had shown more than the sentimental attachment to the plight of minorities that was then common among British and German immigrant artisans. By engineering the acceptance of the United Cigarmakers into the CMIU as Local 144, he had taken a practical interest in organizing both the poor, Bohemian cigarmakers in his own industry, as well as the women who worked in the trade. The early AFL also refused to charter international unions that excluded black workers; Gompers commissioned several black organizers to work in the South, subsequently praising their worth; and he gave strong support to the November 1892 interracial general strike that for a time shut down most industries in New Orleans. "If we fail to organize and recognize the colored wage-workers," wrote Gompers to H. M. Ives on November 10, 1892, "we cannot blame them if they accept our challenge of enmity and do all they can to frustrate our purposes. If we fail to make friends of them, the employing class won't be so shortsighted and /will/ play them against us. Thus if common humanity will not prompt us to have their cooperation, an enlightened self-interest should."

To some extent, liberal attitudes also marked Gompers' early attitudes towards the organization of recent European immigrant workers, although not towards the Chinese, who were almost universally excoriated by white artisans. Yet by 1896 or thereabouts Gompers had agreed to admit into the AFL unions that retained the color line, had abandoned much of his earlier support for female workers, and was expressing both racist and nativist sentiments freely. New peasant immigrants (Italians, Bohemians, Hungarians, Poles, Lithuanians, and Russians, for example) were, unlike northern Europeans, "a heterogeneous stew of divergent and discordant customs, languages, institutions; and they were impossible to organize." And the failure to enroll blacks in large numbers was now attributed not to any

inadequacy on the part of the labor movement, but to the alleged tendency of Afro-American workers to offer themselves spontaneously as strikebreakers.

What explains this reversal of outlook? On this point, perhaps more than on any other, it is difficult to ascertain the personal motivation that lay behind Gompers' change of mind. On the question of organizing blacks and recent immigrants, for example, it might be argued that the period of the 1880s and 1890s was a time of rising Negro-phobia and of nativist sentiment throughout the country, and that in accepting unions that excluded new immigrants and blacks Gompers was simply reflecting the prevailing cultural biases of the white, north European or native American, skilled workers who predominated in the AFL. In the mid-1890s for example, he was frequently criticized for attempting to organize poor black workers alongside of whites in the South, on the grounds that he would thereby alienate the much more important category of white southern artisans.

But such an argument not only ignores the fact that a few years earlier the Knights of Labor—and a few years later, the Industrial Workers of the World (IWW)—succeeded in organizing significant numbers of poor black as well as poor peasant immigrant workers alongside each other in racially integrated unions. It also ignores the point that Gompers' own letter to Ives of November 1892 made plain, that he was aware that the interests of the labor movement would themselves be damaged if he gave in to such narrow, exclusionary policies. The employers would, and did, take full advantage of the AFL's racism and nativism by deliberately exploiting the racist and nativist sentiments present in many white workers. The best that can be said about Gompers' personal views on these matters is that he appears to have been one of those English and German immigrants of the Civil War period, of whom there were many in both of the main political parties, who sincerely believed in the abolition of slavery and in other aspects of political reform, but who continued to regard both blacks and peasant immigrants as intellectually inferior to skilled white workers and as incapable of participating in the benefits of trade unionism. Indeed, he said as much regarding blacks after the turn of the century when he responded to criticism from Booker T. Washington that he had, in a recent speech, "read the Negro out of the labor movement." Not so, replied Gompers. What he had said was that it was difficult to organize Negro workers because they "did not have the same conception of their rights and duties as did the white workers, and were unprepared to fully exercise and enjoy the possibilities existing in trade unionism."

As for the AFL's own exclusionary policies, which Gompers exercised a crucial influence in developing, they were in a sense a logical extension of the high-dues, high-benefit systems that he and Strasser had earlier introduced into the CMIU. For since most women workers, as well as most peasant immigrants and blacks, toiled either in domestic work or in such heavy, unskilled occupations as steel, coal mining, meat packing and common laboring, they were by definition ineligible for admission into the AFL's skilled unions. Thus Gompers managed to avoid confronting the issue directly by pointing to the rationale that lay behind the form of unionism that he did so much to develop. That such a rationale was an extremely slim excuse upon which to depend, however, was amply demonstrated later when the AFL was itself challenged successfully by the Congress of Industrial Organizations (CIO), which managed to incorporate precisely those workers whom Gompers believed were impossible to organize.

A similar retrograde pattern can be seen at work in Gompers' growing preoccupation with trade autonomy and in his opposition to industrial unionism, which became almost an obsession in his later years. Beginning with the Building Trades Department in 1907, the AFL did establish consultative departments within the federation in such industries as railroads and mining to adjudicate jurisdictional disputes between unions. In 1901, in the Scranton Declaration (and with Gompers playing a leading role in the debate), the AFL even conceded to the United Mine Workers the right to organize all workers "in and around the mines," irrespective of their levels of skill. But for the most part it hewed rigidly to the doctrine of trade—which in most instances meant craft—autonomy, despite the fact that technological changes in industry were rendering many distinctions based upon hand skills obsolete. On this issue, as on a number of others in his later years, Gompers' early pragmatism was transformed into blind obstinacy.

The origins of this rigidity can largely be found in the years of instability and trauma that were visited upon the labor movement generally, and upon Gompers personally, by the prolonged period of rivalry for the loyalties of the cigarmakers, which occurred between the late 1870s and the year 1886 when the Cigarmakers International Union finally emerged triumphant in his own trade. In turn, this rivalry involved the far more momentous issue of who would emerge victorious in the struggle between the trades unions and the Knights of Labor for the control of the labor movement, a struggle that was to determine the shape of the entire labor movement until the rise of the CIO. As the Knights' strength grew in the mid-1880s, jurisdictional disputes occurred with increasing frequency between the Knights and a wide range of craft unions, which complained that the Knights failed to respect their picket lines, urged trade union members to desert their organization for Knights of Labor assemblies, and undermined their strength generally. The reverse also occurred, of course.

But it was the bitter dispute that erupted in 1886 between the CMIU, on the one hand, and the Cigarmakers Progressive Union backed by powerful District Assembly 49 of the Knights of Labor in New York, on the other, that ended any apparent prospect of collaboration between the two movements; it also initiated

Gompers' life-long hatred of dual or rival unionism and his preoccupation with the sanctity of craft autonomy. In January 1886 the United Cigar Manufacturers Association of New York locked out approximately fifteen thousand workers in one of the largest disputes in the city's history. In February the association revoked its earlier agreement with the CMIU. Instead, it signed a contract with the Progressives, as well as with District Assembly 49 of the Knights, thereby recognizing the Knight's white union label instead of the CMIU's blue one. Recognition of the union label was a crucial tool in boycotts and organizing work. Seriously alarmed, Gompers was dispatched on a nationwide speaking tour to dramatize the cigarmakers' grievances against the Knights for supporting the Progressives in their challenge to the CMIU's jurisdiction.

A prolonged struggle for control of the American labor movement then followed. It was most acute in New York, where the fight was between District Assembly 49 of the Knights of Labor, the largest in the order, on the one hand, and national unions such as the CMIU, backed by the Printers, the Carpenters, the Iron Moulders, and the Granite Cutters, on the other. Despite efforts at reconciliation, the Knights of Labor General Assembly backed District Assembly 49 against the CMIU. Terence V. Powderly added insult to injury by accusing Gompers of being a drunkard with whom it was impossible to do business. Stung, Gompers replied that Powderly and other leaders of the Knights floated "like scum on the top of a part of the labor movement, continually seeking to divert it to their own ends." Although the CMIU eventually won, it was this conflict more than anything else that led to the final break between the craft unions and the Knights, and to the establishment of the AFL in December 1886.

It would be going too far to say that this dispute alone determined all of Gompers' subsequent attitudes toward trade autonomy and established his hostility towards industrial or broadly based forms of trade unionism that would attempt to incorporate unskilled or semiskilled elements of the labor force. Nevertheless, it was to this 1886 conflict between the craft unions and the Knights of Labor that he repeatedly referred in later years when he sought to justify the principle of craft autonomy and when he excoriated alternative bodies that he considered to be threats to the AFL. What probably clinched the matter for Gompers was the fact that the Progressive Cigarmakers had been influenced by the Lassallean wing of the New York socialist movement. It was as a result of this dispute that the triple evils of dual unionism, jurisdictional poaching, and socialist politics became permanently linked in his mind.

This first came apparent in 1896, when Gompers reacted angrily to the establishment by Daniel DeLeon and other leftist SLP elements of the Socialist Trades and Labor Alliance (STLA). The STLA was set up in December 1895 as a rival body to the AFL to organize workers on a more radical basis than the AFL had been willing to do. The now weakened District Assembly 49 of the Knights of Labor backed the new organization, a fact that infuriated Gompers. But it was the dual unionist or competitive character of the STLA and the support that was given to it by the DeLeonite wing of the SLP that he focused on in his criticisms. A number of local unions attached to the AFL had been "rent asunder," he reported to the December 1896 convention of the federation, "and brother workmen have been organized into hostile camps, to the destruction of their own interests and to the delight of the enemies of labor." Earlier in the year he had condemned the "union wrecking" that, he said, had been "taken up by a wing of the so-called socialist party of New York." Such men as DeLeon, Hugo Vogt, and Lucian Saniel, the chief architects of the STLA, "should be pilloried as the enemies of labor, and held, now and forever, in the contempt they should so justly deserve." This kind of language was henceforth to characterize most of Gompers' references to labor radicals.

Gompers' reaction to the IWW, which was established in 1905 by the Western Federation of Miners, by the followers of Eugene Debs, by disaffected AFL elements, and by what remained of the STLA, was almost identical. It can be questioned whether the IWW was in fact a dual union in the same sense that the STLA had been. Its main aim was to organize the unorganized workers that the AFL had ignored. But by this time Gompers had become so fanatical in his devotion to the idea of trade autonomy that he was unwilling to make the necessary distinction. He denied that industrial unionism was the real purpose of the organization, ordered all AFL affiliates to expel IWW members, and even sanctioned the breaking of IWW strikes. The real and only purpose of the new body was "to divert, pervert, and disrupt the labor movement" in order to promote socialism, he later wrote. The whole venture simply proved that "the trade-union smashers and rammers from without and the 'borers from within' are again joining hands."

By extension, this distrust of SLP support for such bodies as the STLA spilled over into an overall repudiation of independent labor politics, even though the Socialist party of America, which was founded in 1901, specifically rejected the dual unionist policies followed by DeLeon and by the IWW, and sought instead to cultivate the friendship of the existing trade unions. Hence when, after the turn of the century, a conservative Congress refused to adopt legislation favorable to the interests of workers, Gompers and the AFL leadership turned, not to the Socialist party as most European trade union movements would have done, but to the nonpartisan "reward-your-friends, punish-your-enemies" political policy that was henceforth to be the hallmark of the federation's approach. In March 1906 the AFL issued its celebrated Bill of Grievances, demanding among other things an effective eight-hour work law for federal employees, enforcement of the exclusion law against Chinese immigrants, an anti-injunction bill, and protection against the low prices charged for the products of convict labor. In the November 1906 congressional elections, the AFL spent considerable sums of money attempting to defeat Republican Charles E. Littlefield of Maine, a sworn enemy of labor; and in 1908 it presented the same demands to both the Republican and Democratic national conventions. The more favorable response that it received from the Democrats started the labor movement towards de facto support for the Democratic party.

Of course, many other factors besides Gompers' personal predilections account for this swing towards the Democrats. Among them were the traditional support that working-class immigrants had given to the party and the body of favorable labor and social legislation that was enacted by President Woodrow Wilson's first administration between 1912 and 1916. But although the relationship between the AFL and the Democratic party continued to deepen, as far as the AFL was concerned— unlike the later CIO—it was always accompanied by extreme caution about the dangers of the labor movement becoming overly dependent upon the political largesse of the state. This was another reason for Gompers' hostility towards the socialists. The political principle that lay behind this attitude was voluntarism. It derived, in turn, from the antimercantilist tradition that was present, to a greater or lesser degree, in other Anglo-Saxon labor movements as well as in that of the United States. Thus the general idea that informed Gompers' attitude toward political action after 1906 was that the trades unions should only seek "to secure by legislation at the hands of government what they could /not/ accomplish by their own initiative and activities."

Hence Gompers supported federal legislation to limit or control immigration from China and later from Europe, women's suffrage, inspection of factory working conditions, and prohibitions on the sale of convict-made goods. All of these were objectives that the AFL itself could not either initiate or enforce. However, even at the height of the Progressive movement just before the First World War, the AFL consistently opposed the enactment of legislation fixing the hours of male workers in private industry, minimum wage legislation, and anything that smacked of compulsory arbitration. All of these things were better left to the independent power of the trades unions.

Gompers' distrust of state power can also be linked to his post–1900 willingness to collaborate with elements of the business community in ways that he would never have contemplated in his early years. The connection resulted from the fusing of two new developments that by the turn of the century had transformed the workplace environment that Gompers had known as a young man. These were the growth that took place in the size and scale of business corporations and the increasingly successful use that was made by employers of court injunctions to break strikes on the ground that they interfered with interstate commerce or with the operation of free trade. Companies like Standard Oil of New Jersey, U.S. Steel, as well as numerous railroad, coal, and other industrial manufacturers, were now giant corporations with immense financial resources, which could invoke the power of the state to defeat the trades unions. Their political influence was such that they could secure court injunctions forcing union members to desist from striking and summon state and federal troops to protect their property rights and to back up the power of the law.

During this period Gompers did press for legislation that would exempt unions from prosecution under the Sherman Anti-Trust Act. This was successfully achieved, even if only temporarily, with the passage of the 1914 Clayton Act. But the general lesson that Gompers drew from the defeats that labor had suffered in the Homestead, Pullman, and Cripple Creek strikes, defeats that resulted from state or federal intervention on the side of the employers, was not that labor should challenge the corporations in the political field; it was that some kind of accomodation should be made with

them at the workplace. The large, trustified industries, in particular, were too powerful to be challenged directly. They would only tolerate trade unionism, Gompers came to believe, if it was confined mainly to the skilled trades, if it rejected militancy and radicalism, and if it was in general reasonable in its demands. The agency that was to carry out this new policy was the National Civic Federation (NCF), a voluntary association established in 1900 by representatives of labor, capital, and the general public whose purpose was to mediate industrial disputes.

A good example of Gompers' new policy was his handling of the summer 1901 steel strike. This took place in a relatively new, modern industry employing almost 150,000 unskilled and semiskilled Slavic, Italian, and Polish workers in which the Amalgamated Association of Iron, Steel and Tin Workers— the old union of skilled Anglo workers—had only a toehold, but which it was imperative to unionize on a larger scale if the AFL were to grow beyond its narrow constituency of skilled craftsmen.

The strike began when the union attempted to secure union contracts in several of the subsidiary companies of the recently established United States Steel Corporation, which was now the largest single business organization in the United States. At two conferences held between Amalgamated leaders and banking magnate J. P. Morgan and Charles Schwab, who between them controlled U.S. Steel, the steel executives agreed to grant the union wage in the plants already organized, but specified that the Amalgamated was not to organize the nonunion mills. Morgan assured President Shaffer that he was not hostile to organized labor and that he would be willing to sign a contract with the Amalgamated for all of the mills within two years but could not do so just then.

Once its offer had been rejected, however, U.S. Steel began importing strikebreakers to start up the mills. The Amalgamated replied by appealing to Gompers to make the steel strike the central fight for unionism and to call for a conference of the leaders of the appropriate international unions in Pittsburgh. Gompers would not do so, and he refused even to call a meeting of the AFL Executive Council to consider tactics. A compromise was then proposed by the National Civic Federation under which the union scale would be signed for the steel mills that had been organized the previous year, union wages would be paid in the additional mills on strike, and no worker would lose his job because of striking. President John Mitchell also appears to have promised to bring out the United Mine Workers, which had the ability to cut off the fuel supply for steel, on sympathy strike if the employers rejected the offer.

U.S. Steel did reject this compromise offer, the United Mine Workers failed to come out in sympathy, and on September 14, 1901, the Amalgamated was forced to concede defeat. The overall result weakened the Amalgamated even further in the skilled sections of the trade and ended all efforts to organize the great mass of unskilled Slav and other immigrant workers in the industry until 1919. Gompers' conduct in this strike was in some ways understandable. He had warned President Shaffer ahead of time of the dangers of taking on the largest company in the United States without adequate preparation, and he had no power to force the United Mine Workers to come out on sympathy strike.

Yet it is also clear that in his refusal to make the steel strike the central concern of the AFL, in his unwillingness to put even the slightest pressure on John Mitchell to bring out the miners in support, and in his willingness to rely on the National Civic Federation as a genuinely neutral body that could alone bring about a compromise result, Gompers did far less than he could have done to unionize the steel industry. There is even a suggestion in the evidence that under pressure from Mark Hanna, NCF president, Gompers moderated his support for President Shaffer of the Amalgamated because he had favored the establishment of an industrial union in the trade.

There is also little doubt that Gompers' posi-tion was based on several underlying considerations that he did not bring into the open during the controversy: his fear of the steel trust and his readiness, if not eagerness, to accept the professions of the officials of the corporation at face value. Gompers and Mitchell, one historian notes, "prizing union recognition by the leaders of finance and business as their greatest possible achievement, were anxious for a speedy ending of a situation that put labor in an unfavorable light." Gompers was even impressed by J. P. Morgan's avowal of friendship for organized labor in ways that suggest a degree of naiveté more than a little odd for a man of his experience. Ten years later, the investigation of the Stanley congressional committee revealed the true value of such friendship when it published the text of a resolution that had been adopted by U.S. Steel at a directors' meeting just prior to the 1901 strike: "We are unalterably opposed to the extension of labor organization," it read, "and advise subsidiaries to take firm positions /against it/ when these questions come up."

Thus by the time of the First World War, if not before, Samuel Gompers had in many ways come full circle. Beginning in the 1870s as a socialist sympathizer, a believer in the class struggle, and an avowed student of Karl Marx, in the 1890s he insisted that he was not antagonistic to socialism but attacked individual socialists who were hostile to trade unionism as he saw it, or who antagonized it by forming dual unions. By 1903 he had dropped his belief in the class struggle, telling the socialist delegates to the AFL convention of that year: "Economically, you are unsound; socially you are wrong; industrially, you are an impossibility." In 1913 Gompers openly confessed that he was no longer an opponent of the capitalist system in any way, shape, or form. He told a House investigating committee that he had come to the conclusion that "it is our duty to live out our lives as workers in the society in which we live and not work for the downfall or the destruction or the overthrow of that society, but for its fuller development and evolution." In the reference to living out our lives "as workers," there is a faint echo of the Marxist beliefs he once held. But Gompers' insistent disavowal of even the slightest interest in fundamental social change pointed far more insistently towards the narrow, red-baiting, self-righteous patriot who lay upon the flag-draped caisson in San Antonio, Texas, in December 1924, than it did towards the idealistic young radical that he had been in his early years.

Yet there was an alternative to the narrow, craft union policies that Gompers pursued so exclusively in his later years: organization of the mass production industries on the basis of an open, socially progressive, and inclusive form of trade unionism that would have accepted unskilled and semiskilled workers of all races, and of both sexes, into its ranks. It is not difficult, if one accepts the logic of business unionism and focuses upon the policies of a narrow group of trade union leaders, both to find justifications for much of what Gompers stood for and to accept the intellectual rationale that lay behind the Commons-Perlman school of labor writers, who based many of their own ideas on Gompers' achievements. But, as more recent historians have shown, to accept these assumptions is to ignore the opinions of many among the great mass of American workers, both organized and unorganized, who did not share Gompers' opinions. It is also, in an important sense, to misinterpret the American labor tradition itself.

This is so partly because, as I pointed out earlier, the supposed "uniquely American" form of trade unionism that Gompers thought he had discovered in reforming the structure of the Cigarmakers International Union was, in fact, an import from Great Britain. In the second place, the native American tradition of labor reform, which the First International and the group of men among whom Gompers came to maturity so curtly dismissed, did not consist simply of "middle class nostrums." As represented by the National Labor Union, by the Knights of Labor, and by other organizations, it encompassed a wide range of policies, social groups, and methods of labor organizing—

ranging from republican idealism, the mixed trade assembly, and communal resistance to the inequalities created by post–Civil War industry—that were far more "uniquely American" than the alternative model that Gompers himself espoused.

To say this is not to deny the achievements of the American Federation of Labor or of Gompers himself. As the representative of skilled craftsmen, the AFL did much that was indispensable. But with the passage of time, its narrowness of vision became increasingly unrepresentative of the interests of the great mass of unskilled workers, minorities, and factory labor. This becomes particularly clear if we examine the fortunes of the AFL in the period between 1919 and 1924, the last years of Gompers' own life. During the course of the First World War the trade union movement grew dramatically, Gompers became a member of the National War Labor Board, and he was a frequent and influential visitor at the White House. But the years 1919 and 1920 were to represent the high point of the AFL's growth until the late 1930s. By 1921 union membership had fallen from 3,120,000 to just under 3 million. In 1924, the year of Gompers' death, the figure was 2,724,000.

The reasons for this decline were, of course, complex. Some of them, like the Red Scare movement of 1919, which at its height was directed as much against staid craft unionists as it was against supposed Bolsheviks, can in no way be laid at Gompers' feet. Collectively, however, as the most recent commentator on Gompers' life has pointed out, they called into question several of his most cherished principles. As employers all across the country, both large and small, sought to roll back labor's wartime gains, his long-sought policy of seeking acceptance from the corporate community seemed dubious, at best. One result of this, as Gompers pointed out in his own autobiography, was that he was unable to secure even a response to a letter from one of his erstwhile allies in the National Civic Federation, Judge Gary, during the course of the great 1919 steel strike. By 1920 the open shop campaign that business pursued had turned into a frontal attack on the very concept of unionism, against which all of Gompers' pleas for moderation and behind-the-scenes negotiation were powerless.

Much the same thing happened on the political field. With the ending of the First World War and President Wilson's increasing preoccupation with the Versailles peace treaty and his ensuing illness, the AFL lost its most influential Democratic ally. Until 1924 Gompers still received a polite hearing in Democratic party councils. But in that year the party not only nominated a highly conservative presidential candidate, John W. Davis, but it also disregarded virtually all of labor's legislative requests. As a result Gompers belatedly committed his support, and that of organized labor generally, to the independent presidential campaign of the aging Wisconsin senator Robert M. LaFollette. Few people seriously thought that the candidate of the Conference for Progressive Political Action would win, of course. But it was disconcerting that so few urban workers, nationwide, cast their ballots for a candidate who clearly stood for labor's interests.

It is less easy to be critical of Gompers' political policy of "reward-your-friends, punish-your-enemies" than it is of his trade union policies. In the New Deal period, this willingness to support labor's supporters within the Democratic party was probably more advantageous than commitment to an independent party of the working-class would have been. Yet in the latter part of his life both Gompers' industrial and his political policies, not unlike those pursued by Booker T. Washington on behalf of American blacks, betrayed an unfortunate tendency to place too much trust in those leaders of society whom he considered to be labor's friends and not enough trust in the broad masses of the working-class where his own roots lay. In his search for acceptance on behalf of a relatively small—and hence relatively weak—segment of the labor force, he jettisoned the vision of working-class unity that had motivated him in the 1870s and 1880s. Gompers did this not out of any deliberate attempt to practice class collaboration but because he sincerely believed his policies to be in labor's best interests. But in doing so he not only neglected the interests of a large proportion of the American working-class, he also jeopardized much of its as well as his own birthright.

7

THE MILITARY OCCUPATION OF CUBA, 1899–1902: WORKSHOP FOR AMERICAN PROGRESSIVISM

HOWARD GILLETTE, JR.

The years from 1890 to 1920 witnessed a renewed debate by American reformers on the merits of industrial capitalism. As with early nineteenth-century reformers, these latter-day reformers drew upon a wide range of doctrines to attack monopolies, trusts, and large corporations and the social problems such as poverty, government corruption, and industrial pollution that followed in their train. The Progressives, as these new reformers came to be called, offered a solution to mounting social problems that their earlier counterparts would never have countenanced. Recognizing the immense power wielded by corporate capitalism because of its enormous resources and effective bureaucratic organization, Progressives sought a counterweight in the resources and power of government. The notion of government intervention as a means to tame the corporations separated the Progressives from all previous reformers who saw government as a means of insuring the safety and liberty of its citizens and little else.

In articulating their new ideas about the place of government in social reform the Progressives were inspired by their contemporaries in the British social welfare movement and by the success of Bismarck's welfare state in Germany. But as Howard Gillette demonstrates in this essay, many of the ideas of the Progressive reformers had a different origin: they were worked out during the American occupation of Cuba following the Spanish-American War. It was in Cuba, where American administrators exercised virtually unopposed power, that Progressive ideas about civil administration, public schooling, and proper sanitation could be tested and refined without the interference of corporate interests or domestic politics.

From *American Quarterly* 25(4):410–25. Copyright 1973. Reprinted by permission of *American Quarterly,* the author, and the American Studies Association.

The Spanish-American War marked an important turning point in American domestic as well as foreign policy. The intervention on behalf of Cuban independence generated a national sense of mission, not only to uplift the oppressed people of other countries, but also to improve domestic conditions at home. The war and the resulting policy of extraterritorial expansion, according to such a major contributor to progressivism as Herbert Croly "far from hindering the process of domestic amelioration, availed, from the sheer force of the national aspirations it aroused, to give a tremendous impulse to the work of national reform."

The agents of the occupation of Cuba brought the prospects of American civilization—good government, education and business efficiency. In this sense the occupation was profoundly conservative, a reflection of already well-established American values and programs. On the other hand Leonard Wood, the second military governor of the island, established an overall pattern of political action which contrasted sharply with previous reform movements of both populists and Mugwumps. Rejecting both the populist appeal to the masses and the negative Mugwump commitment to laissez-faire and puritan moralism, the Wood administration provided a model of new government powers in the hands of "responsible" leadership. It combined the Mugwump bias for elitism with the belief of populists in government activism. As such it serves as an important, previously neglected, link between old and new reform movements in America. In a real sense the occupation of Cuba served as a workshop for progressivism.

The issues surrounding the early occupation emerged out of the long-term conflict between Mugwump reformers and their opponents. Indeed, John R. Proctor, president of the U.S. Civil Service Commission, could not resist moralizing on Cuba's fate on the occasion of its transfer to American control:

> We do not feel personally responsible for misgovernment in New York or Philadelphia, but every American citizen will feel a personal responsibility for misgovernment in Havana, Santiago, and Manila, and will hold any party to a strict accountability, and any party daring to apply the partisan spoils system to the government of our colonies or dependencies will be hurled from power by the aroused conscience of the American people.

Following as it did the excesses of the Gilded Age, the war inevitably inspired charges from anti-imperialists that it was only the product of greedy business interests wishing to exploit Cuba's natural resources. Such charges made Congress sensitive enough to declare its own good intention through the Teller amendment to the Paris peace treaty: "That the United States hereby disclaims any disposition or intention to exercise sovereignty, jurisdiction, or control over [Cuba] except for the pacification therein and asserts its determination, when that is accomplished, to leave the government of the Island to its people." To insure that the new territory would not be subject to economic exploitation, Congress passed the Foraker Amendment to the Army Appropriations bill in February 1899, prohibiting the granting of franchises or concessions in Cuba to American companies during the period of military occupation. President McKinley himself stressed America's good intentions in an effort to distinguish his foreign policy from the prevailing drive among European nations for colonial possessions. The Spanish territories, McKinley claimed in a recurrent theme of his administration, "have come to us in the providence of God, and we must carry the burden, whatever it may be, in the interest of civilization, humanity and liberty."

Cuba's first military governor, John Brooke, a career soldier who made his reputation in the Spanish War by leading invading columns through the virtually bloodless conquest of Puerto Rico, did his best to effect the outlines of good government promised in Washington. He initiated programs to build new schools and to provide basic sanitation facilities for the island. Among his appointees he counted as military governor of Havana William Ludlow, a man who had already established a credible record in the United States as a good government reformer. During his tenure as director of the Water Department in Philadelphia, according to a New York *Times* report, "political heelers who had won sinecures by carrying their wards were discharged and their places filled by efficient men. Political bosses stood aghast at such independence and after trying all kinds of 'influence' and 'pulls' were compelled to leave the Water Department alone as long as Colonel Ludlow remained at its head." Ludlow expressed his confidence in the effectiveness of transporting America's campaign against corruption to the island, claiming in his first annual report in 1900 that, "For the first time, probably in its history, Havana had an honest and efficient government, clean of bribery and speculation, with revenues honestly collected and faithfully and intelligently expended."

But the problems facing Brooke required more than basic services and clean government. The devastation and near anarchy of the island suggested immediately the need for extensive social, economic and political reconstruction. Yet lacking both administrative experience and any philosophical commitment to government activism, Brooke dampened every effort to provide government services whose need he did not find absolutely compelling. At one point he rejected a plan for long-term low-interest loans to destitute farmers, calling the program a kind of paternalism which would destroy the self-respect of the people.

The prospect for more comprehensive reform was discouraged by the lack of direction from Washington. Despite his repeated promise to carry out an American mission in Cuba, President McKinley outlined no general policy for the island. Henry Adams complained in January 1899, that "the government lets everything drift. It professes earnestly its intention to give Cuba its independence, but refuses to take a step toward it, and allows everyone to act for annexation." Fully a year after the military occupation began, McKinley admitted, "Up to this time we have had no policy in regard to Cuba or our relations therewith, for the simple reason that we have had no time to formulate a policy." Under the circumstances Brooke was forced, as he said, to conduct the government by induction.

Without clear direction from Washington, Brooke lapsed into a narrow strain of reform directed at purifying Cuba's social system. Among his first circulars were orders to abolish gambling, to close business houses on Sunday and to prohibit public games and entertainments on Sunday. In perhaps his most misguided effort at reform he ordered in the interest of public safety the confiscation of all machetes on the island, not realizing that the law, if executed faithfully, would ruin the island's sugar business. Brooke's announced restrictions on theaters and dance halls led the Washington *Post* to editorialize: "Our first duty in Cuba is not morals or customs, but the establishment of institutions of law and order . . . if we begin by interference in their private lives, with puritanical compulsion and missionary irritation, the problem of Cuban rehabilitation will be set back twenty years."

The Brooke administration provoked its first serious internal criticism from Leonard Wood, past commander of the Rough Rider brigade Teddy Roosevelt made famous and military governor of the province of Santiago. As a young activist who felt well-tested by the war, Wood bridled at Brooke's timidity. "The condition of the Island is disheartening," he wrote his friend Roosevelt in August 1899. "I tell you absolutely that no single reform has been initiated which amounts to anything to date." Publicly he made no effort to conceal his discontent, telling a New York *Times* reporter, "The Cuban problem can easily be solved. With the right sort of administration everything could be straightened out in six months. Just now there is too much 'tommyrot.' What is needed is a firm and stable military government in the hands of men who would not hesitate to use severe measures should the occasion arise."

Roosevelt took Wood's complaints seriously and launched a campaign to promote him to Brooke's position. Five days after Wood penned his scathing report on Brooke Roosevelt replied: "Your letter makes me both worried and indignant . . . I am going to show it privately and confidentially to /Secretary of War Elihu/ Root. I do not know what to say. Root is a thoroughly good fellow and I believe he is going to steadily come around to your way of looking at things." As early as July 1 Roosevelt had touted Wood for Military Governor, writing Secretary of State John Hay that he doubted whether "any nation in the world has now or has had within recent time, anyone so nearly approaching the ideal of military administrator of the kind now required in Cuba." Wood, Roosevelt argued, "has a peculiar facility for getting on with the Spaniards and Cubans. They like him, trust him, and down in their hearts are afraid of him." Roosevelt's campaign had its effect, for in December 1899, Wood succeeded to Brooke's position.

Wood accepted his appointment as no ordinary assignment. "He is further impressed with the idea he has a mission—is charged with a great reformation," Brooke's retiring chief of staff noted. Such a mission demanded not just the establishment of civil order as sought by Brooke but reconstruction of the island as a thriving nation state. Though he showed some sensitivity to differences between Latin and Anglo-Saxon cultures, Wood could not resist promoting Americanization of the island—in the administration of justice, the training of police and general administrative practice—where proven methods could speed up goals of efficiency and uplift. As he wrote President McKinley explaining his ultimate objective, "We are going ahead as fast as we can, but we are dealing with a race that has steadily been going down for a hundred years and into which we have got to infuse new life, new principles and new methods of doing things."

Unlike Brooke, Wood established the administrative credibility to effect the changes he sought. He assiduously avoided imposition of puritanical social reforms on the Cuban people. "The main thing," he wrote, "is to avoid the appearance of correcting abuses which do not exist." Instead he emphasized adoption of "a business-like way of doing things," which he had complained was missing from the Brooke administration. His interest in corporate administrative efficiency drew sustenance and support from McKinley's new Secretary of War Elihu Root who had left his job as a New York corporate lawyer to take responsibility both for administering the Spanish possessions and modernizing the Army along efficient corporate lines. Together they shared the goals of an emerging social type in America which stressed organization and efficiency as touchstones of the progress of civilization.

As a start new lines of organization were drawn for the entire administrative system of the island. Wood revamped Brooke's educational program, for example, because it lacked precision. Though Brooke's minister of education succeeded in building new schools and increasing enrollment, he developed no institutional controls over the system. With the application of a new approach fashioned after Ohio law, school administration was divided according to function. A commissioner of education handled all executive matters, including purchasing supplies and making appointments, while a superintendent of schools developed educational policy. Together with six provincial commissioners he formed a board of education authorized to determine and introduce proper methods of teaching in the public schools. Each school district was granted local autonomy, though individual teachers were held responsible to central authority through a system of reports. The school board required teachers to complete reports monthly and yearly. Salaries were withheld for failure to comply. All teachers were also required to spend the first two summers of the American occupation in school and pass a certification exam at the end of their second year. The rigorous system was completely new to Cuba, where no public school system had previously existed and where teaching standards had never been defined.

Next to education, Cuban law was the most important object of Wood's administrative reorganization. In his annual report for 1900, Wood said that no department was "more in need of thorough and radical reform, rigid inspection, and constant supervision," than the department of justice which "was lacking in efficiency, energy and attention to duty." He complained that the Cuban judiciary and legal body had "surrounded itself with a cobweb of tradition and conservatism and adopted a procedure so cumbersome and slow of execution as to render impossible a prompt administration of justice." But he believed progress had been made under his administration. "Incompetent and neglectful individuals have been dismissed, the number of correctional courts has been very greatly increased, the audiencias supplied with necessary material, and very much done to improve the court houses."

Wood also launched a massive program of public works to reconstruct the island's cities. This municipal reform effort started under the crudest conditions. Wood's sanitary engineer in Santiago wrote that when he took office "not a shovel or a broom /was available/, and for several days, pieces of oil cans and brushes of trees, and palm branches, were the only implements available." By the close of 1900 chief engineer William Black could report that the streets of the island's major cities were sprinkled and swept nightly. In 1901 Black reported a wide range of services planned for the island, including new sewer systems; modern street pavements; construction of water mains to new buildings; water pollution controls; public parks; construction of new schools and public buildings; a modern slaughterhouse designed after the best Chicago examples and a system of subways for wires for transmission of electricity for light power, telegraph and telephone service.

The Department of Public Works not only provided a wide range of public services, but under Black it reorganized its internal operation to promote efficient conduct of city business. Cuban street cleaners could no longer be haphazard in their work or their dress. Each man was assigned a particular district responsibility and was uniformed smartly in white cotton-duck suits with brown cord trimmings, white metal badges and brown hats. In addition, the department prepared codes for municipal operations, including a list of plumbing specifications that set standard requirements for every class of pipe and fitting.

In order to institutionalize the improved efficiency of municipal departments in particular, Wood urged adoption of a new city charter in Havana. Soon after his promotion, Wood appointed a commission of American and Cuban experts to draw up a model city charter. The commission was given copies of recent American charters, in which the fundamental principles encouraged were "simplicity, effectiveness, responsibility, and the largest measure of autonomy that could with safety be authorized." Following the argument for home rule in the United States, the new charter prevented the central and provincial governments from intervening in municipal affairs, granting the city control of "all matters within its boundary." Specifically city government was held responsible for "the comfort and health of the inhabitants, and the security of their persons and property." Significantly the charter provided for regulation of all public utilities at a time when municipal reformers in America were attempting to write the same provision into law. The charter also incorporated an order previously adopted on the island which simplified the tax system by eliminating the ill-defined system of shared responsibility between city and province and making a direct connection between the tax rate and benefits received from city government.

The new city charter pointed the way to the best of American municipal reform. It established the dictum, which would be stated most precisely by Herbert Croly, that government must be efficient and to be efficient its powers must equal its responsibilities. Not only was the city authorized to use broad powers in the public interest, it was held responsible to promote that interest. As such, the charter reflected the general enthusiasm for positive government intervention in public affairs shared by Wood, Root, Roosevelt and Croly. Wood worked to define similar powers of public responsibility at a national level in Cuba through the creation of a railroad commission. He was offended, as he said, that the railroads "have always been able to buy the government and run things about as they saw fit." But much more he felt the state had a responsibility to protect public welfare. "I'm going to insist on state intervention in regulating rates," he wrote President Roosevelt in 1902, "when it is evident that such rates are prejudicial to the public interest."

When the railroads balked at possible state regulation Wood received encouragement from E. H. Moseley, Secretary of the U.S. Interstate Commerce Commission. "The demand of the railroads of Cuba that they should be allowed to control at pleasure, consulting their own interest only, the arteries of the internal commerce of the country is preposterous," he wrote Wood in January 1902. "I'm convinced that the railroad commission, composed of men of high character, is determined to follow the reasonable and correct course, dealing fairly with all, and while having the interest of the State and welfare of the people fully in view, do no act of injustice to the railroads."

The Cuban railroad law enacted a month later incorporated all the major features of the Interstate Commerce Act adopted in the United States in 1887. It forbade railroads to engage in discriminatory practices, required them to publish their rate schedules, prohibited them from entering pooling arrangements to keep rates high and declared that rates should be "reasonable and just." The Cuban law attempted to avoid the major pitfall of its predecessor by holding a ruling valid until revoked by the Supreme Court. Under the American law, where the I.C.C. relied on the Supreme Court for enforcement, fifteen of the first sixteen cases appealed had been decided in favor of the railroads against the commission.

Recent scholarship has revealed how legislation for the I.C.C., though stimulated by agrarian discontent, ultimately reflected the concerns of commercial interests, which wished to rationalize the system for their own profits. Taken out of the American context the Cuban reform represented an ideal in itself divorced from the factions which originally shaped the bill. Significantly, Wood gave it new purpose in protecting middle-class producers and planters for whom, he wrote Root, lower rates would be "a very substantial gain."

Indeed Wood built his program around the establishment of a conservative middle-class ruling elite. He distrusted the Cuban politicians who had gained office in the first elections and who, he said, appeared to be "in a certain sense doctors without patients, lawyers without practice and demagogues living in the subscription of the people and their friends." Planters and producers, on the other hand, appealed to him as "an honest, warm-hearted class of people," who were most appreciative of good order and protection of life and property. Wood often called the planter class conservative in a positive sense, consciously identifying them with the better class of citizens in America who unfortunately, he thought, had bypassed public service. He continued to believe, however, that their success, both political and commercial, was essential to the future of Cuba, for ultimately they would have to provide both the tax revenues to pay for needed services on the island and the leadership to effect those services. Wood underscored his belief in working hard for reciprocal trade agreements:

The resources on which Cuba must depend for the income necessary to establish a stable government, requiring, as any government does, good schools, good courts, a system of public works, means of communication, hospitals, charities, etc., are those which will be derived from the sale of her two most stable products, and, if we continue to legislate against these, we cannot, with any degree of sincerity, expect the new government to be able to maintain such conditions as constitute stable government.

Ultimately Wood revealed the kind of commitment to conservative political capitalism which Gabriel Kolko has described as characteristic of progressivism. His hope for Cuba lay in a working relationship of responsible businessmen in both countries. He assigned highest priority to sanitation measures, for instance, largely because he believed adequate safeguards against disease were a prerequisite for American investment in the island. Part of his desire to standardize Cuban law derived from reports from American businessmen that the principal reason for the lack of confidence in Cuban investments was the threat of costly time-consuming litigation in native courts. Wood risked criticism from Cuban patriots for limiting popular suffrage because, as he wrote Root, "if it were known to be a fact that we were going to give universal suffrage, it would stop investments and advancement in this island to an extent which would be disastrous in its results."

Wood clearly opposed outright business exploitation, but he could not avoid a bias for conservative middle-class business ideology. In the final year of his administration he worked actively for a stipulation gained in the controversial Platt Amendment to the Army Appropriations bill which guaranteed the preservation of American commercial interests through the right of intervention. All orders of the military government were granted permanence in Article IV which declared that "all acts of the United States in Cuba during its military occupancy thereof are ratified and validated, and all lawful rights acquired thereunder shall be maintained and protected." Americanization of the island was thus completed, with legal assurance that it would not be quickly or easily overturned.

By every American standard the occupation had been a tremendous success. In guiding Cuba to its independence without succumbing to colonialism, business exploitation or government corruption, Wood rested the worst fears of the Mugwump reformers. Jacob Riis, the New York social reformer, granted the occupation that degree of success, in terms widely adopted by the press at the time:

Cuba is free, and she thanks President Roosevelt for her freedom. But for his insistence that the nation's honor was bound up in the completion of the work his Rough-Riders began at Las Guasimas and on San Juan hill, a cold conspiracy of business greed would have left her in the lurch, to fall by and by reluctantly into our arms, bankrupt and helpless, while the sneer of the cynics that we were plucking that plum for ourselves would have been justified.

Beyond these essentially negative results, however, the administration provided a positive achievement through government activism which separated Wood and his contemporaries from the Mugwumps. Wood himself stressed this activism, in contrast to Brooke's timid administration, in summarizing his record. He had, as he wrote in 1903, completed work "which called for practically a rewriting of the administrative law of the land, including the law of charities, hospitals and public works, sanitary law, school law, and railway law; meeting and controlling the worst possible sanitary conditions; putting the people to school; writing an electoral law and training the people in the use of it, establishing an entirely new system of accounting and auditing." Not without pride he concluded that the work called for and accomplished "the establishment, in a little over three years, in a Latin military colony, in one of the most unhealthy countries of the world, a republic modeled closely upon the lines of our own great Anglo-Saxon republic."

Our understanding of the special nature of the Wood reform ethic is heightened through a brief analysis of its reception in Cuba. For a country whose economic and social identity lay largely in the countryside, Wood could well have concentrated government expenditures in a program of agricultural reconstruction modeled after methods being instituted in the American South and suggested by Governor James Wilson of Matanzas Province. "I do not consider the future of Cuba depends chiefly upon schools, road-making, improved sanitation or judiciary reform," Wilson said. "The best the United States can do for Cuba and the Cubans is to give every opportunity for improving the value of the land by putting it to the best uses. In this way capital could do an immense amount of good here as well as get returns." Wood rejected Wilson's plea, resting his hopes for Cuba's future not in small farms but in the cities. He stressed this urban orientation when he wrote Roosevelt in August 1899, "All we want here are good courts, good schools and all the public work we can pay for. Reform of municipal government and a business way of doing things."

Wood's emphasis on urban development ran counter to established Cuban tradition. While his work in Havana drew praise in America, it received a less welcome reception among Cubans. The Havana ayuntamiento (city council) overwhelmingly rejected the charter commission report, although the proposal purportedly incorporated the best features of American law. According to one councilman, the new plan was but one more of the great many fancies which had been thrust on the Cubans by force.

Beyond Wood's urban orientation lay a bias for government authority which again rankled the Cubans. As governor of Santiago, Wood had gained tremendous popularity by criticizing the centralization of authority in Havana.

When Brooke decreed that all customs revenues would be distributed from Havana, Wood took the case for decentralized distribution to Washington and became a hero among Cubans. Wood's act struck a responsive chord with a people who hoped for a substitution of American decentralized administration for the highly centralized Spanish system. The Spanish law of 1878 governing local administration outwardly allowed local autonomy. But a provision making the alcalde (mayor) removable at will placed the executive authority and the towns generally at the mercy of the central government. The Cubans moved toward greater local independence with the Autonomist Constitution of 1897 which stipulated that the ayuntamientos and not the central government made the final selection of alcaldes.

Wood's reputation as champion of Santiago's independence encouraged the Cubans to believe that he would complete the decentralization begun by the Autonomist Constitution. Wood did encourage municipal autonomy. He eliminated many municipalities which had been created during the war solely to act as agents of the Spanish government, making the remaining cities real functioning units with their own taxing and spending power. But with a lack of administrative experience at the local level, cities repeatedly exceeded their budgets, depending on national revenues to remain solvent. Wood's own personal vigor and the fact that he was so insistent on his directives helped sustain all final authority in Havana. As one sensitive observer of America's overseas policy, Leo S. Rowe, said, "The leaders in the work of civic reorganization were determined to put an end to the highly centralized administration of Spanish times, but in actual development of the system the force of tradition has proved stronger than conscious purpose. Although the municipalities enjoy more extensive powers in law, in fact they remain subservient to the central government."

Wood's authoritarian bent must have reflected a military man's desire to get a job done. He recognized, for instance, no restraints in effecting sanitation measures in Santiago. According to President McKinley's special commissioner to the island, Robert Porter, "The doors of houses had to be smashed in; people making sewers of the thoroughfares were publicly horsewhipped in the streets of Santiago; eminently respectable citizens were forcibly brought before the commanding general and sentenced to aid in cleaning the streets they were in the habit of defiling." As A. Hunter Dupree has pointed out, Wood managed to institute his sanitation program in Cuba because island administrators held powers which "would have been entirely unavailable to the President of the United States had the infected city been New Orleans instead of Havana." Wood himself credited his success in Cuba to the wide scope of his power, indicating that if he were to take a role in administering the Philippines "I should like to have a go at the situation with the same authority I have had here. Without such full authority I believe the Islands will be the burial ground of the reputation of those who go there."

Had Wood shared the philosophical restraints of Brooke or other Mugwump leaders of his generation on the limited use of government power he might not have aroused the kind of opposition in Cuba he did. The important factor for the historian of American reform, however, lies in the example Wood held up to his countrymen back home and its reception there, whatever his own motivations for seeking government authority in Cuba. By carefully selecting among existing precedents in the United States those models which allowed the greatest government activism, Wood presented fellow reformers in America with a new spirit of administrative technique and law. His reforms emphasizing administrative efficiency served as a bridge between Root's reorganization of the Army and Gifford Pinchot's program for a professionally managed forest system and later administrative reforms instituted by Theodore Roosevelt as president.

In a general sense Wood's administration, undertaken as it was in the full glare of national publicity, provided a visibility for reform which had been badly lacking in earlier good government movements. The emergence of Roosevelt, Root and Wood from virtual obscurity to national heroes helped dramatize a new spirit of reform and suggested to the public at large the dawn of a new moral leadership for America. "The war with Spain," Secretary of the Navy William H. Moody claimed in a speech in 1902, "disclosed the enormous resources of this country, its wealth, its power, its strength, but it disclosed more. It disclosed the character of our people, and we know that where the Tafts, and the Roots, and the Days, and the Woods, and the Roosevelts came from, there are many more like them to come to the service of the country when their country calls." Wood's heralded decision to turn down a $25,000-a-year street railway presidency offered during his term as military governor set him apart from public figures of the Gilded Age and gave substance to a new leadership ideal, articulated by Roosevelt as early as 1897 when he was still Assistant Secretary of the Navy that: "The fight well fought, the life honorably lived, the death bravely met—those count far more in building a fine type of temper in a nation than any possible success in the stockmarket, than any possible prosperity in commerce or manufactures."

In a more direct sense the philosophical connection between the occupation and emerging progressivism was tied through personal links, the most important of which was Wood's close relationship with Theodore Roosevelt. Among more specialized progressive leaders, Leo Rowe of the University of Pennsylvania recognized immediately the importance of administrative innovation in the Spanish possessions. Though recognized as an expert on municipal reform in America, Rowe found the study of the Spanish possessions irresistible. He wrote not only extensive articles on the administration of Cuba and the Philippines but also a book on the occupation of Puerto Rico, where he served as chairman of the island's code commission. He predicted in March 1899, that the workshop provided by the Spanish possessions would turn America's political philosophy away from limited protection of individual liberties to one of activist intervention for national development. "The readjustment of the country's international relations, which must follow the recent struggle with Spain, will supply the connecting link between economic and political development," he wrote in *The Forum*. "Its influence, however, will extend far beyond these limits. It will modify our political ideas, develop a broader view of the country's relation to the larger affairs of the world, and react upon domestic politics, with the result of raising the level of public life."

In his urban work Rowe reached theoretical conclusions which Wood coincidentally put into pragmatic effect. In 1897 Rowe argued that even though American cities had reached a nadir in the American experience they would have to serve nonetheless as the chief agent of civilization. The reformer's role, then, lay clearly in upgrading the urban environment, precisely the approach Wood took in Cuba. Indeed, Wood's administration both reflected Rowe's philosophy and gave it sustenance through the apparent triumph of urban-oriented programs to give the island the services sought in America through the city beautiful movement, particularly good schools, grand public buildings and clean streets.

On another level the experiments in the Caribbean served to inspire activists among two other major elements of the emerging reform movement, the journalists who would soon become known as muckrakers and the social welfare activists. Robert Bannister cites the tremendous impact the activism of Wood and Roosevelt had on Ray Stannard Baker in converting him from a Mugwump to a progressive. Indeed Baker seems to have absorbed himself the chief principles of Roosevelt's strenuous life, writing in his journal, "A warrior is not made by the battles he avoids but by the battles he fights." Another entry suggests a parallel drive with Roosevelt, Wood and Rowe to take up the challenge of remaking society: "What we must be thankful for is not perfection, not the solution of all our problems; this condition we can never hope to attain—but let us praise God for the struggle! Completeness we can not attain, but where there is restless activity, there is also health and hope. Not beautification, perfection: that is heaven, but turmoil and struggle, progress; that is human life." For the social reformer Jacob Riis, the example of the American occupation was no less inspiring. "How jolly it is to think of you and Roosevelt being both where you are," he wrote Wood in February 1900. "This is a good world anyway, and the pessimists lie like the Dickens."

Despite our recognition today that Wood's specific programs as well as his desire to civilize Cuba generally reflected already established American values, we should not underestimate the impact of the overall reform effort on the United States. For a country in which administrative reform had not yet emerged as a national goal and in which urban reconstruction remained rather a hope than a reality, Wood's achievement must have provided, as Croly said, a tremendous stimulus for domestic reform. The Cuban occupation provided progressives not only with a programmatic cohesion which had been lacking in earlier reform movements but also the kind of favorable national publicity which could give new efforts momentum at home. The success of the occupation, by American standards, underscored the belief that the United States had fulfilled its mandate to lift the Cuban people into the forward stream of Western civilization, and in so doing, it provided for a new generation of progressives faith in man's ability to remake and reform the world around him.

PART TWO
A
MODERNIZING
PEOPLE

8

A BRIDGE OF BENT BACKS AND LABORING MUSCLES: THE RURAL SOUTH, 1880–1915

JACQUELINE JONES

In the years immediately following the Civil War, southern planters faced an uncertain future. The Union victory ended the slave labor system that planters had relied on since the seventeenth century, and while they were able to forestall a congressional attempt to dispossess former slave owners of their land, that land was useless without the labor that was necessary for growing and harvesting the cotton, sugar, and tobacco crops that were the source of planter profits. Faced with an immediate and pressing need for low-cost labor, between 1865 and 1880 land-owners throughout the South turned to sharecropping and debt peonage as a means to secure a continued supply of agricultural labor. By the end of Reconstruction in 1877, the majority of former slaves, although legally free, were again under the control of white planters.

The working lives of these black sharecroppers were little different from their existence under slavery. This was especially true of freedwomen, who continued to be bound to the double duties of field and household labor long after the end of slavery. Until they abandoned sharecropping and moved northward to take up independent work as laundresses and domestics during World War I, these southern black women lived lives of toil and persistent expectation. Like every member of the sharecropping household, women labored long hours to help the family survive; but as Jacqueline Jones reveals in this essay, they also lived with the hope that their labor would permit their children to escape the economic and social bondage of postwar southern society.

Chapter 3 in Jacqueline Jones, *Labor of Love, Labor of Sorrow: Black Women, Work, and the Family, from Slavery to the Present* (New York: Basic Books, 1985).

For black women in the rural South, the years 1880 to 1915 spanned a period between the Civil War era and the "Great Migration" northward beginning with World War I. Although the physical dimensions of their domestic chores and field work had not changed much since slavery, women during this period toiled with the new hope that their sons and daughters would one day escape from the Cotton South. Maud Lee Bryant, a farm wife in Moncure, North Carolina, spent long days in the fields chopping cotton, wheat, and tobacco, and long nights in the house, washing dishes and clothes, scrubbing floors, and sewing, starching, and ironing. She later recalled, "My main object of working was wanting the children to have a better way of living, that the world might be just a little better because the Lord had me here for something, and I tried to make good out of it, that was my aim." Thus the substance of rural women's work stayed the same compared to earlier generations, while its social context was transformed by the promise, but not necessarily the reality, of freedom.

Black sharecroppers, with the "proverbial unacquisitiveness of the 'rolling stone'," remained outside the mainstream of liberal American society during the years from 1880 to 1915. Their quest for household and group autonomy, like the heavy iron hoes they carried to the cotton fields, represented the tangible legacy of slavery. In an industrializing, urbanizing nation, the former slaves and their children were concentrated in the rural South, and their distinctive way of life became increasingly anomalous within the larger society. Caught in the contradiction of a cash-crop economy based upon a repressive labor system, black households achieved neither consumer status nor total self-sufficiency. Consequently, the lives of black women were fraught with irony; though many had planted, chopped, and picked their share of cotton over the years, they rarely enjoyed the pleasure of a new cotton dress. Though they labored within an agricultural economy, they and their families barely survived on meager, protein-deficient diets. Within individual black households, this tension between commercial and subsistence agriculture helped to shape the sexual division of labor, as wives divided their time among domestic responsibilities, field work, and petty moneymaking activities.

The postbellum plantation economy required a large, subservient work force that reinforced the racial caste system but also undermined the economic status of an increasing number of nonelite whites. By the end of the nineteenth century, nine out of ten Afro-Americans lived in the South, and 80 percent of these resided in rural areas, primarily in the formerly slave Cotton Belt. Blacks represented one-third of the southern population and 40 percent of its farmers and farm laborers, but by no means its only poverty-stricken agricultural group. Up-country yeomen farmers were gradually drawn away from livestock and food production and into the commercial economy after the Civil War. In the process they lost their economic independence to a burgeoning system of financial credit. Yet on a social hierarchy that ranged from planters at the top to small landowners in the middle and various states of tenancy at the bottom—cash renters, share tenants, sharecroppers, and wage laborers—blacks monopolized the very lowliest positions. In 1910 fully nine-tenths of all southern blacks who made their living from the soil worked as tenants, sharecroppers, or contract laborers. Most barely eked out enough in cotton to pay for rent, food, and supplies. They did not own their own equipment, nor could they market their crop independent of the landlord. As the price of cotton declined precipitously near the end of the century, landlords began to insist on a fixed amount of cash—rather than a share of the crop—as payment for rent. Thus individual black households had to bear the brunt of a faltering staple-crop economy.

The black women who emerged from slavery "knew that what they got wasn't what they wanted, it wasn't freedom, really." So they constantly searched for freedom, moving with their families at the end of each year to find better soil or a more reasonable landlord; or, bereft of a husband and grown sons, traveling to a nearby town to locate gainful employment; or raising chickens so they could sell eggs and send their children to school. These women partook of the uniqueness of rural, late nineteenth-century Afro-American culture and at the same time bore the universal burdens and took solace from the universal satisfactions of motherhood. They were the mothers and grandmothers of the early twentieth-century migrants to northern cities, migrants who as young people had been reared in homes with primitive hearths where women of all ages continued to guard the "embers of a smoldering liberty."

THE TRIPLE DUTY OF WIVES, MOTHERS, DAUGHTERS, AND GRANDMOTHERS

For black Americans, the post-Reconstruction era opened inauspiciously. According to Nell Irvin Painter, between 1879 and 1881 as many as twenty thousand rural blacks fled the "young hell" of the Lower South in search of the "promised land" of Kansas. Around this millenarian migration coalesced the major themes of Afro-American history from 1880 to 1915: the forces of terrorism and poverty that enveloped all rural blacks, and the lure of land, education, and "protection for their women" that made them yearn for true freedom. "Rooted in faith and in fear," the Kansas fever exodus consisted primarily of families headed by former slaves desperate to escape neoslavery. Together with their menfolk, then, black women did their best to minimize the control that whites sought to retain over their lives—a "New South" mandate succinctly summarized by the governor of North Carolina in 1883: "Your work is the tilling of the ground, . . . Address yourselves to the work, men and women alike."

In order to understand the roles of black women as workers and household members, it is necessary to examine the methods used by whites to supervise and restrict the options of the family as an economic unit. Although granted relatively more overall freedom than their slave parents, black men and women in the late nineteenth century had only a limited ability to make crucial decisions related to household and farm management. The nature of the sharecropping system meant that economic matters and family affairs overlapped to a considerable degree. Under optimal conditions, each family would have been able to decide for itself how best to use its members' labor, and when or whether to leave one plantation in search of better land or a more favorable contractual arrangement. These conditions rarely pertained in the Cotton South.

By the early twentieth century, some plantations were so large and efficiently managed they resembled agricultural industrial establishments with hired hands rather than a loose conglomeration of independently operated family farms. The degree to which a household was supervised determined its overall status in southern society, and blacks were systematically deprived of self-determination to a greater degree than their poor white counterparts. For example, in an effort to monitor their tenants' work habits, large cotton planters often employed armed "riders" who were "constantly travelling from farm to farm." As agents of the white landowner, these men kept track of the size of each black family and had the authority to order all "working hands" into the fields at any time. Riders dealt with recalcitrant workers by "wearing them out" (that is, inflicting physical punishment). Indeed, a government researcher noted that southern sharecroppers in general were "subjected to quite as complete supervision by the owner, general lessee or hired manager as that to which the wage laborers are subjected on large farms in the North and West, and indeed in the South." The more tenants a planter had, the larger his profit; hence he would more readily withhold food from a family of unsatisfactory workers, or deny its children an opportunity for schooling, than turn them off his land.

The planter thus sought to intervene in the black farmer's attempt to organize the labor of various family members. Usually the father assumed major responsibility for crop production, and he relied on the assistance of his wife and children during planting and harvesting. But, reported Thomas J. Edwards in his 1911 study of Alabama sharecroppers, if the father failed to oversee the satisfactory completion of a chore, then "the landlord compels every member of his family who is able to carry a hoe or plow to clean out the crops." Some very small households counted on relatives and neighbors to help them during these times; others had to pay the expense of extra laborers hired by the landlord to plow, weed, or chop the cotton on their own farms.

Ultimately a white employer controlled not only a family's labor, but also its "furnishings" and food. By combining the roles of landlord and merchant-financier, he could regulate the flow of both cash and supplies to his tenants. Annual interest rates as high as 25 percent (in the form of a lien on the next year's crop) were not unusual, and tenants had little choice but to borrow when they needed to buy seed, fertilizer, and clothes for the children. Some white men, like the planter who forbade sharecroppers on his land to raise hogs so that they would have to buy their salt pork from him, effectively reduced the opportunities for families to provide for their own welfare in the most basic way. To escape this vicious cycle of dependency required a good deal of luck, as well as the cooperation of each household member. The hardworking Pickens family of Arkansas, overwhelmed by debt in 1888, tried desperately to free themselves. Recalled William, the sixth of ten children: ". . . in the ensuing winter Mother cooked and washed and Father felled trees in the icy 'brakes' to make rails and boards /to sell/." Their landlord removed temptation by closing the neighborhood school. Referring to that time, William Pickens remembered many years later that "very small

children can be used to hoe and pick cotton, and I have seen my older sisters drive a plow."

Since tenant-landlord accounts were reckoned at the end of each year, sharecroppers had to remain on a farm until they received payment for their cotton (usually in December) or until they had discharged their debt to their employer. The tendency of families to move whenever they had the opportunity—up to one-third left for another, usually nearby, plantation at the end of any one year—caused apprehension among planters who wanted to count on a stable work force for extended periods of time. In the end, the very measures used to subordinate black farmers served as an impetus for them to migrate—to another county, a nearby town, or, after 1916, a northern city. But until alternative forms of employment became available (the lack of free land and transportation halted the exodus to Kansas after a couple of years), most sharecroppers continued to move around to some extent within the plantation economy, but not out of it. Consequently, the annual December trek of sharecropping families from one plantation to another constituted a significant part of Afro-American community life. Some families "were ever on the move from cabin to cabin," prompting the story about the household whose chickens "regularly presented themselves in the dooryard at Christmastime with their legs crossed for tying up before the next morning. . . ." Within such a circumscribed realm of activity, even a neighboring plantation seemed to beckon with opportunity, or at least the possibility of change.

As productive members of the household economy, black women helped to fulfill the economic as well as the emotional needs of their families, factors to consider whenever a move was contemplated. These needs changed over the life course of individual families and clans. So too did the demands upon women fluctuate in the cabin and out in the cotton field, from season to season and from year to year. Thus the responsibilities of wives and mothers reflected considerations related to their families' immediate daily welfare, the fortunes of their kinfolk, and the staple-crop planting and harvesting cycle. Within this constantly shifting matrix of obligations, black women performed housekeeping and childcare tasks, earned modest sums of cash, and worked in the fields.

In their studies of Afro-American life and culture, historians tend to focus on the nuclear family component. However, it is clear that, in rural southern society, the nuclear family (consisting of two parents and their children) frequently cohabited within a larger, rather flexible household. Moreover, neighboring households were often linked by ties of kinship. These linkages helped to determine very specific (but by no means static) patterns of reciprocal duties among household members, indicating that kinship clusters, rather than nuclear families, defined women's and men's daily labor.

For example, a study of the black population in the Cotton Belt (based upon federal manuscript census data for 1880 and 1900) reveals that the "typical" Afro-American household retained certain structural characteristics throughout this twenty-year period. At the core of this household were both a husband and wife (89.6 percent of all households in the 1880 sample, and 87.8 percent in 1900, were headed by a man; 86.4 percent and 82.5 percent, respectively, included both spouses). The typical household remained nuclear, although extended families (that is, those that included blood relations) increased in importance over time (from 13.6 percent in 1880 to 23 percent in 1900). The average household had between four and five members. Significantly, a crude index of local kinship networks suggests that at least one-third of all families lived near some of their relatives.

Contemporary sources indicate that these networks played a large part in determining where sharecroppers' families moved at the end of the year and where small landowners settled permanently. For example, in-laws and distant cousins might try to induce a newlywed couple to join them by coaxing, "Nate, you a young fellow, you ought to be down here workin." Moreover, the spirit of sharing that informed many small communities meant that a woman's chores extended out of her own household and into the larger community; indeed, some neighborhoods were composed entirely of kin, thereby making family and community virtually congruent. A woman might adopt an orphan or a newborn grandchild whose parents had not married. She and her husband helped out on a nearby farm when their neighbors found themselves shorthanded. She took over the domestic chores of a sister who had just had a baby and consulted with other women in her family about the best remedy for a child wracked by fever. If she was particularly skilled in the art of folk medicine, she might serve as an herb doctor and prescribe cures for her neighbors suffering from anything from a toothache to a heartache.

The needs of her kin had a direct bearing upon the number and ages of the people a woman cooked and washed for under her own roof. The household was in reality a "dynamic process" and not a static entity. Although the pattern changed somewhat during the late nineteenth century, in general the younger the husband, the more likely that he and his wife would live alone with their children. Older couples tended to include relatives to a greater degree than did younger couples. These sketchy data suggest that newlyweds quickly, though not necessarily immediately, established independent households and that years later a husband and wife might welcome kinfolk into their home. Perhaps these relatives worked in the fields, taking the place of older children who had left to begin families of their own. Or they might have needed the care and assistance that only a mature household could provide. In any case, it is clear that the boundaries of a household could expand or contract to fill both economic and social-welfare functions within the black community.

Keeping in mind these transformations that occurred over the course of a generation, it is useful to begin a discussion of the farm wife's daily routine with the experience of a young married couple. She and her husband began their life together with very little in the way of material possessions, and they often had to make do with the "sorriest land"—"Land so doggone thin . . . 'it won't sprout unknown peas.'" At least for the first few years, each new baby (there would probably be five or six who would survive infancy) meant an extra mouth to feed and body to clothe while the number of available "hands" in the family stayed the same. Consequently a young wife had to divide her time between domestic tasks and cotton cultivation, the mainstay of family life; she did "a man's share in the field, and a woman's part at home." As Rossa B. Cooley reported of a South Carolina Sea Island family, "Occupation: Mother, farming and housework. Father, farming."

The primitive conditions under which these women performed household chores means that the term housework—when used in the traditional sense—is somewhat misleading. The size and rudeness of a sharecropper's dwelling made it extremely difficult to keep clean and tidy. Constructed by the white landowner usually many years before, the one- or two-room log or sawn-lumber cabin measured only fifteen or twenty square feet. It lacked glass windows, screens to keep out bugs and flies, running water, sanitary facilities, artificial illumination, cupboard and shelf space, and adequate insulation as well as ventilation. Most of the daily business of living—eating, sleeping, bathing—took place in one room where "stale sickly odors" inevitably accumulated. The ashes from a smoky fire used to prepare the evening meal had barely cooled before the children had to "bundle themselves up as well as they might and sleep on the floor in front of the fireplace," while their parents shared a small bed in the same room. Each modest addition to the cabin increased a family's living space and relative comfort—a lean-to, chicken coop–like kitchen; a wooden floor; efficient chimney; sleeping loft for the children; closets and cupboards; or an extra bedroom.

Farm wives had little in the way of time, money, or incentive to make permanent improvements in or around a cabin the family did not own and hoped to leave in the next year or two anyway. One Alabama mother summed up her frustration this way: "I have done dug holes in de ya/r/d by moonlight mo' dan o/n/ce so dat whah I stay at might hab a rose-bush, but I nebber could be sho' whose ya/r/d it would be de nex' yeah." Yet many women remained sensitive to their domestic environment; if they could not always find time to clean up the mud tracked in from outside each day, still they rearranged the house "very nice to meet the great Easter morning," whitewashed it for a Christmas celebration, dug up flowers in the woods to plant in the yard, or attached brightly colored pictures to the inside walls.

Most families owned few pieces of heavy furniture; modest earnings were often invested in a mule, ox, plow, or wagon rather than domestic furnishings. In any case, a paucity of goods was appreciated when the time came to pick up and move on to another place. Sharecroppers' households also lacked artifacts of middle-class life, such as a wide variety of eating and cooking utensils, books, papers, pencils, bric-a-brac, and clocks. Black rural women relied on a very few pieces of basic equipment in the course of the day; these included a large tub in which to bathe the youngsters and scrub the clothes, a cooking kettle, and a water pail. Their material standard of living was considerably lower than that of midcentury western pioneer families.

The round of daily chores performed by a sharecropper's wife indicates that the arduousness of this way of life bore an inverse relation to its "simplicity." She usually rose with the roosters (about 4 A.M., before other members) to prepare breakfast over an open fire—salt pork (sliced thin and then fried), molasses and fat on cornbread. She either served the meal in the cabin or took it out to family members who were by this time already at work in the field. During the planting season she joined her husband and children outside at tasks assigned on the basis of sex and age. For example, a typical division of labor included a father who "ran furrows" using a plow drawn by a mule or oxen, a small child who followed him dropping seeds or "potato slips" on the ground, and "at each step the mother covering them with a cumbersome hoe or setting out the plants by piercing holes in the ground with a sharp stick, inserting the roots, and packing the earth with deft movements of the hand." Although she knew as much about the growing cycle as her husband, she probably deferred to his judgment when it came to deciding what she needed to do and when. More than one black person remembered a mother who "done anything my daddy told her to do as far as cultivatin a crop out there. . . ."

Harvest time consumed a substantial portion of each year; two to four cotton pickings lasted from August to December. Like planting techniques, picking had remained the same since the earliest days of slavery, and young and old, male and female, performed essentially the same task. During this period in particular, the Cotton South was remarkable for its resistance to technological innovations compared to the industrial section of the Northeast, or commercial agriculture in the Midwest, a fact that weighed heavily on the shoulders of rural black women. Cotton picking was still such a labor-intensive task, few tenant-farm wives could escape its rigors. The importance of this operation to the well-being of the family—the greater the crop, the more favorable their economic situation at the end of the year—necessitated the labor of every able-bodied person and took priority over all but the most vital household chores.

In the sharecropping family, children were a distinct economic asset. In 1880 nine out of ten southern black wives between the ages of twenty-one and thirty had at least one child aged three or under. Just as the agricultural system helped to influence family size, so the growing season affected an expectant mother's ability to refrain from field work. In

1918 a Children's Bureau report noted that "to some extent, the amount of rest a mother can have before and after confinement is determined by the time of year or by the stage of cotton crop upon which depends the livelihood of the family." The birth of a child represented the promise of better times in terms of augmenting the household's labor supply, but for the time being it increased the workload of other family members and placed additional physical demands on the new mother herself.

Compared to slave women, sharecroppers' wives had more flexibility when it came to taking care of their children during the day. Some women managed to hoe and keep an eye on an infant at the same time. But many, like the mother who laid her baby to sleep on a nearby fence rail, only to return and find "a great snake crawling over the child," found it difficult to divide their attention between the two tasks. Slightly older children presented problems of a different sort. For instance, the mother of five-year-old John Coleman had to choose between leaving him to his own devices while she worked in the field—he liked to run off and get into mischief in the creek—and coaxing him to help alongside her, "thinning the cotton or corn . . . picking cotton or peas." At the age of six or seven oldest siblings often remained at home to watch over the younger children while their mother labored "in the crop."

In preparation for the main meal of the day (about 11 A.M.), a woman left the field early to collect firewood (which she might carry home on her back) and fetch water from a stream or well. (If she was lucky, she had children to help her with water-toting, one of the worst forms of domestic drudgery; they would follow along behind her, carrying piggins, pails, or cups according to their size.) The noontime meal often consisted of food left over from breakfast, supplemented (if they were fortunate) by turnip or collard greens from the family garden during the months of summer and early fall. The additional time required to fish, hunt for wild game, and pick berries, and the money needed to purchase additional supplies, meant that many sharecropping families subsisted on a substandard, protein-poor diet of "meat, meal, and molasses," especially in the winter and spring. The decline in black fertility rates during the late nineteenth century and the strikingly high child mortality rates during the same period were probably due at least in part to the poor health of rural women and their families.

In the afternoon, work in the fields resumed. Once again, "the house was left out of order [as it was] in the morning, the cooking things scattered about the hearth just as they were used, and the few dishes on the old table . . . unwashed too." Indeed, travelers and social workers often remarked on the dirty dishes and unmade beds that were the hallmark of a sharecropper's cabin. Sympathetic observers realized that women who spent "twelve hours of the day in the field" could hardly hope to complete certain "homemaking" chores. The routine of meal preparation was repeated in the evening. After she collected firewood, brought up water, and milked the cow, a wife began to prepare the final meal of the day. Once the family had finished eating, she might light a pine knot—"No lamps or oil are used unless some one is sick"—but usually family activity ceased around sunset. After a long day of physical labor, "nature overcomes the strongest and sleep is sought by all of the family"—for some, on mattresses stuffed with corn shucks and pine needles and pillows full of chicken feathers.

Few rural women enjoyed respite from the inexorable demands of day-to-day household tasks or the annual cycle of cotton cultivation. Nursing a newborn child and cooking the family's meals; digging, hoeing, and chopping in the fields—these chores dictated the daily and seasonal rhythms of a black wife's life. But they represented only the barest outline of her domestic obligations. On rainy days, or by the light of a nighttime fire, she sewed quilts and mended clothes. "I worked many hours after they was in bed," recalled one mother of nine; "Plenty of times I've been to bed at three and

four o'clock and get up at five the first one in the morning." During the day she had to carve out time to grind corn for meal, bathe the children, weed the garden, gather eggs, and do the laundry. Periodically she devoted an entire day to making soap out of ashes and lard or helping with the hog butchering.

At this point, it is important to note that, unlike their slave grandmothers, most sharecropping women did not have the necessary equipment to spin cotton into thread and weave thread into cloth; the expense and bulk of spinning wheels and looms precluded household self-sufficiency in the area of textile production. Ironically, then, although the rural black family lived surrounded by raw cotton, its clothing had to be purchased from a local white merchant. A woman's freedom from the seemingly endless chores of spinning and weaving required a family's increased dependence on credit controlled by whites.

Her involvement with very poor women in the Alabama backcountry at the turn of the century convinced social worker Georgia Washington that "the mother has to hustle all through the winter, in order to get anything" for the family. The "wife and children are worked very hard every year" to pay for the bare necessities, but where "the family is large they are only half fed and clothed. . . ." As a result, most wives attempted to supplement the family income in a variety of ways, few of which earned them more than a few extra cents at a time. Some picked and sold berries or peanuts, while others marketed vegetables, eggs, and butter from the family's garden, chickens, and cow. A "midder" (midwife) found that her services were frequently in demand. Part-time laundresses took in washing and worked at home with the assistance of their older children.

Although modest in terms of financial return, these activities were significant because they yielded small amounts of cash for families that had to rely chiefly on credit. Furthermore, they allowed mothers to earn money and simultaneously care for their small children, and provided them with an opportunity to engage in commercial exchange on a limited basis and in the process gain a measure of self-esteem through the use of shrewd trading skills. This form of work contrasted with their husbands' responsibilities for crop production, which included not only field labor but also monthly and annual dealings with white landowner-merchants. Thus men's income-producing activities took place in the larger economic sphere of a regional cotton market, while women worked exclusively within the household and a localized foodstuff and domestic-service economy.

Husbands preferred that their wives not work directly for whites, and, if they had to, that they labor in their own homes (as laundresses, for example) rather than in a white woman's kitchen. Still, out of economic necessity, a mother's money-making efforts could periodically compel her to leave her house. Although relatively few Cotton Belt women worked regularly as servants for whites (4.1 percent in 1880; 9 percent in 1900), some performed day service during the slack season. In addition, if a black household was relatively large and productive (that is, if it included a sufficient number of "hands" to support itself), a woman might hire herself out to a local planter for at least part of the year. In 1910, 27 percent of all black female agricultural laborers earned wages this way. One Alabama mother managed to combine childcare with wage earning; she took her stepson along when she "went and chopped cotton for white folks." He later recalled, "My stepmother wanted my company; but she also wanted to see me eat two good meals" provided each day by the landowner. As three-quarter hands, women could make about 35 cents per day for "full hours in the field."

Children often helped in and around the house; they supplied additional (though somewhat unpredictable) labor and supposedly stayed within their mother's sight and earshot in the process. Youngsters of five or six also worked in the fields, dropping seeds or toting water. As mentioned earlier, white planters often shaped a family's priorities when it came to the use of children as workers; as a general rule, landowners believed that "the raising of children must not interfere with the raising of cotton," and they advanced food to a household in proportion to its "working hands" and not its actual members. W. E. B. DuBois, in his 1899 study, "The Negro in the Black Belt," found sharecroppers' children to be "poorly dressed, sickly, and cross," an indication that poor nutrition combined with hard work took their toll at an early age. Parents at times hired out children to white employers in order to lessen the crowding at home and bring in extra money.

The sexual division of labor between boys and girls became more explicit as they grew older. For example, some families put all their children to work in the fields with the exception of the oldest daughter. Most girls served domestic apprenticeships under their mothers, but at the same time they learned to hoe and pick in the cotton fields and, in some cases, to chop wood and plow (these latter two were usually masculine tasks). In 1900 over half of all Cotton Belt households reported that at least one daughter aged sixteen or less was working as a field laborer. Still, girls probably worked in the fields less often, and in proportionately smaller numbers, than boys, and their parents seemed more willing to allow them to acquire an education; school attendance rates among black females remained higher than those among males throughout the period 1880 to 1915, producing an early form of the "farmer's daughter effect." In the fifteen-to twenty-year age bracket, only seven black males attended school for every ten females. By 1910 literacy rates among young people revealed that girls had surpassed boys in literacy, although the situation was reversed among elderly men and women.

The financial imperatives of sharecropping life produced rates of prolonged dependency for both sexes compared to those of rural wage-earning economies. Black youths who worked on the sugar plantations of Louisiana often grew resentful of having to turn over their wages to their parents, and struck out on their own when they reached the age of fourteen or fifteen. As a result, it was economically feasible for "both boys and girls [to] mate early, take houses, and set up for themselves." On the other hand, sharecroppers' sons could draw upon little in the way of cash resources if they wanted to marry, forcing them "to wait for the home attractions." Men in the Cotton Belt married around age twenty-five, women at age twenty, reflecting, once again, the lessened demands made upon daughters as field workers.

The demographic and economic characteristics of rural black families demonstrate the continuous and pervasive effects of poverty. From 1880 to 1910 the fertility of black women declined by about one-third, due to disease and poor nutrition among females all over the South and their particularly unhealthful living conditions in urban areas. The life expectancy of black men and women at birth was only thirty-three years. If a woman survived until age twenty, she could expect to see one out of three of her children die before its tenth birthday and to die herself (around the age of fifty-four) before the youngest left home. Those women who outlived their husbands faced the exceedingly difficult task of trying to support a farm family on their own. Even women accustomed to plowing with a team of oxen and knowledgeable about the intricacies of cotton cultivation could find the process of bargaining with a white man for seed, supplies, and a sufficient amount of land to be an insurmountable barrier. Many widows relied on the assistance of an older son or other male relative, consolidated their own household with that of neighbors or kin, or moved to the city in search of paid work.

Women headed about 11 percent of all rural black southern households at any one time between 1880 and 1900, but not all of those who managed a farm or supervised the field work of their children were single mothers or widows. Some sharecropping fathers regularly left home to work elsewhere, resulting in a distinction between the "real" (that is, blood) family and the "economic" (cohabitating) household. In the Cotton Belt, men might leave their wives and children to till their land while they hired themselves out to a nearby planter. (In 1910 one-half of all southern black men employed in agriculture earned wages on either a year-round or temporary basis.) This pattern was especially common in areas characterized by noncotton local economies that provided alternative sources of employment for men.

For example, on the South Carolina coast, some black men toiled as day laborers in the rice industry, while others left their farms for Savannah or Charleston in order to earn extra money (usually only a few dollars each week) as stevedores or cotton-gin workers. Phosphate mining in the same area enabled husbands, fathers, and older sons to work together as "dredge han's" and to escape the tedium of rural life. A poor harvest or a natural disaster (like the great hurricane of 1896) affecting the Sea Islands prompted a general exodus of male household members old enough to work for wages; some went north, while most settled for indefinite periods of time in other parts of the South. Sugar plantations (in Louisiana), sawmills and coal mines (in Tennessee), lumbering and turpentine camps (along the Florida and Alabama coast), brickyards, and railroad construction projects provided income for men who sought to work for cash rather than "credit." While the "real" family never changed, then, the "economic" household responded to seasonal opportunities and to its own specific economic needs.

As older children began to leave a mature family, the economic gains achieved at the height of its productivity gradually slipped away. These established households sometimes took in boarders or relatives to offset the loss of departed offspring. There seemed to be no single pattern of either work or dependency among the rural elderly. For instance,

DuBois noted of Black Belt communities in general, "Away down at the edge of the woods will live some grizzle-haired black man, digging wearily in the earth for his last crust; or a swarthy fat auntie, supported in comfort by an absent daughter, or an old couple living half by charity and half by odd jobs."

Widows throughout the South represented extremes of hardship and well-being. An elderly woman living alone sometimes took in a young "mudderless" or "drift" (orphan) for mutual companionship and support. Like Aunt Adelaide, who "received less and less when she needed more and more" once her children left home, some of these women lamented their loss of self-sufficiency: "I ben strong ooman," said Adelaide, "I wuk fo' meself wid me han'. I ben ma/r/sh-cuttin' ooman. I go in de ma/r/sh and cut and carry fo' myself." At the other end of the spectrum was the widow Mrs. Henry; she supported herself by farming and "peddling cakes" until her health failed—or rather, faltered. After that she made a comfortable living selling sweet potatoes, poultry, hogs, and vegetables with the aid of two other women and a child.

Regardless of their physical circumstances, these women formed a bridge of "bent backs and laboring muscles" between "the old African and slavery days, and the sixty difficult years of freedom" for their grandchildren and all younger people in the community. Although men headed individual households, it was not unusual to find an elderly woman presiding over a group of people who in turn cared for her. In Charlotte, North Carolina, the former slave Granny Ann lived alone but "everybody respected" her and "they never would let her cook for herself." She served as spiritual advisor to the neighborhood. To cite another case, according to the 1900 census, Winnie Moore, aged eighty and mother of ten children, lived alone in Perry County, Alabama, with no visible means of support. But at least five nearby households included Moores. Among them was that of John (aged thirty-four) and his wife Sarah (thirty) who had a daughter of twelve named Winnie. Together grandmother and granddaughter Winnie reached from slavery into the twentieth century, and in their lives comingled the anguish of bondage and the ambiguity of freedom.

Although the majority of black rural women were ruled by haggard King Cotton, some followed different seasonal rhythms and work patterns dictated by other forms of commercial enterprise—tobacco and sugar cultivation, truck farming, and oystering. Each of these economies had a distinctive division of labor based on both age and sex. The proximity of processing plants and marketing operations often meant that families employed in such work periodically or in some cases permanently crossed over from agricultural to quasi-industrial labor. For example, in the Piedmont area of Virginia and the Carolinas, and in parts of Kentucky and Tennessee, black people toiled in tobacco fields as hired hands, tenants, or the owners of small family farms. Children performed many of the basic—and most unpleasant—tasks related to the early stages of crop cultivation. Usually boys were hired out for longer periods of time and for a greater variety of operations than were girls. In the tobacco fields closer to home, children's and women's work often overlapped. For example, youngsters of both sexes, together with their mothers, spent long hours stooped over "worming" the plants—that is, examining the underside of each leaf and pinching the head off any worm found there. Conventional wisdom held that "women make better wormers than men, probably because they are more patient and painstaking."

Unlike cotton planters, white tobacco growers after the war resisted the idea of sharecropping for years, and throughout the late nineteenth century many blacks in the "Old Bright" belt of Virginia and North Carolina worked for wages (60 to 70 cents per day). After 1900, when small tenant farms became more common (a trend linked specifically to the emergence of a single-crop commercial economy), women worked in the fields to a greater extent than they had previously. This change suggested that black men in tobacco-growing regions, like Cotton Belt freedmen, preferred that their womenfolk not perform field work for wages under the direct supervision of whites. However, throughout the late nineteenth and early twentieth century, falling tobacco prices caused increasing numbers of farmers to abandon the land and migrate into nearby towns, where both sexes found menial jobs in tobacco-processing establishments.

The sugar plantation economy of Louisiana, described as a "first cousin to slavery," also relied heavily on wage workers during the postbellum period. A persistent labor shortage in the industry between 1880 and 1900 resulted in "chronic labor disturbances" among workers whose wages were set very low (50 cents a day for women; 65 cents for men) by collusive white employers. In the spring and summer, women hoed in the fields; they plowed and ditched infrequently. The terse remarks made by a sugar plantation owner in his diary one day in 1888 revealed that women who worked under a wage (as opposed to family) system of labor organization remained vulnerable to rape and other forms of sexual abuse at the hands of white men: "Young Turcuit /the assistant overseer/ is very objectionable from his 'goings on' with the colored women on the place."

During the grinding season—October through January—hands from all over the state of Louisiana converged on centralized sugar factories. Wages ranged from 25 cents per day for children to 85 cents for women and a dollar for men. Families stayed in company-owned cabins (often converted slave quarters) and made their own decisions about when and how often wives and children should cut cane. Boys began to earn wages around the age of twelve or thirteen, girls not until three or four years later. Women set their own work schedules, much to the disgust of labor-hungry planters. Writing for the Department of Labor in 1902, one investigator found that on the Calumet plantation in St. Mary Parish, "women

make only about half-time. During the cultivating season practically none work on Saturdays and very few on Mondays. They do not work in bad weather. During grinding they lay off on Saturdays, but generally work on Mondays." In this way families managed to maintain domestic priorities within a wage economy.

In the Tidewater region of Virginia around Hampton Roads and Norfolk, black truck farmers cultivated vegetables to be shipped to distant markets. Along the Atlantic coastline from Virginia to Georgia, oystering families included husbands who worked as gatherers and wives as shuckers. In Chatham County, Georgia, for example, fathers and brothers remained in their home villages during the winter harvest season, while their wives and daughters moved to the factory town of Warsaw to find employment in the seafood processing plants. Family members lived together in the off-season when the men fished and the women took in laundry or picked berries to sell.

Despite the variations in these commercial economies, certain patterns of family organization remained characteristic of blacks in the rural South throughout the period from 1880 to 1915. For most households, a single, sudden misfortune—a flood, a summer drought, high prices for fertilizer, the death of a mule or cow—could upset the delicate balance between subsistence and starvation. Husbands and wives, sons and daughters, friends and kinfolk coordinated their labor and shifted their place of residence in order to stave off disaster—a process that was never-ending. Yet even the poorest families sought to preserve a division of labor between the sexes so that fathers assumed primary responsibility for the financial affairs of the household and mothers oversaw domestic chores first and labored as field hands or wage earners when necessary.

WOMEN'S WORK AND ASPIRATIONS

To outsiders, rural life, set within a larger framework of southern economic backwardness, seemed bleak indeed. DuBois himself asserted that the rural black person's "outlook in the majority of cases is hopeless." Perhaps on the surface the struggle for a living was waged "out of grim necessity . . . without query or protest," as he suggested. But below that surface ran a deep current of restlessness among even the least fortunate. In St. Meigs, Alabama, Georgia Washington worked with farm wives who "looked pretty rough on the outside." She soon discovered that these mothers were "dissatisfied themselves and anxious to change things at home and do better, but had no idea how or where to begin." They especially wanted the time and resources "to mend or clean up the children before sending them to school in the morning." According to Washington, their "dissatisfaction" was a hopeful sign, proof that they had not succumbed to a paralyzing fatalism.

Two developments in late nineteenth-century southern society—increasing literacy rates and a general urban in-migration among southern blacks—suggest that at least some families managed to wrench themselves from the past and look to the future. Neither books nor a home in the city would guarantee freedom, but they did afford coming generations a way of life that differed in important respects from the neoslavery of the rural South. Because black girls attended school in greater numbers than boys, and because southern towns had disproportionately large black female populations, it is important to examine the relevance of these developments in regard to Afro-American women and their aspirations for their daughters and sons.

It was not uncommon for sharecroppers' children who acquired some schooling later to credit their mothers with providing them with the opportunity to learn. Speaking from experience, William Pickens declared, "Many an educated Negro owes his enlightenment to the toil and sweat of a mother." The saying "chickens for shoes" referred to women's practice of using the money they earned selling eggs and chickens to buy shoes for their children so that they could attend school in the winter. Rossa

B. Cooley pointed out that some black mothers were particularly concerned about rescuing their daughters from a fate they themselves had endured. For example, born and raised in slavery, the Sea Island woman Chloe had "one idea" for her daughter Clarissa and that was "an education that meant going to school and away from all the drudgery, the chance to wear pretty clothes any day in the week, and as her utmost goal, the Latin and algebra offered by the early Negro schools in their zeal to prove the capacity of liberated blacks." Female college graduates who responded to a survey conducted by Atlanta University researchers in 1900 frequently mentioned the sacrifices of their mothers, who, like Job, were "patience personified."

Frances Harper, a black writer and lecturer, suggested that black mothers "are the levers which move in education. The men talk about it . . . but the women work most for it." She recounted examples of mothers who toiled day and night in the fields and over the washtub in order to send their children to school. One mother "urged her husband to go in debt 500 dollars" for their seven children's education. This emphasis on women's support for schooling raises the question of whether or not mothers and fathers differed in their perception of education and its desirability for their own offspring.

Although girls engaged in some types of field and domestic labor at an early age, we have seen that parents excused them more often and for longer periods of time (compared to their brothers) to attend the neighborhood school. For instance, the George C. Burleson family listed in the 1900 federal manuscript census for Pike County, Alabama, included four children. Ida May, the oldest (aged sixteen), had attended school for six of the previous twelve months. Her younger brother, Clifford (aged eleven) had worked as a farm laborer all year and had not gone to school at all. In 1910 the Bureau of the Census remarked upon higher female literacy rates among the younger generation by observing, "Negro girls and younger women have received at least such elementary school training as is represented by the ability to write, more generally than have Negro boys and men."

If literate persons prized their own skills highly, they might have felt more strongly about enabling their children to learn to read and write. Apparently, in some rural families the different experiences and immediate concerns of fathers compared to mothers prompted conflicting attitudes toward schooling. Perhaps the experiences of Martin V. Washington were not so unusual. Born in 1878 in South Carolina, Washington grew up in a household composed of his parents and ten siblings. His mother had received a grammar-school education, but his father had never gone to school. "Because of the lack of his education," explained Washington, "my father was not anxious for his children to attend school; he preferred to have them work on the farm." On the other hand, his mother, "who knew the value of an education," tried to ensure that all of her children acquired some schooling.

For blacks in the rural South, even a smattering of education could provoke discontent and thereby disrupt family and community life. Martin Washington's father might have feared that his children would move away; Martin himself eventually emigrated to New York City. Nate Shaw put the matter succinctly: "As a whole, if children got book learnin enough they'd jump off of this country; they don't want to plow, don't want no part of no sort of field work." He believed that the "biggest majority" of literate blacks sooner or later moved to town to find a "public job." If education was a means of personal advancement, then it could splinter families, as young people, eager to flee from the routine of rural life, abandoned the farms of their parents.

The Pickens family of South Carolina moved from the country to the village of Pendleton in the late 1880s. The various factors that shaped their decision revealed how considerations related to both work and schooling attracted

people to the towns. (The 1880s represented the peak period of black urban in-migration between 1865 and 1915.) Mrs. Pickens had a great desire "to school the children," but they could hardly attend classes on a regular basis as long as the family's white landlord "would not tolerate a tenant who put his children to school in the farming season." Working together, the Pickenses just barely made ends meet in any case; cotton prices had fallen to the point where a hand earned only 35 or 40 cents a day for picking one hundred pounds.

In Pendleton, the children could attend a better school for longer stretches at a time. Their father relinquished the plow in order to become a "man of all work," and their mother found a job as a cook in a hotel. She preferred this type of employment over field work because it allowed her "somewhat better opportunities" to care for her small children (she probably took them to work with her). William Pickens believed that town life afforded a measure of financial independence for the family, compared to his experiences on a tenant farm where "my father worked while another man reckoned." The young man himself went on to become a scholar and an official of the early National Association for the Advancement of Colored People (NAACP).

By 1910 about 18 percent of the southern black population lived in towns of 2,500 inhabitants or more (an increase of 11 percent over 1860). Since emancipation, small but steadily increasing numbers of former slaves had made their way cityward. As wives, widows, and daughters, black women participated in this gradual migration in disproportionately large numbers. Some women accompanied their husbands to town so that the family as a whole could benefit from the wider variety of jobs available to blacks. Unmarried women—including daughters eager to break away from the "dreary drudgery" of the sharecropper's farm and widows desperate to feed and clothe their children—found an "unlimited field" of jobs, but only in the areas of domestic service and laundering. As a result, all of the major southern cities had an imbalanced sex ratio in favor of women throughout the late nineteenth century. The selection process at work in this population movement, like any other, indicates that black women possessed a spirit of "upward ambition and aspiration" at least equal to that of their menfolk.

Throughout this period, then, some black women demonstrated a restlessness of mind as well as body. In their willingness to move from cabin to cabin and from country to town, they belied the familiar charge that women were more "conservative" than men, less quick to take chances or to abandon the familiar. Perhaps even more dramatic were mothers' attempts to school their children, for in the process they risked losing them. Nate Shaw never went to school because, he thought, "my daddy was scared I'd leave him, so he held me down." Shaw's father had his own priorities, and at least he never had to share the pain felt by a Sea Island mother who read in a note from her self-exiled son, "It pays a man to leave home sometimes, my mother, and he will see more and learn more."

BLACK AND WHITE CULTURE AND MEN AND WOMEN IN THE RURAL SOUTH

Late nineteenth-century middle-class white women derived their status from that of their husbands. Unproductive in the context of a money-oriented, industrializing economy, and formally unable to take part in the nation's political process, they enjoyed financial security only insofar as their spouses were steady and reliable providers. In contrast, black working women in the South had a more equal relationship with their husbands in the sense that the two partners were not separated by extremes of economic power or political rights; black men and women lacked both. Oppression shaped these unions in another way. The overlapping of economic and domestic functions combined with the pressures imposed by a surrounding, hostile white society meant that

black working women were not so dramatically dependent upon their husbands as were middle-class white wives. Within black families and communities, then, public-private, male-female distinctions were less tightly drawn than among middle-class whites. Together, black women and men participated in a rural folk culture based upon group cooperation rather than male competition and the accumulation of goods. The ways in which this culture both resembled and diverged from that of poor whites in the South helps to illuminate the interaction between class and racial factors in shaping the roles of women.

Referring to the world view of Alabama sharecropper Hayes Shaw, Theodore Rosengarten (the biographer-interviewer of Shaw's son Nate) observed that "righteousness consisted in not having so much that it hurt to lose it." Nate himself remembered that his father as a young man had passed up promising opportunities to buy land because "he was blindfolded; he didn't look to the future." Ruled by "them old slavery thoughts," Hayes Shaw knew that

> whenever the colored man prospered too fast in this country under the old rulins, they worked every figure to cut you down, cut your britches off you. So, it . . . weren't no use in climbin too fast; weren't no use in climbin slow, neither, if they was goin to take everything you worked for when you got too high.

Rural black communities that abided by this philosophy sought to achieve self-determination within a limited sphere of action. In this way they insulated themselves from whites and from the disappointment that often accompanied individual self-seeking. They lived like Nate's brother Peter; he "made up his mind that he weren't goin to have anything and after that, why nothin could hurt him."

Northern scholars and journalists, as well as southern planters, charged that rural blacks valued freedom of movement, "furious religious revivals," and community holidays—

"none of which brings them profit of any sort." A Georgia landowner characterized in this way the philosophy of his tenants, who tended to "dismiss further thought of economy" once they had fulfilled their financial obligations to him: *"dum vivimus vivamus"* ("while we are living let us live"). Some white observers seized upon this theme and warned of its ramifications for the future of American society. Within a growing economy based upon the production of consumer goods, black people's apparent willingness to make do with the little they had represented not so much a moral transgression as a threat to employee discipline on the one hand and incentives to buy on the other. Why should a black husband and father work hard if he was "content with a log cabin and a fireplace, and with corn, bacon, and molasses as articles of food"? How would he profit southern or national economic development if he was satisfied with "merely enough to keep soul and body together"? One contemporary scholar suggested that for the average household head to enjoy a higher standard of living "his wants must be diversified"; otherwise he lacked the impulse to make, save, and spend money. Of course the issue was more complex than the "simple needs" or "wants" of blacks would imply. For example, a northern reporter pointed out that the preachers of the New South gospel of wealth inevitably clashed with the majority of white employers who vowed "to do almost anything to keep the Negro on the land and his wife in the kitchen as long as they are obedient and unambitious workers."

Black settlements in remote areas—especially those that remained relatively self-sufficient through hunting and fishing—experienced the mixed blessings of semiautonomy. These communities existed almost wholly outside the larger regional and national economic system. For example, the people of the Sea Islands who "labor only for the fulfillment of the petition, 'Give us this day our daily bread,' and literally 'take no thought for the morrow,' working only when their necessities compel them," revealed the dilemma of a premodern subculture located within an industrial nation. As independent, self-respecting farmers (a proportionately large number owned their own land), the Sea Islanders remained relatively unmolested by whites and managed to preserve African traditions and folkways to a remarkable degree. Their diet, consisting of fowl, fish, shellfish, and fresh vegetables, was nutritionally superior to that of Cotton Belt sharecroppers. Yet these people lacked proper medical care and the most basic household conveniences. (Water-toting women hailed the installation of a water pump in the early twentieth century as "a most spectacular innovation in domestic economy. . . .") Floods and other natural disasters periodically wrought havoc on their way of life, and pushed young people off the islands and into nearby cities, leaving behind primarily the elderly and the blind.

Even rural communities that lacked the almost total isolation of the Sea Islands possessed a strong commitment to corporatism and a concomitant scorn for the hoarding of private possessions. As government researcher J. Bradford Laws wrote disapprovingly of the sugar workers he studied in 1902, "They have an unfortunate notion of generosity, which enables the more worthless to borrow fuel, food, and what not on all hands from the more thrifty." It is clear that these patterns of behavior were determined as much by economic necessity as by cultural "choice." If black household members pooled their energies to make a good crop, and if communities collectively provided for their own welfare, then poverty and oppression ruled out most of the alternative strategies. Individualism was a luxury that sharecroppers simply could not afford.

Rural folk relied on one another to help celebrate the wedding of a young couple, rejoice in a preacher's fervent exhortation, mark the annual closing of the local school, minister to the ill, and bury the dead. Women participated in all these rites and communal events. In addition, they had their own gender-based activities, as well as societies that contributed to the general good of the community. On the Sea Islands, young women would "often take Saturday afternoon as a time for cleaning the yard or the parlor, for ironing their clothes, or for preparing their hair." (Their brothers gathered at a favorite meeting place or organized a "cornfield baseball game.") Quilting brought young and old women together for a daylong festival of sewing, chatting, and feasting. Supported by the modest dues of their members, female voluntary beneficial societies met vital social-welfare needs that individual families could not always afford; these groups helped their members to pay for life insurance, medical care, and burial services. Even the poorest women managed to contribute a few pennies a month and to attend weekly meetings. In turn-of-the-century Alabama, "The woman who is not a member of one of these is pitied and considered rather out of date."

The impulse for mutual solace and support among rural Afro-Americans culminated in their religious institutions and worship services. At monthly meetings women and men met to reaffirm their unique spiritual heritage, to seek comfort, and to comfort one another. Black women found a "psychological center" in religious belief, and the church provided strength for those overcome by the day-to-day business of living. For many weary sharecroppers' wives and mothers, worship services allowed for physical and spiritual release and offered a means of transcending earthly cares in the company of one's friends and family. Faith created "a private world inside the self, sustained by religious sentiment and religious symbolism . . . fashioned to contain the world without." "Spiritual mothers" served as the "main pillars" of Methodist and Baptist churches, but they also exercised religious leadership outside formal institutional boundaries; elderly women in particular commanded respect as the standard-bearers of tradition and as the younger generation's link with its ancestors.

Of course, life in "places behind God's back" was shaped as much by racial prejudice as by black solidarity, and the "ethos of mutuality" that pervaded rural communities did not preclude physical violence or overt conflict between individuals. At times a Saturday night "frolic" ended in a bloody confrontation between two men who sought courage from a whiskey bottle and self-esteem through hand-to-hand conflict. Similarly, oppression could bind a family tightly together, but it could also heighten tensions among people who had few outlets for their rage and frustration. Patterns of domestic conflict reflected both historical injustices and daily family pressures. These forces affected black women and men in different ways.

On a superficial level, the roots of domestic violence are not difficult to recognize or understand. Cramped living quarters and unexpected setbacks provoked the most even-tempered of household heads. Like their slave parents, mothers and fathers often used harsh disciplinary techniques on children, not only to prepare them for life in a white-dominated world where all blacks had to act cautiously, but also to exert rigid control over this one vital facet of domestic life. If whites attempted to cut "the britches off" black fathers and husbands, then these men would try to assert their authority over their households with even greater determination. At times that determination was manifested in violence and brutality.

Hayes Shaw epitomized the sharecropping father who lorded over his wives (he married three times) and children. More than once the Shaw children watched helplessly as their father beat their mother, and they too were "whipped . . . up scandalous" for the slightest infraction. Hayes divided his time between his "outside woman"—an unmarried laundress in the neighborhood—and his "regular" family, and he made no effort to conceal the fact. The Shaw womenfolk were hired out or sent to the fields like children, without daring to protest, while Hayes spent his days in a characteristically masculine fashion—alone, away from the house, hunting. According to Nate Shaw, his "daddy'd have his gun on his shoulder and be off on Sitimachas Creek swamps, huntin," after commanding his wife to "Take that plow! Hoe!" The son remembered with bitterness years later that his stepmother (who had borne his father thirteen children) "put part of a day's work in the field" before she died one night.

Hayes Shaw was undoubtedly an extreme example of a domestic tyrant, but he and other husbands like him inspired white and black women community leaders, educators, and social workers to formulate a critique of Afro-American family life in the late nineteenth century. Sensitive to the economic problems confronted by black marriage partners, these observers charged that black men enjoyed certain male prerogatives without the corresponding striving and ambition that those prerogatives were meant to reward. Juxtaposed with this "irresponsible" man was his wife—no doubt a "real drudge," but certainly "the greatest sufferer from the stress and strain attendant upon the economic conditions" faced by all Afro-Americans. The chief problem seemed to stem from the fact that black women played a prominent role in supporting the family in addition to performing their domestic responsibilities. In the eyes of their critics, black men as a group were not particularly concerned about "getting ahead" in the world and thus fell short of their wives' spirit of industry and self-sacrifice.

White teacher-social workers like Rossa Cooley and Georgia Washington and black writers and educators like Anna J. Cooper, Katherine Davis Tillman, Frances Harper, and Fannie Barrier Williams focused on the domestic achievements of poor women and with varying degrees of subtlety condemned their "worthless" husbands. Their critique of black womanhood marked the emergence of the "black matriarchy thesis," for they suggested that the main problem in Afro-American family life was an "irresponsible" father who took advantage of his "faithful, hardworking women-folks." By the mid-twentieth century sociologists had shifted public attention to the "irresponsible" father's *absence;* the relatively large number of single, working mothers in the nation's urban ghettos seemed to lend additional credence to an argument that originally purported to deal with the problems of rural women. Thus the image of the strong, overburdened black mother persisted through the years, and it was usually accompanied by the implicit assumption that women wielded authority over men and children in Afro-American families.

Yet Hayes Shaw's household was never a "matriarchy." Recent historians who have labeled the postemancipation rural black family "patriarchal" hardly help to clarify the issue. The difficulty in conceptualizing black male-female roles derives from the fact that most observers (whether writing in the nineteenth or twentieth century) have used as their basis for comparison the white middle-class model of family life. Black men headed the vast majority of southern rural families, and they self-consciously ruled their wives and children; hence the use of the term patriarchy to describe family relationships. But these households deviated from the traditional sexual division of labor in the sense that wives worked to supplement the family income, and fathers often lacked the incentive to try to earn money so that they could purchase property or goods and thus advance the family's status. These men worked hard—they had to, in order to survive the ruthlessly exploitative sharecropping system—but most realized that even harder work would not necessarily enable them to escape poverty. Those who confronted this dilemma hardly deserved the epithet "worthless manhood." Still, for the two sexes, relative equality of economic function did not imply equality of domestic authority.

Although a husband and wife each made an essential contribution to the welfare of the household, they were compensated in different ways for their labor. This reward differential reflected their contrasting household responsibilities and produced contrasting attitudes toward work and its personal and social value. As a participant in a staple-crop economy, a black father assumed responsibility for a crop that would be exchanged in the marketplace at the end of the year. He supposedly toiled for future compensation in the form of cash. However, not only did his physical exertion gain him little in the way of immediate reward, in fact he tilled the ground only to repay one debt and to ensure that he would have another in the coming year. Under such conditions, most men took pride in their farming abilities, but worked no more strenuously than was absolutely necessary to satisfy white creditors and keep their own families alive in the process.

Their wives, on the other hand, remained relatively insulated from the inevitable frustrations linked to a future-oriented, market economy. For example, women daily performed discreet tasks that yielded tangible results upon completion. Meal preparation, laundering, egg gathering—these chores had finite boundaries in the course of a day. Childcare was a special case, but it had its own special joys. It was an ongoing responsibility that began when a woman had her first baby and ended only years later when her youngest child left home. On a more mundane level, childcare was a constant preoccupation of mothers during their waking hours, and infants' needs often invaded their sleep. Yet a woman's exclusive authority in this area of domestic life earned her emotional gratification. Her husband hardly derived a similar sense of gratification from his responsibility for the cotton crop; he "earned" only what a white man was willing to pay him. Hence the distinction between work patterns simplistically labeled by some contemporary writers as male "laziness" and female "self-sacrifice" actually represented a complex phenomenon shaped by the different demands made upon black men and women and the degree of personal satisfaction resulting from the fulfillment of those demands.

Poor whites in the late nineteenth-century South were also stigmatized by charges of laziness and lethargy; together black and white sharecroppers and tenants endured a form of opprobrium traditionally directed at working people by their employers and social "betters." Like their black counterparts, propertyless whites valued self-sufficiency over cash-crop tenancy, and they too confronted new class relationships established after the war—relationships that turned on mortgages, credit, and crop liens as much as on race and kinship. By 1900 over one-third of all whites employed in agriculture were tenants, and even small landowners remained perched precariously on the brink of financial disaster, only a drought or a boll weevil plague away from indebtedness. As many as 90 percent of white farmers in Mississippi, Alabama, and Georgia owed money to a local financier at the end of the century. A gradual but significant decrease in domestic food production throughout this period meant that few laborers or tenants regardless of race could feed themselves without purchasing supplies from a planter-merchant. Thus all landless farmers, white and black, confronted uncertainties in a period of declining agricultural prices and general economic hardship. It seems likely then that southern poor people as a group deviated from the predominant (that is, white middle-class northern-industrial) culture, a way of life shaped by the powerful ideology of ambition and personal gain.

A comparison of the experiences of poor white and black women in the rural South suggests that to a great extent, class and gender conjoined to determine what all sharecroppers' wives did and how they did it. For example, data on black and white households in the Cotton South for 1880 and 1900 indicate some striking similarities between the family structures characteristic of the two races. For instance, both types of "average" households possessed a male head, and a male head accompanied by his spouse, in the same proportions. Black and white wives shared the same age patterns relative to their husbands. Though slightly larger, white households had a similar configuration compared to black ones and lived near at least some of their kin to the same extent.

Detailed descriptions of the work of poor white rural women are lacking for the nineteenth century. If we assume, however, that these women were no better off than their daughters and granddaughters who continued to live on farms—and there is no reason to believe that they were—then we can extrapolate material about white tenant-farm women in the 1930s to learn about earlier generations. Margaret Hagood's study *Mothers of the South* (published in 1939), suggests that the basic responsibilities of these women had remained the same over the years. Like black women, poor white farm wives bore the domestic burdens that were endemic to the economic system of southern staple-crop agriculture. They married in their late teens and had an average of six children (although large households of twelve or thirteen were not uncommon). Because the family was constantly in debt to a local merchant, family members felt glad if they broke even at the end of the year. Most women made do with very little cash in piecing together the family's subsistence. They performed all the household chores of washing, sewing, cleaning, cooking, and churning, often with the assistance of their eldest daughter, but a majority also helped out in the cotton or tobacco fields during the busy seasons. Wrote Hagood, "the customary practice is for the father's claim for field work to take precedence over that of the mother for help at the house." These wives often added to the family income with the proceeds they earned from selling eggs, vegetables, or milk. In the Deep South, some couples experienced periodic separations when the wives went off to work temporarily in factories, or when their menfolk found jobs on the levees in the off-season.

In terms of earthly comforts, life offered little more to white tenant-farm wives than it did to blacks; white women too lived in sparsely furnished two- or three-room cabins that lacked running water, and their Cotton Belt families tended to move every three years or so. Mothers were attended by a midwife during childbirth. Predictably, they knew nothing about modern contraceptive techniques, and although they took pride in their child-rearing abilities, they suffered from the consequent drain on their emotional and physical resources. Dreams and fortune-tellers explained the past and predicted the future for many of these illiterate women, but they seemed to lack the religious devotion and denominational loyalties exhibited by black wives and mothers. Undernourished and overworked, they had to remind themselves of the biblical dictate, "Be content with your lot."

In a rural society that honored a code of neighborliness and mutual cooperation, black and white women had few opportunities for interracial contact on any level. Husbands and fathers of both races and all classes observed the ritualized etiquette of southern race relations in the public arena—in town, at the post office, court house, or supply store—but their wives were largely excluded from these encounters. Middle-class white women acted out their own presumptions of racial superiority in their dealings with black servants and laundresses. Tenant-farm wives of course could not afford to employ black women for any length of time or exploit them in a direct way. A few women of the two races did come together in situations that held the promise of enhancing mutual respect and appreciation—for example, when they participated in the Southern Farmers Alliance in the 1880s and 1890s, or when black "grannies" attended white women during childbirth. Yet these opportunities were rare, and for the most part women lacked a formal voice in the politics of interracial protest.

In the end, the fact that the labor of white sharecroppers' wives was so similar to that of their black counterparts is less significant than the social environment in which that work took place. For the outcast group, the preservation of family integrity served as a political statement to the white South. To nurse a child, send a daughter to school, feed a hungry family after a long day at work in the fields, or patch a shirt by the light of a flickering fire—these simple acts of domesticity acquired special significance when performed for a people so beleaguered by human as well as natural forces. If white women also had to make soup out of scraps, at least they and their families remained secure from "bulldosers" (mobs) and Judge Lynch. Finally, and perhaps most important, women of the two races had different things to teach their children about the "southern way of life," its freedoms and its dangers.

Despite the transition in labor organization from slavery to sharecropping, the work of black women in the rural South continued to respond to the same human and seasonal rhythms over the generations. By the early twentieth century, they still structured their labor around household chores and childcare, field and wage work, and community welfare activities. Moreover, emancipation hardly lessened the demands made upon females of all ages; young girls worked alongside their mothers, and elderly women had to provide for themselves and their families as long as they were physically able. Although the specific tasks performed by women reflected constantly changing priorities (determined by the cotton-growing cycle and the size and maturity of individual households), the need for a woman to labor rarely abated in the course of a day, a year, or her lifetime.

In its functional response to unique histori-cal circumstances, the rural black household necessarily differed from the late nineteenth-century middle-class ideal, which assumed that men would engage in individual self-aggrandizement. Furthermore, according to this ideal, women were to remain isolated at home, only indirectly sharing in the larger social values of wealth and power accumulation. In contrast, rural black women labored in harmony with the priorities of cooperation and sharing established by their own communities, even as their husbands were prevented from participating in the cash economy in a way that would answer to white-defined notions of masculinity.

Despite the hard, never-ending work performed by rural women—who, ironically, were labeled part of a "lazy" culture by contemporaries and recent historians alike—they could not entirely compensate for the loss of both a husband (through death or another form of permanent separation) and older sons or male relatives who established households on their own. The sharecropping family strove to maintain a delicate balance between its labor resources and its economic needs, and men, as both negotiators in the public sphere and as field workers, were crucial to that balance. Therefore, during the latter part of the nineteenth century, when the natural selection process endemic to commercial crop agriculture weeded out "unfit" households, it forced single mothers, widows, and unmarried daughters to look cityward. Many of them would discover that while the southern countryside continued to mirror the slave past, in the towns that past was refracted into new shapes and images.

9

WORKING WOMEN, CLASS RELATIONS, AND SUFFRAGE MILITANCE: HARRIOT STANTON BLATCH AND THE NEW YORK WOMAN SUFFRAGE MOVEMENT, 1894–1909

ELLEN CAROL DUBOIS

By the end of the nineteenth century, America's woman suffrage movement had reached a political and organizational stalemate. After a half-century of organizing, petitioning, and campaigning for the right to vote, the American women's movement could count victories only in Wyoming, Utah, Colorado, and a handful of other western states. More critically, their attempt to extend these suffrage victories into established eastern and midwestern states during the 1870s and 1880s had failed completely. With Congress showing little interest in national suffrage and state legislatures closed to suffrage appeals, Elizabeth Cady Stanton and other leaders of the women's movement began a search for new tactics and organizational support.

As many contemporaries understood, the revitalization of the suffrage movement depended on its ability to recruit American's growing body of wage-earning women. This was to be no easy task, however, for women wage-earners were a diverse group that included not only sweatshop and factory workers, but female professionals as well. The problem facing the suffrage movement was finding a way to bring this diverse body together. In this essay, Ellen Carol DuBois follows the career of one imaginative suffrage leader, Harriot Stanton Blatch, as she fought to develop new ways of uniting working women and the suffrage movement. The daughter of Elizabeth Cady Stanton, Blatch was well placed to lead a rejuvenated suffrage movement. But as DuBois reveals, her success among working women required a rejection of her mother's elitist views and rested on her ability to formulate a democratic vision of work as a moral necessity for women as well as men.

From the *Journal of American History* 74:34–58 (1987). Reprinted by permission of Ellen Carol DuBois and the *Journal of American History.*

More than any other period in American reform history, the Progressive Era eludes interpretation. It seems marked by widespread concern for social justice and by extraordinary elitism, by democratization and by increasing social control. The challenge posed to historians is to understand how Progressivism could simultaneously represent gains for the masses and more power for the classes. The traditional way to approach the period has been to study the discrete social programs reformers so energetically pushed in those years, from the abolition of child labor to the Americanization of the immigrants. Recently, historians' emphasis has shifted to politics, where it will probably remain for a time. Historians have begun to recognize that the rules of political life, the nature of American "democracy," were fundamentally reformulated beginning in the Progressive Era, and that such political change shaped the ultimate impact of particular social reforms.

Where were women in all this? The new focus on politics requires a reinterpretation of women's role in Progressivism. As the field of women's history has grown, the importance of women in the Progressive Era has gained notice, but there remains a tendency to concentrate on their roles with respect to social reform. Modern scholarship on the Progressive Era thus retains a separate spheres flavor; women are concerned with social and moral issues, but the world of politics is male. Nowhere is this clearer than in the tendency to minimize, even to omit, the woman suffrage movement from the general literature on the Progressive Era.

Scholarship on woman suffrage is beginning to grow in detail and analytic sophistication, but it has yet to be fully integrated into overviews of the period. Histories that include woman suffrage usually do so in passing, listing it with other constitutional alterations in the electoral process such as the popular election of senators, the initiative, and the referendum. But woman suffrage was a mass movement, and that fact is rarely noticed. Precisely because it was a mass political movement—perhaps the first modern one—woman suffrage may well illuminate Progressive-Era politics, especially the class dynamics underlying their reformulation. When the woman suffrage movement is given its due, we may begin to understand the process by which democratic hope turned into mass political alienation, which is the history of modern American politics.

To illuminate the origin and nature of the woman suffrage movement in the Progressive Era I will examine the politics of Harriot Stanton Blatch. Blatch was the daughter of Elizabeth Cady Stanton, the founding mother of political feminism. Beginning in the early twentieth century, she was a leader in her own right, initially in New York, later nationally. As early as 1903, when politics was still considered something that disreputable men did, like spitting tobacco, Blatch proclaimed: "There are born politicians just as there are born artists, writers, painters. I confess that I should be a politician, that I am not interested in machine politics, but that the devotion to the public cause . . . rather than the individual, appeals to me."

Just as her zest for politics marked Blatch as a new kind of suffragist, so did her efforts to fuse women of different classes into a revitalized suffrage movement. Blatch's emphasis on class was by no means unique; she shared it with other women reformers of her generation. Many historians have treated the theme of class by labeling the organized women's reform movement in the early twentieth century "middle-class." By contrast, I have tried to keep open the question of the class character of women's reform in the Progressive Era by rigorously avoiding the term. Characterizing the early twentieth-century suffrage movement as "middle-class" obscures its most striking element, the new interest in the vote among women at both ends of the class structure. Furthermore, it tends to homogenize the movement. The very term "middle-class" is contradictory, alternatively characterized as people who are not poor, and people who work for a living. By contrast, I have emphasized distinctions between classes and organized my analysis around the relations between them.

No doubt there is some distortion in this framework, particularly for suffragists who worked in occupations like teaching. But there is far greater distortion in using the term "middle class" to describe women like Blatch or Carrie Chapman Catt or Jane Addams. For example, it makes more sense to characterize an unmarried woman with an independent income who was not under financial compulsion to work for her living as "elite," rather than "middle class." The question is not just one of social stratification, but of the place of women in a whole system of class relations. For these new style suffragettes, as for contemporary feminists who write about them, the complex relationship between paid labor, marital status, and women's place in the class structure was a fundamental puzzle. The concept of "middle-class" emerged among early twentieth-century reformers, but may ultimately prove more useful in describing a set of relations *between* classes that was coming into being in those years, than in designating a segment of the social structure.

Blatch, examined as a political strategist and a critic of class relations, is important less as a unique figure than as a representative leader, through whose career the historical forces transforming twentieth-century suffragism can be traced. The scope of her leadership offers clues to the larger movement: She was one of the first to open up suffrage campaigns to working-class women, even as she worked closely with wealthy and influential upper-class women; she pioneered militant street tactics and backroom political lobbying at the same time. Blatch's political evolution reveals close ties between other stirrings among American women in the Progressive Era and the rejuve-

nated suffrage movement. Many of her ideas paralleled Charlotte Perkins Gilman's influential reformulation of women's emancipation in economic terms. Many of Blatch's innovations as a suffragist drew on her prior experience in the Women's Trade Union League. Overall, Blatch's activities suggest that early twentieth-century changes in the American suffrage movement, often traced to the example of militant British suffragettes, had deep, indigenous roots. Among them were the growth of trade unionism among working-class women and professionalism among the elite, changing relations between these classes, and the growing involvement of women of all sorts in political reform.

The suffrage revival began in New York in 1893–1894, as part of a general political reform movement. In the 1890s New York's political reformers were largely upper-class men concerned about political "corruption," which they blamed partly on city Democratic machines and the bosses who ran them, partly on the masses of voting men, ignorant, immigrant, and ripe for political manipulation. Their concern about political corruption and about the consequences of uncontrolled political democracy became the focus of New York's 1894 constitutional convention, which addressed itself largely to "governmental procedures: the rules for filling offices, locating authority and organizing the different branches."

The New York woman suffrage movement, led by Susan B. Anthony, recognized a great opportunity in the constitutional convention of 1894. Focusing on political corruption, Anthony and her allies argued that women were the political reformers' best allies. For while men were already voters and vulnerable to the ethic of partisan loyalty—indeed a man without a party affiliation in the 1890s was damned close to unsexed—everyone knew that women were naturally nonpartisan. Enfranchising women was therefore the solution to the power of party bosses. Suffragists began by trying to get women elected to the constitutional convention itself. Failing this, they worked to convince the convention delegates to include woman suffrage among the proposed amendments.

Anthony planned a house-to-house canvass to collect signatures on a mammoth woman suffrage petition. For the $50,000 she wanted to fund this effort, she approached wealthy women in New York City, including physician Mary Putnam Jacobi, society leader Catherine Palmer (Mrs. Robert) Abbe, social reformer Josephine Shaw Lowell, and philanthropist Olivia (Mrs. Russell) Sage. Several of them were already associated with efforts for the amelioration of working-class women, notably in the recently formed Consumers' League, and Anthony had reason to think they might be ready to advocate woman suffrage.

The elite women were interested in woman suffrage, but they had their own ideas about how to work for it. Instead of funding Anthony's campaign, they formed their own organization. At parlor meetings in the homes of wealthy women, they tried to strike a genteel note, emphasizing that enfranchisement would *not* take women out of their proper sphere and would *not* increase the political power of the lower classes. Eighty-year-old Elizabeth Stanton, observing the campaign from her armchair, thought that "men and women of the conservative stamp of the Sages can aid us greatly at this stage of our movement."

Why did wealthy women first take an active and prominent part in the suffrage movement in the 1890s? In part they shared the perspective of men of their class that the influence of the wealthy in government had to be strengthened; they believed that with the vote they could increase the political power of their class. In a representative argument before the constitutional convention, Jacobi proposed woman suffrage as a response to "the shifting of political power from privileged classes to the masses of men." The disfranchisement of women contributed to this shift because it made all women, "no matter how well born,

how well educated, how intelligent, how rich, how serviceable to the State," the political inferiors of all men, "no matter how base-born, how poverty stricken, how ignorant, how vicious, how brutal." Olivia Sage presented woman suffrage as an antidote to the growing and dangerous "idleness" of elite women, who had forgotten their responsibility to set the moral tone for society.

Yet, the new elite converts also supported woman suffrage on the grounds of changes taking place in women's status, especially within their own class. Jacobi argued that the educational advancement of elite women "and the new activities into which they have been led by it—in the work of charities, in the professions, and in the direction of public education—naturally and logically tend toward the same result, their political equality." She argued that elite women, who had aided the community through organized charity and benevolent activities, should have the same "opportunity to serve the State nobly." Sage was willing to advocate woman suffrage because of women's recent "strides . . . in the acquirement of business methods, in the management of their affairs, in the effective interest they have evinced in civic affairs."

Suffragists like Jacobi and Sage characteristically conflated their class perspective with the role they saw for themselves as women, contending for political leadership not so much on the grounds of their wealth, as of their womanliness. Women, they argued, had the characteristics needed in politics—benevolence, morality, selflessness, and industry; conveniently, they believed that elite women most fully embodied these virtues. Indeed, they liked to believe that women like themselves were elite *because* they were virtuous, not because they were wealthy. The confusion of class and gender coincided with a more general elite ideology that identified the fundamental division in American society not between rich and poor, but between industrious and idle, virtuous and vicious, community-minded and selfish. On these grounds Sage found the purposeless leisure of wealthy women dangerous to the body politic. She believed firmly that the elite, women included, should provide moral—and ultimately political—leadership, but it was important to her that they earn the right to lead.

The problem for elite suffragists was that woman suffrage meant the enfranchisement of working-class, as well as elite, women. Jacobi described a prominent woman who "had interested herself nobly and effectively in public affairs, . . . but preferred not to claim the right /of suffrage/ for herself, lest its concession entail the enfranchisement of ignorant and irresponsible women." An elite antisuffrage organization committed to such views was active in the 1894 campaign as well, led by women of the same class, with many of the same beliefs, as the prosuffrage movement. As Stanton wrote, "The fashionable women are about equally divided between two camps." The antis included prominent society figures Abby Hamlin (Mrs. Lyman) Abbott and Josephine Jewell (Mrs. Arthur) Dodge, as well as Annie Nathan Meyer, founder of Barnard College and member of the Consumers' League. Like the elite suffragists, upper-class antis wanted to insure greater elite influence in politics; but they argued that woman suffrage would decrease elite influence, rather than enhance it.

Elite suffragists' willingness to support woman suffrage rested on their confidence that their class would provide political leadership for all women once they had the vote. Because they expected working-class women to defer to them, they believed that class relations among women would be more cooperative and less antagonistic than among men. Elite women, Jacobi argued before the 1894 convention, would "so guide ignorant women voters that they could be made to counterbalance, when necessary, the votes of ignorant and interested men." Such suffragists assumed that working-class women were too weak, timid, and disorganized to make their own demands. Since early in the nineteenth century, elite women had claimed social and religious

authority on the grounds of their responsibility for the women and children of the poor. They had begun to adapt this tradition to the new conditions of an industrial age, notably in the Consumers' League, formed in response to the pleas of women wage earners for improvement in their working conditions. In fact, elite antis also asserted that they spoke for working-class women, but they contended that working-class women neither needed nor wanted the vote.

From an exclusively elite perspective, the antisuffrage argument was more consistent than the prosuffrage one; woman suffrage undoubtedly meant greater political democracy, which the political reform movement of the 1890s most fundamentally feared. Elite suffragists found themselves organizing their own arguments around weak refutations of the antis' objections. The ideological weakness had political implications. Woman suffrage got no serious hearing in the constitutional convention, and the 1894 constitutional revisions designed to "clean up government" ignored women's plea for political equality.

The episode revealed dilemmas, especially with respect to class relations among women, that a successful suffrage movement would have to address. Elite women had begun to aspire to political roles that led them to support woman suffrage, and the resources they commanded would be crucial to the future success of suffrage efforts. But their attraction to woman suffrage rested on a portrait of working-class women and a system of class relations that had become problematic to a modern industrial society. Could elite women sponsor the entrance of working-class women into politics without risking their influence over them, and perhaps their position of leadership? Might not working-class women assume a newly active, politically autonomous role? The tradition of class relations among women had to be transformed before a thriving and modern woman suffrage movement could be built. Harriot Stanton Blatch had the combination of suffrage convictions and class awareness to lead New York suffragists through that transition.

The 1894 campaign, which confronted suffragists with the issue of class, also drew Blatch actively into the American woman suffrage movement. She had come back from England, where she had lived for many years, to receive a master's degree from Vassar College for her study of the English rural poor. A powerful orator, she was "immediately pressed into service . . . speaking every day," at parlor suffrage meetings, often to replace her aged mother. Like her mother, Blatch was comfortable in upper-class circles; she had married into a wealthy British family. She generally shared the elite perspective of the campaign, assuming that "educated women" would lead their sex. But she disliked the implication that politics could ever become too democratic and, virtually alone among the suffragists, criticized all "those little anti-republican things I hear so often here in America, this talk of the quality of votes." And while other elite suffragists discussed working-class women as domestic servants and shop clerks, Blatch understood the centrality of industrial workers, although her knowledge of them was still primarily academic.

Blatch's disagreements with the elite suffrage framework were highlighted a few months after the constitutional convention in an extraordinary public debate with her mother. In the *Woman's Journal,* Stanton urged that the suffrage movement incorporate an educational restriction into its demand, to respond to "the greatest block in the way of woman's enfranchisement . . . the fear of the 'ignorant vote' being doubled." Her justification for this position, so at odds with the principles of a lifetime, was that the enfranchisement of "educated women" best supplied "the imperative need at the time . . . woman's influence in public life." From England, Blatch wrote a powerful dissent. Challenging the authority of her venerated mother was a dramatic act that—perhaps deliberately—marked

the end of her political daughterhood. She defended both the need and the capacity of the working class to engage in democratic politics. On important questions, "for example . . . the housing of the poor," their opinion was more informed than that of the elite. She also argued that since "the conditions of the poor are so much harder . . . every working man needs the suffrage more than I do." And finally, she insisted on the claims of a group her mother had ignored, working women.

The debate between mother and daughter elegantly symbolizes the degree to which class threatened the continued vitality of the republican tradition of suffragism. Blatch was able to adapt the republican faith to modern class relations, while Stanton was not, partly because of her participation in the British Fabian movement. As a Fabian, Blatch had gained an appreciation for the political intelligence and power of the working class very rare among elite reformers in the U.S. When she insisted that the spirit of democracy was more alive in England than in the U.S., she was undoubtedly thinking of the development of a working-class political movement there.

Over the next few years, Blatch explored basic assumptions of the woman suffrage faith she had inherited in the context of modern class relations. In the process, like other women reformers of her era, such as Charlotte Perkins Gilman, Florence Kelley, Jane Addams, and numerous settlement house residents and supporters of organized labor, she focused on the relation of women and work. She emphasized the productive labor that women performed, both as it contributed to the larger social good and as it created the conditions of freedom and equality for women themselves. Women had always worked, she insisted. The new factor was the shift of women's work from the home to the factory and the office, and from the status of unpaid to paid labor. Sometimes she stressed that women's unpaid domestic labor made an important contribution to society; at other times she stressed that such unpaid work was not valued, but always she emphasized the historical development that was taking women's labor out of the home and into the commercial economy. The question for modern society was not whether women should work, but under what conditions, and with what consequences for their own lives.

Although Blatch was troubled by the wages and working conditions of the laboring poor, her emphasis on work as a means to emancipation led her to regard wage-earning women less as victims to be succored, than as exemplars to their sex. She vigorously denied that women ideally hovered somewhere above the world of work. She had no respect for the "handful of rich women who have no employment other than organizing servants, social functions and charities." Upper-class women, she believed, should also "work," should make an individual contribution to the public good, and where possible should have the value of their labor recognized by being paid for it. As a member of the first generation of college-educated women, she believed that education and professional achievement, rather than wealth and refinement, fitted a woman for social leadership.

Turning away from nineteenth-century definitions of the unity of women that emphasized their place in the home, their motherhood, and their exclusion from the economy, and emphasizing instead the unity that productive work provided for all women, Blatch rewrote feminism in its essentially modern form, around work. She tended to see women's work, including homemaking and child rearing, as a mammoth portion of the world's productive labor, which women collectively accomplished. Thus she retained the concept of "women's work" for the sex as a whole, while vigorously discarding it on the individual level, explicitly challenging the notion that all women had the same tastes and talents.

Her approach to "women's work" led Blatch to believe that the interconnection of women's labor fundamentally shaped relations among them. Here were the most critical aspects of her thought. Much as she admired professional women, she insisted that they recognize the degree to which their success rested on the labor of other women, who cared for their homes and their children. "Whatever merit /their homes/ possess," Blatch wrote, "is largely due to the fact that the actress when on the stage, the doctor when by her patient's side, the writer when at her desk, has a Bridget to do the homebuilding for her." The problem was that the professional woman's labor brought her so much more freedom than the housemaid's labor brought her. "Side by side with the marked improvement in the condition of the well-to-do or educated woman," Blatch observed, "our century shows little or no progress in the condition of the woman of the people." Like her friend Gilman, Blatch urged that professional standards of work—good pay, an emphasis on expertise, the assumption of a lifelong career—be extended to the nursery-maid and the dressmaker, as well as to the lawyer and the journalist. Until such time, the "movement for the emancipation of women /would/ remain . . . a well-dressed movement."

But professional training and better wages alone would not give labor an emancipatory power in the lives of working-class women. Blatch recognized the core of the problem of women's work, especially for working-class women: "How can the duties of mother and wage earner be reconciled?" She believed that wage-earning women had the same desire as professional women to continue to enjoy careers and independence after marriage. "It may be perverse in lowly wage earners to show individuality as if they were rich," Blatch wrote, "but apparently we shall have to accept the fact that all women do not prefer domestic work to all other kinds." But the problem of balancing a career and a homelife was "insoluble—under present conditions—for the women of the people." "The pivotal question for women," she wrote, "is how to organize their work as home-builders and race-builders, how to get that work paid for not in so called protection, but in the currency of the state."

As the female labor force grew in the late

nineteenth century, so did the number of married women workers and demands that they be driven from the labor force. The suffrage movement had traditionally avoided the conflict between work and motherhood by pinning the demand for economic equality on the existence of unmarried women, who had no men to support them. Blatch confronted the problem of work and motherhood more directly. In a 1905 article, she drew from the utopian ideas of William Morris to recommend that married women work in small, worker-owned manufacturing shops where they could have more control over their hours and could bring their children with them. Elsewhere, she argued that the workplace should be reorganized around women's needs, rather than assume the male worker's standards, but she did not specify what that would mean. She never solved the riddle of work and children for women—nor have we—but she knew that the solution could not be to force women to choose between the two nor to banish mothers from the labor force.

Blatch's vision of women in industrial society was democratic—all must work and all must be recognized and rewarded for their work—but it was not an egalitarian approach nor one that recognized most working women's material concerns. According to Blatch, women worked for psychological and ethical reasons, as much as for monetary ones. "As human beings we must have work," she wrote; "we rust out if we have not an opportunity to function on something." She emphasized the common promises and problems work raised in women's lives, not the differences in how they worked, how much individual choice they had, and especially in how much they were paid. She was relatively unconcerned with the way work enabled women to earn their livings. No doubt, her own experience partially explains this. As a young woman fresh out of college in the 1870s, she had dared to imagine that her desire for meaningful work and a role in the world need not deprive her of marriage and motherhood, and it did not.

Despite her marriage, the birth of two children, and the death of one, she never interrupted her political and intellectual labors. But she also never earned her own living, depending instead on the income from her husband's family's business. In later years, she joked about the fact that she was the only "parasite" in the organization of self-supporting women she headed.

But the contradictions in her analysis of the problem of work and women reflected more than her personal situation. There were two problems of work and women: the long-standing exploitation of laboring women of the working classes and the newly expanding place of paid labor in the lives of all women in bourgeois society. While the two processes were not the same, they were related, and women thinkers and activists of the Progressive period struggled to understand how. As more women worked for pay and outside of the home, how would the meaning of "womanhood" change? What would be the difference between "woman" and "man" when as many women as men were paid workers? And what would be the class differences between women if all of them worked? Indeed, would there be any difference between the classes at all, once the woman of leisure no longer existed? Virtually all the efforts to link the gender and class problems of work for woman were incomplete. If Blatch's analysis of work, like Gilman's, shorted the role of class, others' analyses, for instance Florence Kelley's, underplayed what work meant for women as a sex.

Blatch rethought the principles of political equality in the light of her emphasis on women's work. At an 1898 congressional hearing, Blatch hailed "the most convincing argument upon which our future claims must rest—the growing recognition of the economic value of the work of women." Whereas her mother had based her suffragism on the nineteenth-century argument for natural rights and on the individual, Blatch based hers on women's economic contribution and their significance as a group.

The contradictions in Blatch's approach to women and work also emerged in her attempts to link work and the vote. On the one hand, she approached women's political rights as she did their economic emancipation, democratically: Just as all sorts of women must work, all needed the vote. Wealthy women needed the vote because they were taxpayers and had the right to see that their money was not squandered; women industrial workers needed it because their jobs and factories were subject to laws, which they had the right to shape. On the other hand, she recognized the strategic centrality of the enormous class of industrial workers, whose economic role was so important and whose political power was potentially so great. "It is the women of the industrial class," she explained, "the wage-earners, reckoned by the hundreds of thousands, . . . the women whose work has been submitted to a money test, who have been the means of bringing about the altered attitude of public opinion toward woman's work in every sphere of life."

Blatch returned to New York for several extended visits after 1894, and she moved back for good in 1902. She had two purposes. Elizabeth Stanton was dying, and Blatch had come to be with her. Blatch also intended to take a leading role in the New York City suffrage movement. On her deathbed in 1902, Stanton asked Anthony to aid Blatch. However, hampered by Anthony's determination to keep control of the movement, Blatch was not able to make her bid for suffrage leadership until Anthony died, four years later.

Meanwhile, Blatch was excited by other reform efforts, which were beginning to provide the resources for a new kind of suffrage movement. During the first years of the twentieth century two movements contributed to Blatch's political education—a broadened, less socially exclusive campaign against political corruption and a democratized movement for the welfare of working women. By 1907, her combined experience in these two movements enabled her to put her ideas about women and

work into practice within the suffrage movement itself.

Women had become more active in the campaign against political corruption after 1894. In New York City Josephine Shaw Lowell and Mary Putnam Jacobi formed the Woman's Municipal League, which concentrated on educating the public about corruption, in particular the links between the police and organized prostitution. Women were conspicuous in the reform campaigns of Seth Low, who was elected mayor in 1901.

By the early 1900s, moreover, the spirit of political reform in New York City had spread beyond the elite. A left wing of the political reform movement had developed that charged that "Wall Street" was more responsible for political corruption than "the Bowery." Women were active in this wing, and there were women's political organizations with links to the Democratic party and the labor movement, a Women's Henry George Society, and a female wing of William Randolph Hearst's Independence League. The nonelite women in these groups were as politically enthusiastic as the members of the Woman's Municipal League, and considerably less ambivalent about enlarging the electorate. Many of them strongly supported woman suffrage. Beginning in 1905, a group of them organized an Equal Rights League to sponsor mock polling places for women to register their political opinions on election day.

Through the 1900s Blatch dutifully attended suffrage meetings, and without much excitement advocated the municipal suffrage for propertied women favored by the New York movement's leaders after their 1894 defeat. Like many other politically minded women, however, she found her enthusiasm caught by the movement for municipal political reform. She supported Low for mayor in 1901 and believed that his victory demonstrated "how strong woman's power really was when it was aroused." By 1903 she suggested to the National American Woman Suffrage Association (NAWSA) that it set aside agitation for the vote, so that "the women of the organization should use it for one year, nationally and locally, to pursue and punish corruption in politics." She supported the increasing attention given to "the laboring man" in reform political coalitions, but she pointedly observed that "the working woman was never considered."

However, working-class women were emerging as active factors in other women's reform organizations. The crucial arena for this development was the Women's Trade Union League (WTUL), formed in 1902 by a coalition of working-class and elite women to draw wage-earning women into trade unions. The New York chapter was formed in 1905, and Blatch was one of the first elite women to join. The WTUL represented a significant move away from the tradition of elite, ameliorative sisterhood at work in the 1894 campaign for woman suffrage. Like the Consumers' League, it had been formed in response to the request of women wage earners for aid from elite women, but it was an organization of both classes working together. Blatch had never been attracted to the strictly ameliorative tradition of women's reform, and the shift toward a partnership of upper-class and working-class women paralleled her own thinking about the relation between the classes and the role of work in women's lives. She and other elite women in the WTUL found themselves laboring not for working-class women, but with them, and toward a goal of forming unions that did not merely "uplift" working-class women, but empowered them. Instead of being working-class women's protectors, they were their "allies." Instead of speaking on behalf of poor women, they began to hear them speak for themselves. Within the organization wage earners were frequently in conflict with allies. Nonetheless, the league provided them an arena to articulate a working-class feminism related to, but distinct from, that of elite women.

Although prominent as a suffragist, Blatch participated in the WTUL on its own terms, rather than as a colonizer for suffrage. She and two other members assigned to the millinery trade conducted investigations into conditions and organized mass meetings to interest women workers in unions. She sat on the Executive Council from 1906 through 1909 and was often called on to stand in for President Mary Dreier. Her academic knowledge of "the industrial woman" was replaced by direct knowledge of wage-earning women and their working conditions. She was impressed with what she saw of trade unionism, especially its unrelenting "militance." Perhaps most important, she developed working relations with politically sophisticated working-class women, notably Leonora O'Reilly and Rose Schneiderman. Increasingly she believed that the organized power of labor and the enfranchisement of women were closely allied.

Working-class feminists in the league were drawn to ideas like Blatch's—to conceptions of dignity and equality for women in the workplace and to the ethic of self-support and lifelong independence; they wanted to upgrade the condition of wage-earning women so that they, too, could enjoy personal independence on the basis of their labor. On the one hand, they understood why most working-class women would want to leave their hateful jobs upon marriage; on the other, they knew that women as a group, if not the individual worker, were a permanent factor in the modern labor force. Mary Kennedy O'Sullivan of Boston, one of the league's founders, believed that "self support" was a goal for working-class women, but that only trade unions would give the masses of working women the "courage, independence, and self respect" they needed to improve their conditions. She expected "women of opportunity" to help in organizing women workers, because they "owed much to workers who give them a large part of what they have and enjoy," and because "the time has passed when women of opportunity can be self respecting and work *for* others."

Initially, the demand for the vote was less important to such working-class feminists than to the allies. Still, as they began to participate in the organized women's movement on a more equal basis, wage-earning women began to receive serious attention within the woman suffrage movement as well. Beginning about 1905, advocates of trade unionism and the vote for women linked the demands. At the 1906 suffrage convention WTUL member Gertrude Barnum pointed out that "our hope as suffragists lies with these strong working women." Kelley and Addams wrote about the working woman's need for the vote to improve her own conditions. In New York, Blatch called on the established suffrage societies to recognize the importance of the vote to wage-earning women and the importance of wage-earning women to winning the vote. When she realized that existing groups could not adapt to the new challenges, she moved to form her own society.

In January 1907 Blatch declared the formation of a new suffrage organization, the Equality League of Self-Supporting Women. The *New York Times* reported that the two hundred women present at the first meeting included "doctors, lawyers, milliners and shirtmakers." Blatch's decision to establish a suffrage organization that emphasized female "self-support" —lifelong economic independence—grew out of her ideas about work as the basis of women's claim on the state, the leadership role she envisioned for educated professionals, and her discovery of the power and political capacity of trade-union women. The Equality League provided the medium for introducing a new and aggressive style of activism into the suffrage movement—a version of the "militance" Blatch admired among trade unionists.

Initially, Blatch envisioned the Equality League of Self-Supporting Women as the political wing of the Women's Trade Union League. All the industrial workers she recruited were WTUL activists, including O'Reilly, the Equality League's first vice-president, and Schneiderman, its most popular speaker. To welcome working-class women, the Equality League virtually abolished membership fees; the policy

had the added advantage of allowing Blatch to claim every woman who ever attended a league meeting in her estimate of its membership. She also claimed the members of the several trade unions affiliated with the Equality League, such as the bookbinders, overall makers, and cap makers, so that when she went before the New York legislature to demand the vote, she could say that the Equality League represented thousands of wage-earning women.

Blatch wanted the Equality League to connect industrial workers, not with "club women" (her phrase), but with educated, professional workers, who should, she thought, replace benevolent ladies as the leaders of their sex. Such professionals—college educated and often women pioneers in their professions— formed the bulk of the Equality League's active membership. Many were lawyers, for instance, Ida Rauh, Helen Hoy, Madeleine Doty, Jessie Ashley, Adelma Burd, and Bertha Rembaugh. Others were social welfare workers, for instance the Equality League's treasurer, Kate Claghorn, a tenement housing inspector and the highest paid female employee of the New York City government. Blatch's own daughter, Nora, the first woman graduate civil engineer in the United States, worked in the New York City Department of Public Works. Many of these women had inherited incomes and did not work out of economic need, but out of a desire to give serious, public substance to their lives and to make an impact on society. Many of them expressed the determination to maintain economic independence after they married.

Although Blatch brought together trade-union women and college-educated professionals in the Equality League, there were tensions between the classes. The first correspondence between O'Reilly and Barnard graduate Caroline Lexow was full of class suspicion and mutual recrimination. More generally, there were real differences in how and why the two classes of working women demanded the vote. Trade-union feminists wanted the vote so that women industrial workers would have power over the labor laws that directly affected their working lives. Many of the college-educated self-supporters were the designers and administrators of this labor legislation. Several of them were, or aspired to be, government employees, and political power affected their jobs through party patronage. The occupation that might have bridged the differences was teaching. As in other cities, women teachers in New York organized for greater power and equal pay. The Equality League frequently offered aid, but the New York teachers' leaders were relatively conservative and kept their distance from the suffrage movement.

Blatch's special contribution was her understanding of the bonds and common interests uniting industrial and professional women workers. The industrial women admitted the professional ethic, if not the striving careerism, of the educated working women, and the professionals admired the matter-of-fact way wage-earning women went out to work. The fate of the professional woman was closely tied to that of the industrial worker; the cultural regard in which all working women were held affected both. Blatch dramatized that tie when she was refused service at a restaurant because she was unescorted by a man (that is, because she was eating with a woman). The management claimed that its policy aimed to protect "respectable" women, like Blatch, from "objectionable" women, like the common woman worker who went about on her own, whose morals were therefore questionable. Blatch rejected the division between respectable women and working women, pointing out that "there are five million women earning their livelihood in this country, and it seems strange that feudal customs should still exist here."

The dilemma of economically dependent married women was crucial to the future of both classes of working women. Blatch believed that if work was to free women, they could not leave it for dependence on men in marriage. The professional and working-class members of the Equality League shared this belief, one of the distinguishing convictions of their new approach to suffragism. In 1908, Blatch and Mary Dreier chaired a debate about the housewife, sponsored by the WTUL and attended by many Equality League members. Gilman took the Equality Lague position, that the unemployed wife was a "parasite" on her husband, and that all women, married as well as unmarried, should work, "like every other self-respecting being." Anna Howard Shaw argued that women's domestic labor was valuable, even if unpaid, and that the husband was dependent on his wife. A large audience attended, and although they "warmly applauded" Gilman, they preferred Shaw's sentimental construction of the economics of marriage.

A month after the Equality League was formed, Blatch arranged for trade-union women to testify before the New York legislature on behalf of woman suffrage, the first working-class women ever to do so. The New York Woman Suffrage Association was still concentrating on the limited, property-based form of municipal suffrage; in lethargic testimony its leaders admitted that they had "no new arguments to present." Everyone at the hearing agreed that the antis had the better of the argument. The Equality League testimony the next day was in sharp contrast. Clara Silver and Mary Duffy, WTUL activists and organizers in the garment industry, supported full suffrage for all New York women. The very presence of these women before the legislature, and their dignity and intelligence, countered the antis' dire predictions about enfranchising the unfit. Both linked suffrage to their trade-union efforts: While they struggled for equality in unions and in industry, "the state" undermined them, by teaching the lesson of female inferiority to male unionists and bosses. "To be left out by the State just sets up a prejudice against us," Silver explained. "Bosses think and women come to think themselves that they don't count for so much as men."

The formation of the Equality League and its appearance before the New York legislature awakened enthusiasm. Lillie Devereux Blake, whose own suffrage group had tried "one whole Winter . . . to /interest/ the working women" but found that they were "so overworked and so poor that they can do little for us," congratulated Blatch on her apparent success. Helen Marot, organizing secretary for the New York WTUL, praised the Equality League for "realizing the increasing necessity of including working women in the suffrage movement." Blatch, O'Reilly, and Schneiderman were the star speakers at the 1907 New York suffrage convention. "We realize that probably it will not be the educated workers, the college women, the men's association for equal suffrage, but the people who are fighting for industrial freedom who will be our vital force at the finish," proclaimed the newsletter of the NAWSA.

The unique class character of the Equality League encouraged the development of a new style of agitation, more radical than anything practiced in the suffrage movement . . . since Elizabeth Stanton's prime. The immediate source of the change was the Women's Social and Political Union of England (WSPU), led by Blatch's comrade from her Fabian days, Emmeline Pankhurst. Members of the WSPU were just beginning to be arrested for their suffrage protests. At the end of the Equality League's first year, Blatch invited one of the first WSPU prisoners, Anne Cobden-Sanderson, daughter of Richard Cobden, to the U.S. to tell about her experiences, scoring a coup for the Equality League. By emphasizing Cobden-Sanderson's connection with the British Labour party and distributing free platform tickets to trade-union leaders, Blatch was able to get an overflow crowd at Cooper Union, Manhattan's labor temple, two-thirds of them men, many of them trade unionists.

The Equality League's meeting for Cobden-Sanderson offered American audiences their first account of the new radicalism of English suffragists, or as they were beginning to be called, suffragettes. Cobden-Sanderson emphasized the suffragettes' working-class origins. She attributed the revival of the British suffrage movement to Lancashire factory workers; the heroic figure in her account was the working-class suffragette, Annie Kenney, while Christabel Pankhurst, later canonized as the Joan of Arc of British militance, went unnamed. After women factory workers were arrested for trying to see the prime minister, Cobden-Sanderson and other privileged women, who felt they "had not so much to lose as /the workers/ had," decided to join them and get arrested. She spent almost two months in jail, living the life of a common prisoner and coming to a new awareness of the poor and suffering women she saw there. Her simple but moving account conveyed the transcendent impact of the experience.

Cobden-Sanderson's visit to New York catalyzed a great outburst of suffrage energy; in its wake, Blatch and a handful of other new leaders introduced the WSPU tactics into the American movement, and the word *suffragette* became as common in New York as in London. The "militants" became an increasingly distinct wing of the movement in New York and other American cities. But it would be too simple to say that the British example caused the new, more militant phase in the American movement. The developments that were broadening the class basis and the outlook of American suffragism had prepared American women to respond to the heroism of the British militants.

The development of militance in the American suffrage movement was marked by new aggressive tactics practiced by the WSPU, especially open-air meetings and outdoor parades. At this stage in the development of British militance, American suffragists generally admired the heroism of the WSPU martyrs. Therefore, although the press emphasized dissent within the suffrage movement—it always organized its coverage of suffrage around female rivalries of some sort—the new militant activities were well received throughout the movement. And, conversely, even the most daring American suffragettes believed in an American exceptionalism that made it unnecessary to contemplate going to prison, to suffer as did the British militants.

Despite Blatch's later claims, she did not actually introduce the new tactics in New York City. The first open-air meetings were organized immediately after the Cobden-Sanderson visit by a group called the American Suffragettes. Initiated by Bettina Borrman Wells, a visiting member of the WSPU, most of the American Suffragettes membership came from the Equal Rights League, the left-wing municipal reform group that had organized mock polling places in New York since 1905. Feminist egalitarians with radical cultural leanings, its members were actresses, artists, writers, teachers, and social welfare workers—less wealthy versions of the professional self-supporters in the Equality League. Their local leader was a librarian, Maud Malone, whose role in encouraging new suffrage tactics was almost as important as, although less recognized than, Blatch's own.

The American Suffragettes held their first open-air meeting in Madison Square on New Year's Eve, 1907. After that they met in the open at least once a week. Six weeks later, they announced they would hold New York's first all-woman parade. Denied a police permit, they determined to march anyway. The twenty-three women in the "parade" were many times outnumbered by the onlookers, mostly working-class men. In a public school to which they adjourned to make speeches, the American Suffragettes told a sympathetic audience that "the woman who works is the underdog of the world"; thus she needed the vote to defend herself. Socialists and working women rose from the floor to support them. Two years later the Equality League organized a much more successful suffrage parade in New York. Several hundred suffragettes, organized by occupation, marched from Fifty-ninth Street to Union Square. O'Reilly, the featured speaker, made "a tearful plea on behalf of the working girl that drew the first big demonstration of applause from the street crowd."

Perhaps because the American Suffragettes were so active in New York City, Blatch held the Equality League's first open-air meeting in May 1908 upstate. Accompanied by Maud Malone, she organized an inventive "trolley car campaign" between Syracuse and Albany, using the interurban trolleys to go from town to town. The audiences expressed the complex class character of the suffrage movement at that moment. In Syracuse Blatch had her wealthy friend Dora Hazard arrange a meeting among the workers at her husband's factory. She also held a successful outdoor meeting in Troy, home of the Laundry Workers' Union, one of the oldest and most militant independent women's trade unions in the country. Albany was an antisuffrage stronghold, and its mayor tried to prevent the meeting; but Blatch outwitted him. The highlight of the tour was in Poughkeepsie, where Blatch and Inez Milholland, then a student at Vassar College, organized a legendary meeting. Since Vassar's male president forbade any woman suffrage activities on college grounds, Blatch and Milholland defiantly announced they would meet students in a cemetery. Gilman, who was extremely popular among college women, spoke, but it was the passionate trade-union feminist, Schneiderman, who was the star.

Blatch believed that the first function of militant tactics was to gain much-needed publicity for the movement. The mainstream press had long ignored suffrage activities. If an occasional meeting was reported, it was usually buried in a small back-page article, focusing on the absurdity and incompetence of women's efforts to organize a political campaign. Gilded Age suffragists themselves accepted the Victorian convention that respectable women did not court public attention. The Equality League's emphasis on the importance of paid labor for women of all classes struck at the heart of that convention. Blatch understood "the value of publicity or rather the harm of the lack of it." She encouraged open-air meetings and trolley car campaigns because they generated much publicity, which no longer held the conventional horror for her followers.

Militant tactics broke through the "press boycott" by violating standards of respectable femininity, making the cause newsworthy, and embracing the subsequent ridicule and attention. "We . . . believe in standing on street corners and fighting our way to recognition, forcing the men to think about us," an *American Suffragette* manifesto proclaimed. "We glory . . . that we are theatrical." The militant pursuit of publicity was an instant success: Newspaper coverage increased immediately; by 1908 even the sneering *New York Times* reported regularly on suffrage. The more outrageous or controversial the event, the more prominent the coverage. Blatch was often pictured and quoted.

The new methods had a second function; they intensified women's commitment to the movement. Militants expected that overstepping the boundary of respectability would etch suffrage beliefs on women's souls, beyond retraction or modification. Blatch caught the psychology of this process. "Society has taught women self sacrifice and now this force is to be drawn upon in the arduous campaign for their own emancipation," she wrote. "The new methods of agitation, in that they are difficult and disagreeable, lay hold of the imagination and devotion of women, wherein lies the strength of the new appeal, the certainty of victory." Borrman Wells spoke of the "divine spirit of self-sacrifice," which underlay the suffragettes's transgressions against respectability and was the source of the "true inwardness of the movement."

If suffrage militants had a general goal beyond getting the vote, it was to challenge existing standards of femininity. "We must eliminate that abominable word ladylike from our vocabularies," Borrman Wells proclaimed. "We must get out and fight." The new definition of femininity the militants were evolving drew, on the one hand, on traditionally male behaviors, like aggression, fighting, provoca-

tion, and rebelliousness. Blatch was particularly drawn to the "virile" world of politics, which she characterized as a male "sport" she was sure she could master. On the other hand, they undertook a spirited defense of female sexuality, denying that it need be forfeited by women who participated vigorously in public life. "Women are no longer to be considered little tootsey wootseys who have nothing to do but look pretty," suffragette Lydia Commander declared. "They are determined to take an active part in the community and look pretty too." A member of a slightly older generation, Blatch never adopted the modern sexual ethic of the new woman, but she constantly emphasized the fact that women had distinct concerns that had to be accommodated in politics and industry. These two notes—the difference of the sexes and the repressed ability of women for manly activities—existed side by side in the thought of all the suffrage insurgents.

The militant methods, taking suffrage out of the parlors and into the streets, indicated the new significance of working-class women in several ways. Blatch pointed out that the new methods—open-air meetings, newspaper publicity—suited a movement whose members had little money and therefore could not afford to rent halls or publish a newspaper. As a style of protest, "militance" was an import from the labor movement; WTUL organizers had been speaking from street corners for several years. And disrespect for the standards of ladylike respectability showed at least an impatience with rigid standards of class distinction, at most the influence of class-conscious wage-earning women.

Working-class feminists were eager to speak from the militants' platform, as were many Socialists. A Socialist cadre, Dr. Anna Mercy, organized a branch of the American Suffragettes on the Lower East Side, which issued the first suffrage leaflets ever published in Yiddish. Militants also prepared propaganda in German and Italian and, in general, pursued working-class audiences. "Our relation to the State will be determined by the vote of the average man," Blatch asserted. "None but the converted . . . will come to us. We must seek on the highways the unconverted."

However, it would be a mistake to confuse the suffragettes' radicalism with the radicalism of a working-class movement. The ultimate goal of the suffragettes was not a single-class movement, but a universal one, "the union of women of all shades of political thought and of all ranks of society on the single issue of their political enfranchisement." While the Equality League's 1907 hearing before the state legislature highlighted trade-union suffragists, at the 1908 hearing the league also featured elite speakers, in effect deemphasizing the working-class perspective. Militants could neither repudiate the Socialist support they were attracting, and alienate working-class women, nor associate too closely with Socialists and lose access to the wealthy. Blatch—who actually became a Socialist after the suffrage was won—would not arrange for the Socialist party leader Morris Hillquit to join other suffrage speakers at the 1908 legislative hearing. Similarly, the American Suffragettes allowed individual Socialists on their platform but barred Socialist propaganda. Speaking for Socialist women who found the "idea of a 'radical' suffrage movement . . . very alluring," Josephine Conger Kaneko admitted that the suffragettes left her confused.

Moreover, the militant challenge to femininity and the emphasis on publicity introduced a distinctly elite bias; a society matron on an open-air platform made page one while a working girl did not, because society women were obliged by conventions and could outrage by flouting them. In their very desire to redefine femininity, the militants were anxious to stake their claim to it, and it was upper-class women who determined femininity. In Elizabeth Robin's drama about the rise of militance in the British suffrage movement, *The Convert,* the heroine of the title was a beautiful aristocratic woman who became radical when she realized the emptiness of her ladylike existence and the contempt for women obscured by gentlemen's chivalrous gestures. The Equality League brought *The Convert* to New York in 1908 as its first large fund-raising effort; working-class women, as well as elite women, made up the audience. Malone was one of the few militants to recognize and to protest against excessive solicitousness for the elite convert. She resigned from the American Suffragettes when she concluded that they had become interested in attracting "a well-dressed crowd, not the rabble."

Blatch's perspective and associations had always been fundamentally elite. The most well connected of the new militant leaders, she played a major role in bringing the new suffrage propaganda to the attention of upper-class women. She presided over street meetings in fashionable neighborhoods, where reporters commented on the "smart" crowds and described the speakers' outfits in society-page detail. Blatch's first important ally from the Four Hundred was Katherine Duer Mackay, wife of the founder of the International Telephone and Telegraph Company and a famous society beauty. Mackay's suffragism was very ladylike, but other members of her set who followed her into the movement were more drawn to militance. Alva Belmont, a veritable mistress of flamboyance, began her suffrage career as Mackay's protégé. The elitist subtext of militance was a minor theme in 1908 and 1909. But by 1910 becoming a suffragette was proving "fashionable," and upper-class women began to identify with the new suffrage style in significant numbers. By the time suffragette militance became a national movement, its working-class origins and trade-union associations had been submerged, and it was in the hands of women of wealth.

From the beginning, though, class was the contradiction at the suffrage movement's heart. In the campaign of 1894, elite women began to pursue more power for themselves by advocating the suffrage in the name of all women. When Cobden-Sanderson spoke for the Equality League at Cooper Union in 1907, she criticized "idle women of wealth" as the enemies of woman suffrage, and she was wildly applauded. But what did her charge mean? Were all rich women under indictment, or only those who stayed aloof from social responsibility and political activism? Were the militants calling for working-class leadership of the suffrage movement or for cultural changes in bourgeois definitions of womanhood? This ambiguity paralleled the mixed meanings in Blatch's emphasis on working women; it coincided with an implicit tension between the older, elite women's reform traditions and the newer trade-union politics they had helped to usher in; and it was related to a lurking confusion about whether feminism's object was the superfluity of wealthy women or the exploitation of the poor. It would continue to plague suffragism in its final decade, and feminism afterwards, into our own time.

10

JOHN MUIR:
THE MYSTERIES OF MOUNTAINS

PETER WILD

The final phase of America's westward expansion involved the exploration and settlement of the far western frontier. From the end of the Civil War through the early twentieth century, hundreds of thousands of native-born and immigrant Americans flooded into the region between the Rocky Mountains and the Pacific Coast to begin new lives as farmers and small-town businessmen. But unlike America's earlier frontiers, the Far West brought more than farmers and shopkeepers. The region's dense forests and rich mineral deposits also attracted eastern lumber and mining companies intent on exploiting these lucrative natural resources. By the turn of the century, years of unrestricted logging, hydraulic mining, and careless dam-building threatened to destroy the natural beauty of America's last frontier.

This heedless exploitation of the wilderness of the Far West did not go unchallenged, however. Beginning in the 1880s, scientists, naturalists, and government officials joined together in a national conservation movement that sought to preserve the country's wilderness areas for the enjoyment and education of future generations of Americans. If any one man symbolized the conservationist impulse, it was the Scottish immigrant, John Muir. Explorer, nature writer, and general spokesman for wilderness America, Muir played a pivotal role in popularizing the cause of conservation in America. In this biographical essay, Peter Wild traces Muir's love of nature to the restrictions of his early life and follows his efforts to preserve America's wilderness as a counterweight to modern industrial society.

Chapter 3 of Peter Wild, *Pioneer Conservationists of Western America* (Missoula, Mont.: Mountain Press, 1979). Reprinted by permission of Peter Wild and Mountain Press Publishing Co., Inc.

I must explain why it is that at night, in my own house,
Even when no one's asleep, I feel I must whisper.
Thoreau and Wordsworth would call it an act of devotion. . . .

—Reed Whittemore

At sunset in the Sierras some hikers chant John Muir's words: "I am always glad to touch the living rock again and dip my head in high mountain air." To them John Muir is a hero, the high priest of those who escape to the wilderness.

And well he might be. By tradition Americans long for the freedom of wilderness, a wilderness fast disappearing. Muir said that all he needed to flee was to "throw some tea and bread in an old sack and jump over the back fence." How can the schedule-bound and traffic-weary commuter not envy the man who, as Yosemite's cliffs collapsed around him, rushed into the night shouting, "A noble earthquake, a noble earthquake!" At times he seems one of the daring Americans who, we like to imagine, led us West through our short history. We prefer our heroes dressed in a simple guise, but with a vigor and joie de vivre just beyond our ken.

The danger is that Muir tends to become lost in his mythology, some of it of his own making. A closer look shows him a complex man, like others capable of gloom and hesitation. After years of private struggle and doubt, he beat his conflicting practical and mystical bents into an unusually consistent and powerful personality. Yet the most dramatic events of his life are indeed telling, though often not fully appreciated.

One of the most famous of these, a catastrophe that ended in a spiritual change, occurred in 1867. While he adjusted a new belt in an Indianapolis carriage factory, a file flew from his hand, blinding his right eye. Soon after, the other eye went dark as though in sympathetic reaction. For weeks he lay in agony: "My days were terrible beyond what I can tell, and my nights were if possible more terrible. Frightful dreams exhausted and terrified me." Muir was twenty-nine, an age of trial and decision for many prophets.

Up to this time, chances for a lucrative but unsatisfying career as an inventor contended with his love of extended wanderings through the woods. In his blindness he saw an answer: if his eyes healed he would give up tinkering with man's inventions and devote his life to "the study of the inventions of God." As he tossed in his room, slowly his sight returned. Significantly, he described his deliverance in religious terms: "Now had I arisen from the grave. The cup is removed, and I am alive!" From then on he would consistently equate God with light.

Likeable and talented, Muir was asked by his employers Osgood & Smith to stay on. However, a promotion to foreman, a raise, shorter hours, and a future partnership couldn't sway him. Lifting his pack containing a change of underwear and a few favorite books, he was off. His goal was to walk the thousand miles across the South—no mean feat in the bandit-ridden forests after the Civil War—to the tip of Florida, and from there to hitch a ride by boat to the Amazon. In the words of his biographer, Linnie Wolfe, he was resolved to become "one of God's fools." Yet as dramatic as the file incident might appear, the resulting conversion was neither simple nor complete. The five-month trip provided him with the time and space to mull over conflicts that had troubled him since childhood.

John Muir was born in Dunbar, Scotland, in 1838. Over the years his father's zealousness crossed the blurred line into a religious fanaticism the merchant brought with him when he settled his family in America. Daniel Muir sat in his homestead reading the Bible while his sons labored in the Wisconsin fields. When they returned weary at the end of the day, he beat them for sins they might have committed. To him books, paintings—even an adequate diet—smacked of the Devil. Precocious John, however, discovered that he could do with only a few hours sleep; in the darkness of early morning he'd secretly crawl down into the cellar to read and to whittle a variety of curious clocks.

Though Daniel scowled when he found out about the inventions, neighbors urged his son to exhibit them at the State Agricultural Fair. At the age of twenty-two, suffering his father's parting anger, John shouldered his pack stuffed with strange devices and headed for the state capital. There in the Temple of Art, Madison's citizens marveled at the youth from the backwoods, whose early-rising machine whirred and creaked to propel the reluctant sleeper out of bed.

But Muir found more than local fame in Madison. Like many an aspiring American youth, he strolled with opening eyes among the buildings of the nearby university, envious of the students who had stepped into a larger world of intellectual opportunity. Sometime later he enrolled with money earned from odd jobs, to spend two and a half pleasant years at the University of Wisconsin. There, after glimpsing the cosmos through his courses, he amused the other students with the devices that clicked and wheezed through their bizarre paces in his room at North Hall.

Restlessness overtook him in the spring of 1863, and he wandered through Canada, then back again into the Midwest. He was by now in his mid-twenties, a late bloomer tinged with guilt that he hadn't done more with his life. Far from being simply an enjoyable interim, however, the time spent in Madison would change and serve him more profoundly than he realized. In the frontier's atmosphere of intellectual democracy, Muir had made friends. His professors ignored the long hair and careless dress of the country boy and offered him confidence in his eccentric development. Dr. Ezra Carr and his wife Jeanne had graciously opened their Madison home and their private

library to Muir. On the scientific side, Professor Carr instilled his students with Louis Agassiz's theory that a great Ice Age had carved out much of the northern hemisphere's topography. This grounding in science would result in Muir's first public controversy and his fame in California's Sierras. As for philosophy, both Carr and his wife were self-appointed missionaries of Ralph Waldo Emerson's transcendental ideas. They believed that through the oneness of nature a person could arrive intuitively at spiritual truth, if not ecstasy. It was just what young Muir needed to assuage his guilt and to justify wandering as a spiritual adventure.

And so with his boyhood and Madison as backgrounds, the dropout sat writing in his notebook among the palmettos and sand dunes of Florida's west coast, recording his thoughts and working his philosophical and personal conflicts into a unified view, the basis for future publications. He saw nature as a whole, a unity in flux. Man should stand in nature's temple, witnessing the eternal "morning of creation" occurring all about him. Emerson would have applauded the imagery, yet Muir went beyond the Concord philosopher. Unlike the flights of the cerebral Emerson, Muir's arose from perceptions grounded in science and elemental experiences in nature. Whether collecting specimens or hanging perilously by his fingertips from some yet unclimbed peak, he recognized that "a heart like our own must be beating in every crystal and cell" of the surrounding wilderness. Muir's ability to survive, botanize, and philosophize in the wilds was a rare power.

As his thinking developed, he realized—as Emerson did not—that if nature is a holy place, then civilization, with its sheep, axes, and dynamite, is the infidel, the wrecker in the temple. As Thomas Lyon has pointed out, the view represents a reversal of Muir's boyhood Calvinism. God, not the Devil, is to be found in the wilderness. Nature, not man, is the center of a timeless universe. With this in mind, Muir set his spiritual sights south on the Amazon basin; there he could glory in a nature steaming and writhing in the speeded-up processes of the jungle. But the semitropical winds already had blown him ill. Wracked by malaria, he turned back at Havana, Cuba, in hopes that the Sierra cold would purge his blood. The retreat made all the difference to a beginning conservation movement that as yet had no heroes.

In the early spring of 1868, the former inventor stepped off the boat in San Francisco. All around him that bustling city of commerce—a commerce based largely on resources hauled out of the interior—displayed "the gobble gobble school of economics." In a typical Muir scene, he told of stopping a carpenter to ask the fastest way out of town. Puzzled, the workman inquired where he wanted to go. Muir replied, "Anywhere that is wild." About the time that John Wesley Powell was bounding through the unknown Grand Canyon in his little boat, Muir was beginning a decade of Sierra exploration.

At first he supported himself by coming down out of the mountains to work on sheep ranches. The job disgusted him, and he branded the bleating, overgrazing creatures, degenerate cousins of the noble bighorns living high in his range of light, "hooved locusts." Eventually he chose Yosemite as a home base. Though accessible only by foot or horse, the striking canyon scenery attracted the more rugged variety of tourist. Muir took a job operating the sawmill for one of the two expanding hotels—with the stipulation that he would work only on wind-downed logs. On the sunny side of the valley, the sawyer built a little cabin for himself, complete with a wild fern growing inside and a brook running through it. Except for intermittent concessions to working for a few supplies, he was at peace, free to wander and enjoy the unexplored peaks.

Despite his pleasure in solitude, it should not be supposed that Muir was a cranky malcontent. Though he could chide people with his Scottish humor, he enjoyed company; if he had any social fault beyond his slipshod dress, it was his garrulousness. When in the mood around a camp fire, Muir could hold forth on the glories of the surroundings long after foot-weary companions wished they were in their sleeping bags. Even before he was stirring up the public in print, with the help of friends he had become something of a celebrity, something of the "John of the Mountains" figure that persists to this day. Professor and Mrs. Carr of Madison days had moved to the University of California. They sent a stream of vacationing writers and scientists—many of them eminent personages from the East—knocking on the Hutchings Hotel door, asking to be shown Yosemite's wonders by the only authority on them, ragtag John Muir. He more than satisfied tourist expectations of a romantic character of the Wild West.

As he befriended these Eastern visitors, the amateur naturalist made connections that would serve him in future conservation battles. He guided scientific expeditions and showed off the valley to his aging Concord guru. Emerson added the young transcendentalist to his list of "My Men," but he seemed a little taken aback by all the wilderness, so much more wild than his modest Massachusetts woods. Whether intentionally or not, Muir charmed Viscountess Thérèse Yelverton, victim of a scandalous English divorce tangle, who viewed him as a transcendental noble savage. She wanted him to run away with her to Hong Kong, but to his credit he gently turned her aside. However, she continued the romance on a unilateral basis, writing the novel *Zanita*, which featured John Muir as its Pre-Raphaelite hero.

More importantly, in later years he camped out with President Theodore Roosevelt, who happened to be scanning the nation for places to preserve. In his boyish enthusiasm, TR declared that he had a "bully" time with Muir—a man who if pressed would admit that in attempting to scale Mount Whitney he had danced the Highland fling all night to keep from freezing in the −22° cold. Yet California, the bellwether of America, was fast filling with settlers and developers. John Muir's rugged peace could not last long. In one of several striking shifts in his life, he exchanged it for a public career as a writer and for a reputation that holds to this day as the nation's foremost protector of wilderness.

As a late bloomer, John Muir wrote his first article at the age of thirty-four, his first book at fifty-six. Drawing heavily from the journals kept throughout his adult life, he tended to poeticize the facts. Then, too, his mysticism slowed him down; he found his adventures so spiritually satisfying that writing about them gave only a secondary thrill. "Ink cannot tell the glow that lights me at this moment in turning to the mountains," he explained. On the other hand, his beliefs eventually compelled him to write in defense of nature; and, when the writing fire burned in him, he was far more than the reluctant author. A scientific wrangle provided the first spark.

California's State Geologist, Josiah D. Whitney, applied the popular cataclysmic theory of geology to Yosemite. Basically, Whitney maintained that in a dramatic shift of the earth's crust the floor had suddenly fallen out of the valley, creating the present gorge. Schooled in Agassiz's contrary glacial theory and believing in the slow processes of nature espoused by Emerson, Muir viewed Whitney's pronouncement as an affront. By the early 1870's proprietary feelings about the Sierras ran deep in Muir. He, after all, knew his "range of light" far better than any geologist, regardless of his lack of degrees and professional standing. Glaciers grinding over eons had carved out Yosemite, not a super earthquake. As it turned out, Muir happened to be right, though there was at least as much emotion as science on both sides of the debate.

Urged by visiting scientists supporting his minority opinion, he sent off "Yosemite Glaciers." When the New York *Tribune* not only published the article but paid him for the effort, it set the practical side of his Scottish mind to whirling. At the time, journalism offered far more lucrative returns than it does today; writing might be an alternative to his periodic bondage at the sawmill—as well as a vehicle for rebuffing exploiters. Boosted by influential

contacts, his articles, both celebrating his country and warning the public of its imminent demise, won the praise and concern of readers of the *Overland Monthly, Harper's,* and the *National Geographic.* Unlike many of the nature writers of the time, Muir grounded his rhapsody in the details of personal experience. He took readers with him from one detailed Sierra adventure to the next. Here he is edging along a cliff face to get a grand view of plunging Yosemite Creek:

> . . . the slope beside it looked dangerously smooth and steep, and the swift roaring flood beneath, overhead, and beside me was very nerve-trying. I therefore concluded not to venture farther, but did nevertheless. Tufts of artemisia were growing in clefts of the rock near by, and I filled my mouth with the bitter leaves, hoping they might help to prevent giddiness. Then, with a caution not known in ordinary circumstances, I crept down safely to the little edge, got my heels well planted on it, then shuffled in a horizontal direction twenty or thirty feet until close to the out-plunging current, which, by the time it had descended thus far, was already white. Here I obtained a perfectly free view down into the heart of the snowy, chanting throng of comet-like streamers, into which the body of the fall soon separates.

It is perhaps a bit difficult for an age sated with television spectacles to appreciate the impact of his revelations, based on the union of the physical and spiritual. Upon considering a new Muir manuscript, one editor declared that he almost felt as if he had found religion. On the mystical side, the poetry of Muir's words had the ecstatic ring of a man who was "on the side of the angels and Thoreau," as Herbert Smith describes him. Muir was having the best of two worlds: new economic freedom allowed him to garner material for magazines while he enjoyed trips to Utah, Nevada, and Alaska.

Yet there was a hitch; at the age of forty, "John of the Mountains" longed for a home life. Again his friends came into play, this time in match-making. Jeanne Carr introduced Muir to Louie Wanda Strentzel, eligible daughter of a wealthy medical doctor exiled from Poland. The match was not as unlikely as it first sounds. Despite his wanderings, Muir could carry himself like a gentleman; by this time he was a writer of some note; he knew the value of money and had $1,000 in the bank. It took patience and subtle urgings on the part of Mrs. Carr, but in the middle of April, 1880, John Muir married Louie Strentzel. The groom's literary abilities lapsed into cliché, however, when he expressed his genuine domestic joy: "I am now the happiest man in the world!"

For a wedding present, Dr. Strentzel gave his new son-in-law an orchard and a house in Martinez, across the bay from San Francisco. Perhaps middle-aged Muir needed a rest from freezing on mountaintops and eating monk's fare from a bread bag. Whatever the case, his old farming instinct asserted itself. With the exception of significant trips to Alaska, in the next few years he stayed fairly close to home, laboring in the vineyards that provided the modest fortune that would support his final and most important years of activism. To his credit, though Muir showed astute business sense, he also was generous with his money, supporting relatives, giving heavily to charity. "We all loved him," said a friend, "for his thoughtfulness for others." And Muir loved the banter and refuge of a comfortable household, one much different from that of his severe childhood.

John Muir's grapevines prospered, but his health and writing, cut off from the strength of the Sierras, suffered. In a way that might not be fashionable today, his wife rearranged her life to deal with the problem. Louie insisted that he spend July through October, the slack season for orchardmen in Contra Costa County, trying to regain his vital contact with the mountains. Though she loved music, when he was laboring in his study, she kept her piano closed. Editors hadn't forgotten Muir; joined by his wife, they connived to get him out into the wilderness and his pen working again.

In time they succeeded in rebaptizing Muir with his old power—redoubled when Robert Underwood Johnson of *Century Magazine* took him on a camping trip to see what unrestrained sheep and lumbermen had done to his beloved Yosemite. The plots of his friends worked just in time; the 1880's and 1890's marked the first cohesion and substantial victories of the early conservation movement. Pen in hand and backed by Johnson, the aging mountain man stood at its forefront. In 1890 the Eastern press reprinted his articles "Treasures of the Yosemite" and "Features of the Proposed Yosemite National Park." Telegrams and letters flooded Congressmen's offices. Saving Muir's old stamping grounds became a cause celebre of national proportions. Congress reacted to the outcry for government preservation—a novel idea. Forced by popular pressure to ignore commercial interests opposing the plan, it created Yosemite National Park and provided a cavalry detachment to patrol the area. Muir and Johnson took advantage of the public's ire at its loss of scenic places and of its hope for saving what remained of them. Through writing and lobbying, in the same year they compelled a publicity-conscious Congress to add Sequoia and General Grant to the growing list of National Parks.

Things were going well for conservation. Supported by a core group of activists, including the young forester Gifford Pinchot in the East, the Enabling Act of 1891 allowed timberlands to be set aside by executive order. Before he left office, President Harrison created the forerunners of the National Forests by designating 13,000,000 acres of public land as Forest Reserves. Through these years, editor Johnson continued to be the man behind the somewhat shy John Muir. Individual concerns, however deep, could be effective in the political maelstrom only through united effort, Johnson urged. In 1892 Muir gathered a number of prominent Californians into a San Francisco law office to incorporate the Sierra Club, an organization Muir led until his death. One of the earliest citizen groups of its kind, the Club continues in the tradition of its founder to "explore, enjoy, and preserve" the country's resources. To support the movement, Muir was writing, writing—*The Mountains of California* (1894), *Our National Parks* (1901), *My First Summer in the Sierra* (1911)—for a public that looked to the written word as a guide for its judgments.

Yet in the seesaw of politics, for a time it looked as if the new Forest Reserve system—if not the new National Parks—might be lost. Those whose livelihoods depended on exploiting the natural heritage were quick to call in political debts and mount an effective counterattack. By then, however, other magazines followed the example of *Century* with strong stands for conservation. And from John Muir's pen came prose with a stentorian thunder that echoed the fire and brimstone of his childhood. Readers opening the August, 1897, issue of the *Atlantic Monthly* found both their religion and patriotism at the stake:

> The forests of America, however slighted by man, must have been a great delight to God; for they were the best he ever planted. The whole continent was a garden, and from the beginning it seemed to be favored above all the other wild parks and gardens of the globe. . . . Everywhere, everywhere over all the blessed continent, there were beauty, and melody, and kindly, wholesome, foodful abundance.

Muir knew his rhetoric. After presenting an historical survey of America's forests, comparing their abuse with the stewardship of Germany, France, and Switzerland, he concluded with a poetic appeal for firm government action:

> Any fool can destroy trees. They cannot run away; and if they could, they would still be destroyed,—chased and hunted down as long as fun or a dollar could be got out of their bark hides. . . . Through all the wonderful, eventful centuries since Christ's time—and long before

that—God has cared for these trees, saved them from drought, disease, avalanches, and a thousand straining, leveling tempests and floods; but he cannot save them from fools,—only Uncle Sam can do that.

Only ignorance and greed could challenge Muir's plea. There were successes—passage of the Lacey Antiquities Act of 1906, for example. Its provisions allowed creation of National Monuments by Presidential decree. Because of Muir's urging, Roosevelt set aside Petrified Forest and parts of the Grand Canyon. And Muir, at the age of seventy-four, would fulfill his youthful urge to explore the Amazon. But in the last years John Muir fought his most significant and agonizing battle—and lost.

In 1913, after years of bitter feuding, Congress voted to dam the Hetch Hetchy Valley, fifteen miles northwest of Yosemite, in order to provide water and power for San Francisco. Like so many plans touted by politicians as cure-alls, Hetch Hetchy proved a miserable, unnecessary boondoggle, a windfall for a few, with the public paying the bills. It hurt Muir that his friend and ally of the past, Forest Service Chief Gifford Pinchot—his eye always on use rather than preservation—joined its loudest promoters. Worse still, the Hetch Hetchy project violated the purpose of a National Park. Muir knew that it was a commercial wedge into an ideal, a wedge that has since been sunk into other parks. In Wolfe's words, Muir "was a prophet of the shape of things to come."

Yet to a reform-minded nation, the lost Hetch Hetchy Valley, whose beauty had once rivaled Yosemite's, became a symbol, part of John Muir's legacy. Stung by its mistake, Congress three years later passed a comprehensive National Parks bill. In 1914 "John of the Mountains" died, but he had shown the way to Aldo Leopold, Enos Mills, and Stephen Mather—and to thousands of others.

11

W. E. B. DU BOIS: PROTAGONIST OF THE AFRO-AMERICAN PROTEST

ELLIOTT RUDWICK

By the beginning of the twentieth century many African Americans and their leaders despaired of ever achieving equality in American society. In the South, where the majority of blacks lived before World War I, disfranchisement, the legal discrimination of Black Codes, the terrorism of lynchings, and the intimidation and violence of the Klu Klux Klan served notice that white society meant to keep black Americans separate and unequal. The manifest racial discrimination which southern blacks encountered when they traveled north only served to reinforce the conclusion that the Fourteenth and Fifteenth Amendments to the Constitution, which guaranteed black citizenship and voting rights, were hollow phrases that would never be realized in practice.

It was against this background of profound racial domination that black leaders argued over the proper course to be taken by their people. Two of the most famous and powerful of these leaders were Booker T. Washington and W. E. B. Du Bois. Faced with the fact of deep-seated racial antagonism, Washington urged his people to forget integration into white society and to concentrate their energies on the intellectual, moral, and economic development of their race. To accomplish these goals, Washington founded the Tuskegee Institute to train young black people in the skills needed to meet the demands of a modern business-oriented society. With great success, Washington appealed to the giants of the financial and business world for funds to build and operate Tuskegee and to make it a shining example of black abilities in a hostile white world.

Not all black leaders were willing to follow the path marked out by Washington, however. As Elliott Rudwick points out in this essay, resistance to Washington's accommodation with American racism became manifest in the rise of the Niagara Movement and the founding of the National Association for the Advancement of Colored People (NAACP) early in the twentieth century. At the center of this opposition was the man who both organized the Niagara Movement and helped to found the NAACP, W. E. B. Du Bois. From 1903 until his death in 1963, Du Bois was the nation's foremost advocate of the active integration of black people into the mainstream of American life.

Chapter 4 in John Hope Franklin and August Meier, eds., *Black Leaders of the Twentieth Century* (Urbana, Ill.: University of Illinois Press, 1982). Reprinted by permission of Elliott Rudwick and University of Illinois Press.

During the nineteenth century and the early decades of the twentieth, when blacks were virtually powerless, propagandists like Frederick Douglass, Booker T. Washington, and W. E. B. Du Bois naturally loomed large in the pantheon of black leaders. The term propagandist—used here in its neutral meaning as denoting one who employs symbols to influence the feelings and behavior of an audience—is a particularly apt description of the role played by Du Bois, the leading black intellectual and the most important black protest spokesman in the first half of the twentieth century. As platform lecturer and particularly as editor of several publications, Du Bois was a caustic and prophetic voice, telling whites that racist social institutions oppressed blacks and telling blacks that change in their subordinate status was impossible unless they demanded it insistently and continuously. Du Bois himself in his noted autobiographical work, *Dusk of Dawn,* aptly evaluated his principal contribution when he wrote of "my role as a master of propaganda."

Central to Du Bois's role as a propagandist were the ideologies that he articulated. And Du Bois's ideas reflected most of the diverse themes in black thinking about how to assault the bastions of prejudice and discrimination. Most important, he articulated the blacks' desire for full participation in the larger American society and demanded "the abolition of all caste distinctions based simply on race and color." On the other hand, he also exhibited a nationalist side—a strong sense of group pride, advocacy of racial unity, and a profound identification with blacks in other parts of the world. As he said in one of his oft-quoted statements,

> One ever feels his twoness—an American, a Negro; two souls, two thoughts, two unreconciled strivings; two warring ideals in one dark body, whose dogged strength alone keeps it from being torn asunder. The history of the American Negro is the history of this strife—this longing to attain self-conscious manhood,

> to merge his double self into a better and truer self. In this merging he wishes neither of the older selves to be lost. . . . He simply wishes to make it possible for a man to be both a Negro and an American, without being cursed and spit upon by his fellows, without having the doors of opportunity closed roughly in his face.

In addition Du Bois was both a pioneering advocate of black capitalism, and later was one of the country's most prominent black Marxists. Essentially a protest leader he was also criticized at times for enunciating tactics of accommodation. An elitist who stressed the leadership role of a college-educated Talented Tenth, he articulated a fervent commitment to the welfare of the black masses.

Given the persistent and intransigent nature of the American race system, which proved quite impervious to black attacks, Du Bois in his speeches and writings moved from one proposed solution to another, and the salience of various parts of his philosophy changed as his perceptions of the needs and strategies of black America shifted over time. Aloof and autonomous in his personality, Du Bois did not hesitate to depart markedly from whatever was the current mainstream of black thinking when he perceived that the conventional wisdom being enunciated by black spokesmen was proving inadequate to the task of advancing the race. His willingness to seek different solutions often placed him well in advance of his contemporaries, and this, combined with a strong-willed, even arrogant personality made his career as black leader essentially a series of stormy conflicts.

Thus Du Bois first achieved his role as a major black leader in the controversy that arose over the program of Booker T. Washington, the most prominent and influential black leader at the opening of the twentieth century. Amidst the wave of lynchings, disfranchisement, and segregation laws, Washington, seeking the goodwill of powerful whites, taught blacks not to protest against discrimination, but to elevate themselves through industrial education, hard work, and property accumulation; then, they would ultimately obtain recognition of their citizenship rights. At first Du Bois agreed with this gradualist strategy, but in 1903 with the publication of his most influential book, *Souls of Black Folk,* he became the chief leader of the onslaught against Washington that polarized the black community into two wings—the "conservative" supporters of Washington and his "radical" critics. For Du Bois, the blacks' only effective way to open the doors of opportunity was to adopt tactics of militant protest and agitation; by employing this style of propaganda, he made a key contribution to the evolution of black protest in the twentieth century—and to the civil rights movement.

Du Bois's background helps explain his divergence from the Washingtonian philosophy. From a young age, Du Bois saw himself as a future race leader, part of an elite corps of black college graduates dedicated to advancing the welfare of black people. The Tuskegean deprecated Du Bois's perspective, and although other factors were involved in the disagreement between the two men, a central issue in what became a titanic leadership struggle was Washington's denigration of the Du Boisian commitment to higher education.

Du Bois was born in Great Barrington, Massachusetts in 1868, and his sense of special mission to free black America had appeared even before his graduation at twenty from Fisk University, one of the leading black institutions of higher education. Committed to a platform of racial unity, Du Bois, while still an undergraduate, was earnestly lecturing fellow students that as "destined leaders of a noble people," they must dedicate themselves to the black masses. He declared to his classmates: "I am a Negro; and I glory in the name! . . . From all the recollections dear to my boyhood have I come here /to Fisk/, . . . to join hands with this, my people." Du Bois felt that a college degree was important because it equipped black youth with knowledge and wisdom essential to serve the race.

The first application of Du Bois's ideas about the role of an educated elite took the form of scientific investigations that were intended to advance the cause of social reform. In 1895 Du Bois became the first black to receive a Ph.D. from Harvard University, and utilizing his broad training in the social sciences, he published *The Philadelphia Negro* in 1899, the first in-depth case study of a black community in the United States. By then as a professor at Atlanta University, he had begun to publish annual sociological investigations about living conditions among blacks. Du Bois at this point in his career passionately believed that social science would provide white America's leaders with the knowledge necessary to eliminate discrimination and solve the race problem. At the same time he had seen much value in Washington's program. But with his sociological publications virtually ignored by influential reformers, and with the Negroes' status deteriorating under Washington's ascendancy, Du Bois gradually came to the conclusion that only through agitation and protest could social change ever come.

The unbridgeable differences that thus appeared between Washington's accommodating stance and Du Bois's advocacy of militant protest were rooted in personality incompatibility as well as irreconcilable emphases regarding the solution of the race problem. Du Bois felt awkward and uneasy with Washington, who, in turn, considered him haughty and arrogant and who appeared jealous of highly educated blacks with Ivy League degrees and cultural advantages. But the more serious barrier to a trusting relationship lay beyond personality. Where the heart of Du Bois's solution to the race problem lay in the hopes for the Talented Tenth—the college-trained leadership cadre responsible for elevating blacks economically and culturally—Washington was the preeminent black advocate of industrial education. Beyond this and other ideological concerns lay certain very practical conflicts: that with the popularity of industrial education the needy black colleges were slighted by the philanthropists, and that the Tuskegean—while decrying black political participation—acted as a White House broker for black appointees. Increasingly, Du Bois became incensed that Washington was using connections with the powerful to build up his own Tuskegee Machine while doing little to disturb the caste barriers that were causing devastating problems for blacks.

In 1903 Du Bois took the crucial step that led to his command of a movement dedicated to reducing Washington's influence and to raising black consciousness against the caste system. For the very first time, the Atlanta professor publicly denounced the Tuskegean for condoning white racism and for shifting to blacks the major blame for their deprivation. Charging that the accommodationist Tuskegean had brought together the South, the North, and the blacks in a monumental compromise that "practically accepted the alleged inferiority of the Negro," Du Bois declared that social justice could not be achieved through flattering racist whites; that blacks could not gain their rights by voluntarily tossing them away or by constantly belittling themselves; and that what was needed was a clamorous protest against oppression. Du Bois's critical analysis of Washington's leadership was later credited by James Weldon Johnson with effecting "a coalescence of the more radical elements . . . thereby creating a split of the race into two contending camps." Yet the camps were not evenly matched; Washington had the support of most articulate blacks and among most of those whites who displayed any interest in black advancement, and in successive battles the Du Bois forces were outmaneuvered by the wily Tuskegean.

An example of Washington's maneuvering and Du Bois's impotence was the 1904 Carnegie Hall Conference, which the Tuskegean arranged with money from white philanthropists. On the surface Washington wished to convene representatives of the two contending camps to construct a mutually acceptable platform. Washington was determined that the majority

of the conferees would be under his control, but made sufficient conciliatory gestures to Du Bois so that the latter agreed to help draw up the list of participants. Du Bois suspected Washington's motives, but convinced himself that if the "radicals" caucused beforehand and came armed with documented evidence against Washington, the latter would be so overwhelmed that he would accede to the adoption of a militant racial program. Thus Du Bois bombarded his associates with confidential memos, urging them to "hammer at" Washington's record and make the conference's "main issue" Washington's accommodation to white supremacists. Du Bois also circulated the platform for radical uplift that would form the basis of his activities as a protest leader during the next thirty years: "full political rights on the same terms as other Americans; higher education of selected Negro youth; industrial education for the masses; common school training for every Negro child; a stoppage to the campaign of self-depreciation; a careful study of the real conditions of the Negro; a national Negro periodical; . . . the raising of a defense fund; a judicious fight in the courts for civil rights."

But for all of his preconference planning, Du Bois had paid insufficient attention to the fact that Washington controlled more than enough votes to dominate the proceedings. And Washington's performance was clever—first backing a statement of principles that accorded with Du Bois's views and then manipulating the selection of the Committee of Twelve that was to carry on the conference's work. Subsequently, when this committee issued conciliatory statements downplaying black higher education and the importance of the franchise, Du Bois angrily resigned. Although his action was interpreted by some black editors as selfishness and immaturity and by sympathetic whites like New York *Evening Post* editor Oswald Garrison Villard as "a great mistake," the Atlanta professor had concluded that a viable coalition with the Tuskegean was impossible.

For the black "radicals" these events of

1903–4 propelled Du Bois into the limelight as a militant leader. Now he created two tasks for himself: to expose Washington's "veiled surrender" to the race's enemies and to organize a new black rights movement. More clearly than before, Du Bois perceived the enormous influence of his adversary. Washington's power within the black community—which was more than any other black man had previously possessed—derived from his popularity with influential white politicians and philanthropists. Moreover, to millions of whites he was the only bona fide interpreter of black wishes. Washington virtually controlled the major sources of philanthropy for black schools; he had influential connections in the black church, black press, and other race institutions; and ambitious blacks found it difficult to get ahead without his approval.

Nevertheless Du Bois initiated a frontal assault on this Tuskegee Machine in 1905, publicly charging that Washington was imposing thought control inside black America through payments of "hush money" to certain editors. More important, Du Bois was already meeting privately with fellow "radicals" in several cities, exploring the extent of potential support for a militant anti-Washington movement dedicated to protesting this accommodation to white supremacy and segregation. Yet Du Bois had to ponder the chances of survival for an organization that challenged Washington. Could it accomplish anything constructive if nearly all influential whites and the most powerful among the blacks opposed its ideas? Might a militant protest prove counterproductive by arousing a white backlash? And could Du Bois answer Washington's charge that black intellectuals were merely status-hungry elitists far removed from the black masses?

Responding to Du Bois's call, twenty-nine delegates, who had been carefully screened to eliminate "bought" and "hidebound" Washingtonians, met on the Canadian side of Niagara Falls in July 1905. The Niagara Movement, whose tiny membership was drawn chiefly from the ranks of northern college-educated

professional men, held annual meetings for the next five years. The chief function of these gatherings was to issue declarations of protest to white America. On every basic issue the Niagara men stood in direct contrast to Washington—denouncing the inequities of the separate-but-equal doctrine, the unfairness of the disfranchisement laws, and the notion that blacks were contentedly climbing from slavery by "natural and gradual processes." Niagara platforms—in whose formulation Du Bois played the most prominent role—were sharp and vigorous, clearly telling whites that they had caused the "Negro problem" and insisting that blacks should unequivocally protest. The Niagara men declared in 1905: "We repudiate the monstrous doctrine that the oppressor should be the sole authority as to the rights of the oppressed. . . . The Negro race in America, stolen, ravished, and degraded, struggling up through difficulties and oppression, needs sympathy and receives criticism, needs help and is given hindrance, needs protection and is given mob-violence, needs justice and is given charity, needs leadership and is given cowardice and apology, needs bread and is given a stone. . . . we do not hesitate to complain and to complain loudly and insistently. To ignore, overlook, or apologize for these wrongs is to prove ourselves unworthy of freedom. Persistent manly agitation is the way to liberty."

While articulating the anger of a small group of black intellectuals, the leaders of the Niagara Movement like Du Bois said they wanted to be "in close touch with the people and with intimate knowledge of their thoughts and feelings." Clearly the Atlanta professor hoped that his propaganda would both raise the consciousness of the black millions and awaken the complacent whites. And in view of the Tuskegee Machine's influence with the mass media, both black and white, not surprisingly two basic Niagara principles were "freedom of speech and criticism" and "an unfettered and unsubsidized press." As it turned out, Du Bois was very proficient at composing annual Addresses to the Nation, but powerless at removing the barriers that prevented the messages from being widely heard.

From the day of its inception Washington plotted the destruction of the Niagara Movement. He and his associates used political patronage to strengthen their hand, and they even considered the idea of having leading Niagara men fired from their federal jobs. The public speeches of key Niagara people like Du Bois were regularly monitored, and Washington, acting through his private secretary Emmett Scott, even planted spies to report what was transpiring at the organization's conventions. Yet these cloak-and-dagger operations could hardly have produced enough significant information to justify all the trouble, and the Washingtonians were far more effective in stymying the movement through their influence over the black press. Usually black editors were counseled to ignore Niagara, but for a period Scott decided that it would be more damaging if the race press would "hammer" the movement. The Tuskegean himself justified these maneuvers on the grounds that Niagara's leaders were not honest "gentlemen," and he even went so far as to subsidize key black journals in cities where his opponents were especially active.

In the large northern centers Washington had considerable contacts among white editors who easily concluded that the Niagara Movement was potentially damaging to harmonious race relations. Thus they followed the strong suggestions of Washington and his agents to ignore the activities of Du Bois and his group. Since the Tuskegean was assumed to be the blacks' only "real leader," white editors found nothing incongruous about giving the Niagara Movement the silent treatment. Indeed with the saintly image that Washington cultivated in the white media, the Niagara Movement's anti-Washington stance was beyond their comprehension. In 1906 the editor of the prominent white weekly, the *Outlook,* contrasted the pronouncements of the Tuskegean's National Negro Business League with the recent Niagara manifesto, and Washington's "pacific" group was praised because it demanded more of blacks themselves, while Du Bois's "assertive" group unreasonably demanded more of whites on behalf of blacks— to the latter's moral detriment. The Business League was lauded for focusing on achieving an "inch of progress" rather than strangling itself in a "yard of faultfinding" as the Niagara Movement was doing. Washington's supporters in the black press made even more invidious contrasts. Thus the New York *Age* asserted that blacks needed "something cheerful," which the Tuskegean offered the masses, rather than the "lugubrious" and "bitter" commentary of Niagara's jealous "aggregation of soreheads."

Despite these highly personal attacks, the Tuskegeans were correct about the lack of accomplishments of the Niagara Movement, whose local branches were usually inactive or ineffective. The Illinois unit futilely tried to mobilize when the Negrophobic *Clansman* opened at a Chicago theater, while the Massachusetts branch lobbied unsuccessfully to prevent the state legislature from appropriating tax dollars for Virginia's segregated exposition celebrating the three hundredth anniversary of the founding of Jamestown. The Niagara Movement's weakness existed less because of its leaders than because of the nation's racist social climate. Epitomizing the steady deterioration in race relations and the Niagara Movement's inability to do anything about it were the eruption in 1906 of a race riot in Atlanta, the city where Du Bois lived and worked, and later in the same year the serious miscarriage of justice at Brownsville, Texas, where despite inadequate evidence, three companies of black soldiers were dishonorably discharged on unproven charges of "shooting up" the Texas town. Helplessly the Niagara Movement issued an "Address to the World" attacking President Theodore Roosevelt (to whom enfranchised blacks had long given political allegiance) for his unfair treatment of the soldiers.

The 1907 Niagara conference was very depressing, with Du Bois himself conceding his own "inexperience" as a leader and admitting that the movement was now operating with "less momentum" and with considerable "internal strain." Indeed during the conclave he had a serious falling-out with Boston *Guardian* editor William Monroe Trotter, one of the earliest and most prominent critics of Washington. With this controversy further damaging the Movement's morale, the organization limped along; most of its 400 members even declined to pay the modest annual dues. When the fourth annual conference opened in 1908 soon after the Springfield, Illinois, race riot, the small band of black militants faced its own impotence and the powerlessness of a race that could not count on the authorities for protection even in the North. The leaders could only curse the "Negro haters of America" and remind blacks that they possessed the right to use guns against white mobs.

While the Niagara Movement was thus falling apart, Du Bois, undoubtedly to compensate for the organization's inability to obtain publicity, managed to implement his long-held dream of editing a militant "national Negro magazine" that would be a vehicle for his agitation. Although an earlier effort to publish a periodical of "new race consciousness," the *Moon,* had failed after a brief existence, Du Bois and two associates (F. H. M. Murray and L. M. Hershaw, both civil servants in Washington) had in 1907 started publishing *Horizon,* the Niagara Movement's unofficial organ. As Du Bois informed the *Horizon*'s early subscribers, "We need a journal, not as a matter of business, but as a matter of spiritual life and death." The journal enunciated the Niagara Movement's philosophy and sought to convert the slight voting power of northern Negroes into a racial asset. Preaching that blacks owed nothing to the Republicans, it condemned the GOP and hammered away at the theme that Secretary of War William Howard Taft (associated with Roosevelt in the Brownsville injustice and a veteran apologist for the southern caste system as well as a denigrator of

higher education for blacks) had to be prevented from reaching the White House in 1908 as Roosevelt's successor. But the Tuskegee Machine, operating on the Republicans' behalf, flailed away at Du Bois's political defection to the Democrats; to the disappointment of the editors of *Horizon,* on election day most black voters made Washington's choice their own. Not surprisingly, Du Bois's two colleagues on the *Horizon* had placed their government jobs in jeopardy because of their service to the race. Charles W. Anderson, who as collector of Internal Revenue in New York was a prominent Republican politician in the Tuskegee Machine, tried to persuade the president to fire the pair.

Given the temper of the times and the power of the Tuskegean, Du Bois found himself frustrated. He discovered that there were not enough blacks willing and able to make the magazine self-supporting, and for a while he and his two associates underwrote the deficit. In 1910 both the *Horizon* and the Niagara Movement finally died. Although Du Bois declared himself pleased that there was now within the race "increasing spiritual unrest, sterner impatience with cowardice and deeper determination to be men at any cost," obviously much more work remained to educate blacks away from the accommodation to white supremacy that the Washingtonians preached. While there was no doubt that the Tuskegean had seriously weakened Niagara, it is important to reemphasize that the movement's basic problem was the nation's virulent racism that had catapulted a leader like Washington into power. Even if Du Bois had demonstrated superlative leadership skills, Niagara's program of uncompromising protest for equal treatment was too far ahead of white public opinion, and this fact damaged the movement's propaganda campaign. Of course, Du Bois's personality exacerbated the problem and made it difficult for him to be a successful organizational leader. As he later freely conceded, he appeared "aristocratic and aloof," and his "natural reticence" and "hatred of forwardness" were serious impediments. Although Du Bois "hated the role" of being Niagara's top leader, Washington, in contrast, thrived in his leadership position, operating facilely as a diplomat, politician, and tactician. Given Du Bois's insensitivity to interpersonal problems and his inadequacy in handling them, his signal contribution to Niagara had been as a propagandist, writing manifestos, articles, and speeches, always showing whites that racism pervaded their social institutions and showing blacks the importance of vigorous protest. Far ahead of his time, virtually a voice in the wilderness, Du Bois articulated better than any of his contemporaries the hope for equal citizenship rights that American blacks never relinquished.

With the Niagara Movement hovering near death, it was clear that the resources to make the black protest movement viable would have to be found elsewhere. Du Bois and other leading "radicals" had been in touch with the small number of prominent whites who were becoming disillusioned with Washington's accommodationist platform. Du Bois concluded that an interracial protest movement was essential, considering the devastating problems that his black movement had experienced and the increased resources and legitimization that prominent whites could provide. It was the mob violence at Springfield in 1908 that finally convinced this group of whites of the absolute necessity of forming an interracial protest organization possessing the aims or goals of the Niagara Movement. Through publicity directed at the whole nation, through litigation in the courts and lobbying in the legislature, this new organization called the National Association for the Advancement of Colored People hoped to topple the walls of race discrimination. Du Bois became the principal black founder and the most prominent Niagara veteran connected with the NAACP.

Although the membership was overwhelmingly black, for nearly a decade the NAACP was largely white-funded and white-dominated, and Du Bois was the only black in its inner circle. He performed a very significant role in the organization—serving as the embodiment of militant protest, the link to the small band of black "radicals," and the symbol to the public of demonstrably successful interracial cooperation. Beyond these contributions lay his more significant asset to the NAACP as its chief propagandist. As director of Publicity and Research, he founded the *Crisis* in 1910 and edited this influential NAACP official organ for a quarter-century.

In many ways Du Bois was all that the white founders had hoped for. It is true that he was not intimately involved in the administrative work of the NAACP, and only on rare occasions did he even attempt to influence policy. He quite consciously confined himself to his work as *Crisis* editor and saw his role as being a molder of public opinion—chiefly among blacks. As *Crisis* editor he recorded and supported the NAACP program for constitutional rights; he stirred up intellectual controversies, commented on current events related to the race problem, and provided arguments for racial equalitarianism. His expressions of protest were clearly, sharply, and often dramatically written, in sentences sometimes so aphoristic that black readers cherished them: *"I am resolved to be quiet and law abiding, but to refuse to cringe in body or in soul, to resent deliberate insult, and to assert my just rights in the face of wanton aggression."* "Oppression costs the oppressor too much if the oppressed stand up and protest." "Agitate, then, brother; protest, reveal the truth and refuse to be silenced." "A moment's let up, a moment's acquiescence, means a chance for the wolves of prejudice to get at our necks." The reverence that many black families had for the magazine was described by the writer, J. Saunders Redding, who recollected that in his boyhood home the only periodical that the children could not touch was the *Crisis,* which "was strictly inviolate until my father himself had unwrapped and read it—often . . . aloud" to the family.

At last Du Bois had fulfilled the vision that had inspired him for so many years. The *Crisis* was his opportunity to edit a national black journal of opinion to which people would listen. As early as 1913, when the NAACP could scarcely attract 3,000 members, the circulation of the *Crisis*—chiefly among blacks—reached 30,000. Clearly Du Bois was making a considerable impact. Yet given his personality and his deep-seated desire for autonomy, the public image of harmony within the NAACP was belied by the battling that erupted between Du Bois and certain key board members.

The basic problem involved how much independence Du Bois as the only board member who was also a paid NAACP executive would have in operating the organization's official magazine, and what contributions to other NAACP activities were required of him. Du Bois, who was frequently unavailable for organizational chores like writing pamphlets, regarded the *Crisis* as "the only work" in the NAACP "which attracts me." In fact, he believed that the *Crisis,* rather than serving the NAACP as its interpreter to the public, was the one vehicle—through raising the consciousness of thousands of blacks—that could "make the NAACP *possible."* Demanding "independence of action" in running the *Crisis,* Du Bois was determined "to prove the possibilities of a Negro magazine," and he clashed with two successive white board chairmen—Villard (who was dictatorial and seemed at times subtly prejudiced) and Joel Spingarn (whom Du Bois described as a "knight" untarnished by any racist tendencies). To these board chairmen, faced with the problem of stretching limited funds to cover such vital activities as branch development and legal redress, the *Crisis* did not have the same priority that it had for Du Bois. And when the *Crisis* editor published materials that the other NAACP leaders felt were tactically ill advised and even harmful to the organization, open conflict resulted.

Villard was determined that the *Crisis* editor like other paid executives should be subordinated to the board chairman. Moreover, he resented that although the magazine was the property of the NAACP, and despite its large circulation not self-supporting, Du Bois wanted to "carry it around in his pocket." In protest Villard resigned as chairman in late 1913, being replaced by Spingarn—but the board struggle with the editor continued. Spingarn was more understanding than Villard and wanted to see a black editor like Du Bois exercise maximum influence, but he also believed that Du Bois's difficult personality produced situations that damaged the organization. Indeed there were even times when the NAACP, in its drive for black support, was acutely embarrassed by the editor's attacks on black ministers, journalists, and educators. For example, in 1912 Du Bois had indicted the Negro churches: "the paths and the higher places are choked with pretentious ill-trained men . . . in far too many cases with men dishonest and otherwise immoral." Two years later at a time when the NAACP desperately needed support from the black press, Du Bois fired a volley against these weeklies, claiming that many were not "worth reprinting or even reading" because their editors were venal, empty-headed, or ungrammatical. The barrage did not go unanswered, and Du Bois created a serious public relations problem for the NAACP.

Du Bois's original indiscretion had been precipitated by his acute sensitivity to a black newspaper's comment that the *Crisis* was financially dependent on an NAACP subsidy. Moreover the subsidy was one that the NAACP found it hard to afford, especially with a recent recession sharply reducing the organization's income. Nonetheless, Spingarn and the board reluctantly acceded to Du Bois's demands for more staff and office space—at a time when the national administrative office with fund-raising responsibilities shouldered by a small staff was forced to accept budgetary cuts. Because of such incidents, Spingarn, although having the highest respect for Du Bois, like Villard, eventually concluded that the *Crisis* editor was exercising too much autonomy and reluctantly announced his own intention to resign as chairman. Yet in the end Spingarn had too much admiration for Du Bois's contributions to make more than a gentle rebuke. In 1916 he and the board agreed that the *Crisis* under Du Bois could not simply be a house organ and that its editorials must be permitted to represent Du Bois's opinions within the framework of broad NAACP policy.

By 1916 in the wake of Washington's death, Du Bois became the nation's most prominent black leader, freed now from the heavy burden of competing with the Tuskegean. To the end the *Crisis* editor had remained Washington's most implacable foe among NAACP leaders. Even before Washington's death, a noticeable shift in sentiment had begun among leading blacks, which was reflected in the successful attempts to organize NAACP branches. This shift reflected not only the growing stature of Du Bois and the NAACP, but changing social conditions as well. With increasing urbanization and educational attainment and with more migration to the North, growing numbers of blacks by World War I were embracing Du Bois's doctrine of agitation and protest.

Ironically, with the passing of Washington from the scene and the decline of Tuskegee's influence, Du Bois and the NAACP now occupied a centrist rather than a "radical" role in the black community, and the editor of the *Crisis* even found himself on occasion attacked for conservatism and lack of militancy. To some extent Du Bois made himself vulnerable on this score, since during World War I he muted his criticism. Hopeful that with the return of peace blacks would be rewarded for their contributions to the war that was supposed "to make the world safe for democracy," he had urged blacks to "forget our special grievances" and "close ranks" with fellow white Americans in the battle against the country's European enemies. Not only did a number of black editors openly criticize Du Bois for this stand, but during the war and postwar years the young socialist A. Philip Randolph stridently condemned the NAACP spokesman as a "hand-picked, me-too-boss, hat-in-hand, sycophant, lick spittling" Negro.

For his part, Du Bois, disillusioned by the new spurt in racism and the resurgence of mob violence that followed the war, composed some of the most ringingly militant editorials of his career. Enraged when he discovered evidence that black soldiers who had risked their lives in Europe were discriminated against by the American military establishment there, Du Bois documented these facts in a special *Crisis* issue that also featured an editorial, "Returning Soldiers": "By the God of Heaven, we are cowards and jackasses if now that the war is over, we do not marshal every ounce of our brain and brawn to fight a sterner, longer, more unbending battle against the forces of hell in our own land. *We return. We return from fighting. We return fighting.* Make way for Democracy! We saved it in France, and by the Great Jehovah, we will save it in the United States of America, or know the reason why."

This particular number of the *Crisis,* which sold 100,000 copies, was not only widely discussed among blacks but created a furor outside the race. To say that certain U.S. government officials were alarmed is putting it mildly. The Post Office Department held up the copies while debating whether to allow them through the mails. Representative James Byrnes of South Carolina, epitomizing the sentiment of many in Congress, delivered a speech charging that Du Bois and other black newsmen had precipitated the postwar rioting. Although white mobs had caused most of the bloodshed, Byrnes singled out "Returning Soldiers" as the inspiration for black violence, holding that Du Bois should be indicted for having encouraged resistance to the government. Du Bois's fury continued unabated, and he warned blacks again to arm themselves against white mobs. The Justice Department, also anxious about "Returning Soldiers," investigated the *Crisis,* Randolph's *Messenger,* and other black periodicals. Noting that blacks like Du Bois had counseled retaliatory violence against white attackers, the department reported that black newsmen were actually "antagonistic to the white race and openly defiantly assertive of [their] own equality and even superiority."

As noted earlier, there had always been a strong nationalist strain in Du Bois's thinking, and in the postwar era this aspect of his propaganda became the focus of another controversy—his acrimonious struggle with the famous black separatist leader, Marcus Garvey. The most influential aspect of Du Bois's nationalism had been his pioneering advocacy of Pan-Africanism, the belief that all people of African descent had common interests and should unite in the struggle for their freedom. Moreover, he articulated both a cultural nationalism encouraging the development of black literature and art and an economic nationalism urging blacks to create a separate "group economy."

All of these themes had been expressed much earlier. Thus in an 1897 paper aptly entitled "The Conservation of Races," Du Bois enunciated the doctrine of "Pan-Negroism"—that regardless of what nation they lived in, Africans and their descendants had a common identity and should feel an emotional commitment to one another. American blacks, the vanguard of blacks the world over, should have a special attachment to Africa as the race's "greater fatherland." Arguing that "the Negro people as a race have a contribution to make to civilization and humanity, which no other race can make," he maintained that blacks possessed "a distinct mission as a race . . . to soften the whiteness" of an uninspiring materialistic Teutonic culture that seemed to dominate the world. Accordingly, Du Bois argued that Afro-Americans should maintain their group identity and institutions; for them salvation would come only from an educated elite who would chart the way to cultural and economic elevation, teaching the doctrine that blacks "MUST DO FOR THEMSELVES," by developing their own businesses, newspapers, schools, and welfare institutions.

Later Du Bois used the *Crisis* as a vehicle for cultural nationalism. Calling for the systematic cultivation of all kinds of black art forms, he proudly presented works by young black novelists, essayists, painters, and poets, and in the early 1920s he proposed an Institute of Negro Literature and Art. Determined to harness the race's creative strivings, he told defeatists, "Off with these thought-chains and inchoate soul-shrinkings, and let us train ourselves to see beauty in black." Blacks were "a different kind" of people, possessing the spirit and power to build a "new and great Negro ethos." The race, armed with "group ideals," could bring forth a flood of artistic and literary creation based on themes in black life and black history. Above all, blacks could enrich themselves and America only by defining their own standards of beauty, rather than permitting whites to define them.

The *Crisis* also taught lessons in economic nationalism. Early in his life Du Bois had made bourgeois pleas for black capitalist enterprises based on the Negro market, but after coming under Socialist influences during his leadership of the Niagara Movement, he began advocating black consumers' and producers' cooperatives as a basic weapon for fighting discrimination and poverty. Du Bois devoted considerable space in the *Crisis* to stimulate readers to open cooperative stores, and in 1918 he helped form the Negro Cooperative Guild, which hoped to set up retail stores, cooperative warehouses, and even banks. Du Bois believed that white racism, by reducing the range of black incomes, had unintentionally made a socialized black economy feasible. Blacks, rather than aspiring to be rapacious millionaires, would find it satisfying to be "consecrated" workers devoted to "social service" for the race. Du Bois saw no reason why this "closed economic circle" could not encompass a complex racial manufacturing-distributive system, with profits reinvested in useful race projects like large housing developments. Moreover, a black cooperative system could be extended to race members in far off places like Africa.

Du Bois's cultural nationalism was intimately related to the stirrings among black intellectuals and artists known as the Harlem Renaissance, but his quasi-socialistic brand of economic nationalism was never widely accepted. Even his more influential Pan-Africanism was really not a central element in Afro-American thinking at that period. Du Bois had probably been the first black American to develop explicitly the concept of Pan-Africanism; certainly of all the black American intellectuals, he was the one most deeply identified with Africa itself—at a time when most Afro-Americans were embarrassed by the "primitiveness" of their ancestral societies. In 1900 Du Bois had been a leader in the first Pan-African Conference, and as chairman of its "Committee on the Address to the Nations of the World," he called for the creation of "a great central Negro State of the World" in Africa, which would raise the status of blacks wherever they lived. No sooner had World War I ended when, amidst the discussion of European imperialism and the disposition of the German colonies in Africa, Du Bois again took up the Pan-African theme and convened four Pan-African congresses in Europe and the United States between 1919 and 1927. Urging the recognition of the "absolute equality of races" and the end of imperialist exploitation of blacks everywhere, these conclaves focused on racial developments in Africa and were, in fact, a concrete application of his notion that black intellectuals should lead the race into the future.

His nationalist Pan-African Movement shared several parallels with the integrationist Niagara Movement: it was dominated by Du Bois's towering personality; it attracted only a very small segment of the Talented Tenth; it suffered from serious internal schisms; it exemplified his strength as a propagandist leader and his weakness as an organizational leader; it clashed sharply with a popular black spokesman of the period; and yet it was important as an ideological forerunner of very significant future developments among Afro-Americans.

When Du Bois revived the Pan-African Movement in 1919, he had hoped that the NAACP would be a base of grass-roots support. But neither the black middle and upper classes who were the readers of the *Crisis* and the backbone of the NAACP's supporters nor the masses of the black poor rallied to it. The NAACP contributed only token funds and considered the movement UNIA incompatible with its basic thrust. Since Du Bois largely isolated himself from the machinery of the NAACP and was not essentially an organizational leader, he did almost nothing to convince the board to adopt his cause as their own. Certainly Du Bois did not try to alter the thinking of the leadership in conferences with key officials or in board meetings. Nor did he seek to organize NAACP branch officials behind the Pan-African Movement. Characteristically, he attempted to proselytize through *Crisis* editorials and seemed satisfied to persuade the NAACP to make occasional official statements (which he wrote) supporting his views on Africa.

Like the Niagara Movement, these Pan-African congresses were beset by insuperable external and internal problems. Basically in an imperialist age Du Bois lacked bargaining power to pressure the European nations to liberate their subject peoples. Impotent, the Pan-African Movement could assume only a conciliatory stance and produce respectful petitions that obtained for Du Bois a hearing from minor officials. Still, conciliation won permission to hold the Pan-African Congress in places like London, Paris, and Brussels. Conciliation also gained the support of influential Africans like Blaise Diagne, a Senegalese representative in France's Chamber of Deputies, but such friends did not prove to be anticolonialists, and this fact precipitated a serious split within Du Bois's movement.

Yet in a period dominated by rampant imperialism a confrontational approach, such as Garvey's nationalist Universal Negro Improvement Association (UNIA), got no further than Du Bois did. But Garvey succeeded in causing considerable problems for Du Bois and his movement. Originally Du Bois had been impressed by Garvey's Black Star Steamship Line, the company founded in 1919 to link blacks in

Africa and the New World. Hoping for Garvey's cooperation, he thought that the UNIA might bring to fruition his own Pan-Africanist dreams. But Du Bois soon decided that the line was being financially mismanaged and that Garvey was self-destructive in defiantly threatening the imperialist nations while being powerless to back up the threats. For their part, Garvey and his associates decided that Du Bois was merely a jealous rival, and an "aristocratic" Uncle Tom "controlled" by white money—in fact, the *Crisis* editor was pronounced "more of a white man than a Negro." Besides being subjected to this sort of criticism from the Garveyites, Du Bois was bombarded by white journalists who confused his movement with the UNIA and queried the *Crisis* editor about plans to expel whites from Africa. During the early 1920s, when the UNIA attracted hundreds of thousands of followers, the Pan-African Congress barely managed to stay alive, and as with the Niagara Movement most members did little, not even paying their annual dues. Moreover, the problem of inactivity was exacerbated by the serious split between the French and American members. Finally in futility Du Bois announced that if the Afro-American Talented Tenth did not rally around the movement he was ready to give it up, and although another Pan-African Congress was held in 1927, it was a perfunctory affair, and Du Bois's hopes were unrealized again. (As "elder statesman" of the movement, he was later associated with the post–World War II Fifth Pan-African Congress held in England in 1945.)

Regardless of his differences with the NAACP on Pan-Africa and other matters, Du Bois usually could be counted upon to defend the organization publicly. Thus in 1921 when the *Crisis* exonerated the board of charges of undemocratic domination, its editor declared, "It is foolish for us to give up this practical program." But behind the scenes, however, the potential for serious disruption was inherent in the ongoing problem of competition for scarce resources. Money difficulties became even more acute during the 1920s because the circulation of the *Crisis* fell drastically, from over 100,000 in 1919 to about 30,000 in 1930. Du Bois expected the board to cover the deficit, and the board did so, although his colleagues would undoubtedly have been more agreeable to providing additional money had Du Bois been willing to make the *Crisis* more decidedly the house organ of the NAACP and to devote more pages to the organization's national projects as well as branch activities. But Du Bois found that route unpalatable—he still insisted that he must "blaze a trail" and perform "a work of education and ideal beyond the practical steps of the N.A.A.C.P."

At the end of the 1920s the financial crunch facing the *Crisis* set the stage for a serious, in one sense fatal, conflict between Du Bois and new NAACP Executive Secretary Walter White. White disliked Du Bois intensely and believed that the *Crisis* had become the NAACP's rather superfluous tail; for Du Bois, of course, it was still the other way around. In 1929 White protested that Du Bois's requests for ever-larger subsidies were being granted only at the expense of a weakened administrative office and were becoming a luxury that could be afforded no longer. But the board managed to find the money until the Great Depression set in, when its members paid more attention to White's admonitions that scarce dollars could be better spent on antilynching campaigns, court cases, and legislative lobbying.

Du Bois's problem was that as the Depression deepened, White's powers grew not only in the administrative office but also in matters directly affecting the *Crisis*. Thus in 1931, after the magazine lost another several thousand dollars (although the NAACP was paying Du Bois's entire salary), the Crisis Publishing Company was organized (with White on the board of directors) as a legal maneuver to limit the NAACP's liability for the obligations of the *Crisis*. Du Bois fought back, ostensibly to overhaul the NAACP's structure but actually to strip

White of much of his power. First the *Crisis* editor informed the board that its members were undemocratically chosen since the rank-and-file throughout the country had no voice in the selection process. Then in 1932 he went public with his charges and called for transferring the central office's power to the branches; simultaneously he urged that the NAACP adopt a program that would replace the "mere negative attempt to avoid segregation and discrimination." In his solution to the many problems posed by the Depression, Du Bois went beyond the NAACP's official program of protecting constitutional rights and revived his old dream for systematic "voluntary segregation" in the form of a separate black cooperative economy. "That race pride and race loyalty, Negro ideals and Negro unity have a place and function today, the NAACP never has denied and never can deny!" Refusing to accept Du Bois's distinction between enforced and voluntary separation, White and Spingarn challenged the *Crisis* editor, contending that he was undermining the decades-long struggle against segregation. White declared that blacks "must, without yielding, continue the grim struggle *for* integration" and stop the damage that Du Bois was inflicting on the organization. The whole debate degenerated into bitter personal recriminations between White and the *Crisis* editor. Defeated, Du Bois resigned in 1934 and returned to his old professorship at Atlanta University.

Neither inside nor outside the NAACP had there been any groundswell of support for Du Bois's position. The Talented Tenth by and large was marching to a different drummer. Black intellectuals like the sociologist E. Franklin Frazier, the political scientist Ralph Bunche, and the former NAACP Executive Secretary James Weldon Johnson all repudiated his separatism, arguing that an all-black economy in an era of black powerlessness could easily be destroyed by "the legal and police forces of the state /which/ would inevitably be aligned against them." Most critics actually viewed Du Bois's call as retrogression, a return to Washington's accommodationist apologia for segregation.

Thus Du Bois had created serious problems for himself. His "voluntary segregation" campaign put him outside the mainstream of the civil rights movement in the mid-1930s, and in severing his *Crisis* ties he had given up the platform that was essential for his role as propagandist. Although he remained a venerated symbol, he had lost his position of effective leadership. No longer was he the molder and shaper of Negro opinion that he had been since the early part of the century.

During the 1940s Du Bois downplayed the plan for a separate economy, but he gradually identified himself with pro-Russian causes, thus drifting further from the main currents of black thinking at the time. In 1951 he was tried in federal court on charges of being an unregistered agent of a foreign power, and although the judge directed an acquittal, Du Bois became so thoroughly disillusioned about the United States that in 1961 he officially joined the Communist party and moved to Ghana.

Du Bois continued to write and lecture until the end of his life, but the output of his last three decades had slight impact among his black American contemporaries. Then, ironically, shortly after his departure from the United States, Du Bois's reputation soared, and he was transformed into a prophet. In the early 1960s the militant integrationist phase of the black direct-action protest movement was building toward its climax, and his enormous contributions became widely recognized and revered among young activists. Du Bois died on the very day that one-quarter of a million people gathered at the March on Washington—August 27, 1963. Moments before the mammoth march departed from the Washington Monument, the vast assemblage stood bowed in silent tribute at the announcement of his death. Later at the Lincoln Memorial Roy Wilkins, now executive secretary of the NAACP, referred to Du Bois's vast contributions to the long struggle for black freedom. Then a few years afterward, with the decline of militant integrationism and the ascendancy of the Black Power Era with its separatist thrust, the relevance of his nationalist writings became widely appreciated.

W. E. B. Du Bois, the propagandist, had now become symbol and prophet, and events both in the United States and abroad vindicated the celebrated words he had used in *Souls of Black Folk* in 1903: "The problem of the Twentieth Century is the problem of the color line."

12

PUBLIC OPINION AND CIVIL LIBERTIES IN WARTIME, 1917–1919

O. A. HILTON

Of the many problems that war presents to liberal democratic societies, none has proved more difficult to solve than the wartime protection of civil liberties. As many writers have observed, war requires a total and unquestioning commitment of a nation's people and resources. Yet at the same time, liberal democracies rest on the individual and collective right to dissent and reject such total commitment. These issues have been raised in each of America's wars from the Revolution to Vietnam, and in each case the question of dissent has been answered with a combination of government suppression and private intimidation. In this essay, O. A. Hilton surveys the role public opinion played in enforcing consent during World War I. At the beginning of the war in 1914 many groups, including the Non-Partisan League and Eugene V. Debs's Socialist party, worked to prevent American involvement in the European conflict. But once the United States entered the war in 1917, all talk of pacifism and noninvolvement was quickly labeled unpatriotic and seditious. As Hilton points out, extralegal state and local groups often took on the mantle of authority during the war in their private campaign to suppress dissent and enforce commitment to the war effort.

From the *Southwestern Social Science Quarterly* 28:201–24 (1947). Reprinted with the permission of the University of Texas Press.

The influence of public opinion in extending or restricting civil liberties has long been recognized by students of law and government. But so long as government was weak and its administrative functions poorly organized, the potentialities of propaganda not recognized and public opinion divided, interferences with personal liberties were usually sporadic in character and probably did not affect the foundations of constitutional government.

The years of the First World War probably furnish the most profitable period in our history to observe the relationship between public opinion and the restrictions upon individual liberties which had been commonly regarded as automatically protected by the Bill of Rights. During the period, almost every conceivable form of propaganda and coercion was employed on a scale sufficiently wide to be noticeable. Public opinion became highly unified, and one might almost say that it was nearly hysterical at times. These events were concentrated within a short period, so that the war years furnish a kaleidoscopic view of experiences which at other times would require years of history to unroll.

The techniques of the control of public opinion were but dimly understood in 1917, and probably no one at the outset had any conception of an overall pattern which could be employed effectively. But in this time of crisis and emotional stimulation a pattern does emerge through the fact that from time to time, and in one section of the country or another, every means then known was tried in swaying public opinion and in silencing those whose views differed radically from the unified majority.

—1—

Within a few months after the Declaration of War on April 6, 1917, the use of pressure tactics to coerce the minority into line had reached a high state of refinement. At the center of the periphery of pressure groups was the state council of defense with its county and local councils. Usually it was closely allied with the state units of the federal agencies, such as the Liberty Loan Committee, Food and Fuel Administrators, and the like. Some of the councils were statutory bodies, but slightly more than half of them were created simply by appointment of the governor, and hence had no more actual authority than he was able to delegate to them. On the whole, however, any distinction between the statutory and non-statutory councils is largely an artificial one. In general, one might say that lack of legal authority was no great handicap to a determined state council which understood the potentialities inherent in the war psychosis.

This power was recognized quite generally, and occasionally is stated naively. For example, the South Dakota Council of Defense sent a circular letter to the county councils in which it made specific reference to the fact that some persons had refused to subscribe to the amount of Liberty Bonds which had been apportioned to them by committees. "Such persons," the letter stated, "come under our classification as slackers," and where they can afford to take a certain amount of bonds "can justly be suspicioned as being in opposition to the policy of our government." And more specifically the letter went on to state that: *"There is no law upon our statute books governing such cases, but in these times there is a recognition of authority that has the right and power to inquire into the general conditions and reasons. . . ."* The county councils were advised to subpoena the delinquents and interrogate them about their ability to buy bonds.

The same attitude was shown in a smaller sphere by the chairman of one county council in Oklahoma, who announced that he was going to make it his duty to determine what securities were necessary to the conduct of the war. Salesmen for those which were not would find other jobs or be asked to leave the county. He stated that until the legislature enacted laws to weed out "unnecessary and unreliable corporations," which he was sure would be done at the next session, "it is the duty of patriotic men of Oklahoma to defend their neighbors against misguidance."

The operations of the Food Administration reflect much the same point of view. From the official history of the Food Administration, we quote:

> The *penalties* for the violation of the law against profiteering *were stricken out by Congress,* and therefore legal action became a matter of withdrawal of license or some public expression of contrition or some sale of food at nominal consideration to the government departments such as the Army or Navy or the Grain Corporation. Such contributions to the Red Cross and other charities exceeded $500,-000, and the value of the food sold to government departments at a nominal consideration exceeded $1,000,000. The flour millers entered into agreement to turn over any profits in excess of agreed amount by a nominal sale to the Grain Corporation, and such receipts exceeded $6,000,000. All together, *8,800 cases were handled* by the Enforcement Division in Washington *in which some penalty was inflicted.*

In other words, the agency deemed certain controls to be necessary although Congress had refused to provide these through authorizing penalties, and consequently the administrators must find some means of enforcing their edicts. This they did either by bringing public pressure to bear so strongly on offenders that the latter dared not disobey the orders of the food administrators and paid fines to the Red Cross or other agencies, or by compelling the wholesalers and jobbers to refuse to sell to offending retailers under threat of having their licenses revoked.

Whether in relation to financial drives, food, or unpopular utterances, pressure and intimidation were widely used with little regard to legal or constitutional rights, or their implications for the democracy we claimed to be fighting a war to preserve. Certain so-called Russian colonies in South Dakota, which were incorporated for religious purposes, refused to buy Liberty Bonds. It was charged that a local Liberty Loan committee, upon the colonists' refusal to purchase bonds, seized some of their stock and sold it at public auction. Apparently the group ultimately gave way under pressure, agreed to dissolve, and invest the proceeds of the communal property sale in bonds, which would be divided among the members according to a disposition to be made by the state council of defense.

The New Mexico Council sent a circular letter to the county councils which strongly hinted that they should follow the example of the Guadaloupe County Council. The latter had sent letters to individuals informing them that they had uttered remarks unbecoming to a person "enjoying the Liberty and Protection of the United States," and "emphatically that such conduct will not be tolerated." Furthermore, a second complaint would bring such remedy "as is necessary to counteract seditious conduct, and we are acting under orders given us by the Governor. . . ." The offender was also reminded that he would "be kept under surveillance from this time on, and our action depends entirely upon your department."

In many places census cards were used on which were listed the wealth of the individual (usually estimated, although sometimes obtained by canvass,) his investment in Liberty Bonds and War Savings Stamps, contributions to the Red Cross, Y.M.C.A., and other agencies, as well as other information. From these the councils, Liberty Loan committees and other war boards arranged individual quotas and determined whether a man was doing his "fair share." The following extract from a report of the War Service Board of Council Bluffs, Iowa, on the Second Liberty Loan illustrates the effectiveness of the assessment method. "One township in this county, whose quota was $50,-000, reported but $15,000, was shown the light, made a recanvass and returned triumphantly in a few days with $67,000 having simply made an assessment of so much per acre on every farm and gone out and collected it."

In many communities, including Council

Bluffs, above mentioned, "courts" were set up before which were brought those who refused to accept the quotas fixed for them, and also in many cases those who had made utterances which jarred the sensibilities of the patriots or perhaps those who had actually uttered seditious remarks, though these were more likely to be reported to federal authorities. Legal appearing summons, which of course had no legal status whatever, were probably sufficient to convince most offenders that they should surrender to the demands made upon them when they appeared before the "court." Certain communities, of which Milwaukee would be a good example, were particularly sensitive to the reputations they had in other parts of the country and used arbitrary means to raise more funds than their quotas called for, in order to prove their patriotism. Other towns threatened to place the names of recalcitrants on a Dishonor Roll which would be exhibited in a prominent place. To classify a merchant as a "pro-German" or a "slacker" was sufficient to ruin his business in many localities; and refusal to take the amount fixed might place him in one or another category. Stories of merchants appearing in the morning to find their store fronts painted yellow were not too uncommon over the country. While in many cases such jobs may have been the work of hoodlums of rather tender age, nevertheless the value of such acts to competitors is obvious.

In the Northwest the Nonpartisan League had a phenomenal growth among the farmers just preceding the entry of the United States into the war and during the first few months of hostilities. Its grievances were chiefly economic and were directed against the millers and other middlemen. The League regarded the old parties as being aligned with the "vested" interests and turned to politics to secure control entirely. Its program was a form of agrarian socialism, and hence it was rather natural that the League leaders should have had something of the same attitude toward the war that many members of the Socialist Party had, i. e., it was a rich man's war and a poor man's fight. This attitude was not expressed clearly, however; instead the League demanded reforms of the tax structure and other changes which opponents claimed was for the purpose of dividing the people in their support of the war. Though its grievances were chiefly economic in character, its questioning of motives in the war and methods of paying for it made its patriotism and loyalty subject to grave doubts by its enemies. The rapid growth of the League in Minnesota and its political activities threatened to end the conservative Republican control of the state government in the fall election of 1918. Urban interests in many Minnesota towns took a most intolerant stand against the League organizers. The Minnesota Commission of Public Safety, probably the most powerful state council in the nation, accepted the view that the organization was disloyal; but instead of trying to persuade the members to change their views they attempted to crush the League—and succeeded to a remarkable degree.

The Wilson administration became convinced that the situation in the Northwest was dangerous. The administration leaders feared an explosion might occur in the Northwest, particularly in Minnesota, unless measures were taken to settle the grievances and change the attitude of the farmers. Consequently, through the Committee on Public Information and the Council of National Defense, plans were made to route speakers through the section under the auspices of the Nonpartisan League. The Public Safety Commission refused to permit them to speak under such auspices, but asked to use the speakers themselves. Though perhaps maintaining an officially correct position, the Safety Commission indirectly encouraged the use of force and other arbitrary tactics against the League. The files of the Safety Commission contain many accounts of actions by the county commissions and peace officers prohibiting or breaking up Nonpartisan League meetings. Instead of repudiating such tactics, the State Commission followed some such procedure as the following. A county commission of public safety would notify the state body that A. C. Townley, or another of the leaders, was scheduled to address a meeting in a certain town at a specified date, and inquire if the Commission could prevent it. The Safety Commission would reply that it had no power to prevent the meeting, but would then cite the provisions of the Minnesota statutes which provided that the sheriff of a county had authority to prevent any meeting which in his opinion would result in violence and disorder. With that broad hint, it was rather easy to make arrangements which would insure that disorder would result, and to persuade the sheriff that the meeting should be prohibited. In one case, Mr. Townley was notified not to speak in the county and was informed that "if you persist in trying to talk here we have made arrangements with our Mayor who has given orders to the police force not to interfere if small boys (and others) use ancient eggs and other missiles wherewith to punctuate your discourse."

The Montana State Council ordered the public schools to cease using a textbook on Ancient History written by Professor Willis Mason West, because he gave too favorable a treatment of the Teutonic tribes prior to the year 812 A.D. At the time, West was assisting the Committee on Public Information. The Oklahoma Council prohibited travelling shows from exhibiting in the state. The Texas Council instructed the county councils to discourage the use of trading stamps by merchants, although there was no state statute covering such action. Many state councils agitated against the German language and in several cases openly, or in effect, prohibited its use in the schools or other public places. The Governor of Iowa prohibited the use of all languages except English in schools and churches and in conversations in public places. The South Dakota Council prohibited the use of German in public places, with one exception—it would issue permits for its use at funerals.

Although there is no record of its actual use, the potentialities of utilizing the legal machinery for intimidation are illustrated by the following incident. An Iowa lawyer who was "chairman of the Waterloo Council of Defense; one of the judges of the American Defense Society branch, viz: Waterloo Vigilance Corps, and Judge Advocate of the Waterloo Service League," and whose duties in all of these organizations was "to pass upon the loyalty of suspected persons," complained to the United States District Attorney that his organizations were having considerable difficulty with the disloyal because they could not enforce their judgments. He was certain that disloyalty was increasing, and that the law was inadequate to deal with pro-Germans. Since it seemed impossible to get evidence upon which to convict the culprits he suggested that if the latter were put under heavy bond to appear before grand juries, or in default were committed, "such pro-German influence would soon subside." The District Attorney promised the "Judge" that if he had a "real objectionable man . . . and there is a 'peg' at all upon which to hang a charge I will institute the proceedings." Ultimately the correspondence reached the Department of Justice which referred it to the Council of National Defense. The latter informed the "Judge" that the District Attorney could, of course, have anyone arrested for violation of the Espionage Act, and he would then be held upon bail for indictment. "Whether the Federal District Attorney will issue such warrants of arrest without having proofs sufficient in his judgment to bring about conviction rests in his discretion. There is nothing in the law which prohibits him from such action; on the other hand, there is nothing which compels him to take this action."

The state councils frequently represented the most intolerant points of view. By warring on the German press and language, circulating loyalty pledges, helping to spread fear of spy activities, and encouraging or condoning excesses of the extremists, they aided in arousing the sort of spirit which made it unwise in some sections even to have a dachshund trailing one's heels. They became imbued with a sense of their own power and duty which transcended legal limitations, and which only the rash or the extremely courageous dared to challenge.

But not all forms of pressure are traceable to the councils. They were of all kinds and emanated from many sources: individual and group, conscious and unconscious, organized and unorganized. For example, M. S. Eccles of Logan, Utah, complained to the United States Forestry Service that men who were making great profits through permits to graze their cattle on the Cache National Forest refused to purchase more than a fifty or one-hundred dollar Liberty Bond. He requested that something be done to exclude them from the range unless they showed a "better attitude," and allow patriotic cattlemen to have the fall privileges. The Forestry Service replied that "other things being equal" the Department of Agriculture would "give preference to persons who have subscribed for Liberty Bonds to an amount considered reasonable."

—2—

In time of war or other crisis, when public opinion is largely unified and emotions rather than reason so greatly influence human attitudes and conduct, intimidation by mob action may become widespread. The spirit of the great West is portrayed by the secretary of one of the New England State Councils of Defense, who was sent by the National Council on a trip to check up on the western councils and hold patriotic rallies. Of Butte, Montana, he wrote:

> The spirit of Butte is fine, so far as I could gather. Indeed the workman who is not behind the war seems to be a sort of scab. Certain whilom vocal and influential citizens of Butte, who had exhibited pro-German and Anti-War sentiments, have been used for decorative purposes in connection with bridges, trestles and lampposts and other objects in the bleak landscape. The men of Butte are of a practical turn of mind.

He was even more delighted with Nevada, and gave the following as a rough paraphrase of a report made to the Governor by one of the sheriffs.

> I regret to report to your excellency that on such and such a date such and such a person was forcibly taken from my possession by parties unknown. He was placed on trial before an improvised tribunal and found guilty of lukewarmness toward the cause of the United States and her Allies. Thereupon, your Excellency, I regret to report to you that said unknown persons proceeded to strip said party to the waist and applied to his person a coating of black substance, which I am told was tar. Thereafter, they applied to the surface thus covered, a coating which, I am told, was feathers; whereupon they forcibly applied to his person the toe of their boots and instructed him to leave the country, telling him that if he ever came back they would lynch him—and if he does, by God, Governor, *we will!*

> Governor Boyle said he thought some of the boys were "pulling a little rough stuff," but it all helped the cause.

While it is unlikely a western sheriff would have used such indirect language, the description could be applied to other sections of the country.

Law observance perhaps has never been the most striking quality of the American people, but during the World War it reached a new low in the use of violence in dealing with individuals and certain groups. Once an individual or group was identified with pro-German leanings or utterances, interested parties could organize a mob to take summary action against them. In the summer of 1921, the writer was in a small Nebraska town in which a large proportion of the population was of German nationality. Some of the older people still would not converse in English (if they could) with a stranger, even after having gone through the rigors of war treatment. In reply to a question as to how they handled the German group during the war, a young business man replied in effect: "Oh, we didn't have much trouble with them. If one of them got too obstreperous, we would just ride him up and down the street on a rail, and make him kneel and kiss the flag. Or if he was too bad, we might add a coat of tar and feathers. After that he wouldn't give any more trouble." . . . In such simple ways as this were loyal citizens to be made of the disloyal.

Mob violence occurred in many widely separated places, but probably was most prevalent in the Middle West and Rocky Mountain regions. One of the most notorious incidents occurred in Illinois, when, following his acquittal on charges of violation of the Epsionage Act, Robert Paul Praeger was seized by a mob and lynched. The Reverend Herbert Bigelow, later a member of Congress from Ohio, was kidnapped and horsewhipped by a mob in Kentucky. The I.W.W.'s suffered from mob violence in many places. Vigilantes rounded up about 1,200 persons around Bisbee and Jerome, Arizona, loaded them on cattle cars and shipped them out in the desert. Many were not I. W. W.'s, but all might have perished from hunger and thirst if supplies had not been sent from United States Army stores. Frank Little was hanged from a trestle at Butte, Montana. Seventeen men who were charged with being I. W. W.'s were taken from the police of Tulsa, Oklahoma, by a hooded mob of "Knights of Liberty" who beat them, poured hot tar on their wounds and drove them from the city. The I. W. W. headquarters in Los Angeles was wrecked by a mob. These are only a few examples of the many which could be cited of mob violence.

Apparently there is a widespread assumption that democracy is of and in itself a form of government which will assure justice to everyone. The framers of the Constitution had no such illusions, nor did those who led the fight for the first ten amendments. As a matter of fact a democracy, or what passes for a democracy in the common though loose terminology of the present day, may be the most tyrannical of governments. Under favorable circum-stances, at least, unscrupulous politicians and interested propagandists can play upon the emotions of the crowd and sway it almost to hysteria. Under the spell of such feeling the people may demand more stringent legislation, and failing that, resort to illegal methods of silencing the opposition and thus force the government to decree as illegal the very acts the mobs have been punishing by summary action. There had been disrespect for law, outbreaks of one sort or another, and decided tendencies for citizens to take the law into their own hands before the war, of course. But during this period there was an extensive disregard for the limitations of law, even among the "best" citizens of American communities. It extended to, and often was fostered by official bodies representing the state or federal governments. These bodies no doubt believed that they were above the law.

Through propaganda and the whole effects of the war, the great majority of the people became convinced that we were fighting a holy war in which democracy, freedom, Christianity, and "all that we hold near and dear" were at stake. Probably most people would have agreed with Arthur Train who wrote for the National Security League:

> If Germany wins the war the United States will either be paying tribute to the Kaiser or German soldiers will be bayoneting American girls and women in Jersey City rather than take the trouble to shoot them.

The crusading spirit seldom begets tolerance.

—3—

The prevalence of war emotions was reflected in a widespread fear that swarms of German spies were infesting the country. The fear arose and grew despite lack of evidence, and in spite of the large array of federal, state and local investigative and enforcement officers. If one tasted grit while eating oysters, a German spy had put ground glass in the food. An outbreak of anthrax in cattle was caused by German spies planting the germs. Fireflies flickering their luminous tails over the swamps at nightfall were giving signals to German spies.

The emotional state indicated by the spy mania, as well as the lure which secret organizations have for Americans, resulted in the creation of several private organizations for suppressing sedition and apprehending spies, all of them an "outgrowth of good motives and manned by a high type of citizens." The most noted of these was the American Protective League, which secured the recognition of the Department of Justice. It enrolled some 250,-000 citizens in the grim business of spying on their neighbors for evidence of sedition and treason, rifling their office correspondence and searching their homes without benefit of search warrants—but in the name of patriotism and national defense. John Lord O'Brian, Chief of the War Emergency Division of the Department of Justice, paid tribute to the work of the organized spy-chasers in awakening the country to the dangers of "insidious propaganda," but, he says, "no other cause contributed so much to the oppression of innocent men as the systematic and indiscriminate agitation against what was claimed to be an all-pervasive system of German espionage." He was also unpleasantly impressed by "the insistent desire of a very large number of highly intelligent men and women to become arms of the Secret Service and to devote their time to the patriotic purpose of pursuing spies." George Creel summed up the espionage situation in the following language: "Never was a country so thoroughly counter-espionaged. Not a pin dropped in the home of any one with a foreign name but that it rang like thunder on the inner ear of some listening sleuth." The fact that the spy scare was largely a figment of the collective imagination was an irrelevant matter at the time. The importance of the phenomenon lies in the fact that it increased the attitude of intolerance of the people toward any who were not of the "100 percenters," and

added to the persecution of innocent men and women."

—4—

Considering the state of the public mind it is not surprising that legislation was enacted which granted far-reaching powers to government, that administrative officials sought means of extending their powers in ways which would seem questionable in more normal times, and that the courts were frequently extreme in interpreting the laws and in upholding the administrative decisions of executive officials. Prosecutions for treason were instituted but no convictions were obtained. Naturalization papers were revoked, even in the cases of citizens who had been naturalized two or three decades earlier. The Threats Against the President Act, as the courts interpreted it, came near to creating a crime of *lèse majesté*. Several states passed sedition acts. These arts, however, illustrate few features of the influence of public opinion upon civil liberties that are not indicated by the Espionage and the Trading with the Enemy Acts, and in the interest of brevity may be omitted from this discussion.

The Espionage Act was the most important war time statute for curbing ideas and their utterance. Because of a stringent censorship provision which President Wilson insisted upon having incorporated, the Espionage Bill precipitated a long and acrimonious debate that revealed how lightly some members of Congress regarded the constitutional guarantees of individual rights if these promised to restrain at all the war-making powers of government. Many Congressmen indicated their complete willingness to abrogate the First Amendment for the duration of the war, with little discussion of the possible effects of such action upon our own democracy, when, according to the popular view, we were fighting the war to make the world safe for democracy. Legal maxims were cited to support the contention that in time of war the Constitution is suspended to the extent that acts committed in violation of it are acquiesced in by the people.

The opponents of a censorship centered their arguments largely on the contention that the Constitution prohibited Congress from putting previous restraint on speech or the press. As with libel, there was freedom to express whatever seemed pertinent, but the press or the speaker could then be held accountable. The provisions of the act indicate that this interpretation was adopted in the final draft of the bill.

The Espionage Act was an omnibus bill which covered many features of the war situation. Only Titles I and XII apply to this discussion. Section 3 of Title I provided that:

> Whoever, when the United States is at war, shall willfully make or convey false reports or false statements with intent to interfere with the operation or success of the military or naval forces of the United States or to promote the success of its enemies, and whoever, when the United States is at war, shall willfully cause or attempt to cause insubordination, disloyalty, mutiny, or refusal of duty, in the military or naval forces of the United States, or shall willfully obstruct the recruiting or enlistment service of the United States, to the injury of the service or of the United States, shall be punished by a fine of not more than $10,000 or imprisonment for not more than twenty years, or both.

Thus the Espionage Act was intended to and did operate against organized propaganda, deliberately organized and intentionally carried on. It was not intended to reach those who made impulsive and casual remarks which, though arousing the ire of super-patriots, particularly, were not made with intent to interfere with the operation of the military and naval services, cause insubordination, or obstruct the recruiting service. It is quite likely, however, that many persons actually opposed to the war did push their activities to the very limits of the statute, but took care not to go beyond. To the non-legal minds of extremists,

however, every utterance in the nature of criticism was a violation of the statute, particularly if it were uttered by someone with a foreign-sounding name or someone identified with one of the radical organizations, or by someone personally offensive. Many self-appointed guardians of the patriotism of their respective communities sent accounts of every suspected case to the nearest federal district attorney. Failing to get action there, they put pressure upon their state council of defense or upon the Council of National Defense. As a last resort, and sometimes at a first resort, they organized mobs to beat the offender, tar and feather him and make him kiss the flag—and in some cases had recourse to lynching. Some district attorneys were severely criticized, it appears, because they refused to bring action in cases which were exasperating to the patriots, but which did not fall within the prohibitions of the law. Influential citizens wanted anyone who was guilty of an offensive statement about the war incarcerated for the duration.

John Lord O'Brian has stated that on the whole the courts were fair and impartial in hearing cases under the war statutes. In a general way, he probably is correct. On the other hand, particularly after the enactment of the Sedition Act, he complained of the great number of complaints which flooded the Department of Justice, and deplored the tendency of so many people to dignify with demands for prosecutions incidents which were hardly more than saloon squabbles or neighborhood quarrels. About two weeks before the Armistice, the Attorney General attempted to curb the tendency of certain district attorneys to cater to the super-patriots by urging indictments in some cases not justified by law. He issued instructions that the evidence must be submitted to the Justice Department for decisions before instituting action against anyone under the war statutes. Evidence was unearthed later, however, which showed that some of the district attorneys disregarded the instructions. And since even the Department of Justice reported many of the more extreme cases in its *Interpretations of War Statutes* bulletins, so as to indicate to the district attorneys the extent to which the law could be used for curbing agitation and talk, it does not seem unfair to outline here the extremes of law enforcement, and the prejudices of the judges and juries. This subject of law enforcement, particularly of the Espionage act, has been discussed elsewhere more than any other matter treated in this article; hence it will be covered briefly and with little attempt to portray the intricacies of the facts of the cases themselves.

The provisions of the Espionage Act were broad and vague. Clearly the law did not cover every criticism of government or lack of sympathy with the war. Consequently, much depended upon whether the court construed the law strictly as it does the usual criminal statute or whether it construed it loosely. Only a succession of court decisions made under pressure of public opinion could fully confuse the issue as to what were the ultimate limitations upon civil liberties under the law. Early in the war Judge Learned Hand had attempted to lay down an objective standard by which the law could be interpreted. He held that "if one stops short of urging upon others that it is their duty or their interest to resist the law," one could not be held for its violation. Otherwise, the court stated, "I can see no escape from the conclusion that under this section every political agitation which can be shown to be apt to create a seditious temper is illegal," and he was confident that by the language used "Congress had no such revolutionary purpose in view." In reversing Judge Hand, the Circuit Court of Appeals denied that his interpretation was correct, and declared that even if there was any doubt of the guilt of the defendant the case would be governed by the principle that the ruling of an administrative department must stand unless clearly wrong.

The crucial test of violation of the act was intent—the intent with which the accused spoke the words or committed the acts complained of. Since most of the courts took the attitude that anything which tended to dampen the war enthusiasm was a violation of the law, and that success was not necessary to constitute a violation, the question of intent became a mere formula. It is a well-known rule of criminal law that a person is presumed to intend the reasonable and natural consequences of his acts. But even at best the test is vague, and when public opinion is aroused and emotionally tense, it is an extremely tenuous doctrine for the protection of rights of those who hold unpopular economic and political doctrines.

Extraneous matter was often introduced in trials to show the motive or intent which actuated the accused. The anti-war Platform and other Socialist documents were introduced in a number of cases. Statements made before the enactment of the Espionage Act, or even before the declaration of war, were allowed in evidence. Within certain limits such evidence was valuable to the jury in determining the mental attitude, and hence the motives, of the defendant. But it placed a great burden on the jury. If the defendant was connected with such an unpopular organization as the Socialist Party or the I. W. W., he was likely to be convicted, because of his views on economic and industrial matters, or for membership in a certain group, rather than for the specific charges in the indictment.

To attribute the war to financial interests and for the benefit of the profiteers fell within the prohibitions of the law. And the President's War Message to Congress and the Declaration of War were accepted as evidence of the falsity of statements which blamed the war upon economic or capitalistic factors. Yet historians later recognized that economic entanglements were one factor in involving us. It is also a matter of common knowledge that unconscionable profiteering did take place. In at least one case the jury was instructed to determine from its own general knowledge the truth or falsity of such statements. Those who have followed the controversy among historians and the voluminous literature on the causes of American intervention will recognize the absurdity of such procedure.

Under the provisions regarding insubordination in the military and naval forces, few were convicted for actually urging men to evade the draft or not to enlist. Most convictions were for "expressions of opinion about the merit and conduct of the war." It was not necessary for the offender to speak in the presence of men of military age. One person was convicted for utterances against the Canadian Army. The Red Cross and the Y. M. C. A. fell within the prohibitions of the statute because civilian and military efforts were so related that a limited definition of the term "military and naval forces" could not be drawn. The law prohibited making false statements with intent to influence hearers so as to "dampen their ardor in the war . . . deter them from subscribing to bonds," or to giving their loyal support to the war activities of the country.

Many of the judges showed a confident omniscience as to the complex series of events which brought on the war. They often failed to recognize the limitations of a jury of twelve good men and true whose knowledge of history was sketchy at best and highly distorted by the widely disseminated war time propaganda. One may ask where the judges and juries obtained knowledge which was superior to that of the radicals who held objectionable views about the war. One cannot be sure, but presumably from the same source that most of us at the time got what we thought were absolute facts and truths on the causes and issues of the war—principally from the American and British propaganda machines, official and unofficial. In other words, the courts were simply reflecting in a large measure the intolerance of an aroused public opinion which refused to permit any questioning of the purity of American motives. And it may be remarked in passing that curiously enough Americans have fought for liberty, freedom and democracy for ourselves and others, and for American "rights," but have refused to consciously recognize economic causation, even when it was obvious. One may wonder if this is not a form of compensation for the high degree of eco-

nomic causation which really does provide so significant a motivating force in our culture.

So long as the Department of Justice refuses to permit researchers to examine its archives of the World War I period, a principal source of information is lacking as to the influence of public opinion on the enactment of the Sedition Act. But from other sources it is obvious that one reason for the support accorded this extreme measure was the demand for legal authority to reach, by the more orderly processes of law, the type of agitation which aroused some mobs to commit violence upon the person of the disturbers of the mental equilibrium of the patriots. Despite the severity with which the Espionage Act was enforced, it did not prohibit the utterance of many offensive words and sentiments which irritated the patriots no end. It was argued that a large part of the instances of mob violence was due to the "inadequacy" of existing law, which meant in effect that because citizens exercised certain rights which were legal in themselves but were an affront to others, such persons must be punished by mobs because there was no law which could be invoked against them. The remedy was simple: make such offenses punishable by law and reach the offenders by regular legal processes. Extremist patriotic organizations led in the hue and cry. One of these, the American Defense Society, circulated petitions through state defense councils and by other means demanding that Congress enact a law which would provide punishment for publication of statements of a "seditious or disloyal nature," and citing with approval the Montana State sedition law. This Montana statute was used by Congress as a guide in preparing its own bill. Nearly all of the acts committed by the mobs were considered as outside the scope of the federal law. It is doubtful whether convictions could have been obtained from juries anyway, even if the Department of Justice had been able to compel local authorities to bring actions against members of the mobs.

The Attorney General, with the concurrence of the Secretary of the Treasury, submitted a proposed bill amending Title I, Section 3, of the Espionage Act to include in its prohibitions efforts intentionally made for the purpose of discrediting and interfering with the flotation of government war loans, and to clarify the last section regarding obstruction of the recruiting and enlistment service. The Senate Committee on the Judiciary, however, acting on its own initiative "decided upon a course which resulted in the declaration by Congress of a changed and different policy aimed at the suppression of all utterances of a disloyal character." The interpretation of the meaning of the term "utterances of a disloyal character" may depend upon and vary with time and place, but there can be little doubt that the Sedition Bill prohibited the type of utterances which had been arousing patriots over the country.

Space does not permit of an extended discussion of the new law, and coming as late in the war as it did, after so many offenders had been silenced by other means, it does not appear that the law was widely used after all. As an example of the extent to which it could be applied, the most noted is the Abrams case. The defendants referred to themselves variously as "rebels," "revolutionists," "anarchists," and "socialists," all terms which in that day aroused fear and animosity in the breast of every "right-thinking" American. None believed in the form of government of the United States and none was a citizen. They had published a number of leaflets denouncing the United States for sending aid to the White Russians against the Bolsheviks. Technically the United States was not at war with Russia, and hence the war statutes, it might be thought, would not apply. The defendants had declared, and no evidence was introduced to the contrary, that they had no desire to see Germany win the war. Yet three defendants were sentenced to twenty years and one to fifteen years, and the decision was affirmed by the United States Supreme Court.

The inadequacies of the jury system in free speech cases was well demonstrated during the war. In his report for 1919, the Attorney General stated that: "The care used by the department in its desire to do nothing to interfere with the legitimate exercise of the right of free speech is shown by the fact that in practically every case convictions were secured and substantial sentences imposed." This statement may be, and probably is, a perversion of the proper order of cause and effect, for, as stated by O'Brian,

> It has been quite unnecessary to urge upon the United States attorneys the importance of prosecuting vigorously, and there has been little difficulty in securing convictions from juries. On the contrary, it has been necessary at all times to exercise caution in order to secure to defendants accused of disloyalty the safeguards of fair and impartial trial.

Casting aside the element of excited public opinion, it is obvious that a juryman's judgment of the "remote political and economic effects" of a publication or speech involving the issue of loyalty or the doctrines of socialism is more easily warped by his own views, his cultural and social background, than in ordinary criminal cases. An unsympathetic critic of the Espionage Act and its enforcement stated that:

> A jury of a man's peers in a free speech case means a jury of one hundred per cent Americans who are also one hundred per cent conservative and one hundred per cent ignorant of the most elementary theories of socialism, industrial unionism, the labor movement, and social betterment in general. The very ideals of socialism and communism in their most pacifist forms shock an average jury to such an extent that they mistake the shock itself for force and violence.

On March 24, 1929, the *Chicago Tribune* published an editorial entitled "Gentlemen of the Jury," in which it was stated that "The jury is simply a sample of public opinion." In time of emotional excitation, at least, the aptness of the statement is obvious. In effect, the jury returns to the functions it had in its early origins in England where it was a body representative of the hundreds when the royal justice held court in the shire. In time of excitement the jury represents the dominant viewpoint of the community. Unless checked by the cool conduct and instructions of the judge, a verdict may be arrived at unconsciously through emotions and prejudices, rather than on the basis of the evidence presented. Under such circumstances the utmost responsibility rests upon the judge, not only for what he says to the jury but for what he does not say or for his attitude toward the defendant; or even for his attitude toward witnesses professing to hold beliefs similar to those of the defendants.

It is probable that the judges were unprejudiced in the great majority of cases and deserve high praise for enjoining upon juries a dispassionate consideration of the evidence. Others, however, lectured the juries upon internationalism, Bolshevism, socialism, democracy, patriotism and love of country; defended the governments of England and France, and the righteousness of American participation in the war; and impressed upon them the necessity of suppressing traitors and treasonable utterances. In some cases, judges submitted opinions to the jury as statements of fact and then denounced the opinions in vigorous language. Free speech as guaranteed in the First Amendment was not regarded as a positive protection, nor was it clearly defined. The courts in Espionage Act cases repeated "Freedom of speech does not mean license" so much that it became a hackneyed phrase, but it was of little help to a jury in determining a man's constitutional rights.

The war was over and most of the district court cases disposed of before the United States Supreme Court passed upon the Espionage Act and cases arising under it. Of the cases which it accepted for review, at least seven were affirmed and six reversed on error. In only one of the latter did the court give a written opinion. This was the Victor Berger

case, and the reversal was based upon the refusal of Judge Landis to vacate the bench upon a petition of prejudice. Petitions for writs of certiorari were refused in at least five cases.

The first two cases, *Schenk* v. *U.S.* and *Sugarman* v. *U.S.,* presented no very great legal difficulties, since the defendants had in effect urged upon men subject to the draft to oppose it. Aside from formally declaring the Espionage Act constitutional, the Schenk case is important in the history of free speech for the oft cited "clear and present danger" test given by Justice Holmes, who wrote the opinion. The court recognized the vital importance of circumstances in determining the rights of men. Under certain conditions the defendants "would have been within their constitutional rights" in doing the acts complained of. But "The most stringent protection of free speech would not protect a man in falsely shouting fire in a theatre and causing a panic." "The question in every case is whether the words used are used in such circumstances and are of such a nature as to create a clear and present danger that they will bring about the substantive evils that Congress has a right to prevent. It is a question of proximity and degree." There was more question as to the guilt of Jacob Frohwerk, publisher of the *Missouri Staats Zeitung,* and Eugene V. Debs, but the court maintained its unity. Justice Holmes, who wrote the opinion in the Frohwerk case, intimated that if the evidence had been better prepared and more fully presented, the lower court might have been reversed. But on the existing record it was not possible to say that the intent of the editors was not as charged. The conviction of Eugene V. Debs has been criticized both on grounds of public policy and law. The wisdom of making Debs a martyr in the eyes of his numerous followers certainly was open to question. But except for the fact that the lower court had permitted to be introduced in evidence so much extraneous matter, including the St. Louis Platform and the records and convictions of five Socialists whom

Debs had defended, the Supreme Court's decision should have been expected. Debs had invited conviction by addressing the jury himself and admitting that he abhorred war and had obstructed the war.

In the other three cases the Court split, with Justices Holmes and Brandeis dissenting in each case and Justice Clark joining them in one case. The majority of the court failed to follow the "clear and present danger" test laid down in the Schenk case. Of course, minority decisions do not make the law, unless they later become majority opinions. Our civil rights are what the legislative bodies and the courts say they are in a given instance. Since these bodies are composed of men who are fallible and subject to the same currents as the majority of the people, the nature of the rights will vary somewhat as prevailing philosophies change, particularly whenever an emotionally aroused public opinion attains a large degree of unity in a given direction. But, except for the Schenk case, it is only in the minority decisions in the cases above mentioned that one finds any discussion of the fundamental rights of free speech. In the decade of the 1930's, however, under the leadership of Charles Evans Hughes as Chief Justice, the Supreme Court in several notable decisions came to accept the definitions laid down by Justices Brandeis and Holmes in the Espionage Act cases.

Motives are often complex and the controlling one may not always be realized by the individual concerned. Whether the left-wing Socialists, for example, were dominated primarily by opposition to the government and a desire to obstruct its prosecution of the war, or by a desire to further the cause of Socialism by their propaganda may not always be clear. The evidence does not indicate that the leaders were pro-German in sympathy, but of course their stand was one which would attract alien sympathizers to their banner. Such close distinctions are not likely to be drawn in time of war, and under the doctrine of constructive intent it is not necessary to make them. Justice Brandeis believed in the Pierce case that the primary motive of the defendants was to aid the cause of Socialism, but seven of his colleagues believed otherwise.

Like the historians and propagandists of the war period, the courts disregarded the lessons of history in convicting offenders who honestly attributed bad motives to the United States in the war. As a matter of fact, both the Socialists and pro-war propagandists presented distorted views of the causes and issues of the war; however, the Socialist viewpoint was hardly more unrealistic in one direction than that of the Committee on Public Information in another. As pointed out by Justice Brandeis, also in the Pierce case, the causes of war are complex and are the results of many conditions and motives. He said:

> Historians rarely agree in their judgment as to what was the determining factor in a particular war, even when they write under circumstances where detachment and the availability of evidence from all sources minimize their prejudice and other sources of error. For individuals, and classes of individuals attach significance to those things which are significant to them ... One finds the determining cause for war in a great man, another in an idea, a belief, an economic necessity, a trade advantage, a sinister machination, or an accident.

Whether judges were influenced by public pressure to extend their interpretation of the law far beyond what Congress had intended, or whether through associations and propaganda they had become merely "samples" of public opinion, is a question which is not necessary for us to answer. Sufficient it is to recognize that the courts and other public officials do not dwell in ivory towers apart from the world; and hence our judicial system is not of itself sufficient protection of rights guaranteed by the Constitution. Only the people can protect those rights. Only through a realization on the part of the majority that tolerance toward unpopular ideas is necessary to preserve civil liberties, and through defending those who have their rights threatened, can liberty be protected and assured. Too often, it appears, when the majority is large, it is willing to discard the safeguards of freedom already established in order to reach those whom it would silence, without thought of the danger that when once removed, these safeguards may never be restored. It fails to recognize, also, that the persecutors in the one instance may be the persecuted in the other, because the winds of public opinion have shifted, or because once the safeguards are loosed those who have control of the machinery of government may act without legal restraint.

13

WHAT THE DEPRESSION DID TO PEOPLE

EDWARD R. ELLIS

The American economy has a long history of cyclical recessions and depressions dating back to the eighteenth century. But none of the depressions could compare in severity or longevity to that which struck Americans between 1929 and 1941. Following a decade of unprecedented prosperity, which saw the rapid expansion of consumer goods production and the introduction of consumer credit to pay for it, the Great Depression took Americans by surprise. What had gone wrong?

Modern historians and economists now view the Depression as the consequence of underconsumption, that is, the overproduction of goods for sale and the lack of buyers with sufficient wages to purchase them. But to the unemployed workers, the dispossessed farmers, and their families, the Depression, whatever its cause, was the most disastrous event of their lives. By 1931 over 11 million workers, nearly a third of the labor force, were unemployed, and average farm income had declined to 60 percent of 1929 levels. In this essay Edward Ellis provides a wide panorama of life during the Depression, surveying its effects on the rich as well as the poor. Whatever their social class, he finds the Great Depression scarred the lives and shaped the outlook of everyone who lived through it.

The Depression smashed into the nation with such fury that men groped for superlatives to express its impact and meaning.

Edmund Wilson compared it to an earthquake. It was "like the explosion of a bomb dropped in the midst of society," according to the Social Science Research Council Committee on Studies in Social Aspects of the Depression.

Alfred E. Smith said the Depression was equivalent to war, while Supreme Court Justice Louis D. Brandeis and Bernard Baruch declared that it was worse than war. Philip La Follette, the governor of Wisconsin, said: "We are in the midst of the greatest domestic crisis since the Civil War." Governor Roosevelt agreed in these words: "Not since the dark days of the Sixties have the people of this state and nation faced problems as grave, situations as difficult, suffering as severe." A jobless textile worker told Louis Adamic: "I wish there would be war again." In a war against a foreign enemy all Americans might at least have felt united by a common purpose, and production would have boomed.

Poor and rich alike felt anxious and helpless.

Steel magnate Charles M. Schwab, despite his millions and the security of his Manhattan palace, freely confessed: "I'm afraid. Every man is afraid." J. David Stern, a wealthy newspaper publisher, became so terrified that he later wrote in his autobiography: "I sat in my back office, trying to figure out what to do. To be explicit, I sat in my private bathroom. My bowels were loose from fear." Calvin Coolidge dolorously told a friend: "I can see nothing to give ground for hope."

Herbert C. Pell, a rich man with a country estate near Governor Roosevelt's, said the country was doomed unless it could free itself from the rich, who have "shown no realization that what you call free enterprise means anything but greed." Marriner Eccles, a banker and economist who had *not* lost his fortune, wrote that "I awoke to find myself at the bottom of a pit without any known means of scal-

ing its sheer sides." According to Dwight W. Morrow, a Morgan associate, diplomat and Senator: "Most of my friends think the world is coming to an end—that is, the world as we know it." Reinhold Niebuhr, the learned and liberal clergyman, said that rich "men and women speculated in drawing-rooms on the best kind of poison as a means to oblivion from the horrors of revolution."

In Youngstown, Ohio, a friend of Mayor Joseph L. Heffernan stood beside the mayor's desk and said: "My wife is frantic. After working at the steel mill for twenty-five years I've lost my job and I'm too old to get other work. If you can't do something for me, I'm going to kill myself." Governor Gifford Pinchot of Pennsylvania got a letter from a jobless man who said: "I cannot stand it any longer." Gan Kolski, an unemployed Polish artist from Greenwich Village, leaped to his death from the George Washington Bridge, leaving this note: "To All: If you cannot hear the cry of starving millions, listen to the dead, brothers. Your economic system is dead."

An architect, Hugh Ferriss, stood on the parapet of a tall building in Manhattan and thought to himself that the nearby skyscrapers seemed like monuments to the rugged individualism of the past. Thomas Wolfe wrote: "I believe that we are lost here in America, but I believe we shall be found," Democratic Senator Thomas Gore of Oklahoma called the Depression an economic disease. Henry Ford, on the other hand, said the Depression was "a wholesome thing in general."

Obviously, the essence of a depression is widespread unemployment. In one of the most fatuous remarks on record, Calvin Coolidge said: "The final solution of unemployment is work." He might have added that water is wet. Senator Robert Wagner of New York called unemployment inexcusable.

A decade before the Crash the British statesman David Lloyd George had said: "Unemployment, with its injustice for the man who seeks and thirsts for employment, who begs for labour and cannot get it, and who is punished for failure he is not responsible for by the starvation of his children—that torture is something that private enterprise ought to remedy for its own sake." Winston Churchill now used the same key word, "torture," in a similar comment: "This problem of unemployment is the most torturing that can be presented to a civilized society."

Before Roosevelt became President and named Frances Perkins his secretary of labor, she was so pessimistic that she said publicly it might take a quarter century to solve the unemployment problem. A Pennsylvania commission studied 31,159 workless men and then reported that the typical unemployed man was thirty-six years old, native-born, physically fit and with a good previous work record. This finding contradicted Henry Ford's belief that the unemployed did not want to work.

However, the Pennsylvania study was *not* typical of the unemployed across the entire nation. Negroes and aliens were the last hired and the first fired. Young men and women were graduated from high schools and colleges into a world without jobs. Mississippi's demagogic governor and sometime Senator, Theodore G. Bilbo, vowed the unemployment problem could be solved by shipping 12,000,000 American blacks to Africa. The United Spanish War Veterans, for their part, urged the deportation of 10,000,000 aliens—or nearly 6,000,000 more than the actual number of aliens in the United States. Some noncitizens, unable to find work here, voluntarily returned to their homelands. With the deepening of the Depression, immigration dropped until something strange happened in the year 1932: More than three times as many persons left this country as entered it. No longer was America the Promised Land.

The Depression changed people's values and thus changed society.

The Chamber of Commerce syndrome of the Twenties became a mockery in the Thirties. Business leaders lost their prestige, for now it had become apparent to all Americans that these big shots did not know what they were talking about when they said again and again and again that everything would be all right if it were just left to them. Worship of big business was succeeded by greater concern for human values. The optimism of the speculative decade was replaced by the pessimism of the hungry decade, by anguished interest in the problem of having enough food on the table.

People eager to make a big killing in the stock market had paid scant attention to politics, but now they wondered about their elected representatives and the kind of political system that could permit such a catastrophe to happen. Indifference gave way to political and social consciousness. Dorothy Parker, the sophisticate and wit, cried: "There is no longer I. There is WE. The day of the individual is dead." Quentin N. Burdick, who became a Senator from North Dakota, said long after the Depression: "I guess I acquired a social conscience during those bad days, and ever since I've had the desire to work toward bettering the living conditions of the people." Sylvia Porter, who developed into a financial columnist, said that while at Hunter College she switched from English to economics because of "an overwhelming curiosity to know why everything was crashing around me and why people were losing their jobs."

People lost their houses and apartments.

Franklin D. Roosevelt said: "One of the major disasters of the continued depression was the loss of hundreds of thousands of homes each year from foreclosure. The annual average loss of urban homes by foreclosure in the United States in normal times was 78,000. By 1932 this had increased to 273,000. By the middle of 1933, foreclosures had advanced to more than 1,000 a day."

In New York City, which had more apartments than private houses, there were almost 200,000 evictions in the year 1931. During the first three weeks of the following year there were more than 60,000 other evictions. One judge handled, or tried to handle, 425 eviction cases in a single day! On February 2, 1932, the New York *Times* described the eviction of three families in the Bronx:

Probably because of the cold, the crowd numbered only about 1,000, although in unruliness it equalled the throng of 4,000 that stormed the police in the first disorder of a similar nature on January 22. On Thursday a dozen more families are to be evicted unless they pay back rents.

Inspector Joseph Leonary deployed a force of fifty detectives and mounted and foot patrolmen through the street as Marshal Louis Novick led ten furniture movers in to the building. Their appearance was the signal for a great clamor. Women shrieked from the windows, the different sections of the crowd hissed and booed and shouted invectives. Fighting began simultaneously in the house and in the street. The marshal's men were rushed on the stairs and only got to work after the policemen had driven the tenants back into their apartments.

In that part of New York City known as Sunnyside, Queens, many homeowners were unable to meet mortgage payments and were soon ordered to vacate. Eviction notices were met with collective action, the residents barricading their doors with sandbags and barbed wire, flinging pepper and flour at sheriffs who tried to force their way inside. However, it was a losing battle; more than 60 percent of Sunnyside's householders lost their homes through foreclosure.

Harlem Negroes invented a new way to get enough money to pay their rent. This, as it came to be called, was the house-rent party. A family would announce that on Saturday night or Thursday night they would welcome anyone and everyone to their home for an evening of fun. Sometimes they would print and distribute cards such as this: "There'll be plenty of pig feet / And lots of gin; / Jus' ring the bell / An' come on in." Saturday night, of course, is the usual time for partying, while Thursday was chosen because this was the

only free night for sleep-in black domestics who worked for white people. Admission to a house-rent party cost 15 cents, but more money could be spent inside. A festive mood was established by placing a red bulb in a light socket, by serving food consisting of chitterlings and pigs' feet and by setting out a jug of corn liquor. These parties often went on until daybreak, and the next day the landlord got his rent. The innovation spread to black ghettos in other big cities across the land, and some white people began imitating the Negroes.

In Chicago a crowd of Negroes gathered in front of the door of a tenement house to prevent the landlord's agent from evicting a neighborhood family, and they continued to stand there hour after hour, singing hymns. A Chicago municipal employee named James D. O'Reilly saw his home auctioned off because he had failed to pay $34 in city taxes at the very time the city owed him $850 in unpaid salary.

A social worker described one pathetic event: "Mrs. Green left her five small children alone one morning while she went to have her grocery order filled. While she was away the constable arrived and padlocked her house with the children inside. When she came back she heard the six-weeks-old baby crying. She did not dare to touch the padlock for fear of being arrested, but she found a window open and climbed in and nursed the baby and then climbed out and appealed to the police to let her children out."

In widespread areas of Philadelphia no rent was paid at all. In this City of Brotherly Love evictions were exceedingly common—as many as 1,300 a month. Children, who saw their parents' distress, made a game of evictions. In a day-care center they piled all the doll furniture in first one corner and then another. One tot explained to a teacher: "We ain't got no money for the rent, so we's moved into a new house. Then we got the constable on us, so we's moving' again."

In millions of apartments, tension mounted and tempers flared toward the end of each month, when the rent was due. Robert Bendiner, in his book *Just Around the Corner,* wrote about conditions in New York City:

Evictions and frequent moves to take advantage of the apartment market were as common in middle-income Washington Heights as in the poor areas of town, and apartment hopping became rather a way of life. My own family moved six times in seven years. . . . Crises occurred monthly, and several times we were saved from eviction by pawning leftover valuables or by my mother's rich talent for cajoling landlords. On one more than routinely desperate occasion she resorted to the extreme device of having one of us enlarge a hole in the bathroom ceiling and then irately demanding repairs before another dollar of rent should be forthcoming.

In moving from one place to another, some families left their furniture behind because it had been bought on the installment plan and they were unable to meet further payments. Time-payment furniture firms owned warehouses that became crammed with tables and chairs and other items reclaimed from families without money. Whenever a marshal, sheriff or constable evicted a family from a house or apartment, the landlord would simply dump the furniture on the sidewalk. If the installment company failed to pick it up, each article would soon be carried away by needy neighbors.

What happened to people after they were dispossessed? Many doubled up with relatives—or even tripled up, until ten or twelve people were crammed into three or four rooms. Human beings are like porcupines: they like to huddle close enough to feel one another's warmth, but they dislike getting so close that the quills begin pricking. Now, in teeming proximity to one another, the quills pricked, and relatives quarreled bitterly.

The Depression strained the family structure and sometimes shattered it. Well-integrated families closed ranks in the face of this common danger and became ever more monolithic. Loosely knit families, on the other hand, fell apart when the pressures on them became too great.

After a man lost his job, he would trudge from factory to factory, office to office, seeking other employment, but after weeks of repeated rejections he would lose heart, mutely denounce himself as a poor provider, shed his self-respect and stay at home. Here he found himself unwelcome and underfoot, the target of puzzled glances from his children and hostile looks from his wife. In the early part of the Depression some women simply could not understand that jobs were unavailable; instead, they felt there was something wrong with their men. In Philadelphia one unemployed man begged a social worker: "Have you anybody you can send around to tell my wife you have no job to give me? She thinks I don't want to work."

The idle man found himself a displaced person in the household, which is woman's domain, and in nameless guilt he crept about uneasily, always finding himself in the way. He got on his wife's nerves and she on his, until tension broke in endless wrangles. If the man tried to help by washing dishes and making beds, he lost status in the eyes of the rest of the family.

The Depression castrated some men by dethroning them from their position as the breadwinner and the head of the family. Ashamed, confused and resentful, they became sexually impotent. In Western culture a man tends to think of himself in terms of the work he does, this self-identity being what Jung calls his persona. Man does. Woman is. To rob a man of his work was to rob him of his idea of himself, leaving him empty and without much reason for living. The displacement of the man as the head of the family and the way some women moved in to fill this vacuum were described sensitively by John Steinbeck in his novel *The Grapes of Wrath.* This great book tells the story of the flight of the Joad family from the dust bowl of Oklahoma to the green valleys of California:

"We got nothin', now," Pa said. "Comin' a long time—no work, no crops. What we gonna do then? How we gonna git stuff to eat? . . . Git so I hate to think. Go diggin' back to a ol' time to keep from thinkin'. Seems like our life's over an' done."

"No, it ain't," Ma smiled. "It ain't, Pa. An' that's one more thing a woman knows. I noticed that. Man, he lives in jerks—baby born an' a man dies, an' that's a jerk—gets a farm an' loses his farm, an' that's a jerk. Woman, it's all one flow, like a stream, little eddies, little waterfalls, but the river, it goes right on. Woman looks at it like that. We ain't gonna die out. People is goin' on—changin' a little maybe, but goin' right on."

Some adolescent girls felt their fathers' agony and tried to comfort them with lavish expressions of love, much to the embarrassment of the man and the uneasiness of his wife. This did emotional damage to father, mother and the young girl, whose fixation on her father retarded her normal interest in boys her own age.

Strife between parents, together with the realization that it cost money to marry and have babies, resulted in a decision by many young people to postpone their weddings. One young man joined the Communist Party and swore he never would marry or have children under "the present system." Unable to repress their human needs, however, young men and women made love secretly and guiltily, regarding pregnancy as a disaster. Despite an increase in the sale of contraceptives, the abortion rate rose, and so did venereal disease. The birthrate dropped.

It has been estimated that the Depression postponed 800,000 marriages that would have occurred sooner if it had not been for hard times. Margaret Mead, the noted anthropologist, argued that there was nothing wrong about letting girls support their lovers so they could marry sooner. Surprisingly, there even was a decline in marriages among members of the *Social Register.* Liberals and feminists pointed out that half of all births were in fami-

lies on relief or with incomes of less than $1,000 a year; they strongly advocated birth control. Who could afford babies when a sixty-one-piece layette cost all of $7.70? Gasps of horror arose when it was reported in Illinois that a sixteenth child had been born to a family on relief.

Housewives suffered as acutely as their husbands. Many had to send their kids to live with relatives or friends. Others took part-time jobs, while a few wives actually became temporary whores to earn enough money to keep the family going. Lacking money for streetcars and buses, without the means to buy clothes to keep them looking attractive, they remained cooped up in their homes until their nerves screamed and they had nervous breakdowns.

All too often their men simply deserted them. A California woman said: "My husband went north about three months ago to try his luck. The first month he wrote pretty regularly. . . . For five weeks we have had no word from him. . . . Don't know where he is or what he is up to."

A young man who lived in the French Quarter of New Orleans was solicited by five prostitutes during a ten-block stroll, each woman asking only 50 cents. In Houston a relief worker, curious about how the people were getting along, was approached by one girl after another. For the benefit of an insistent streetwalker, the man turned his pockets inside out to prove that he had no money. Looking at him ruefully, she said: "It doesn't cost much—only a dime!"

The close relationship between poverty and morals shocked Franklin D. Roosevelt, who told reporters about an investigator who went to southeastern Kentucky: "She got into one of those mining towns," Roosevelt said, "and started to walk up the alley. There was a group of miners sitting in front of the shacks, and they pulled down their caps over their faces. As soon as she caught sight of that she walked up and said, 'What are you pulling your caps down for?' They said, 'Oh, it is all right.' 'Why pull your caps down?' They said, 'It is sort of a custom because so many of the women have not got enough clothes to cover them.' "

The Depression made changes in the country's physical appearance.

Fewer pedestrians were to be seen on the streets since many men did not go to work and women shopped less frequently; for lack of warm clothing and fuel, many people stayed in bed most of the day during winter. The air became cleaner over industrial cities, for there was less smoke from factory chimneys. The downtown business districts of most cities had long rows of empty shops and offices. Trains were shorter, and only rarely did one see a Pullman car. However, gas stations multiplied because millions of Americans drove their battered family cars here and there in endless quest of work. In conflicting attempts to solve their problems, farmers moved into town while city folks moved into the country to build their own houses and grow their own food. More and more blacks were seen in northern cities as desperate Negroes fled from the hopeless South. Telephones were taken out of homes, and mail deliveries were lighter. Houses and stores, parks and fences sagged and lapsed into unpainted, flaked ugliness for want of money to make repairs.

In his novel called *You Can't Go Home Again,* Thomas Wolfe described a comfort station in front of New York City Hall:

... One descended to this place down a steep flight of stairs from the street, and on bitter nights he would find the place crowded with homeless men who had sought refuge there. Some were those shambling hulks that one sees everywhere, in Paris as well as in New York. ... But most of them were just flotsam of the general ruin of the time—honest, descent, middle-aged men with faces seamed by toil and want, and young men, many of them mere boys in their teens, with thick, unkempt hair. These were the wanderers from town to town, the riders of freight trains, the thumbers of rides on highways, the uprooted, unwanted male population of America. They drifted across the land and gathered in the big cities when winter came, hungry, defeated, empty, hopeless, restless, driven by they knew not what, always on the move, looking everywhere for work, for the bare crumbs to support their miserable lives, and finding neither work nor crumbs. Here in New York, to this obscene meeting place, these derelicts came, drawn into a common stew of rest and warmth and a little surcease from their desperation.

Heywood Broun devoted a column to a description of a slum in San Antonio, Texas:

... The Church of Guadalupe stands upon the fringe of what had been described to me as the most fearsome slum in all America. It covers four square miles. At first I thought that the extreme description might have been dictated by local pride. It was my notion to protest and say, "Why, we in New York City know worse than that." But after we had gone up the third back alley I had to confess defeat gracefully.

You can see shacks as bad as these in several States, but I do not know of any place where they have been so ingeniously huddled together. This is flat, sprawling country, and there is much of it, and so it seems devilish that one crazy combination of old lumber and stray tin should be set as a flap upon the side of another equally discreditable. I did not quite comprehend the character of the alley until I discovered that what I took to be a toolhouse was a residence for a family of eleven people.

And these are not squatter dwellings. People pay rent for them, just as if a few rickety boards and a leaky roof constituted a house. They even have evictions and go through the solemn and obscene farce of removing a bed and a frying pan as indication that the landlord's two-dollars-and-a-half rent has not been forthcoming. ...

Back at the Church of Guadalupe, the priest said, "I have other letters from those who fight federal housing because they like their rents." He tossed over an anonymous message, which read, "I could start a story that there is a priest who writes love letters to young girls and gives jewels to women of his congregation."

"Doesn't this worry you?" one of us asked.

"No," said the priest. "Last month we buried thirty-nine persons, mostly children, from this little church alone.

"I am worried," he said, "about people starving to death."

Louis Adamic and his wife were living with her mother in New York City in January, 1932. Born in Yugoslavia, now a naturalized American, he was a writer, a tall young man with a look of eager curiosity in his eyes. One cold morning at seven forty-five the doorbell rang, and Adamic, thinking it was the postman, opened the front door. In his book called *My America,* he told what happened next.

There stood a girl of ten and a boy of eight. They had schoolbooks in their arms, and their clothing was patched and clean, but hardly warm enough for winter weather. In a voice strangely old for her age, the girl said: "Excuse me, mister, but we have no eats in our house and my mother she said I should take my brother before we go to school and ring a doorbell in some house"—she swallowed heavily and took a deep breath—"and ask you to give us . . . something . . . to eat."

"Come in," Adamic said. A strange sensation swept over him. He had heard that kids were ringing doorbells and asking for food in the Bronx, in Harlem and in Brooklyn, but he had not really believed it.

His wife and her mother gave the children some food. The girl ate slowly. Her brother bolted his portion, quickly and greedily.

"He ate a banana yesterday afternoon," said his sister, "but it wasn't ripe enough or something', and it made him sick and he didn't eat anything since. He's always like this when he's hungry and we gotta ring doorbells."

"Do you often ring doorbells?"

"When we have no eats at home."

"What made you ring our bell?"

"I don't know," the girl answered. "I just did."

Her name was Mary, and her brother's name was Jimmie. They lived in a poor neighborhood five blocks away.

Mary said: "We used to live on the fourth floor upstairs and we had three rooms and a kitchen and bath, but now we have only one room downstairs. In back."

"Why did you move downstairs?"

The boy winced.

"My father," said the girl. "He lost his job when the panic came. That was two years ago. I was eight and Jimmie was six. My father he tried to get work, but he couldn't, the depression was so bad. But he called it the panic."

Adamic and the two women were astonished at her vocabulary: "panic" . . . "depression."

"What kind of work did your father do?"

"Painter and paperhanger. Before things got so bad, he always had jobs when his work was in season, and he was good to us—my mother says so, too. Then, after he couldn't get any more jobs, he got mean and he yelled at my mother. He couldn't sleep nights and he walked up and down and talked, and sometimes he hollered and we couldn't sleep, either."

"Was he a union man?"

"No, he didn't belong to no union."

"What did your father holler about?"

"He called my mother bad names."

At this point in the conversation, Adamic wrote, the little girl hesitated, and her brother winced again. Then she continued: "Uh . . . he was angry because my mother, before she married him, she was in love with another man and almost married him. But my mother says it wasn't my father's fault he acted mean like he did. He was mean because he had no job and we had no money."

"Where's your father now?"

"We don't know. He went away four months ago, right after Labor Day, and he never came back, so we had to move downstairs. The landlord didn't want to throw us out, so he told my mother to move in downstairs."

Between sips of milk the girl said her mother did household work whenever she could find a job, but earned very little money this way. A charity organization had been giving her $2.85 a week, but lately it had stopped. Mary did not know why. Her mother had applied for home relief, but had not yet received anything from that source.

The boy stopped eating, turned to his sister and muttered: "You talk too much! I told you not to talk!"

The girl fell silent.

Adamic said: "It's really our fault, Jimmie. We're asking too many questions."

The little boy glared and said: "Yeah!"

In Detroit someone gave another little girl a nickel, which seemed like such a fortune to her that she agonized three full days about how best to spend it.

In Erie, Pennsylvania, a seven-year-old boy named Tom received a tiny yellow chick as an Easter present. Using some old chicken wire, he built a coop for his pet beneath the back step to the house and fed and tended it carefully. His father was an unemployed molder, and the family often ate nothing but beans. Time passed. Now the little chick had grown into a full-sized chicken. One day Tom's father announced that the boy's pet would have to be killed and served for Sunday dinner, since everyone was hungry. Tom screamed in horrified protest but was unable to prevent his father from taking his chicken into the backyard and chopping off its head. Later that day the family sat around the table feasting on fowl, while the boy hunched in his chair, sobbing.

There was another boy who never forgot a scene from his childhood days during the Depression. He lived in a small town in Iowa. Every so often a train would stop there for a few minutes, and a man would get out carrying bags of buttons. He would distribute these buttons to waiting farmers and their wives, collect the cards to which they had sewn other buttons, pay them a meager sum for their labor, get back into the train and depart. This trivial piecework provided them with the only income they could get.

President Hoover was foolish enough to let himself be photographed on the White House lawn feeding his dog. This picture did not sit well with Americans who were hungry, suffering from malnutrition or even starving to death. Several times Hoover denied that there was widespread undernourishment in the nation, but he depended on unreliable statistics. Comedian Groucho Marx, who was closer to the people, said he knew things were bad when "the pigeons started feeding the people in Central Park." However, it was no laughing matter.

In Oklahoma City a newspaper reporter was assigned to cover state relief headquarters. Walking into the building one morning, he ran into a young man he had met through his landlady. This fellow offered the reporter some candy. The reporter did not want the candy but accepted it lest he hurt the other's feelings. As they stood and chewed, a social worker approached them.

"We don't allow any eating in here," she said.

The reporter, who thought she was jesting, made a wisecrack.

"We don't allow any eating in here," she repeated sternly. "Some of these applicants haven't had any breakfast. We make it a rule among ourselves never to eat or to drink Cokes in front of them."

Ashamed of himself, the reporter mumbled an apology and slunk behind a beaver-board wall. He wanted to throw away the morsel of candy remaining in his hand but felt that this would be even more sinful with hungry people so near.

Arthur Brisbane, the rich columnist and editor, walked into a Manhattan restaurant and ordered two lamb chops. When he had finished the first one, he looked longingly at the second but was too full to eat it, too. After much thought he summoned a waiter.

"What happens if I don't eat this chop?" Brisbane asked. "Will you take it back?"

"No, sir. We can't do that, sir."

"But what will you do with it? Will it be thrown away?"

"Not at all, sir. We give the leftovers to poor people."

Brisbane sighed in relief, nodded approvingly, paid his check and left.

In 1933 the Children's Bureau reported that one out of every five children in the nation was not getting enough of the right things to eat. A teacher in a coal-mining town asked a little girl in her classroom whether she was ill. The child said: "No. I'm all right. I'm just hungry." The teacher urged her to go home and eat something. The girl said: "I can't This is my sister's day to eat." In the House of Representatives, during a debate about appropriations for Indians living on reservations, a Congressman said that eleven cents a day was enough to feed an Indian child. A Senate subcommittee learned that the president of a textile firm had told his workers they should be able to live on six cents a day.

AFL President William Green said: "I warn the people who are exploiting the workers that they can only drive them so far before they will turn on them and destroy them. They are taking no account of the history of nations in which governments have been overturned. Revolutions grow out of the depths of hunger."

Sidney Hillman, president of the Amalgamated Clothing Workers of America, appeared at a Senate hearing in 1932 and was told that it was not yet time to give federal relief. Angrily, he cried: "I would ask by what standards are we to gauge that time! Must we have hundreds of thousands of people actually dead and dying from starvation? Must we have bread riots? What is necessary to convince them that there is a need for federal and speedy relief?"

The Communists took up the slogan: "Starve or fight!"

At the University of Pennsylvania a prim audience was shocked to hear Daniel Willard, president of the B & O Railroad, say: "While I do not like to say so, I would be less than candid if I did not say that in such circumstances I would steal before I would starve."

Obviously, less fortunate Americans agreed.

Petty thievery soared. Children hung around grocery stores begging for food. Customers emerging from groceries had bundles snatched from their arms by hungry kids, who ran home with the food or ducked into alleys to gobble it as fast as they could. Small retail stores had their windows smashed and their display goods stolen. Grown men, in groups of two and three, walked into chain store markets, ordered all the food they could carry and then quietly walked out without paying for it. Chain store managers did not always report these incidents to the police for fear that publicity would encourage this sort of intimidation. For the same reason the newspapers engaged in a tacit conspiracy of silence.

However, newspapers did not mind reporting that in Manhattan a debutante supper for 600 guests at the Ritz-Carlton cost $4,750. On nearby Park Avenue, beggars were so numerous that a well-dressed man might be asked for money four or five times in a ten-block stroll. President Hoover not only denied that anyone was starving, but said: "The hoboes, for example, are better fed than they ever have been. One hobo in New York got ten meals in one day."

People of means thought up ways to protect themselves from panhandlers and from begging letters. Boston's mayor, James M. Curley had a male secretary named Stan Wilcox, who was adept at brushing off approaches. Whenever a beggar asked if he had a quarter, Wilcox would reply: "Heavens, no! I wouldn't dream of taking a drink at this hour!" Alfred E. Smith received the following letter from Milwaukee: "This is unusual, but I am in need. Would you send me $2,500, as this is the amount I am in need of. I will give you as collateral my word of honor that I will repay you if possible. If not, let the good Lord repay you and he will also pay better interest."

Governor Gifford Pinchot of Pennsylvania flatly declared that starvation was widespread. Among the many pathetic letters he received was this one: "There are nine of us in the family. My father is out of work for a couple of months and we haven't got a thing eat *[sic]* in the house. Mother is getting $12 a month of the county. If mother don't get more help we will have to starve to death. I am a little girl 10 years old. I go to school every day. My other sister hain't got any shoes or clothes to wear to go to school. My mother goes in her bare feet and she crys every night that we don't have the help. I guess that is all, hoping to hear from you."

Bernard Baruch, who felt burdened by the thought of his wealth, got a desperate letter from his cousin, Fay Allen Des Portes, who lived in his home state of South Carolina. "The horrible part of the whole situation," she wrote to him, "is these poor starving people here in our midst. The banks can't let anyone have money, the merchants are all broke; the farmers can't let the poor Negroes on the farm have anything to eat. I don't know what is going to happen. I have about four hundred Negroes that are as absolutely dependent upon me as my two little boys, but I can't help them any more and God knows what is going to happen to them."

John L. Lewis, president of the United Mine Workers, once said to a group of mine operators: "Gentlemen, I speak to you for my people. I speak to you for the miners' families in the broad Ohio valley, the Pennsylvania mountains and the black West Virginia hills. There, the shanties lean over as if intoxicated by the smoke fumes of the mine dumps. But the more pretentious ones boast a porch, with the banisters broken here and there, presenting the aspect of a snaggle-toothed child. Some of the windows are wide open to flies, which can feast nearby on garbage and answer the family dinner call in double-quick time. But there is no dinner call. The little children are gathered around a bare table without anything to eat. Their mothers are saying, 'We want bread.'"

A writer named Jonathan Norton Leonard described the plight of Pennsylvania miners who had been put out of company villages after losing a strike: "Reporters from the more liberal metropolitan papers found thousands of them huddled on the mountainsides, crowded three or four families together in one-room shacks, living on dandelion and wild weedroots. Half of them were sick, but no local doctor would care for the evicted strikers. All of them were hungry and many were dying of those providential diseases which enable welfare workers to claim that no one has starved."

In 1931 four New York City hospitals reported 95 deaths from starvation. Two years later the New York City Welfare Council said that 29 persons had died from starvation, more than 50 others had been treated for starvation, while an additional 110 individuals—most of them children—had perished of malnutrition. In one routine report the council gave this picture of the plight of one family in the Brownsville section of Brooklyn: "Family reported starving by neighbors. Investigator found five small children at home while mother was out looking for vegetables under pushcarts. Family had moved into one room. Father sleeping at Municipal Lodging House because he could get more to eat there than at home and frequently brought food home from there in pockets for children and wife. Only other food they had for weeks came from pushcarts."

A family of fourteen was on relief in Kewanee, Illinois, the hog-raising center of the Midwest. The family was given $3 worth of groceries a week, and of course this food soon ran out. After giving the last crumbs to the children, the adults would exist on nothing but hot water until they received their next grocery allotment.

In Chicago a committee investigated city garbage dumps and then reported: "Around the truck which was unloading garbage and other refuse were about 35 men, women and children. As soon as the truck pulled away from the pile all of them started digging with sticks, some with their hands, grabbing bits of food and vegetables."

Edmund Wilson described another Chicago scene: "A private incinerator at Thirty-fifth and La Salle Streets which disposes of garbage from restaurants and hotels, has been regularly visited by people, in groups of as many as twenty at a time, who pounce upon anything that looks edible before it is thrown into the furnace. The women complained to investigators that the men took unfair advantage by jumping on the truck before it was unloaded; but a code was eventually established which provided that different sets of people should come at different times every day, so that everybody would be given a chance."

A ballad called "Starvation Blues" was sung by some of the poor people of America during the Depression.

Prentice Murphy, director of the Children's Bureau of Philadelphia, told a Senate committee: "If the modern state is to rest upon a firm foundation, its citizens must not be allowed to starve. Some of them do. They do not die quickly. You can starve for a long time without dying."

Scientists agree that a person can starve a long time without dying, but this is what it is like to starve to death: After a few days without food the stomach cramps and bloats up. Later it shrinks in size. At first a starving child will cry and eat anything to ease hunger pains—stuffing his mouth with rags, clay, chalk, straw, twigs, berries and even poisonous weeds. Then, as the child weakens, his cries change to whimpers. He feels nauseated. All the fat is being burned from his body. This burning produces acidosis. The fruity odor of acetone can be smelled on the breath, and it also appears in the urine. When starvation reaches this point, nature becomes kinder. The child grows listless and sleepy. The bulging eyes are sad and dull. Now body proteins have been depleted, while the water and electrolyte balance has been destroyed. Degeneration of the vital organs, such as the liver and kidneys, proceeds in earnest. By this time the child lacks all resistance to diseases and may be killed by some infection.

John Steinbeck has told how he survived the early part of the Depression before he became a famous author. "I had two assets," he wrote. "My father owned a tiny three-room cottage in Pacific Grove in California, and he let me live in it without rent. That was the first safety. Pacific Grove is on the ocean. That was the second. People in inland cities or in the closed and shuttered industrial cemeteries had greater problems than I. Given the sea, a man must be very stupid to starve. That great reservoir is always available. I took a large part of my protein food from the ocean.

"Firewood to keep warm floated on the beach daily, needing only handsaw and ax. A small garden of black soil came with the cottage. In northern California you can raise vegetables of some kind all year long. I never peeled a potato without planting the skins. Kale, lettuce, chard, turnips, carrots and onions rotated in the little garden. In the tide pools of the bay, mussels were available and crabs and abalones and that shiny kelp called sea lettuce. With a line and pole, blue cod, rock cod, perch, sea trout, sculpin could be caught."

The sale of flower seeds shot up as Americans, tired of the ugliness of their lives, turned to the beauty of homegrown flowers. As might have been expected, there was widespread cultivation of vegetable gardens. Many did this on their own, while others received official encouragement. Big railroads rented garden plots for their workers. The United States Steel Corporation used social workers and faculty members of Indiana University to develop an extensive garden project for its workers in Gary, Indiana. In New York State, in the summer of 1933, jobless men and women were tending 65,000 gardens. The city of Detroit provided tools and seed for "thrift gardens" on empty lots, an idea which Mayor Frank Murphy said he had borrowed from Hazen S. Pingree. During the Panic of 1893 Pingree had been the mayor of Detroit, and confronted with a city of jobless men, he provided them with gardens to cultivate—"Pingree's Potato Patches" receiving national attention.

Now, in the present emergency, Henry Ford ordered all his workmen to dig in vegetable gardens or be fired. Out of his imperious command there developed what the Scripps-Howard Washington *News* called 50,000 "shotgun gardens." Rough-grained Harry Bennett, chief of Ford's private police, supervised this vast project and kept a filing system on all Ford employees. If a man had no garden in his own backyard or on some neighborhood lot, he was assigned a patch of earth somewhere on Ford's 4,000 acres of farmland around Dearborn, Michigan. Each workman had to pay fifty cents to have his strip plowed.

More than one-third of the men employed in Ford's Dearborn plant lived 10 to 20 miles away, and some protested that since they did not own a car they would have to spend an extra two hours daily just traveling to and from their allotted patches. A Bennett henchman would snarl: "Why don't-cha buy a car? You're makin' 'em, ain't-cha?" Bone-weary workmen who simply couldn't muster the energy to toil on their garden plots soon were brought into line by Bennett's personal deputy, Norman Selby, the former boxer "Kid McCoy."

In the spring of 1932 the Community Council of Philadelphia ran out of private funds for the relief of needy families. Eleven days elapsed before this relief work could be resumed with public funds, and many families received no help during this interim. A study was made to find out what had happened when food orders stopped.

One woman borrowed 50 cents from a friend and bought stale bread at 3½ cents per loaf. Except for one or two meals, this was all she could serve her family throughout those eleven days.

A pregnant mother and her three children could afford only two meals a day. At eleven o'clock in the morning she would serve breakfast, which consisted of cocoa, bread and butter. This left everyone so hungry that the mother began advancing the time of their evening meal, which was just one can of soup.

Another woman scoured the docks, picking up vegetables that fell from produce wagons. Fish vendors sometimes gave her a fish at the end of the day. On two separate occasions her family went without food for a day and a half.

On the day the food orders stopped, one family ate nothing all day. At nine o'clock that night the mother went to a friend's house and begged for a loaf of bread. Later she got two days' work at 75 cents a day. With this pittance she bought a little meat. Then, adding vegetables picked up off the street, she made a stew which she cooked over and over again each day to prevent spoilage.

One family ate nothing but potatoes, rice, bread and coffee, and for one and a half days they were totally without food.

Hunting jackrabbits to feed the family became a way of life among farmers and ranchers. This gave birth to a Depression joke reported by John Steinbeck in *The Grapes of Wrath.* One man said to another: "Depression is over. I seen a jackrabbit, an' they wasn't nobody after him." The second man said: "That ain't the reason. Can't afford to kill jackrabbits no more. Catch'em and milk'em and turn'em loose. One you seen prob'ly gone dry."

Audie Murphy was born on a Texas farm five years before the Crash, the son of very poor parents. Almost as soon as he could walk, he began hunting game for the family. Since shells were expensive, every shot had to count. Aware of this, Audie Murphy developed into an expert marksman—so expert that when he was a GI during World War II, he killed 240 Nazis and emerged as the most decorated American soldier of the war.

Wheat growers, bankrupted by drought, talked about heading for Alaska to kill moose to fill their growling bellies. In the timberlands of the great Northwest some desperate men set forest fires so that they would be hired to extinguish them, while in big cities other men prayed for heavy snowfalls to provide them with shoveling jobs. When some Pittsburgh steel mills reopened briefly, the steelworkers called back to their jobs were too weak from hunger to be able to work.

At the age of eleven Cesar Chavez, who later won renown as a Mexican-American labor leader, fished and cut mustard greens to help keep his family from starving.

Charles H. Percy, who wound up a multimillionaire and a United States Senator, never forgot what it was like to be a poor boy in Chicago during the Depression: "I remember a great feeling of shame when the welfare truck pulled up to our house. And you talk about cheating! Once they delivered us 100 pounds of sugar by mistake. My father wanted to return it, but my mother said, 'God willed us to have it,' and she wouldn't give it up." She swapped some of the sugar for flour and helped tide the family over by baking cookies that little Chuck Percy peddled door to door.

Americans under the stress of the Depression behaved with a dignity that varied in terms of their religious backgrounds, their mental images of themselves and their rigidity or flexibility. Brittle people snapped, while the pliant bent and survived.

In Georgia a blind Negro refused all relief, harnessed himself to a plow like a mule and tilled the fields, day after day. In Pittsburgh a father with starving children stole a loaf of bread from a neighbor, was caught, hanged himself in shame. In Youngstown, Ohio, a father, mother and their four sons preferred to starve rather than accept charity. Before they died, their condition was discovered by a neighbor who happened to be a newspaper reporter. They were existing on fried flour and water.

Charles Wayne also lived in Youngstown. He had been a hot mill worker for the Republic Iron and Steel Company until he was laid off. For the next two years he was unable to get any kind of work. Now a fifty-seven-year-old man, workless, hopeless, unable to feed his wife and ten children, he climbed onto a bridge one morning. He took off his coat, folded it neatly, then jumped into the swirling Mahoning River below. Instinct caused him to swim a few strokes, but then he gave up and let himself drown. Later his wife sobbed to reporters: "We were about to lose our home and the gas and electric companies had threatened to shut off the service."

An elderly man receiving $15-a-week relief money for his large family went out each day, without being asked, to sweep the streets of his village. "I want to do something," he said, "in return for what I get." A graduate of the Harvard Law School, now old and almost deaf, gladly took a $15-a-week job as assistant caretaker at a small park.

Rather than accept charity, a New York dentist and his wife killed themselves with gas. He left this note: "The entire blame for this tragedy rests with the City of New York or whoever it is that allows free dental work in the hospital. We want to get out of the way before we are forced to accept relief money. The City of New York is not to touch our bodies. We have a horror of charity burial. We have put the last of our money in the hands of a friend who will turn it over to my brother."

John Steinbeck wrote: "Only illness frightened us. You have to have money to be sick—or did then. And dentistry also was out of the question, with the result that my teeth went badly to pieces. Without dough you couldn't have a tooth filled."

Shoes were a problem. Upon reaching home, poor people took off their shoes to save wear and tear. Middle-class people bought do-it-yourself shoe-repair kits. Those unable to afford the kits would resole their shoes with strips of rubber cut from old tires. Some wore ordinary rubbers over shoes with holes in their bottoms. A miner's son, Jack Conroy, told what a hole in a shoe could mean to a man walking the streets looking for work: "Maybe it starts with a little hole in the sole; and then the slush of the pavements oozes in, gumming sox and balling between your toes. Concrete whets Woolworth sox like a file, and if you turn the heel on top and tear a pasteboard inner sole, it won't help much. There are the tacks, too. You get to avoiding high places and curbstones because that jabs the point right into the heel. Soon the tack has calloused a furrowed hole, and you don't notice it unless you strike something unusually high or solid, or forget and walk flat-footed. You pass a thousand shoe-shops where a tack might be bent down, but you can't pull off a shoe and ask to have *that* done—for nothing."

Keeping clean was also a problem, since soap cost money. Steinbeck washed his linen with soap made from pork fat, wood ashes and salt, but it took a lot of sunning to get the smell out of sheets. As the sale of soap declined across the nation, its production was reduced. Procter & Gamble did not lay off its workers, as it might have done under the circumstances, but put them to work cutting grass, painting fences and repairing factories until soap production began to rise again.

Steinbeck wrote a short story called "Daughter" about a sharecropper who shot and killed his own daughter because he had no food to give her. This could not be shrugged off as mere fiction, for in Carlisle, Pennsylvania, a starving man named Elmo Noakes actually suffocated his three small daughters rather than see them starve.

The Depression scarred many young men and women who later became celebrities or who already were well known. Jack Dempsey, former heavy-weight boxing champion of the world, became so strapped for money that at the age of thirty-six he got himself sufficiently back into shape to fight fifty-six exhibition bouts. Babe Ruth, always a big spender, tried to supplement his income by opening a haberdashery on Broadway but lost his own shirt after five months.

Clifford Odets wrote his first play while living on ten cents a day. Lillian Hellman, who later became a renowned playwright, earned $50 a week as a script reader for Metro-Goldwyn-Mayer. William Inge, who also won fame as a playwright, acted in tent shows during the Depression, long afterward recalling: "We actors considered ourselves fortunate if we earned five dollars a week. Sometimes the farmers of Kansas would bring in flour and

meat as barter for admission to Saturday matinees."

Songwriter Frank Loesser learned from his parents that they had lost all their money. He took any job he could get, including screwing the tops on bottles of an insecticide. He also worked as a spotter for a chain of restaurants, getting seventy-five cents a day plus the cost of each meal for reporting on the food and service. Later he reminisced: "I used to eat twelve times a day. When you're poor, you're always hungry from walking around so much."

Danny Thomas performed in saloons, but finally even this kind of work came to an end. The chance of getting another job seemed so slim that he considered giving up show business. In desperation, he prayed to St. Jude, the patron saint of the hopeless, and the next day he landed a job in Chicago that proved to be the turning point of his career.

Ralph Bellamy almost starved to death in the basement of a Greenwich Village apartment. Cary Grant was working in Hollywood as an extra. Dana Andrews worked four years as a gas station attendant in Van Nuys, California. Robert Young was employed as a soda jerk, grease monkey and truck driver. Ray Milland, living on credit in Hollywood, was about to go to work in a garage when he landed a part in a movie called *Bolero*. In Chireno, Texas, a twelve-year-old girl named Lucille Ann Collier began dancing professionally to help the family finances; later she grew into a long-legged beauty and won fame under the name of Ann Miller. In the Bronx a four-year-old girl named Anna Maria Italiano sang for WPA men working on a nearby project; today she is known as Anne Bancroft.

Victor Mature set out for Hollywood in 1935 at the age of seventeen, with $40 in cash and a car loaded with candy and chewing gum. He drove for five days and slept in his automobile each night, and by the time he reached the film capital he was almost broke. To his father in Louisville he wired: ARRIVED HERE WITH 11 CENTS. His father, an Austrian scissors grinder who had taken up refrigerator selling, wired back:

FORTY-THREE YEARS AGO I ARRIVED IN NEW YORK WITH FIVE CENTS. I COULD NOT EVEN SPEAK ENGLISH. YOU ARE SIX CENTS UP ON ME.

The effect of the Depression on Hollywood extras was told by Grover Jones to an amused courtroom in a trial concerning Metro-Gold-wyn-Mayer. Jones, once an extra and then a scriptwriter, gave this entertaining testimony: "They wanted eighty Indians, and I got the job only because I knew how to put on what they called bolamania—burnt umber and raw umber mixed. But they made me a chief. That meant I didn't have to go naked. I could wear a suit, you see. And at that time I was convinced I was fairly smart. So there were now eighty-one Indians. I had never seen a camera during all those months, because I was always in the background, waiting over in back of the hill for the call to come over the hill on the horses to rescue the child. And I had never been on horses. So we sat on these horses, each confiding in the other, and none of them had ever been on horses, except we were all hungry. Finally the man said, 'Now look, when you hear shooting I want you all to come over the hills, and I want some of you to fall off the horses.' Well, in those days they paid three dollars extra for a man who would fall off a horse, because it is quite a stunt. So we waited until finally we got the call to come over the hill, and somebody shot a gun off—and eighty-one Indians fell off their horses."

There was nothing surprising about the fact that men would risk injury or death by falling off a horse to earn an extra $3 a day. People felt that if they could just live through the Depression, they could endure anything else life had to offer. To *endure* was the main thing. Many took pay cuts without a murmur. A young man just out of college with a Bachelor of Journalism degree accepted a job on a newspaper at exactly *nothing* per week; a month later he was grateful to be put on the payroll at $15. Graduate engineers worked as office boys. College graduates of various kinds ran elevators in department stores. Unemployed architects turned out jigsaw puzzles. One jobless drafts-man, Alfred Butts, used his spare time to invent the game of Scrabble.

Young men who might have grown into greatness chose, instead, to seek the security of civil service jobs, becoming policemen, firemen, garbage collectors. Fewer sailors deserted from the Navy. Enlistments rose in all branches of the nation's military establishment. When Congress voted a 10 percent pay cut for all federal employees, President Hoover secretly asked the Senate to make an exception for soldiers and sailors, because he did not wish to rely on disgruntled troops in case of internal trouble.

Women and children toiled for almost nothing in the sweatshops of New York City, welfare workers reporting these grim examples:

· A woman crocheted hats for 40 cents a dozen and was able to make only two dozen per week.
· An apron girl, paid 2½ cents per apron, earned 20 cents a day.
· A slipper liner was paid 21 cents for every seventy-two pairs of slippers she lined, and if she turned out one slipper every forty-five seconds she could earn $1.05 in a nine-hour day.
· A girl got half a cent for each pair of pants she threaded and sponged, making $2.78 a week.

Connecticut's state commissioner of labor said that some sweatshops in that state paid girls between 60 cents and $1.10 for a fifty-five-hour week. In Pennsylvania men working in sawmills were paid 5 cents an hour, men in tile and brick manufacturing got 6 cents per hour, while construction workers earned 7½ cents an hour. In Detroit the Briggs Manufacturing Company paid men 10 cents and women 4 cents an hour, causing auto workers to chant: "If poison doesn't work, try Briggs!" Also in Detroit, the Hudson Motor Car Company called back a small-parts assembler and then kept her waiting three days for a half hour of work, forcing her to spend 60 cents in carfare to earn 28 cents.

Two Marine fishermen put out to sea at four o'clock one morning and did not return to port until five o'clock that afternoon. During this long day of toil they caught 200 pounds of hake and 80 pounds of haddock. They burned up eight gallons of gas at 19 cents a gallon and used 100 pounds of bait costing two cents a pound. For their catch they were paid one cent a pound for the hake and four cents a pound for the haddock. Thus they earned less than two cents an hour for their day's work.

Meantime, Henry Ford was declaring: "Many families were not so badly off as they thought; they needed guidance in the management of their resources and opportunities." Ford needed no guidance. He managed to transfer 41½ percent of stock in the Ford Motor Company to his son, Edsel, without paying a cent in inheritance or estate taxes.

Ford, who liked to boast that he always had to work, declared in 1930 that "the very poor are recruited almost solely from the people who refuse to think and therefore refuse to work diligently." Roger W. Babson, the statistician, pontificated two years later: "Better business will come when the unemployed change their attitude toward life." Most rich men were quick to moralize.

The concept of hard work was central to capitalism and the Protestant ethic. Americans had been raised on a diet of aphorisms praising work and self-reliance. Benjamin Franklin said: "God helps them that help themselves." The Bible insisted: "In the sweat of thy face shalt thou eat bread." Thomas Carlyle said: "All work, even cotton-spinning, is noble; work alone is noble." Elizabeth Barrett Browning wrote: "Whoever fears God, fears to sit at ease." It was either Bishop Richard Cumberland or George Whitefield (no one is sure) who first said: "Better to wear out than to rust out." Most Americans agreed, but now in these Depression times men did sit at home and rust,

through no fault of their own, losing the fine edge of their skills.

Idle, dispirited, hungry, defeated, withdrawn, brooding—people began to feel that somehow they were to blame for everything, that somehow, somewhere, they had failed. Maybe the Depression was punishment for their sins. After all, Protestant Episcopal Bishop John P. Tyler attributed it to the lack of religion. Perhaps Christians, if they wished to be good Christians, should bow to fate by accepting Christ's words that "to everyone that hath shall be given; and from him that hath not, even that which he hath shall be taken from him." But some found it difficult to find comfort in a sermon preached by the Reverend William S. Blackshear, an Episcopalian clergyman, in the bleak year of 1932. Blackshear said in part: "Christ was happy to be at the banquets of the rich. It was at such a place that the woman broke the vial of costly ointment and anointed His feet. There were those who cried out for the improvident and rebuked the woman, saying that this should have been converted into cash and given to the poor. It was then that Christ spoke on the economic plan, 'The poor ye have always with you.' "

This kind of sermon, representing conservative Protestantism, offended liberal clergymen. Forced by the Depression to rethink their values, they began searching for a new theology. Some began with the premise that if the church were to serve any purpose or perform realistically, it had to divorce itself from economic and political values. This developing viewpoint was expressed with crystal clarity by H. Richard Niebuhr, a pastor and a brother of Reinhold Niebuhr. He wrote:

The church is in bondage to capitalism. Capitalism in its contemporary form is more than a system of ownership and distribution of economic goods. It is a faith and a way of life. It is faith in wealth as the source of all life's blessings and as the savior of man from his deepest misery. It is the doctrine that man's most important activity is the production of economic goods and that all other things are dependent upon this. On the basis of this initial idolatry it develops a morality in which economic worth becomes the standard by which to measure all other values and the economic virtues take precedence over courage, temperance, wisdom and justice, over charity, humility and fidelity. Hence nature, love, life, truth, beauty and justice are exploited or made the servants of the high economic good. Everything, including the lives of workers, is made a utility, is desecrated and ultimately destroyed. . . .

Other dissenters noted the supremacy of capitalism over every other value in the fact that church property was exempt from taxation. State constitutions and special statutes declared that no real estate taxes could be levied on church-owned properties, such as the church building itself, parochial schools, parsonages, the parish house and cemeteries. Why? A Missouri Supreme Court decision said that "no argument is necessary to show that church purposes are public purposes."

But was this really true? The United States of America was a Christian nation nominally, but not legally. No single religion, sect or church was recognized as the established church. Although the phrase "separation of church and state" does not appear in the Constitution of the United States or in that of any state but Utah, the idea for which it stands is found in the constitutional provisions against religious tests and in the words of the First Amendment: "Congress shall make no law respecting an establishment of religion. . . ."

During the Depression some liberal Christians, agnostics, atheists and others fretted about the special status given churches and church property. A few scholars recalled that President Ulysses S. Grant had said: "I would suggest the taxation of all property equally, whether church or corporation, exempting only the last resting place of the dead, and possibly, with proper restrictions, church edifices." Dissenters objected on principle to the exemption of church property, regarded this as an indirect subsidy by the state to religion and pointed out that personal taxes might be less if churches bore their share of the tax burden.

They got nowhere. At the core of capitalism was the belief that God looked with favor on the rich. This idea had been expressed as long ago as 1732 by one of J. P. Morgan's ancestors, the Reverend Joseph Morgan, who sermonized: "Each man coveting to make himself rich, carries on the Publick Good: Thus God in His Wisdom and Mercy turns our wickedness to Publick Benefit. . . . A rich Man is a great friend of the Publick, while he aims at nothing but serving himself. God will have us live by helping one another; and since Love will not do it, Covetousness shall."

J. P. Morgan himself flatly told a Senate committee: "If you destroy the leisure class you destroy civilization." When reporters pressed for a definition of the leisure class, Morgan said it included all who could afford a maid. In 1931, according to *Fortune* magazine, there still were 1,000,000 families with servants. One wealthy family announced that it had solved its Depression problem by discharging fifteen of its twenty servants—although the family members showed no curiosity or concern about the fate of the unemployed fifteen.

John Jacob Astor came of age in 1933 and thereupon inherited about $4 million. Nonetheless, he dabbled at a job in a downtown Manhattan brokerage house. Before long he quit with the explanation: "I didn't finish until five o'clock and by the time I got uptown it was six. And then I had to get up early the next morning." At a later date Astor was employed briefly by a shipping firm, and when he quit this second job, he commented: "I have discovered that work interferes with leisure." He was a representative of that leisure class which Morgan felt must be maintained to save civilization.

When Dwight Morrow was running for governor of New Jersey, he said: "There is something about too much prosperity that ruins the fiber of the people. The men and women that built this country, that founded it, were people that were reared in adversity." Morrow made this statement and died before Adolf Hitler declared: "It was poverty that made me strong." Joseph P. Kennedy, a busy member of the leisure class, felt that the rich had to make some sacrifices. Writing about the Depression, Kennedy said: "I am not ashamed to record that in those days I felt and said I would be willing to part with half of what I had if I could be sure of keeping, under law and order, the other half."

One member of the enormously wealthy Du Pont family seems to have been out of touch with reality. An advertising agency wanted his company to sponsor a Sunday afternoon radio program, but this Du Pont rejected the idea, saying: "At three o'clock on Sunday afternoons everybody is playing polo."

Everybody except the millions of Americans gobbling the last morsel of food from their plates in the fear that it might be their last meal—a habit that persisted in some people down through the next three decades. As Sinclair Lewis commented in his novel *It Can't Happen Here,* people were so confused, insecure and frustrated that they hardly could do anything more permanent than shaving or eating breakfast. They were tortured with feelings of inadequacy and guilt.

A young Alabama school teacher with eight years of tenure was fired after the Wall Street Crash. Eager to work, willing to take any job however low in the social scale, she became a maid in a private home. However, upon learning that she would be expected to work seven days a week, getting room and board but no wages, she quit. Then she took a job in a convalescent home which paid her room and board and $3 a week, but soon the home closed for lack of funds. The gentle schoolteacher completely lost faith in herself, confessing to a caseworker: "If, with all the advantages I've had, I can't make a living, then I'm just no good, I guess!"

Forty experienced secretaries found work after being unemployed a year, but the first few days on the job they were unable to take dictation from their bosses without weeping from sheer nervousness. After seeking employment for a long time, a man finally landed a job and became so overwrought with joy that he died of excitement. A corporation executive was given the nasty chore of firing several hundred men. A kind and compassionate person, he insisted on talking to each of them personally and asking what plans each had for the future. In a few months the executive's hair had turned gray.

The Depression began to erode freedom.

Some Americans, a little more secure than others, asked harsh questions. How about fingerprinting everyone on relief? Was it proper for a man on relief to own a car—even if he needed it to try to find work? Wasn't it wrong to sell liquor to the head of a family on relief? Did anyone owning a life insurance policy deserve relief? Should reliefers be allowed to vote? Did they deserve citizenship?

In New Orleans a federal judge denied citizenship to four qualified persons because they were on relief and therefore, in the judge's words, "unable financially to contribute to the support of the government." In California another judge withheld citizenship from Jacob Hullen; in response to the judge's questions Hullen had said he believed in municipal or federal ownership of public utilities.

In New York City, one cold and rainy day, the police arrested 38 men who had taken shelter in the Pennsylvania Railroad's ferry terminal on Cortlandt Street. All were marched to the nearest police station. Fifteen of them, able to prove that they had a few nickels and dimes in their pockets, were released. The other 23 men, who did not have a cent on them, were led before a magistrate, who sentenced them to jail for vagrancy. Newspaper stories about this obvious injustice raised such a hullabaloo, however, that the 23 prisoners soon were freed.

Robert Morss Lovett, a professor of English literature at the University of Chicago, wrote in his autobiography:

An example of the injustice meted out to for-eign-born workers involved a Yugoslav named Perkovitch. When conditions were at their worst in 1932–33 the unemployed on the West Side [of Chicago] were in the habit of crossing the city to the South Side where food was some-times available from bakeries, disposing of yes-terday's bake, and where, at least, the garbage was more lavish.

One morning these itinerants were picked up by the police and held at the station house on the absurd pretext that a revolution was planned. Perkovitch told me that he and about one hundred others were kept in the basement all day without food. Once a lieutenant with a bodyguard of patrolmen raged through the room, striking and kicking the men in an ec-stasy of sadism. At six the prisoners were re-leased with no charges.

Paul D. Preacher, the town marshal of Jonesboro, Arkansas, arrested a group of Negro men without cause and forced them to work on his farm. A federal grand jury indicted him under Title 18 of the Anti-Slavery Act of 1866 for "causing Negroes to be held as slaves" on a cotton plantation. This was the first case ever tried under the slavery statute. A county grand jury absolved Peacher, but the federal Department of Justice would not drop the case. Now the marshal was forced to stand trial—this time before a *federal* jury. Taking the witness chair in his own behalf, he denied that he had done anything wrong. However, the jury disagreed with him and found him guilty. Peacher was sentenced to two years in prison and fined $3,500. He appealed, lost his appeal, paid the fine and accepted a two-year probationary sentence.

Someone asked Eugene Talmadge, the gov-ernor of Georgia, what he would do about the millions of unemployed Americans. Talmadge snarled: "Let'em starve!" It made him happy when the city fathers of Atlanta put unwanted nonresidents in chain gangs. When some tex-tile workers went on strike in Georgia the gov-ernor had barbed-wire concentration camps built and threw pickets into them. Frank Hague, the mayor and ruthless boss of Jersey City, called for the erection in Alaska of a con-centration camp for native "Reds."

Wise and temperate men worried about the growing loss of liberty in America, the land of the free and the home of the brave. George Boas, a professor of philosophy, sadly said: "It is taken for granted that democracy is bad and that it is dying." Will Durant, busy writing his many-volumed *Story of Civilization,* asked rhetorically: "Why is it that Democracy has fallen so rapidly from the high prestige which it had at the Armistice?"

14

THE NEW DEAL: THE CONSERVATIVE ACHIEVEMENTS OF LIBERAL REFORM

BARTON BERNSTEIN

Most historians view Franklin D. Roosevelt's New Deal as a watershed in American history. In a sharp break with the past, they argue, Roosevelt and his advisors began to fashion a distinctively American welfare state to combat the worst abuses of the Depression. The New Deal record was an impressive one: it established price supports in agriculture, fashioned a National Recovery Administration to direct new industrial growth, provided jobs for the unemployed through the Civilian Conservation Corps and the Works Progress Administration, insured bank deposits, and established social welfare programs through the Social Security Administration. The New Deal, these historians claim, tamed capitalism and paved the way for further liberal reforms during the next two decades.

Not all historians agree with this interpretation however. As Barton J. Bernstein suggests in this essay, the New Deal can be seen as something less than revolutionary. The principle of government involvement in the economy and the idea of a welfare state emerged in the 1880s and was foreshadowed in the progressive movement at the turn of the century. New Deal reforms were important, but it can be argued that they did more to help the middle and upper classes than the poor. And the evidence clearly demonstrates that it was World War II, not the New Deal, that rescued America from the Depression. For Bernstein the New Deal was not always the watershed that historians have made it. If it brought the power of the state into social reform, he argues, it was only in order to save capitalism.

Reprinted from *Towards a New Past: Dissenting Essays in American History,* edited by Barton Bernstein. Copyright © 1968 by Random House, Inc. Reprinted by permission of Pantheon Books, a division of Random House, Inc.

Writing from a liberal democratic consensus, many American historians in the past two decades have praised the Roosevelt administration for its nonideological flexibility and for its far-ranging reforms. To many historians, particularly those who reached intellectual maturity during the depression, the government's accomplishments, as well as the drama and passion, marked the decade as a watershed, as a dividing line in the American past.

Enamored of Franklin D. Roosevelt and recalling the bitter opposition to welfare measures and restraints upon business, many liberal historians have emphasized the New Deal's discontinuity with the immediate past. For them there was a "Roosevelt Revolution," or at the very least a dramatic achievement of a beneficent liberalism which had developed in fits and spurts during the preceding three decades. Rejecting earlier interpretations which viewed the New Deal as socialism or state capitalism, they have also disregarded theories of syndicalism or of corporate liberalism. The New Deal has generally commanded their approval for such laws or institutions as minimum wages, public housing, farm assistance, the Tennessee Valley Authority, the Wagner Act, more progressive taxation, and social security. For most liberal historians the New Deal meant the replenishment of democracy, the rescuing of the federal government from the clutches of big business, the significant redistribution of political power. Breaking with laissez faire, the new administration, according to these interpretations, marked the end of the passive or impartial state and the beginning of positive government, of the interventionist state acting to offset concentrations of private power, and affirming the rights and responding to the needs of the unprivileged.

From the perspective of the late 1960s these themes no longer seem adequate to characterize the New Deal. The liberal reforms of the New Deal did not transform the American system; they conserved and protected American corporate capitalism, occasionally by absorbing parts of threatening programs. There was no significant redistribution of power in American society, only limited recognition of other organized groups, seldom of unorganized peoples. Neither the bolder programs advanced by New Dealers nor the final legislation greatly extended the beneficence of government beyond the middle classes or drew upon the wealth of the few for the needs of the many. Designed to maintain the American system, liberal activity was directed toward essentially conservative goals. Experimentalism was most frequently limited to means; seldom did it extend to ends. Never questioning private enterprise, it operated within safe channels, far short of Marxism or even of native American radicalisms that offered structural critiques and structural solutions.

All of this is not to deny the changes wrought by the New Deal—the extension of welfare programs, the growth of federal power, the strengthening of the executive, even the narrowing of property rights. But it is to assert that the elements of continuity are stronger, that the magnitude of change has been exaggerated. The New Deal failed to solve the problem of depression, it failed to raise the impoverished, it failed to redistribute income, it failed to extend equality and generally countenanced racial discrimination and segregation. It failed generally to make business more responsible to the social welfare or to threaten business's pre-eminent political power. In this sense, the New Deal, despite the shifts in tone and spirit from the earlier decade, was profoundly conservative and continuous with the 1920s.

Rather than understanding the 1920s as a "return to normalcy," the period is more properly interpreted by focusing on the continuation of progressive impulses, demands often frustrated by the rivalry of interest groups, sometimes blocked by the resistance of Harding and Coolidge, and occasionally by Hoover. Through these years while agriculture and labor struggled to secure advantages from the federal government, big business flourished.

Praised for creating American prosperity, business leaders easily convinced the nation that they were socially responsible, that they were fulfilling the needs of the public. Benefitting from earlier legislation that had promoted economic rationalization and stability, they were opponents of federal benefits to other groups but seldom proponents of laissez faire.

In no way did the election of Herbert Hoover in 1928 seem to challenge the New Era. An heir of Wilson, Hoover promised an even closer relationship with big business and moved beyond Harding and Coolidge by affirming federal responsibility for prosperity. As Secretary of Commerce, Hoover had opposed unbridled competition and had transformed his department into a vigorous friend of business. Sponsoring trade associations, he promoted industrial self-regulation and the increased rationalization of business. He had also expanded foreign trade, endorsed the regulation of new forms of communications, encouraged relief in disasters, and recommended public works to offset economic declines.

By training and experience, few men in American political life seemed better prepared than Hoover to cope with the depression. Responding promptly to the crisis, he acted to stabilize the economy and secured the agreement of businessmen to maintain production and wage rates. Unwilling to let the economy "go through the wringer," the President requested easier money, self-liquidating public works, lower personal and corporate income taxes, and stronger commodity stabilization corporations. In reviewing these unprecedented actions, Walter Lippmann wrote, "The national government undertook to make the whole economic order operate prosperously."

But these efforts proved inadequate. The tax cut benefitted the wealthy and failed to raise effective demand. The public works were insufficient. The commodity stabilization corporations soon ran out of funds, and agricultural prices kept plummeting. Businessmen cut back production, dismissed employees, and

finally cut wages. As unemployment grew, Hoover struggled to inspire confidence, but his words seemed hollow and his understanding of the depression limited. Blaming the collapse on European failures, he could not admit that American capitalism had failed. When prodded by Congress to increase public works, to provide direct relief, and to further unbalance the budget, he doggedly resisted. Additional deficits would destroy business confidence, he feared, and relief would erode the principles of individual and local responsibility. Clinging to faith in voluntarism, Hoover also briefly rebuffed the efforts by financiers to secure the Reconstruction Finance Corporation (RFC). Finally endorsing the RFC, he also supported expanded lending by Federal Land Banks, recommended home-loan banks, and even approved small federal loans (usually inadequate) to states needing funds for relief. In this burst of activity, the President had moved to the very limits of his ideology.

Restricted by his progressive background and insensitive to politics and public opinion, he stopped far short of the state corporatism urged by some businessmen and politicians. With capitalism crumbling he had acted vigorously to save it, but he would not yield to the representatives of business or disadvantaged groups who wished to alter the government. He was reluctant to use the federal power to achieve through compulsion what could not be realized through voluntary means. Proclaiming a false independence, he did not understand that his government already represented business interests; hence, he rejected policies that would openly place the power of the state in the hands of business or that would permit the formation of a syndicalist state in which power might be exercised (in the words of William Appleman Williams) "by a relatively few leaders of each functional bloc formed and operating as an oligarchy."

Even though constitutional scruples restricted his efforts, Hoover did more than any previous American president to combat depression. He "abandoned the principles of laissez faire in relation to the business cycle, established the conviction that prosperity and depression can be publicly controlled by political action, and drove out of the public consciousness the old idea that depressions must be overcome by private adjustment," wrote Walter Lippmann. Rather than the last of the old presidents, Herbert Hoover was the first of the new.

A charismatic leader and a brilliant politician, his successor expanded federal activities on the basis of Hoover's efforts. Using the federal government to stabilize the economy and advance the interests of the groups, Franklin D. Roosevelt directed the campaign to save large-scale corporate capitalism. Though recognizing new political interests and extending benefits to them, his New Deal never effectively challenged big business or the organization of the economy. In providing assistance to the needy and by rescuing them from starvation, Roosevelt's humane efforts also protected the established system: he sapped organized radicalism of its waning strength and of its potential constituency among the unorganized and discontented. Sensitive to public opinion and fearful of radicalism, Roosevelt acted from a mixture of motives that rendered his liberalism cautious and limited, his experimentalism narrow. Despite the flurry of activity, his government was more vigorous and flexible about means than goals, and the goals were more conservative than historians usually acknowledge.

Roosevelt's response to the banking crisis emphasizes the conservatism of his administration and its self-conscious avoidance of more radical means that might have transformed American capitalism. Entering the White House when banks were failing and Americans had lost faith in the financial system, the President could have nationalized it— "without a word of protest," judged Senator Bronson Cutting. "If ever there was a moment when things hung in the balance," later wrote Raymond Moley, a member of the original

"brain trust," "it was on March 5, 1933—when unorthodoxy would have drained the last remaining strength of the capitalistic system." To save the system, Roosevelt relied upon collaboration between bankers and Hoover's Treasury officials to prepare legislation extending federal assistance to banking. So great was the demand for action that House members, voting even without copies, passed it unanimously, and the Senate, despite objections by a few Progressives, approved it the same evening. "The President," remarked a cynical congressman, "drove the money-changers out of the Capitol on March 4th—and they were all back on the 9th."

Undoubtedly the most dramatic example of Roosevelt's early conservative approach to recovery was the National Recovery Administration (NRA). It was based on the War Industries Board (WIB) which had provided the model for the campaign of Bernard Baruch, General Hugh Johnson, and other former WIB officials during the twenties to limit competition through industrial self-regulation under federal sanction. As trade associations flourished during the decade, the FTC encouraged "codes of fair competition" and some industries even tried to set prices and restrict production. Operating without the force of law, these agreements broke down. When the depression struck, industrial pleas for regulation increased. After the Great Crash, important business leaders including Henry I. Harriman of the Chamber of Commerce and Gerard Swope of General Electric called for suspension of antitrust laws and federal organization of business collaboration. Joining them were labor leaders, particularly those in "sick" industries—John L. Lewis of the United Mine Workers and Sidney Hillman of Amalgamated Clothing Workers.

Designed largely for industrial recovery, the NRA legislation provided for minimum wages and maximum hours. It also made concessions to pro-labor congressmen and labor leaders who demanded some specific benefits for unions—recognition of the worker's right to organization and to collective bargaining. In practice, though, the much-heralded Section 7a was a disappointment to most friends of labor. (For the shrewd Lewis, however, it became a mandate to organize: "The President wants you to join a union.") To many frustrated workers and their disgusted leaders, NRA became "National Run Around." The clause, unionists found (in the words of Brookings economists), "had the practical effect of placing NRA on the side of anti-union employers in their struggle against trade unions. . . . [It] thus threw its weight against labor in the balance of bargaining power." And while some far-sighted industrialists feared radicalism and hoped to forestall it by incorporating unions into the economic system, most preferred to leave their workers unorganized or in company unions. To many businessmen, large and independent unions as such seemed a radical threat to the system of business control.

Not only did the NRA provide fewer advantages than unionists had anticipated, but it also failed as a recovery measure. It probably even retarded recovery by supporting restrictionism and price increases, concluded a Brookings study. Placing effective power for code-writing in big business, NRA injured small businesses and contributed to the concentration of American industry. It was not the government-business partnership as envisaged by Adolf A. Berle, Jr., nor government managed as Rexford Tugwell had hoped, but rather, business managed, as Raymond Moley had desired. Calling NRA "industrial self-government," its director, General Hugh Johnson, had explained that "NRA is exactly what industry organized in trade associations makes it." Despite the annoyance of some big businessmen with Section 7a, the NRA reaffirmed and consolidated their power at a time when the public was critical of industrialists and financiers.

Viewing the economy as a "concert of organized interests," the New Deal also provided benefits for farmers—the Agricultural Adjustment Act. Reflecting the political power of larger commercial farmers and accepting restrictionist economics, the measure assumed that the agricultural problem was overproduction, not underconsumption. Financed by a processing tax designed to raise prices to parity, payments encouraged restricted production and cutbacks in farm labor. With benefits accruing chiefly to the larger owners, they frequently removed from production the lands of sharecroppers and tenant farmers, and "tractored" them and hired hands off the land. In assisting agriculture, the AAA, like the NRA, sacrificed the interests of the marginal and the unrecognized to the welfare of those with greater political and economic power.

In large measure, the early New Deal of the NRA and AAA was a "broker state." Though the government served as a mediator of interests and sometimes imposed its will in divisive situations, it was generally the servant of powerful groups. "Like the mercantilists, the New Dealers protected vested interests with the authority of the state," acknowledges William Leuchtenburg. But it was some improvement over the 1920s when business was the only interest capable of imposing its will on the government. While extending to other groups the benefits of the state, the New Deal, however, continued to recognize the pre-eminence of business interests.

The politics of the broker state also heralded the way of the future—of continued corporate dominance in a political structure where other groups agreed generally on corporate capitalism and squabbled only about the size of the shares. Delighted by this increased participation and the absorption of dissident groups, many liberals did not understand the dangers in the emerging organization of politics. They had too much faith in representative institutions and in associations to foresee the perils—of leaders not representing their constituents, of bureaucracy diffusing responsibility, of officials serving their own interests. Failing to perceive the dangers in the emerging structure, most liberals agreed with Senator Robert Wagner of New York: "In order that the strong may not take advantage of the weak, every group must be equally strong." His advice then seemed appropriate for organizing labor, but it neglected the problems of unrepresentative leadership and of the many millions to be left beyond organization.

In dealing with the organized interests, the President acted frequently as a broker, but his government did not simply express the vectors of external forces. The New Deal state was too complex, too loose, and some of Roosevelt's subordinates were following their own inclinations and pushing the government in directions of their own design. The President would also depart from his role as a broker and act to secure programs he desired. As a skilled politician, he could split coalitions, divert the interests of groups, or place the prestige of his office on the side of desired legislation.

In seeking to protect the stock market, for example, Roosevelt endorsed the Securities and Exchange measure (of 1934), despite the opposition of many in the New York financial community. His advisers split the opposition. Rallying to support the administration were the out-of-town exchanges, representatives of the large commission houses, including James Forrestal of Dillon, Read, and Robert Lovett of Brown Brothers, Harriman, and such commission brokers as E. A. Pierce and Paul Shields. Opposed to the Wall Street "old guard" and their companies, this group included those who wished to avoid more radical legislation, as well as others who had wanted earlier to place trading practices under federal legislation which they could influence.

Though the law restored confidence in the securities market and protected capitalism, it alarmed some businessmen and contributed to the false belief that the New Deal was threatening business. But it was not the disaffection of a portion of the business community, not the creation of the Liberty League, that menaced the broker state. Rather it was the threat of the Left—expressed, for example, in such overwrought statements as Minnesota Governor Floyd Olson's: "I am not a liberal

. . . I am a radical. . . . I am not satisfied with hanging a laurel wreath on burglars and thieves . . . and calling them code authorities or something else." While Olson, along with some others who succumbed to the rhetoric of militancy, would back down and soften their meaning, their words dramatized real grievances: the failure of the early New Deal to end misery, to re-create prosperity. The New Deal excluded too many. Its programs were inadequate. While Roosevelt reluctantly endorsed relief and went beyond Hoover in support of public works, he too preferred self-liquidating projects, desired a balanced budget, and resisted spending the huge sums required to lift the nation out of depression.

For millions suffering in a nation wracked by poverty, the promises of the Left seemed attractive. Capitalizing on the misery, Huey Long offered Americans a "Share Our Wealth" program—a welfare state with prosperity, not subsistence, for the disadvantaged, those neglected by most politicians. "Every Man a King": pensions for the elderly, college for the deserving, homes and cars for families—that was the promise of American life. Also proposing minimum wages, increased public works, shorter work weeks, and a generous farm program, he demanded a "soak-the-rich" tax program. Despite the economic defects of his plan, Long was no hayseed, and his forays into the East revealed support far beyond the bayous and hamlets of his native South. In California discontent was so great that Upton Sinclair, food faddist and former socialist, captured the Democratic nomination for governor on a platform of "production-for-use"—factories and farms for the unemployed. "In a cooperative society," promised Sinclair, "every man, woman, and child would have the equivalent of $5,000 a year income from labor of the able-bodied young men for three or four hours per day." More challenging to Roosevelt was Francis Townsend's plan—monthly payments of $200 to those past sixty who retired and promised to spend the stipend within thirty days.

Another enemy of the New Deal was Father Coughlin, the popular radio priest, who had broken with Roosevelt and formed a National Union for Social Justice to lead the way to a corporate society beyond capitalism.

To a troubled nation offered "redemption" by the Left, there was also painful evidence that the social fabric was tearing—law was breaking down. When the truckers in Minneapolis struck, the police provoked an incident and shot sixty-seven people, some in the back. Covering the tragedy, Eric Sevareid, then a young reporter, wrote, "I understood deep in my bones and blood what fascism was." In San Francisco union leaders embittered by police brutality led a general strike and aroused national fears of class warfare. Elsewhere, in textile mills from Rhode Island to Georgia, in cities like Des Moines and Toledo, New York and Philadelphia, there were brutality and violence, sometimes bayonets and tear gas.

Challenged by the Left, and with the new Congress more liberal and more willing to spend, Roosevelt turned to disarm the discontent. "Boys—this is our hour," confided Harry Hopkins. "We've got to get everything we want—a works program, social security, wages and hours, everything—now or never. Get your minds to work on developing a complete ticket to provide security for all the folks of this country up and down and across the board." Hopkins and the associates he addressed were not radicals: they did not seek to transform the system, only to make it more humane. They, too, wished to preserve large-scale corporate capitalism, but unlike Roosevelt or Moley, they were prepared for more vigorous action. Their commitment to reform was greater, their tolerance for injustice far less. Joining them in pushing the New Deal left were the leaders of industrial unions, who, while also not wishing to transform the system, sought for workingmen higher wages, better conditions, stronger and larger unions, and for themselves a place closer to the fulcrum of power.

The problems of organized labor, however, neither aroused Roosevelt's humanitarianism nor suggested possibilities of reshaping the political coalition. When asked during the NRA about employee representation, he had replied that workers could select anyone they wished—the Ahkoond of Swat, a union, even the Royal Geographical Society. As a paternalist, viewing himself (in the words of James MacGregor Burns) as a "partisan and benefactor" of workers, he would not understand the objections to company unions or to multiple unionism under NRA. Nor did he foresee the political dividends that support of independent unions could yield to his party. Though presiding over the reshaping of politics (which would extend the channels of power to some of the discontented and redirect their efforts to competition within a limited framework), he was not its architect, and he was unable clearly to see or understand the unfolding design.

When Senator Wagner submitted his labor relations bill, he received no assistance from the President and even struggled to prevent Roosevelt from joining the opposition. The President "never lifted a finger," recalls Miss Perkins. ("I, myself, had very little sympathy with the bill," she wrote.) But after the measure easily passed the Senate and seemed likely to win the House's endorsement, Roosevelt reversed himself. Three days before the Supreme Court invalidated the NRA, including the legal support for unionization, Roosevelt came out for the bill. Placing it on his "must" list, he may have hoped to influence the final provisions and turn an administration defeat into victory.

Responding to the threat from the left, Roosevelt also moved during the Second Hundred Days to secure laws regulating banking, raising taxes, dissolving utility-holding companies, and creating social security. Building on the efforts of states during the Progressive Era, the Social Security Act marked the movement toward the welfare state, but the core of the measure, the old-age provision, was more important as a landmark than for its substance. While establishing a federal-state system of unemployment compensation, the government, by making workers contribute to their old-age insurance, denied its financial responsibility for the elderly. The act excluded more than a fifth of the labor force leaving, among others, more than five million farm laborers and domestics without coverage.

Though Roosevelt criticized the tax laws for not preventing "an unjust concentration of wealth and economic power," his own tax measure would not have significantly redistributed wealth. Yet his message provoked an "amen" from Huey Long and protests from businessmen. Retreating from his promises, Roosevelt failed to support the bill, and it succumbed to conservative forces. They removed the inheritance tax and greatly reduced the proposed corporate and individual levies. The final law did not "soak the rich." But it did engender deep resentment among the wealthy for increasing taxes on gifts and estates, imposing an excess-profits tax (which Roosevelt had not requested), and raising surtaxes. When combined with such regressive levies as social security and local taxes, however, the Wealth Tax of 1935 did not drain wealth from higher-income groups, and the top one percent even increased their shares during the New Deal years.

Those historians who have characterized the events of 1935 as the beginning of a second New Deal have imposed a pattern on those years which most participants did not then discern. In moving to social security, guarantees of collective bargaining, utility regulation, and progressive taxation, the government did advance the nation toward greater liberalism, but the shift was exaggerated and most of the measures accomplished far less than either friends or foes suggested. Certainly, despite a mild bill authorizing destruction of utilities-holding companies, there was no effort to atomize business, no real threat to concentration.

Nor were so many powerful businessmen disaffected by the New Deal. Though the smaller businessmen who filled the ranks of the Chamber of Commerce resented the federal bureaucracy and the benefits to labor and thus criticized NRA, representatives of big business found the agency useful and opposed a return to unrestricted competition. In 1935, members of the Business Advisory Council—including Henry Harriman, outgoing president of the Chamber, Thomas Watson of International Business Machines, Walter Gifford of American Telephone and Telegraph, Gerard Swope of General Electric, Winthrop Aldrich of the Chase National Bank, and W. Averell Harriman of Union Pacific—vigorously endorsed a two-year renewal of NRA.

When the Supreme Court in 1935 declared the "hot" oil clause and then NRA unconstitutional, the administration moved to measures known as the "little NRA." Reestablishing regulations in bituminous coal and oil, the New Deal also checked wholesale price discrimination and legalized "fair trade" practices. Though Roosevelt never acted to revive the NRA, he periodically contemplated its restoration. In the so-called second New Deal, as in the "first," government remained largely the benefactor of big business, and some more advanced businessmen realized this.

Roosevelt could attack the "economic royalists" and endorse the TNEC investigation of economic concentration, but he was unprepared to resist the basic demands of big business. While there was ambiguity in his treatment of oligopoly, it was more the confusion of means than of ends, for his tactics were never likely to impair concentration. Even the antitrust program under Thurman Arnold, concludes Frank Freidel, was "intended less to bust the trusts than to forestall too drastic legislation." Operating through consent degrees and designed to reduce prices to the consumer, the program frequently "allowed industries to function much as they had in NRA days." In effect, then, throughout its variations, the New Deal had sought to cooperate with business.

Though vigorous in rhetoric and experimental in tone, the New Deal was narrow in its goals and wary of bold economic reform.

Roosevelt's sense of what was politically desirable was frequently more restricted than others' views of what was possible and necessary. Roosevelt's limits were those of ideology; they were not inherent in experimentalism. For while the President explored the narrow center, and some New Dealers considered bolder possibilities, John Dewey, the philosopher of experimentalism, moved far beyond the New Deal and sought to reshape the system. Liberalism, he warned, "must now become radical. . . . For the gulf between what the actual situation makes possible and the actual state itself is so great that it cannot be bridged by piecemeal policies undertaken *ad hoc.*" The boundaries of New Deal experimentalism, as Howard Zinn has emphasized, could extend far beyond Roosevelt's cautious ventures. Operating within very safe channels, Roosevelt not only avoided Marxism and the socialization of property, but he also stopped far short of other possibilities—communal direction of production or the organized distribution of surplus. The President and many of his associates were doctrinaires of the center, and their maneuvers in social reform were limited to cautious excursions.

Usually opportunistic and frequently shifting, the New Deal was restricted by its ideology. It ran out of fuel not because of the conservative opposition, but because it ran out of ideas. Acknowledging the end in 1939, Roosevelt proclaimed, "We have now passed the period of internal conflict in the launching of our program of social reform. Our full energies may now be released to invigorate the processes of recovery in order to preserve our reforms. . . ."

The sad truth was that the heralded reforms were severely limited, that inequality continued, that efforts at recovery had failed. Millions had come to accept the depression as a way of life. A decade after the Great Crash, when millions were still unemployed, Fiorello LaGuardia recommended that "we accept the inevitable, that we are now in a new normal." "It was reasonable to expect a probable minimum of 4,000,000 to 5,000,000 unemployed," Harry Hopkins had concluded. Even that level was never reached, for business would not spend and Roosevelt refused to countenance the necessary expenditures. "It was in economics that our troubles lay," Tugwell wrote. "For their solution his /Roosevelt's/ progressivism, his new deal was pathetically insufficient. . . ."

Clinging to faith in fiscal orthodoxy even when engaged in deficit spending, Roosevelt had been unwilling to greatly unbalance the budget. Having pledged in his first campaign to cut expenditures and to restore the balanced budget, the President had at first adopted recovery programs that would not drain government finances. Despite a burst of activity under the Civil Works Administration during the first winter, public works expenditures were frequently slow and cautious. Shifting from direct relief, which Roosevelt (like Hoover) considered "a narcotic, a subtle destroyer of the human spirit," the government moved to work relief. ("It saves his skill. It gives him a chance to do something socially useful," said Hopkins.) By 1937 the government had poured enough money into the economy to spur production to within 10 percent of 1929 levels, but unemployment still hovered over seven million. Yet so eager was the President to balance the budget that he cut expenditures for public works and relief, and plunged the economy into a greater depression. While renewing expenditures, Roosevelt remained cautious in his fiscal policy, and the nation still had almost nine million unemployed in 1939. After nearly six years of struggling with the depression, the Roosevelt administration could not lead the nation to recovery, but it had relieved suffering. In most of America, starvation was no longer possible. Perhaps that was the most humane achievement of the New Deal.

Its efforts on behalf of humane *reform* were generally faltering and shallow, of more value to the middle classes, of less value to organized workers, of even less to the marginal men. In conception and in practice, seemingly humane efforts revealed the shortcomings of American liberalism. For example, public housing, praised as evidence of the federal government's concern for the poor, was limited in scope (to 180,000 units) and unfortunate in results. It usually meant the consolidation of ghettos, the robbing of men of their dignity, the treatment of men as wards with few rights. And slum clearance came to mean "Negro clearance" and removal of the other poor. Of much of this liberal reformers were unaware, and some of the problems can be traced to the structure of bureaucracy and to the selection of government personnel and social workers who disliked the poor. But the liberal conceptions, it can be argued, were also flawed for there was no willingness to consult the poor, nor to encourage their participation. Liberalism was elitist. Seeking to build America in their own image, liberals wanted to create an environment which they thought would restructure character and personality more appropriate to white, middle-class America.

While slum dwellers received little besides relief from the New Deal, and their needs were frequently misunderstood, Negroes as a group received even less assistance—less than they needed and sometimes even less than their proportion in the population would have justified. Under the NRA they were frequently dismissed and their wages were sometimes below the legal minimum. The Civilian Conservation Corps left them "forgotten" men—excluded, discriminated against, segregated. In general, what the Negroes gained—relief, WPA jobs, equal pay on some federal projects—was granted them as poor people, not as Negroes. To many black men the distinction was unimportant, for no government had ever given them so much. "My friends, go home and turn Lincoln's picture to the wall," a Negro publisher told his race. "That debt has been payed in full."

Bestowing recognition on some Negro leaders, the New Deal appointed them to agencies as advisers—the "black cabinet." Probably more dramatic was the advocacy of Negro rights by Eleanor Roosevelt. Some whites like Harold Ickes and Aubrey Williams even struggled cautiously to break down segregation. But segregation did not yield, and Washington itself remained a segregated city. The white South was never challenged, the Fourteenth Amendment never used to assist Negroes. Never would Roosevelt expend political capital in an assault upon the American caste system. Despite the efforts of the NAACP to dramatize the Negroes' plight as second-class citizens, subject to brutality and often without legal protection, Roosevelt would not endorse the anti-lynching bill. ("No government pretending to be civilized can go on condoning such atrocities," H. L. Mencken testified. "Either it must make every possible effort to put them down or it must suffer the scorn and contempt of Christendom.") Unwilling to risk schism with Southerners ruling committees, Roosevelt capitulated to the forces of racism.

Even less bold than in economic reform, the New Deal left intact the race relations of America. Yet its belated and cautious recognition of the black man was great enough to woo Negro leaders and even to court the masses. One of the bitter ironies of these years is that a New Dealer could tell the NAACP in 1936: "Under our new conception of democracy, the Negro will be given the chance to which he is entitled. . . ." But it was true, Ickes emphasized, that "The greatest advance /since Reconstruction/ toward assuring the Negro that degree of justice to which he is entitled and that equality of opportunity under the law which is implicit in his American citizenship, has been made since Franklin D. Roosevelt was sworn in as President. . . ."

It was not in the cities and not among the Negroes but in rural America that [the] Roosevelt administration made its (philosophically) boldest efforts: creation of the Tennessee Valley Authority and the later attempt to construct seven little valley authorities. Though conservation was not a new federal policy and government-owned utilities were sanctioned by municipal experience, federal activity in this area constituted a challenge to corporate enterprise and an expression of concern about the poor. A valuable example of regional planning and a contribution to regional prosperity, TVA still fell far short of expectations. The agency soon retreated from social planning. ("From 1936 on," wrote Tugwell, "the TVA should have been called the Tennessee Valley Power Production and Flood Control Corporation.") Fearful of antagonizing the powerful interests, its agricultural program neglected the tenants and the sharecroppers.

To urban workingmen the New Deal offered some, but limited, material benefits. Though the government had instituted contributory social security and unemployment insurance, its much-heralded Fair Labor Standards Act, while prohibiting child labor, was a greater disappointment. It exempted millions from its wages-and-hours provisions. So unsatisfactory was the measure that one congressman cynically suggested, "Within 90 days after appointment of the administrator, she should report to Congress whether anyone is subject to this bill." Requiring a minimum of twenty-five cents an hour ($11 a week for 44 hours), it raised the wages of only about a half-million at a time when nearly twelve million workers in interstate commerce were earning less than forty cents an hour.

More important than these limited measures was the administration's support, albeit belated, of the organization of labor and the right of collective bargaining. Slightly increasing organized workers' share of the national income, the new industrial unions extended job security to millions who were previously subject to the whim of management. Unionization freed them from the perils of a free market.

By assisting labor, as well as agriculture, the New Deal started the institutionalization of larger interest groups into a new political economy. Joining business as tentative junior partners, they shared the consensus on the value of large-scale corporate capitalism, and were permitted to participate in the competition for the division of shares. While failing to redistribute income, the New Deal modified the political structure at the price of excluding many from the process of decision making. To many what was offered in fact was symbolic representation, formal representation. It was not the industrial workers necessarily who were recognized, but their unions and leaders; it was not even the farmers, but their organizations and leaders. While this was not a conscious design, it was the predictable result of conscious policies. It could not have been easily avoided, for it was part of the price paid by a large society unwilling to consider radical new designs for the distribution of power and wealth.

In the deepest sense, this new form of representation was rooted in the liberal's failure to endorse a meaningful egalitarianism which would provide actual equality of opportunity. It was also the limited concern with equality and justice that accounted for the shallow efforts of the New Deal and left so many Americans behind. The New Deal was neither a "third American Revolution," as Carl Degler suggests, nor even a "half-way revolution," as William Leuchtenburg concludes. Not only was the extension of representation to new groups less than full-fledged partnership, but the New Deal neglected many Americans—sharecroppers, tenant farmers, migratory workers and farm laborers, slum dwellers, unskilled workers, and the unemployed Negroes. They were left outside the new order. As Roosevelt asserted in 1937 (in a classic understatement), one third of the nation was "ill-nourished, ill-clad, ill-housed."

Yet, by the power of rhetoric and through the appeals of political organization, the Roosevelt government managed to win or retain the allegiance of these peoples. Perhaps this is one of the crueller ironies of liberal politics, that the marginal men trapped in hopelessness were seduced by rhetoric, by the style and movement, by the symbolism of efforts seldom reaching beyond words. In acting to protect the institution of private property and in advancing the interests of corporate capitalism, the New Deal assisted the middle and upper sectors of society. It protected them, sometimes, even at the cost of injuring the lower sectors. Seldom did it bestow much of substance upon the lower classes. Never did the New Deal seek to organize these groups into independent political forces. Seldom did it risk antagonizing established interests. For some this would constitute a puzzling defect of liberalism; for some, the failure to achieve true liberalism. To others it would emphasize the inherent shortcomings of American liberal democracy. As the nation prepared for war, liberalism, by accepting private property and federal assistance to corporate capitalism, was not prepared effectively to reduce inequities, to redistribute political power, or to extend equality from promise to reality.

PART THREE

A
RESILIENT
PEOPLE

15

THE DECISION FOR MASS EVACUATION OF THE JAPANESE-AMERICANS

ROGER DANIELS

From 1939, when World War II broke out in Europe, to December 1941, mainstream opinion in America was avowedly isolationist. The war was widely thought to be a European concern, the price that European states had to pay for their "corrupt" system of power politics. But when Japanese naval aircraft attacked and destroyed much of the American fleet at Pearl Harbor on December 7, 1941, popular isolationism quickly changed to demands for prompt retaliation.

In Washington, Franklin D. Roosevelt responded quickly to the Japanese attack, asking Congress on December 9 for a declaration of war. But America was militarily unprepared to proceed against the Japanese, for much of its Pacific forces had been destroyed at Pearl Harbor. Moreover, America's European allies were in desperate straits by 1942; excepting Switzerland, Luxembourg, and Sweden, all of continental Europe was under Axis control and Germany was poised for a major assault upon a staggering Britain.

Faced with this situation, Roosevelt saw America's first duty as the rescue of Britain and the defeat of the fascist forces in Europe. Only then, reasoned Roosevelt, would the United States have sufficient time to arm itself for a concentrated campaign against Japan. But while he developed this European strategy, Roosevelt also had to respond to the growing public clamor for an immediate military response to the Japanese attack.

Caught between these conflicting demands, Roosevelt looked to symbolic attacks against the Japanese to satisfy domestic demands and to gain support for his war strategy. Thus, in early 1942, Roosevelt authorized air raids on Tokyo, and in February of the same year he signed an executive order giving the Army authority to remove all people of Japanese descent, many of whom were American citizens, from the western United States. In this essay, Roger Daniels traces the ways in which government officials conspired to deprive thousands of Japanese-Americans of their constitutional rights.

Chapter 3 in Roger Daniels, *Concentration Camps, North America: Japanese in the United States and Canada During World War II* (Malabar, Fla.: Robert E. Krieger, 1981). Reprinted by permission of the author.

December 1941 was a month of calamities which saw West Coast opinion harden against the Japanese; during January, as the war news got worse and worse and it became apparent that the Japanese audacity at Pearl Harbor would not be quickly avenged, the national climate of opinion, and Congressional opinion in particular, began to veer toward the West Coast view. That this climate had to be created is shown by an examination of the *Congressional Record.* Not only was there no concerted strong feeling exhibited against the Japanese Americans, but in the first weeks after Pearl Harbor members of the California delegation defended them publicly. (The only trace of hostility shown by a California solon in early December was a telephone call that the junior senator, Democrat Sheridan Downey, made to the Army on the night of December 7 suggesting that De Witt prompt Governor Olson to declare some sort of curfew on "Japs.") On December 10, for example, Bertrand W. Gearhart, a four-term Republican congressman from Fresno and an officer of the American Legion, read a telegram professing loyalty to the United States from an Issei leader in his district whom Gearhart described as an "American patriot." Five days later, when John Rankin (D-Miss.), the leading nativist in the lower house, called for "deporting every Jap who claims, or has claimed, Japanese citizenship, or sympathizes with Japan in this war," he was answered by another Californian, Leland M. Ford, a Santa Monica Republican:

> These people are American-born. They cannot be deported . . . whether we like it or whether we do not. This is their country. . . . /When/ they join the armed forces . . . they must take this oath of allegiance . . . and I see no particular reason at this particular time why they should not. I believe that every one of these people should make a clear, clean acknowledgment.

Despite the lack of Congressional concern, by the end of December momentum was gathering for more drastic action against the Japanese and against enemy aliens generally. On December 30 the Justice Department made the first of many concessions to the military, concessions that had little to do either with due process or the realities of the situation. On that date Attorney General Biddle informed the Provost Marshal General's office that he had authorized the issuance of search warrants for any house in which an enemy alien lived, merely on the representation that there was reasonable cause to believe that there was contraband on the premises. Contraband had already been defined to include anything that might be used as a weapon, any explosive (many Issei farmers used dynamite to clear stumps), radio transmitters, any radio that had a shortwave band, and all but the simplest cameras. For the next few months thousands of houses where Japanese lived were subjected to random search. Although much "contraband" was found (most of it in two Issei-owned sporting goods stores), the FBI itself later stipulated that none of it was sinister in nature and reported that there was no evidence at all that any of it was intended for subversive use. But the mere fact of these searches, widely reported in the press, added to the suspicion with which the Japanese were viewed. These searches, like so much of the anti-Japanese movement, were part of a self-fulfilling prophecy: one is suspicious of the Japanese, so one searches their houses; the mere fact of the search, when noticed ("the FBI went through those Jap houses on the other side of town"), creates more suspicion.

For individual Japanese families, these searches intensified the insecurity and terror they already felt. One fifteen-year-old girl in San Jose, California reported what must have been an all-too-routine occurrence:

> One day I came home from school to find the two F.B.I. men at our front door. They asked permission to search the house. One man looked through the front rooms, while the other searched the back rooms. Trembling with fright, I followed and watched each of the men

look around. The investigators examined the mattresses, and the dresser and looked under the beds. The gas range, piano and sofa were thoroughly inspected. Since I was the only one at home, the F.B.I. questioned me, but did not procure sufficient evidence of Fifth Columnists in our family. This made me very happy, even if they did mess up the house.

Concurrent with its more stringent search order, the Department of Justice and the Provost Marshal General's office decided to send representatives to De Witt's headquarters in San Francisco; the two men sent—James Rowe, Jr., Assistant Attorney General and a former Presidential assistant, and Major (later Colonel) Karl R. Bendetsen, chief of the Aliens Division, Provost Marshal General's office— were key and mutually antagonistic figures in the bureaucratic struggle over the fate of the West Coast Japanese. Rowe, during his short visit in California, exercised a moderating influence on the cautious General De Witt, who often seemed to be the creature of the last strong personality with whom he had contact. Bendetsen represented a chief (Gullion) who wanted not only exclusion of the Japanese from the West Coast but also the transfer of supervisory authority over all enemy aliens in the United States from the civilian control of the Department of Justice to the military control of his office. Bendetsen soon became the voice of General De Witt in matters concerning aliens, and was well rewarded for his efforts. A graduate of Stanford Law School, he had gone on to active duty as a captain in 1940, and in the process of evacuating the Japanese he would gain his colonel's eagles before he turned thirty-five. After Bendetsen's arrival, Gullion arranged with De Witt that the West Coast commander go out of normal channels and deal directly with the Provost Marshal on matters concerning aliens. The result of this seemingly routine bureaucratic shuffle was highly significant; as Stetson Conn has pointed out, the consequence of this arrangement was that "the responsible Army command head-

quarters in Washington /that is, Chief of Staff George C. Marshall and his immediate staff/ had little to do during January and February 1942 with the plans and decisions for Japanese evacuation."

Telephone conversations and correspondence between De Witt's headquarters and the Provost Marshal General's office in late December and early January reveal the tremendous pressures that the soldiers were putting on the civilians. According to General Gullion, the Justice Department's representatives, James Rowe, Jr., and Edward J. Ennis, were apologetic about the slowness of the Justice Department, an apparent criticism of their chief, the Attorney General. At about the same time Gullion was complaining that "the Attorney General is not functioning" and threatened to have Secretary Stimson complain to the President. De Witt was, as usual, vacillating. Within the same week he told the Provost Marshal General's office that "it would be better if . . . this thing worked through the civil channels," but a few days later insisted that "I don't want to go after this thing piecemeal. I want to do it on a mass basis, all at the same time."

The arrival of Bendetsen at De Witt's San Francisco headquarters seemed to strengthen the West Coast commander's resolve. Before Bendetsen left Washington he had drafted an Executive Order transferring authority over aliens to the War Department, but the Provost Marshal General's office felt that since the Justice Department's representatives were so apologetic, it "wasn't quite fair" to take over without giving them a chance to come up to the Army's standards. Shortly after his arrival in San Francisco, Bendetsen drafted a memo that quickly became the guideline for De Witt's policy. It called for an immediate and complete registration of all alien enemies, who were to be photographed and fingerprinted. These records were to be kept in duplicate, one set to be kept in the community in which the alien resided, the other in a central office. The purpose was to set up what Bendetsen called a "Pass and Permit System." Doubtful that the Attorney General would agree to this, Bendetsen's memo concluded with what had become the refrain of the Provost Marshal General's men: if Justice won't do it, the War Department must.

The next day, January 4, in a conference at his Presidio headquarters attended by Rowe, Bendetsen, and representatives of other federal departments and officials in local government, De Witt made some of his position clear, stressing, as he always did to civilians, what he called the military necessity.

> We are at war and this area—eight states—has been designated as a theater of operations. I have approximately 240,000 men at my disposal. . . . /There are/ approximately 288,000 enemy aliens . . . which we have to watch. . . . I have little confidence that the enemy aliens are law-abiding or loyal in any sense of the word. Some of them yes; many, no. Particularly the Japanese. I have no confidence in their loyalty whatsoever. I am speaking now of the native born Japanese—117,000–and 42,000 in California alone.

One result of this conference was that the Department of Justice agreed to go further than it had previously: enemy aliens were to be re-registered under its auspices, the FBI would conduct large-scale "spot" raids, something De Witt was particularly eager for, and, most significantly, a large number of restricted, or Category A, zones would be established around crucial military and defense installations on the Pacific Coast. Entry to these zones would be on a pass basis. Assistant Secretary of War John J. McCloy later described this program as "the best way to solve" the West Coast alien problem.

> . . . establish limited restricted areas around the airplane plants, the forts and other important military installations . . . we might call these military reservations in substance and exclude everyone—whites, yellows, blacks, greens— from that area and then license back into the area those whom we felt there was no danger

to be expected from . . . then we can cover the legal situation . . . in spite of the constitution. . . . You may, by that process, eliminate all the Japs /alien and citizen/ but you might conceivably permit some to come back whom you are quite certain are free from any suspicion.

In addition to the Category A zones, there were to be Category B zones, consisting of the rest of the coastal area, in which enemy aliens and citizen Japanese would be allowed to live and work under rigidly prescribed conditions. Although De Witt and the other Army people were constantly complaining about the slowness of the Justice Department, they quickly found that setting up these zones was easier said than done. De Witt did not forward his first recommendations for Category A areas to the War Department until January 21, more than two weeks after the San Francisco conference.

On January 16 Representative Leland Ford, the Santa Monica Republican who had opposed stern treatment for the Japanese on the floor of the House in mid-December, had changed his mind. Ford had received a number of telegrams and letters from California suggesting removal of Japanese from vital coastal areas—the earliest seems to have been a January 6 telegram from Mexican American movie star Leo Carillo—and by mid-January had come around to their point of view. He urged Secretary of War Henry L. Stimson to have "all Japanese, whether citizens or not, . . . placed in inland concentration camps." Arguing that native-born Japanese either were or were not loyal to the United States, Ford developed a simple test for loyalty: any Japanese willing to go to a concentration camp was a patriot; therefore it followed that unwillingness to go was a proof of disloyalty to the United States. Stimson and his staff mulled over this letter for ten days, and then replied (in a letter drafted by Bendetsen, now back from the Pacific Coast) giving the congressman a certain amount of encouragement. "The internment of over a hundred thousand people," Stimson wrote, "involves many complex considerations." The basic responsibility, Stimson pointed out, putting the finger on his Cabinet colleague Francis Biddle, has been delegated to the Attorney General. Nevertheless, the Secretary continued, "the Army is prepared to provide internment facilities in the interior to the extent necessary." Assuring Ford that the Army was aware of the dangers on the Pacific Coast, Stimson informed him that the military were submitting suggestions to the Justice Department, and advised him to present his views to the Attorney General.

The same day that Ford wrote Stimson, January 16, another federal department became involved in the fate of the West Coast Japanese. Agriculture Secretary Claude Wickard, chiefly concerned with increasing farm production—"Food Can Win the War" was his line—called a meeting in his office at which the War, Labor, Navy, Justice, and Treasury Departments were represented. He had become alarmed over investigative reports from his agents on the West Coast, who were concerned both about the fate of the Japanese and the threat to food production. Wickard had been informed that although violence against the Japanese farmers was an isolated phenomenon, greatly exaggerated by the press, nevertheless it was quite clear that the Japanese rural population was "terrified."

> They do not leave their homes at night, and will not, even in the daytime, enter certain areas populated by Filipinos. The police authorities are probably not sympathetic to the Japanese and are giving them only the minimum protection. Investigation of actual attacks on Japanese have been merely perfunctory and no prosecutions have been initiated.

The federal officials then concluded that the whole "propaganda campaign" against the Japanese was essentially a conspiracy designed to place Japanese-owned and leased farm lands into white hands; the real aim was to "eliminate Japanese competition." Wickard's West Coast representatives urged him to take positive steps both to maintain agricultural production and to preserve and protect the property and persons of the Japanese farmers.

Wickard's action was not exactly along the lines recommended by the men in the field. He did urge immediate federal action "so that the supply of vegetables for the military forces and the civilian population will not be needlessly curtailed." But Wickard also felt that the fears and suspicions of the general public—particularly the West Coast public—should be taken into account. He seemed to envision a sort of large agricultural reservation in the central valleys of California on which the Japanese could "carry on their normal farming operations" after being removed from "all strategic areas." In this way, Wickard felt, the country could protect itself from "possible subversive Japanese activities," provide "limited protection to all Japanese whose conduct is above suspicion," and at the same time "avoid incidents that might provide an excuse for cruel treatment for our people in Japanese occupied territory." As for the agricultural lands in the coastal area which the Japanese had tilled, Wickard suggested that Mexicans might be brought in to replace them.

Also, by mid-January, the urban Japanese, if not terrorized as were their rural cousins, were feeling more and more hopeless and demoralized. An occasional militant like James Y. Sakamoto, a Japanese American Citizen League (JACL) official in Seattle, could indignantly protest against Representative Ford's evacuation proposal which went out on the Associated Press wire on January 21.

"This is our country," Sakamoto pointed out, "we were born and raised here . . . have made our homes here . . . /and/ we are ready to give our lives, if necessary, to defend the United States." Ford's drastic measures, he insisted, were not in the best interests of the nation. But even a Nisei leader like Sakamoto felt compelled to admit that there was some kind of subversive danger from the older generation of Japanese. The Seattle Nisei, he stated, were "actively cooperating" with the authorities "to uncover all subversive activity in our midst" and, if necessary, he concluded, the Nisei were "ready to stand as protective custodians over our parent generation to guard against danger to the United States arising from their midst." One of the standard complaints quite properly raised by Americans in denouncing totalitarian regimes is that their police states turn children against their parents; it is rarely remarked that, in this instance at least, such too was the function of American democracy.

But for those really in charge, the agonizing distinctions between father and son, between alien and citizen, were essentially irrelevant. By mid-January, perhaps as a way of answering the points made by Representative Ford, Chief of Staff George C. Marshall ordered the Provost Marshal General's office to prepare a memorandum on the West Coast Japanese situation. Bendetsen, the natural drafter for such a report, called General De Witt to ask what his attitude would be if "the Department of Justice still fails to do what we think they ought to do?" De Witt, who felt that things would work out, was nevertheless apprehensive about the continuing potentialities for sabotage and other subversive activities. "We know," he told Bendetsen, "that they are communicating at sea. . . ." De Witt actually knew no such thing, as no evidence existed of such communication, but he undoubtedly believed it. Then, in a classic leap in what Richard Hofstadter has styled the paranoid style, the West Coast commander insisted that "the fact that we have had /not even/ sporadic attempts at sabotage clearly means that control is being exercised somewhere." Here then was the "heads I win, tails you lose" situation in which this one Army officer was able to place more than 100,000 innocent people. There had been no acts of sabotage, no real evidence of subversion, despite the voices that De Witt kept hearing at sea. Yet, according to this military logician, there was a conspiracy afoot not to commit sabotage until America dropped its guard. Ergo, evacuate

them quickly before the conspiracy is put into operation.

The next day, January 25, the long-awaited report on the attack on Pearl Harbor made by the official committee of inquiry headed by Supreme Court Justice Owen J. Roberts was released to the press just in time for the Sunday morning papers, though it is dated two days earlier. In addition to its indictment of the general conditions of unreadiness in the Hawaiian command, the board reported, falsely, as it turned out, that the attack was greatly abetted by Japanese spies, some of whom were described as "persons having no open relations with the Japanese foreign service." It went on to criticize the laxity of counterespionage activity in the Islands, and implied that a too close adherence to the Constitution had seriously inhibited the work of the Federal Bureau of Investigation. The publication of the report was naturally a sensation; it greatly stimulated already prevalent rumors that linked the disaster to wholly imaginary fifth column activities by resident Japanese. Perhaps the most popular was the yarn that University of California class rings had been found on the fingers of Japanese pilots shot down in the raid. Even more ridiculous was the story that the attacking pilots had been aided by arrows, pointing at Pearl Harbor, which had been hacked into the cane fields the night before by Japanese workers. The absurdity of this device—a large natural harbor containing dozens of war vessels, large and small, is highly visible from the air— seems to have occurred to few. The Roberts Report provided a field day for those who had long urged more repressive measures and a more effective secret police unfettered by constitutional restrictions. Congressmen like Martin Dies of Texas, then head of the House Committee on Un-American Activities, insisted, in and out of Congress, that if only people had listened to them, the disaster at Pearl Harbor could have been averted. More significantly, it gave an additional argument to those who were pressing for preventive detention and must have given pause to some who had been urging restraint.

On January 25 Secretary Stimson forwarded to Attorney General Biddle recommendations that General De Witt had made four days earlier, calling for total exclusion of enemy aliens from eighty-six Category A zones and close control of enemy aliens in eight Category B zones on a pass and permit system. As this proposal involved only aliens, the Justice Department quickly agreed and made the first public, official announcement of a mass evacuation on January 29, to be effective almost a month later, on February 24. This relatively modest proposal would have moved only about 7000 aliens in all, and fewer than 3000 of these would have been Japanese. At about the same time it announced the appointment of Tom C. Clark (who later became Attorney General under Truman and then an Associate Justice of the Supreme Court) as Coordinator of the Alien Enemy Control Program within the Western Defense Command. Clark flew to the West Coast the next day.

A few days before Stimson's recommendation to Biddle, the top echelons of military command, for the first time, began to become aware of the kinds of proposals that were emanating from De Witt's headquarters. General Mark W. Clark (then a brigadier on the General Staff and later a major commander in the European Theater) was instructed to prepare a memorandum for the President on the subject of "enemy aliens" in the Western Theater of Operations. The day after Stimson's letter to Biddle requesting the announcement of Category A and B areas, General Clark recommended that no memorandum be sent unless the Attorney General's action should "not be all that is desired." Clark's memorandum was read by Chief of Staff George C. Marshall, who noted on it "hold for me until Feb. 1." The top brass was satisfied with a very modest program, involving the forced removal, without detention, of a very few aliens. Clark's memorandum made no mention of citizens at all.

But if the top brass were satisfied, De Witt,

Bendetsen, and Gullion were not. And neither were the leading public officials in California. On January 27 De Witt had a conference with Governor Culbert Olson and related to Washington, probably accurately:

> There's a tremendous volume of public opinion now developing against the Japanese of all classes, that is aliens and non-aliens, to get them off the land, and in Southern California around Los Angeles—in that area too—they want and they are bringing pressure on the government to move all the Japanese out. As a matter of fact, it's not being instigated or developed by people who are not thinking but by the best people of California. Since the publication of the Roberts Report they feel that they are living in the midst of a lot of enemies. They don't trust the Japanese, none of them.

Two days later, De Witt talked with Olson's Republican Attorney General Earl Warren. (De Witt thought his name was Warner.) The California Attorney General, who was then preparing to run for governor against Olson in November, was in thorough agreement with his rival that the Japanese ought to be removed. This was not surprising. Warren was heir to a long anti-Japanese tradition in California politics and the protégé of U. S. Webb, a long-time Attorney General of California (1902–1939) and the author of the 1913 California Alien Land Act. Warren had been intimately associated with the most influential nativist group in the state, the Joint Immigration Committee, but shortly after he became Attorney General in 1939 he prudently arranged to have his name taken off the Committee's letterhead, although he continued to meet with them and receive copies of all documents and notices. Because of his later prominence, some have tried to make too much of Warren's very minor role in pressing for an evacuation. He did add his voice, but it was not yet a very strong one and it is almost inconceivable that, had any other politician held his post, essentially the same result would not have ensued.

On the very day of Biddle's formal announcement of the A and B zones, De Wit and Bendetsen worked out a more sweeping scheme, which Bendetsen would present to an informal but influential meeting of congressmen the next day. After a rambling conversation—De Witt was rarely either concise or precise—Bendetsen, always the lawyer in uniform, summed it up neatly:

Bendetsen: . . . As I understand it, from your viewpoint summarizing our conversation, you are of the opinion that there will have to be an evacuation on the west coast, not only of Japanese aliens but also of Japanese citizens, that is, you would include citizens along with alien enemies, and that if you had the power of requisition over all other Federal agencies, if you were requested you would be willing on the coast to accept responsibility for the alien enemy program.

De Witt: Yes I would. And I think it's got to come sooner or later.

Bendetsen: Yes sir, I do too, and I think the subject may be discussed tomorrow at the congressional delegation meeting.

De Witt: Well, you've got my viewpoint. You have it exactly.

The next day, January 30, the Japanese question was discussed in two important meetings, one in the White House and one on Capitol Hill. In the Cabinet meeting fears were expressed about the potentially dangerous situation in Hawaii. General Marshall penned a short memo to General Dwight D. Eisenhower, then a member of his staff, telling him that Stimson was concerned about "dangerous Japanese in Hawaii." Justice Roberts had told the War Secretary that "this point was regarded by his board as most serious." Several Cabinet members, but particularly Navy Secretary Frank Knox, were greatly disturbed at what they considered the laxity with which the Hawaiian Japanese were treated. As early as December 19, a previous Cabinet meeting had

decided that all Japanese aliens in the Hawaiian Islands should be interned, and put on some island other than Oahu, where the major military installations were located.

At the other end of Pennsylvania Avenue, the focus was on the West Coast Japanese. Bendetsen, along with Rowe and Ennis from the Justice Department, attended a meeting of the Pacific Coast House delegation. (A joint meeting between the congressmen and the six senators was already scheduled for the following Monday.) The subject was what to do about the Japanese. Although Bendetsen officially reported to his superiors that he "was present as an observer," it is clear from his telephone conversations with General De Witt, both before and after the meeting, that he went as an advocate for the policies that he and his boss, General Gullion, had been proposing. Bendetsen called De Witt right after the meeting and told him what they both considered good news.

> They asked me to state what the position of the War Department was. I stated that I could not speak for the War Department. . . . They asked me for my own views and I stated that the position of the War Department was this: that we did not seek control of the program, that we preferred it be handled by the civil agencies. However, the War Department would be entirely willing, I believed, /to assume/ the responsibility provided they accorded the War Department, and the Secretary of War, and the military commander under him, full authority to require the services of any federal agency, and required that that federal agency was required to respond.

De Witt liked this. "That's good," he responded. "I'm glad to see that action is being taken . . . that someone in authority begins to see the problem." What he particularly liked was the delegation to himself of full power over civilian agencies. He had had problems with civilians already, particularly civilians in the Federal Bureau of Investigation whose West Coast agents, as we have seen, refused to respond positively to De Witt's imaginary alarms and excursions. As De Witt envisioned it, "Mr. [J. Edgar] Hoover himself as head of the F.B.I. would have to function under the War Department exactly as he is functioning under the Department of Justice."

Bendetsen, naturally, encouraged De Witt to grab for power. "Opinion is beginning to become irresistible, and I think that anything you recommend will be strongly backed up . . . by the public." De Witt and Bendetsen agreed that protestations of loyalty from the Nisei were utterly worthless. As De Witt put it:

> "There are going to be a lot of Japs who are going to say, 'Oh, yes, we want to go, we're good Americans and we want to do everything you say,' but those are the fellows I suspect the most."
>
> "Definitely," Bendetsen agreed. "The ones who are giving you only lip service are the ones always to be suspected."

The Congressional recommendations were immediately sent to Secretary Stimson by the senior California representative, Clarence Lea, a Santa Rosa Democrat first elected in 1916. Although they did not specifically call for removal of American citizens of Japanese ancestry, the delegation did ask that mass evacuation proceed for "all enemy aliens and their families," which would have included most of the Nisei. Later the same day, Provost Marshal General Gullion called De Witt to get some details straight. He was chiefly interested in how far De Witt proposed to move the evacuees. De Witt did not know, but he did point out to Gullion that within California "one group wanted to move them entirely out of the state," whereas another wanted "them to be left in California." After receiving these assurances from De Witt, Gullion began to wonder where the Army was going to put 100,000 people, and, perhaps for the first time, fleetingly realized that "a resettlement proposition is quite a proposition." The following day, Bendetsen, acting for his chief, had the Adjutant General

dispatch telegrams to Corps Area commanders throughout the nation asking them about possible locations for large numbers of evacuees. Bendetsen suggested some possible sites: "agricultural experimental farms, prison farms, migratory labor camps, pauper farms, state parks, abandoned CCC camps, fairgrounds."

By the end of the month De Witt was able to make his position a little clearer. When Bendetsen asked whether or not he contemplated moving citizens, De Witt was emphatic.

> I include all Germans, all Italians who are alien enemies and all Japanese who are native-born or foreign born . . . evacuate enemy aliens in large groups at the earliest possible date . . . sentiment is being given too much importance. . . . I think we might as well eliminate talk of resettlement and handle these people as they should be handled . . . put them to work in internment camps. . . . I place the following priority. . . . First the Japanese, all prices [?sic] . . . as the most dangerous . . . the next group, the Germans . . . the third group, the Italians. . . . We've waited too long as it is. Get them all out.

On Sunday, February 1, exactly eight weeks after Pearl Harbor, Assistant Secretary of War John J. McCloy, Gullion, and Bendetsen went to a meeting in Attorney General Francis Biddle's office. Biddle, who was seconded by James Rowe, Jr., Edward J. Ennis, and J. Edgar Hoover, had been concerned about the increasing pressure for mass evacuation, both from the military and from Congress, and about a crescendo of press criticism directed at his "pussyfooting," some of which was undoubtedly inspired by the military. Biddle presented the Army men with a draft of what he hoped would be a joint press release. Its crucial sentences, which the military refused to agree to, were

> The Department of War and the Department of Justice are in agreement that the present military situation does not *at this time* [my emphasis] require the removal of American citizens of

the Japanese race. The Secretary of War, General De Witt, the Attorney General, and the Director of the Federal Bureau of Investigation believe that appropriate steps have been and are being taken.

Biddle informed McCloy and the others that he was opposed to mass evacuation and that the Justice Department would have nothing to do with it. Rowe, remembering his early January visit to De Witt's headquarters, said that the West Coast commander had been opposed to mass evacuation then and wondered what had changed his mind. According to Gullion, Rowe, after some uncomplimentary remarks about Bendetsen, complained about the hysterical tone of the protests from the West Coast, argued that the western congressmen were "just nuts" on the subject, and maintained that there was "no evidence whatsoever of any reason for disturbing citizens." Then Biddle insisted that the Justice Department would have nothing at all to do with any interference with civilians. Gullion, admittedly "a little sore," said: "Well, listen, Mr. Biddle, do you mean to tell me if the Army, the men on the ground, determine it is a military necessity to move citizens, Jap citizens, that you won't help us?"

After Biddle restated his position, McCloy, again according to Gullion, said to the Attorney General: "You are putting a Wall Street lawyer in a helluva box, but if it is a question of the safety of the country /and/ the Constitution. . . . Why the Constitution is just a scrap of paper to me."

As the meeting broke up, it was agreed that the Army people would check with the "man on the ground," General De Witt. As soon as they got back to their office, Gullion and Bendetsen made a joint phone call to the West Coast commander. They read him the proposed press release and, when the crucial sentences were reached, De Witt responded immediately: "I wouldn't agree to that." When asked specifically whom he did want to evacuate, the answer was "those

people who are aliens and who are Japs of American citizenship." Then Gullion cautioned De Witt:

> Now I might suggest, General, Mr. McCloy was in the conference and he will probably be in any subsequent conference . . . he has not had all the benefit of conversations we have had with you—if you could give us something, not only in conversation but a written thing . . . stating your position.

De Witt agreed to do this. Then Bendetsen summarized the Justice Department's point of view:

> . . . they say . . . if we recommend and it is determined that there should be an evacuation of citizens, they said hands off, that is the Army's job . . . they agree with us that it is possible from . . . a legal standpoint. . . . They agree with us that /the licensing theory/ could be . . . the legal basis for exclusion. . . . However we insist that we could also say that while all whites could remain, Japs can't, if we think there is military necessity for that. They apparently want us to join with them so that if anything happens they would be able to say "this was the military recommendation."

De Witt stated, "they are trying to cover themselves and lull the populace into a false sense of security."

When questioned about the details of the evacuation, De Witt blustered: "I haven't gone into the details of it, but Hell, it would be no job as far as the evacuation was concerned to move 100,000 people."

Actually, of course, it was a tremendous job, and even in such a relatively simple matter as the designation of Category A (prohibited to aliens) and Category B (restricted to aliens) zones, De Witt's staff had botched the job. Bendetsen had to call Western Defense Command headquarters and point out that although they had permitted limited use by enemy aliens of the San Francisco–Oakland Bay Bridge (the bridge itself was Category B), all the approaches to the bridge were classified Category A, and thus prohibited.

Two days after the conference in Biddle's office both Assistant Secretary of War McCloy and General George C. Marshall made separate calls to De Witt. McCloy, and presumably Stimson and Marshall, had become concerned that De Witt and the Provost Marshal's office were committing the Army to a policy that the policy makers had not yet agreed to. McCloy was blunt:

> . . . the Army, that means you in the area, should not take the position, even in your conversations with political figures out there [favoring] a wholesale withdrawal of Japanese citizens and aliens from the Coast. . . . We have about reached the point where we feel that perhaps the best solution of it is to limit the withdrawal to certain prohibited areas.

Then, incredibly to anyone who has read the transcripts of his conversations with Gullion and Bendetsen (which were apparently not then available to McCloy), General De Witt denied that he had done any such thing: "Mr. Secretary . . . I haven't taken any position."

This, of course, was a palpable lie. What the cautious commander knew, however, was that he had never put any recommendations on paper, and that General Gullion was not likely to produce the telephone transcripts because they showed him and his subordinates pressing for a policy that had not yet been officially sanctioned.

General Marshall's call was terse and businesslike; the extract of it which he furnished to the Secretary of War is worth quoting in full, both because of what it does and what it does not say.

Marshall:	Is there anything you want to say now about anything else? Of course we're on an open phone.
De Witt:	We're on an open phone, but George I can talk a little about this alien situation out here.

Marshall:	Yes.
De Witt:	I had a conference yesterday [February 2] with the Governor [Olson] and several representatives of the Department of Justice [Tom C. Clark] and the Department of Agriculture with a view to removal of the Japanese from where they are now living to other portions of the state.
Marshall:	Yes.
De Witt:	And the Governor thinks it can be satisfactorily handled without having a resettlement somewhere in the central part of the United States and removing them entirely from the state of California. As you know the people out here are very much disturbed over these aliens, and want to get them out of the several communities.
Marshall:	Yes.
De Witt:	And I've agreed that if they can get them out of the areas limited as the combat zone, that it would be satisfactory. That would take them about 100 to 150 miles from the coast, and they're going to do that I think. They're working on it.
Marshall:	Thank you.
De Witt:	The Department [of Justice] has a representative out here and the Department of Agriculture, and they think the plan is an excellent one. I'm only concerned with getting them away from around these aircraft factories and other places.
Marshall:	Yes. Anything else?
De Witt:	No, that's all.
Marshall:	Well, good luck.

That same day, February 3, there was an hour-and-a-half meeting between Stimson, McCloy, Gullion, and Bendetsen. (It is not clear whether the phone conversations between McCloy and De Witt and Marshall and De Witt preceded, followed or straddled this meeting.) The next day Provost Marshal Gullion reported, somewhat dejectedly: ". . . the two Secretaries [Stimson and McCloy] are against any mass movement. They are pretty much against it. And they are also pretty much against interfering with citizens unless it can be done legally."

What had apparently happened was that De Witt, understanding from the McCloy and Marshall phone calls that the War Department was, as he put it, "afraid that I was going to get into a political mess," and under great pressure from Governor Olson and Tom C. Clark to allow a limited, voluntary, compromise evacuation within California, trimmed his position accordingly. Clark, a strong and vigorous personality, seemed to have great influence over the general, who described him as "a fine fellow . . . the most cooperative and forceful man I have ever had to deal with. He attacks a problem better than any civilian I have ever had contact with."

Clark was clearly playing an independent role, and his position was somewhere between that of the Provost Marshal's office and that held by his own chief, the Attorney General. The plan that he sponsored or supported in the February 2 conference in Sacramento with Governor Olson and De Witt called for a conference between Governor Olson and leading Japanese Americans which would result in a voluntary resettlement in the central valleys of California where the Japanese could augment agricultural production. As De Witt explained the Clark-Olson plan to an unhappy Gullion:

Well, I tell you, they are solving the problem here very satisfactorily. . . . I have agreed to accept any plan they propose to put those people, Japanese Americans and Japanese who are in Category A area in the Category B area on farms. . . . We haven't got anything to do with it except they are consulting me to see what areas I will let them go into. . . . Mr. Clark is very much in favor of it . . . the people are going to handle it locally through the Governor and they are going to move those people to arable and tillable land. They are going to keep them in the state. They don't want to bring in a lot of negroes and mexicans and let them take their place. . . . They just want to put them on the land

out of the cities where they can raise vegetables like they are doing now.

The Provost Marshal General's men were disgusted with this turn of events. Not only were their plans being thwarted by the civilians who ran the Army—Stimson and McCloy, who were thinking in terms of creating "Jap-less" islands of security around a few key installations like the Consolidated-Vultee aircraft plant in San Diego, the Lockheed and North American plants in Los Angeles, and the Boeing plant in Seattle—but even their former ally, General De Witt, the all-important man on the ground who alone could make authoritative statements about "military necessity," had now deserted their cause. As Colonel Archer Lerch, Gullion's deputy, put it:

I think I detect a decided weakening on the part of Gen. De Witt, which I think is most unfortunate. . . . The idea suggested to Gen. De Witt in his conference with Gov. Olson, that a satisfactory solution must be reached through a conference between the Governor and leading Jap-Americans, savors too much of the spirit of Rotary and overlooks the necessary cold-bloodedness of war.

If pressure for evacuation within the Army seemed to be weakening, stronger and stronger outside forces were being brought into play. On February 2 and 3, in separate meetings, representatives and senators from all three Pacific Coast states agreed to coordinate their efforts. Serving as coordinator of these anti-Japanese efforts was Senator Hiram W. Johnson of California, who, in the mid-1920s, had masterminded a similar joint Congressional effort which brought about elimination of a Japanese quota in the Immigration Act of 1924. Johnson was actually more concerned about the defense of the West Coast—he feared a Japanese invasion—and complained bitterly to one of his political intimates that "the keenness of interest in the Japanese question far overshadowed the general proposition of our preparedness."

Back in California, Governor Culbert Olson went on the air on February 4; his speech could only have further inflamed public opinion. Disseminating false information that probably came from his conference two days previously with General De Witt and Tom Clark, he warned the already frightened people of California that

> it is known that there are Japanese residents of California who have sought to aid the Japanese enemy by way of communicating information, or have shown indications of preparation for fifth column activities.

Loyal Japanese, he insisted, could best prove their loyalty by cooperating with whatever the authorities asked them to do. Then, in a vain attempt to reassure the public, he went on to say that everything would be all right. He told of his conference with De Witt and announced, without of course giving any specifics, that

> general plans /have been/ agreed upon for the movement and placement of the entire adult Japanese population in California at productive and useful employment within the borders of our state, and under such surveillance and protection . . . as shall be deemed necessary.

The next day the mayor of Los Angeles, Fletcher Bowron, outdid the governor in attempting to arouse passions. After pointing out that the largest concentration of Japanese was in Los Angeles, he turned on the venom:

> Right here in our own city are those who may spring to action at an appointed time in accordance with a prearranged plan wherein each of our little Japanese friends will know his part in the event of any possible attempted invasion or air raid.

He then argued that not only Japanese aliens but citizens of Japanese descent, some of whom were "unquestionably . . . loyal," represented a threat to Los Angeles. Disloyal Nisei, he argued, would loudly proclaim their patriotism. "Of course they would try to fool us. They did in Honolulu and in Manila, and we may expect it in California." Bowron's answer, of course, was mass internment for all Japanese, citizens and aliens alike. From favorable references to Tom Clark, he seems to have been willing to go along with the De Witt–Olson–Clark plan of labor camps within California. Bowron also tried to take care of constitutional and ethical scruples:

> If we can send our own young men to war, it is nothing less than sickly sentimentality to say that we will do injustice to American-born Japanese to merely put them in a place of safety so that they can do no harm. . . . We /in Los Angeles/ are the ones who will be the human sacrifices if the perfidy that characterized the attack on Pearl Harbor is ever duplicated on the American continent.

In a follow-up statement the next day, Bowron put forth the interesting proposition that one of the major reasons that Japanese could not be trusted was that Californians had discriminated against them:

> The Japanese, because they are unassimilable, because the aliens have been denied the right to own real property in California, because of /immigration discrimination against them/, because of the marked differences in appearance between Japanese and Caucasians, because of the generations of training and philosophy that makes them Japanese and nothing else—all of these contributing factors set the Japanese apart as a race, regardless of how many generations have been born in America. Undoubtedly many of them intend to be loyal, but only each individual can know his own intentions, and when the final test comes, who can say but that "blood will tell"? We cannot run the risk of another Pearl Harbor episode in Southern California.

And, that same week, in Sacramento, Attorney General Earl Warren presided over a meeting of some one hundred and fifty law enforcement officers, mostly sheriffs and district attorneys. According to a federal official who attended the meeting:

In his opening remarks, Mr. Warren cautioned against hysteria but then proceeded to outline his remarks in such a fashion as to encourage hysterical thinking. . . . Mr. /Isidore/ Dockweiler, Los Angeles District Attorney . . . , asserted that the United States Supreme Court had been packed with leftist and other extreme advocates of civil liberty and that it was time for the people of California to disregard the law, if necessary, to secure their protection. Mr. Dockweiler finally worked himself into such a state of hysteria that he was called to order by Mr. Warren. . . . The meeting loudly applauded the statement that the people of California had no trust in the ability and willingness of the Federal Government to proceed against enemy aliens. One high official was heard to state that he favored shooting on sight all Japanese residents of the state.

Despite relative calm in the press until the end of January, a government intelligence agency (the civilian Office of Government Reports) informed Washington that "word of mouth discussions /continue/ with a surprisingly large number of people expressing themselves as in favor of sending all Japanese to concentration camps." By the end of January, the press "flared up again" with demands growing "that positive action be taken by the Federal Government. This awakening of the press has increased the verbal discussions that never ceased." By early February the Los Angeles *Times,* never friendly to the Japanese Americans, as we have seen, could no longer find human terms to describe them. All Japanese Americans, the *Times* insisted editorially, were at least potentially enemies: "A viper is nonetheless a viper wherever the egg is hatched—so a Japanese-American, born of Japanese parents—grows up to be a Japanese, not an American."

Henry McLemore, the nationally syndicated columnist, put into words the extreme reaction against Attorney General Francis Biddle, whom Californians (probably with some prompting from the military and militant congressmen) had made the chief target of their ire. Biddle, McLemore reported, couldn't even win election as "third assistant dog catcher" in California. "Californians have the feeling," he explained, "that he is the one in charge of the Japanese menace, and that he is handling it with all the severity of Lord Fauntleroy."

With this kind of encouragement in the background, Provost Marshal Gullion and his associates continued to press for mass action against the West Coast Japanese despite the fact that the officers of General Headquarters, directly under Marshall, were now trying to moderate anti-Japanese sentiment among members of Congress. On February 4, an impressive array of military personnel attended the meeting of West Coast congressmen: Admiral Harold R. Stark, Chief of Naval Operations; Brigadier General Mark W. Clark of General Headquarters (who had become Marshall's "expert" on the West Coast Japanese, even though just hours before he was to appear at the meeting he had to ask Bendetsen, "Now what is this Nisei?"); Colonel Hoyt S. Vandenberg of the Army Air Corps; and Colonel Wilton B. Persons, Chief of the (Congressional) Liaison Branch. According to Colonel Persons' report, Senator Rufus Holman of Oregon was the chief spokesman, and in pressing for an evacuation, he stressed the point that the people on the West Coast were "alarmed and terrified as to their person, their employment, and their homes." Clark then gave the congressmen the first truly military appraisal of the situation that they had received. Summarizing General Headquarters' findings, he told them that they were "unduly alarmed" and speculated that, at worst, there might be a sporadic air raid or a commando attack or two, and that while an attack on Alaska "was not a fantastic idea," there was no likelihood of a real onslaught on the West Coast states.

The day after General Clark's moderate presentation, the Provost Marshal began to try to bring Assistant Secretary of War McCloy around to his point of view. On February 5 he wrote McCloy that although De Witt had changed his mind, he (Gullion) was still of the view that mass evacuation was necessary. The De Witt–Olson–Tom Clark idea of voluntary cooperation with Japanese American leaders, the Provost Marshal General denounced as "dangerous to rely upon. . . ." In a more detailed memo the following day (February 6) he warned McCloy of the possible grave consequences of inaction:

> If our production for war is seriously delayed by sabotage in the West Coastal states, we very possibly shall lose the war. . . . From reliable reports from military and other sources, the danger of Japanese inspired sabotage is great. . . . No half-way measures based upon considerations of economic disturbance, humanitarianism, or fear of retaliation will suffice. Such measures will be "too little or too late."

This shrewd appeal—"too little and too late" was a journalistic slogan that all too accurately described the general tenor of anti-Axis military efforts to that date—was followed by a concrete program that had been drawn up by Gullion and Bendetsen, and that the Provost Marshal General formally recommended. Somewhat short of total evacuation, it still would have involved moving the vast majority of West Coast Japanese. The plan consisted of four steps, as follows:

> *Step 1.* Declare restricted areas from which all alien enemies are barred. *[This had already been done by Biddle, although it would not go into effect until February 24.]*
>
> *Step 2.* Internment east of the Sierra Nevadas of *all* Japanese aliens, accompanied by such citizen members of their families as may volunteer for internment. *[Since a majority of the Nisei were minors this would have included most of the citizen generation.]*
>
> *Step 3.* The pass and permit system for "military reservations." *[This would result, according to Gullion, in excluding citizens of Japanese extraction, "without raising too many legal questions."]*

> *Step 4.* Resettlement. *[Neither Gullion nor anyone else, as we shall see, had worked this out in any detail. According to the Provost Marshal General, it was "merely an idea and not an essential part of the plan."]*

By February 10, however, Gullion and Bendetsen, the latter now back on the West Coast to strengthen General De Witt's resolve, seemed to have convinced McCloy, somehow, that a mass evacuation was necessary, although Secretary Stimson still clung to the idea of creating islands around strategic locations, an idea that the Provost Marshal General's men were sure he had gotten from General Stilwell. Bendetsen insisted that safety "islands" would not prevent sabotage: "if they wanted to sabotage that area, they could set the outside area on fire. They could still cut water lines and power lines." According to Bendetsen he had been over that ground twice with McCloy, who seemed to agree, and who had told Bendetsen that he would call him back after he had had another talk with the Secretary.

The next day, February 11, 1942, was the real day of decision as far as the Japanese Americans were concerned. Sometime in the early afternoon, Secretary Stimson telephoned Franklin Roosevelt at the White House. Shortly after that call, McCloy phoned Bendetsen at the Presidio to tell him the good news. According to McCloy:

> . . . we talked to the President and the President, in substance, says go ahead and do anything you think necessary . . . if it involves citizens, we will take care of them too. He says there will probably be some repercussions, but it has got to be dictated by military necessity, but as he puts it, "Be as reasonable as you can."

McCloy went on to say that he thought the President would sign an executive order giving the Army the authority to evacuate. He also indicated there was at least some residual reluctance on the part of Secretary Stimson, who wanted to make a start in Los Angeles, concentrating on areas around the big bomber plants. McCloy indicated that he thought he could convince the Secretary that the limited plan was not practicable. In his conversation with McCloy, Bendetsen had talked about evacuating some 61,000 people, but in talking to Gullion about an hour later, he spoke of evacuating approximately 101,000 people.

By February 11 the Provost Marshal's men had the situation all their own way. Assistant Secretary McCloy, who had been "pretty much against" their view just a week before, had been converted, and through him, Secretary Stimson and the President, although the latter probably did not take too much persuading. Bendetsen was again in San Francisco, and helping General De Witt draft what the Western Defense commander called "the plan that Mr. McCloy wanted me to submit." Although, in retrospect, it seems clear that the struggle for mass evacuation was over by then, not all the participants knew it yet.

Among those in the dark were the staff at General Headquarters, particularly General Mark Clark who had been assigned to make the official military report on the advisability of mass evacuation. Early on February 12 he called De Witt, and when told that an evacuation, to include citizens of Japanese descent, was in the works, he expressed disbelief. His own official memorandum, completed at about that time, had reached opposite conclusions, and deserves quoting at length, because it alone represents official military thinking on the subject.

General Clark's report concluded:

I cannot agree with the wisdom of such a mass exodus for the following reasons:

(a) We will never have a perfect defense against sabotage except at the expense of other equally important efforts. The situation with regards to protecting establishments from sabotage is analogous to protecting them from air attack by antiaircraft and barrage balloons. We will never have enough of these means to fully

protect these establishments. Why, then, should we make great sacrifices in other efforts in order to make them secure from sabotage?

(b) We must weigh the advantages and disadvantages of such a wholesale solution to this problem. We must not permit our entire offensive effort to be sabotaged in an effort to protect all establishments from ground sabotage.

I recommend the following approach to this problem:

(a) Ascertain and designate the critical installations to be protected in each area and list them according to their importance.

(b) Make up our minds as to what means are available for such protection and apply that protection as far as it will go to the most critical objectives, leaving the ones of lesser importance for future consideration, or lesser protection.

(c) Select the most critical ones to be protected and delimit the essential areas around them for their protection.

(d) Eject all enemy aliens from those areas and permit entrance of others by pass only.

(e) Only such installations as can be physically protected in that manner should be included in this category. For example, it is practicable to do this in the case of the Boeing Plant, Bremerton Navy Yard and many other similar vital installations. In other words we are biting off a little at a time in the solution of the problem.

(f) Civilian police should be used to the maximum in effecting this protection.

(g) Federal Bureau of Investigation should be greatly augmented in counter-subversive activity.

(h) Raids should be used freely and frequently.

(i) Ring leaders and suspects should be interned liberally.

(j) This alien group should be made to understand through publicity that the first overt act on their part will bring a wave of countermeasures which will make the historical efforts of the vigilantes look puny in comparison.

It is estimated that to evacuate large numbers of this group will require one soldier to 4 or 5 aliens. This would require between 10,000 and 15,000 soldiers to guard the group during their internment, to say nothing of the continuing burden of protecting the installations. I feel that this problem must be attacked in a sensible manner. We must admit that we are taking some chances just as we take other chances in war. We must determine what are our really critical installations, give them thorough protection and leave the others to incidental means in the hope that we will not lose too many of them—and above all keep our eye on the ball—that is, the creating and training of an offensive army.

Here was truly "stern military necessity." The General Staff officer, who probably reflected Marshall's real view, would have moved very few Japanese, not because he was a defender of civil liberty, or even understood what the probabilities for sabotage really were, but because, it did not seem to him, on balance, that the "protection" which total evacuation would provide was worth its cost in military manpower and energy. But military views, as we have seen, were not the determinants of policy; political views were. The real architects of policy were the lawyers in uniform, Gullion and Bendetsen. Their most highly placed supporters, McCloy and Stimson, were two Republican, Wall Street lawyers.

Very late in the game, and often after the fact, a very few New Dealers tried to influence the President to take a more consistently democratic approach to the Japanese. On February 3 Archibald MacLeish, then Director of the Office of Facts and Figures, a predecessor of the Office of War Information, wrote one of Roosevelt's confidential secretaries suggesting that the President might want to try to hold down passions on the West Coast. His office, he said, was "trying to keep down the pressure out there." He enclosed, for the President, a statement of Woodrow Wilson's that he thought might be useful. During the other world war, Wilson had said, in a statement highly appropriate to the West Coast situation:

> . . . I can never accept any man as a champion of liberty either for ourselves or for the world who does not reverence and obey the laws of our beloved land, whose laws we ourselves have made. He has adopted the standards of the enemies of his country, whom he affects to despise.

Getting no response from the White House, MacLeish tried the Army six days later. "Dear Jack," the libertarian poet wrote McCloy, "In my opinion great care should be taken not to reach a grave decision in the present situation on the representations of officials and pressure groups alone. The decision may have far-reaching effects."

MacLeish's efforts were, of course, fruitless. Much more influential was the authoritarian voice of America's chief pundit, Walter Lippmann. Writing from San Francisco in a column published on February 12, the usually detached observer who has so often been on the unpopular side of issues, was, in this instance, merely an extension of the mass West Coast mind. In an essay entitled "The Fifth Column on the Coast," Lippmann wrote:

> . . . the Pacific Coast is in imminent danger of a combined attack from within and without. . . . It is a fact that the Japanese navy has been reconnoitering the coast more or less continuously. . . . There is an assumption /in Washington/ that a citizen may not be interfered with unless he has committed an overt act. . . . The Pacific Coast is officially a combat zone: Some part of it may at any moment be a battlefield. And nobody ought to be on a battlefield who has no good reason for being there. There is plenty of room elsewhere for him to exercise his rights.

The pundit's thinkpiece drew a lot of notice. Westbrook Pegler, delighted at finding a respectable man urging what he had long urged, chortled:

Do you get what he says? This is a high-grade fellow with a heavy sense of responsibility. . . . The Japanese in California should be under armed guard to the last man and woman right now /even Pegler didn't like to talk about children/—and to hell with habeas corpus until the danger is over. . . . If it isn't true, we can take it out on Lippmann, but on his reputation I will bet it is all true.

In the War Department, Marshall sent a copy of Lippmann's column to Stimson, and Stimson sent it to McCoy, and it was undoubtedly read in the White House. It was read in the Justice Department too. Long-suffering Attorney General Francis Biddle, former law clerk to Justice Holmes, civil libertarian and New Dealer, was finally stirred to respond by Lippmann's column. In his memoirs, published in 1962, deeply regretting the whole affair, Biddle wrote:

> . . . if, instead of dealing almost exclusively with McCloy and Bendetsen, I had urged /Stimson/ to resist the pressure of his subordinates, the result might have been different. But I was new to the Cabinet, and disinclined to insist on my view to an elder statesman whose wisdom and integrity I greatly respected.

What Biddle did not reveal, however, was that he himself had given Stimson a kind of green light. In a letter written on February 12, the Attorney General voiced his distaste for the proposed evacuation, particularly of citizens, but assured Stimson that

> I have no doubt that the Army can legally, at any time, evacuate all persons in a specified territory if such action is deemed essential from a military point of view. . . . No legal problem arises when Japanese citizens are evacuated, but American citizens of Japanese origin could not, in my opinion, be singled out of an area and evacuated with the other Japanese.

Then Biddle, Philadelphia lawyer that he was, told Stimson how he thought it could be done.

However, the result might be accomplished by evacuating all persons in the area and then licensing back those whom the military authorities thought were not objectionable from a military point of view.

Five days later, on February 17, Biddle addressed a memorandum to the President, a memorandum that was, in effect, a last-gasp effort to stop the mass evacuation that was being planned. Biddle apparently was unaware that Roosevelt had given Stimson and McCloy the go-ahead signal almost a week before. The Attorney General opened with a statement about the various West Coast pressure groups and congressmen who were urging the evacuation. He then singled out Lippmann and Pegler, and argued that their concern about imminent invasion and sabotage was not borne out by the facts. Biddle then maintained, rather curiously, that "there /was/ no dispute between the War, Navy and Justice Departments," and warned that the evacuation of 93,000 Japanese in California would disrupt agriculture, require thousands of troops, tie up transportation, and raise very difficult questions of resettlement. Then, in an apparent approval of evacuation, Biddle wrote, "If complete confusion and lowering of morale is to be avoided, so large a job must be done after careful planning."

Then, in a parting blast, directed specifically at Lippmann, Biddle attacked columnists acting as "Armchair Strategists and Junior G-Men," suggested that they were essentially "shouting FIRE! in a crowded theater," and warned that if . . . riots occurred, Lippmann and the others would bear a heavy responsibility.

But Biddle could have directed his attack much closer to home. Not only his Cabinet colleagues but some of his subordinates were doing more than shouting. Three days before the Attorney General's letter, Tom C. Clark, of his staff, assured a Los Angeles press conference that the federal government would soon evacuate over 200,000 enemy aliens and their children, including all American-born Japanese, from areas in California vital to national defense.

On February 13, the Pacific Coast Congressional delegation forwarded to the President a recommendation for evacuation that was fully in line with what Stimson and McCloy were proposing. They recommended, unanimously:

> the immediate evacuation of all persons of Japanese lineage and all others, aliens and citizens alike, whose presence shall be deemed dangerous or inimical to the defense of the United States from all strategic areas . . . such areas /should/ be enlarged as expeditiously as possible until they shall encompass the entire strategic areas of the states of California, Oregon and Washington, and the Territory of Alaska.

Finally, on Thursday, February 19, 1942, a day that should live in infamy, Franklin D. Roosevelt signed an Executive Order that gave the Army, through the Secretary of War, the authority that Gullion and Bendetsen had sought so long. Using as justification a military necessity for "the successful prosecution of the war," the President empowered the military to designate "military areas" from which "any or all persons may be excluded" and to provide for such persons "transportation, food, shelter, and other accommodations as may be necessary . . . until other arrangements are made." The words Japanese or Japanese Americans never even appear in the order; but it was they, and they alone, who felt its sting.

The myth of military necessity was used as a fig leaf for a particular variant of American racism. On the very day that the President signed the order, a conference at General Headquarters heard and approved an opposite opinion. Army Intelligence reported, officially, that it believed "mass evacuation unnecessary." In this instance, at least, the military mind was superior to the political: the soldiers who opposed the evacuation were right and the politicians who proposed it were wrong. But, why did it happen?

Two major theories have been propounded

by scholars which ought to be examined. Almost as the evacuation was taking place, administrators and faculty at the University of California at Berkeley took steps to set up a scholarly study of the relocation in all its aspects. With generous foundation support and with the cooperation of some of the federal officials most responsible for the decision (for example, John J. McCloy), the "Japanese American Evacuation and Resettlement Study" was set up under the directorship of Dorothy Swaine Thomas, then a University of California Professor of Rural Sociology and a skilled demographer. Her staff included a broad spectrum of social scientists, but curiously did not include either professional historians or archivists. Professor Thomas' own volumes did not seek to determine responsibility for the evacuation, but two volumes that flowed out of the project did: Morton Grodzins, *Americans Betrayed* (Chicago, 1949) and Jacobus tenBroek, Edward N. Barnhart, and Floyd Matson, *Prejudice, War, and the Constitution* (Berkeley and Los Angeles, 1954). Grodzins felt that the major cause of the evacuation was the pressure exerted by special interest groups within California and on the Pacific Coast generally. The "western group," he wrote, "was successful in having a program molded to its own immediate advantage made national policy." Professors tenBroek, Barnhart, and Matson vigorously disputed the Grodzins thesis: for them, the responsibility was General De Witt's, and, they argued, his decision was based essentially on his "military estimate of the situation."

Five years later a professional historian, Stetson Conn, then a civilian historian for the Department of the Army and later the Army's Chief of Military History, published an authoritative account of what really happened, as far as the military was concerned. He found in the contemporary evidence "little support for the argument that military necessity required a mass evacuation" and pointed, accurately, to the machinations of Gullion and Bendetsen and their success in bending the civilian heads of the War Department to their will.

The question that remains to be answered

is why the recommendation of Stimson and McCloy was accepted by the nation. Grodzins' pressure groups were, of course, important, but even more important than the peculiar racism of a region was the general racist character of American society. The decision to evacuate the Japanese was popular, not only in California and the West, but in the entire nation, although only on the West Coast was it a major issue in early 1942.

The leader of the nation, was, in the final analysis, responsible. It was Franklin Roosevelt, who in one short telephone call, passed the decision-making power to two men who had never been elected to any office, saying only, with the politician's charm and equivocation: "Be as reasonable as you can." Why did he agree? Probably for two reasons: in the first place, it was expedient; in the second place, Roosevelt himself harbored deeply felt anti-Japanese prejudices.

As to expediency, it is important to remember what the war news was like in early 1942. It was a very bad time for the military fortunes of the United States and its allies. The Japanese had landed on the island of Singapore on February 8, on New Britain on the 9th, and were advancing rapidly in Burma. Roosevelt was concerned, first of all with winning the war, and secondly with unity at home, so that he, unlike his former chief, Woodrow Wilson, could win the peace with the advice and consent of the Senate. He could read the Congressional signs well and knew that cracking down on the Japanese Americans would be popular both on the Hill and in the country generally. And the last thing he wanted was a rift with establishment Republicans like Stimson and McCloy; New Dealers like Biddle and MacLeish could be counted on not to rock the boat.

But, in addition, Franklin Roosevelt was himself convinced that Japanese, alien and citizen, were dangerous to American security. He, along with several members of his Cabinet and circle of advisers, persistently pushed for mass internment of the Hawaiian Japanese-Americans long after the military had wisely rejected such a policy. And there was a kind of rationale

for such a policy. If Japanese were a threat to security in California, where they represented fewer than 2 percent of the population, certainly in wartorn Hawaii, where they were more than a third of the population, they should have constituted a real menace. But it is one thing to incarcerate a tiny element of the population, as was done on the West Coast, and quite another to put away a sizable fraction of the whole. Apart from the sheer size of the problem, relatively and absolutely, there was the question of the disruption that such a mass evacuation would cause in the local economy. Referring to Oahu alone, Lieutenant General Delos C. Emmons, the Army commander there, pointed out to the War Department in January 1942 that Japanese provided the bulk of the main island's skilled labor force and were indispensable unless replaced by an equivalent labor force from the mainland. In addition, the logistical problems of internment in the islands were so great that Emmons recommended that any evacuation and relocation be to the mainland.

At the Cabinet level, however, different views were held. On February 27, for example, Navy Secretary Knox, the most vocal Japanophobe in the Cabinet, suggested rounding up all the Japanese on Oahu and putting them under Army guard on the neighboring island of Molokai, better known as a leper colony. Stimson concurred as to the danger, but insisted that if they were to be moved they be sent to the states. (The shipping situation, for all practical purposes, made this impossible.) The President, according to Stimson, clearly favored Knox's plan. The President and his Navy Secretary continued to press for this policy well into 1942, but eventually were forestalled by a strongly worded joint recommendation to the contrary signed by both Chief of Staff Marshall and Chief of Naval Operations Admiral Ernest J. King. In other words, real rather than imaginary military necessity governed in Hawaii. Although Hawaii was the first real theater of war, fewer than 2000 of the territory's 150,000 Japanese were ever deprived of their liberty.

16

THE ATOMIC BOMB AND THE ORIGINS OF THE COLD WAR

MARTIN J. SHERWIN

International politics has always created strange alliances, but none as unique as that of the Big Three during World War II. Faced with a powerful and successful Fascist onslaught, Stalin joined forces with Churchill and Roosevelt to defeat German hopes for domination in Europe. Thus were joined one of Britain's most conservative politicians, a reforming American president, and the leader of the Communist world.

What united these three improbable allies, however, was not merely the German war threat. From 1942 onward these three leaders were increasingly concerned with the shape of the postwar world and with establishing and maintaining their respective spheres of influence within it. Breaking with the American isolationist past, Roosevelt joined with Churchill and Stalin in secret agreements designed to partition the world, dividing it into Russian and Anglo-American zones where each was to have military and political control.

As Martin Sherwin demonstrates in this essay, however, relations between the Big Three were not always free of conflict. One of the most divisive issues faced by this alliance was the question of the atomic bomb. Since the early 1940s, when British and American intelligence operatives reported German experiments with nuclear weaponry, British and American scientists had been engaged in their own intensive nuclear program. The critical question, as Sherwin points out, was who among the Allies was to share in the knowledge and production of the Allies' atomic bomb. It was Churchill and Roosevelt's decision to exclude Stalin from their atomic club, he argues, that precipitated the climate of distrust that characterized the Cold War following World War II.

From *American Historical Review* 78:945–68 (1973). Reprinted by permission of the author.

During the Second World War the atomic bomb was seen and valued as a potential rather than an actual instrument of policy. Responsible officials believed that its impact on diplomacy had to await its development and, perhaps, even a demonstration of its power. As Henry L. Stimson, the secretary of war, observed in his memoirs: "The bomb as a merely probable weapon had seemed a weak reed on which to rely, but the bomb as a colossal reality was very different." That policy makers considered this difference before Hiroshima has been well documented, but whether they based wartime diplomatic policies upon an anticipated successful demonstration of the bomb's power remains a source of controversy. Two questions delineate the issues in this debate. First, did the development of the atomic bomb affect the way American policy makers conducted diplomacy with the Soviet Union? Second, did diplomatic considerations related to the Soviet Union influence the decision to use the atomic bomb against Japan?

These important questions relating the atomic bomb to American diplomacy, and ultimately to the origins of the cold war, have been addressed almost exclusively to the formulation of policy during the early months of the Truman administration. As a result, two anterior questions of equal importance, questions with implications for those already posed, have been overlooked. Did diplomatic considerations related to Soviet postwar behavior influence the formulation of Roosevelt's atomic-energy policies? What effect did the atomic legacy Truman inherited have on the diplomatic and atomic-energy policies of his administration?

To comprehend the nature of the relationship between atomic-energy and diplomatic policies that developed during the war, the bomb must be seen as policy makers saw it before Hiroshima, as a weapon that might be used to control postwar diplomacy. For this task our present view is conceptually inadequate. After more than a quarter century of experience we understand, as wartime policy makers did not, the bomb's limitations as a diplomatic instrument. To appreciate the profound influence of the unchallenged wartime assumption about the bomb's impact on diplomacy we must recognize the postwar purposes for which policy makers and their advisers believed the bomb could be used. In this effort Churchill's expectations must be scrutinized as carefully as Roosevelt's and scientists' ideas must be considered along with those of politicians. Truman's decision to use the atomic bomb against Japan must be evaluated in the light of Roosevelt's atomic legacy, and the problems of impending peace must be considered along with the exigencies of war. To isolate the basic atomic-energy policy alternatives that emerged during the war requires that we first ask whether alternatives were, in fact, recognized.

What emerges most clearly from a close examination of wartime formulation of atomic-energy policy is the conclusion that policy makers never seriously questioned the assumption that the atomic bomb should be used against Germany or Japan. From October 9, 1941, the time of the first meeting to organize the atomic-energy project, Stimson, Roosevelt, and other members of the "top policy group" conceived of the development of the atomic bomb as an essential part of the total war effort. Though the suggestion to build the bomb was initially made by scientists who feared that Germany might develop the weapon first, those with political responsibility for prosecuting the war accepted the circumstances of the bomb's creation as sufficient justification for its use against any enemy.

Having nurtured this point of view during the war, Stimson charged those who later criticized the use of the bomb with two errors. First, these critics asked the wrong question: it was not whether surrender could have been obtained without using the bomb but whether a different diplomatic and military course from that followed by the Truman administration would have achieved an earlier surrender. Second, the basic assumption of these critics was false: the idea that American policy should have been based primarily on a desire not to employ the bomb seemed as "irresponsible" as a policy controlled by a positive desire to use it. The war, not the bomb, Stimson argued, had been the primary focus of his attention; as secretary of war his responsibilities permitted no alternative.

Stimson's own wartime diary nevertheless indicates that from 1941 on, the problems associated with the atomic bomb moved steadily closer to the center of his own and Roosevelt's concerns. As the war progressed, the implications of the weapon's development became diplomatic as well as military, postwar as well as wartime. Recognizing that a monopoly of the atomic bomb gave the United States a powerful new military advantage, Roosevelt and Stimson became increasingly anxious to convert it to diplomatic advantage. In December 1944 they spoke of using the "secret" of the atomic bomb as a means of obtaining a *quid pro quo* from the Soviet Union. But viewing the bomb as a potential instrument of diplomacy, they were not moved to formulate a concrete plan for carrying out this exchange before the bomb was used. The bomb had "this unique peculiarity," Stimson noted several months later in his diary; "Success is 99% assured, yet only by the first actual war trial of the weapon can the actual certainty be fixed." Whether or not the specter of postwar Soviet ambitions created "a positive desire" to ascertain the bomb's power, until that decision was executed "atomic diplomacy" remained an idea that never crystallized into policy.

Although Roosevelt left no definitive statement assigning a postwar role to the atomic bomb, his expectations for its potential diplomatic value can be recalled from the existing record. An analysis of the policies he chose from among the alternatives he faced suggests that the potential diplomatic value of the bomb began to shape his atomic-energy policies as early as 1943. He may have been cautious about counting on the bomb as a reality during the war, but he nevertheless consistently chose policy alternatives that would promote the postwar diplomatic potential of the bomb if the predictions of scientists proved true. These policies were based on the assumption that the bomb could be used effectively to secure postwar diplomatic aims; and this assumption was carried over from the Roosevelt to the Truman administration.

Despite general agreement that the bomb would be an extraordinarily important diplomatic factor after the war, those closely associated with its development did not agree on how to use it most effectively as an instrument of diplomacy. Convinced that wartime atomic-energy policies would have postwar diplomatic consequences, several scientists advised Roosevelt to adopt policies aimed at achieving a postwar international control system. Churchill, on the other hand, urged the president to maintain the Anglo-American atomic monopoly as a diplomatic counter against the postwar ambitions of other nations—particularly against the Soviet Union. Roosevelt fashioned his atomic-energy policies from the choices he made between these conflicting recommendations. In 1943 he rejected the counsel of his science advisers and began to consider the diplomatic component of atomic-energy policy in consultation with Churchill alone. This decision-making procedure and Roosevelt's untimely death have left his motives ambiguous. Nevertheless it is clear that he pursued policies consistent with Churchill's monopolistic, anti-Soviet views.

The findings of this study thus raise serious questions concerning generalizations historians have commonly made about Roosevelt's diplomacy: that it was consistent with his public reputation for cooperation and conciliation; that he was naive with respect to postwar Soviet behavior; that, like Wilson, he believed in collective security as an effective guarantor of national safety; and that he made every possible effort to assure that the Soviet Union and its allies would continue to function as postwar partners. Although this article does not dispute the view that Roosevelt desired amicable postwar relations with the Soviet Union, or even that he worked hard to achieve them, it does suggest that historians have exaggerated his confidence in (and perhaps his commitment to) such an outcome. His most secret and among his most important long-range decisions—those responsible for prescribing a diplomatic role for the atomic bomb—reflected his lack of confidence. Finally, in light of this study's conclusions, the widely held assumption that Truman's attitude toward the atomic bomb was substantially different from Roosevelt's must also be revised.

Like the Grand Alliance itself, the Anglo-American atomic-energy partnership was forged by the war and its exigencies. The threat of a German atomic bomb precipitated a hasty marriage of convenience between British research and American resources. When scientists in Britain proposed a theory that explained how an atomic bomb might quickly be built, policy makers had to assume that German scientists were building one. "If such an explosive were made," Vannevar Bush, the director of the Office of Scientific Research and Development, told Roosevelt in July 1941, "it would be thousands of times more powerful than existing explosives, and its use might be determining." Roosevelt assumed nothing less. Even before the atomic-energy project was fully organized he assigned it the highest priority. He wanted the program "pushed not only in regard to development, but also with due regard to time. This is very much of the essence," he told Bush in March 1942. "We both felt painfully the dangers of doing nothing," Churchill recalled, referring to an early wartime discussion with Roosevelt about the bomb.

The high stakes at issue during the war did not prevent officials in Great Britain or the United States from considering the postwar implications of their atomic-energy decisions. As early as 1941, during the debate over whether to join the United States in an atomic-energy partnership, members of the British government's atomic-energy committee argued that the matter "was so important for the future that work should proceed in Britain." Weighing the obvious difficulties of proceeding alone against the possible advantages of working with the United States, Sir John Anderson, then lord president of the council and the minister responsible for atomic-energy research, advocated the partnership. As he explained to Churchill, by working closely with the Americans British scientists would be able "to take up the work again /after the war/, not where we left off, but where the combined effort had by then brought it."

As early as October 1942 Roosevelt's science advisers exhibited a similar concern with the potential postwar value of atomic energy. After conducting a full-scale review of the atomic-energy project, James B. Conant, the president of Harvard University and Bush's deputy, recommended discontinuing the Anglo-American partnership "as far as development and manufacture is concerned." Conant had in mind three considerations when he suggested a more limited arrangement with the British: first, the project had been transferred from scientific to military control; second, the United States was doing almost all the developmental work; and third, security dictated "moving in a direction of holding much more closely the information about the development of this program." Under these conditions it was difficult, Conant observed, "to see how a joint British-American project could be sponsored in this country." What prompted Conant's recommendations, however, was his suspicion—soon to be shared by other senior atomic-energy administrators—that the British were rather more concerned with information for postwar industrial purposes than for wartime use. What right did the British have to the fruits of American labor? "We were doing nine-tenths of the work," Stimson told Roosevelt in October. By December 1942 there was general agreement among the president's atomic-energy advisers that the British no longer had a valid claim to all atomic-energy information.

Conant's arguments and suggestions for a more limited partnership were incorporated into a "Report to the President by the Military Policy Committee." Roosevelt approved the recommendations on December 28. Early in January the British were officially informed that the rules governing the Anglo-American atomic-energy partnership had been altered on "orders from the top."

By approving the policy of "restricted interchange" Roosevelt undermined a major incentive for British cooperation. It is not surprising, therefore, that Churchill took up the matter directly with the president and with Harry Hopkins, "Roosevelt's own, personal Foreign Office." The prime minister's initial response to the new policy reflected his determination to have it reversed: "That we should each work separately," he threatened, "would be a sombre decision."

Conant and Bush understood the implications of Churchill's intervention and sought to counter its effect. "It is our duty," Conant wrote Bush, "to see to it that the President of the United States, in writing, is informed of what is involved in these decisions." Their memorandums no longer concentrated on tortuous discussions differentiating between the scientific research and the manufacturing stages of the bomb's development but focused on what to Conant was "the major consideration . . . that of *national security and postwar strategic significance.*" Information on manufacturing an atomic bomb, Conant noted, was a "military secret which is in a totally different class from anything the world has ever seen if the potentialities of this project are realized." To provide the British with detailed knowledge about the construction of a bomb "might be the equivalent to joint occupation of a fortress or strategic harbor in perpetuity." Though British and American atomic-energy policies might coincide during the war, Conant and Bush expected them to conflict afterward.

The controversy over the policy of "restricted interchange" of atomic-energy information shifted attention to postwar diplomatic considerations. As Bush wrote to Hopkins, "We can hardly give away the fruits of our developments as a part of postwar planning except on the basis of some overall agreement on that subject, which agreement does not now exist." The central issue was clearly drawn. The atomic-energy policy of the United States was related to the very fabric of Anglo-American postwar relations and, as Churchill would insist, to postwar relations between each of them and the Soviet Union. Just as the possibility of British postwar commercial competition had played a major role in shaping the U.S. policy of restricted interchange, the specter of Soviet postwar military power played a major role in shaping the prime minister's attitude toward atomic-energy policies in 1943.

"We cannot," Sir John Anderson wrote Churchill, "afford after the war to face the future without this weapon and rely entirely on America should Russia or some other power develop it." The prime minister agreed. The atomic bomb was an instrument of postwar diplomacy that Britain had to have. He could cite numerous reasons for his determination to acquire an independent atomic arsenal after the war, but Great Britain's postwar military-diplomatic position with respect to the Soviet Union invariably led the list. When Bush and Stimson visited London in July, Churchill told them quite frankly that he was "vitally interested in the possession of all [atomic-energy] information because this will be necessary for Britain's independence in the future as well as for success during the war." Nor was Churchill evasive about his reasoning: "It would never do to have Germany or Russia win the race for something which might be used for international blackmail," he stated bluntly and then pointed out that "Russia might be in a position to accomplish this result unless we worked together." In Washington, two months earlier, Churchill's science adviser Lord Cherwell had told Bush and Hopkins virtually the same thing. The British government, Cherwell stated, was considering "the whole [atomic-energy] affair on an after-the-war military basis." It intended, he said, "to manufacture and produce the weapon." Prior to the convening of the Quebec Conference, Anderson explained his own and Churchill's view of the bomb to the Canadian prime minister, Mackenzie King. The British knew, Anderson said, "that both Germany and Russia were working on the same thing," which, he noted, "would be a terrific factor in the postwar world as giving an absolute control to whatever country possessed the secret." Convinced that the British attitude toward the bomb would undermine any possibility of postwar cooperation with the Soviet Union, Bush and Conant vigorously continued to oppose any revival of the Anglo-American atomic-energy partnership.

On July 20, however, Roosevelt chose to accept a recommendation from Hopkins to restore full partnership, and he ordered Bush to "renew, in an inclusive manner, the full exchange of information with the British." A garbled trans-Atlantic cable to Bush reading "review" rather than "renew" gave him the opportunity to continue his negotiations in London with Churchill and thereby to modify the president's order. But Bush could not alter Roosevelt's intentions. On August 19, at the Quebec Conference, the president and the prime minister agreed that the British would share the atomic bomb. Despite Bush's negotiations with Churchill, the Quebec Agreement revived the principle of an Anglo-American atomic-energy partnership, albeit the British were reinstated as junior rather than equal partners.

The president's decision was not a casual one taken in ignorance. As the official history of the Atomic Energy Commission notes: "Both Roosevelt and Churchill knew that the stake of their diplomacy was a technological breakthrough so revolutionary that it transcended in importance even the bloody work of carrying the war to the heartland of the Nazi foe." The president had been informed of Churchill's position as well as of Bush's and Conant's. But how much closer Roosevelt was to Churchill than to his own advisers at this time is sug-

gested by a report written after the war by General Leslie R. Groves, military director of the atomic-energy project. "It is not known what if any Americans President Roosevelt consulted at Quebec," Groves wrote. "It is doubtful if there were any. All that is known is that the Quebec Agreement was signed by President Roosevelt and that, as finally signed, it agreed practically in toto with the version presented by Sir John Anderson to Dr. Bush in Washington a few weeks earlier."

The debate that preceded the Quebec Agreement is noteworthy for yet another reason: it led to a new relationship between Roosevelt and his atomic-energy advisers. After August 1943 the president did not consult with them about the diplomatic aspects of atomic-energy policy. Though he responded politely when they offered their views, he acted decisively only in consultation with Churchill. Bush and Conant appear to have lost a large measure of their influence because they had used it to oppose Churchill's position. What they did not suspect was the extent to which the president had come to share the prime minister's view.

It can be argued that Roosevelt, the political pragmatist, renewed the wartime atomic-energy partnership to keep relations with the British harmonious rather than disrupt them on the basis of a postwar issue. Indeed it seems logical that the president took this consideration into account. But it must also be recognized that he was perfectly comfortable with the concept Churchill advocated—that military power was a prerequisite to successful postwar diplomacy. As early as August 1941, during the Atlantic Conference, Roosevelt had rejected the idea that an "effective international organization" could be relied upon to keep the peace; an Anglo-American international police force would be far more effective, he told Churchill. By the spring of 1942 the concept had broadened: the two "policemen" became four, and the idea was added that every other nation would be totally disarmed. "The Four Policemen" would have "to build up a reservoir of force so powerful that no aggressor would dare to challenge it," Roosevelt told Arthur Sweetser, an ardent internationalist. Violators first would be quarantined, and, if they persisted in their disruptive activities, bombed at the rate of a city a day until they agreed to behave. The president told Molotov about this idea in May, and in November he repeated it to Clark Eichelberger, who was coordinating the activities of the American internationalists. A year later, at the Teheran Conference, Roosevelt again discussed his idea, this time with Stalin. As Robert A. Divine has noted: "Roosevelt's concept of big power domination remained the central idea in his approach to international organization throughout World War II."

Precisely how Roosevelt expected to integrate the atomic bomb into his plans for keeping the peace in the postwar world is not clear. However, against the background of his atomic-energy policy decisions of 1943 and his peace-keeping concepts, his actions in 1944 suggest that he intended to take full advantage of the bomb's potential as a postwar instrument of Anglo-American diplomacy. If Roosevelt thought the bomb could be used to create a more peaceful world order, he seems to have considered the threat of its power more effective than any opportunities it offered for international cooperation. If Roosevelt was less worried than Churchill about Soviet postwar ambitions, he was no less determined than the prime minister to avoid any commitments to the Soviets for the international control of atomic energy. There could still be four policemen, but only two of them would have the bomb.

The atomic-energy policies Roosevelt pursued during the remainder of his life reinforce this interpretation of his ideas for the postwar period. The following three questions offer a useful framework for analyzing his intentions. Did Roosevelt make any additional agreements with Churchill that would further support the view that he intended to maintain an Anglo-American monopoly after the war? Did

Roosevelt demonstrate any interest in the international control of atomic energy? Was Roosevelt aware that an effort to maintain an Anglo-American monopoly of the atomic bomb might lead to a postwar atomic arms race with the Soviet Union?

An examination of the wartime activities of the eminent Danish physicist, Niels Bohr, who arrived in America early in 1944 as a consultant to the atomic-bomb project, will help answer these questions. "Officially and secretly he came to help the technical enterprise," noted J. Robert Oppenheimer, the director of the Los Alamos atomic-bomb laboratory, but "most secretly of all . . . he came to advance his case and his cause." Bohr was convinced that a postwar atomic armaments race with the Soviet Union was inevitable unless Roosevelt and Churchill initiated efforts during the war to establish the international control of atomic energy. Bohr's attempts to promote this idea in the United States were aided by Justice Felix Frankfurter.

Bohr and Frankfurter were old acquaintances. They had first met in 1933 at Oxford and then in 1939 on several occasions in London and the United States. At these meetings Bohr had been impressed by the breadth of Frankfurter's interests and, perhaps, overimpressed with his influence on Roosevelt. In 1944 the Danish minister to the United States brought them together, once again, at his home in Washington. Frankfurter, who appears to have suspected why Bohr had come to America and why this meeting had been arranged, had learned about the atomic-bomb project earlier in the war when, as he told the story, several troubled scientists had sought his advice on a matter of "greatest importance." He therefore invited Bohr to lunch in his chambers and, by dropping hints about his knowledge, encouraged Bohr to discuss the issue.

After listening to Bohr's analysis of the postwar alternatives—an atomic armaments race or some form of international control—Frankfurter saw Roosevelt. Bohr had persuaded him, Frankfurter reported, that disastrous consequences would result if Russia learned on her own about the atomic-bomb project. Frankfurter suggested that it was a matter of great importance that the president explore the possibility of seeking an effective arrangement with the Soviets for controlling the bomb. He also noted that Bohr, whose knowledge of Soviet science was extensive, believed that the Russians had the capability to build their own atomic weapons. If the international control of atomic energy was not discussed among the Allies during the war, an atomic arms race between the Allies would almost certainly develop after the war. It seemed imperative, therefore, that Roosevelt consider approaching Stalin with a proposal as soon as possible.

Frankfurter discussed these points with the president for an hour and a half, and he left feeling that Roosevelt was "plainly impressed by my account of the matter." When Frankfurter had suggested that the solution to this problem might be more important than all the plans for a world organization, Roosevelt had agreed. Moreover he had authorized Frankfurter to tell Bohr, who was scheduled to return to England, that he might inform "our friends in London that the President was most eager to explore the proper safeguards in relation to X [the atomic bomb]." Roosevelt also told Frankfurter that the problem of the atomic bomb "worried him to death" and that he was very eager for all the help he could have in dealing with it.

The alternatives placed before Roosevelt posed a difficult dilemma. On the one hand, he could continue to exclude the Soviet government from any official information about the development of the bomb, a policy that would probably strengthen America's postwar military-diplomatic position. But such a policy would also encourage Soviet mistrust of Anglo-American intentions and was bound to make postwar cooperation more difficult. On the other hand, Roosevelt could use the atomic-bomb project as an instrument of cooperation by informing Stalin of the American government's intention of cooperating in the development of a plan for the international control of atomic weapons, an objective that might never be achieved.

Either choice involved serious risks. Roosevelt had to balance the diplomatic advantages of being well ahead of the Soviet Union in atomic-energy production after the war against the advantages of initiating wartime negotiations for postwar cooperation. The issue here, it must be emphasized, is not whether the initiative Bohr suggested would have led to successful international control, but rather whether Roosevelt demonstrated any serious interest in laying the groundwork for such a policy.

Several considerations indicate that Roosevelt was already committed to a course of action that precluded Bohr's internationalist approach. First, Frankfurter appears to have been misled. Though Roosevelt's response had been characteristically agreeable, he did not mention Bohr's ideas to his atomic-energy advisers until September 1944, when he told Bush that he was very disturbed that Frankfurter had learned about the project. Roosevelt knew at this time, moreover, that the Soviets were finding out on their own about the development of the atomic bomb. Security personnel had reported an active Communist cell in the Radiation Laboratory at the University of California. Their reports indicated that at least one scientist at Berkeley was selling information to Russian agents. "They [Soviet agents] are already getting information about vital secrets and sending them to Russia," Stimson told the president on September 9, 1943. If Roosevelt was indeed worried to death about the effect the atomic bomb could have on Soviet-American postwar relations, he took no action to remove the potential danger, nor did he make any effort to explore the possibility of encouraging Soviet postwar cooperation on this problem. The available evidence indicates that he never discussed the merits of the international control of atomic energy with his advisers after this first or any subsequent meeting with Frankfurter.

How is the president's policy of neither discussing international control nor promoting the idea to be explained if not by an intention to use the bomb as an instrument of Anglo-American postwar diplomacy? Perhaps his concern for maintaining the tightest possible secrecy against German espionage led him to oppose any discussion about the project. Or he may have concluded, after considering Bohr's analysis, that Soviet suspicion and mistrust would be further aroused if Stalin were informed of the existence of the project without receiving detailed information about the bomb's construction. The possibility also exists that Roosevelt believed that neither Congress nor the American public would approve of a policy giving the Soviet Union any measure of control over the new weapon. Finally Roosevelt might have thought that the spring of 1944 was not the proper moment for such an initiative.

Though it would be unreasonable to state categorically that these considerations did not contribute to his decision, they appear to have been secondary. Roosevelt was clearly, and properly, concerned about secrecy, but the most important secret with respect to Soviet-American relations was that the United States was developing an atomic bomb. And that secret, he was aware, already had been passed on to Moscow. Soviet mistrust of Anglo-American postwar intentions could only be exacerbated by continuing the existing policy. Moreover an attempt to initiate planning for international control of atomic energy would not have required the revelation of technical secrets. Nor is it sufficient to cite Roosevelt's well-known sensitivity to domestic politics as an explanation for his atomic-energy policies. He was willing to take enormous political risks, as he did at Yalta, to support his diplomatic objectives.

Had Roosevelt avoided all postwar atomic-energy commitments, his lack of support for international control could have been interpreted as an attempt to reserve his opinion on the best course to follow. But he had made

commitments in 1943 supporting Churchill's monopolistic, anti-Soviet position, and he continued to make others in 1944. On June 13, for example, Roosevelt and Churchill signed an Agreement and Declaration of Trust, specifying that the United States and Great Britain would cooperate in seeking to control available supplies of uranium and thorium ore both during and after the war. This commitment, taken against the background of Roosevelt's peace-keeping ideas and his other commitments, suggests that the president's attitude toward the international control of atomic energy was similar to the prime minister's.

Churchill had dismissed out of hand the concept of international control when Bohr talked with him about it in May 1944. Their meeting was not long under way before Churchill lost interest and became involved in an argument with Lord Cherwell, who was also present. Bohr, left out of the discussion, was frustrated and depressed; he was unable to return the conversation to what he considered the most important diplomatic problem of the war. When the allotted half hour elapsed, Bohr asked if he might send the prime minister a memorandum on the subject. A letter from Niels Bohr, Churchill bitingly replied, was always welcome, but he hoped it would deal with a subject other than politics. As Bohr described their meeting: "We did not even speak the same language."

Churchill rejected the assumption upon which Bohr's views were founded—that international control of atomic energy could be used as a cornerstone for constructing a peaceful world order. An atomic monopoly would be a significant diplomatic advantage in postwar diplomacy, and Churchill did not believe that anything useful could be gained by surrendering this advantage. The argument that a new weapon created a unique opportunity to refashion international affairs ignored every lesson Churchill read into history. "You can be quite sure," he would write in a memorandum less than a year later, "that any power that gets hold of the secret will try to make the article and this touches the existence of human society. This matter is out of all relation to anything else that exists in the world, and I could not think of participating in any disclosure to third or fourth parties at the present time."

Several months after Bohr met Churchill, Frankfurter arranged a meeting between Bohr and Roosevelt. Their discussion lasted an hour and a half. Roosevelt told Bohr that contact with the Soviet Union along the lines he suggested had to be tried. The president also said he was optimistic that such an initiative would have a "good result." In his opinion Stalin was enough of a realist to understand the revolutionary importance of this development and its consequences. The president also expressed confidence that the prime minister would eventually share these views. They had disagreed in the past, he told Bohr, but they had always succeeded in resolving their differences.

Roosevelt's enthusiasm for Bohr's ideas was more apparent than real. The president did not mention them to anyone until he met with Churchill at Hyde Park on September 18, following the second wartime conference at Quebec. The decisions reached on atomic energy at Hyde Park were summarized and documented in an *aide-mémoire* signed by Roosevelt and Churchill on September 19, 1944. The agreement bears the markings of Churchill's attitude toward the atomic bomb and his poor opinion of Bohr. "Enquiries should be made," the last paragraph reads, "regarding the activities of Professor Bohr and steps taken to ensure that he is responsible for no leakage of information particularly to the Russians." If Bohr's activities prompted Roosevelt to suspect his loyalty, there can be no doubt that Churchill encouraged the president's suspicions. Atomic energy and Britain's future position as a world power had become part of a single equation for the prime minister. Bohr's ideas, like the earlier idea of restricted interchange, threatened the continuation of the Anglo-American atomic-energy partnership.

With such great stakes at issue Churchill did not hesitate to discredit Bohr along with his ideas. "It seems to me," Churchill wrote to Cherwell soon after Hyde Park, "Bohr ought to be confined or at any rate made to see that he is very near the edge of mortal crimes."

The *aide-mémoire* also contained an explicit rejection of any wartime efforts toward international control: "The suggestion that the world should be informed regarding tube alloys /the atomic bomb/, with a view to an international agreement regarding its control and use, is not accepted. The matter should continue to be regarded as of the utmost secrecy." But Bohr had never suggested that the world be informed about the atomic bomb. He had argued in memorandums and in person that peace was not possible unless the Soviet government—not the world—was officially notified only about the project's existence before the time when any discussion would appear coercive rather than friendly.

It was the second paragraph, however, that revealed the full extent of Roosevelt's agreement with Churchill's point of view. "Full collaboration between the United States and the British Government in developing tube alloys for military and commercial purposes," it noted, "should continue after the defeat of Japan unless and until terminated by joint agreement." Finally the *aide-mémoire* offers some insight into Roosevelt's intentions for the military use of the weapon in the war: "When a bomb is finally available, it might perhaps, after mature consideration, be used against the Japanese, who should be warned that this bombardment will be repeated until they surrender."

Within the context of the complex problem of the origins of the cold war the Hyde Park meeting is far more important than historians of the war generally have recognized. Overshadowed by the Second Quebec Conference on one side and by the drama of Yalta on the other, its significance often has been overlooked. But the agreements reached in September 1944 reflect a set of attitudes, aims, and assumptions that guided the relationship between the atomic bomb and American diplomacy during the Roosevelt administration and, through the transfer of its atomic legacy, during the Truman administration as well. Two alternatives had been recognized long before Roosevelt and Churchill met in 1944 at Hyde Park: the bomb could have been used to initiate a diplomatic effort to work out a system for its international control, or it could remain isolated during the war from any cooperative initiatives and held in reserve should cooperation fail. Roosevelt consistently favored the latter alternative. An insight into his reasoning is found in a memorandum Bush wrote following a conversation with Roosevelt several days after the Hyde Park meeting: "The President evidently thought he could join with Churchill in bringing about a US-UK postwar agreement on this subject /the atomic bomb/ by which it would be held closely and presumably to control the peace of the world." By 1944 Roosevelt's earlier musings about the four policemen had faded into the background. But the idea behind it, the concept of controlling the peace of the world by amassing overwhelming military power, appears to have remained a prominent feature of his postwar plans.

In the seven months between his meeting with Churchill in September and his death the following April Roosevelt did not alter his atomic-energy policies. Nor did he reverse his earlier decision not to take his advisers into his confidence about diplomatic issues related to the new weapon. They were never told about the Hyde Park agreements, nor were they able to discuss with him their ideas for the postwar handling of atomic-energy affairs. Though officially uninformed, Bush suspected that Roosevelt had made a commitment to continue the atomic-energy partnership exclusively with the British after the war, and he, as well as Conant, opposed the idea. They believed such a policy "might well lead to extraordinary efforts on the part of Russia to establish its own position in the field secretly,

and might lead to a clash, say 20 years from now." Unable to reach the president directly, they sought to influence his policies through Stimson, whose access to Roosevelt's office (though not to his thoughts on atomic energy) was better than their own.

Summarizing their views on September 30 for the secretary of war, Bush and Conant predicted that an atomic bomb equivalent to from one to ten thousand tons of high explosive could be "demonstrated" before August 1, 1945. They doubted that the present American and British monopoly could be maintained for more than three or four years, and they pointed out that any nation with good technical and scientific resources could catch up; accidents of research, moreover, might even put some other nation ahead. In addition atomic bombs were only the first step along the road of nuclear weapons technology. In the not-too-distant future loomed the awesome prospect of a weapon perhaps a thousand times more destructive—the hydrogen bomb. Every major center of population in the world would then lie at the mercy of a nation that struck first in war. Security therefore could be found neither in secrecy nor even in the control of raw materials, for the supply of heavy hydrogen was practically unlimited.

These predictions by Bush and Conant were more specific than Bohr's, but not dissimilar. They, too, believed that a nuclear arms race could be prevented only through international control. Their efforts were directed, however, toward abrogating existing agreements with the British rather than toward initiating new agreements with the Soviets. Like Bohr they based their hope for Stalin's eventual cooperation on his desire to avoid the circumstances that could lead to a nuclear war. But while Bohr urged Roosevelt to approach Stalin with the carrot of international control before the bomb became a reality, Bush and Conant were inclined to delay such an approach until the bomb was demonstrated, until it was clear that without international control the new weapon could be used as a terribly effective stick.

In their attempt to persuade Roosevelt to their point of view Bush and Conant failed. But their efforts were not in vain. By March 1945 Stimson shared their concerns, and he agreed that peace without international control was a forlorn hope. Postwar problems relating to the atomic bomb "went right down to the bottom facts of human nature, morals and government, and it is by far the most searching and important thing that I have had to do since I have been here in the office of Secretary of War," Stimson wrote on March 5. Ten days later he presented his views on postwar atomic-energy policy to Roosevelt. This was their last meeting. In less than a month a new president took the oath of office.

Harry S. Truman inherited a set of military and diplomatic atomic-energy policies that included partially formulated intentions, several commitments to Churchill, and the assumption that the bomb would be a legitimate weapon to be used against Japan. But no policy was definitely settled. According to the Quebec Agreement the president had the option of deciding the future of the commercial aspects of the atomic-energy partnership according to his own estimate of what was fair. Although the policy of "utmost secrecy" had been confirmed at Hyde Park the previous September, Roosevelt had not informed his atomic-energy advisers about the *aide-mémoire* he and Churchill signed. Although the assumption that the bomb would be used in the war was shared by those privy to its development, assumptions formulated early in the war were not necessarily valid at its conclusion. Yet Truman was bound to the past by his own uncertain position and by the prestige of his predecessor. Since Roosevelt had refused to open negotiations with the Soviet government for the international control of atomic energy, and since he had never expressed any objection to the wartime use of the bomb, it would have required considerable political courage and confidence for Truman to alter those policies. Moreover it would have required the encouragement of his advisers, for under the circum-

stances the most serious constraint on the new president's choices was his dependence upon advice. So Truman's atomic legacy, while it included several options, did not necessarily entail complete freedom to choose from among all the possible alternatives.

"I think it is very important that I should have a talk with you as soon as possible on a highly secret matter," Stimson wrote to Truman on April 24. It has "such a bearing on our present foreign relations and has such an important effect upon all my thinking in this field that I think you ought to know about it without further delay." Stimson had been preparing to brief Truman on the atomic bomb for almost ten days, but in the preceding twenty-four hours he had been seized by a sense of urgency. Relations with the Soviet Union had declined precipitously during the past week, the result, he thought, of the failure of the State Department to settle the major problems between the Allies before going ahead with the San Francisco Conference on the United Nations Organization. The secretary of state, Edward R. Stettinius, Jr., along with the department's Soviet specialists, now felt "compelled to bull the thing through." To get out of the "mess" they had created, Stimson wrote in his diary, they were urging Truman to get tough with the Russians. He had. Twenty-four hours earlier the president met with the Soviet foreign minister, V. M. Molotov, and "with rather brutal frankness" accused his government of breaking the Yalta Agreement. Molotov was furious. "I have never been talked to like that in my life," he told the president before leaving.

With a memorandum on the "political aspects of the S-1 *[atomic bomb's]* performance" in hand and General Groves in reserve, Stimson went to the White House on April 25. The document he carried was the distillation of numerous decisions already taken, each one the product of attitudes that developed along with the new weapon. The secretary himself was not entirely aware of how various forces had shaped these decisions: the recommendations of Bush and Conant, the policies Roosevelt had followed, the uncertainties inherent in the wartime alliance, the oppressive concern for secrecy, and his own inclination to consider long-range implications. It was a curious document. Though its language revealed Stimson's sensitivity to the historic significance of the atomic bomb, he did not question the wisdom of using it against Japan. Nor did he suggest any concrete steps for developing a postwar policy. His objective was to inform Truman of the salient problems: the possibility of an atomic arms race, the danger of atomic war, and the necessity for international control if the United Nations Organization was to work. "If the problem of the proper use of this weapon can be solved," he wrote, "we would have the opportunity to bring the world into a pattern in which the peace of the world and our civilizations can be saved." To cope with this difficult challenge Stimson suggested the "establishment of a select committee" to consider the postwar problems inherent in the development of the bomb. If his presentation was the "forceful statement" of the problem that historians of the Atomic Energy Commission have described it as being, its force inhered in the problem itself, not in any bold formulations or initiatives he offered toward a solution. If, as another historian has claimed, this meeting led to a "strategy of delayed showdown," requiring "the delay of all disputes with Russia until the atomic bomb had been demonstrated," there is no evidence in the extant records of the meeting that Stimson had such a strategy in mind or that Truman misunderstood the secretary's views.

What emerges from a careful reading of Stimson's diary, his memorandum of April 25 to Truman, a summary by Groves of the meeting, and Truman's recollections is an argument for overall caution in American diplomatic relations with the Soviet Union: it was an argument against any showdown. Since the atomic bomb was potentially the most dangerous issue facing the postwar world and since the most desirable resolution of the problem was some form of international control, Soviet cooperation had to be secured. It was imprudent, Stimson suggested, to pursue a policy that would preclude the possibility of international cooperation on atomic-energy matters after the war ended. Truman's overall impression of Stimson's argument was that the secretary of war was "at least as much concerned with the role of the atomic bomb in the shaping of history as in its capacity to shorten the war." These were indeed Stimson's dual concerns on April 25, and he could see no conflict between them.

Despite the profound consequences Stimson attributed to the development of the new weapon, he had not suggested that Truman reconsider its use against Japan. Nor had he thought to mention the possibility that chances of securing Soviet postwar cooperation might be diminished if Stalin did not receive a commitment to international control prior to an attack. The question of why these alternatives were overlooked naturally arises. Perhaps what Frankfurter once referred to as Stimson's habit of setting "his mind at one thing like the needle of an old victrola caught in a single groove" may help to explain his not mentioning these possibilities. Yet Bush and Conant never raised them either. Even Niels Bohr had made a clear distinction between the bomb's wartime use and its postwar impact on diplomacy. "What role it /the atomic bomb/ may play in the present war," Bohr had written to Roosevelt in July 1944, was a question "quite apart" from the overriding concern: the need to avoid an atomic arms race.

The preoccupation with winning the war obviously helped to create this seeming dichotomy between the wartime use of the bomb and the potential postwar diplomatic problems with the Soviet Union raised by its development. But a closer look at how Bohr and Stimson each defined the nature of the diplomatic problem created by the bomb suggests that for the secretary of war and his advisers (and ultimately for the president they advised) there was no dichotomy at all. Bohr apprehended the meaning of the new weapon even before it was developed, and he had no doubt that scientists in the Soviet Union would also understand its profound implications for the postwar world. He was also certain that they would interpret the meaning of the development to Stalin just as scientists in the United States and Great Britain had explained it to Roosevelt and Churchill. Thus the diplomatic problem, as Bohr analyzed it, was not the need to convince Stalin that the atomic bomb was an unprecedented weapon that threatened the life of the world but the need to assure the Soviet leader that he had nothing to fear from the circumstances of its development. By informing Stalin during the war that the United States intended to cooperate with him in neutralizing the bomb through international control, Bohr reasoned that its wartime use could be considered apart from postwar problems.

Stimson approached the problem rather differently. Although he believed that the bomb "might even mean the doom of civilization or it might mean the perfection of civilization" he was less confident than Bohr that the weapon in an undeveloped state could be used as an effective instrument of diplomacy. Until its "actual certainty /was/ fixed," Stimson considered any prior approach to Stalin as premature. But as the uncertainties of impending peace became more apparent and worrisome, Stimson, Truman, and the secretary of state-designate, James F. Byrnes, began to think of the bomb as something of a diplomatic panacea for their postwar problems. Byrnes had told Truman in April that the bomb "might well put us in a position to dictate our own terms at the end of the war." By June, Truman and Stimson were discussing "further *quid pro quos* which should be established in consideration for our taking them /the Soviet Union/ into /atomic-energy/ partnership." Assuming that the bomb's impact on diplomacy would be immediate and extraordinary, they agreed on no less than "the settlement of the Polish, Rumanian, Yugoslavian, and Manchurian problems." But they also concluded that no

revelation would be made "to Russia or anyone else until the first bomb had been successfully laid on Japan." Truman and Stimson based their expectations on how they saw and valued the bomb; its use against Japan, they reasoned, would transfer this view to the Soviet Union.

Was an implicit warning to Moscow, then, the principal reason for deciding to use the atomic bomb against Japan? In light of the ambiguity of the available evidence the question defies an unequivocal answer. What can be said with certainty is that Truman, Stimson, Byrnes, and several others involved in the decision consciously considered two effects of a combat demonstration of the bomb's power: first, the impact of the atomic attack on Japan's leaders, who might be persuaded thereby to end the war; and second, the impact of that attack on the Soviet Union's leaders, who might then prove to be more cooperative. But if the assumption that the bomb might bring the war to a rapid conclusion was the principal motive for using the atomic bomb, the expectation that its use would also inhibit Soviet diplomatic ambitions clearly discouraged any inclination to question that assumption.

Policy makers were not alone in expecting a military demonstration of the bomb to have a salubrious effect on international affairs. James Conant, for example, believed that such a demonstration would further the prospects for international control. "President Conant has written me," Stimson informed the news commentator Raymond Swing in February 1947, "that one of the principal reasons he had for advising me that the bomb must be used was that that was the only way to awaken the world to the necessity of abolishing war altogether." And the director of the atomic-energy laboratory at the University of Chicago made the same point to Stimson in June 1945: "If the bomb were not used in the present war," Arthur Compton noted, "the world would have no adequate warning as to what was to be expected if war should break out again." Even Edward Teller, who has publicly decried the attack on Hiroshima and declared his early opposition to it, adopted a similar position in July 1945. "Our only hope is in getting the facts of our results before the people," he wrote to his colleague, Leo Szilard, who was circulating a petition among scientists opposing the bomb's use. "This might help to convince everybody that the next war would be fatal," Teller noted. "For this purpose actual combat use might even be the best thing."

Thus by the end of the war the most influential and widely accepted attitude toward the bomb was a logical extension of how the weapon was seen and valued earlier—as a potential instrument of diplomacy. Caught between the remnants of war and the uncertainties of peace, scientists as well as policy makers were trapped by the logic of their own unquestioned assumptions. By the summer of 1945 not only the conclusion of the war but the organization of an acceptable peace seemed to depend upon the success of the atomic attacks against Japan. When news of the successful atomic test of July 16 reached the president at the Potsdam Conference, he was visibly elated. Stimson noted that Truman "was tremendously pepped up by it and spoke to me of it again and again when I saw him. He said it gave him an entirely new feeling of confidence." The day after receiving the complete report of the test Truman altered his negotiating style. According to Churchill the president "got to the meeting after having read this report [and] he was a changed man. He told the Russians just where they got on and off and generally bossed the whole meeting." After the plenary session on July 24 Truman "casually mentioned to Stalin" that the United States had "a new weapon of unusual destructive force." Truman took this step in response to a recommendation by the Interim Committee, a group of political and scientific advisers organized by Stimson in May 1945 to advise the president on atomic-energy policy. But it is an unavoidable conclusion that what the president told the premier followed the letter of the recommendation rather than its spirit, which embodied

the hope that an overture to Stalin would initiate the process toward international control. In less than three weeks the new weapon's destructive potential would be demonstrated to the world. Stalin would then be forced to reconsider his diplomatic goals. It is no wonder that upon learning of the raid against Hiroshima Truman exclaimed: "This is the greatest thing in history."

As Stimson had expected, as a colossal reality the bomb was very different. But had American diplomacy been altered by it? Those who conducted diplomacy became more confident, more certain that through the accomplishments of American science, technology, and industry the "new world" could be made into one better than the old. But just how the atomic bomb would be used to help accomplish this ideal remained unclear. Three months and one day after Hiroshima was bombed Bush wrote that the whole matter of international relations on atomic energy "is in a thoroughly chaotic condition." The wartime relationship between atomic-energy policy and diplomacy had been based upon the simple assumption that the Soviet government would surrender important geographical, political, and ideological objectives in exchange for the neutralization of the new weapon. As a result of policies based on this assumption American diplomacy and prestige suffered grievously: an opportunity to gauge the Soviet Union's response during the war to the international control of atomic energy was missed, and an atomic-energy policy for dealing with the Soviet government after the war was ignored. Instead of promoting American postwar aims, wartime atomic-energy policies made them more difficult to achieve. As a group of scientists at the University of Chicago's atomic-energy laboratory presciently warned the government in June 1945: "It may be difficult to persuade the world that a nation which was capable of secretly preparing and suddenly releasing a weapon as indiscriminate as the [German] rocket bomb and a million times more destructive, is to be trusted in its proclaimed desire of having such weapons abolished by international agreement." This reasoning, however, flowed from alternative assumptions formulated during the closing months of the war by scientists far removed from the wartime policy-making process. Hiroshima and Nagasaki, the culmination of that process, became the symbols of a new American barbarism, reinforcing charges, with dramatic circumstantial evidence, that the policies of the United States contributed to the origins of the cold war.

17

FROM HARLEM TO MONTGOMERY: THE BUS BOYCOTTS AND LEADERSHIP OF ADAM CLAYTON POWELL, JR., AND MARTIN LUTHER KING, JR.

DOMINIC J. CAPECI, JR.

One of the most dramatic and important social movements of the twentieth century was the civil rights movement of the 1950s and 1960s. After centuries of servitude, discrimination, and oppression, black Americans began a campaign to gain a measure of economic, political, and social equality that had been denied them by white America.

Although attention is easily drawn to the Montgomery, Alabama, bus boycott of 1956, to the march on Washington and Martin Luther King's "I Have A Dream" speech of 1963, and to the final passage of the Civil Rights and Voting Rights Acts of 1964 and 1965, the success of the modern civil rights movement rests on the firm foundation of earlier struggles for black equality. A continuous movement for black equality, however, is the product of the twentieth century. Beginning with W. E. B. Du Bois's Niagara Movement and the founding of the NAACP and Urban League early in the century, black Americans and their liberal white supporters were able to maintain an organized response to the predominant racism of American society.

But, as Dominic Capeci points out, it is easy to forget the less publicized local battles for black equality in the glare of dramatic national battles. It was, however, from local struggles, such as the Harlem bus boycott of 1941 and the more recent Memphis sanitation worker's strike of 1968, that a feeling of power, and with it the ability to change social conditions, developed among black Americans. It was these local struggles, Capeci argues, that provided the basis for successful campaigns on the national level.

From *The Historian* 41:721–37 (1979). Reprinted by permission.

While much has been written about Martin Luther King, Jr., and the Montgomery Bus Boycott of 1956, historians have ignored Adam Clayton Powell, Jr., and the Harlem Bus Boycott of 1941. The two boycotts were marked by similar leadership and occurred in decades of despair but in periods of major socioeconomic change. Although it was much smaller in size and more local in impact, a study of the Harlem boycott yields important information on Powell's leadership before his political career and, more significantly, on earlier protest philosophies and tactics. A comparison of the boycotts reveals both the continuity and unity in black protest and leadership and the diversity that marks different eras and locales.

Though Powell and King came of age in different generations and regions, they experienced similar formative influences that ultimately led them to nonviolent protest. Both were named after their fathers, each of whom had risen from sharecropping to become renowned Baptist ministers in Harlem and Atlanta, respectively. Reverend Adam Clayton Powell, Sr., and Reverend Martin Luther King, Sr., were assertive, protective parents. Thus young Powell was spoiled "utterly and completely," while King, Jr., enjoyed life's comforts in "an extraordinarily peaceful and protected way." Both were precocious, entering college in their mid-teens and earning advanced degrees in religion. More significant, both underwent serious racial and religious growing pains. As a youngster, Powell had been roughed up by blacks for being "white" and by whites for being "colored." Later at Colgate University he passed for white until his father came to lecture on race relations. The negative reaction of Powell's white roommate to his true identity was a "tremendous" shock. Perhaps the trauma was almost as great as the earlier, unexpected death of his sister Blanche, which triggered in Powell a religious reaction: "The church was a fraud, my father the leading perpetrator, my mother a stupid rubber stamp." King, too, was scarred during his early years. When the mother of his white playmates

informed King (then six years old) that as they grew older they could no longer play together, he ran home crying. Although never estranged from his father, as a teenager King considered the church irrelevant and wondered whether religion "could serve as a vehicle for modern thinking."

As young adults, Powell and King overcame these problems. At Colgate, Powell experienced a revelation, which led to his ordination in 1931. He served as assistant pastor of his father's Abyssinian Baptist Church and earned a master's degree in religious education at Columbia University. In 1937, he succeeded his father as pastor. Adopting the elder Powell's commitment to the social gospel, he forged his congregation into "a mighty weapon" and led numerous nonviolent direct action protests for black employment opportunities during the Great Depression. As part of the larger "Jobs-for-Negroes" movement, Powell joined with Reverend William Lloyd Imes of the St. James Presbyterian Church and A. Philip Randolph of the Brotherhood of Sleeping Car Porters to organize the Greater New York Coordinating Committee for Employment. By 1941 Powell overestimated that four years of picketing by the committee had brought Harlem "ten thousand jobs." This commitment and leadership earned him enormous popularity and, among church women, the title "Mr. Jesus."

King matured along similar lines, for Dr. Benjamin E. Mays and others at Morehouse College successfully molded his concept of religion. King was ordained and became the assistant pastor at his father's Ebenezer Baptist Church. He then attended Crozer Theological Seminary and received a doctorate in theology from Boston College. Although the elder King was only infrequently involved in organized protest, he and Alberta King had instilled dignity and pride in their son. King remembered his father admonishing a policeman for calling him "boy"; pointing to his son, the elder King ejaculated, "That's a boy there. I'm Reverend King." Eventually, King drew on nonviolent direct action for the Montgomery boycott and became immensely popular. "L. L. J.," or "Little Lord Jesus" as church women called him, had moved to the center stage of black leadership.

While Powell and King, then, experienced similar upbringings, a comparison of the bus boycotts in Harlem and Montgomery provides an opportunity to analyze their leadership, protest philosophies, and tactics.

The Harlem bus boycott of 1941 was prompted by black degradation, rising expectations, and a heritage of black protest. Throughout the 1930s, black New Yorkers subsisted on marginal economic levels. As late as 1940, 40 percent of the city's black population received relief or federal monies for temporary jobs. Moreover, most blacks were relegated to menial positions. In Harlem, the largest black community of over two hundred thousand persons, hope was generated, nevertheless, as black leaders and white officials—like Mayor Fiorello H. La Guardia—pressed for change and as World War II held out promise for greater black employment opportunities.

Blacks had a longstanding grievance against the Fifth Avenue Coach Company and the New York Omnibus Corporation. In 1935, the Mayor's Commission on Conditions in Harlem reported that the Coach Company was "fixed in its policy of the exclusion of Negroes from employment." At the time of the bus boycott six years later, the Coach Company and the Omnibus Corporation together employed only sixteen blacks, mostly as janitors, none as drivers or mechanics, out of a labor force of thirty-five hundred persons. Hence, on March 10, 1941, when the Transportation Workers Union (TWU), under the leadership of Michael J. Quill, went on strike against the bus companies, black leaders moved quickly to the union's support. The National Negro Congress, for example, "wholeheartedly" supported the strike, which lasted for twelve days and halted the service of thirteen hundred buses.

Under Roger Straugh's leadership, the Harlem Labor Union (HLU) began picketing local bus stops before the TWU strike had ended, demanding the employment of black bus drivers and mechanics. The Greater New York Co-ordinating Committee for Employment led by Powell and the Manhattan Council of the National Negro Congress directed by Hope R. Stevens joined with HLU to form the United Bus Strike Committee (UBSC). The formal boycott, however, did not begin until March 24, four days after TWU had agreed to arbitration and two days after bus service had resumed. Moreover, Powell emerged as the spokesman for the boycotters, providing, in Urban Leaguer Elmer A. Carter's estimation, "dynamic leadership."

Before the boycott began, Powell received a quid pro quo from Quill. In return for black support of the TWU strike, the boycott would receive union backing. Later, on March 24, Quill assured Powell that blacks employed by the bus companies would be considered for union membership so long as they had clean records and had never been scabs. That evening, over fifteen hundred persons gathered at the Abyssinian Baptist Church and agreed to boycott the buses until blacks were hired as drivers and mechanics.

Powell's tactics drew from the Jobs-for-Negroes movement, in which many members of the United Bus Strike Committee had participated. Picket lines surrounded Harlem's bus stops, soup kitchens fed volunteers, and black chauffeurs and mechanics were registered. An "emergency jitney service" of privately owned automobiles transported some boycotters, but the key to the boycott's success was New York City's subway system and taxi companies which provided efficient, relatively inexpensive alternative transportation. Before the boycott terminated, volunteers painted placards, donated approximately $500, and gave the use of their automobiles. The month-long campaign kept sixty thousand persons off the buses each day at a loss of $3,000 in daily fares. It also drew together five hundred persons from various backgrounds and both races, as bandleaders, ministers, postal clerks, housewives, beauticians, and nurses walked the picket line. Celebrities, like musician Duke Ellington, actively supported the boycott.

Well aware of the significance of the church in black society, Powell made the Abyssinian Baptist Church one of two boycott headquarters. It was the location of the first and second boycott rallies. It provided volunteers experienced in protest, communications, and physical resources and, of course, became the base of Powell's operations and the center of his power.

Powell stressed the philosophy of nonviolent direct action. Blacks were to use only peaceful, legal avenues of redress. By appealing to "the Grace of God" and "the power of the masses," Powell combined religious and political themes; this combination of righteousness and self-help would enable "a black boy . . . to roll a bus up Seventh Avenue." Picket lines, as well as Powell's rhetoric, however, implied militancy. Those flouting the boycott, he declared, should be converted, "one way or another." Three years after the boycott, Powell summarized his nonviolent, though strident, philosophy in *Marching Blacks:* "No blows, no violence, but the steady unrelenting pressure of an increasing horde of people who knew they were right" would bring change.

The boycott was threatened first by violence and then by a misleading newspaper story. Following a UBSC rally at the Abyssinian Baptist Church on March 31, individuals hurled objects at several buses along Lenox Avenue. Fifty patrolmen dispersed those responsible, some of whom had attended the rally. "FEAR ANOTHER HARLEM RIOT," screamed the *Age*'s headlines. Of more concern to Powell and others was the *Amsterdam News* story of April 5. It announced that the bus companies had agreed to employ over two hundred black drivers and mechanics, providing that TWU waive the seniority rights of more than three hundred former bus employees waiting to be rehired. Such an agreement had been discussed, but no final decision had been reached. UBSC leaders moved quickly to maintain the boycott. They labeled the story "a lie,"

reorganized pickets, distributed leaflets, asked ministers to inform their congregations of "the true facts," and planned a mass meeting.

Despite crisis, the boycott and negotiations continued. Once Ritchie agreed to hire blacks, the major obstacle was TWU seniority policies. On April 17, Powell informed five thousand persons at the Golden Gate Ballroom that an agreement was imminent. Signed twelve days later, the agreement waived the seniority rights of all except ninety-one TWU drivers furloughed by the bus companies; after these men were reinstated, one hundred black drivers were to be hired. The next seventy mechanics employed would also be black, and thereafter, blacks and whites would be taken on alternately until 17 percent of the companies' labor force—exclusive of clerical staff— was black. This quota represented the percentage of black residents in Manhattan. Black workers would be enrolled as TWU members, although the bus companies exercised "sole discretion as to the type of Negro employees to be hired." The agreement would not take precedence over prior management-labor commitments provided they were nondiscriminatory. Of course, all boycott activities would cease. Powell declared that the agreement was made possible by new TWU contracts providing shorter hours and by additional municipal franchises enabling the bus companies to employ three hundred more persons.

Several factors made the Harlem boycott successful. Powell's agreement with Quill prevented bus company officials from playing blacks against whites in the TWU strike and the bus boycott. Throughout the strike, Quill raised the possibility of the bus companies employing strikebreakers. Blacks traditionally had been exploited as scabs, and some of the bus terminals were strategically located in Harlem. Indeed, at least one Harlem correspondent informed Mayor La Guardia that two thousand black men could "start the bus lines in 5, 10, or 20 hours." Powell's agreement significantly reduced the possibility of TWU's strike being broken by force, and reciprocally, it assured that the bus boycott would not fail because of traditional union opposition toward blacks.

Powell's agreement with Quill also held out the hope that blacks would support labor in the upcoming subway negotiations between La Guardia and TWU leaders. During the previous June, the municipal government had bought and unified the Brooklyn-Manhattan Transit Corporation and the Interborough Rapid Transit Company, which had been operated by TWU and the Brotherhood of Locomotive Engineers. When La Guardia contended that neither the right to strike nor a closed shop could be permitted among civil service employees, labor officials reported that the mayor had reneged on his obligations and anticipated a precedent-breaking conflict with the municipal government when the original contract expired on June 20, 1941. TWU leaders believed that mayoral reference to the bus strike as "bullheaded, obstinate and stupid" was designed to weaken their position in the coming subway negotiations. Obviously, public opinion would be crucial in that dispute. Hence, some blacks, like the *Age* editor, saw TWU support for the bus boycott as a trade-off for black support in the forthcoming union battle with the mayor.

Changing opinions and the impact of World War II helped make the Powell-Quill agreement possible. The racial attitudes of TWU leaders had been improving since 1938 when the union unsuccessfully sent blacks to be employed as drivers at the World's Fair. By World War II, Powell understood how uncomfortable society was in opposing a totalitarian, racist Nazi regime while practicing racial discrimination. "America," he stated later, "could not defeat Hitler abroad without defeating Hitlerism at home." Of equal importance, TWU leadership could pare seniority lists by three hundred unemployed members and make room for black employees because defense orders stimulated the economy and selective service calls reduced union ranks. According to the

Afro-American editor, the difficulty in finding bus drivers and mechanics provided blacks with unforeseen opportunities.

The boycott assured those opportunities. By early May, seven black mechanics had been hired by the bus companies and ten blacks were expected to begin chauffeur training within a week. Six months later, forty-three blacks had been employed in various classifications, including mechanic's helpers. Finally, on February 1, 1942, after all the ninety-odd furloughed white operators had been given opportunity for reemployment, the first ten black drivers employed by the Coach Company and the Omnibus Corporation began their routes.

That victory was historical. It drew blacks, labor, and management together in a successful effort to break down discriminatory employment practices in privately owned bus companies, and indirectly, it accelerated a similar trend that had already begun in the municipally owned transportation systems under La Guardia's leadership. The boycott also held out promise for "Negro-labor solidarity." Moreover, it effectively utilized the tactics and philosophies of the Jobs-for-Negroes movement, focused on the concept of equal opportunity, established the idea of a quota system, and provided safeguards for protecting blacks in their newly won jobs. All these elements were also attempted in the 1930s and 1960s, indicating the continuum in black protest that links militant means with traditional ends and nonviolent direct action tactics with greater participation in larger society. By exploiting both TWU ambitions and war manpower exigencies, Powell, Straugh, and Stevens created numerous jobs for black workers. But it was Powell who played the leading role, as he had done for the past decade, speaking out and organizing protests that brought approximately seventeen hundred jobs to Harlem. Exactly because of that record, blacks enthusiastically supported his successful candidacy for City Council in November 1941. His delivery of tangible gains merits mention, for as councilman and later, congressman he had the reputation for imparting only catharsis to his constituents. Finally, Powell's boycott sparked other protests; numerous blacks agreed with the editor of the *Pittsburgh Courier,* who said, "If this can be done in New York, it can be done in other cities." Indeed, in May the National Association for the Advancement of Colored People launched a nationwide picket campaign against defense industries that held government contracts but refused to hire blacks; Powell journeyed to Chicago to help the Negro Labor Relations League launch a jobs campaign; and the Colored Clerks Circle of St. Louis prepared to boycott a local cleaning company. Official entry of the United States into World War II prevented the emergence of what might have been widespread black protest akin to that of the 1950s and 1960s.

Nearly fifteen years later, when Rosa Parks refused to give up her seat to a white passenger on the Montgomery Bus Line, another phase of black protest began. It was led by Martin Luther King, Jr., who was unknown and inexperienced when leadership of the Montgomery Improvement Association was thrust on him in December of 1955. When he arrived in Montgomery during the previous year to accept the pastorate of the Dexter Avenue Baptist Church, it was "the cradle of the Confederacy." Of one hundred and thirty thousand residents, blacks comprised 40 percent. Segregated and scattered throughout the city, they were exploited economically and lacked even the semblance of geographic, political, or social unity. Jim Crow practices prevailed, particularly on the bus lines where operators possessed police powers for enforcing segregation. A long history of passenger abuse by bus drivers was well known to blacks who had been beaten, ridiculed, and stranded. Coretta Scott King accurately contended that black passengers were treated worse than cattle, "for nobody insults a cow." Earlier efforts to protest this treatment had failed because of black disunity and white power.

Juxtaposed to years of degradation, however, were rising expectations. If the United

States Supreme Court's decision against segregated public school systems in *Brown* v. *Topeka* (1954) did not affect Montgomery immediately, it signaled a major change in race relations. More immediate, however, was the emergence of what King termed "a brand new Negro" whose struggle for dignity was obstructed by self-deceiving whites who continued to live in the past. Hence some blacks and many whites were surprised when the arrest of Rosa Parks triggered protest. During the eighteen years that he had lived in the South, columnist Carl Rowan "had never seen such spirit among a group of Negroes."

That spirit was mobilized by the Montgomery Improvement Association (MIA) which grew out of the efforts of E. D. Nixon, a pullman porter who presided over the local NAACP, and Jo Ann Robinson, an English professor at Alabama State College and president of the Women's Political Council. They arranged a meeting of black ministers, who adopted Reverend Ralph Abernathy's idea of the MIA, elected King as its president, and organized a mass meeting of black residents. On Sunday, December 5, over four thousand people crammed into the Holt Street Baptist Church to endorse a boycott until the bus lines guaranteed (1) courteous treatment, (2) a first-come-first-served seating arrangement (blacks in the rear, whites in the front), and (3) employment of black operators on predominantly black routes. Moderate, mostly symbolic, alterations in the Jim Crow system were sought.

The MIA tactics resembled those of earlier black protest movements, including Powell's. As Lawrence D. Reddick has pointed out, Montgomery was "ideally fitted" for a bus boycott: its sizable black population comprised 70 percent of all bus passengers, while its layout of 27.9 square miles enabled residents to reach most places by foot. An effective boycott, however, needed alternative means of transportation. In its initial stages, black cab companies agreed to carry black passengers for the price of the ten cents bus fare. A car pool supplemented the taxi service, becoming the major mode of transportation after municipal officials outlawed the lower taxi fares. Over three hundred automobiles moved in and out of forty-eight dispatch and forty-two collection stations. Financial support originated among the protestors, but as their efforts drew national and international attention, donations came from various sources. In one year, the MIA had spent $225,000. From December 5, 1955, to December 21, 1956, the boycott cost the Montgomery Bus Lines over a quarter of a million dollars in fares, the City of Montgomery several thousand dollars in taxes, and the downtown white merchants several million dollars in business. It also boosted black businesses and reduced the social distance between classes within the black society.

It was no coincidence that the protest spirit emanated from the church, southern black society's most independent institution and primary means of communication. It became routine for blacks to share a ride or walk daily and attend mass meetings at a different church each Monday and Thursday. The boycott became inseparable from the secular and religious life of black society, maximizing the participation of everyone from domestic to clergymen. Not surprisingly, church-owned vehicles in the car pool were dubbed 'rolling churches'.

Emphasizing the concepts of love and justice, King forged a philosophy of nonviolent direct action, stressing self-help, condemning violence, focusing on evil—rather than evil-doers—and espousing "love for America and the democratic way of life." He realized the limits of black power, the history of white repression, and the need for legitimacy in the eyes of white America. Perhaps for these reasons, MIA leaders originally sought a first-come-first-served seating arrangement "under segregation" and watched those blacks who might have resorted to violence. Both the demands for desegregation in seating arrangements and the Gandhian dimension of King's philosophy evolved after the boycott had begun. Nonviolence, already implicit in the Christian teaching that underlay the boycott, was formally articulated by King as a result of the influences of Bayard Rustin and the Reverend Glenn E. Smiley of the Fellowship of Reconciliation.

Despite solid organization and philosophical appeal, the boycott confronted several problems. King later admitted having been "scared to death by threats against myself and my family." Indeed, on January 30, 1956, as Coretta King and baby Yolanda inhabited the premises, the King home was bombed. In addition, King had to deal with a legal system that sanctioned Jim Crow. As a result of Title 14, Section 54, of the Alabama Code prohibiting boycotts, King and eighty-eight others were convicted of unlawful activities. Later the car pool was halted by court injunction. What saved the boycott was the slow wit of the municipal officials and the federal injunction banning segregated buses which was upheld by the United States Supreme Court. Nor did the boycott receive meaningful support from the white community. A handful of whites, like Reverend Robert Graetz, pastor of the black Lutheran Trinity Church, "paid dearly" for participating in the boycott. Other whites assisted the protest unwittingly by chauffeuring their domestics to and from work. For the most part, however, whites either opposed the boycott or, if sympathetic to it, were afraid to say so publicly.

Internal pressures also proved troublesome. Early in the boycott, as abusive phone calls, long hours of work, and relentless efforts to maintain unity began to mount, King despaired and confided in God, "I've come to the point where I can't face it alone." At this time King experienced a revelation, which enabled him "to face anything." Jealousy on the part of some black ministers threatened the boycott periodically. The gravest incident occurred on January 21 when King was informed that Mayor W. A. Gayle and three black ministers had agreed on a settlement to end the boycott. That evening and the following Sunday morning, MIA leaders successfully alerted the black community to this hoax.

These pressures notwithstanding, the boycott was successful, with support coming from numerous quarters. Congressman Adam Clayton Powell, Jr., for example, pressed President Dwight D. Eisenhower to protect the eighty-odd blacks indicted for boycott activities. When Eisenhower refused to comply, Powell publicly chided him for "trying to wash his hands like Pilate of the blood of innocent men and women in the Southland." He then organized a "National Deliverance Day of Prayer" for March 28, which was commemorated in several cities, including Atlanta, Chicago, and New York. Powell collected and sent $2,500 to MIA. Early the next month, he asked all members of the House of Representatives for contributions to help rebuild seven black churches in Montgomery that had been bombed by terrorists, and later recorded that only two Congressmen honored his request. Before the year ended, he and several other nationally known blacks spoke in Montgomery. In sum, the Montgomery bus boycott brought to the surface black awareness that had been stirring since World War II.

As significant was the recent shift in the United States Supreme Court under Chief Justice Earl Warren. Just as Mayor Gayle had deduced that the boycott could be crushed by enjoining the car pool for being unlicensed, the higher court upheld a United States District Court decision that laws in Alabama requiring segregation on buses were unconstitutional. This decision of November 13, 1956, meant victory for MIA, but King continued the boycott until a federal order arrived in Montgomery six weeks later; on December 21, MIA leaders rode the bus in victory.

That victory sparked the Civil Rights Movement. The Montgomery bus boycott provided a leader in King, a philosophy in nonviolence, a tactic in direct action, and, as important, a tangible triumph. Blacks were poised for change, needing, in Lerone Bennett's worlds, "an act to give them power over their fears." The boycott, of course, did much more, for under King's leadership it achieved legitimacy and prepared both races for a prolonged assault on inequality. That King succeeded in the South, and succeeded with the United States Supreme Court's assistance, underscored a major theme for the coming decade. That the Montgomery City Bus Line so adamantly and successfully refused any agreement regarding the hiring of black bus drivers indicated both the obstacles and limits for changes that lay ahead. Nevertheless, the boycott spawned the Southern Christian Leadership Conference, "a sustaining mechanism," and elevated the struggle for racial equality to the national level.

The Harlem boycott of 1941 came nowhere near achieving this, for it was much smaller and failed to sustain a national protest movement. Nor was it supported throughout the black community. Yet similarities between it and the Montgomery experience abound, particularly those dealing with leadership. Powell and King came from deeply Christian, middle-class families that provided physical security while imposing high parental expectations. As precocious youngsters, both Powell and King experienced anxiety and guilt. Each questioned his father's vocation, perhaps feeling incapable of living up to the parental reputation or, as most likely in Powell's case, repressing hostility toward a domineering father. Each tried to escape: Powell by passing for white and King by engaging in masochistic tendencies. (King jumped out of an upstairs window once, blaming himself for an accident involving his grandmother; at another time, he blamed himself for being at a parade when she died of illness.) As young adults, however, both men sublimated this inner turmoil and embraced the church and their fathers, becoming independent from the latter, yet reflecting them. Perhaps, as psychoanalyst Erich Fromm has theorized about other historical figures, their long-sought-after personal independence emerged in their struggle for collective black liberation.

Powell and King believed that collective liberation could only come through the black church with its "enormous reservoirs of psychic and social strength." Such liberation would free both races, for blacks possessed the divinely inspired mission of achieving equality through the redemption of white society. As the largest black Protestant church in the United States, the Abyssinian Baptist Church boasted a membership of thousands, which provided Powell with impressive human and financial resources. King's Dexter Avenue Baptist Church, however, was more representative of black congregations, comprising one thousand persons and limited finances. In order to be effective, Powell and King successfully established coalitions with other religious and secular groups.

If the church became the vehicle for change, it was black folk religion that provided the sinew for protest. Powell and, more directly King, converted traditional black religiosity into "a passion for justice." Speaking to northern, urban congregations, Powell, avoided "Valley-and-Dry-Bones sermons," stressing instead "nicely chosen Negro idioms about every day issues." Powell could be moved by his own words and weep publicly. King spoke a more "religious language" that struck at the heart of southern black culture. Reverend Andrew Young, a member of the Southern Christian Leadership Conference, observed that no one could have mobilized black southerners by arguing about segregation and integration, but when King preached about "leaving the slavery of Egypt" or "dry bones rising again" everybody understood his language. Both Powell and King possessed what historian Joseph R. Washington, Jr., has called "that Baptist hum which makes what is said only as important as how it is said." The inflections of their voices, the cadence of their deliveries, the nuances of their messages, the animation of their gestures were eagerly anticipated and instinctively understood by multitudes who shared a special cultural and historical relationship with their preachers. Powell and King, then, mobilized black people and became their surrogates, "interpreting their innermost feelings, their passions, their yearnings" as well as channeling their emotions into viable protest.

Protestant theology and Gandhian tactics provided the means by which Powell and King could channel the passion for justice. Both men advocated the social gospel, contending that any religion ignoring the socioeconomic conditions that shackle humanity was, in King's rhetoric, "a dry-as-dust religion." Nonviolent direct action was not a new tactic in black protest, but it was one that permitted Powell, King, and their supporters to become social gospel activists. Following King's successful boycott, blacks increasingly favored an active role by the church in social and political issues during the years 1957 to 1968.

If the boycotts shared a similar religious heritage, they also reflect the respective personality characterizations of Powell and King. Political scientist Hanes Walton, Jr., notes that Powell used nonviolence for practical reasons as "a potent, energetic tool," while King embraced it as "an end in itself, endowed with superior moral qualities." Powell did not advocate violence, but on occasion his rhetoric was intimidating and implied the use of intimidation. King, of course, would tolerate no such deviation from passive resistance. King's commitment notwithstanding, Powell more accurately reflected the reasons for which blacks utilized nonviolent direct action. In the aftermath of the Montgomery boycott, for example, over 70 percent of the black respondents surveyed in that city recognized the usefulness of nonviolence since black people lacked the "power to use violence successfully." According to sociologist E. Franklin Frazier, "Gandhism as a philosophy and a way of life is completely alien to the Negro"; black religious heritage accounts for the presence of nonviolent direct action in the civil rights movement.

That King much more than Powell envisaged—as did Mahatma Gandhi—"a life of service to humanity on a level which called for a self-discipline of rare order" was partly due to socioecological factors. Even in 1941, Harlem, the "Negro Mecca" of the world, was a more secure environment for black people than was Montgomery fifteen years later. Powell had been raised in that security and had successfully used the avenues of redress that were available in the North. King had been brought up in southern segregation, where survival depended upon staying in one's place and where protest efforts had little result. Powell never experienced the pressures and fears that haunted King daily; Powell had enemies, but none who threatened his family or bombed his home. Exactly because of his own background and fears, King understood the need to allay southern white fears if blacks were to avoid pogroms and race relations were to progress: "If you truly love and respect an opponent, you respect his fears too."

King's upbringing emphasized inner control, the kind that enabled him to bear parental whippings with "stoic impassivity." Reverend King, Sr., stressed discipline, and the precarious social environs demanded self-regulation. Hence King originally questioned the emotionalism in the black church and later, in the boycott, took great pains to direct it into safe arenas. Finally, the religious and secular elements in the southern black church appear to have been much more interdependent than elsewhere, which partly accounts for King's commitment to nonviolence as a way of life. This commitment may have been—as in Gandhi's experience—marked by ambivalence, for King stressed love partly for the purpose of controlling hate (perhaps his own). In Powell's case, the opposite was true. As a child, he was spoiled, and lived in an environment that did not demand inner control for survival. He never led a humble life but, rather, publicly flouted the racial mores of white society. Nor was his religion as all-encompassing as King's; it was more secular and compartmentalized, reflecting the tremendous impact that migration and urbanization had had upon the northern black church. Powell released anger more directly by stressing direct action, while King tended to displace it by putting emphasis on

nonviolence or, more precisely, on what Gandhi called Satyagraha—love-force. It is, then, no coincidence that Powell later singled out Marcus Garvey as the greatest mass leader, demonstrated his independence by clearly identifying an enemy, and spoke militantly of change. King, however, referred only to Booker T. Washington in his first major address in the boycott—"Let no man pull you so low as to make you hate him," stressed racial reconciliation by describing forces of evil, and prayed for opponents. Hence it is not surprising that the name of Powell's organization, the United Bus Strike Committee, projected an assertive, challenging image and that the Harlem boycott focused on the tangible bread-and-butter issue of jobs. By contrast, King's efforts emphasized uplift, as implied in the title, Montgomery Improvement Association, and sought more symbolic, civil rights objectives.

Powell had undertaken the Harlem boycott as his last major protest as a social gospel activist at the end of the Jobs-for-Negroes campaign. He would soon begin a political career as councilman in New York City, and World War II would soon reduce protest to rhetoric as black leaders feared that their efforts would be labeled traitorous. King was thrust into the Montgomery boycott, his first meaningful protest, which began the civil rights movement. Larger and more significant historically than anything that Powell had done, King embraced that movement and its principles until they died together on April 4, 1968. While the contributions of King are obvious, those of Powell have been forgotten by many. Nevertheless, King knew of Powell's efforts. "Before some of us were born, before some of us could walk or talk," King recalled in the 1960s, "Adam Powell wrote *Marching Blacks,* the charter of the black revolution that is taking place today." One can imagine Powell, in his accustomed modesty, ejaculating an "Amen."

18

THE DRIVE-IN CULTURE OF CONTEMPORARY AMERICA

KENNETH T. JACKSON

Nothing has so transformed the landscape and architecture of America as the automobile. At the beginning of the twentieth century, the automobile was a plaything of the rich, but by the end of World War II, a majority of Americans owned automobiles, and the proportion has grown ever since. As more and more Americans purchased cars in the postwar decades and as an increasing proportion of the nation's manufactured goods was transported by highway instead of rail, entirely new kinds of industries emerged to service an increasingly motorized society.

In this essay, Kenneth T. Jackson documents the tremendous impact of the automobile and truck on contemporary America. From the interstate highway system inaugurated during the Eisenhower administration to such innovations as shopping centers, motels, and service stations, "automobility" has done much to turn America into a service society. But, Jackson suggests, this 30-year trend may be coming to an end. A countertrend has recently emerged, he tells us, in which central cities are increasingly being revitalized as living and shopping spaces, while the corporate consolidation of the gasoline, motel, and retail sales industries has led to the closing of independent service stations and many other artifacts of the early automobile age. If he is correct, the next decades may usher in yet another phase in America's constantly changing architectural landscape.

Chapter 14 in Kenneth T. Jackson, *Crabgrass Frontier: The Suburbanization of the United States*

The postwar years brought unprecedented prosperity to the United States, as color televisions, stereo systems, frost-free freezers, electric blenders, and automatic garbage disposals became basic equipment in the middle-class American home. But the best symbol of individual success and identity was a sleek, air-conditioned, high-powered, personal statement on wheels. Between 1950 and 1980, when the American population increased by 50 percent, the number of their automobiles increased by 200 percent. In high school the most important rite of passage came to be the earning of a driver's license and the freedom to press an accelerator to the floor. Educational administrators across the country had to make parking space for hundreds of student vehicles. A car became one's identity, and the important question was: "What does he drive?" Not only teenagers, but also millions of older persons literally defined themselves in terms of the number, cost, style, and horsepower of their vehicles. "Escape," thinks a character in a novel by Joyce Carol Oates. "As long as he had his own car he was an American and could not die."

Unfortunately, Americans did die, often behind the wheel. On September 9, 1899, as he was stepping off a streetcar at 74th Street and Central Park West in New York, Henry H. Bliss was struck and killed by a motor vehicle, thus becoming the first fatality in the long war between flesh and steel. Thereafter, the carnage increased almost annually until Americans were sustaining about 50,000 traffic deaths and about 2 million nonfatal injuries per year. Automobility proved to be far more deadly than war for the United States. It was as if a Pearl Harbor attack took place on the highways every two weeks, with crashes becoming so commonplace that an entire industry sprang up to provide medical, legal, and insurance services for the victims.

The environmental cost was almost as high as the human toll. In 1984 the 159 million cars, trucks, and buses on the nation's roads were guzzling millions of barrels of oil every day, causing traffic jams that shattered nerves and clogged the cities they were supposed to open up and turning much of the countryside to pavement. Not surprisingly, when gasoline shortages created long lines at the pumps in 1974 and 1979, behavioral scientists noted that many people experienced anger, depression, frustration, and insecurity, as well as a formidable sense of loss.

Such reactions were possible because the automobile and the suburb have combined to create a drive-in culture that is part of the daily experience of most Americans. Because of unemployment and war, per capita motor-vehicle ownership was stable (at about 30 million vehicles) between 1930 and 1948, and as late as 1950 (when registrations had jumped to 49 million) an astonishing 41 percent of all American families and a majority of working-class families still did not own a car. Postwar prosperity and rising real wages, however, made possible vastly higher market penetration, and by 1984 there were about seventy motor vehicles for every one hundred citizens, and more cars than either households or workers. Schaeffer and Sclar have argued that high auto ownership is the result of real economic needs rather than some "love affair" with private transportation. Moreover, the American people have proven to be no more prone to motor vehicle purchases than the citizens of other lands. After World War II, the Europeans and the Japanese began to catch up, and by 1980 both had achieved the same level of automobile ownership that the United States had reached in 1950. In automotive technology, American dominance slipped away in the postwar years as German, Swedish, and Japanese engineers pioneered the development of diesel engines, front-wheel drives, disc brakes, fuel-injection, and rotary engines.

Although it is not accurate to speak of a uniquely American love affair with the automobile, and although John B. Rae claimed too much when he wrote in 1971 that "modern suburbia is a creature of the automobile and could not exist without it," the motor vehicle has fundamentally restructured the pattern of everyday life in the United States. As a young man, Lewis Mumford advised his countrymen to "forget the damned motor car and build cities for lovers and friends." As it was, of course, the nation followed a different pattern. Writing in the *American Builder* in 1929, the critic Willard Morgan noted that the building of drive-in structures to serve a motor-driven population had ushered in "a completely new architectural form."

THE INTERSTATE HIGHWAY

The most popular exhibit at the New York World's Fair in 1939 was General Motors' "Futurama." Looking twenty-five years ahead, it offered a "magic Aladdin-like flight through time and space." Fair-goers stood in hour-long lines, waiting to travel on a moving sidewalk above a huge model created by designer Norman Bel Geddes. Miniature superhighways with 50,000 automated cars wove past model farms en route to model cities. Five million persons peered eventually at such novelties as elevated freeways, expressway traffic moving at 100 miles per hour, and "modern and efficient city planning—breath-taking architecture—each city block a complete unit in itself (with) broad, one-way thoroughfares—space, sunshine, light, and air." The message of "Futurama" was as impressive as its millions of model parts: "The job of building the future is one which will demand our best energies, our most fruitful imagination; and that with it will come greater opportunities for all."

The promise of a national system of impressive roadways attracted a diverse group of lobbyists, including the Automobile Manufacturers Association, state-highway administrators, motor-bus operators, the American Trucking Association, and even the American Parking Association—for the more cars on the road, the more cars would be parked at the end of the journey. Truck companies, for example, promoted legislation to spend state gasoline taxes on highways, rather than on schools, hospitals, welfare, or public transit. In 1943 these groups came together as the American Road Builders Association, with General Motors as the largest contributor, to form a lobbying enterprise second only to that of the munitions industry. By the mid-1950s, it had become one of the most broad-based of all pressure groups, consisting of the oil, rubber, asphalt, and construction industries; the car dealers and renters; the trucking and bus concerns; the banks and advertising agencies that depended upon the companies involved; and the labor unions. On the local level, professional real-estate groups and home-builders associations joined the movement in the hope that highways would cause a spurt in housing turnover and a jump in prices. They envisaged no mere widening of existing roads, but the creation of an entirely new superhighway system and the initiation of the largest peacetime construction project in history.

The highway lobby inaugurated a comprehensive public relations program in 1953 by sponsoring a national essay contest on the need for better roads. The winner of the $25,-000 grand prize was Robert Moses, the greatest builder the world has yet known and a passionate advocate of the urban expressway. The title of his work was "How to Plan and Pay for Better Highways." As his biographer Robert A. Caro has noted, Moses was "the world's most vocal, effective and prestigious apologist for the automobile," and he did more than any other single urban official to encourage more hesitant officials to launch major road-building efforts in their cities.

The Cold War provided an additional stimulus to the campaign for more elaborate expressways. In 1951 the *Bulletin of the Atomic Scientists* devoted an entire issue to "Defense through Decentralization." Their argument was simple. To avoid national destruction in a nuclear attack, the United States should disperse existing large cities into smaller settlements. The ideal model was a depopulated urban core surrounded by satellite cities and low-density suburbs.

Sensitive to mounting political pressure, President Dwight Eisenhower appointed a committee in 1954 to "study" the nation's highway requirements. Its conclusions were foregone, in part because the chairman was Lucius D. Clay, a member of the board of directors of General Motors. The committee considered no alternative to a massive highway system, and it suggested a major redirection of national policy to benefit the car and the truck. The Interstate Highway Act became law in 1956, when the Congress provided for a 41,000-mile (eventually expanded to a 42,500-mile) system, with the federal government paying 90 percent of the cost. President Eisenhower gave four reasons for signing the measure: current highways were unsafe; cars too often became snarled in traffic jams; poor roads saddled business with high costs for transportation; and modern highways were needed because "in case of atomic attack on our key cities, the road net must permit quick evacuation of target areas." Not a single word was said about the impact of highways on cities and suburbs, although the concrete thoroughfares and the thirty-five-ton tractor-trailers which used them encouraged the continued outward movement of industries toward the beltways and interchanges. Moreover, the interstate system helped continue the downward spiral of public transportation and virtually guaranteed that future urban growth would perpetuate a centerless sprawl. Soon after the bill was passed by the Senate, Lewis Mumford wrote sadly: "When the American people, through their Congress, voted a little while ago for a $26 billion highway program, the most charitable thing to assume is that they hadn't the faintest notion of what they were doing."

Once begun, the Interstate Highway System of the United States became a concrete colossus that grew bigger with every passing year. The secret of its success lay in the principle of non-divertibility of highway revenues collected from gasoline taxes. The Highway Trust Fund, as it was called, was to be held separately from general taxes. Although no less a

personage than Winston Churchill called the idea of a non-divertible road fund "nonsense," "absurd," and "an outrage upon . . . common sense," the trust fund had powerful friends in the United States, and it easily swept all opposition before it. Unlike European governments, Washington used taxes to support the highway infrastructure while refusing assistance to railroads. According to Senator Gaylord Nelson of Wisconsin, 75 percent of government expenditures for transportation in the United States in the postwar generation went for highways as opposed to 1 percent for urban mass transit.

The inevitable result of the bias in American transport funding, a bias that existed for a generation before the Interstate Highway program was initiated, is that the United States now has the world's best road system and very nearly its worst public-transit offerings. Los Angeles, in particular, provides the nation's most dramatic example of urban sprawl tailored to the mobility of the automobile. Its vast, amorphous conglomeration of housing tracts, shopping centers, industrial parks, freeways, and independent towns blend into each other in a seamless fabric of concrete and asphalt, and nothing over the years has succeeded in gluing this automobile-oriented civilization into any kind of cohesion—save that of individual routine. Los Angeles's basic shape comes from three factors, all of which long preceded the freeway system. The first was cheap land (in the 1920s rather than 1970s) and the desire for single-family houses. In 1950, for example, nearly two-thirds of all the dwelling units in the Los Angeles area were fully detached, a much higher percentage than in Chicago (28 percent), New York City (20 percent), or Philadelphia (15 percent), and its residential density was the lowest of major cities. The second was the dispersed location of its oil fields and refineries, which led to the creation of industrial suburbs like Whittier and Fullerton and of residential suburbs like La Habra, which housed oil workers and their families. The third was its once excellent mass-transit system, which at its peak included more than 1,100 miles of track and constituted the largest electric interurban railway in the world.

The Pacific Electric Company collapsed in the 1920s, however, and since that time Los Angeles has been more dependent upon the private automobile than other large American cities. Beginning in 1942, the Los Angeles Chamber of Commerce, the automobile club, and elected officials met regularly to plan for a region-wide expressway network. They succeeded, and southern California's fabled 715 miles of freeways now constitute a grid that channels virtually all traffic and sets many communal boundaries. They are the primary form of transportation for most residents, who seem to regard time spent in their cars as more pleasurable than time walking to, waiting for, or riding on the bus. More than a third of the Los Angeles area is consumed by highways, parking lots, and interchanges, and in the downtown section this proportion rises to two-thirds. Not surprisingly, efforts to restore the region's public transportation to excellence have thus far failed. In 1976, for example, the state of California attempted to discourage single-passenger automobiles by reserving one lane in each direction on the Santa Monica Freeway for express buses and car pools. An emotional explosion ensued that dominated radio talk shows and television news, and Los Angeles' so-called "diamond lanes" were soon abolished.

More recently, southern California has followed the growing national enthusiasm for rail transit, and Los Angeles broke ground in 1984 for an 18-mile, $3.3 billion subway that will cut underneath the densely built, heavily trafficked Wilshire Boulevard corridor, cut through Hollywood, and end up in the residential San Fernando Valley. The underground will hopefully be the centerpiece of an eventual 160-mile network, second in size in the United States only to New York City's.

THE GARAGE

The drive-in structure that is closest to the hearts, bodies, and cars of the American family is the garage. It is the link between the home and the outside world. The word is French, meaning storage space, but its transformation into a multi-purpose enclosure internally integrated with the dwelling is distinctively American.

In the streetcar era, curbs had been unbroken and driveways were almost unknown. A family wealthy enough to have a horse and carriage would have stored such possessions either in a public livery stable or in a private structure at the rear of the property. The owners of the first automobiles were usually sufficiently affluent to maintain a private stable. The first cars, therefore, which were open to the elements, often found lodging in a corner of the stable, side by side with the carriages they were soon to replace. These early accommodations for the automobile were often provided with gasoline tanks, for filling stations at the time were few and far between. This and the fact that cars often caught fire were good and sufficient reasons to keep the motor vehicles away from the family.

After World War I, house plans of the expensive variety began to include garages, and by the mid-1920s driveways were commonplace and garages had become important selling points. The popular 1928 *Home Builders* pattern book offered designs for fifty garages in wood, Tudor, and brick varieties. In affluent sections, such large and efficiently planned structures included housing above for the family chauffeur. In less pretentious neighborhoods, the small, single-purpose garages were scarcely larger than the vehicles themselves, and they were simply portable and prefabricated structures, similar to those in Quebec today, that were camouflaged with greenery and trellises. As one architect complained in 1924: "The majority of owners are really ashamed of their garages and really endeavor to keep them from view," and he implored his readers to build a garage "that may be worthy of standing alongside your house." Although there was a tendency to move garages closer to the house, they typically remained at the rear of the property before 1925, often with access via an alley which ran parallel to the street. The car was still thought of as something similar to a horse—dependable and important, but not something that one needed to be close to in the evening.

By 1935, however, the garage was beginning to merge into the house itself, and in 1937 the *Architectural Record* noted that "the garage has become a very essential part of the residence." The tendency accelerated after World War II, as alleys went the way of the horse-drawn wagon, as property widths more often exceeded fifty feet, and as the car became not only a status symbol, but almost a member of the family, to be cared for and sheltered. The introduction of a canopied and unenclosed structure called a "car port" represented an inexpensive solution to the problem, particularly in mild climates, but in the 1950s the enclosed garage was back in favor and a necessity even in a tract house. Easy access to the automobile became a key aspect of residential design, and not only for the well-to-do. By the 1960s garages often occupied about 400 square feet (about one-third that of the house itself) and usually contained space for two automobiles and a variety of lawn and woodworking tools. Offering direct access to the house (a conveniently placed door usually led directly into the kitchen), the garage had become an integrated part of the dwelling, and it dominated the front facades of new houses. In California garages and driveways were often so prominent that the house could almost be described as accessory to the garage. Few people, however, went to the extremes common in England, where the automobile was often so precious that living rooms were often converted to garages.

THE MOTEL

As the United States became a rubber-tire civilization, a new kind of roadside architecture was created to convey an instantly recognizable image to the fast-moving traveler. Criticized as tasteless, cheap, forgettable, and flimsy by most commentators, drive-in struc-

tures did attract the attention of some talent architects, most notably Los Angeles's Richard Neutra. For him, the automobile symbolized modernity, and its design paralleled his own ideals of precision and efficiency. This correlation between the structure and the car began to be celebrated in the late 1960s and 1970s when architects Robert Venturi, Denise Scott Brown, and Steven Izenour developed such concepts as "architecture as symbol" and the "architecture of communication." Their book, *Learning from Las Vegas,* was instrumental in encouraging a shift in taste from general condemnation to appreciation of the commercial strip and especially of the huge and garish signs which were easily recognized by passing motorists.

A ubiquitous example of the drive-in culture is the motel. In the middle of the nineteenth century, every city, every county seat, every aspiring mining town, every wide place in the road with aspirations to larger size, had to have a hotel. Whether such structures were grand palaces on the order of Boston's Tremont House or New York's Fifth Avenue Hotel, or whether they were jerry-built shacks, they were typically located at the center of the business district, at the focal point of community activities. To a considerable extent, the hotel was the place for informal social interaction and business, and the very heart and soul of the city.

Between 1910 and 1920, however, increasing numbers of traveling motorists created a market for overnight accommodation along the highways. The first tourists simply camped wherever they chose along the road. By 1924, several thousand municipal campgrounds were opened which offered cold water spigots and outdoor privies. Next came the "cabin camps," which consisted of tiny, white clapboard cottages arranged in a semicircle and often set in a grove of trees. Initially called "tourist courts," these establishments were cheap, convenient, and informal, and by 1926 there were an estimated two thousand of them, mostly in the West and in Florida.

Soon after clean linens and comfortable

rooms became available along the nation's highways, it became apparent that overnight travelers were not the only, or even the largest, pool of customers. Convenience and privacy were especially appealing to couples seeking a romantic retreat. A well-publicized Southern Methodist University study in 1935 reported that 75 percent of Dallas area motel business consisted of one man and one woman remaining for only a short stay. Whatever the motivation of patrons, the success of the new-style hotels prompted Sinclair Lewis to predict in 1920:

> Somewhere in these states there is a young man who is going to become rich. He is going to start a chain of small, clean, pleasant hotels, standardized and nationally advertised, along every important motor route in the country. He is not going to waste money on glit and onyx, but he is going to have agreeable clerks, good coffee, endurable mattresses and good lighting.

It was not until 1952 that Kemmons Wilson and Wallace E. Johnson opened their first "Holiday Inn" on Summer Avenue in Memphis. But long before that, in 1926, a San Luis Obispo, California, proprietor had coined a new word, "motel," to describe an establishment that allowed a guest to park his car just outside his room. New terminology did not immediately erase the unsavory image of the roadside establishments, however. In 1940 FBI Director J. Edgar Hoover declared that most motels were assignation camps and hideouts for criminals. Perhaps he was thinking of Bonnie and Clyde, who had a brief encounter with the law at the Red Crown Cabin Camp near Platte City, Missouri, one evening in July of 1933. Many of Hoover's "dens of vice" were once decent places that, unable to keep up, turned to the "hot pillow trade." Some Texas cabins, said the FBI director, were rented as many as sixteen times a night, while establishments elsewhere did business by the hour, with "a knock on the door when the hour was up."

Motels began to thrive after World War II,

when the typical establishment was larger and more expensive than the earlier cabins. Major chains set standards for prices, services, and respectability that the traveling public could depend on. As early as 1948, there were 26,000 self-styled motels in the United States. Hard-won respectability attracted more middle-class families, and by 1960 there were 60,000 such places, a figure that doubled again by 1972. By that time an old hotel was closing somewhere in downtown America every thirty hours. And somewhere in suburban America, a plastic and glass Shangri La was rising to take its place.

Typical of the inner-city hotels was the Heritage in Detroit. The big bands once played on its roof, and aspiring socialites enjoyed crepe-thin pancakes. In 1975 a disillusioned former employee gestured futilely, "It's dying; the whole place is dying," as the famed hotel closed its doors. By 1984 about fifty historic establishments in downtown areas, such as the Peabody in Memphis, the Mayflower in Washington, the Galvez in Houston, the Menger in San Antonio, and the Biltmore in Providence were reopening with antique-filled rooms and oak-paneled bars. But the trend remained with the standard, two-story motel.

THE DRIVE-IN THEATER

The downtown movie theaters and old vaudeville houses faced a similar challenge from the automobile. In 1933 Richard M. Hollinshead set up a 16-mm projector in front of his garage in Riverton, New Jersey, and then settled down to watch a movie. Recognizing a nation addicted to the motorcar when he saw one, Hollinshead and Willis Smith opened the world's first drive-in movie in a forty-car parking lot in Camden on June 6, 1933. Hollinshead profited only slightly from his brainchild, however, because in 1938 the United States Supreme Court refused to hear his appeal against Loew's Theaters, thus accepting the argument that the drive-in movie was not a patentable item. The idea never caught on in Europe, but by 1958 more than four thousand outdoor screens dotted the American landscape. Because drive-ins offered bargain-basement prices and double or triple bills, the theaters tended to favor movies that were either second-run or second-rate. Horror films and teenage romance were the order of the night, as *Beach Blanket Bingo* or *Invasion of the Body Snatchers* typified the offerings. Pundits often commented that there was a better show in the cars than on the screen.

In the 1960s and 1970s the drive-in movie began to slip in popularity. Rising fuel costs and a season that lasted only six months contributed to the problem, but skyrocketing land values were the main factor. When drive-ins were originally opened, they were typically out in the hinterlands. When subdivisions and shopping malls came closer, the drive-ins could not match the potential returns from other forms of investments. According to the National Association of Theater Owners, only 2,935 open-air theaters still operated in the United States in 1983, even though the total number of commercial movie screens in the nation, 18,772, was at a 35-year high. The increase was picked up not by the downtown and the neighborhood theaters, but by new multi-screen cinemas in shopping centers. Realizing that the large parking lots of indoor malls were relatively empty in the evening, shopping center moguls came to regard theaters as an important part of a successful retailing mix.

THE GASOLINE SERVICE STATION

The purchase of gasoline in the United States has thus far passed through five distinct epochs. The first stage was clearly the worst for the motorist, who had to buy fuel by the bucketful at a livery stable, repair shop, or dry goods store. Occasionally, vendors sold gasoline from small tank cars which they pushed up and down the streets. In any event, the automobile owner had to pour gasoline from a bucket through a funnel into his tank. The entire procedure was inefficient, smelly, wasteful, and occasionally dangerous.

The second stage began about 1905, when C. H. Laessig of St. Louis equipped a hot-water heater with a glass gauge and a garden hose and turned the whole thing on its end. With this simple maneuver, he invented an easy way to transfer gasoline from a storage tank to an automobile without using a bucket. Later in the same year, Sylvanus F. Bowser invented a gasoline pump which automatically measured the outflow. The entire assembly was labeled a "filling station." At this stage, which lasted until about 1920, such an apparatus consisted of a single pump outside a retail store which was primarily engaged in other businesses and which provided precious few services for the motorist. Many were located on the edge of town for safety and to be near the bulk stations; those few stations in the heart of the city did not even afford the luxury of off-street parking.

Between 1920 and 1950, service stations entered into a third phase and became, as a group, one of the most widespread kinds of commercial buildings in the United States. Providing under one roof all the functions of gasoline distribution and normal automotive maintenance, these full-service structures were often built in the form of little colonial houses, Greek temples, Chinese pagodas, and Art Deco palaces. Many were local landmarks and a source of community pride. One cartoonist in the 1920s mocked such structures with a drawing in which a newcomer to town confused the gas station with the state capitol. Grandiose at the time, many of them molder today—deserted, forlorn structures with weeds growing in the concrete where gasoline pumps once stood. Their bays stand empty and silent, rendered that way by changing economics, changing styles, and changing consumer preferences.

After 1935 the gasoline station evolved again, this time into a more homogeneous entity that was standardized across the entire country and that reflected the mass-marketing techniques of billion-dollar oil companies. Some of the more familiar designs were innovative or memorable, such as the drumlike Mobil station by New York architect Frederick Frost, which featured a dramatically curving facade while conveying the corporate identity. Another popular service station style was the Texaco design of Walter Dorwin Teague—a smooth white exterior with elegant trim and the familiar red star and bold red lettering. Whatever the product or design, the stations tended to be operated by a single entrepreneur and represented an important part of small business in American life.

The fifth stage of gasoline-station development began in the 1970s, with the slow demise of the traditional service-station businessman. New gasoline outlets were of two types. The first was the super station, often owned and operated by the oil companies themselves. Most featured a combination of self-service and full-service pumping consoles, as well as fully equipped "car care centers." Service areas were separated from the pumping sections so that the two functions would not interfere with each other. Mechanics never broke off work to sell gas.

The more pervasive second type might be termed the "mini-mart station." The operators of such establishments have now gone full circle since the early twentieth century. Typically, they know nothing about automobiles and expect the customers themselves to pump the gasoline. Thus, "the man who wears the star" has given way to the teenager who sells six-packs, bags of ice, and pre-prepared sandwiches.

THE SHOPPING CENTER

Large-scale retailing, long associated with central business districts, began moving away from the urban cores between the world wars. The first experiments to capture the growing suburban retail markets were made by major department stores in New York and Chicago in the 1920s, with Robert E. Wood, Sears's vice

president in charge of factories and retail stores, as the leader of the movement. A student of population trends, Wood decided in 1925 that motor-vehicle registrations had outstripped the parking space available in metropolitan cores, and he insisted that Sears's new "A" stores (their other retail outlets were much smaller) be located in low-density areas which would offer the advantages of lower rentals and yet, because of the automobile, be within reach of potential customers. With the exception of Sears's flagship store on State Street in Chicago (which was itself closed in 1983), Woods's dictum of ample free parking was rigorously followed throughout the United States. Early examples of the formula were the Pico Boulevard store in Los Angeles and the Crosstown store in Memphis. A revolution in retailing followed. Writing in the *American Builder* in 1929, the critic Willard Morgan found it natural that traffic congestion at the center would drive thousands of prospective customers to turn instead to suburban marketing centers.

Another threat to the primacy of the central business district was the "string street" or "shopping strip," which emerged in the 1920s and which were designed to serve vehicular rather than pedestrian traffic. These bypass roads encouraged city dwellers with cars to patronize businesses on the outskirts of town. Short parades of shops could already have been found near the streetcar and rapid transit stops, but, as has been noted, these new retailing thoroughfares generally radiated out from the city business district toward low-density, residential areas, functionally dominating the urban street system. They were the prototypes for the familiar highway strips of the 1980s which stretch far into the countryside.

Sears's big stores were initially isolated from other stores, while the retail establishments of highway strips were rarely unified into a coordinated whole. The multiple-store shopping center with free, off-street parking represented the ultimate retail adaptation to the requirements of automobility. Although the *Guinness Book of World Records* lists the

Roland Park Shopping Center (1896) as the world's first shopping center, the first of the modern variety was Country Club Plaza in Kansas City. It was the effort of a single entrepreneur, Jesse Clyde Nichols, who put together a concentration of retail stores, and used leasing policy to determine the composition of stores in the concentration. By doing that, Nichols created the idea of the planned regional shopping center.

Begun in 1923 in a Spanish-Moorish style with red tile roofs and little towers—its Giralda Tower is actually a replica of the original in Seville—Country Club Plaza featured waterfalls, fountains, flowers, tree-lined walks, and expensive landscaping. As the first automobile-oriented shopping center, it offered extensive parking lots behind ornamented brick walls. Most buildings were two stories high, with the second-floor offices typically occupied by physicians, dentists, and attorneys, whose presence would help stimulate a constant flow of well-heeled visitors. An enormous commercial success, Country Club Plaza stood in organic harmony with the prairie surroundings, and it soon became the hub of Kansas City's business and cultural activities.

Nichols's Country Club Plaza generated considerable favorable publicity after it became fully operational in 1925, and by the mid-1930s the concept of the planned shopping center, as a concentration of a number of businesses under one management and with convenient parking facilities, was well known and was recognized as the best method of serving the growing market of drive-in customers. But the Great Depression and World War II had a chilling effect on private construction, and as late as 1946 there were only eight shopping centers in the entire United States. They included Upper Darby Center in West Philadelphia (1927); Suburban Square in Ardmore, Pennsylvania (1928); Highland Park Shopping Village outside Dallas (1931); River Oaks in Houston (1937); Hampton Village in St. Louis (1941); Colony in Toledo (1944); Shirlington in Arlington, Virginia (1944); and Belleview Square in

Seattle (1946). Importantly, however, they provided many of the amenities that shoppers would take for granted half a century later. In 1931, for example, Highland Park Village outside Dallas offered department, drug, and food stores, as well as banks, a theater, beauty and barber shops, offices, studios, and parking for seven hundred cars. The Spanish architecture was uniform throughout, and the rental charge include a maintenance fee to insure that the property was adequately cared for during the term of the lease.

The first major planned retail shopping center in the world went up in Raleigh, North Carolina in 1949, the brainchild of Homer Hoyt, a well-known author and demographer best known for his sector model of urban growth. Thereafter, the shopping-center idea caught on rapidly in the United States and less rapidly in Canada, where the first shopping center— Dixie Plaza near Toronto—did not open until 1954. The most successful early examples, such as Poplar Plaza in Memphis, offered at least thirty small retailers, one large department store, and parking for five hundred or more cars. By 1984 the nation's 20,000 large shopping centers accounted for almost two-thirds of all retail trade, and even in relatively centralized cities like New York, Boston, and San Francisco downtown merchants adapted to the suburban shift. Easy facilities for parking gave such collections of stores decisive advantages over central city establishments.

The concept of the enclosed, climate-controlled mall, first introduced at the Southdale Shopping Center near Minneapolis in 1956, added to the suburban advantage. A few of the indoor malls, such as the mammoth Midtown Plaza in Rochester, New York, were located downtown, but more typical were Paramus Park and Bergen Mall in New Jersey; Woodfield Mall in Schaumburg outside Chicago; King's Plaza and Cross County outside Gotham; and Raleigh Mall in Memphis—all of which were located on outlying highways and all of which attracted shoppers from trading areas of a hundred square miles and more. Edward J.

Bartolo, Sr., a self-made millionaire and workaholic, operated from a base in Youngstown, Ohio, to become the most prominent mall developer in the United States, but large insurance companies, especially the Equitable Life Assurance Society, increasingly sought high yields as shopping-center landlords.

During the 1970s, a new phenomenon—the super regional mall—added a more elaborate twist to suburban shopping. Prototypical of the new breed was Tyson's Corner, on the Washington Beltway in Fairfax County, Virginia. Anchored by Bloomingdale's, it did over $165 million in business in 1983 and provided employment to more than 14,000 persons. Even larger was Long Island's Roosevelt Field, a 180-store, 2.2 million square foot mega-mall that attracted 275,000 visitors a week and did $230 million in business in 1980. Most elaborate of all was Houston's Galleria, a world-famed setting for 240 prestigious boutiques, a quartet of cinemas, 26 restaurants, an olympic-sized ice-skating pavilion, and two luxury hotels. There were few windows in these mausoleums of merchandising, and clocks were rarely seen—just as in gambling casinos.

Boosters of such mega-malls argue that they are taking the place of the old central business districts and becoming the identifiable collecting points for the rootless families of the newer areas. As weekend and afternoon attractions, they have a special lure for teenagers, who often go there on shopping dates or to see the opposite sex. As one official noted in 1971: "These malls are now their street corners. The new shopping centers have killed the little merchant, closed most movies, and are now supplanting the older shopping centers in the suburbs." They are also especially attractive to mothers with young children and to the elderly, many of whom visit regularly to get out of the house without having to worry about crime or inclement weather.

In reality, even the largest malls are almost the opposite of downtown areas because they are self-contained and because they impose a uniformity of tastes and interests. They cater exclusively to middle-class tastes and contain no unsavory bars or pornography shops, no threatening-looking characters, no litter, no rain, and no excessive heat or cold. As Anthony Zube-Jackson has noted, their emphasis on cleanliness and safety is symptomatic of a very lopsided view of urban culture.

Despite their blandness, the shopping malls and the drive-in culture of which they are a part have clearly eclipsed the traditional central business districts, and in many medium-sized cities the last of the downtown department stores has already closed. The drive-in blight that killed them, like the Dutch Elm disease that ravaged Eastern towns in years past, has played hopscotch from one town to another, bringing down institutions that had once appeared invincible. The targets of this scourge, however, were not trees, but businesses, specifically the once-mighty department stores that anchored many a Main Street.

The most famous retailing victim of the drive-in culture thus far has been the stately J. L. Hudson Company of Detroit. It was a simple fact that all roads in the Motor City led to Hudson's. Featuring tall chandeliers, wood-paneled corridors, and brass-buttoned doormen, the 25-story, full-square-block emporium at its height ranked with Macy's in New York and Marshall Field in Chicago as one of the country's three largest stores. After 1950, however, the once-proud store was choked by its own branches, all of them in outlying shopping centers. As soon as Hudson's opened Northland, its biggest suburban outlet and one of the earliest in the nation, sales downtown began to fall. They declined from a peak in 1953 of $153 million to $45 million in 1981. Finally, in 1981, the downtown landmark closed its doors for good. Hudson's was a victim of the product that made Detroit: the car.

In a Christmastime obituary for Detroit's most famous retailer, a WWJ radio commentator maintained that white flight to the suburbs, hastened by the Motor City's 1967 race riot, helped deal Hudson's a mortal blow. Actually, the 91-year-old store was killed by the free parking, easy accessibility, and controlled environment of the mega-malls.

By the 1960s, the primary rival to the shopping center as the locus of brief, informal communication and interaction had become the highway strip, with its flashing neon signs and tacky automobile showrooms. Especially in medium-sized cities, the vitality after dark is concentrated in the shopping malls or along the highway, not along Main Street.

THE HOUSE TRAILER AND MOBILE HOME

The phenomenon of a nation on wheels is perhaps best symbolized by the uniquely American development of the mobile home. "Trailers are here to stay," predicted the writer Howard O'Brien in 1936. Although in its infancy at that time, the mobile-home industry has flourished in the United States. The house trailer itself came into existence in the teens of this century as an individually designed variation on a truck or a car, and it began to be produced commercially in the 1920s. Originally, trailers were designed to travel, and they were used primarily for vacation purposes. During the Great Depression of the 1930s, however, many people, especially salesmen, entertainers, construction workers, and farm laborers, were forced into a nomadic way of life as they searched for work, any work. They found that these temporary trailers on rubber tires provided the necessary shelter while also meeting their economic and migratory requirements. Meanwhile, Wally Byam and other designers were streamlining the mobile home into the classic tear-drop form made famous by Airstream.

During World War II, the United States government got into the act by purchasing tens of thousands of trailers for war workers and by forbidding their sale to the general public. By 1943 the National Housing Agency alone owned 35,000 of the aluminum boxes, and more than 60 percent of the nation's 200,000 mobile homes were in defense areas. The government also built prefabricated homes without wheels near weapons factories. The ticky-tacky quality of these prefabricated shanty towns gave prefabs a lingering bad image, which remained after the war, when trailers found a growing market among migratory farm workers and military personnel, both of whom had to move frequently.

Not until the mid-1950s did the term "mobile home" begin to refer to a place where respectable people could marry, mature, and die. By then it was less a "mobile" than a "manufactured" home. No longer a trailer, it became a modern industrialized residence with almost all the accoutrements of a normal house. By the late 1950s, widths were increased to ten feet, the Federal Housing Administration (FHA) began to recognize the mobile home as a type of housing suitable for mortgage insurance, and the maturities on sales contracts were increased from three to five years.

In the 1960s, twelve-foot widths were introduced, and then fourteen, and manufacturers began to add fireplaces, skylights, and cathedral ceilings. In 1967 two trailers were attached side by side to form the first "double wide." These new dimensions allowed for a greater variety of room arrangement and became particularly attractive to retired persons with fixed incomes. They also made the homes less mobile. By 1979 even the single-width "trailer" could be seventeen feet wide (by about sixty feet long), and according to the Manufactured Housing Institute, fewer than 2 percent were ever being moved from their original site. Partly as a result of this increasing permanence, individual communities and the courts began to define the structures as real property and thus subject to real-estate taxes rather than as motor vehicles subject only to license fees.

Although it continued to be popularly perceived as a shabby substitute for "stick" housing (a derogatory word used to describe the ordinary American balloon-frame dwelling), the residence on wheels reflected American values and industrial practices. Built with easily machined and processed materials, such as sheet metal and plastic, it represented a total consumer package, complete with interior furnishings, carpets, and appliances. More importantly, it provided a suburban type alternative to the inner-city housing that would otherwise have been available to blue-collar workers, newly married couples, and retired persons. After 1965 the production of factory-made housing (the term preferred by the industry) rarely fell below 200,000 per year, and in Florida, Wyoming, and Montana they typically accounted for more than a quarter of all new housing units. By 1979 manufactured housing was a $3.1 billion industry, and the nation counted more than ten million mobile-home dwellers. These figures exclude the "motor homes" made popular by Winnebago in the 1970s, the modular homes that are built on a floor system like a conventional house, and the prefabricated houses for which parts are built in a factory and shipped in sections to be assembled on the site.

A DRIVE-IN SOCIETY

Drive-in motels, drive-in movies, and drive-in shopping facilities were only a few of the many new institutions that followed in the exhaust of the internal-combustion engine. By 1984 mom-and-pop grocery stores had given way almost everywhere to supermarkets, most banks had drive-in windows, and a few funeral homes were making it possible for mourners to view the deceased, sign the register, and pay their respects without emerging from their cars. Odessa Community College in Texas even opened a drive-through registration window.

Particularly pervasive were fast-food franchises, which not only decimated the family-style restaurants but cut deeply into grocery store sales. In 1915 James G. Huneker, a raconteur whose tales of early twentieth-century American life were compiled as *New Cosmopolis,* complained of the infusion of cheap, quick-fire "food hells," and of the replacement of relaxed dining with "canned music and au-

tomatic lunch taverns." With the automobile came the notion of "grabbing" something to eat. The first drive-in restaurant, Royce Hailey's Pig Stand, opened in Dallas in 1921, and later in the decade, the first fast-food franchise, "White Tower," decided that families touring in motorcars needed convenient meals along the way. The places had to look clean, so they were painted white. They had to be familiar, so a minimal menu was standardized at every outlet. To catch the eye, they were built like little castles, replete with fake ramparts and turrets. And to forestall any problem with a land lease, the little white castles were built to be moveable.

The biggest restaurant operation of all began in 1954, when Ray A. Kroc, a Chicago area milkshake-machine salesman, joined forces with Richard and Maurice McDonald, the owners of a fast-food emporium in San Bernardino, California. In 1955 the first of Mr. Kroc's "McDonald's" outlets was opened in Des Plaines, a Chicago suburb long famous as the site of an annual Methodist encampment. The second and third, both in California, opened later in 1955. Within five years, there were 228 golden arches drive-ins selling hamburgers for 15 cents, french fries for 10 cents, and milkshakes for 20 cents. In 1961 Kroc bought out the McDonald brothers, and in the next twenty years this son of an unsuccessful realtor whose family came from Bohemia built an empire of 7,500 outlets and amassed a family fortune in excess of $500 million. Appropriately headquartered in suburban Oak Brook, Illinois, the McDonald's enterprise is based on free parking and drive-in access, and its methods have been copied by dozens of imitators. Late in 1984, on an interstate highway north of Minneapolis, McDonald's began construction of the most complete drive-in complex in the world. To be called McStop, it will feature a motel, gas station, convenience store, and, of course, a McDonald's restaurant.

Even church pews occasionally were replaced by the automobile. In early 1955, in suburban Garden Grove, California, the Reverend

Robert Schuller, a member of the Reformed Church in America, began his ministry on a shoestring. With no sanctuary and virtually no money, he rented the Orange Drive-In movie theater on Sunday mornings and delivered his sermons while standing on top of the concession stand. The parishioners listened through speakers available at each parking space. What began as a necessity became a virtue when Schuller began attracting communicants who were more comfortable and receptive in their vehicles than in a pew. Word of the experiment—"Worship as you are . . . In the family car"—spread, the congregation grew, and in 1956 Schuller constructed a modest edifice for indoor services and administrative needs. But the Drive-in Church, as it was then called, continued to offer religious inspiration for automobile-bound parishioners, and in succeeding sanctuaries facilities were always included for those who did not want a "walk-in" church. By 1969 he had six thousand members in his church, and architect Richard Neutra had designed a huge, star-shaped "Tower of Power," situated appropriately on twenty-two acres just past Disneyland on the Santa Ana Freeway. It looked like and was called "a shopping center for Jesus Christ."

In 1980 a "Crystal Cathedral" was dedicated on the grounds. Designed by Philip Johnson, the $26 million structure is one of the most impressive and gargantuan religious buildings on earth. More than 125 feet high and 415 feet wide, its interior is a stunning cavern without columns, clad in over 10,000 panes of transparent glass. Yet the drive-in feature remains. Instead of separate services for his indoor and outdoor followers, Schuller broadcasts his message over the radio from an indoor/outdoor pulpit. At the beginning of each session, two 90-foot glass walls swing open so that the minister can be seen by drive-in worshippers. Traditionalists come inside the 3,000-seat "Crystal Cathedral," while those who remain in the "pews from Detroit" are directed to the announcement: "If you have a car radio, please turn to 540 on your dial for this service.

If you do not have a radio, please park by the amplifiers in the back row." The appeal has been enormously successful. By 1984 Schuller's Garden Grove Community Church claimed to be the largest walk-in, drive-in church in the world. Its Sunday broadcasts were viewed by an estimated one million Californians and commanded the nation's highest ratings for religious programming.

THE CENTERLESS CITY

More than anyplace else, California became the symbol of the postwar suburban culture. It pioneered the booms in sports cars, foreign cars, vans, and motor homes, and by 1984 its 26 million citizens owned almost 19 million motor vehicles and had access to the world's most extensive freeway system. The result has been a new type of centerless city, best exemplified by once sleepy and out-of-the-way Orange County, just south and east of Los Angeles. After Walt Disney came down from Hollywood, bought out the ranchers, and opened Disneyland in 1955, Orange County began to evolve from a rural backwater into a suburb and then into a collection of medium and small towns. It had never had a true urban focus, in large part because its oil-producing sections each spawned independent suburban centers, none of which was particularly dominant over the others. The tradition continued when the area became a subdivider's dream in the 1960s and 1970s. By 1980 there were 26 Orange County cities, none with more than 225,000 residents. Like the begats of the Book of Genesis, they merged and multiplied into a huge agglomeration of two million people with its own Census Bureau metropolitan area designation—Anaheim, Santa Ana, Garden Grove. Unlike the traditional American metropolitan region, however, Orange County lacked a commutation focus, a place that could obviously be accepted as the center of local life. Instead, the experience of a local resident was typical: "I live in Garden Grove, work in Irvine, shop in Santa Ana, go to the dentist in Anaheim, my husband works in Long Beach, and I used to be the president of the League of Women Voters in Fullerton."

A centerless city also developed in Santa Clara County, which lies forty-five miles south of San Francisco and which is best known as the home of "Silicon Valley." Stretching from Palo Alto on the north to the garlic and lettuce fields of Gilroy to the south, Santa Clara County has the world's most extensive concentration of electronics concerns. In 1940, however, it was best known for prunes and apricots, and it was not until after World War II that its largest city, San Jose, also became the nation's largest suburb. With fewer than 70,000 residents in 1940, San Jose exploded to 636,000 by 1980, superseding San Francisco as the region's largest municipality. As the automobile-based circulation system matured, the county's spacious orchards were easily developed, and bulldozers uprooted fruit trees for shopping centers and streets. Home builders, encouraged by a San Jose city government that annexed new territory at a rapid pace and borrowed heavily to build new utilities and schools on the fringes of town, moved farther and farther into the rural outskirts. Dozens of semiconductor and aerospace companies expanded and built plants there. In time, this brought twice-daily ordeals of bumper-to-bumper traffic on congested freeways. The driving time of some six-mile commutes lengthened to forty-five minutes, and the hills grew hazy behind the smog. As Santa Clara County became a national symbol of the excesses of uncontrolled growth, its residents began to fear that the high-technology superstars were generating jobs and taxes, but that the jobs attracted more people, and the taxes failed to cover the costs of new roads, schools, sewers, and expanded police and fire departments.

The numbers were larger in California, but the pattern was the same on the edges of every American city, from Buffalo Grove and Schaumburg near Chicago, to Germantown and Collierville near Memphis, to Creve Couer and Ladue near St. Louis. And perhaps more important than the growing number of people living outside of city boundaries was the sheer physical sprawl of metropolitan areas. Between 1950 and 1970, the urbanized area of Washington, D.C., grew from 181 to 523 square miles, of Miami from 116 to 429, while in the larger megalopolises of New York, Chicago, and Los Angeles, the region of settlement was measured in the thousands of square miles.

THE DECENTRALIZATION OF FACTORIES AND OFFICES

The deconcentration of post-World War II American cities was not simply a matter of split-level homes and neighborhood schools. It involved almost every facet of national life, from manufacturing to shopping to professional services. Most importantly, it involved the location of the workplace, and the erosion of the concept of suburb as a place from which wage-earners commuted daily to jobs in the center. So far had the trend progressed by 1970 that in nine of the fifteen largest metropolitan areas suburbs were the principle sources of employment, and in some cities, like San Francisco, almost three-fourths of all work trips were by people who neither lived nor worked in the core city. In Wilmington, Delaware, 66 percent of area jobs in 1940 were in the core city; by 1970, the figure had fallen below one quarter. And despite the fact that Manhattan contained the world's highest concentration of office space and business activity, in 1970, about 78 percent of the residents in the New York suburbs also worked in the suburbs. Many outlying communities thus achieved a kind of autonomy from the older downtown areas. A new "Americanism" even entered the language—"beltway"—to describe the broad expressways that encircled every important city by 1975 and that attracted employers of every description.

Manufacturing is now among the most dispersed of non-residential activities. As the proportion of industrial jobs in the United

States work force fell from 29 percent to 23 percent of the total in the 1970s, those manufacturing enterprises that survived often relocated either to the suburbs or to the lower-cost South and West. Even tertiary industries, which do not utilize assembly-line processes and which require less flat space than larger factories, have adapted to the internal-combustion engine with peripheral sites. As early as 1963, industrial employment in the United States was more than half suburban based, and by 1981, about two-thirds of all manufacturing activity took place in the "industrial parks" and new physical plants of the suburbs. The transition has been especially hard on older workshop cities, where venerable factories are abandoned as employers are lured outward by the promise of open land, easy access to interstate highways, and federal investment tax credits. Between 1970 and 1980, for example, Philadelphia lost 140,-000 jobs, many of them with the closing down or moving away of such Quaker City mainstays as Philco-Ford, Cuneo Eastern Press, Midvale Heppenstall Steel, Bayuk Cigar, Eaton and Cooper Industries' Plumb Tool Division, and the Container Corporation.

Office functions, once thought to be securely anchored to the streets of big cities, have followed the suburban trend. In the nineteenth century, businesses tried to keep all their operations under one centralized roof. It was the most efficient way to run a company when the mails were slow and uncertain and communication among employees was limited to the distance that a human voice could carry. More recently, the economics of real estate and a revolution in communications have changed these circumstances, and many companies are now balkanizing their accounting departments, data-processing divisions, and billing departments. Just as insurance companies, branch banks, regional sales staffs, and doctors offices have reduced their costs and presumably increased their accessibility by moving to suburban locations, so also have back-office functions been splitting away from front offices and moving away from central business districts.

Corporate headquarters relocations have been particularly well-publicized. Although the publishing firm of Doubleday and Company moved to quiet Garden City on Long Island in 1910 and Reader's Digest shifted to Pleasantville, New York, in Westchester County in 1936, the overall trend of corporate movement was toward central business districts until about 1950. The outward trend began in earnest in 1954, when the General Foods Corporation moved its home office from midtown Manhattan to a spacious, low-slung campus surrounded by acres of trees and free parking in suburban White Plains. The exodus reached a peak between 1955 and 1980, when, arguing, "It's an altogether more pleasant way of life for all," more than fifty corporations, including such giants as International Business Machines, Gulf Oil, Texaco, Union Carbide, General Telephone, American Cyanamid, Xerox, Pepsico, U. S. Tobacco, Cheeseborough Ponds, Nestlé, American Can, Singer, Champion International, and Olin, abandoned their headquarters in New York City.

Because Manhattan remained the dominant center of the nation's corporate and financial life, most companies simply moved within the region to more bucolic surroundings, principally in one of three small areas: a strip of central Westchester County from the Hudson River past White Plains to the Connecticut border, the downtown of Stamford and adjacent Greenwich in Fairfield County, Connecticut, and a narrow slice through the heartland of Morris and Somerset counties in New Jersey. All three areas built more than 16 million square feet of office space between 1972 and 1985, or more than exists in all but a handful of American cities.

The trend was particularly strong toward Connecticut, where executives could have the benefit of Gotham's business and cultural advantages without the bother of New York State's income taxes. In 1960 when the first urban renewal plans were drawn up for downtown Stamford, no consideration was given to building any commercial office space there. In the next three decades, however, while the original proposals were delayed by community resistance, Stamford's urban-renewal plans were redrawn to reflect changes in corporate attitudes toward relocating out of Gotham and into more comfortable suburban locations. For Stamford the delay was beneficial. When companies began their Manhattan exodus, Stamford had available space downtown. By 1984 Fairfield County was the third leading corporate headquarters site in the United States, after only New York City and Chicago.

Several studies have pointed out that the most important variable in determining the direction of a corporate shift was the location of the home and country club of the chief executive officer of the particular company. In fact, top officers were often the only ones to benefit from the suburban shifts. When A & W Beverages made the move from Manhattan to White Plains early in 1984, the company lost its entire support staff in the transition and had to spend a small fortune on severance costs. "Some of these people had been with us for many years, so we had to ask ourselves what we should do with loyal and good workers who will no longer have a job," said Craig Honeycutt, director of personnel for A & W, about the employees who quit rather than commute from Manhattan, Brooklyn, or New Jersey to White Plains.

Because the construction of suburban office headquarters tends to be expensive, the purpose of most such moves is to improve employee morale and productivity as much as to reduce costs. To this end, a company typically hires a well-known architect to design a rustic complex on the model of a college campus or a self-contained village. Free parking and easy access to interstate highways presumably make possible a longer work day, while stone piazzas, landscaped gardens, impressive sculpture, and splashing water fountains, as well as gymnasiums, showers, and saunas presumably

make possible a more relaxed one. Company-owned cafeterias replace the downtown restaurants, shopping districts, and even noontime concerts of the city centers. To some employees the result is "close to perfect." Others find the campus environment boring and bemoan that "the main thing of interest out here is what's new in the gift shop."

Corporate relocation in the postwar period has been overwhelmingly a city-to-suburb phenomenon rather than a regional shift. The move of Gulf Oil to Houston and of American Airlines to Dallas, both from New York, were exceptions to this general rule. Only occasionally have large firms shifted both from a city to a suburb and from one region to another. The Johns-Manville Company, which transferred in the 1970s from a Manhattan office tower to a sleek and gleeming spaceship-style structure in the midst of a 10,000-acre ranch in the foothills of the Rocky Mountains, is a clear exception. Perhaps coincidentally the Johns-Manville Corporation was saved from bankruptcy in 1982 only by the intervention of a court.

Since World War II, the American people have experienced a transformation of the man-made environment around them. Commercial, residential, and industrial structures have been redesigned to fit the needs of the motorist rather than the pedestrian. Garish signs, large parking lots, one-way streets, drive-in windows, and throw-away fast-food buildings—all associated with the world of suburbia—have replaced the slower-paced, neighborhood-oriented institutions of an earlier generation. Some observers of the automobile revolution have argued that the car has created a new and better urban environment and that the change in spatial scale, based upon swift transportation, has formed a new kind of organic entity, speeding up personal communication and rendering obsolete the older urban settings. Lewis Mumford, writing from his small-town retreat in Amenia, New York, has emphatically disagreed. His prize-winning book, *The City in History,* was a celebration of the medieval community and an excoriation of "the formless urban exudation" that he saw American cities becoming. He noted that the automobile megalopolis was not a final stage in city development but an anticity which "annihilates the city whenever it collides with it."

The most damning indictment of private transportation remains, however, the 1958 work of the acid-tongued John Keats, *The Insolent Chariots.* He forcefully argued, as have others since that time, that highway engineers were wrong in constantly calling for more lanes of concrete to accommodate yet more lines of automobiles. Instead, Keats's position was that motorcars actually created the demand for more highways, which in turn increased the need for more vehicles, and so on ad infinitum. More ominously, he surmised, public expenditures for the automobile culture diverted funds from mass transit and needed social services.

The automobile lobby swept everything and everybody before it, however, and it was not until the first oil boycott of 1973 that Americans would seriously ponder the full implications of their drive-in culture. Especially in the 1950s, expressways represented progress and modernity, and mayors and public officials stumbled over themselves in seeking federal largesse for more and wider roads. Only a few people realized that high-speed roads accelerated deconcentration, displaced inner-city residents, contributed to the decay of central business districts, and hastened the deterioration of existing transportation systems. As Raymond Tucker, mayor of St. Louis and former president of the American Municipal Association, put it, "The plain fact of the matter is that we just cannot build enough lanes of highways to move all of our people by private automobile and create enough parking space to store the cars without completely paving over our cities and removing all of the . . . economic, social, and cultural establishments that the people were trying to reach in the first place."

Because structures built to accommodate the demands of the automobile are likely to have an ephemeral life, it is a mistake for cities to duplicate suburban conditions. In 1973 a RAND study of St. Louis suggested as an alternative strategy that the city become "one of many large suburban centers of economic and residential life" rather than try to revive traditional central city functions. Such advice is for those who study statistics rather than cities. Too late, municipal leaders will realize that a slavish duplication of suburbia destroys the urban fabric that makes cities interesting. Memphis's Union Avenue, once a grand boulevard lined with the homes of the well-to-do, has recently fallen victim to the drive-in culture. In 1979 one of the last surviving landmarks, an elegant stone mansion, was leveled to make room for yet another fast-food outlet. Within three years, the plastic-and-glass hamburger emporium was bankrupt, but the scar on Union Avenue remained.

There are some signs that the halcyon days of the drive-in culture and automobile are behind us. More than one hundred thousand gasoline stations, or about one-third of the American total, have been eliminated in the last decade. Empty tourist courts and boarded-up motels are reminders that the fast pace of change can make commercial structures obsolete within a quarter-century of their erection. Even that suburban bellwether, the shopping center, which revolutionized merchandising after World War II, has come to seem small and out-of-date as newer covered malls attract both the trendy and the family trade. Some older centers have been recycled as bowling alleys or industrial buildings, and some have been remodeled to appeal to larger tenants and better-heeled customers. But others stand forlorn and boarded up. Similarly, the characteristic fast-food emporiums of the 1950s, with uniformed "car hops" who took orders at the automobile window, are now relics of the past. One of the survivors, Delores Drive-In, which opened in Beverly Hills in 1946, was recently proposed as an historic landmark, a sure sign that the species is in danger.

19

CESAR CHAVEZ AND THE UNIONIZATION OF CALIFORNIA FARM WORKERS

CLETUS E. DANIEL

In the course of the late nineteenth and twentieth centuries, skilled craftsmen, semiskilled machine operators, and clerical workers formed unions to represent and protect their interests as workers. Employers fought bitterly against these unions until the post-World War II era, when collective bargaining became a widely accepted standard for employer-employee relations. This new era of industrial relations was also facilitated by the role that the federal government played in stabilizing these relations. Beginning with the establishment of the National Labor Relations Board in 1935, the federal government became increasingly involved in every aspect of industrial relations until today labor law constitutes a separate field of legal scholarship and practice.

Yet in spite of widespread unionization and the involvement of government in labor relations, many sectors of the labor force were left unprotected. One of the largest groups of these forgotten workers was America's agricultural laborers. Not only were agricultural laborers thought to be unorganizable because of their migratory status, but the National Labor Relations Act specifically excluded agricultural workers from its statutes. Ignored by the union movement and the government as well, agricultural workers were left at the mercy of growers who cared little for their welfare. It was not surprising, then, that in his classic exposé of postwar American poverty, *The Other America* (1963), Michael Harrington found migratory agricultural workers to be among the poorest of America's poor. Migrating from state to state as they followed the harvest season, living without adequate housing, food, or medical care and paid the lowest wages of any American labor group, these workers lived a life of extreme deprivation and poverty amid widespread American prosperity. In this essay, Cletus E. Daniel tells the story of one of America's most unique unions, the United Farm Workers of America, and Cesar Chavez, the man who organized the union against seemingly insurmountable odds.

Chapter 15 in Melvyn Dubofsky and Warren Van Tine, eds., *Labor Leaders in America* (Urbana, Ill.: University of Illinois Press, 1987). Reprinted by permission of Cletus E. Daniel and University of Illinois Press.

It was, Cesar Chavez later wrote, "the strangest meeting in the history of California agriculture." Speaking by telephone from his cluttered headquarters in La Paz to Jerry Brown, the new governor of California, Chavez had been asked to repeat for the benefit of farm employers crowded into Brown's Sacramento office the farmworker leader's acceptance of a farm labor bill to which they had already assented. And as the employers heard Chavez's voice repeating the statement of acceptance he had just made to the governor, they broke into wide smiles and spontaneous applause.

That representatives of the most powerful special interest group in California history should have thus expressed their delight at the prospect of realizing still another of their legislative goals does not account for Chavez's assertion of the meeting's strange character. These were, after all, men long accustomed to having their way in matters of farm labor legislation. What was strange about that meeting on May 5, 1975, was that the state's leading farm employers should have derived such apparent relief and satisfaction from hearing the president of the United Farm Workers of America, AFL-CIO, agree to a legislative proposal designed to afford farmworkers an opportunity to escape their historic powerlessness through unionism and collective bargaining.

Beyond investing the state's farmworkers with rights that those who labored for wages on the land had always been denied, the passage of California's Agricultural Labor Relations Act (ALRA) was a seismic event, one that shattered the foundation upon which rural class relations had rested for a century and more. For the state's agribusinessmen, whose tradition it had been to rule the bounteous fields and orchards of California with a degree of authority and control more appropriate to potentates than mere employers, supporting the ALRA was less an act of culpable treason against their collective heritage than one of grudging resignation in the face of a suddenly irrelevant past and an apparently inescapable future. For the state's farmworkers, whose in-

voluntary custom it had always been to surrender themselves to a system of industrialized farming that made a captive peasantry of them, the new law made possible what only the boldest among them had dared to image: a role equal to the employer's in determining terms and conditions of employment. Yet if the ALRA's enactment was a victory of unprecedented dimensions for California farmworkers as a class, it was a still greater personal triumph for Cesar Chavez.

More than any other labor leader of his time, and perhaps in the whole history of American labor, Cesar Chavez leads a union that is an extension of his own values, experience, and personality. This singular unity of man and movement has found its most forceful and enduring expression in the unprecedented economic and political power that has accrued to the membership of the United Farm Workers (UFW) under Chavez's intense and unrelenting tutelage. Indeed, since 1965, when Chavez led his then small following into a bitter struggle against grape growers around the lower San Joaquin valley town of Delano, the UFW has, despite the many crises that have punctuated its brief but turbulent career, compiled a record of achievement that rivals the accomplishments of the most formidable industrial unions of the 1930s.

While this personal domination may well be the essential source of the UFW's extraordinary success, it has also posed risks for the union. For just as Chavez's strengths manifest themselves in the character of his leadership, so, too, must his weaknesses. Certainly the UFW's somewhat confused sense of its transcending mission—whether to be a trade union or a social movement; whether to focus on narrow economic gains or to pursue broader political goals—reflects in some degree Chavez's personal ambivalence toward both the ultimate purpose of worker organization and the fundamental objective of his own prolonged activism.

Had his adult life followed the pattern of his early youth, Cesar Chavez need not have concerned himself with the task of liberating California farmworkers from an exploitive labor system that had entombed a succession of Chinese, Japanese, Filipino, Mexican, and other non-Anglo immigrants for more than a hundred years. Born on March 31, 1927, the second child of Librado and Juana Chavez, Cesar Estrada Chavez started his life sharing little beyond language and a diffuse ethnic heritage with the Chicano—Mexican and Mexican-American—workers who constitute nearly the entire membership of the United Farm Workers of America. Named after his paternal grandfather Cesario, who had homesteaded the family's small farm in the north Gila River valley near Yuma three years before Arizona attained statehood, Chavez enjoyed during his youth the kind of close and stable family life that farmworkers caught in the relentless currents of the western migrant stream longed for but rarely attained. And although farming on a small scale afforded few material rewards even as it demanded hard and unending physical labor, it fostered in Chavez an appreciation of independence and personal sovereignty that helps to account for the special force and steadfastness of his later rebellion against the oppressive dependence into which workers descended when they joined the ranks of California's agricultural labor force.

It is more than a little ironic that until 1939, when unpaid taxes put the family's farm on the auction black, Chavez could have more reasonably aspired to a future as a landowner than as a farmworker. "If we had stayed there," he later said of the family's farm, "possibly I would have been a grower. God writes in exceedingly crooked lines."

The full significance of the family's eviction from the rambling adobe ranch house that had provided not only shelter but also a sense of place and social perspective was not at once apparent to an eleven year old. The deeper meaning of the family's loss was something that accumulated in Chavez's mind only as his subsequent personal experience in the mi-grant stream disclosed the full spectrum of emotional and material hardship attending a life set adrift from the roots that had nurtured it. At age eleven the sight of a bulldozer effortlessly destroying in a few minutes what the family had struggled over nearly three generations to build was meaning enough. The land's new owner, an Anglo grower impatient to claim his prize, dispatched the bulldozer that became for Chavez a graphic and enduring symbol of the power that the "haves" employ against the "have-nots" in industrialized agriculture. "It was a monstrous thing," he recalled: "Its motor blotted out the sound of crickets and bullfrogs and the buzzing of the flies. As the tractor moved along, it tore up the soil, leveling it, and destroying the trees, pushing them over like they were nothing. . . . And each tree, of course, means quite a bit to you when you're young. They are a part of you. We grew up there, saw them every day, and they were alive, they were friends. When we saw the bulldozer just uprooting those trees, it was tearing at us too."

The experience of the Chavez family fell into that category of minor tragedy whose cumulative influence lent an aura of catastrophe to the greater part of the depression decade. The scene became sickeningly familiar in the 1930s: a beleaguered farm family bidding a poignant farewell to a failed past; setting out for California with little enthusiasm and even less money toward a future that usually had nothing but desperation to commend it.

"When we were pushed off our land," Chavez said, "all we could take with us was what we could jam into the old Studebaker or pile on its roof and fenders, mostly clothes and bedding. . . . I realized something was happening because my mother was crying, but I didn't realize the import of it at the time. When we left the farm, our whole life was upset, turned upside down. We have been part of a very stable community, and we were about to become migratory workers."

Yet if Chavez's experience was in some

ways similar to that of the dispossessed dust-bowl migrant whose pilgrimage to California was also less an act of hope than of despair, it was fundamentally unlike that of even the most destitute Anglo—John Steinbeck's generic "Okie"—because of virulent racial attitudes among the state's white majority that tended to define all persons "of color" as unequal. For the Chavez family, whose standing as landowners in a region populated by people mainly like themselves had insulated them from many of the meanest forms of racism, following the crops in California as undifferentiated members of a brown-skinned peasantry afforded an unwelcome education. To the familiar varieties of racial humiliation and mistreatment—being physically punished by an Anglo teacher for lapsing into your native tongue; being in the presence of Anglos who talked about you as if you were an inanimate object—were added some new and more abrasive forms: being rousted by border patrolmen who automatically regarded you as a "wetback" until you proved otherwise; being denied service at a restaurant or made to sit in the "Mexican only" seats at the local movie house; being stopped and searched by the police for no reason other than your skin color announced your powerlessness to resist; being cheated by an employer who smugly assumed that you probably wouldn't object because Mexicans were naturally docile.

But, if because of such treatment Chavez came to fear and dislike Anglos—*gringos* or *gabachos* in the pejorative lexicon of the barrio—he also came to understand that while considerations of race and ethnicity compounded the plight of farmworkers, their mistreatment was rooted ultimately in the economics of industrialized agriculture. As the family traveled the state from one crop to the next, one hovel to the next, trying desperately to survive on the meager earnings of parents and children alike, Chavez quickly learned that Chicano labor contractors and Japanese growers exploited migrants as readily as did Anglo employers. And, although the complex dynamics of California's rural political economy might still have eluded him, Chavez instinctively understood that farmworkers would cease to be victims only when they discovered the means to take control of their own lives.

The realization that unionism must be that means came later. Unlike the typical Chicano family in the migrant stream, however, the Chavez family included among its otherwise meager possessions a powerful legacy of the independent life it had earlier known, one that revealed itself in a stubborn disinclination to tolerate conspicuous injustices. "I don't want to suggest we were that radical," Chavez later said, "but I know we were probably one of the strikingest families in California, the first ones to leave the fields if anyone shouted "Huelga!"—which is Spanish for "Strike!" . . . If any family felt something was wrong and stopped working, we immediately joined them even if we didn't know them. And if the grower didn't correct what was wrong, then they would leave, and we'd leave."

Chavez had no trouble identifying the source of the family's instinctive militancy. "We were," he insisted, "constantly fighting against things that most people would probably accept because they didn't have that kind of life we had in the beginning, that strong family life and family ties which we would not let anyone break." When confronted by an injustice, there "was no question. Our dignity meant more than money."

Although the United Cannery, Agricultural, Packing and Allied Workers of America, a CIO-affiliated union, was conducting sporadic organizing drives among California farmworkers when Chavez and his family joined the state's farm labor force at the end of the 1930s, he was too young and untutored to appreciate "anything of the real guts of unions." Yet because his father harbored a strong, if unstudied, conviction that unionism was a manly act of resistance to the employers' authority, Chavez's attitude toward unions quickly progressed from vague approval to ardent endorsement. His earliest participation in a union-led struggle did not occur until the late 1940s, when the AFL's National Farm Labor Union conducted a series of ultimately futile strikes in the San Joaquin valley. This experience, which left Chavez with an acute sense of frustration and disappointment as the strike inevitably withered in the face of overwhelming employer power, also produced a brief but equally keen feeling of exhilaration because it afforded an opportunity to vent the rebelliousness that an expanding consciousness of his own social and occupational captivity awakened within him. Yet to the extent that unionism demands the subordination of individual aspirations to a depersonalized common denomination of the group's desires, Chavez was not in his youth the stuff of which confirmed trade unionists are made. More than most young migrant workers, whose ineluctable discontent was not heightened further by the memory of an idealized past, Chavez hoped to escape his socioeconomic predicament rather than simply moderate the harsh forces that governed it.

To be a migrant worker, however, was to learn the hard way that avenues of escape were more readily imagined than traveled. As ardently as the Chavez family sought a way out of the migrant orbit, they spent the early 1940s moving from valley to valley, from harvest to harvest, powerless to fend off the corrosive effects of their involuntary transiency. Beyond denying them the elementary amenities of a humane existence—a decent home, sufficient food, adequate clothing—the demands of migrant life also conspired to deny the Chavez children the educations that their parents valiantly struggled to ensure. For Cesar school became a "nightmare," a dispiriting succession of inhospitable places ruled by Anglo teachers and administrators whose often undisguised contempt for migrant children prompted him to drop out after the eighth grade.

Chavez's inevitable confrontation with the fact of his personal powerlessness fostered a sense of anger and frustration that revealed itself in a tendency to reject many of the most visible symbols of his cultural heritage. This brief episode of open rebellion against the culture of his parents, which dates from the family's decision to settle down in Delano in late 1943 until he reluctantly joined the navy a year later, was generally benign: *mariachis* were rejected in favor of Duke Ellington; his mother's *dichos* and *consejós*—the bits of Mexican folk wisdom passed from one generation to the next—lost out to less culture-bound values; religious customs rooted in the rigid doctrines of the Catholic church gave way to a fuzzy existentialism. In its most extreme form, this rebelliousness led Chavez to affect the distinctive style of a *pachuco,* although he never really ventured beyond dress into the more antisocial ways in which that phenomenon of youthful rebellion manifested itself in the activities of Mexican gangs in urban areas like Los Angeles and San Jose. In the end, Chavez reacted most decisively against the debilitating circumstances of his life by joining the navy, a reluctant decision whose redeeming value was that it offered a means of escape, a way "to get away from farm labor."

The two years he spent in the navy ("the worst of my life") proved to be no more than a respite from farm labor. If Chavez had hoped to acquire a trade while in the service, he soon discovered that the same considerations of race and ethnicity that placed strict limits on what non-Anglos could reasonably aspire to achieve at home operated with equal efficiency in the navy to keep them in the least desirable jobs. Without the training that might have allowed him to break out of the cycle of poverty and oppression that the labor system of industrialized agriculture fueled, Chavez returned to Delano in 1946 to the only work he knew.

Finding work had always been a problem for farmworkers due to a chronic oversupply of agricultural labor in California. The problem became even more acute for migrant families after the war because agribusiness interests succeeded in their political campaign to extend the so-called *Bracero* program,* a treaty arrangement dating from 1942 that permitted farm employers in California and the Southwest to import Mexican nationals under contract to alleviate real and imagined wartime labor shortages.

For Chavez, the struggle to earn a living took on special urgency following his marriage in 1948 to Helen Fabela, a Delano girl whom he had first met when his family made one of its periodic migrations through the area in search of work. Being the daughter of farmworkers, and thus knowing all too well the hardships that attended a family life predicated upon the irregular earnings of agricultural work, did nothing to cushion the hard times that lay ahead for Helen Chavez and her new husband, a twenty-one-year-old disaffected farm laborer without discernable prospects.

Chavez met the challenge of making a living, which multiplied with the arrival of a new baby during each of the first three years of marriage, in the only way he knew: he took any job available, wherever it was available. Not until 1952, when he finally landed a job in a San Jose lumberyard, was Chavez able to have the settled life that he and Helen craved. The Mexican barrio in San Jose, known to its impoverished inhabitants as Sal Si Puedes—literally "get out if you can"—was a few square blocks of ramshackle houses occupied by discouraged parents and angry children who, in their desperation to do just what the neighborhood's morbid nickname advised, too often sought ways out that led to prison rather than to opportunity. Long before it became home to Chavez and his family, Sal Si Puedes had earned a reputation among the sociologists who regularly scouted its mean streets as a virtual laboratory of urban social pathology. In the early 1950s, however, the area also attracted two men determined in their separate ways to alleviate the powerlessness of its residents rather than to document or measure it. More than any others, these two activists, one a young Catholic priest, the other a veteran community organizer, assumed unwitting responsibility for the education of Cesar Chavez.

When Father Donald McDonnell established his small mission church in Sal Si Puedes, he resolved to attend to both the spiritual need of his destitute parishioners and their education in those doctrines of the Catholic church relating to the inherence rights of labor. To Cesar Chavez, the teachings of the church, the rituals and catechism that he absorbed as an obligation of culture rather than a voluntary and knowing act of religious faith, had never seemed to have more than tangential relevance to the hard-edged world that poor people confronted in their daily lives. But in the militant example and activist pedagogy of Father McDonnell, Chavez discovered a new dimension of Catholicism that excited him precisely because it was relevant to his immediate circumstances. "Actually," he later said, "my education started when I met Father Donald McDonnell. . . . We had long talks about farm workers. I knew a lot about the work, but I didn't know anything about economics, and I learned quite a bit from him. He had a picture of a worker's shanty and a picture of a grower's mansion; a picture of a labor camp and a picture of a high-priced building in San Francisco owned by the same grower. When things were pointed out to me, I began to see. . . . Everything he said was aimed at ways to solve the injustice." Chavez's appetite for the social gospel that McDonnell espoused was insatiable: "[He] sat with me past midnight telling me about social justice and the Church's stand on farm labor and reading from the encyclicals of Pope Leo XIII in which he upheld labor unions. I would do anything to get the Father to tell me more about labor history. I began going to the

---

*The *Bracero* program—the word root means "arm" in Spanish—continued in force until the end of 1964, when political pressures finally led the federal government to abolish this "emergency" measure.

bracero camps with him to help with Mass, to the city jail with him to talk to prisoners, anything to be with him so that he could tell me more about the farm labor movement."

More than anyone else, Father McDonnell awoke Chavez to a world of pertinent ideas that would become the essential source of his personal philosophy; introduced him to a pantheon of crusaders for social justice (Gandhi among them) whose heroic exertions would supply the inspiration for his own crusade to empower farmworkers. Yet the crucial task of instructing Chavez in the practical means by which his nascent idealism might achieve concrete expression was brilliantly discharged by Fred Ross, an indefatigable organizer who had spent the better part of his adult life roaming California trying to show the victims of economic, racial, and ethnic discrimination how they might resist further abuse and degradation through organization.

Drawn to Sal Si Puedes by the palpable misery of its Chicano inhabitants, Ross began to conduct the series of informal house meetings through which he hoped to establish a local chapter of the Community Service Organization (CSO), a self-help group that operated under the sponsorship of radical activist Saul Alinsky's Chicago-based Industrial Areas Foundation. Always on the lookout for the natural leaders in the communities he sought to organize, Ross at once saw in Chavez, despite his outwardly shy and self-conscious demeanor, the telltale signs of a born organizer. "At the very first meeting," Ross recalled: "I was very much impressed with Cesar. I could tell he was intensely interested, a kind of burning interest rather than one of those inflammatory things that lasts one night and is then forgotten. He asked many questions, part of it to see if I really knew, putting me to the test. But it was much more than that." Ross also discovered that Chavez was an exceedingly quick study: "He understood it almost immediately, as soon as I drew the picture. He got the point—the whole question of power and the development of power within the group. He made the con-

nections very quickly between the civic weakness of the group and the social neglect in the barrio, and also conversely, what could be done about that social neglect once the power was developed." "I kept a diary in those days," Ross said later. "And the first night I met Cesar, I wrote in it, 'I think I've found the guy I'm looking for.' It was obvious even then."

The confidence that Ross expressed in Chavez's leadership potential was immediately confirmed. Assigned to the CSO voter registration project in San Jose, Chavez displayed a natural aptitude for the work; so much in fact that Ross turned over control of the entire drive to him. And if his style of leadership proved somewhat unconventional, his tactical sense was unerring. While Ross had relied upon local college students to serve as registrars for the campaign, Chavez felt more could be gained by using people from the barrio. "Instead of recruiting college guys," he said, "I got all my friends, my beer-drinking friends. With them it wasn't a question of civic duty, they helped me because of friendship, and because it was fun." With nearly six thousand new voters registered by the time the campaign ended, Chavez's reputation as an organizer was established.

As exhilarated as he was by the challenge of organizing, Chavez was also sobered by the personal attacks that the local political establishment unleashed against anyone who presumed to alter the balance of power in the ghetto. Since it was the heyday of McCarthyism, the charge most frequently lodged against him was that he was a Communist. It seemed not to matter that such charges were preposterous. Even the vaguest suggestion of radicalism was enough to cause the more cautious members of the Chicano community to regard Chavez with growing suspicion. "The Chicanos," he said, "wouldn't talk to me. They were afraid. The newspaper had a lot of influence during those McCarthy days. Anyone who organized or worked for civil rights were called a Communist. Anyone who talked about police brutality was called a Communist."

Everywhere I went to organize they would bluntly ask, "Are you a Communist?"

I would answer, "No."

"How do we know?"

"You don't know. You know because I tell you."

And we would go around and around on that. If it was somebody who was being smart, I'd tell them to go to hell, but if it was somebody that I wanted to organize, I would have to go through an explanation.

Before long, however, Chavez became an expert in turning the cultural tendencies of his Chicano neighbors to his own advantage. When his detractors wrapped themselves in the flag, Chavez countered, with the help of Father McDonnell and other sympathetic priests, by cloaking himself in the respectability of the Catholic church. "I found out," he recalled with apparent satisfaction, "that when they learned I was close to the church, they wouldn't question me so much. So I'd get the priests to come out and give me their blessing. In those days, if a priest said something to the Mexicans, they would say fine. It's different now."

In the course of raising the civic consciousness of others, Chavez broadened and deepened his own previously neglected education. "I began to grow and to see a lot of things that I hadn't seen before," he said. "My eyes opened, and I paid more attention to political and social events." And though his emergence as a trade union activist was still years away, Chavez the community organizer felt a sufficient affinity with his counterparts in the labor field that he adopted as texts for his self-education "biographies of labor organizers like John L. Lewis and Eugene Debs and the Knights of Labor."

After watching his protégé in action for only a few months, Fred Ross persuaded Saul Alinsky that the CSO should employ the talents of so able an organizer on a full-time basis. Becoming a professional organizer, however,

was a prospect that frightened Chavez nearly as much as it excited him. Helping Fred Ross was one thing, organizing on his own among strangers was quite another. Yet in the end, his desire to oppose what seemed unjust outweighed his fears.

From the end of 1952 until he quit the organization ten years later to build a union among farmworkers, the CSO was Chavez's life. He approached the work of helping the poor to help themselves in the only way his nature allowed, with a single-mindedness that made everything else in his life—home, family, personal gain—secondary. For Chavez, nothing short of total immersion in the work of forcing change was enough. If his wife inherited virtually the entire responsibility for raising their children (who were to number eight in all), if his children became resentful at being left to grow up without a father who was readily accessible to them, if he was himself forced to abandon any semblance of personal life, Chavez remained unshaken in his belief that the promotion of the greater good made every such sacrifice necessary and worthwhile.

The years he spent as an organizer for the CSO brought Chavez into contact, and usually conflict, with the whole range of public and private authorities to which the poor were accountable and by which they were controlled. The problems he handled were seldom other than mundane, yet each in its own way confirmed the collective impotence of those who populated the Chicano ghettos that became his special province. "They'd bring their personal problems," Chavez said of his CSO clients: "They were many. They might need a letter written or someone to interpret for them at the welfare department, the doctor's office, or the police. Maybe they were not getting enough welfare aid, or their check was taken away, or their kids were thrown out of school. Maybe they had been taken by a crooked salesman selling fences, aluminum siding, or freezers that hold food for a month."

In the beginning, helping people to deal with problems they felt otherwise powerless to resolve was an end in itself. In time, however, Chavez saw that if his service work was going to produce a legacy of activist sentiment in Chicano neighborhoods, it was necessary to recast what had typically been an act of unconditional assistance into a mutually beneficial transaction. And, when he discovered that those whom he was serving were not just willing, but eager, to return the favor, Chavez made that volition the basis upon which he helped to build the CSO into the most formidable Mexican-American political organization in the state. "Once I realized helping people was an organizing technique," he said, "I increased that work. I was willing to work day and night and to go to hell and back for people—provided they also did something for the CSO in return. I never felt bad asking for that . . . because I wasn't asking for something for myself. For a long time we didn't know how to put that work together into an organization. But we learned after a while—we learned how to help people by making them responsible."

Because agricultural labor constituted a main source of economic opportunity in most Chicano communities, many of those whom Chavez recruited into the CSO were farmworkers. Not until 1958, however, did Chavez take his first halting steps toward making work and its discontents the essential focus of his organizing activities. This gradual shift from community to labor organization occurred over a period of several months as Chavez struggled to establish a CSO chapter in Oxnard, a leading citrus growing region north of Los Angeles. Asked by Saul Alinsky to organize the local Chicano community in order that it might support the flagging efforts of the United Packinghouse Workers to win labor contracts covering the region's citrus-packing sheds, Chavez embarked upon his task intending to exploit the same assortment of grievances that festered in barrios throughout the state.

His new clients, however, had other ideas. From the beginning, whenever he sought to impress his agenda upon local citizens, they interrupted with their own: a concern that they were being denied jobs because growers in the region relied almost entirely on braceros to meet their needs for farm labor. It proved to be an issue that simply would not go away. "At every house meeting," Chavez recalled, "they hit me with the bracero problem, but I would dodge it. I just didn't fathom how big that problem was. I would say, 'Well, you know, we really can't do anything about that, but it's a bad problem. Something should be done.' " An apparently artless dodger, he was, in the end, forced to make the bracero problem the focus of his campaign. "Finally," he admitted, "I decided this was the issue I had to tackle. The fact that braceros were also farmworkers didn't bother me. . . . The jobs belonged to local workers. The braceros were brought only for exploitation. They were just instruments for the growers. Braceros didn't make any money, and they were exploited viciously, forced to work under conditions the local people wouldn't tolerate. If the braceros spoke up, if they made the minimal complaints, they'd be shipped back to Mexico."

In attacking Oxnard's bracero problem, Chavez and his followers confronted the integrated power of the agribusiness establishment in its most forceful and resilient aspect. While farm employers around Oxnard and throughout the state were permitted under federal regulations to employ braceros only when they had exhausted the available pool of local farmworkers, they had long operated on the basis of a collusive arrangement with the California Farm Placement Service that allowed them to import Mexican nationals without regard to labor market conditions in the region.

Although Chavez and the large CSO membership he rallied behind him sought nothing more than compliance with existing rules regarding the employment of braceros, the thirteen-month struggle that followed brought them into bitter conflicts with politically influential employers, state farm placement bureaucrats, and federal labor department officials. Yet through the use of picket lines, marches, rallies, and a variety of innovative agitational techniques that reduced the Farm Placement Service to almost total paralysis, Chavez and his militant following had by the end of 1959 won a victory so complete that farm employers in the region were recruiting their labor through a local CSO headquarters that operated as a hiring hall.

Chavez emerged from the Oxnard campaign convinced that work-related issues had greater potential as a basis for organizing Chicanos than any that he had earlier stressed. The response to his organizing drive in Oxnard was overwhelming, and he saw at once "the difference between that CSO chapter and any other CSO up to that point was that jobs were the main issue." And at the same juncture, he said: "I began to see the potential of organizing the Union."

What Chavez saw with such clarity, however, the elected leadership of the CSO, drawn almost exclusively from the small but influential ranks of middle-class Chicanos, was unwilling even to imagine. Determined that the CSO would remain a civic organization, the leadership decisively rejected Chavez's proposal to transform the Oxnard chapter into a farmworker's union. "We had won a victory," Chavez bitterly recalled, "but I didn't realize how short-lived it would be. We could have built a union there, but the CSO wouldn't approve. In fact, the whole project soon fell apart. I wanted to go for a strike and get some contracts, but the CSO wouldn't let me. . . . If I had had the support of the CSO, I would have built a union there. If anyone from labor had come, we could have had a union. I think if the Union of Organized Devils of America had come, I would have joined them, I was so frustrated."

Even though he remained with the CSO for two years following his defeat over the issues of unionism, Chavez's devotion to the organization waned as his determination to organize farmworkers increased. Finally, when the CSO once again rejected the idea of unionism at its annual convention in 1962, Chavez decided that he had had enough. He resigned as the convention ended and left the organization on his thirty-fifth birthday. "I've heard people say," he later explained, "that because I was thirty-five, I was getting worried, as I hadn't done too much with my life. But I wasn't worried. I didn't even consider thirty-five to be old. I didn't care about that. I just knew we needed a Union. . . . What I didn't know was that we would go through hell because it was an all but impossible task."

Based on the often heroic, but inevitably futile, efforts of those who had earlier dared to challenge the monolithic power of industrialized agriculture in California—the Industrial Workers of the World before World War I; the communist-led Cannery and Agricultural Workers Industrial Union during the early 1930s; the CIO in the late thirties; the AFL in the 1940s; and a rich variety of independent ethnic unions over the better part of a century— Chavez's assertion that organizing the state's farmworkers was "an all but impossible task" hardly overstated the case. Farm employers, assisted by a supporting cast representing nearly every form of public and private power in the state, had beaten back every attempt by workers to gain power while assiduously cultivating a public image of themselves as beleaguered yeomen valiantly struggling against the erosive forces of modernity, including unionism, to preserve the nation's Jeffersonian heritage.

To the task of contesting the immense power and redoubtable prestige of the agribusiness nexus, Chavez brought nothing more or less than an intensity of purpose that bordered on fanaticism. And while he would have rejected the disdain that the remark reflected, Chavez was in essential agreement with the cynical AFL official who declared in 1935: "Only fanatics are willing to live in shacks or tents and get their heads broken in the interest of migratory labor." In Chavez's view, nothing less than fanaticism would suffice if farmworkers were to be emancipated from a system of wage slavery that had endured for a century. When a reporter observed during one of the UFW's later struggles that he "sounded like a fanatic," Chavez readily admitted the charge. "I am," he confessed. "There's nothing wrong with being a fanatic. Those are the only ones that get things done."

In many ways, Chavez's supreme accomplishment as an organizer came long before he signed up his first farmworker. Attracting disciples willing to embrace the idea of a farmworkers' movement with a passion, single-mindedness, and spirit of sacrifice equal to his own was at once Chavez's greatest challenge and his finest achievement. By the fall of 1962, when he formally established the National Farm Workers Association (NFWA) in a derelict Fresno theater, Chavez had rallied to "La Causa"—the iconographic designation soon adopted by the faithful—an impressive roster of "co-fanatics": Dolores Huerta, a small, youthful-looking mother of six (she would have ten in all) whose willingness to do battle with Chavez over union tactics was exceeded only by her fierce loyalty to him; Gilbert Padilla, like Huerta another CSO veteran, whose activism was rooted in a hatred for the migrant system that derived from personal experience; Wayne Hartimire and Jim Drake, two young Anglo ministers who were to make the California Migrant Ministry a virtual subsidiary of the union; Manuel Chavez, an especially resourceful organizer who reluctantly gave up a well-paying job to join the union when the guilt his cousin Cesar heaped upon him for not joining became unbearable. Most important, there was Helen Chavez, whose willingness to sacrifice so much of what mattered most to her, including first claim on her husband's devotion, revealed the depth of her own commitment to farmworker organization.

Working out of Delano, which became the union's first headquarters, Chavez began the slow and often discouraging process of organizing farm laborers whose strong belief in the rightness of his union-building mission was tempered by an even deeper conviction that "it couldn't be done, that the growers were too powerful." With financial resources consisting of a small savings account, gifts and loans from relatives, and the modest wages Helen earned by returning to the fields, the cost of Chavez's stubborn idealism to himself and his family was measured in material deprivation and emotional tumult. Had he been willing to accept financial assistance from such sources as the United Packinghouse Workers or the Agricultural Workers Organizing Committee (AWOC), a would-be farmworkers' union established in 1959 by the AFL-CIO, the worst hardships that awaited Chavez and his loyalists might have been eased or eliminated. Yet, following a line of reasoning that was in some ways reminiscent of the voluntarist logic of earlier trade unionists, Chavez insisted that a farmworkers' union capable of forging the will and stamina required to breach the awesome power of agribusiness could only be built on the sacrifice and suffering of its own membership.

During the NFWA's formative years there was more than enough sacrifice and suffering to go around. But due to the services it provided to farmworkers and the promise of a better life it embodied, the union slowly won the allegiance of a small but dedicated membership scattered through the San Joaquin valley. By the spring of 1965, when the union called its first strike, a brief walkout by rose grafters in Kern County that won higher wages but no contract, Chavez's obsession was on its way to becoming a functioning reality.

Despite the studied deliberateness of its leaders, however, the struggle that catapulted the union to national attention, and invested its mission with the same moral authority that liberal and left-wing activists of the 1960s attributed to the decade's stormy civil rights, antipoverty, and antiwar movements, began in the fall of 1965 as a reluctant gesture of solidarity with an AWOC local whose mainly Filipino membership was on strike against grape growers around Delano. Given the demonstrated ineptitude of the old-time trade unionists who directed the AFL-CIO's organizing efforts among California farmworkers, Chavez had reason to hesitate before committing his still small and untested membership to the support of an AWOC strike. But the strike was being led by Larry Itliong, a Filipino veteran of earlier agricultural strikes and the ablest of the AWOC organizers, and Chavez did not have it in him to ignore a just cause. "At the time," he recalled, "we had about twelve hundred members, but only about two hundred were paying dues. I didn't feel we were ready for a strike—I figured it would be a couple more years before we would be—but I also knew we weren't going to break a strike." The formal decision to support AWOC, made at a boisterous mass meeting held in Delano's Catholic church on September 16 (the day Mexicans celebrate the end of Spanish colonial rule), produced twenty-seven hundred workers willing to sign union cards authorizing the NFWA to represent them in dealing with area grape growers.

The Delano strike, which soon widened beyond the table grape growers who were its initial targets to include the state's major wineries, was a painful five-year struggle destined to test not only the durability of agricultural unionism in California but also the wisdom and resourcefulness of Chavez's leadership. Because growers had little difficulty in recruiting scabs to take the place of strikers, Chavez recognized immediately that a strike could not deny employers the labor they required to cultivate and harvest their crops. Even so, picket lines went up on the first day of the strike and were maintained with unfailing devotion week after week, month after month. Chavez emphasized the need for picketing because he believed that no experience promoted a keener sense of solidarity or afforded strikers a more graphic and compelling illustration of the struggle's essential character. "Unless you have been on a picket line," he said, "you just can't understand the feeling you get there, seeing the conflict at its two most acid ends. It's a confrontation that's vivid. It's a real education." It was an education, however, for which pickets often paid a high price: threats, physical intimidation, and outright violence at the

hands of growers and their agents and arbitrary arrests and harassment by local lawmen who made no effort to mask their pro-employer sympathies. Yet, no matter how great the provocation, no matter how extreme the violence directed against them, strikers were sworn by Chavez not to use violence. Chavez's unwavering commitment to nonviolence was compounded from equal measures of his mother's teachings, the affecting example of St. Francis of Assissi, and the moral philosophy of Gandhi. In the end, though, it was the power of nonviolence as a tactical method that appealed to him. Convinced that the farmworkers' greatest asset was the inherent justice of their cause, Chavez believed that the task of communicating the essential virtue of the union's struggle to potential supporters, and to the general public, would be subverted if strikers resorted to violence. "If someone commits violence against us," Chavez argued, "it is much better—if we can—not to react against the violence, but to react in such a way as to get closer to our goal. People don't like to see a nonviolent movement subjected to violence. . . . That's the key point we have going for us. . . . By some strange chemistry, every time the opposition commits an unjust act against our hopes and aspirations, we get tenfold paid back in benefits."

Winning and sustaining public sympathy, as well as the active support of labor, church, student, civic, and political organizations, was indispensable to the success of the Delano struggles because the inefficacy of conventional strike tactics led Chavez to adopt the economic boycott as the union's primary weapon in fighting employers. Newly sensitized to issues of social justice by the civil rights struggles that reverberated across the country, liberals and leftists enthusiastically embraced the union's cause, endorsing its successive boycotts and not infrequently showing up in Delano to bear personal witness to the unfolding drama of the grape strike. Many unions—from dockworkers who refused to handle scab grapes to autoworkers, whose president, Walter Reuther, not only pledged generous financial assistance to the strikers but also traveled to Delano to join their picket lines—also supported the NFWA. Even the AFL-CIO, which had been sponsoring the rival Agricultural Workers Organizing Committee, ended up embracing the NFWA when Bill Kircher, the federation's national organizing director, concluded that the future of farmworker unionism lay with Chavez and his ragtag following rather than with the more fastidious, but less effective, AWOC. Kircher's assessment of the situation also led him to urge a merger of the UFWA and AWOC. And although their long-standing suspicion of "Big Labor" impelled many of the Anglo volunteers who had joined his movement to oppose the idea, Chavez and the union's farmworker membership recognized that the respectability and financial strength to be gained from such a merger outweighed any loss of independence that AFL-CIO affiliation might entail. With Chavez at its helm and Larry Itliong as its second-in-command, the United Farm Workers Organizing Committee (UFWOC) was formally chartered by the AFL-CIO in August 1966.

The public backing the farmworkers attracted, including that of Senator Robert F. Kennedy, who became an outspoken supporter of the union when the Senate Subcommittee on Migratory Labor held its highly publicized hearings in Delano during the spring of 1966, indicated that large segments of the American people believed that grape strikers occupied the moral "high ground" in their dispute with farm employers. To an important degree, however, public support for the farmworkers' cause also reflected a willingness among many Americans to believe and trust in Cesar Chavez personally; to see in the style and content of his public "persona" those qualities of integrity, selflessness, and moral rectitude that made his cause theirs whether or not they truly understood it. And if Chavez was more embarrassed than flattered by such adoration, he was also enough of an opportunist to see that when liberals from New York to Hollywood made him the human repository of their own unrequited idealism or proclaimed his sainthood, it benefited farmworkers.

"Alone, the farm workers have no economic power," Chavez once observed, "but with the help of the public they can develop the economic power to counter that of the growers." The truth of that maxim was first revealed in April 1966, when a national boycott campaign against its product line of wines and spirits caused Schenley Industries, which had 5,000 acres of vineyards in the San Joaquin valley, to recognize the farmworkers' union and enter into contract negotiations. For Chavez, who received the news as he and a small band of union loyalists were nearing the end of an arduous, but exceedingly well-publicized, 300-mile march from Delano to Sacramento, Schenley's capitulation was "the first major proof of the power of the boycott."

Chavez's tactical genius, and the power of a national (and later international) boycott apparatus that transformed an otherwise local dispute into a topic of keen interest and passionate debate in communities across the country, prompted one winery after another to choose accommodation over further conflict. For two of the biggest wine grape growers, however, the prospect of acquiescing to UFWOC's brand of militant unionism was so loathsome that they resolved to court a more palatable alternative: the giant International Brotherhood of Teamsters. And although they had no apparent support among farmworkers in the region, the Teamsters, under the cynical and oportunistic leadership of William Grami, organizing director of the union's western conference, eagerly sought to prove that theirs was indeed the type of "businesslike" labor organization which anti-union farm employers could tolerate. Yet as good as the idea first seemed to the DiGiorgio Fruit Corporation and then to Perelli-Minetti Vineyards, consummating such a mischievous liaison with the Teamsters proved impossible. In the end, neither the companies nor the Teamsters had the will to persist in the face of intensified UFWOC boycotts, angry condemnations by the labor movement, and a rising tide of public disapproval. The controversy was finally resolved through secret ballot elections, which resulted in expressions of overwhelming support for Chavez and UFWOC.

The victories won during the first two years of the Delano struggle, while they propelled the cause of farmworker organization far beyond the boundaries of any previous advance, left Chavez and his followers still needing to overcome table grape growers in the San Joaquin and Coachella valleys before the union could claim real institutional durability. The state's table grape industry, comprised for the most part of family farms whose hardworking owners typically viewed unionism as an assault on their personal independence as well as a threat to their prerogatives as employers, remained unalterably opposed to UFWOC's demands long after California's largest wineries had acceded to them. Thus when Chavez made them the main targets of the union's campaign toward the end of 1967, table grape growers fought back with a ferocity and tactical ingenuity that announced their determination to resist unionism at whatever cost.

While the boycott continued to serve as the union's most effective weapon, especially after employers persuaded compliant local judges to issue injunctions severely restricting picketing and other direct action in the strike region, the slowness with which it operated to prod recalcitrant growers toward the bargaining table produced in farmworkers and volunteers alike an impatience that reduced both morale and discipline. It also undermined La Causa's commitment to nonviolence. "There came a point in 1968," Chavez recalled, "when we were in danger of losing. . . . Because of a sudden increase in violence against us, and an apparent lack of progress after more than two years of striking, there were those who felt that the time had come to overcome violence by violence. . . . There was demoralization in the ranks, people becoming desperate, more and more talk about violence. People meant it, even when they talked to me. They would say, 'Hey, we've got to burn these sons of bitches down. We've got to kill a few of them.' "

In responding to the crisis, Chavez chose a method of restoring discipline and morale that was as risky and unusual as it was revealing of the singular character of his leadership. He decided to fast. The fast, which continued for twenty-five painful days before it was finally broken at a moving outdoor mass in Delano that included Robert Kennedy among its celebrants, was more than an act of personal penance. "I thought I had to bring the Movement to a halt," Chavez explained, "do something that would force them and me to deal with the whole question of violence and ourselves. We had to stop long enough to take account of what we were doing." Although the fast's religious overtones offended the secular sensibilities of many of his followers, it was more a political than a devotional act; an intrepid and dramatic, if manipulative, device by which Chavez established a compelling standard of personal sacrifice against which his supporters might measure their own commitment and dedication to La Causa, and thus their allegiance to its leader. The power of guilt as a disciplinary tool was something Chavez well understood from his study of life and philosophy of Gandhi, and he was never reluctant to use it himself. "One of his little techniques," Fred Ross said of Chavez's style of leadership, "has always been to shame people into doing something by letting them know how hard he and others were working, and how it was going to hurt other people if they didn't help too."

Those in the union who were closest to Chavez, whatever their initial reservations, found the fast's effect undeniably therapeutic. Jerry Cohen, the union's able young attorney, while convinced that it had been "a fantastic gamble," was deeply impressed by "what a great organizing tool the fast was." "Before the fast," Cohen noted, "there were nine ranch committees [the rough equivalent of locals within the UFW's structure], one for each winery. The fast, for the first time, made a union out of those ranch committees. . . . Everybody worked together." Dolores Huerta also recognized the curative power of Chavez's ordeal. "Prior to that fast," she insisted, "there had been a lot of bickering and backbiting and fighting and little attempts at violence. But Cesar brought everybody together and really established himself as a leader of the farm workers."

While a chronic back ailment, apparently exacerbated by his fast and a schedule that often required him to work twenty hours a day, slowed Chavez's pace during much of 1968 and 1969, the steadily more punishing economic effects of the grape boycott finally began to erode the confidence and weaken the resistance of growers. With the assistance of a committee of strongly pro-union Catholic bishops who had volunteered to mediate the conflict, negotiations between the union and the first defectors from the growers' ranks finally began in the spring of 1970. And by the end of July, when the most obdurate growers in the Delano area collapsed under the combined weight of a continuing boycott and their own mounting weariness, Chavez and his tenacious followers had finally accomplished what five years before seemed impossible to all but the most sanguine forecasters.

The union's victory, which extended to eighty-five percent of the state's table grape industry, resulted in contracts that provided for substantial wage increases and employer contributions to UFWOC's health and welfare and economic development funds. Even more important, however, were the noneconomic provisions: union-run hiring halls that gave UFWOC control over the distribution of available work; grievance machinery that rescued the individual farmworker from the arbitrary authority of the boss; restrictions on the use of pesticides that endangered the health of workers; in short, provisions for the emancipation of workers from the century-old dictatorship of California agribusiness.

After five years of struggle and sacrifice, of anguish and uncertainty, Chavez and his fol-

lowers wanted nothing so much as an opportunity to recuperate from their ordeal and to savor their victory. It was not to be. On the day before the union concluded its negotiations with Delano grape growers, Chavez received the distressing news that lettuce growers in the Salinas and Santa Maria valleys, knowing that they would be the next targets of UFWOC's organizing campaign, had signed contracts providing for the Teamsters' union to represent their field workers. In keeping with the pattern of the Teamsters' involvement with agricultural field labor, no one bothered to consult the Chicano workers whose incessant stopping and bending, whose painful contortions in the service of the hated short-handle hoe, made possible the growers' proud boast that the Salinas valley was the "salad bowl of the nation."

Except for one contract, which the union acquired in 1961 through a collusive agreement with a lettuce grower scheming to break a strike by the Agricultural Workers Organizing Committee, the Teamsters had been content to limit their interest to the truck drivers, boxmakers, and packing-shed workers of the vegetable industry. The Teamsters' decision to expand their jurisdiction to include field labor was a frontal assault on UFWOC. Still weary from the Delano struggle and confronting the complex job of implementing the union's newly won contracts, Chavez and his staff rushed to Salinas in order to meet the challenge.

If William Grami and his Teamsters cohorts discovered that the specter of a UFWOC organizing drive put Anglo lettuce growers in an unusually accommodating frame of mind, they found that Chicano farmworkers in the Salinas and Santa Maria valleys were unwilling to accept a union other than of their own choosing, especially after Chavez launched his boisterous counterattack. As thousands of defiant workers walked off their jobs rather than join a union of the employers' choice, the Teamsters' hierarchy, inundated by a rising tide of liberal and labor criticism, decided that

Grami's tactics were inopportune from a public relations standpoint, and therefore ordered him to undo his now inexpedient handiwork. Grami dutifully, if reluctantly, invited Chavez to meet with him, and the two men quickly worked out an agreement providing the UFWOC would have exclusive jurisdiction over field labor, and that the Teamsters would renounce their contracts with lettuce growers and defer to the workers' true preference in bargaining agents. For a few of the largest growers in the Salinas valley, those who felt most vulnerable to the boycott Chavez had threatened, abandoning Teamsters contracts in favor of agreements with UFWOC provided a welcome escape from a misadventure. Yet when the Teamsters asserted that they were "honor bound" to respect the wishes of 170 growers who refused to void their contracts, Chavez had no choice but to resume hostilities.

Although the more than five thousand workers who responded to UFWOC's renewed strike call brought great enthusiasm and energy to the union's rallies, marches, and picket lines, their capacity to disrupt the fall lettuce harvest declined as the influence exerted by a ready supply of job-hungry *green carders* (Mexican nationals with work permits) combined with aggressive strikebreaking by violence-prone Teamsters "guards," hostile police, politically influential employers, and injunction-happy local judges. As strike activities diminished and boycott operations intensified, employers obtained a court order declaring both types of union pressure illegal under a state law banning jurisdictional strikes.* Chavez later spent three weeks in jail for instructing his followers to ignore the order, but the publicity and additional support his brief imprisonment generated made it one of the few positive developments in an otherwise discouraging slide into adversity.

The challenge presented by the Teamsters-grower alliance in the lettuce industry forced UFWOC to divert precious resources into the reconstruction of its far-flung boycott network. It also distracted Chavez and his most competent aides at a time when the union was in the process of transforming itself from an organization expert in agitation into one equipped to administer contracts covering thousands of workers in the grape industry. Meeting the demands of the hiring hall and the grievance process, which were the union's greatest potential sources of institutional strength, also became its most worrisome and debilitating problem as ranch committees composed of rank-and-file members struggled against their own inexperience, and sometimes powerful tendencies toward vindictiveness, favoritism, and a residual servility, to satisfy the labor requirements of employers and to protect the contractual rights of their fellow workers.

Although Chavez instituted an administrative training program designed by his old mentor Fred Ross, he rejected an AFL-CIO offer of assistance because of his stubborn conviction that a genuinely democratic union must entrust its operation to its own members even at the risk of organizational inefficiency and incompetence. And when he shifted the union's headquarters fifty miles southeast of Delano to an abandoned tuberculosis sanitorium in the Tehachapi Mountains that he called La Paz—short for Nuestra Senora de la Paz (Our Lady of Peace)—Chavez claimed the move was prompted by a concern that his easy accessibility to members of the union's ranch committees discouraged self-reliance. "It was my idea to leave for La Paz," he explained, "because I wanted to remove my presence from Delano, so they could develop their own leadership, because if I am there, they wouldn't make the decisions themselves. They'd come to me." But the move intensified suspicions of internal

---

*Two years later the California State Supreme Court overturned the order, citing the collusive relationship between the employers and the Teamsters and the latter's lack of support among farmworkers at the time the contracts were signed.

critics like Larry Itliong, who left the union partly because Chavez's physical isolation from the membership seemed to enhance the influence of the Anglo "intellectuals" while diminishing that of the rank and file. The greatest barrier to broadening the union's leadership and administrative operation, however, was posed neither by geography nor the influence of Anglo volunteers, but by Chavez himself, whose devotion to the ideal of decentralization was seldom matched by an equal disposition to delegate authority to others. Journalist Ron Taylor, who observed Chavez's style of leadership at close range, wrote: "He conceptually saw a union run in the most democratic terms, but in practice he had a difficult time trying to maintain his own distance; his tendencies were to step in and make decisions. . . . Even though he had removed himself from Delano, he maintained a close supervision over it, and all of the other field offices. Through frequent staff meetings and meetings of the executive board, he developed his own personal involvement with the tiniest of union details."

If Chavez's deficiencies as an administrator troubled sympathetic AFL-CIO officials like Bill Kircher, they tended to reinforce the suspicion privately harbored by such trade-union traditionalists as federation president George Meany that viable organization was probably beyond the compass of farmworkers, no matter how driven and charismatic their leader. Indeed, what appeared to be at the root of Meany's personal skepticism was Chavez's eccentric style of leadership and somewhat alien trade union philosophy: his well-advertised idealism, which uncharitably rendered was a species of mere self-righteousness; his overweening presence, which seemingly engendered an unhealthy cult of personality; his extravagant sense of mission, which left outsiders wondering whether his was a labor or a social movement; his apparently congenital aversion to compromise, which, in Meany's view, negated the AFL-CIO's repeated efforts to negotiate a settlement of UFWOC's jurisdictional dispute with the Teamsters. None of these reservations was enough to keep the AFL-CIO in early 1972 from changing the union's status from that of organizing committee to full-fledged affiliate—the United Farm Workers of America—but in combination they were apparently enough to persuade Meany that Chavez was no longer deserving of the same levels of financial and organizational support previously contributed by the federation.

Yet if trade union administration of an appropriately conventional style was not his forte, Chavez demonstrated during the course of several legislative battles in 1971 and 1972 that his talents as a political organizer and tactician were exceptional. When the Oregon legislature passed an anti-union bill sponsored by the American Farm Bureau Federation, Chavez and his followers, in only a week's time, persuaded the governor to veto it. Shortly thereafter, Chavez initiated a far more ambitious campaign to recall the governor of Arizona for signing a similar grower-backed bill into law. And while the recall drive ultimately bogged down in a tangle of legal disputes, Chavez's success in registering nearly one hundred thousand mostly poor, mostly Chicano voters fostered fundamental changes in the political balance of power in Arizona.

It was in California, however, that the UFW afforded its opponents the most impressive demonstration of La Causa's political sophistication and clout, and Chavez revealed to friends and foes alike that his ability to influence public debate extended well beyond the normal boundaries of trade union leadership. With the backing of the state's agribusiness establishment, the California Farm Bureau launched during 1972 a well-financed initiative drive—popularly known as Proposition 22—designed to eliminate the threat of unionism by banning nearly every effective weapon available to the UFW, including the boycott. Having failed the year before to win legislative approval for an equally tough anti-union measure, farm employers were confident that they could persuade the citizens of California, as they had so often before, that protecting the state's highly profitable agricultural industry was in the public interest. Aware that the UFW could not survive under the restrictive conditions that Proposition 22 contemplated, but without the financial resources needed to counter the growers' expensive media campaign, Chavez and his aides masterfully deployed what they did have: an aroused and resourceful membership. In the end, the growers' financial power proved to be no match for the UFW's people power. In defeating Proposition 22 by a decisive margin—58 percent to 42 percent—the UFW not only eliminated the immediate threat facing the union, but also announced to growers in terms too emphatic to ignore that the time was past when farm employers could rely upon their political power to keep farmworkers in their place.

The political battles that occupied Chavez and the UFW during much of 1972 involved issues so central to the union's existence that they could not be avoided. But even in the course of winning its political fights with agribusiness, the union lost ground on other equally crucial fronts. Organizing activities all but ceased as the UFW turned its attention to political action, and further efforts aimed at alleviating the administrative problems that plagued the union's operation in the grape industry and increasing the pressures on Salinas valley lettuce growers were neglected. At the beginning of 1973 the UFW was in the paradoxical situation of being at the height of its political strength while its vulnerability as a union was increasing.

Just how vulnerable the union was became apparent as the contracts it had negotiated in 1970 with Coachella valley grape growers came up for renewal. Chavez had heard rumors that the Teamsters were planning to challenge the UFW in the region, but not until growers made plain their intention to reclaim complete control over the hiring, dispatching, and disciplining of workers did he suspect that a deal was already in the making. The UFW retained the allegiance of a vast majority of the industry's workers, but neither the growers

nor the Teamsters seemed to care. As soon as the UFW contracts expired, all but two growers announced that they had signed new four-year agreements with the Teamsters. Hiring halls, grievance procedures, and protections against dangerous pesticides disappeared along with the workers' right to a union of their own choice.

Unlike their earlier forays into agriculture, which reflected the opportunism of lower level functionaries interested in advancing their own careers, the Teamsters' move into the grape industry was only the leading edge of a grandiose new strategy by the union's top leadership to rescue farm employers from the UFW in return for the exclusive right to represent farmworkers. Teamsters president Frank Fitzsimmons, with the strong encouragement of the Nixon administration, had suggested such an arrangement late in 1972 when he appeared as the featured speaker at the annual convention of the American Farm Bureau Federation. The Teamsters provided further evidence of their revived interest in agriculture by announcing a few weeks later that the union had renegotiated contracts with 170 growers operating in the Salinas, Santa Maria, and Imperial valleys even though the existing five-year agreement still had nearly three years to run.

The Teamsters' special appeal to California's agribusiness community was obvious: while the UFW insisted that farm employers share power with their workers, Teamsters contracts required only a sharing of the industry's wealth in the form of higher wages and other economic benefits. That the Teamsters never contemplated a kind of unionism that would permit Chicano farmworkers to gain a measure of control over their own lives was confirmed by Einar Mohn, director of the Western Conference of Teamsters, who said shortly after the union announced its coup in the grape industry: "We have to have them in the union for a while. It will be a couple of years before they can start having membership meetings, before we can use the farm workers' ideas in the union. I'm not sure how effective a union can be when it is composed of Mexican-Americans and Mexican nationals with temporary visas. Maybe as agriculture becomes more sophisticated, more mechanized, with fewer transients, fewer green carders, and as jobs become more attractive to whites, then we can build a union that can have structures and that can negotiate from strength and have membership participation."

In the face of the Teamsters onslaught, the UFW, reinforced by familiar coalition of religious, student, liberal, and labor volunteers, resorted to its customary arsenal: picket lines, rallies, marches, boycotts, and appeals to the public's sense of justice. Yet with hundreds of beefy Teamster goons conducting a reign of terror through the region, and UFW activists being jailed by the hundreds for violating court orders prohibiting virtually every form of resistance and protest the union employed, the Chavez forces never had a chance of winning back what they had lost in the Coachella valley, or of stopping the Teamsters when they later moved in on the UFW's remaining contracts with Delano-area table grape growers and the state's major wineries. George Meany, who described the Teamsters' raids as "the most vicious strikebreaking, union-busting effort I've seen in my lifetime," persuaded the AFL-CIO executive council to contribute $1.6 million to the UFW's support. But the money could only ease the union's predicament, not solve it. After five months of bitter struggle, more than thirty-five hundred arrests, innumerable assaults, and the violent deaths of two members—one at the hands of a deputy sheriff who claimed that his victim was "resisting arrest," the other at the hands of a gun-toting young strikebreaker who said he felt menaced by pickets—Chavez, his union in ruins, called off any further direct action in favor of the UFW's most effective weapon: the boycott. The UFW, which only a year before had more than one hundred fifty contracts and nearly forty thousand members, was reduced by September 1973 to a mere handful of contracts and perhaps one-quarter of its earlier membership.

In the wake of the UFW's stunning defeat in the grape industry, writing the union's obituary became a favorite position not only of its long-time adversaries but of some of its traditional sympathizers as well. Most acknowledged the irresistible pressures that a Teamsters-grower alliance unleashed against the union, but many also found fault with the leadership of Cesar Chavez, especially his real or imagined failure to progress from unruly visionary to orderly trade unionist. Chavez's "charisma," said one sympathizer, was no longer "as marketable a commodity as it once was." Another observer concluded that "the charisma and the cause are wearing thin." The "priests and nuns" were losing interest; "the rad-chics from New York's Sutton Place to San Francisco's Nob Hill are bored with it all." "I admire him," George Meany said of Chavez: "He's consistent, and I think he's dedicated. I think he's an idealist. I thinks he's a bit of a dreamer. But the thing that I'm disappointed about Cesar is that he never got to the point that he could develop a real viable union in the sense of what we think of as a viable union."

Yet if Chavez left something to be desired as a union administrator, his alleged deficiencies scarcely explained the UFW's precipitous descent. The union's battered condition was not a product of its failure to behave conventionally, or of Chavez's disinclination to abandon his assertedly quixotic proclivities in favor of the pure and simple ethic that informed the thinking and demeanor of the more typical trade union leader. Rather, the UFW's sudden decline was, for the most part, not of its own making: grape growers had never resigned themselves to sharing power with their workers, and when the Teamsters proffered an alternative brand of unionism that did not impinge upon their essential prerogatives they happily embraced it.

It was precisely because Chavez was "a bit of a dreamer" that the idea of farmworker organization gathered the initial force necessary to overcome the previously insurmountable opposition of employers, and it was because he remained stubbornly devoted to his dream even in the face of the UFW's disheartening setbacks that those who had rushed to speak eulogies over the momentarily prostrated union were ultimately proven wrong. The resources available to him after the debacle of 1973 were only a fraction of what they had been, but Chavez retained both the loyalty of his most able assistants and his own exceptional talents as an organizer and agitator. As the nationwide boycotts he revived against grape and lettuce growers and the country's largest wine producers, the E. and J. Gallo Wineries, slowly gained momentum during 1974, Chavez reminded his Teamsters-employer adversaries in the only language they seemed to understand that the UFW was not going away no matter how diligently they conspired to that end.

The same message was communicated through the union's greatly intensified political activity in 1974. The union relentlessly lobbied the state assembly to win passage of a farm labor bill providing for secret-ballot union-representation elections. Although it later died in the agribusiness-dominated senate, Chavez still demonstrated that the UFW had lost none of its political prowess. The union also brought considerable pressures to bear on Democratic gubernatorial nominee Jerry Brown to win a promise that, if elected, he would make the passage of an acceptable farm labor bill one of his top legislative priorities. The UFW had no real hope of achieving its legislative aim as long as the anti-union administration of Governor Ronald Reagan dominated the state government, but in the youthful Brown, who had actively supported the UFW's grape boycotts while he was a seminary student, Chavez recognized a potential ally.

Because they could not have the kind of explicitly anti-union law they had promoted through their unavailing campaign in support of Proposition 22, the state's farm employers, in a significant reversal of their longstanding position, sought to undermine the UFW by joining with both the Teamsters and AFL-CIO in support of federal legislation extending the National Labor Relations Act (NLRA) to in-

clude farmworkers. Chavez, who had years before supported such an extension, strongly opposed NLRA coverage for farmworkers both because of its diminished effectiveness in guaranteeing workers' rights and because it banned the secondary boycotts upon which the UFW had become so dependent.

With Brown's election in November 1974, a legislative solution to the conflict that had convulsed the state's agricultural labor relations for nearly a decade appeared to be at hand. But given the mutual rancor and distrust that existed between farm employers and Teamsters on the one hand and Chavez and his followers on the other, drafting legislation compelling enough in its composition to induce compromises required both unfailing patience and an uncommon talent for legerdemain. Brown, however, was persuaded that a combination of good will and resolve could produce such a "vehicle for compromise." The new governor recognized that almost ten years of constant hostilities had not only rendered the combatants less intransigent, but had also created public enthusiasm for legislation that might restore labor peace to California's fields and vineyards.

Though none of the parties affected by Brown's compromise bill was fully satisfied in the end, each found reasons to support it. For the Teamsters' union, whose reputation as labor's pariah was reinforced by its anti-UFW machinations, supporting the Agricultural Labor Relations bill was a belated act of image polishing. For the state's agribusinessmen, who were finally discovering that preemptive arrangements with the Teamsters would not protect them from the UFW's seemingly inexhaustible boycott organizers, accepting Brown's proposal promised to restore order to their long unsettled industry. For the UFW, whose leaders were hopeful that legislation might do for La Causa what it had earlier done for the civil rights movement, going along with the governor's bill was a calculated risk that had to be taken.

The Agricultural Labor Relations Act, which went into effect during the fall harvest season of 1975, established a five-member Agricultural Labor Relations Board (ALRB) to implement the law, the most important provisions of which guaranteed the right of farmworkers to organize and bargain collectively through representatives chosen by secret-ballot elections. The ALRB, which faced problems not unlike those confronted by the National Labor Relations Board forty years earlier, was forced to operate under exceedingly difficult circumstances, particularly after disgruntled growers provoked a bitter year-long political confrontation with the UFW by blocking the special appropriations the agency needed to support its heavier than expected workload. Yet despite attacks from all sides, an inexperienced staff, and the administrative miscarriages that inevitably attended the discharging of so controversial and exceptional a mandate, the ALRB doggedly pursued the law's essential intention of ensuring that farmworkers were free to decide questions of union affiliation without undue interference.

Whereas Chavez was often frustrated by the ALRB's plodding pace and periodic bungling, and at times criticized its operation in language as caustic and intemperate as that used by the most aggrieved farm employer, he considered the law a "godsend . . . without question the best law for workers—any workers—in the entire country." Chavez and the UFW, notwithstanding their sporadic fulminations, had good reasons to consider the ALRA in providential terms. Within two years of its passage, the UFW, with a membership approaching forty thousand, had regained its position as the dominant union in California agriculture. Even more important, the union's success persuaded the Teamsters, who had faltered badly in the heated competition for the allegiance of farmworkers, to sign a five-year pact that effectively ceded jurisdiction over agricultural labor to the UFW.* The ALRA became, in short, the means by which the UFW accomplished its own resurrection, the instrument by which

Cesar Chavez redeemed his stewardship of La Causa.

But for the tenacious idealism and organizational virtuosity of Cesar Chavez, there is no reason to believe that the circumstances which fostered the ALRA's enactment would have arisen. Before he arrived on the scene, agribusinessmen in California were as secure in their power and authority as any employers in the country. Yet only ten years after Chavez and his followers first challenged their supremacy, farm employers were acquiescing to a law that augured the demolition of their one-hundred-year-old dominion over labor.

The law, however, imposed obligations as great as the benefits it promised. Beyond forcing the UFW to prove that the support it had always claimed to enjoy among farmworkers was actual rather than imagined, the ALRA had also challenged the capacity of Chavez and his lieutenants to take their organization into a new and different phase, one that rewarded abilities more closely associated with conventional trade union leadership than with the boycotting, marching, and other forms of social proselytism that the UFW had emphasized up to that time. Once the ALRA created the machinery whereby farmworkers might secure their rights to organize and bargain collectively, the conflicts that remained between themselves and employers had much less to do with elemental questions of justice than with arguable issues of economic equity and job control. The law enabled the UFW to make its presence felt in California's industrialized agriculture; it did not ensure that the union would either prevail in the short run or endure in the long run.

As from the beginning, the UFW's future as an organization is inextricably linked to Cesar Chavez's success as a leader. And since 1975 the union's record testifies to a mixed performance on Chavez's part. After reaching a membership of approximately fifty thousand by the late 1970s, the union has slowly dwindled in

---

*Early in 1982 the pact was extended for another five-year period.

size, comprising roughly forty thousand members by the early 1980s, nearly all of whom, except for isolated outposts in Florida, Arizona, and a couple of other states, are confined to California. The union's continuing failure to make greater headway among the 200,000 farmworkers who are potential members in California alone is attributable, in part, to the growing sophistication of employers in countering the UFW's appeal to workers through voluntary improvements in wages and conditions; to the entry into the farm labor force of workers without strong emotional ties to or knowledge of the heroic struggles of the past; and to the inability of an increasingly politicized ALRB to enforce the letter and the spirit of its mandate in a timely fashion, especially following the election in 1984 of a governor allied with the union's fiercest opponents.

It is also the case, however, that the UFW's drift from vitality toward apparent stagnation is partially rooted in a web of complex factors related to the sometimes contradictory leadership of Cesar Chavez: a sincere devotion to democratic unionism that is undermined by a tendency to regard all internal dissidents as traitors at best and anti-union conspirators at worst; a professed desire to make the UFW a rank-and-file union governed from the bottom up that is contradicted by a strong inclination to concentrate authority in his own hands and those of close family members; a commitment to professionalize the administration of the UFW that is impeded by a reliance on volunteerism so unyielding as to have caused many of the union's most loyal and efficient staff members to quit.

In fairness, however, Chavez's performance must be assessed on a basis that encompasses far more than the normal categories of trade union leadership. For unlike most American labor leaders, who had stood apart from the traditions of their European counterparts by insisting that unionism is an end in itself, Chavez has, in his own somewhat idiosyncratic way, remained determined to use the UFW and the heightened political consciousness of his Chicano loyalists as a means for promoting changes more fundamental than those attainable through collective bargaining and other conventional avenues of trade union activism. In defining the UFW's singular mission, Chavez once declared: "As a continuation of our struggle, I think that we can develop economic power and put it in the hands of the people so they can have more control of their own lives, and then begin to change the system. We want radical change. Nothing short of radical change is going to have any impact on our lives or our problems. We want sufficient power to control our own destinies. This is our struggle. It's a lifetime job. The work for social change and against social injustice is never ended."

When measured against the magnitude of his proposed enterprise, and against his extraordinary achievements on behalf of workers who were among the most powerless and degraded in America prior to his emergence, Chavez's real and alleged deficiencies in guiding the UFW across the hostile terrain of California's industrialized agriculture in no way detract from his standing as the most accomplished and far-sighted labor leader of his generation. Whether or not he has it in him to be more than a labor leader, to turn the UFW into an instrument of changes still more profound and far-reaching than it has already brought about, remains to be proven.

The history of American labor is littered with the wreckage of workers' organizations—the Knights of Labor and the Industrial Workers of the World among them—that tried and failed to combine the immediate purposes of trade unionism with an ultimate ambition to alter the fundamental structure of American society. Indeed, in an era when many labor leaders are preoccupied with nothing so much as the survival of their organizations, Chavez's pledge before the UFW's 1983 convention to lead the union in new and even bolder assaults against the economic and political status quo seems distinctly unrealistic. Unrealistic, that is, until one recalls the implausibility of what he has already accomplished.

20

THE PAUL ROBESON–JACKIE ROBINSON SAGA: A POLITICAL COLLISION

RONALD A. SMITH

The post–World War II years have been dominated by the geopolitical and ideological contest between the United States and the Soviet Union known as the Cold War. Beginning during World War II itself, the Cold War made its first public appearance with Winston Churchill's "Iron Curtain" speech of 1946. That speech, which warned Americans of the imminent threat that Soviet communism posed to the "free world," joined with Harry Truman's Cold War policies to create an atmosphere of tension and misunderstanding in Soviet-American relations.

It was in this atmosphere of profound international distrust and domestic anxiety that the House Un-American Activities Committee began its search for evidence of "Communist" infiltration of American organizations and institutions. Directing most of its attention to organizations and individuals critical of various aspects of American society, the House committee effectively used the national media to convince the public that lawful dissent was tantamount to treason. Employing deceit, innuendo, falsification, and badgering, the House Un-American Activities Committee called scores of Americans before its hearings to ferret out what it claimed were Communists in all walks of life.

One of the most dramatic appearances before the House committee was that of Jackie Robinson in the spring of 1949. Called before the committee to neutralize Paul Robeson's recent denunciation of American race relations, the hearings brought the man who had desegregated baseball before it to testify against one of America's foremost black actors. As Ronald A. Smith argues in this essay, the Robeson-Robinson saga was part of a larger debate within Afro-American society over the most effective means to bring about the end of racial segregation. Although both men agreed about the need to end segregation, Robeson took a less accommodative and more critical view of American race relations. In an atmosphere of mounting anti-Communist hysteria, Robeson's brief remark comparing American and Soviet attitudes toward blacks was enough to have him condemned by the House Committee and branded as an internal threat to American society. In the years following the committee hearing, Jackie Robinson's moderate path led him to prosperity and public acclaim, while Paul Robeson never recovered from the financial and public loss caused by the House hearings.

From *Journal of Sport History* 6:5–27 (1979). Reprinted by permission of Ronald A. Smith and *Journal of Sport History*.

Time: October 21, 1947, nearly two years before the collision

Locale: Washington, D.C., U.S. House of Representatives

Scene: Hearings of the House Un-American Activities Committee Regarding the Communist Infiltration of the Motion Picture Industry

Main Performers: Congressman Richard M. Nixon (R), California

Actor Adolphe Menjou

————

Nixon: (Questioning his Committee's subpoenaed guest) Other than belonging to a communist-front organization, do you, Mr. Menjou, have "tests which you would apply which would indicate to you that people acted like communists?"

Menjou: "Well, I think attending any meetings at which Mr. Paul Robeson appeared and applauding or listening to his Communist songs in America. . . ."

****

Time: One and one-half years later, April 19, 1949

Locale: Paris, France

Scene: World Congress of the Partisans of Peace

Main Performer: Singer, actor, and ex-athlete Paul Robeson

Robeson: (Standing tall and addressing the Congress) "It is unthinkable that American Negroes would go to war on behalf of those who have oppressed us for generations against a country /the USSR/ which in one generation has raised our people to the full dignity of mankind."

****

Time: Three months later, July 18, 1949

Locale: Washington, D.C., U.S. House of Representatives

Scene: Hearings of the House Un-American Activities Committee Regarding Communist Infiltration of Minority Groups

Main Performers: Congressman Morgan Moulder (D), Missouri

Professional baseball player Jackie Robinson

————

Moulder: Mr. Robinson, this hearing regarding communist infiltration of minority groups is being conducted "to give an opportunity to you and others to combat the idea Paul Robeson has given by his statements."

Robinson: Thank you Congressman Moulder for this opportunity. "Paul Robeson's statement in Paris to the effect that American Negroes would refuse to fight in any way against Russia . . . sounds very silly to me. . . . I've got too much invested for my wife and child and myself in the future of this country . . . to throw it away because of a siren song sung in bass."

Moulder: "I think you have rendered a great service to your country and to your people and we are proud of you and congratulate you upon being the great success that you are in this great country of ours."

****

Two Afro-American performing heroes, Paul Robeson and Jackie Robinson, collided politically during the turbulent anti-communist days of the early Cold War era. The House Un-American Activities Committee erected a stage for star athletic performer Jackie Robinson, the twentieth century desegregator of professional baseball. At the same time it attempted to construct the political gallows for ex-athletic great and premier singer and actor, Paul Robeson, who was praising the Soviet Union's race relations as he fought for the rights of blacks in America. The political collision of two black heroes tells us much about the nature of American society and of the place of sport and the performing arts during the precipitous years of the communist-hunting post-World War II era. For symbolic reasons, Jackie Robinson was asked by government officials to help obliterate Paul Robeson's leadership role among Americans. So successful were Robinson and others that for a generation Paul Robeson remained for most Americans a non-person.

It is ironic that Paul Robeson (1898–1976), who had been involved himself in the desegregation of professional baseball, should have the desegregator, Jackie Robinson (1919–1972), play an important role in Robeson's departure from the public forum. Robeson, who was over fifty years old when the confrontation occurred, was a product of the latter nineteenth and early twentieth centuries. The fact that Robeson's early life and career took place in the depths of Jim Crowism in America may help explain why he developed certain racial and political positions perceived as radical and became a target for Robinson and others in the desegregation movement of the Cold War Years.

ROBESON AND JIM CROW

Paul Robeson was born the same decade that baseball, then the unquestioned national pastime, rid itself of all blacks playing the professional game. At about the same time, the League of American Wheelmen, a key amateur bicycle association, inserted a whites-only clause in its constitution; John L. Sullivan, the first great American boxing champion, refused to fight blacks; and the newly formed Jockey Club of New York began to restrict the licensing of black jockeys. Two years before the birth of Robeson, the historic 1896 Supreme Court *Plessy* v. *Ferguson* "separate but equal" decision judicially sanctioned the segregation of blacks from whites. This was followed during Robeson's first year by Supreme Court decisions to uphold literacy tests and poll-tax qualifications for voting; policies devised to keep the Negro out of politics. Justice Henry Brown rationalized these decisions when he wrote in the *Plessy* decision: "If one race be inferior to the other socially, the Constitution of the United States cannot put them on the same plane...." It would have been natural for blacks born at the time to be socialized in believing that they were inferior. Even the evolu-

tionary theory of natural selection, struggle for existence, and survival of the fittest indicated to many Americans that blacks were placed low on the evolutionary ladder.

The belief in the racial inferiority of blacks at the time of Robeson's birth influenced the racial question in at least two important ways. First, Jim Crow laws multiplied greatly so that in the leisure domain, recreational facilities such as swimming pools, playgrounds, and public parks were segregated, though almost never equally. Especially in the South, laws mandated separate entrances, ticket windows, and seating arrangements and created such curiosities as an Oklahoma ban on blacks and whites fishing together in the same boat and a Birmingham, Alabama ordinance prohibiting racially mixed play at dominoes or checkers. Second, the hue and cry of voices proclaiming racial superiority of whites affected the way blacks thought of themselves. Increasingly, Negro leaders and masses turned toward an accommodation with the Jim Crow system rather than protest against it. The dominant Negro leader of the turn-of-the-century America, Booker T. Washington, led the way toward accommodation with the whites. In his famous Atlanta Compromise speech in 1895, Washington held up his hands, fingers outstretched, to a mixed crowd of blacks and whites, and proclaimed that "in all things that are purely social we can be as separate as the fingers...." Washington believed that it was more valuable for blacks to prove their worth by their own productivity than to demand either political or social rights.

If most blacks became accommodated to the unjust system, some, such as W. E. B. Du Bois, the historian and social critic, attacked racial prejudice where they found it. Du Bois criticized Booker T. Washington's views arguing that they represented "in Negro thought the old attitude of adjustment and submission ... /which/ practically accepts the alleged inferiority of the Negro races." Du Bois called for "work, culture, liberty,—all these we need, not singly but together, not successively but together, each growing and aiding each, and all striving toward that vaster ideal that swims before the Negro people, the ideal of human brotherhood, gained through the unifying ideal of Race...." Said Du Bois: "All that makes life worth living—Liberty, Justice, and Right, [should not be] marked 'For White People Only.' "

Paul Robeson was raised with beliefs more in sympathy with Du Bois than with Washington. From an early time, his preacher-father, a former runaway slave, ingrained in the boy a sense of pride and worth as a black man. He soon found that in mental and physical qualities he was superior to most whites. As one of only three blacks graduating from his high school in Somerville, New Jersey, Robeson scholastically headed his class of 250 students. He was a skilled debator in his high school, was a soloist of the glee club, acted in the drama club, and excelled in several sports. During his senior year he achieved the highest score on a statewide examination for a scholarship to attend Rutgers College. From that day on, he later recalled, "Equality might be denied but I *knew* I was not inferior."

ROBESON AND ROBINSON IN THE 1920S AND 1930S

Indeed, Robeson was not inferior physically or mentally, and he showed remarkable abilities during his college years and after. He was an all-American football player at Rutgers in 1917 and 1918, and was called the greatest defensive end of all time by Walter Camp, the so-called father of American football. Robeson won twelve varsity letters in football, basketball, baseball, and track and field. He led his class academically and was elected to Phi Beta Kappa in his junior year. After college, he played professional football on the first championship team of what today is the National Football League. He took a law degree at Columbia University, before becoming a Shakespearean actor and a world renowned singer. Yet, by the 1960s and 1970s, he had become for most, a forgotten man. While Jackie Robinson was generally recognized for desegregating professional baseball, Robeson was not widely remembered even among blacks.

Jackie Robinson was born on a share-cropper farm in Cairo, Georgia in 1919, the year Babe Ruth was sold to the New York Yankees and the Black Sox scandal took place. The same year saw Jack Dempsey winning the heavyweight boxing championship and immediately announcing that he would pay "no attention to Negro challengers." Both Robeson and Robinson grew up in a Jim Crow society in which social and legal separation was readily apparent.

While Jackie Robinson moved to southern California with his mother and older brothers and sisters in 1920, Paul Robeson attended Columbia Law School. On weekends, he traveled to Ohio and played football with another black, Fritz Pollard, on the championship Akron Pros. Later, as he was completing his law degree, he competed for the Milwaukee Badgers in the fledgling National Football League. Upon graduation from Columbia, the American Bar Association denied him membership, and he suffered other severe limitations on his chosen profession. He soon withdrew from law practice and launched an acting and singing career. The summer before his last term at Columbia Law School, he had toured Great Britain singing and acting in a play titled *Voodoo*. By the mid-1920s, Robeson starred in Eugene O'Neill's plays, *The Emperor Jones* and *All God's Chillun Got Wings*. Robeson portrayed a black man who married a white women in *All God's Chillun*. Reaction to his involvement in a racially mixed drama in Jim Crow America included hate mail and threats to both Robeson and playwright O'Neill from the Ku Klux Klan and individuals with equally harsh racist feelings. Favorable audience reaction and reviews, however, brought Robeson recognition among both whites and blacks. He gained further public recognition from musical concerts featuring his rich voice singing Negro spirituals.

Robeson spent increasing periods of time in Europe and England in the 1920s and 1930s. Especially in London he found less racial hatred and greater personal freedom than in America. Becoming more politically aware as areas of the world moved toward fascism during the 1930s, Robeson began to question the imperialistic policies of European nations and America toward colonial Africa, of fascist Italy toward Ethiopia, and of Nazi Germany toward the Spanish Civil War. By the mid-to-late 1930s, Robeson took the side of those who favored freedom for blacks in Africa. He campaigned for the Republican cause against totalitarian Franco in Spain, and deeply opposed fascism in Italy and especially in Germany. In Nazi Germany in 1934, on his way to Russia to confer with a film director, Robeson was threatened and racially abused by German storm troopers near Berlin.

In Moscow, Robeson was greatly impressed with the Russian people and what he considered their lack of racial prejudice. He wrote: "I, the son of a slave, walk this earth in complete dignity." From that point on, Robeson continued his praise of the Soviet Union while speaking out against fascist thought wherever he found it. He found much to criticize in America. Two decades later he would testify before the House of Representatives Committee on Un-American Activities, stating:

I would say in Russia I felt for the first time a full human being, and no colored prejudice like in Mississippi and no colored prejudice like in Washington and it was the first time I felt like a human being, where I did not feel the pressure of color as I feel in this committee today.

In September, 1939, Paul Robeson returned to live in the United States after spending most of the previous twelve years abroad. This was the same month that Jackie Robinson began attending college at UCLA after first going to Pasadena Junior College. Unlike Robeson who attended Rutgers as the only black on campus and the first to participate in athletics, Robin-son had as a teammate on the football squad the Negro Kenny Washington, possibly the most outstanding football player in America that year. Like Robeson, Robinson lettered in each of four sports, football, basketball, baseball, and track and field. Besides being an outstanding back in football, he led his team in scoring in basketball and won the Pacific Coast title in the broad jump. In baseball, he played shortstop while displaying exceptional speed and daring on the base paths.

During the time Robinson starred in athletics at UCLA, Robeson was attaining new heights of popularity as a singer and actor. When the United States entered World War II as an ally of the Soviet Union, little was said about Robeson's praise of life in the Soviet Union—most saw him as a strong opponent of fascism. He helped conduct war bond drives as he continued to sing Russian folk songs and speak out for black rights everywhere. Like a number of civil rights leaders, he saw World War II as having a positive effect in breaking down Jim Crow laws and customs. Robeson even had a part in the attempt to desegregate professional baseball in the midst of the war.

WORLD WAR II AND ROBESON'S INVOLVEMENT IN BASEBALL DESEGREGATION

Segregation existed in professional baseball during World War II as it had for more than a half-century when it had first drawn the color line. It seemed hypocritical to Robeson and others that America would fight to end the myth of Aryan supremacy in Germany while the nation preserved its own myth of racial supremacy at home. A movement to end baseball segregation began soon after Pearl Harbor. It is not surprising that the American Communist Party took a lead in the agitation for integrating baseball and in accepting any role Paul Robeson would play in it.

The American Communist Party organ, the *Daily Worker*, had called for breaking the color line in the 1930s, but in early 1942 its sports editor, Lester Rodney, began attacking the Commissioner of Baseball, Kenesaw Mountain Landis, for not eliminating Jim Crowism in America's most visible sport. After the great black pitcher Satchel Paige and his Kansas City Monarchs defeated a group of Major Leaguers, who were in military service and headed by pitcher Dizzy Dean, Rodney wrote contemptuously:

> Can you read, Judge Landis? . . . The Stars could get only two hits off Satchel Paige in seven innings of trying. Why does your silence keep him and other Negro stars from taking their rightful place in our national pastime at a time when we are at war and Negro and white are fighting and dying together to end Hitlerism?

The *Daily Worker* quoted Jimmy Dykes, manager of the Chicago White Sox, as saying to Jackie Robinson, the young Negro shortstop: "I'd love to have you on my team and so would all the other big league managers. But it's not up to us. Get after Landis." To a similar statement, Commissioner Landis replied that if any managers "want to sign one, or 25 Negro players, it is all right with me. That is the business of the managers and the club owners." Arguing against the entry of blacks in baseball was Larry McPhail, president of the Brooklyn Dodgers. He stated that the lack of Negroes in organized baseball "is not due to racial discrimination," but rather that "Negro baseball leagues might be wrecked if the major leagues raid these clubs and grab a few outstanding players." This argument of ruining black baseball by desegregating white baseball was likely more economically than altruistically derived, for Major League owners profited from the existence of Negro teams which rented their parks.

Pressure to change baseball's six decades of segregation continued to be exerted during the first summer of America's entry into World War II. There was one report of a heated discussion of club owners over blacks in baseball at the time of the Major League All-Star game

and of the meeting transcripts being ordered destroyed. That same summer the president of the Pittsburgh Pirates announced that blacks would be given tryouts for his team. There is, however, no evidence that blacks of the stature of Josh Gibson, a catcher, or Sammy Bankhead, an outfielder, of the nearby Homestead Grays Negro team—or any other—were given the opportunity. Thirty-five year old Satchel Paige, the best known and highest paid black player of the times, indicated that he would only come into white baseball if it were on a team of all blacks because the racial tension in both the South and the North would be too high if a white team were desegregated. A writer from Los Angeles mocked the scene: "Let the Negro have his name in the casualty lists of Pearl Harbor or Bataan or Midway. But, for heavensakes, let's keep his name out of the boxscores." Indeed, the old argument of possible race riots, as had occurred after the Jack Johnson-Jim Jeffries Great White Hope fight of 1910, was still brought up in discussions of desegregation in American sport.

Agitation continued into 1943, eventually involving Paul Robeson. A resolution was introduced in the New York State legislature protesting the unwritten ban against blacks in baseball, and Brooklyn's communist councilman, Peter V. Cocchione, introduced a resolution calling for desegregation of baseball. The Negro Publishers Association became involved and requested Commissioner Landis to discuss the question of blacks in organized baseball at the annual meeting of Major League teams. The Commissioner agreed, and for the first time in its history professional baseball officially examined the desegregation issue in its December meeting. Eight black newspapermen and Paul Robeson attended the meeting. Robeson's presence dominated the session.

Robeson was one of three blacks to address the club owners. He was introduced by Landis who said that he had brought Robeson to the meeting "because you all know him. You all know that he is a great man in public life, a great American" Robeson told the owners: "I come here as an American and former athlete. I come because I feel this problem deeply." He expressed his belief that the time had come for baseball to change its attitude toward the Negro and told them he had become the first black actor to play in Shakespeare's *Othello* on Broadway less than two months before. He declared that if he could be a black in an otherwise all-white play, then a Negro in a white cast should no longer be incredible to baseball owners. Robeson said that though he understood the owner's fears of racial disturbance if baseball were desegregated, "my football experience showed me such fears are groundless." When he finished, the owners gave him what a black writer called a "rousing ovation," but the owners neither questioned Robeson nor the other two speakers. Landis did reiterate a previous statement that "each club is entirely free to employ Negro players to any extent it pleases and the matter is solely for each club's decision without any restrictions whatsoever."

One club owner, Philip K. Wrigley of the Chicago Cubs, did not believe that the middle of World War II was the time to hire blacks in baseball, but said that he would consider hiring a scout to pursue a talent search for future Negro players. Wrigley showed his understanding of baseball when he observed that the sport was not progressive and only accepted something new after everyone else had already adopted it. "Baseball hesitates to break a custom," Wrigley told a Chicago delegation for baseball integration in late 1943, "whether it is using Negro players or removing the traditional sleeve out of uniforms." Whether baseball was conservative or not, there was great social pressure to keep the "National Pastime" free of blacks. The problem of bringing blacks into baseball was enormous when one considers that in the midst of World War II, both the American and National League teams from St. Louis prevented black spectators from purchasing tickets for any section of their stadiums except the bleachers. Allowing blacks to sit in the grandstand seemed minute compared to allowing them to play on the field. To this sentiment Robeson countered that the temper of the Negro had changed, that the Negro was fighting "a world-wide war for the right of people to be free, and he will resist any attempt to keep him tied down to a reactionary status quo."

ROBINSON DESEGREGATES BASEBALL

Blacks did not break the color barrier in baseball during World War II, but there is little doubt that the war was a catalyst in bringing about black entry into both professional baseball (closed to Negroes since the 1880s) and professional football (closed to Negroes since 1933). Near the close of the war, the *New York Times* editorialized: "If we are willing to let Negroes as soldiers fight wars on our team, we should not ask questions about color in the great American game." Economic and political pressure as well as moral pressure was being exerted. In Boston, city councilman Isadore Munchnick threatened to cancel Sunday permits to the Boston Red Sox and the Boston Braves Major League teams unless both clubs agreed to end discrimination against Negroes. Munchnick agreed to withdraw his motion after the Boston clubs verbally assented to give equal opportunity to blacks. In mid-April, Jackie Robinson and two others were given "tryouts" by the Red Sox although all three blacks agreed that there was no intent by the Boston team to sign any of them. After the tryouts, one of the three, Sam Jethroe, told black sportswriter Wendell Smith of the *Pittsburgh Courier:* "We'll hear from the Red Sox like we'll hear from Adolph Hitler." The Secretary of the Negro National League said the tryouts in Boston were a travesty, "the most humiliating experience Negro baseball has yet suffered from white organized baseball." Jackie Robinson was more circumspect. "We can consider ourselves pioneers," commented Robinson. "Even if they don't accept us, we are doing our part and, if possible, making the way easier for those who follow. Some day some Negro player will get a break. We want to help make that day a reality."

Pressure to desegregate baseball was occurring elsewhere, mostly in the state of New York. Vito Marcantonio, the only U.S. Congressman of the left wing American Labor Party, asked the Interstate Commerce Committee to hold a hearing on discrimination in baseball. He also conferred with the New York baseball clubs asking them to break the color line. One club owner, Branch Rickey of the Brooklyn Dodgers, voluntarily gave a tryout to two Negroes. The tryout of these well-travelled Negroes, Terris McDuffie (thirty-six years old) and Dave Thomas (thirty-nine years old), could not be seen as highly promising for blacks as neither had had a good record in the Negro league the previous year. McDuffie had a losing record as a pitcher, and Thomas batted only .248 in 1944. It appeared that voluntary tryouts such as Rickey's might become mandatory in the near future. The New York state Fair Employment Practices Bill had recently passed and had forbidden discrimination in employment on the basis of race, color, or creed. If this were applied to baseball, it might be shown that baseball owners in New York City had not given equal opportunity to blacks. Larry McPhail, by then owner of the New York Yankees, rhetorically asked to "name me the colored players today who have the qualifications for a career in the major leagues, or in the minors, for that matter!" The same day Jackie Robinson opened the season at shortstop for the Kansas City Monarchs of the Negro American League. Several months later and just two days before Japan surrendered ending World War II, Branch Rickey was appointed by Mayor LaGuardia of New York City to a Committee of Ten which was established to study racial discrimination in baseball. The little publicized Committee of Ten worked rapidly and concluded in November of 1945 with two special points. The report emphasized that no racial differences in baseball

skill existed between blacks and whites and that action, not silence, was needed to end sixty years of segregation. "The time is never ripe for social reform," the report stressed, the Major Leagues must act soon.

Branch Rickey had already begun to act by quietly beginning his quest to find the right player to break the discrimination policy. He had done this before the LaGuardia Committee of Ten had been announced. Using subterfuge to accomplish his desegregation plan, Rickey announced in the spring of 1945 the formation of a six team, black baseball league including his own team, the Brooklyn Brown Dodgers. The Brown Dodgers were used as a front to cover his talent search—a quest which determined that Jackie Robinson should be the first black to enter organized baseball in the twentieth century. Robinson had been chosen because he was an outstanding athlete, and it was done with the knowledge that his highly competitive nature would make him stand up and fight for his rights as an individual. Robinson had stood up against racism as a young boy, during his college career, and while he was in military service during World War II. While stationed at a Southern military camp, Robinson was court-martialed and later acquitted for challenging the Jim Crow tradition which dictated that blacks should sit in the rear of a military bus.

While Jackie Robinson endured the torture of desegregating organized baseball, Paul Robeson entered the post-World War II era criticizing American racial policies and praising those of the socialistic Soviet Union. Robeson had noted during the war the influence that he believed would be brought on the United States' racial policies from abroad. "We in America," Robeson said, "criticize many nations. We know that international conscience has great influence in spite of wars. One important part of the solution of the Negro problem here will be the pressure of other countries on America from the outside." These were prophetic remarks in light of the effect of the Cold War politics on breaking down America's Jim

Crow policies in the 1950s and 1960s. After World War II, Robeson was much involved in that external influence, probably giving it more visible support than any other black American. His outspoken stance for black rights and his pro-communist ideology created a furor wherever he went as America turned to a hate-Russia campaign in the post-war era.

Jackie Robinson, unlike Robeson, was restrained from certain actions for the first several years in the Brooklyn Dodger organization as Branch Rickey believed that his venture in race relations would fail if Robinson reacted outwardly to racial slurs. Robinson gave his assurance that he would not retaliate against insults from players nor complain to umpires; he promised not to make public endorsements, write newspaper or magazine articles, frequent night spots, or accept social invitations from whites or blacks. He was also warned by heavyweight boxing champion Joe Louis, who himself had been cautioned, not to get cocky so that whites might call him an "uppity nigger." During his first year with the Dodgers he received death threats against himself and his family while he stoically took verbal abuse, the worst from manager Ben Chapman and his Philadelphia Phillies. A challenge by the St. Louis Cardinals to boycott the Brooklyn Dodgers if Robinson played was cut short by league president Ford Frick who warned the Cardinals that those who took part would be suspended, and Frick added bluntly: "I don't care if it wrecks the National League for five years." Later, the Cardinals Enos Slaughter and Joe Garagiola spiked Robinson, maliciously, Robinson believed. Nevertheless, he became Rookie of the Year and helped Brooklyn reach the World Series. Thus, Robinson came into the Major Leagues under rules created to make him more acceptable to whites, something Robeson would not have done at that time in his life.

As Jackie Robinson attempted to make his impact in baseball with his base hits and effective fielding, Paul Robeson plowed forth on his own crusade. The day after Robinson made his first Major League base hit, Robeson's scheduled concert appearance in Peoria, Illinois, was unanimously banned by the city council. Not long after that incident, the Albany, New York Board of Education withdrew permission previously granted to Robeson for a concert in its school auditorium. Said a board member: "The color of Paul Robeson's skin has nothing to do with this case, but the color of his ideologies has." Retorted Robeson: "Whether I am a communist or a communist sympathizer is irrelevant. The question is whether American citizens, regardless of their political beliefs or sympathies, may enjoy their constitutional rights." The Albany case was eventually taken to the New York Supreme Court, which granted Robeson the right to sing in the Albany school. Robeson gave his concert, and that same day Jackie Robinson revealed hate letters written to him threatening his life if he did not quit baseball.

THE ROBESON-ROBINSON POLITICAL CONFRONTATION

It was in context of Robinson's desegregation of baseball under white terms and Robeson's stand for human rights under free political terms that a collision arose between Robinson and Robeson. The catalyst was the House Un-American Activities Committee (HUAC) of the United States Congress. In the late 1930s, HUAC had been established principally to investigate fascist and communist activities. It became an inquisitorial committee which ferreted out political deviants for public exposure and ridicule. Organizations and individuals which HUAC considered heretical were singled out to be destroyed or at least immobilized. Extended hearings were conducted in which accused and accusers were questioned at length. One historian has written that the accused would leave HUAC hearings "with a mark of Cain," while the accuser would depart "the tribunal with a halo of potential market value." Another has concluded that HUAC's "endless harassment of individuals for disagreeable opinions and actions has created anxiety, revulsion, indignation, /and/ outrage. . . ."

Paul Robeson was one of HUAC's targets. He had been chastised previously by HUAC, but in 1949 the Committee, representing American fear of and hysteria over the Cold War political left, attacked Robeson violently. This vendetta came as a result of a comment made by Robeson at the World Congress of Partisans held in Paris, France on April 20, 1949. Robeson, along with W. E. B. Du Bois, directed the American delegation to the communist-led meeting. Both men spoke to the 1800 delegates from about sixty nations, and both condemned America's international actions. It was Robeson, however, whose rhetoric drew the attention of the American press and the ire of governmental officials. One of Robeson's unwritten statements caught the ear of the press:

> It is unthinkable that American Negroes would go to war on behalf of those who have oppressed us for generations against the Soviet Union which in one generation has raised our people to full human dignity.

The next day the nation's newspapers reported Robeson's remarks indicating that blacks would never fight against the Soviet Union. As one Negro leader, Lester B. Granger, commented: "A nation-wide 9-day sensation was manufactured." Most black leaders were quick to castigate Robeson for his Paris speech. "We American Negroes," declared Max Yergan, a black who had once led the Council of African Affairs with Robeson, "can be deeply grateful Mr. Paul Robeson did not speak for us in Paris a few days ago." Exclaimed Walter White, head of the National Association for the Advancement of Colored People: "We will not shirk equal responsibilities. . . . We will meet the responsibilities imposed upon all America." Robeson is "an ingrate" chided Dr. Channing Tobias, a member of the NAACP board of directors. Wrote Mary McLeod Bethune, President of the National Council of Negro Women: "I am chagrined at

his presumption. . . . I think he has missed his cue and has entered the stage during the wrong scene." Edgar G. Brown, Director of the National Negro Council, went further by calling Robeson's speech communist propaganda while quoting Stephen Decatur's "In peace and war—my country, right or wrong." To all of this a black columnist stated that "we all know that our professional leaders had to say officially that Paul does not speak for Negroes as a group." He then criticized others for joining the bandwagon which he believed was essentially saying, "Deed, Boss, that bad old Paul ain't speaking for me and you know I'll fight for democracy, if I ain't been lynched first."

Newspapers intended for a Negro audience were almost as unequivocal in their stands against Robeson as were white newspapers and black leaders, and their immediate reaction to Robeson's Paris statement clearly showed that Robeson did not speak for all American blacks, probably not even most blacks. The *Pittsburgh Courier* editorialized that Robeson's declaration that blacks would never fight the Soviets was a "pathetic statement." The *Chicago Defender* snapped "Nuts to Mr. Robeson," and the less hostile *Philadelphia Afro-American* stressed that "Robeson does not speak for us and millions of other colored people." Some black columnists, though, sided with Robeson. This was only natural, for at the time Robeson spoke in Paris, lynchings were still prevalent in the South while anti-lynching bills before Congress died; Jim Crow conditions existed in the nation's capital; segregation continued in the military; and the Ku Klux Klan persisted in America. One writer, while condemning Robeson's "fat-heated" statement about fighting the Soviets, nevertheless commented that the "racial consciousness of Americans sorely needs to be stirred up." Another believed that the "fear of Russia and of communism, as well as outside criticism of the United States, have been the Negro's greatest benefactor in recent years." Few took the stance of Robeson's friend, W. E. B. Du Bois, who praised Robeson and condemned the "sheep-like disposition, inevitably born of slavery" which Negroes showed in following white leadership.

Most reaction by both blacks and whites was hostile to Robeson, but there was an uneasy feeling exposed in the American press that there was some truth to what Robeson was saying. Would blacks fight for America in a war against the Soviet Union? In a sample of whites in several Northern cities, over 50 percent questioned Negro's loyalty to America. Members of HUAC, who had used Robeson previously as a favorite target, believed that they could attack the problem positively and leftist Paul Robeson negatively at the same time. They would conduct a hearing on the communist infiltration of minority groups and invite prominent blacks to testify about Negro loyalty and Robeson's disloyalty. Invited to testify before HUAC, among others, were Lester Granger, National Urban League head; Dr. Charles S. Johnson, President of Fisk College; Thomas W. Young, Negro publisher; and Clarence Clark, a disabled Negro veteran of World War II. Of greatest importance because of his popular stature as desegregator of America's "National Pastime," was the invitation sent to Jackie Robinson. Chairman of HUAC, John S. Wood of Georgia, telegrammed Robinson asking him to testify before his Committee "to give the lie" to statements by Paul Robeson.

By 1949, Jackie Robinson was probably the best known black in America with the possible exception of Joe Louis and Paul Robeson. At the time of the HUAC hearings on communist infiltration of minority groups, Robinson was leading the National League in batting with a .360 average and was also the top vote getter in the annual all-star balloting in his league. It was not unexpected that HUAC would ask a black of Robinson's public exposure to testify against another prominent black. According to Alvin Stokes, a black investigator for HUAC, the Committee felt it was necessary to get someone of the popular stature of Robinson to discredit Robeson.

The decision to speak out against Robeson was not an easy one for Robinson. He recounted his dilemma. If he testified he might merely be the black pawn in a white man's game which pitted one black against another, and he might be considered a "traitor" to his own people. If he did not testify he feared that Robeson's statement might discredit all blacks in the eyes of whites. At that time, Robinson had faith that whites would ultimately render justice to blacks. He chose to testify before HUAC. With advice from Branch Rickey and Lester Granger, Robinson prepared a statement which he delivered before HUAC on July 18, 1949.

Seated before the Committee, Robinson testified, rather naively but with good effect, that baseball was "as far removed from politics as anybody can possibly imagine." Referring to Robeson's statement which he had been called upon by HUAC "to combat," Robinson said:

> I can't speak for any 15,000,000 people any more than any other one person can, but I know that I've got too much invested for my wife and child and myself in the future of this country, and I and other Americans of many races and faiths have too much invested in our country's welfare, for any of us to throw it away because of a siren song sung in bass.

Robinson continued:

> But that doesn't mean that we're going to stop fighting race discrimination in this country until we've got it licked. It means that we're going to fight it all the harder because our stake in the future is so big. We can win our fight without the Communists and we don't want their help.

With those strong words he closed his testimony. Earlier in his statements he had qualified his harsh remarks by stating that Robeson should have a "right to his personal views, and if he wants to sound silly when he expresses them in public, that is his business and not mine." Acknowledging that Robeson was "still a famous ex-athlete and a great singer and actor," Robinson said that "Negroes were stirred up long before there was a Communist party and they'll stay stirred up long after the party has disappeared—unless Jim Crow has disappeared by then as well." Robinson saw progress, though slow, in black rights, pointing out that there were only seven blacks out of 400 Major League players and that only three of the sixteen Major League teams were desegregated. "We're going to keep on making progress," Robinson told the probers, "until we go the rest of the way in wiping Jim Crow out of American sports."

Robinson's testimony against Robeson was predictably praised by HUAC, which for the first time that year allowed motion and still photographers free access in the room during Robinson's testimony. The Committee obviously knew the publicity value of a sports performer well-known to Americans. Major newspapers emphasized the anti-Robeson comments of Robinson while giving little space to the pro-civil rights statements of the all-star second baseman. Newspaper accounts accomplished HUAC's objective of discrediting Robeson's Paris statement. Headlines of "ROBESON SILLY, JACKIE ROBINSON TELLS RED QUIZ" and "DODGER STAR RAPS ROBESON 'SIREN SONG' " appeared in leading Chicago and Philadelphia newspapers. The *New York Times* editorialized: "Jackie Robinson scored four hits and no errors" testifying before HUAC, while the *Washington Post* editor praised Robinson and denigrated Robeson for his "insulting libels."

Opinions expressed by blacks were not as consistent. First, some blacks were suspicious of HUAC, questioning why it had never thoroughly investigated the Ku Klux Klan or any other American fascist group. They also distrusted HUAC because its committee chair had been held by Southern racists of the likes of Martin Dies (Texas) and John Rankin (Mississippi). Commented one black writer: "How come your committee can investigate everything from Reds to second basemen, and can't investigate the Ku Klux Klan?" Second, one of their own black heroes Paul Robeson, even

though tainted, was being attacked by the white establishment. However, questionable were some of Robeson's beliefs, he was one of their own. While major white newspapers were cheering Robinson for castigating Robeson, black papers were generally cheering Robinson for advocating black civil rights and criticizing HUAC's investigation for dividing blacks against each other. "LYNCHERS OUR CHIEF ENEMY JACKIE TELLS 'RED' PROBERS" headlined the *Philadelphia Afro-American*. One of its writers claimed that the hearings were a "witchhunt." Meanwhile a Pittsburgh writer asserted that Robinson had been a "stooge" for HUAC and had put Negroes on the defensive, hamstringing the civil rights movements. Others, too, criticized Robinson. A woman from the west coast chided Robinson claiming that "the habit of 'bad mouthing' is a slavery trait and should have been outgrown ere this time." An angry individual from Boston wrote that "Paul Robeson was fighting for his people's rights when Jackie Robinson was in knee pants." If HUAC had been successful in creating a negative climate around Robeson's name, it had also created division among blacks over two of their heroes.

A POSTSCRIPT TO THE ROBESON-ROBINSON SAGA

The Robeson-Robinson confrontation added to the mounting pressure in America to cleanse itself of any sympathy for the Soviet Union. Robeson soon began his rapid decline to near oblivion. A Robeson concert in Peekskill, New York later in the summer of 1949, brought about a united effort by several military veterans groups to stop it. Concert-goers were prevented from attending the first concert attempt, and after it was given a week later, a riot resulted with hundreds injured, numerous autos and buses wrecked, and crosses burned as if it were a Ku Klux Klan rally. Concert managers soon refused to book him, and his recordings were often taken out of record shops. There was even a move by Rutgers University alumni to remove his name from the college rolls. The *American Sports Annual* deleted Robeson's name from its list of football all-American selections for the years 1917 and 1918. The Federal Bureau of Investigation continually harassed Robeson, and the Secretary of State, John Foster Dulles, had his passport cancelled—two methods used by the federal government to deny Robeson personal freedom and economic independence. The vicious attacks upon Robeson were part of the hysteria created out of the Cold War ideology of the post-World War II era. It was the same hysteria which gave rise to the demogogic character of Joseph McCarthy, who as Senator used character assassination involving the issue of communism in his rise to prominence around 1950.

By the mid-1950s, the anti-communist excesses diminished considerably. Though HUAC was still active, the Senate's censuring of McCarthy helped to control the most outrageous charges of communism in America. Robeson was still effectively blacklisted in America, however, and the denial of a passport for almost a decade placed him in a difficult economic position. He, like the Communist Party which had been legislated out of existence, was successfully silenced. But the question of equal political and social rights for blacks, for which Robeson had been active for a generation, was beginning to come to a head. The landmark Supreme Court decision of 1954, *Brown* v. *Board of Education*, overturned the earlier "separate but equal" decision. Other court actions and federal legislation soon brought resistance and physical confrontation as America faced the proposition of equal rights for all its citizens regardless of race.

Jackie Robinson increasingly spoke out for black rights and, like Robeson before him, was classified by some as an "uppity nigger." Unlike Robeson, Robinson kept his remarks within a more conservative framework. When Robinson announced publicly after the 1956 baseball season that he was retiring from baseball, he wrote:

I don't regret any part of these last 10 years. There's no reason why I should. Because of baseball I met a man like Branch Rickey and was given the opportunity to break the major-league color line. Because of baseball, I was able to speak on behalf of Negro Americans before the House Un-American Activities Committee and rebuke Paul Robeson for saying most of us Negroes would not fight for our country in a war against Russia.

Robinson soon joined the National Association for the Advancement of Colored People, and he contributed effectively as a fund raiser. A decade later he withdrew as a protest against its inflexible and conservative nature. Yet Robinson actively campaigned in the 1960 presidential election for Richard Nixon. Nixon had no strong civil rights record, and he had, like Senator Joe McCarthy, used character assassination and the communist issue to promote his popularity. Robinson eventually became disillusioned with Nixon. He also became more pessimistic about the status of American race relations.

Although Jackie Robinson never became reconciled to the beliefs of Paul Robeson, he saw something more positive in Robeson shortly before his own death. Writing in his autobiography published in 1972, titled *I Never Had It Made*, Robinson stated that he never regretted his statements about Robeson made two decades before. "But," Robinson wrote:

I have grown wiser and closer to painful truths about America's destructiveness. And I do have increased respect for Paul Robeson who, over a span of that twenty years, sacrificed himself, his career, and the wealth and comfort he once enjoyed because, I believe, he was sincerely trying to help his people.

When Jackie Robinson died on October 24, 1972, his place in history was almost assured. Paul Robeson died on January 23, 1976. Because he had tied the black rights movement in America to what he considered was a positive Soviet racial policy, he had become a political leper and was in almost total eclipse in the 1950s and 1960s. There was, indeed, a curtain of silence surrounding him. By the 1970s, and especially after his death, a growing number of individuals began to see greatness in Robeson. Even politicians, who often fear to speak out on controversial individuals and issues, began to speak of Robeson's historic concern for humanity. One of the outspoken was Congressman Andrew Young, a black who later became Ambassador to the United Nations under President Jimmy Carter. He wrote:

> Paul Robeson was the hero of my youth. . . . I can never forget the strength of conviction that helped strengthen our backs and set our feet in the path of self-liberation as a people. Paul loved people of all colors and of many nations. He loved justice, freedom, and compassion. He had no tolerance for injustice, oppression, or tyranny. Few men in their lifetime bequeath a legacy to the living.

If both Paul Robeson and Jackie Robinson, as performers, were on the cutting edge of racial reform in America, it appears that they were approaching change from different direc-

tions. Robeson wanted reform on his own terms, not necessarily those of white society. Robinson was more willing to compromise with white society for a time to accomplish positive racial goals and his own advancement. Robeson was more idealistic and unyielding, and because of it he was politically, economically, and socially alienated from the greater American society. Robinson was more realistic and pragmatic, and he fared far better socially and financially than did Robeson. What was common to both Robeson and Robinson was that they were both black performers, one an ex-athlete and an actor and singer and the other solely an athlete, who in their own ways fought for equal rights for blacks. Robinson's position as desegregator of professional baseball seems assured. Robeson's status as a crusader for black rights everywhere seems likely to rise with time. If "men will judge men by their souls and not by their skins," as W. E. B. Du Bois advocated in the early twentieth century, it appears that both Paul Robeson and Jackie Robinson, despite their acknowledged differences, will be judged not only as athletic and performing champions but as leaders in race relations as well.

21

FAMILY VIOLENCE AS HISTORY AND POLITICS, 1875–1985

LINDA GORDON

One of the most important contributions made by the contemporary women's movement has been our enhanced awareness of the incidence and dynamics of family violence throughout the nation. As the problem began to be recognized during the late 1970s and 1980s, social scientists and policymakers began to ask historical questions: Was domestic violence more prevalent today than in the past? Was child and wife abuse related to periods of social dislocation such as industrialization or urbanization? Did people in past times view violence in similar ways? Although these were recognized as important questions, historians found themselves unprepared to offer answers because they, too, had not yet come to view family violence as a significant problem.

In this essay, Linda Gordon inaugurates the historical study of family violence in modern America. Drawing upon the case records of social welfare agencies to reveal the inner workings of poorer American families, Gordon finds that the definition of domestic violence itself has been "constructed" differently over time by social workers, by the fears of middle-class society, and by the victims themselves. The problem of domestic violence, she concludes, cannot be understood apart from an understanding of what Americans have thought and believed about normative family life in this century.

This article is taken from a lecture delivered April 1988, on material covered in Linda Gordon's book on family violence, *Heroes of Their Own Lives: The Politics and History of Family Violence* (New York: Viking/Penguin, 1988). Detailed references may be found there and have been eliminated here. Reprinted by permission of the author.

In the past few decades many Americans have come to understand that family violence is a *social* problem. This has been a very important breakthrough. A century of romanticizing family life, of peddling the myth that "normal" family life is peaceful and harmonious, has led to embarrassment and shame about family violence. The result has been to punish doubly the victims of family violence by forcing them to hide their problems and to blame themselves. Sometimes even the aggressors in family violence have benefitted from this new understanding that they are not unique, allowing them to ask for help.

However, another aspect of family violence has not been understood: that it is an historical and a political problem. Most writing about child abuse proceeds as if it is obvious and unarguable what child abuse *is.* By contrast, an historical view shows that, for example, some forms of today's child abuse were yesterday's whipping; one family's child neglect is another family's standard. Without historical analysis of how family violence was constructed as a social problem, increasing concern about it is taken to mean that the incidence of family violence itself is increasing. In fact there is no conclusive evidence about trends in family violence over time. Furthermore, family violence studies today are isolated from the contributions of family history, about change and cultural variation in family patterns.

Family violence is political in a double sense. First, the very definition of what constitutes unacceptable domestic violence developed and then changed according to political moods and the force of certain political movements. Second, family conflicts were political with respect to familial power relations. By and large domestic violence grew out of intrafamily power struggles in which valuable resources and benefits were at issue. Men fought to enforce their dominance and privilege; women to get what they wanted for themselves and their children. Family violence is also influenced by extrafamilial social change and social conflict. Children were influenced by new cultural patterns which offered autonomy and values alien to their parents, and the latter fought to hold their children to more traditional norms of family life. One aspect of social change in particular—the increasing independence of women and privilege of children—has been experienced and fought out within the family in a particularly acute way.

One of the best sources for studying family violence are the case records of social-work agencies. Bias infects these records, to be sure. The agency "clients" were almost exclusively poor, largely Catholic immigrants, and predominantly female. The charity workers, later professional social workers, were well educated, were at first exclusively and later predominantly white native-born Protestants, and their leadership was exclusively male. These workers were the authors of the case records, and their views of clients were often disdainful, paternalistic at best, ignorant and obtuse in many cases. Yet ironically this very bias helps us understand family violence. The bias shows that family violence cannot be conceived as an objective, static problem, and forces us to realize that the very concept of family violence is a product of conflict and negotiation between people genuinely suffering from domestic violence and social control agents attempting to change the behavior of people they consider unruly and deviant.

Three major themes arise from an examination of the case records. First, family violence was originally constructed as a social problem in the 1870s in response to complex historical changes. Second, in the century since its first recognition as a social problem, the campaign against family violence has had different meanings related to changing political and social contexts. Third, these meanings always represented a negotiation between the needs of clients, usually the women and children victims of such violence, and the social-control agendas of child-welfare agencies.

Child abuse was "discovered" as a social problem in the 1870s. We can be certain that many children had been mistreated by parents before this, but not until this decade was there a widespread alarm about it. As a result, organizations, usually called Societies for the Prevention of Cruelty to Children (SPCCs) were established throughout the United States and Europe. Many new social conditions contributed to this concern, particularly the wretched conditions of urban poverty and unemployment in growing industrial cities.

The women's rights movement exerted a major political influence on the SPCCs. In fact, every time child welfare movements have arisen, every time there have been concerns with the sufferings of children and demands for greater social responsibility for children—whether the immediate demand was education or health or welfare—feminism has been influential. There are several reasons for this. One is that women have been responsible for child-raising in most societies, and that women far more than men have tended to internalize the needs of children, to be able to see children as subjects and not merely objects. A second reason is that feminist movements have had an interest in criticizing the oppression that takes place within the family, opening the family to scrutiny. As heads of families, many men have benefitted from the privacy that families provide them and have been resistant to criticizing intrafamily relations. Third, the women's rights movement of the nineteenth century, like that of today, extended its critique of male domination to social and cultural violence in general and to corporal punishment in particular. As women demanded more autonomy in their role as child-raisers in the nineteenth century, they also mounted a propaganda campaign arguing for more "tender" methods of disciplining children and against the heavy use of physical coercion.

The anti–child-abuse campaign was anti-patriarchal in its very conception. A word about the definition of patriarchy is necessary here. In the 1970s a new definition of that term came into use: patriarchy became a synonym for male supremacy, for "sexism." In its earlier, historical and more specific sense, patriarchy

referred to a family form in which fathers had control over all other family members—children, women, and servants—a control which flowed from the fathers' monopolization of economic resources. The patriarchal family presupposed a family mode of production, as among peasants, artisans or farmers, in which individuals did not work individually as wage laborers. That historical patriarchy defined a set of parent-child relations as much as it did relations between the sexes, for the children rarely had opportunities for economic independence except by inheriting the family property, trade or craft.

Thus, the claim of an organization such as an SPCC to speak on behalf of children's rights, its claim to the license to intervene in parental treatment of children, was an attack on patriarchal power, and very much one of the contributions of the nineteenth-century women's rights movement. At the same time, the anti–child-abuse movement had class and cultural meanings that were by no means so progressive. Agencies like the SPCCs were attempting to impose elite, white Protestant values on working-class immigrant families. For example, the Massachusetts Society for Prevention of Cruelty to Children (MSPCC) attempted to enforce norms of proper parenting that were not only alien to the cultural legacy of their "clients" but also flew in the face of many of the economic necessities of their lives. MSPCC agents prosecuted cases in which cruelty to children was caused, in their view, by children's labor: girls doing housework and child care, often required to stay home from school by their parents; boys and girls working in shops, peddling on the streets; boys working for organ grinders or lying about their ages to enlist in the navy. In the pre-World War I era, the enemy of the truant officers was usually parents, not children. To immigrants from peasant backgrounds it seemed irrational and blasphemous that adult women should work while able-bodied children should be idle. In another example of cultural disagreement, the MSPCC was opposed to the common immigrant practice of leaving children unattended, and allowing them to play and wander in the streets. This violated the Society's norm of domesticity for women and children; proper middle-class children in those days did not—at least not in the cities—play outside without being attended.

The style of mothering and fathering that charity and social workers imposed was new. Mothers were supposed to be tender, gentle, to protect their children from immoral influences. The "child savers" considered yelling, rude language, or sexually explicit talk to be forms of cruelty to children. Fathers were to provide models of emotional containment, to be relatively uninvolved with children; their failure to provide was often interpreted as a character flaw, no matter what the evidence of widespread, structural unemployment.

The MSPCC's model of parenting at the turn of the century had little room for cultural variety. The agency staff, for example, hated the eternal cabbage of Irish cooking, and the garlic and olive oil of Italian cooking, considering this food unhealthy, overstimulating, aphrodisiacal. They were unable to distinguish alcoholics and heavy drinkers from moderate wine and beer drinkers, and they believed that any woman who touched even a drop of spirits was a degenerate and unfit parent. The agents specifically associated many of these forms of depravity with Catholicism. Agents were convinced of the subnormal intelligence of most immigrant and especially non-English-speaking clients, and the agents' comments and expectations in this early period could easily be transposed for similar views of blacks in the mid-twentieth century. Particularly these child welfare specialists misunderstood and disapproved of non-nuclear child-raising patterns: children raised by grandmothers, complex households composed of children from several different marriages (or, worse, out-of-wedlock relationships) and children sent temporarily to other households.

The peasant backgrounds of so many of the "hyphenated" Americans created a situation in which ethnic bias could not easily be separated from class bias. Class misunderstanding, moreover, took a form specific to urban capitalism: a failure to grasp the actual economic circumstances of this immigrant proletariat and subproletariat. Unemployment was not yet understood to be a structural characteristic of industrial capitalism. Nor were disease, overcrowding, crime and—above all—dependence understood as part of the system. For social workers they were more often personal failings.

Given these biases, it is not surprising that some cases of cruelty to children arose from disagreement about proper child-raising, and that others arose from the inevitable cruelties of poverty—many of them experienced by parents as well, such as disease and malnutrition, children left unattended while their parents worked, children not warmly dressed, houses without heat, bedding crawling with vermin, unchanged diapers, injuries left without medical treatment. But at the same time it would be a great mistake to conclude that family violence was only a figment of cultural bias or an inevitable result of poverty. On the contrary, the evidence indicates that family violence was experienced as a problem by its participants who—despite their awareness of the discrimination they were likely to encounter at the hands of the SPCCs—eagerly sought the help of these agencies.

From very early on in the history of these agencies, the major sources of complaints were family members themselves, primarily women and secondarily children. For women and children, the oppressiveness of the class discrimination they experienced from the agencies was by no means always worse than the oppression they experienced within their families from husbands, mothers, or fathers. Women manipulated agencies concerned with child abuse to get help against wife abuse. Moreover, in child-abuse cases we see women's own violence, quite in contrast to the nineteenth-century feminist image of women as naturally tender and peaceful, and women's self-criticism of themselves as child-raisers, again in contrast to the feminist view of women as natural mothers. Some of that self-criticism was a self-destructive guilt, but some of it was instead an honest expression of frustration that they were unable to live up to their standards for good motherhood. Child protection agencies may have seen themselves as teaching good standards to poor and ignorant parents, but in fact they were encountering people with their own strong views about good family life, who hoped to use these agencies in their own interest.

It was in this context of class, ethnic, and gender conflict that family violence was first defined. Family violence has been defined outside a context of political and social conflict. In every time period, family violence has been defined and treated in a complex negotiation, involving charity and professional workers and the fears of the social groups they represented, and the needs of family violence victims, women and children, looking for help.

PERIODIZATION

This historical construction of family violence can be traced through five approximate, overlapping periods.

1. The late nineteenth century, when family violence agencies were part of the general charity organization, moral reform movement.
2. The Progressive Era of the early twentieth century, when family violence was assimilated to an environmentalist analysis and reform program.
3. The Great Depression of the 1930s, when intrafamily violence was radically deemphasized in favor of amelioration of economic hardship.
4. The 1940s and 1950s, when psychiatric categories and intensely "pro-family" values dominated the social work approach to family problems.
5. The 1960s and 1970s, when feminist and

youth movements began a critique of the family which forced open doors that hid family problems in various closets.

NINETEENTH-CENTURY CHILD SAVING

Nineteenth-century definitions of domestic violence mirrored the values of the social movements that produced them. They reflected the emphasis on illegitimate male power characteristic of feminists, as well as the moralism and class arrogance of campaigns to help the poor. Cruel parents, both in SPCC rhetoric and in the labeling SPCC agents used, were mainly drunkards, and drunkards were mainly immigrants. Male cruelty was depicted as sexual and physical violence resulting from drink. The image of maternal cruelty was a negligent mother, lying abed in a drunken stupor while her children cried for food.

Because of the emphasis on drink, and the envisioning of cruelty to children as something that the immigrant poor did, never the respectable classes, even antifeminist moral reformers could include wife-beating within the jurisdiction of the SPCCs without taking the feminist message to heart. In practice, however, the inclusion of wife-beating was mainly accomplished by the demands of the poor client mothers. These often accused their husbands of child-beating in order to draw agency workers into their homes to witness violence against women.

Moreover, up to at least 1910, child-protection agencies identified and prosecuted many incest cases, virtually all of them attacks by men on girls. Incest was well known not only to all child-welfare workers but to the public as a major category of family violence. Its causes and patterns were attributed to male depravity in the same manner as wife beating.

THE PROGRESSIVE ERA

Social work as a whole was becoming professionalized during the Progressive era, rejecting its previous association with upper-class charity volunteers. In theory its diagnoses became scientific and environmentalist. These changes in professional discourse have led some historians to assume that nineteenth-century class and ethnic bias diminished, but a closer look casts doubt. Blaming cruel behavior on the environment did not produce a more respectful attitude towards different cultures, and certainly no humility about the role of professionals in prescribing the correct reform program. At the same time the Progressive reformers' belief in governmental intervention increased the power of child-protection agencies to determine arbitrarily what constituted inadequate child-raising and when parental custody of children could be severed.

The most important operative change in child-protection work was the discovery of child neglect (as opposed to abuse) as the major category of improper parenting. Many sorts of stress—poverty, unemployment, illness, alcoholism—contributed to child neglect. So did intrafamily problems, such as marital violence and single motherhood. Indeed, single mothers were so overrepresented in child neglect cases that this might be described as the first "discovery" of woman-headed households as a social problem.

Yet in their conflicts with social workers, many so-called neglectful parents were influential in teaching social workers about child neglect and its remedies. These mothers barraged child welfare agencies with demands for help, for child care, for relief, for collection of child support payments. They were often victimized by their search for help, losing their children because they confessed their own "negligence" to powerful agencies. But in taking that risk they contributed their views of what were minimal standards for children and demonstrated that the poor, drunk, and "depraved" were by no means without aspirations for their children.

The responses of parents also helped expose a contradiction in child-protection work which was discovered in this period and continues to the present: the difficulty in distinguishing culpable parental negligence from the inevitable results of poverty. As some social workers began to admit this difficulty, they met a fundamental contradiction in "scientific" child-protection work: the notion of child neglect implies a commitment to guarantee a minimal standard of living for all children. Yet this goal clashed with the principles of private child-raising, an economic system based on free enterprise, and the norm of economic autonomy for each family—a system that defined public aid as a necessary evil that should be kept to a minimum and made as uncomfortable as possible for recipients. The resulting solutions created one of the bitterest ironies of child-protection work: the usual solutions involved taking children away from parents rather than helping parents, despite an ideology that children need mothers. Thus the social worker penalized not only the culprits but the victims.

The Progressive era produced a cover-up of wife beating as a form of family violence. The old feminist diatribes against drunken, brutal men came to seem moralistic and unscientific. Instead marital violence was portrayed as mutual, resulting from environmental stress, lack of education or lack of mental hygiene. In many cases, social work agencies undertook regular supervision of immigrant households, attempting to "Americanize" them through instruction in "proper" child care and housekeeping methods.

The cover-up extended to that other highly gendered form of family violence, incest. In a pattern familiar to those who have followed the public alarm about sexual assault of children in the 1980s, in the decades from 1910 to 1930 sexual assault by strangers was emphasized and incest—that is, sexual assault within the family—deemphasized. Sexual assaults were blamed on "dirty old men," who were considered sick. This paralleled, of course, the decline of a feminist analysis of male domination in the family. Incest and sexual abuse were fit into a new category, sexual delinquency. In this new understanding, the victims, almost always girls, were labeled as sexually deviant and criminal, even when they had been raped or mistreated at young ages, and were often incarcerated in industrial schools.

THE GREAT DEPRESSION

One of the major characteristics of Depression-era social work was a policy of defending the "conventional" nuclear family. This meant working against all centrifugal forces in the family, at the expense of asking women and children to suppress their own aspirations. The great advances in provision of general welfare necessitated by the massive unemployment of the 1930s have tended to occlude other dimensions in which social policy at that time moved in a conservative direction. In treatment of conflict between the sexes, Depression-era family violence agencies strengthened still further the Progressive-era tendency to deemphasize male violence as a significant family problem. A sympathy arose for the unemployed husband and for the stress and role conflict that frequently engendered his violence. Remarkably less sympathy was expressed for the situation of working mothers doing double days in the attempts to hold their families together. Indeed, women were consistently held responsible for the treatment of children and the general mood of the family, as men were not. The preferred treatment for family violence were reconciliation and economic aid. The very meaning of family violence had shifted: it was seen as a product of forces outside the family.

Indeed, violence altogether was deemphasized, and the SPCCs devoted themselves primarily to child neglect, defined in turn primarily as physical deprivation. Child-protection workers became clients' advocates to relief agencies. These changing definitions were expressions not only of the ideology of the social-work establishment, but also of clients' demands. In the Depression clients were more effective at doing what they had so often tried

before—forcing agencies to go beyond their own jurisdictions, to see the impossibility of solving violence problems through counseling or punishment while ignoring poverty. But relief alone was no answer to family violence. Poverty creates stress but does not cause family violence. After all, most poor children are neither abused nor neglected. While the economic relief offered by New Deal agencies certainly contributed to family wellbeing and therefore to family harmony, the victims of family violence may have suffered the more because of the widespread denial of child abuse and wife-beating.

WORLD WAR II AND THE 1950S

Social-work policy through the 1940s and 1950s continued to emphasize the need to preserve the conventional nuclear family and to deny evidence of its imperfections. These decades represented a low point in public awareness of family violence problems and in the status of child-protection work within the social work profession. Family case workers were, however, no longer reluctant to inquire into the roots of intrafamily conflict, but did so now in psychiatric categories. The goal of the new psychiatric therapy was individual maturity, and this was often measured by the patient's ability to adjust to a nuclear family life. The roots of most interpersonal problems were sought in individual "complexes," not in cultural attributes or economic problems. The most notorious example of the psychiatrization of family violence work was in the blaming of wives for their abuse by husbands—again, a double standard in setting requirements for individual responsibility for their actions. The "nagging wife" of traditional patriarchal folklore was now transformed into a woman of complex mental ailments: failure to accept her own femininity and attempting to compete with her husband; frustration as a result of her own frigidity; a need to control resulting from her own sexual repression; masochism; failure to achieve full genital sexuality. These neuroses could not be cured by relying on friends but required diagnosis and treatment by professionals. Moreover, these neuroses demanded treatment not of the assailant but of the victim.

The psychiatrization of family violence work also affected problems with children. Child neglect cases were increasingly seen as products not of poverty but of neurotic rejection or negligence. Indeed, social workers now created a new category of cruelty to children: emotional neglect. This was a gendered form of child abuse that only mothers could inflict. Emotional neglect as a category allowed the mystification of incest in a new way, the "discovery" of emotional incest, or seductiveness, between mother and child. Thus, child-protection policies that rarely admitted the occurrence of actual sexual molestation of children nevertheless evinced interest in symbolic sexual behavior involving intimate emotional relations indulged in by women.

Delinquency was still a major category for social workers, with greater interest now in boys' gang and criminal behavior as well as girls' sexual behavior. Here too women were blamed. Delinquency was less often interpreted as environmentally caused than in the Progressive era and much more as the result of intrafamily patterns. Working mothers were the main culprits, with far less attention to abusive fathers.

THE 1960S AND 1970S

In the 1960s family violence was rediscovered and reinvented in a new social context. Professionally, the first wave of reformers concerned with cruelty to children had been charity volunteers, later social workers, who used the issue in building their group prestige. Child abuse was an effective fund-raising issue. The MSPCC, for example, was, until at least 1920, one of the best endowed, most upper-class charities in Boston. Later child-protection work helped in the development of the new social-work profession. Family violence was defined in terms of problems that social work could solve. In the 1960s, by contrast, child abuse was seized upon by doctors, particularly pediatricians and psychiatrists, who medicalized its diagnosis and treatment. A second context of the rediscovery and redefinition of family violence in the last few decades was the civil rights, antiwar, student, and women's movements, all of them challenging family norms in different ways. Indeed, the issue of family violence offers another vantage point from which to evaluate the influence of the social movements of the 1960s, often underestimated when that influence is measured strictly in terms of institutional or legislative change. Combined, these movements raised critical questions about the sanctity of family privacy, the privileged position of the male head of family, and the importance of family togetherness at all costs. The movements created an atmosphere in which child abuse, wife-beating and incest could be pulled out of the closet. The atmosphere was pervaded by a critique of more accepted forms of violence as well: cultural, military and political. Wife-beating, for example, is now viewed by an increasing segment of the population, including professionals and law-enforcement officials, as entirely unacceptable in all circumstances. Anger against child abuse shades into a critique of military aggression and media macho, into a rejection of all physical punishment, and into demands for better social supports for child-raising.

In challenging the ideology of separate public and private spheres, the new social movements of the 1950s, 1960s, and 1970s also challenged the power of professionals to define and then cure social problems. An antiauthoritarian interpretive framework stimulated collective citizens' action on family violence. Self-help projects such as battered women's shelters and Parents Anonymous competed with professionals in aiding victims. These projects render evident what was previously disguised—the role of victims, or "clients," in defining the problem and the remedies.

By tracing attitudes towards family violence through five periods, we can see that it is a problem inseparable from the family norms of a whole society or from the overall political conflicts in that society. It is a changing historical and cultural issue, not a biological or sociobiological universal. About some individual cases of family violence there may be general agreement on standards and definitions, but as a public issue, family violence has been a virtual lightning rod for different social and political perspectives. First defined as a social problem in the 1870s, an era of a powerful women's rights movement, campaigns against child abuse and wife-beating have tended to lose momentum and support, even to disappear altogether, when feminist influence has been in decline. In such periods family togetherness is often sought at the expense of individual rights and by ignoring intrafamily problems, rather than by exposing and attacking them. Alternatively, family violence problems were redefined as if they were outside the family in order to present myths of the harmony of the normative family. Such a redefinition may be happening now. Historically campaigns against family violence have had multiple functions: alleviating suffering, instilling and enforcing dominant norms of proper family life, and helping to strengthen professional social control methods.

22

THE VIETNAM WAR, THE LIBERALS, AND THE OVERTHROW OF LBJ

ALLEN J. MATUSOW

The Vietnam War dominated much of American life in the decade between 1964 and 1974. With an active draft supplying the bulk of the quarter of a million American troops and advisers fighting in Vietnam, three presidents—Kennedy, Johnson, and Nixon—sought to project American military power into Southeast Asia in an effort to "contain communism."

Between 1954, when the United States assumed the role of supporter of the corrupt but anti-Communist South Vietnamese regime, and the early 1960s American involvement in Vietnam was limited to small numbers of military and civilian advisers. But beginning in 1962, when President John F. Kennedy created the Green Berets, a special counterinsurgency force, American involvement in the region took the path of escalation. Slowly at first, but with increasing speed after the mid-1960s, the American military presence grew until daily reports from the war zone dominated the nightly television news.

As the war continued, with little evidence of success or purpose, growing numbers of Americans began to question the propriety of the war. At the same time, students and other Americans, including many church leaders, organized the most effective antiwar movement in American history. By the late 1960s antiwar protest took on epic proportions as tens of thousands of Americans—men and women, young and old alike—marched across the country to end the war and bring American troops home.

One of the Vietnam War's more famous casualties was President Lyndon Johnson. In the arrogance of his belief that he could convert the peasants of Vietnam into his image of upwardly mobile American farmers, Johnson escalated U.S. involvement on an unprecedented scale. Mindless of local conditions and the history of the Vietnamese people, Johnson and his advisors committed billions of dollars to a war that many military analysts agreed could not be won. As Allen J. Matusow shows in this essay, Johnson's arrogance cost him the support of American liberals and ultimately the presidency itself.

From Allen J. Matusow, *The Unraveling of America: A History of Liberalism in the 1960s* (New York: Harper & Row, 1984). Copyright 1984 © by Allen J. Matusow. Reprinted by permission of Harper & Row, Publishers, Inc.

In April 1965, three months after Lyndon Johnson made his decision to bomb North Vietnam, Democratic Senator Wayne Morse of Oregon predicted that Johnson's war policy would send him "out of office the most discredited President in the history of the nation." Given the popularity of both the war and the president at the time, Morse's prophecy seemed absurd on its face. But, as Vietnam dragged on month after month, it did indeed become an acid eroding Johnson's political base, until in the end it destroyed his presidency. The first constituency to be alienated by Vietnam—and the most dangerous opponent of Johnson's war policy—proved to be the liberal intellectuals.

At first glance the split between the president and the intellectuals seemed surprising. He was, after all, attempting to govern in the liberal tradition not only in his conduct of domestic policy but in foreign affairs as well. They must hate him, he came to believe, not really for anything he did but because of who he was—a crude Texas cowboy without a Harvard degree. What he failed to understand was that his liberalism and theirs—apparently so similar in 1964—thereafter rapidly diverged, his remaining rooted in the ideas of the 1950s, theirs moving far beyond.

The root of the difficulty was the breakup of the Cold War consensus. In the 1950s, of course, liberal intellectuals typically had embraced the Cold War as a holy crusade, becoming in the process staunch defenders of the American way of life. Even after Sputnik in 1957, when the intellectuals began denouncing the nation for its materialism and complacency, they did so primarily to goad the people into greater sacrifice for the struggle against world Communism. The first sign of restlessness began to appear around 1960. That was the year, for example, when Norman Podhoretz, a New York intellectual who had been a dutiful Cold War liberal but now felt the old ideas going stale, "going dead," became editor of the influential magazine *Commentary*. Daring to open his early issues to dissident voices,

he discovered among the intellectuals who wrote for his magazine and read it "a hunger for something new and something radical." Radicalism was hardly the term to describe the outlook of the intellectuals in the Kennedy era, but they were more open to novelty, more willing to acknowledge the flaws in American society, than they had been for years. In 1963, when Kennedy and Khrushchev moved toward détente following the Cuban missile crisis, the international tension that for so long had sustained the Cold War mentality began to dissipate, the old obsession to bore. Liberal intellectuals supported Johnson's 1964 presidential campaign because they believed he shared not only their renewed commitment to social justice but their growing willingness to reach an accommodation with the Russians.

Strains in Johnson's relations with the liberals first appeared in February 1965 when Johnson launched his air war over North Vietnam. Immediately the *New Republic*, a leading journal of liberal opinion, and the Americans for Democratic Action (ADA), the leading liberal organization, condemned the bombing and called for a negotiated settlement. Johnson was perplexed by the criticism since he correctly believed that he was merely applying in Vietnam the doctrine of containment so recently espoused by the liberals themselves. He did not grasp that that doctrine had suddenly fallen from fashion. Among the prominent liberal intellectuals who attempted to account for the shifting views of their community were Hans Morgenthau, an academic specialist in foreign affairs, member of the ADA board, and an early and formidable war critic; Reinhold Niebuhr, the renowned theologian and a founder of ADA, ailing but still influential; Arthur Schlesinger, Jr., a historian, former White House aide to Kennedy and Johnson, half-hearted defender of the war in 1965, but a leading foe by 1966; John Kenneth Galbraith, the Harvard economist, Kennedy's ambassador to India, and in 1967 the ADA chairman; Richard Goodwin, a precocious speech writer for Johnson till September 1965, and a war critic by the following spring; and Richard Rovere, the prestigious political correspondent of *The New Yorker*, a late but important convert to the dove side of the war argument.

The liberal intellectuals did not apologize for their past support of the Cold War. So long as Communist parties everywhere had subordinated themselves to the malign purposes of the Soviet Union, every Communist gain threatened American security. But times had changed, the liberals said. The Communist world was now "polycentric" (many-centered), a situation resulting from the Sino-Soviet split and the emergence of conflicting national aspirations among Communist states. Wrote Schlesinger, "Communism is no longer a unified, coordinated, centralized conspiracy." According to Rovere, since Tito's break with Stalin in 1948, the U.S. should have known that "international Communism" was a myth, "that national interest was more powerful than ideology, and that while we might on occasion find it advisable to resist the outward thrust of certain Communist nations, it made absolutely no sense to have a foreign policy directed against an alliance that did not exist." In short, it was no longer necessary to oppose every Communist initiative on every part of the globe.

With the exception of Morgenthau, who favored recognizing spheres of influence, these intellectuals continued to advocate containing China. But they denied that the war in Vietnam followed logically from this policy. Secretary of State Dean Rusk's opinion to the contrary, China was not the enemy there. The war in South Vietnam, they argued, was primarily a civil war, pitting indigenous revolutionaries against the corrupt and repressive regime in Saigon. If the Communists won, Vietnam might well become a bulwark against the spread of Chinese influence in the region. As a practical matter, the U.S. could not win. Escalation on the ground in the South could easily be offset by the enemy and would do nothing to remedy the defects of the Saigon government. Bombing the North would merely strengthen the

enemy's will to fight. If Johnson proceeded on the course of escalation, he would destroy the country he was trying to save or else provoke war with China.

The war, the liberals said, was not a result of American imperialism but a mistake of policy deriving from obsolete assumptions about international Communism. Unfortunately, it was a mistake not easily remedied. Liberals rejected unilateral withdrawal on the grounds that it would mean abandonment of America's friends in the South, a blow to U.S. prestige, and maybe even the rise at home of a new Joe McCarthy to exploit the frustrations attending defeat. The liberal solution was a negotiated settlement—the middle course, they called it. Stop the foolish bombing in the North, since Hanoi demanded it as a precondition for negotiations. Convince Ho Chi Minh that the U.S. could not be dislodged by force. Offer the Vietcong a seat at the conference table and a role in the postwar political life of South Vietnam. It was possible, of course, that negotiations would fail. In that event, said Galbraith, "We must be prepared to defend for the time being the limited areas that are now secure." Indeed, on close inspection, it turned out that the liberals were waist deep in the Big Muddy along with LBJ and were no more certain than he of getting back to shore. The difference was that they thought the war was all a big mistake, and he was there on principle.

As opposition to the war among the intellectuals mounted, so did their impatience with the administration's response to the great racial and urban crisis that was tearing the country apart. As they never would have done during the American celebration that had characterized the heyday of the Cold War, liberals were now earnestly discussing the menace of corporate monopoly, redistribution of income, and a Marshall Plan for the cities. In its January 1967 issue *Commentary* ran both a long article by Theodore Draper attacking Johnson's foreign policy for its "willingness to use and abuse naked military power" and an essay by the Keynesian economist Robert Lekachman summarizing the case of many liberal intellectuals against the president's domestic policies. Lekachman wrote:

> Possibly Mr. Johnson went just about as far as a conservative politician in a conservative, racist country could have gone. The Great Society has distributed the nation's income even less equally than it was distributed before 1960. It has enlarged the prestige and influence of the business community. It has lost its token bouts with racism and poverty. The Great Society, never a giant step beyond the New Deal which was President Johnson's youthful inspiration, has ground to a halt far short of a massive attack on urban blight, far short of the full integration of Negroes into American society, and far short of a genuine assault upon poverty and deprivation.

Where liberal intellectuals led, liberal politicians usually followed. But politicians skeptical of the war in Vietnam initially hesitated to tangle with a president to whom most were bound by ties of party loyalty and whose vindictive character was legend. In 1965 even senators held their tongues, excepting of course Oregon's Wayne Morse and Alaska's Ernest Gruening, the lone opponents of the 1964 Gulf of Tonkin Resolution. Among those who privately worried but publicly acquiesced in Johnson's war policy were Senators Mike Mansfield, George McGovern, Frank Church, Joseph Clark, Eugene McCarthy, and J. William Fulbright. Fulbright was the pivotal figure. If he moved into the open against Johnson, the rest would follow.

A senator from the ex-Confederate state of Arkansas, Fulbright was a gentleman of inherited wealth, excellent education, and illiberal record on matters of race and social reform. But for more than twenty years, on matters of foreign policy, Fulbright had been the leading spokesman in Congress for the views of the liberal community. Though he had had his share of arguments with presidents, he was by nature a contemplative rather than a combative man, a Senate club member who played by the rules. Fulbright's early opinions on Vietnam were hardly heretical. In March 1964, in a wide-ranging speech attacking Cold War mythology, he paused over Vietnam long enough to make a few hawkish observations. The allies were too weak militarily to obtain "the independence of a non-Communist South Vietnam" through negotiations, he said. The only "realistic options" were to hasten the buildup of the regime in the South or to expand the war, "either by the direct commitment of large numbers of American troops or by equipping the South Vietnamese Army to attack North Vietnamese territory." In August 1964 Fulbright sponsored the Gulf of Tonkin Resolution, which gave Johnson authority to expand the war.

For reasons unknown, Fulbright had second thoughts about escalation once it actually began. Publicly in the spring of 1965 he backed Johnson's policy, though he called for a temporary bombing halt to induce Hanoi to negotiate. Privately, he warned his old friend in the White House against waging war on North Vietnam and tempted him with the vision of a Communist Vietnam hostile to China. Johnson seemed bored by Fulbright's conversation. Fulbright gave a Senate speech in June that both criticized the bombing and praised Johnson's statesmanship. In July Johnson began the massive infusion of ground troops into South Vietnam.

Fulbright's first real attack on the Johnson administration was occasioned not by Vietnam but by policy in the Dominican Republic. In April 1965 Johnson sent U.S. troops into the midst of a developing civil war, ostensibly to protect Americans but really to prevent a possible Communist takeover. Fulbright brooded over this intervention, held secret hearings on it, and finally in September delivered a powerful Senate speech attacking the administration's conduct as ruthless and lacking in candor. The president promptly ended all pretense of consulting the chairman of the Foreign Relations Committee and cut him socially.

As Fulbright edged toward open rebellion

on the issue of the war, so did the other Senate doves, almost all of whom were liberal Democrats. This was probably one reason why Johnson halted the bombing of North Vietnam on Christmas Eve, 1965, and launched a well-advertised peace offensive allegedly to persuade Hanoi to negotiate. The State Department moved closer to Hanoi's conditions for negotiations in early January, and both sides scaled down ground action in South Vietnam. Diplomats in several capitals worked to bring the wary antagonists together. But on January 24, 1966, Johnson hinted to a group of congressional leaders that he might soon resume the bombing. Two days later fifteen senators, all of them liberal Democrats, sent a letter to Johnson urging him to continue the pause. Fulbright and Mansfield did not sign but were on record with similar views. On January 29, Johnson ordered the air attack to recommence. The episode convinced many liberals that Johnson's talk about peace masked his private determination to win total military victory.

In February 1966 Fulbright held televised hearings on the war. The scholar-diplomat George Kennan and the retired general James Gavin argued the case against it on grounds of American self-interest. Dean Rusk and General Maxwell Taylor parried the thrusts of liberal committee members now openly critical of Johnson's policy. Neither side drew blood in debate, but by helping legitimize dissent, the Fulbright hearings were a net loss for Johnson. Fulbright, meantime, was reading, talking to experts, and rethinking first principles. In the spring of 1966 he took to the lecture platform to hurl thunderbolts at orthodoxy. Revised and published as a book later in the year, Fulbright's lectures were a critique of American foreign policy far more advanced than any yet produced by the liberal academicians.

"Gradually but unmistakably America is showing signs of that arrogance of power which has afflicted, weakened, and in some cases destroyed great nations in the past," Fulbright said. Harnessing her might to a crusading ideology, America had overextended herself abroad and was neglecting vital tasks at home. Americans meant well overseas, Fulbright conceded, but they often did more harm than good, especially in the Third World. A conservative people, Americans supported necessary social revolutions in traditional societies only if they were peaceful, that is, in "our own shining image." To violent revolutions, which "seem to promise greater and faster results," Americans reacted with automatic hostility or panic. Fulbright was hardly an apologist for revolutions, but neither would he oppose them, even if they were led by Communists. Fulbright dared to find much that was praiseworthy in Castro's Cuba and even extended sympathy to the aims of the Chinese revolutionaries, whose regime he would recognize de facto. In Vietnam, he said, the U.S. had blundered into a war against Communism in the only country in the world "which won freedom from colonial rule under communist leadership." Fulbright favored a negotiated settlement that would provide self-determination for South Vietnam through the mechanism of a referendum.

President Johnson had expected his main trouble to come from hawks who wanted to escalate faster than he did. Stung by the sweeping attacks of Fulbright and other doves, he resorted to a scoundrel's last refuge. Before a friendly audience of Democratic politicians in Chicago mid-May 1966, Johnson defended the war as a patriotic effort to secure lasting peace by punishing aggression and then said, "There will be some 'Nervous Nellies' and some who will become frustrated and bothered and break ranks under the strain, and some will turn on their leaders, and on their country, and on our own fighting men. . . . But I have not the slightest doubt that the courage and the dedication and the good sense of the wise American people will ultimately prevail." The attack failed to silence the critics. The majority of the people still backed the war, but not with the passion aroused by wars of the past. Fulbright continued to assault the premises of American foreign policy and, indirectly, the president who was acting on them. Confronted with irreconcilable views of world politics, members of the liberal public in ever-increasing numbers deserted the president and sided with the senator.

To make matters worse for Johnson, he faced a personal as well as an intellectual challenge to his party leadership. When Robert Kennedy emerged from mourning in early 1964, he discovered a remarkable fact. Despite his squeaky voice, diffident public manner, private shyness, and reputation as a ruthless backroom operator, he was the sole beneficiary of his brother's political estate. In him resided the hopes of millions who believed in the myth of Camelot and longed for a Kennedy restoration. Robert Kennedy believed the myth himself and shared the longing. Lyndon Johnson, however, despised Kennedy personally and made himself the great obstacle to the younger man's ambitions. After Johnson denied him the vice-presidential nomination in 1964, Kennedy repaired to New York, where he successfully ran for the Senate. Soon there grew up around him what the political columnists called the Kennedy party—Kennedy loyalists still in the bureaucracy, some senators, New Frontiersmen out of favor, and lesser politicians, lawyers, and professors scattered around the country. Most of the Kennedy loyalists were liberals, but by no means all liberals were Kennedy loyalists. Robert Kennedy, after all, had been an ally of Joe McCarthy, an advocate of wiretapping, too zealous a pursuer of the Teamster chief Jimmy Hoffa, and a frequent offender of liberal sensibilities. But liberals unhappy with Johnson needed a popular leader, and Kennedy needed to broaden his party base. The one issue guaranteed to bring them together was Vietnam.

The issue posed problems for Kennedy. As a Cabinet officer, he had been an enthusiastic student of guerrilla warfare and strong supporter of his brother's counterinsurgency program in South Vietnam. When Johnson escalated in 1965, Kennedy questioned less the attempt to rescue South Vietnam by force of arms than the tendency to subordinate political to military considerations in fighting the war. Speaking at the graduation ceremony of the International Police Academy in July, he said, "I think the history of the last 20 years demonstrates beyond doubt that our approach to revolutionary war must be political—political first, political last, political always." To avoid offending Johnson, he excised from his prepared text the view that "victory in a revolutionary war is won not by escalation but by de-escalation." Kennedy waited one whole year after escalation before putting real distance between his position and Johnson's. It bothered Kennedy that, when Fulbright asked Rusk during the televised hearings of February 1966 to state the options other than "surrender or annihilation" that he was offering the Vietcong, Rusk had replied, "They do have an alternative of quitting, of stopping being an agent of Hanoi and receiving men and arms from the North." The war could go on forever if this was the American requirement for peace. So Kennedy decided to propose another option. On February 19, 1966, he became the first senator to suggest a negotiated settlement that would give the Vietcong "a share of power and responsibility"—in what he did not say. Assuming he meant the government of Vietnam, the administration dismissed the idea contemptuously. Kennedy's proposal, said Vice President Humphrey, would be like putting "a fox in the chicken coop" or "an arsonist in a fire department." Kennedy spent the next week clarifying and qualifying, and though he retreated some, he was clearly moving toward the peace wing of his party.

Strange things were happening to Bobby Kennedy. Perhaps prolonged grief deepened his social sympathies, perhaps he was trying in his own life to vindicate his brother's legend—or outdo it. Whatever the cause, Kennedy plunged into the currents of change that were swirling through America in the mid-1960s, currents that were altering the perspective of liberalism and passing Johnson by. Kennedy opened a running dialogue with students, made a friend of Tom Hayden, felt the yearnings of the poor and the black for power and dignity, and took unnecessary political risks. Blood donations for the Vietcong? Burial for a Communist war hero in Arlington Cemetery? Why not? he asked. Kennedy went to South Africa in mid-1966 to aid the opponents of apartheid. He attacked administration witnesses at Senate hearings in August for unresponsiveness to the poor. He flew to California to stand with Cesar Chavez in his fight to unionize the grape pickers. A man who risked his life scaling mountains and defying tropical storms on the Amazon, Kennedy was becoming an existentialist in politics, defining himself in action and moving where his heart told him to go.

As Kennedy and Johnson edged closer toward political combat, their personal relations worsened. In February 1967 *Newsweek* erroneously reported that Kennedy had brought back from a recent trip to Paris a peace feeler from Hanoi. The story enraged Johnson, who, believing it was planted by Kennedy, called him to the White House for a tongue lashing. According to *Time*'s colorful account, Johnson told Kennedy, "If you keep talking like this, you won't have a political future in this country within six months," warned him that "the blood of American boys will be on your hands," and concluded, "I never want to see you again." Uncowed, Kennedy called Johnson an s.o.b. and told him, "I don't have to sit here and take that—." Whether Kennedy really used vulgarity was a matter of some dispute, but there was no doubt that the gist of the conversation had been accurately reported. Less than a month later (March 2, 1967) Kennedy gave a major Senate speech calling for a halt to the bombing and a compromise settlement through negotiations. A few party malcontents, especially in the liberal wing, permitted themselves a small hope that maybe the crown prince of the Democratic party would claim his inheritance sooner than expected.

In the summer of 1967 gloom descended on the camp of the liberals. In August Johnson sent 45,000 more troops to Vietnam and asked for higher taxes to finance the war. And, though Defense Secretary Robert McNamara himself voiced public criticism of the bombing, day after day the bombs continued to fall. Liberals who had once viewed it merely as politically stupid watched in horror as the carnage mounted and now pronounced the war morally wrong as well. Meanwhile domestic insurrectionaries were gutting great American cities, the War on Poverty was bogging down, and the long-awaited white backlash finally arrived. Among those surrendering to despair that summer was Senator Fulbright. Speaking to the American Bar Association in August, he said, "How can we commend democratic social reform to Latin America when Newark, Detroit, and Milwaukee are providing explosive evidence of our own inadequate efforts at democratic social reform? How can we commend the free enterprise system to Asians and Africans when in our own country it has produced vast, chaotic, noisy, dangerous and dirty urban complexes while poisoning the very air and land and water?" Fulbright called the war "unnecessary and immoral" and blamed it for aggravating grave domestic problems. The country "sickens for lack of moral leadership," he said, and only the idealistic young may save us from the "false and dangerous dream of an imperial destiny."

Fulbright's charges about the damage done at home by the war were confirmed in the autumn. Driven by hatred of the war, new left students began acting out their guerrilla fantasies, and major campuses were threatened by chaos. No less disturbing to liberals was the fever of discontent rising in intellectual circles. Some of the nation's most brilliant writers and artists were concluding, as had their counterparts in France during the Algerian war, that they now had no choice but to resist the state.

From the beginning a minority of the nation's intellectual elite—call them radicals—saw the war as more than a blunder in judgment. Most of these radicals had life histories punctuated by episodes of dissent but had stayed aloof from politics during the Cold War. Vietnam brought them back to political awareness and gave focus to their inchoate alienation. To people like the novelists Norman Mailer and Mary McCarthy, the critics Susan Sontag and Dwight Macdonald, *New York Review of Books* editor Robert Silvers, the linguist Noam Chomsky, the anarchist writer Paul Goodman, and the poet Robert Lowell, America appeared to be in the hands of a technological elite that was debauching the American landscape and lusting after world dominion. Morally revolted by the imperial war against the peasants of Vietnam, the radicals found traditional politics insufficient to express their opposition. The war was a matter of conscience, and good men would act accordingly.

Their first impulse was to avoid complicity with the crime. Thus when Johnson invited a group of writers and artists to participate in a White House Festival of the Arts in June 1965, Robert Lowell refused to come. Scion of a distinguished American family, perhaps the best of living American poets, and a draft resister in World War II, Lowell sent a letter to the president, saying, "Every serious artist knows that he cannot enjoy public celebration without making subtle public commitments. . . . We are in danger of imperceptibly becoming an explosive and suddenly chauvinistic nation, and we may even be drifting on our way to the last nuclear ruin. . . . At this anguished, delicate and perhaps determining moment, I feel I am serving you and our country best by not taking part." Robert Silvers took the lead in circulating a statement in support of his friend Lowell and in two days attracted the signatures of twenty of the nation's most prominent writers and artists, among them Hannah Arendt, Lillian Hellman, Alfred Kazin, Dwight Macdonald, Bernard Malamud, Mary McCarthy, William Styron, and Robert Penn Warren. Johnson was so angry at "these people," these "sonsofbitches" that he almost canceled the festival.

By 1967 the radicals were obsessed by the war and frustrated by their impotence to affect its course. The government was unmoved by protest, the people were uninformed and apathetic, and American technology was tearing Vietnam apart. What, then, was their responsibility? Noam Chomsky explored this problem in February 1967 in the *New York Review*, which had become the favorite journal of the radicals. By virtue of their training and leisure, intellectuals had a greater responsibility than ordinary citizens for the actions of the state, Chomsky said. It was their special responsibility "to speak the truth and to expose lies." But the "free-floating intellectual" who had performed this function in the past was being replaced by the "scholar-expert" who lied for the government or constructed "value-free technologies" to keep the existing social order functioning smoothly. Chomsky not only enjoined the intellectuals once again "to seek the truth lying behind the veil of distortion"; he concluded by quoting an essay written twenty years before by Dwight Macdonald, an essay that implied that in time of crisis exposing lies might not be enough. "Only those who are willing to resist authority themselves when it conflicts too intolerably with their personal moral code," Macdonald had written, "only they have the right to condemn." Chomsky's article was immediately recognized as an important intellectual event. Along with the radical students, radical intellectuals were moving "from protest to resistance."

The move toward resistance accelerated through 1967. Chomsky announced in the *New York Review* that for the second consecutive year he was withholding half his income taxes to protest the war. Paul Goodman invited federal prosecution by acknowledging his efforts to aid and abet draft resistance. Mary McCarthy, back from a trip to Vietnam, said that "to be in the town jail, as Thoreau knew, can relieve any sense of imaginary imprisonment." On the cover of its issue of August 24, 1967, the *New York Review* put a diagram of a Molotov cocktail, while inside Andrew Kopkind, in the midst of dismissing Martin Luther

King for having failed to make a revolution, wrote, "Morality, like politics, starts at the barrel of a gun." (Some intellectuals never forgave the *New York Review* for that one.) On October 12, 1967, the *New York Review* published a statement signed by 121 intellectuals and entitled "A Call to Resist Illegitimate Authority." The statement denounced the war on legal and moral grounds and pledged the signers to raise funds "to organize draft resistance unions, to supply legal defense and bail, to support families and otherwise aid resistance to the war in whatever ways may seem appropriate."

A few days later Stop the Draft Week began. This was an event whose possibilities excited radical intellectuals as well as radical students. Paul Goodman kicked the week off with a speech at the State Department before an audience of big business executives. "You are the military industrial of the United States, the most dangerous body of men at the present in the world," Goodman declaimed. On Friday, October 20, 1967, Lowell and Mailer spoke on the steps of the Justice Department prior to the efforts of the Reverend William Sloane Coffin to deliver to the government draft cards collected from draft resisters across the country earlier in the week. (This occasion provided evidence for later federal charges of criminal conspiracy against Coffin, Dr. Benjamin Spock, and three other antiwar activists.) Saturday began with speeches at the Lincoln Memorial ("remorseless, amplified harangues for peace," Lowell called them), and then the march across the bridge toward the Pentagon. Lowell, Mailer, and Macdonald, described by Mailer as "America's best poet? and best novelist??, and best critic???," walked to the battle together. Lowell wrote of the marchers that they were

> . . . like green Union recruits
> for the first Bull Run, sped by photographers,
> the notables, the girls . . . fear, glory, chaos,
> rout . . .
> our green army staggered out on the
>   miles-long green fields,

> met by the other army, the Martian, the ape,
>   the hero,
> his new-fangled rifle, his green new steel
>   helmet.

At the Pentagon Mailer was arrested, much to his satisfaction, but Lowell and Macdonald failed of their object. Noam Chomsky, also present, had not intended to participate in civil disobedience, feeling its purpose in this occasion too vague to make a point. Swept up by the events of the day, Chomsky found himself at the very walls of the fortress, making a speech. When a line of soldiers began marching toward him, he spontaneously sat down. Chomsky spent the night in jail with Mailer.

In his brilliant book *The Armies of the Night*, Mailer probed for the meaning of these apocalyptic events. For him the siege of the Pentagon was a rite of passage for the student rebels, for the intellectuals, for himself. The few hundred fearful youths who sat on the Pentagon steps till dawn on Sunday were a "refrain from all the great American rites of passage when men and women manacled themselves to a lost and painful principle and survived a day, a night, a week, a month, a year." The battle at the Pentagon was a pale rite of passage, he thought, compared to that of the immigrants packed in steerage, Rogers and Clark, the Americans "at Sutter's Mill, at Gettysburg, the Alamo, the Klondike, the Argonne, Normandy, Pusan." But it was a true rite of passage nonetheless, the survivors having been reborn and rededicated to great purpose. On departing from jail Sunday morning, Mailer felt as Christians must "when they spoke of Christ within them." For Mailer and many other radical intellectuals, American institutions seemed so illegitimate that a moral man could find redemption only in resisting them. As for the liberals, they could only wonder what would happen to America if Lyndon Johnson was not stopped.

Signs of a liberal revolt against Johnson's renomination were plentiful in the fall of 1967. Reform Democrats in New York, the liberal California Democratic Council, party factions in Minnesota, Michigan, Wisconsin, and else-where were preparing to oppose him. In late September the ADA national board implicitly came out against him by promising to back the candidate who offered "the best prospect for a settlement of the Vietnam conflict." The *New Republic* explicitly rejected his candidacy in an editorial that same week. And Allard Lowen-stein, thirty-eight-year-old liberal activist and ADA vice-chairman, opened an office in Wash-ington and began organizing a movement on campuses, in the peace movement, and among dissident Democratic politicians to "dump Johnson."

Lowenstein wanted Robert Kennedy to be his candidate. And the existentialist Bobby was tempted. Kennedy worried about the frustra-tion building up in the antiwar movement and had himself come to view the war as morally repugnant. "We're killing South Vietnamese, we're killing women, we're killing innocent people because we don't want to have the war fought on American soil, or because they're 12,000 miles away and they might get 11,000 miles away," he said on *Face the Nation* late in November 1967. But Bobby the professional hated losing, and in his view he could not de-feat Johnson in a fight for the nomination, and neither could anybody else. On that same TV program he stated flatly that he would not be a candidate. If he were, he said, "it would im-mediately become a personality struggle," and the real issues would be obscured. Asked about some other Democrat, such as Senator Eugene McCarthy of Minnesota, taking on the president, Kennedy replied, "There could be a healthy element in that." He would endorse neither Johnson nor McCarthy but support whoever was the eventual party nominee.

Eugene McCarthy had become convinced that someone would have to raise the issue of the war in the party primaries in 1968. When Kennedy and other leading doves rejected Lowenstein's pleas to be the candidate, McCarthy agreed to run. Explaining his pur-pose at a press conference on November 30,

1967, he said, "There is growing evidence of a deepening moral crisis in America—discon-tent and frustration and a disposition to take extralegal if not illegal actions to manifest pro-test. I am hopeful that this challenge . . . may alleviate at least in some degree this sense of political helplessness and restore to many peo-ple a belief in the processes of American poli-tics and of American government." In other words, McCarthy was offering his candidacy as an alternative to radicalism.

Only an unusual politician would undertake what no one else would dare. In truth McCarthy, who had spent eight months of his youth as a novice in a Benedictine monastery, was in the political world but not of it. He was a senator bored by the Senate, an office seeker who disdained intrigue and self-advertisement, a professional who valued honor more than influence. In recent years he had seemed more interested in Thomistic theology and writing poetry than in the business of government. His career, it appeared, would not fulfill its early promise. But the political crisis in the United States in late 1967 provided McCarthy with an opportunity perfectly suited to his self-concep-tion. Like his hero Thomas More, he would play the martyr in a historic confrontation be-tween conscience and power.

McCarthy's candidacy prospered beyond anyone's expectation, even his own. Though Johnson's rating on the Gallup poll was only 41 percent in November, the professionals were mesmerized by the cliché that no president could be denied renomination by his own party. The war was the biggest cause of John-son's unpopularity. Hawks and doves dis-agreed on how best to end the war but other-wise had much in common: both disliked the war, wanted its early termination, and tended to blame Lyndon Johnson for dragging it on. It was the public's declining confidence in John-son's ability to conclude the war that made him vulnerable to McCarthy's candidacy.

What little confidence still existed in the president's war leadership was shattered on

January 31, 1968, when the Vietnamese Communists launched a massive attack in the midst of a truce called for the Tet holiday. Sixty-seven thousand enemy troops invaded more than one hundred of South Vietnam's cities and towns. The allies recaptured most urban areas after a few days and inflicted huge casualties on the attackers. But the Tet Offensive had astounded military men by its scope and daring. It showed that no place in South Vietnam was secure, not even the American embassy, whose walls had been breached in the first hours of the attack. And it temporarily derailed the pacification program in the countryside by drawing allied troops into the cities. Coming after recent administration assurances that the war was being won, the Tet Offensive dealt Johnson's credibility its crowning blow. When he and the U.S. commander in Vietnam, General William Westmoreland, issued victory statements after the offensive ended, few took them seriously, though militarily they were right. The chief political casualty of the Tet Offensive, therefore, was Lyndon Johnson.

In the six weeks after Tet, such pillars of establishment opinion as Walter Cronkite, *Newsweek*, the *Wall Street Journal*, and NBC News gave way and called for de-escalation. High officials in the government finally dared express their private doubts bout the war to the president. The Gallup poll reported a seismic shift in public opinion: in February self-described hawks had outnumbered doves 60 percent to 24 percent; in March it was hawks 41 percent, doves 42 percent. And on March 10, two days before the New Hampshire primary, the *New York Times* set off waves of national anxiety by reporting a secret request from the generals to the president for 206,000 more troops for the war.

Meanwhile, in New Hampshire, the first primary state, McCarthy was proving an eccentric candidate. A lazy campaigner, he often did not return phone calls, would not court potential contributors, and avoided local politicians. His manner on the stump was uninspired, and even his references to the war were low-key. (McCarthy opposed unilateral withdrawal and advocated a negotiated settlement.) But McCarthy had an insight denied to his detractors: he mattered less in this campaign than the movement he represented. At the climax of the campaign there were so many student volunteers in the tiny state (3,000, or one for every 25 Democratic voters) that McCarthy's lieutenants begged potential workers to stay home. Scrubbed and shaven, the students ran a canvassing operation that was the envy of the professionals. Even McCarthy's peculiar style proved to be an asset. At a time when the country was fed up with politicians, shrill voices, and the hard sell, there was something reassuring in McCarthy's unhurried, dignified manner. He did not frighten people. He seemed safe.

Governor John W. King, one of the inept managers of Johnson's write-in campaign in New Hampshire, said in the beginning that McCarthy would get 5 percent of the vote. McCarthy himself predicted 30 percent. On March 12, 1968, 49 percent of New Hampshire's Democratic voters wrote in the name of the president of the United States, and 42 percent marked their ballots for a senator of whom days before few had heard. Poll data showed that more McCarthy voters in New Hampshire were hawks than doves. McCarthy's remarkable showing, then, was not a victory for peace, merely proof that Lyndon Johnson, who could neither pacify the ghetto, speak the plain truth, lick inflation, nor above all end the war, was a mighty unpopular president indeed.

McCarthy had done more than demonstrate Johnson's vulnerability. As he had hoped, his candidacy drained off some of the discontent flowing into illegal protest. Thousands of students who might otherwise have joined SDS got "clean for Gene." Intellectuals who had flirted with resistance a few months before became the senator's avid fans. McCarthy's traveling companion through much of New Hampshire was Robert Lowell—a symbolic relationship whose significance was probably lost on neither of these famous poets.

It had been a hard winter for Robert Kennedy. He realized after the Tet Offensive that his refusal to run had been a mistake. Throughout February 1968, while McCarthy's New Hampshire campaign was getting started, Kennedy and his advisers wrestled again with the problem of his candidacy. Kennedy was ready to go early in March and set in motion machinery for a campaign. But still he found reason to delay a public announcement. By the time he declared on March 16, 1968, the results of the New Hampshire primary had already electrified the country. Much of the constituency that would have been his now belonged to McCarthy. Lyndon Johnson, however, took Kennedy's candidacy more seriously than McCarthy's. He knew, even if the students did not, that Kennedy was the one man in the party who might beat him.

McCarthy refused to step aside for Kennedy and moved on to the Wisconsin primary, whose date was April 2. Early in March the president's men in Wisconsin had been confident of victory. But McCarthy arrived with more students, money, and prestige than he had had in New Hampshire, and by mid-month the Johnson managers knew their man was in trouble. On March 28 Postmaster Larry O'Brien, an old political pro, returned from a look around the state to tell Johnson that his cause there was hopeless.

While the political storms raged around them, Johnson and his advisers were deep into a momentous review of war policy. General Earl Wheeler, chairman of the Joint Chiefs of Staff, had blundered in late February when he privately requested 206,000 additional troops for Vietnam. Since General Westmoreland was in no danger of being overrun, there was never much chance that Johnson would dispatch massive reinforcements. The tax money to pay for escalation was not there, and neither was the political support. Wheeler's request had one unintended result. By asking so much, it forced policy makers to resolve the basic ambiguity that had characterized America's policy since 1965. Militarily, Johnson had been seeking victory over the Vietcong. Diplomatically, he paid lip service to a negotiated settlement, which implied compromise. Since his generals were in effect telling him that they needed more troops than he could furnish to win, Johnson had no choice now except to opt for negotiation. Accounts differ on how Johnson reached this conclusion in March 1968. But in the end those of his advisers urging some steps in the direction of de-escalation prevailed. On March 31 Johnson went on television to announce that he was stopping the bombing over most of North Vietnam and would end it entirely if Hanoi demonstrated comparable restraint. Johnson called on the North Vietnamese to respond to his partial bombing halt by accepting his invitation to negotiate. A few days later they did so.

Johnson announced another decision in this speech. For some time he had been dropping hints among friends and advisers that he might not run in 1968. Only at the last minute did he determine not to make his 1968 State of the Union Message the occasion for announcing his retirement. But his mood seemed to change after that, and he took steps to organize a re-election campaign. Even after the ambush in New Hampshire, Johnson authorized Larry O'Brien to meet with Cabinet officers and give them marching orders for the political battle ahead.

Though most Johnson intimates believed he would run, he had compelling reasons not to. Exhausted, haunted by fear of another heart attack, bitter at the vilification he had suffered, the man had had enough. "The only difference between the [John F.] Kennedy assassination and mine," he said in this period, "is that I am alive and it has been more tortuous." There were other reasons too. Politically he faced a Congress opposed to his programs, a public that had lost confidence in his leadership, a defeat at the hands of McCarthy in the Wisconsin primary, and an uncertain contest with

Robert Kennedy. On the diplomatic front, he wished to take a step toward peace, which his opponents, domestic and foreign, would probably dismiss as insincere if he remained a potential candidate. In his speech of March 31, Johnson spoke of "division in the American house" and declared his intention to keep the presidency above partisanship in this election year. "Accordingly," he told a stunned nation, "I shall not seek, and I will not accept, the nomination of my party for another term as your President." The liberals, with an assist from the peace movement, the attackers of Tet, and war-weariness, had dumped Johnson.